1795

MACROECONOMICS:
measurement, theory, and policy

MICHAEL C. LOVELL
WESLEYAN UNIVERSITY

macro-
economics:
measurement,
theory,
& policy

JOHN WILEY & SONS, INC. New York·London·Sydney·Toronto

15.47

Library of Congress Cataloging in Publication Data:

Lovell, Michael C   1930-
  Macroeconomics.

  Includes bibliographical references and index.
  1.   Macroeconomics.   I.   Title.

HB171.5.L79   339   75-2001
ISBN 0-471-54850-2

Printed in the United States of America

10 9 8 7 6 5 4 3

for my family

preface

In this textbook I have tried to capture the excitement of an intellectual revolution. It may not be revolutionary to change from "Classical" to "Keynesian," "Neoclassical," and "Monetarist" viewpoints, for paradigm shifts of this kind have been characteristic of economics since its inception. Furthermore, it is not revolutionary to have a substantial increase in the size of the economics profession for, with considerable regularity, the number of professional economists and their research output have doubled about every 15 years for most of the past century. But there has been a revolution in terms of the data base available for the business analyst who is interested in forecasting the business cycle and the academic economist who is dedicated to the task of evaluating economic policy. There has also been an econometric revolution, taking the form of fundamental improvements in the statistical techniques specifically designed for analyzing economic data. And the computer revolution makes it possible to execute the computations required in subjecting economic data series to statistical analysis and in simulating the effects of alternative economic policies. Since progress in economics requires that theoretical and empirical analyses interact (like the left foot and right foot in walking), it is fortunate that the data, the econometric, and the computer revolutions have been matched by substantial progress in the involvement of applied mathematicians in the study of economic theory. But as vital as these revolutions have been, the most fundamental change has been a policy revolution; more than ever, governments have become committed to the application of the fruits of economic research to the task of achieving full employment, price stability, and balance of payments equilibrium.

In writing this book I have found that there is a temptation, as in the classroom, to provide a sugar-coated pill of easily digested, packaged answers to issues that are inherently controversial. In resisting the temptation I have tried to convey a great deal of the controversy that permeates professional economic thought. I not only have tried to reveal how economists pursue their research interests, but I have tried to explain why debate persists and to comment on some of the obstacles involved in attempting to resolve questions of controversy.

Studying economics is not like studying spelling, because there are no "right" answers to memorize. Although economics, like other social sciences, has a specialized language, we cannot learn the subject simply by enlarging our vocabulary by glancing through a dictionary of economics.

The thing that distinguishes the professional economist from the layman is not his vocabulary. And the economist is not unique in his interest in such problems as inflation, growth, and unemployment; these macroeconomic issues are of universal concern. Instead, the economist is distinguished by how he *thinks* about the problems. He must know more facts than the man in the street, and he must also use a specialized kit of analytical tools.

This textbook provides a sequence of tools for analyzing economic illnesses and evaluating their remedies. Let me warn you, however, that even with the aid of the best instructor, you cannot learn macroeconomics by scanning these pages. You not only must review the key concepts after reading each chapter, but you must take a pencil and graph paper and make sure that you can reconstruct the argument. You must work through a sample of the problem exercises at the end of each chapter. You must question the assumptions underlying the argument, and you must determine how the conclusions of the analysis can be modified when certain assumptions are changed or relaxed. Many of you will find that your understanding is greatly enhanced by focusing on a specialized research topic of particular interest; several topics are suggested in the text and exercises. It will be particularly instructive to dig out your own data from the government documents listed in the appendix to Chapter 2.

PRODUCT DIFFERENTIATION

This book is differentiated from its competitors in several respects. Instead of the usual chapters on national income accounting, greater emphasis is placed on measuring unemployment and the rate of inflation. Key national income concepts are introduced as they arise in the course of the argument. (Students might review the presentation in their introductory text.) In developing the theory of income determination the weaknesses in the link between GNP and disposable income are stressed. Emphasis is placed on the positive act of spending instead of on the passive act of saving in explaining the multiplier process. Balanced budget and foreign trade multiplier concepts are explored. The *IS-LM* apparatus is developed without resorting to "fourquadrant" Hicksian-type diagrams; instead, a series of flowcharts, culminating with Figure 8.1, illustrates how the basic equations that constitute the building blocks of a sequence of models fit together. A detailed analysis of aggregate demand and supply facilitates a comparison of "Classical" and "Keynesian" viewpoints. The influence of money is carefully evaluated in the extensive analysis of the business cycle. The discussion of econometric models in Chapter 17 gives a convenient summary of the analysis in earlier chapters. And in the discussion of growth and technological change, an atypical presentation of the Neoclassical growth model emphasizes population problems and diminishing returns.

LEVEL OF ANALYSIS

Economic problems are not easy problems, and they are important enough to demand sophisticated treatment with advanced mathematical and statistical techniques. In the classroom, however, I always find a great diversity among students in both quantitative interests and experience. This textbook provides an appropriate compromise between oversimplification of the material and intimidation of the reader. Throughout, there are a variety of exercises and appendices that cater to a diverse audience. Students, with no college mathematics, who have completed at least one semester of economics will find the book understandable. (The material marked with a dagger in the contents can be skipped by anyone not interested in mathematical details.) This does not mean that equations have been spared; reliance exclusively on graphs would frustrate students who have a working knowledge of the calculus. Indeed, calculus is used in certain points of the analysis, but it is accompanied with a verbal interpretation so that those who are unfamiliar with calculus can follow the argument. Students with a stronger background will find sufficient challenge in the more advanced problems that appear at the end of most chapters. The appendixes provide a flexibility in meeting the specialized needs and interests of individual readers. Some will find that Appendix 2.C gives a helpful review of compound interest, logarithms, and semi-logarithmic growth charts, but others already will be well grounded in these topics. Students not familiar with production functions or regression analysis, may find that the appendixes which give brief introductions to these topics are interesting and helpful. Other appendixes explore more esoteric topics that will interest students with a stronger background in mathematics and statistics. For example, students with a working knowledge of matrix algebra may find the discussion of input-output analysis in the appendix to Chapter 4 particularly stimulating. Furthermore, those familiar with computers will find ample exercises that show how to write programs for simulating the business cycle.

ORGANIZATION AND COVERAGE

The field of macroeconomics is now so broad that it cannot be covered in a single volume, but I have tried to achieve a breadth of coverage even when it meant that many topics could not be explored with the depth that they deserve. In my own teaching I have found that the current business situation has influenced the way in which I allocate time to the business cycle, inflation, and balance of payments problems. My assignments have been influenced partly by the divergent backgrounds of my students at different institutions. Consequently, this book is intended to allow for maximum flexibility. Depending on student interests and background, certain sections may be scanned while others deserve more intensive study. Instructors who have less time available for analytical discussion because they want to rely on outside readings in focusing on current policy issues may restrict their students' attention to the core sections identified by asterisks in the table of contents. If you focus on the *core sections*, you will find that you can skip over other parts of the text without a loss of continuity, and the core sections will make minimal demands on the students quantitative background.

The order in which macroeconomic topics are introduced is a matter of personal taste, judgment, and logic. The chapters are arranged in a way that I have found to be most helpful for my students; the majority of instructors will probably want to follow the same sequence. However, there is room for considerable flexibility. For example, the discussion of the methodology of macroeconomics appears in the first chapter because I find it helpful to examine these issues at the beginning of the course; but many instructors may postpone this noncore section until a discussion of a controversial issue, such as the perennial debate over the relative importance of monetary and fiscal policy. Also, Chapters 6 and 7, on investment and the IS schedule, can be read before the discussion of money in Chapter 5. Chapter 9 on the balance of payments may be omitted, since it is not in the *core*, or it may be postponed until after Chapter 10. An instructor who wants to review the effects of fiscal and monetary policy at the end of the course may conclude with Chapter 17, which summarizes the effects of fiscal and monetary policy with the aid of a comprehensive discussion of the Fed-MIT econometric model.

ACKNOWLEDGMENTS

I have incurred many debts in writing this book. I thank my students at Yale, Carnegie-Mellon, and Wesleyan for their perceptive comments during the formative stage. I am grateful for constructive suggestions by Locke Anderson, William Brainard, F. Trenery Dolbear, James Hansen, Rita E. Hauser, R. Ivan Lovell, Charles Miller, Marnie W. Mueller, and R. L. Teigen. Norma Ziker typed several chapters of the manuscript when I was at Carnegie-Mellon University. I especially thank Joan Halberg for her patience in preparing the manuscript for publication.

Michael C. Lovell

contents

Chapter 1   Introduction   1

   *1.1   The Politics of Macroeconomics   1
   1.2   The Methodology of Macroeconomics   6
   *1.3   The Plan of This Book   11
   *1.4   A Guide for the Reader   12

**PART I   UNEMPLOYMENT AND THE ELEMENTARY   15
THEORY OF INCOME DETERMINATION**

Chapter 2   The Unemployment Gap   17

   *2.1   Measuring Unemployment   17
   *2.2   The Social Costs of Unemployment   17
   *2.3   The Target Unemployment Rate   22
   *2.4   Unemployment and the GNP Gap   25
   Appendix 2.A   Guide to Sources of Economic Data   35
   Appendix 2.B   On Errors of Measurement   36
      2.B.1   Revisions of the GNP Accounts   37
      2.B.2   The Statistical Discrepancy   39
      2.B.3   Sampling Error in the Unemployment Estimates   39
      2.B.4   Regional Unemployment Estimates   40
      2.B.5   On Defining Unemployment   40
   Appendix 2.C   Semilogarithmic (Ratio) Charts, Geometric   42
   Growth, and Compound Interest—A Survey
      2.C.1   Arithmetic versus Geometric Growth   42
      2.C.2   Exponents and Logarithms   44
      2.C.3   Geometric Growth and Semilogarithmic Charts   45
      2.C.4   Natural Logarithms and the Continuous   46
      Compounding of Interest

* denotes key sections constituting the basic core of the book.
† indicates optional mathematical material.

Chapter 3   Elementary Multiplier Theory   48

*3.1   Introduction   48
*3.2   An Identity and Two Behavioral Equations   49
*3.3   Rounds of Induced Expenditure—The Kahn Multiplier   60
*3.4   Graphical Analysis of the Multiplier   64
*3.5   A Family of Multipliers   68
    a. Effects of Increased Government Spending
    b. Effects of a Tax Cut   c. The Balanced-
    Budget Multiplier   d. The Paradox of Thrift
    e. A Simplification
3.6   Evaluating Tax Policy: The Full-Employment Budget   76
    a. Graphical Analysis   b. Algebraic Analy-
    sis of the GNP—Disposable Income Gap
*3.7   A Caveat   82
Appendix 3.A   Multisector Multipliers   89
3.A.1   Introduction   89
3.A.2   The Foreign Trade Multiplier   89
3.A.3   Input-Output Analysis—A Two-Industry Example   92
3.A.4   Input-Output Applications   95
†3.A.5   Matrix Analysis   100
    a. Price Implications   b. Viable So-
    lutions, A Theorem   c. Material Bal-
    ance in Planned Economies

Chapter 4   Consumption   105

*4.1   Introduction   105
*4.2   Consumption and the Distribution of Income   109
4.3   The Life-Cycle Hypothesis   117
4.4   Consumption and the Rate of Interest   122
4.5   Inertia and Expectations: Distributed Lag Analysis of   125
    Consumption
4.6   Wealth, Income, and Consumption   131
4.7   Liquid Assets and the "Wealth" Effect of Price and   134
    Interest Rate Changes
*4.8   Policy Implications   136
Appendix 4.A   The Method of Least Squares   142
4.A.1   Introduction   142
†4.A.2   Descriptive Statistics   142

†4.A.3   Statistical Inference   146

Appendix 4.B   Some Consumption Function Estimates   148

PART II   MONEY AND THE PACE OF ECONOMIC   151
ACTIVITY

Chapter 5   Money and the Economy: An Overview   153

*5.1   What Money Is   153
*5.2   The Quantity Theory of Money   156
*5.3   The Transactions Demand for Money   161
*5.4   Precautionary and Speculative Balances   165
*5.5   Three Perspectives on the Demand for Money—   175
        Derivation of the *LM* Curve
*5.6   The Role of Money: An Agenda   179

Appendix 5.A   The Demand for Money, An Empirical   183
Illustration

Appendix 5.B   Portfolio Selection and the Demand for Money 184
5.B.1   Risk and Return   184
†5.B.2   Efficient Portfolios: A Numerical Example   186
†5.B.3   Risk: Quadratic Utility and Variance   191

Chapter 6   Investment and the Rate of Interest   193

*6.1   The Decision to Invest   193
*6.2   The Accelerator   193
*6.3   The Cost of Funds and the Marginal Efficiency of   198
        Investment
6.4   Empirical Evidence   202
*6.5   Regulating the Pace of Investment   204

Chapter 7   Investment, the Multiplier, and Stagnation: 210
The *IS* Schedule

*7.1   The Interest Rate and the Determination of Output   210
*7.2   Derivation of the *IS* Curve   212
*7.3   The Stagnation Thesis   215

Chapter 8   Monetary Policy and the Determination of GNP   220

*8.1   Alternative Control Strategies   220
*8.2   The *IS-LM* Apparatus   220
*8.3   Fiscal versus Monetary Policy   222

Chapter 9   Balance of Payments Equilibrium and Full Employment   232

    9.1   The Balance of Payments   232
    9.2   Analysis   237
    9.3   Theory and Practice   240
        a. The Gold Standard   b. Operation Twist
        c. Currency Devaluation   d. Flexible
        Exchange Rates

Chapter 10   On Monetary Policy   250

    *10.1   The Lender of Last Resort   250
    *10.2   Reserve Requirements, the Discount Rate, and Open   252
        Market Operations
    10.3   Bank Transactions and Reserve Posture   257
        a. Loans   b. Check Clearing
        c. Currency Drain   d. Federal Funds
        Market   e. Buying Government Securities
        f. Government Expenditures   g. Open
        Market Operations
    10.4   The Money Supply Expansion Coefficient   263
    10.5   Excess Reserves, Interest Rates, and the Money Supply   267
    *10.6   Evaluating Central Bank Performance   270
        a. The Real-Bills Doctrine   b. Financing
        War   c. Ratification of the 1964 Tax Cut

PART III   MONETARY POLICY AND THE PRICE LEVEL   279

Chapter 11   Inflation and Deflation   281

    *11.1   What It Is   281
    *11.2   Living with Inflation—And Who Gets Hurt   285
    11.3   Measuring Inflation   292
    *11.4   Types of Inflation: Remedies and Panaceas   300
        a. Wage-Push and Cost-Push Inflation
        b. Wage and Price Controls   c. Demand-
        Pull Inflation and the Inflationary Gap
        d. Monetary Policy   e. Monetary
        Conversion
    *11.5   Studying Inflation   309
    Appendix 11.A   Index Numbers   313
        11.A.1   Introduction   313

11.A.2   A Production Index   313

11.A.3   Price Indices   316

Chapter 12   Aggregate Demand and Supply   318

*12.1   Overview of a Sequence of Models   318

12.2   Aggregate Demand and Prices   320

12.3   Output and the Real Wage   321

12.4   Rigid Money Wages and Aggregate Supply   325

12.5   Interaction of Aggregate Demand and Supply   328

   a. Price-output Response to $M_s{}^n$ and G
   b. Wage-Push Inflation   c. Market
   Imperfections and Cost-Push Inflation
   d. Technological Change

12.6   The "Classical World" of Flexible Money Wages   336

12.7   The Great Debate   340

†**Appendix 12.A**   Production Functions   349

Chapter 13   Dynamic Aspects of Inflation and Deflation   352

*13.1   Statics and Dynamics   352

*13.2   Wage Changes, Productivity, and Inflation   352

*13.3   The "Phillips Curve," an Empirical Relationship   358

13.4   The Pace of Inflation and Effective Demand   366

   a. Consumption Spending   b. Investment
   Spending   c. The Demand for Money
   d. Determining the Speed of Inflation

13.5   Forced Saving   375

PART IV   THE BUSINESS CYCLE AND ECONOMIC   383
FORECASTING

Chapter 14   The Business Cycle: An Overview   385

*14.1   Introduction   385

*14.2   A Capsule History of the Business Cycle   385

*14.3   Barometric Forecasting of the Cycle   390

   a. NBER indicators   b. Diffusion indices
   c. Anticipatory Data   d. Summary

*14.4   The Scope of the Business Cycle Theory   399

Chapter 15   Simple Dynamics of the Business Cycle   405

*15.1   Introduction   405

*15.2   Multiplier-Accelerator Interaction   406

15.3   Equilibrium Output   409

15.4   Modes of Dynamic Behavior   410

15.5   Automatic Stabilizers and Tax Adjustments   415

†**Appendix 15.A**   Solution of Linear Difference Equations   424

    †15.A.1   Introduction   424

    †15.A.2   Solution of First-Order Difference Equations   425

    †15.A.3   Second Order Linear Difference Equations   426

             *a. Distinct Real Roots   b. Identical
             Roots   c. Complex Roots*

†**Appendix 15.B**   Graphical Analysis of Second-Order   433
    Difference Equations

    †15.B.1   Cycles   433

             *a. Oscillatory Behavior (imaginary
             roots)   b. Sawtooth cycles
             (negative real roots)*

    †15.B.2   Iso-Stability Triangles   434

    †15.B.3   Iso-Frequency Curves   436

Chapter 16   A Portfolio of Cycle Models   437

    *16.1   Catalog   437

    16.2   Money and the Business Cycle   437

           *a. Alternative Simulations, An Exercise in
           Comparative Dynamics   b. Model Details
           c. Analysis of the Dynamic Properties of
           the Model   d. A More Responsive
           Monetary Policy*

    16.3   The Inventory Cycle   447

           *a. Behavioral Assumptions   b. Dynamic
           Properties*

    Appendix 16.A   Optimal Linear Decision Rules   460

        16.A.1   Introduction   460

        †16.A.2   Some Simple Examples   460

                 *a. Adjustment Costs   b. Control
                 Costs   c. Adjustment and Control
                 Costs*

        †16.A.3   Certainty Equivalence   465

        16.A.4   Summary and Implications   466

    †**Appendix 16.B**   Stochastic Difference Equations   469

Chapter 17   Macroeconometric Models   472

  *17.1   History   472

  *17.2   The Federal Reserve Board—MIT Econometric Model   473

    *a. Consumption-Inventory Block b. The
Investment Block c. The Financial Block
d. The Three Blocks Combined
e. Critique*

  *17.3   Achievement and Prospects   485

PART VI GROWTH AND TECHNOLOGICAL CHANGE   493

Chapter 18   Characteristics of the Growth Process   495

  *18.1   Introduction   495

  *18.2   The Burden of the Debt   496

  *18.3   The Warranted Rate of Growth   499

  †18.4   On the Sources of Capacity Growth   502

    *a. The Estimation Procedure b. Results
Qualifications, and Elaborations*

Chapter 19   Growth Under Full Employment   511

  *19.1   Introduction   511

   19.2   Assumptions   512

   19.3   Full-Employment Growth Equilibrium   514

  †19.4   Stability of the Full-Employment Growth Path   518

  †19.5   Wage, Price, and Monetary Adjustment for Full-   521
Employment Growth

    *a. The wage rate b. The interest rate
c. Monetary Policy for Full-Employment
Growth d. An Optimal Propensity to
Save e. Adjustment to Accelerating
Technological Change and Population
Growth*

Index   533

introduction

*1.1 THE POLITICS OF MACROECONOMICS

The dread specter of inflation and balance of payments disequilibrium, the task of adjusting to the implications of technological change and achieving rapid economic growth, the recurrence of unemployment and the persistence of the business cycle—all these are vital macroeconomic problems. A glance at this volume's table of contents indicates the many issues that concern the student of macroeconomics. These are problems that can arouse the politician—and perhaps they should. Certainly, the sizable bipartisan majorities in both houses of Congress that supported the passage the *Employment Act of 1946* thought such problems constituted a legitimate concern of government. The legislation, which culminated a heated debate in Congress on the problems of adjusting from a wartime to a peacetime economy, opened with the following declaration of policy.

"The Congress declares that it is the continuing policy and responsibility of the Federal Government to use all practicable means consistent with its needs and obligations and other essential considerations of national policy with the assistance and cooperation of industry, agriculture, labor, and State and local governments to coordinate and utilize all its plans, functions, and resources, for the purpose of creating and maintaining, in a manner calculated to foster and promote free competitive enterprise and the general welfare, conditions under which there will be afforded useful employment opportunities, including self-employment, for those able, willing, and seeking to work, and to promote maximum employment, production, and purchasing power."

In subsequent years candidates for national office, regardless of party, have seldom failed to reassert the extent of the economic responsibilities of the federal government—and usually the politician's rhetoric has been more decisive than the stilted language of the Employment Act of 1946.

President Kennedy, speaking at the 1962 Yale University commencement, declared:[1]

"The national interest lies in high employment and steady expansion of output, in stable prices and a strong dollar. The declaration of such objectives is easy; their attainment in an intricate and interdependent economy and world is a little more

---

[1] Commencement speech delivered at Yale University, June 11, 1962.

1

difficult. To attain them, we require not some automatic response but hard thought. What we need is not labels and cliches but more basic discussion of the sophisticated and technical questions involved in keeping a great economic machinery moving ahead."

And these targets were no longer a matter of partisan politics; Richard M. Nixon regarded the high levels of unemployment that plagued our economy when the voters went to the polls in the 1960 presidential election as a major factor contributing to his narrow defeat by Kennedy.[2]

A careful statistical study by Gerald H. Kramer of voting behavior in congressional elections in the United States from 1896 to 1964 revealed:[3]

"Economic fluctuations, in particular, are important influences on Congressional elections, with economic upturn helping the Congressional candidates of the incumbent party, and economic decline benefiting the opposition. In quantitative terms, a 10% decrease in per capita real personal income would cost the incumbent administration 4 or 5 percent of the Congressional vote, other things being equal. . . . [E]conomic fluctuations can account for something like half the variance of the Congressional vote, over the period considered. Of the economic variables considered, real personal income seems to be the most important; with real income held constant, changes in unemployment or the rate of inflation have no significant independent effects."

The Employment Act of 1946 does more than reassert the scope of governmental concern in matters economic. It places on the President a major responsibility for the diagnosis of pressing economic problems and the prescription of appropriate remedies. Specifically, the President is required at the start of each year to transmit to the Congress an *Economic Report* discussing current economic conditions and specifying programs that will contribute to a healthy economy. The three-member Council of Economic Advisers established by the Employment Act serves as a source of professional advice to the President on issues of economic policy. The Joint Economic Committee of the Congress was created to conduct hearings in overseeing the activities of the executive branch in economic matters.

[2] As Vice-President under President Eisenhower, Nixon had unsuccessfully pushed for a tax cut in 1958; he supported more vigorous measures to counter the 1960 recession. For a discussion of the economic views of Richard Nixon while Vice President, see Herbert Stein, *The Fiscal Revolution in America*, Chicago: University of Chicago Press, 1969, pp. 370–371. When Nixon won the election of 1968, Stein was appointed Chairman of President Nixon's Task Force on Fiscal and Budget Policy and was later appointed Chairman of the Council of Economic Advisers.

[3] "Short-Term Fluctuations in U.S. Voting Behavior, 1886–1964," *American Political Science Review*, Vol. 65, 1971, pp. 140–141. Kramer reports that presidential elections are substantially less responsive to economic conditions.

The Employment Act was partly the product of acrimonious debate. An earlier bill, introduced as "The *Full*-Employment Act of 1945," had stressed the responsibility of the federal government "to provide such volume of federal investment and expenditure as may be needed to assure continuing *full*-employment." While only a few opponents of the bill were prepared to argue that "depressions are inevitable under the free enterprise system and the price we pay for freedom," Ohio Senator Robert A. Taft was frightened by the possibility of continued deficit spending and an ever growing national debt. The compromise provided by the Employment Act of 1946 was characterized by Representative Celler of New York as "something written by the best minds of the 18th century," while Representative Bender of Ohio complained: "The bill is not a full-employment bill and does not assure anybody anything. Basically, then, the bill is a fraud."

Even with the best of good intentions, no legislative body can simply abolish such economic problems as unemployment. At best, it may be possible to create institutions that will insure that the recommendations of the best minds of the economics profession are followed. But, of course, the best professional opinion may not be enough. After all, the best doctors do not save every patient—even when their advice is followed. We will see that in many respects the knowledge of economists concerning the causes and cures of economic ills is indeed quite primitive.

There are some 18,000 members of the American Economic Association, some 18,000 purveyors of economic wisdom. No President has had difficulty finding volunteers willing to serve on his Council of Economic Advisers, although some may have found it easier than others. But it is said that economists seldom agree, and perhaps it was George Bernard Shaw who was so unkind as to suggest that "if all economists were laid end to end they would never reach a conclusion." There is a tremendous temptation to soft pedal the extent of disagreement and to search for topics indicating consensus within the economics profession. That consensus is often lacking on key policy issues is suggested by a poll of university economists conducted in 1966 by the Chase Manhattan Bank.[4] Among other questions, the Chase Manhattan Bank asked the economists whether they favored the "wage-price guideposts" as a technique for holding the line on prices. This was a critical political question because the guideposts constituted a key element in the New Economics instituted during the Kennedy administration. The poll revealed that 50% of the economists favored the

[4] *The Chase Manhattan Bank News Letter*, June 1966, reported on their poll of 500 university and 300 business economists. The sample was drawn from a handbook of the American Economic Association and the membership directory of the National Association of Business Economists.

technique, and 50% were opposed.[5] Doesn't this suggest that a student assigned at random would have an even chance of finding his professor advocating wage-price guideposts as an antiinflationary technique for controlling inflation? And *if* economic advisors were picked at random, key elements of our economic policy might also be a random phenomenon.

Does this constitute an exaggerated picture of the extent to which economists disagree? Professor Paul A. Samuelson of the Massachusetts Institute of Technology argued in a 1968 issue of *Newsweek*:[6]

"It is not really true that economists can never agree. Last week more than 1,200 economists . . . signed what may be a historically significant petition. The time has come, these economists stated, . . . to introduce in the American System a 'negative income tax.' . . . Economists are virtually unanimous on this matter. . . ."

But we must not exaggerate the degree of consensus behind the negative income tax, a program to modify the mechanism by which the government now collects tax revenue from people with incomes above a minimum level so as to provide financial assistance—a negative tax with no strings attached—to people with poverty incomes. Professor Milton Friedman of the University of Chicago explained in a follow-up *Newsweek* column that the apparent degree of consensus was in fact misleading.[7]

"In large part, it reflects the use of the same term to describe very different plans. . . . I found it impossible to join in sponsoring the petition or even to sign it because I did not agree with the plan it advocated or the arguments it represented."

And Friedman is one of the architects of the negative income tax! The negative income tax and wage-price guideposts are only two examples illustrating the extent to which disagreement and dissension characterize professional economic opinion. Indeed, it may even be safe to say that the range of opinion among economic professionals is no narrower than the range of views held by the general public. Economists argue about how much unemployment should be tolerated in order to limit inflationary pressure and control the balance of payments deficit. In addition to arguing about which problems deserve highest priority, there is also disagreement concerning the most appropriate remedies. Many economists stress the importance of fiscal policy—adjustments in tax rates and changes in the magnitude of government spending. Others regard monetary policy

[5] A Harris Survey reported in the October 12, 1966, *New York Times* revealed that 71% of the general public said they would vote for a candidate who favored more wage and price controls; 21% were against more controls; and 8% were indifferent. Thus, on this issue at least, professional economists were more conservative than the average citizen.

[6] *Newsweek*, June 10, 1968, p. 76.

[7] *Newsweek*, September 16, 1968, p. 86.

as the strongest lever for controlling the pace of economic activity. While economists disagree about means and ends, probably a majority of the profession is convinced that active government intervention in the functioning of the economy is required. Nonetheless, many renowned members of the profession do not hesitate to voice concern about the dangers of discretionary intervention in the marketplace. Thus Friedman argues:[8]

"History suggests that the real problem is to keep the Fed[eral Reserve System], operating on the wrong premises, from doing precisely the wrong thing, from pouring gas on a fire. . . . [W]e can take discretionary power away from the Fed and make it into a system that operates according to rules. . . ."

Although many economists complain that the government does not apply sound economic principles in managing its responsibilities, it may be that in practice both politicians and the public are overly confident in the ability of professional economists to prescribe appropriate remedies for avoiding economic ills.[9]

Economists are occasionally asked whether there could ever be another great depression such as the one that followed the stock market crash of 1929 and led to 25% of the labor force being unemployed by 1933. It is both fun and instructive for the economist to reverse the question, to ask John Q. Public about the likelihood of such a calamitous event. Professor George Katona of the University of Michigan did just that in a survey conducted in 1965, and he was surprised to find that a remarkable 46% of his sample forecast that the United States would never again have a recession of even the mild 1960 variety. And when Katona asked the optimists why they were so confident, the general response was that " 'they' have learned how to avoid recessions."[10] Presumably, by "they" the optimists were referring to the economists in Washington who are charged with stabilizing the economy. That the confidence might have been misplaced is suggested by the fact that William McChesney Martin who, as Chairman of the Federal Reserve Board, had primary responsibility for the execution of monetary policy, was warning in 1965 that in many respects economic conditions were remarkably similar to the situation just prior to

---

[8] Interview of Milton Friedman in *Playboy*, February 1973, p. 53.

[9] But, of course, economics is not the only field divided by professional controversy. To cite one example, in testimony before the Monopoly Subcommittee of the Senate's Select Committee on Small Business, Dr. Dale Console testified, "The chances that an average patient will get the right drug, in the right amount, at the right time, is on the order of 50 percent." He went on to state that the prescribing habits of physicians are subject to marked variability, ranging from the occasional prescriber who writes about 150 prescriptions a year to the heavy prescriber who writes as many as 100 prescriptions a week. This physician's testimony was reported in the *New York Times*, June 8, 1969, p. 40.

[10] As reported in *Time*, January 8, 1965, p. 59.

the 1929 stock market crash.[11] And, if the 1966 Chase Manhattan Bank poll of professional economic opinion is to be believed, only a minute portion of the experts regard recessions as an anachronism deserving discussion only by the economic historian instead of as a prospect for the future. Specifically, 93% of university economists polled in 1966 thought that the business cycle was *not* dead.[12]

While the persistence of the business cycle may be attributed partly to a failure of governmental agencies to abide by the dictates of economic principles, macroeconomic problems remain with us largely because of the limited nature of our knowledge. Before proceeding to a discussion of what economists know, it is necessary to study the sources of economic knowledge; we must consider the methodology of macroeconomics.

1.2   THE METHODOLOGY OF MACROECONOMICS

When first exposed to the study of economics, skeptical students are often dismayed to find that ours is not an "experimental science." The evidence that economists have to work with is provided primarily by observing actual economic behavior. The skillful chemist and the psychologist are both concerned with problems of "experimental design." In contrast, the economist usually does not have the opportunity to design experiments; obviously, the costs of experimenting on the national economy are prohibitive. The economist observes the world as it is; his data are generated in "nature's laboratory."

We do observe the results of nature's experiments, and the research efforts of economists have been revolutionized within the last quarter century as a result of the avalanche of data that has become available on the behavior of the national economy. Indeed, without careful organization and compilation of data sources, we would be in danger of inundation by the wealth of observations. But there are several reasons why measurement in itself cannot suffice to generate answers to fundamental questions of macroeconomic policy.

Nature does not conduct controlled experiments. In medical research it is customary to contrast the behavior of a sample subjected to treatment with the behavior of a second sample reserved for purposes of control. In the field of economics we have no "control group." Quite the contrary, at any point of time a host of changing factors makes it difficult to isolate the

[11] Does Monetary History Repeat Itself?", address before the Commencement Day Luncheon of the Alumni Federation of Columbia University, June 1, 1965, as reprinted in *Economic Analysis and Policy*, Joseph, Seeber, and Bach, editors, 2nd edition, Prentice-Hall, 1966.

[12] *Chase Manhattan Bank News Letter*, June 1966.

effects of a particular change. For example, efforts at a postmortem evaluation of the extent to which the tax cut of 1964 actually stimulated the economy are partially confounded by the fact that changes were simultaneously taking place in the money supply. *Post hoc ergo propter hoc* is the Achilles heel of the armchair economist who attempts to reach policy conclusions on the basis of simpleminded casual empiricism. The facts do *not* speak for themselves.

Theory is needed, first of all, in order to decide what facts are relevant to the analysis. What, if not economic theory, can guide in the selection of the facts to be considered? Such a wealth of information now exists, indicated by the scope of the data sources listed in the appendix to the next chapter, that it is impossible for any one scholar to study the economy without guidance as to what is "relevant" or "important." Any investigator, at least implicitly, is guided by a theory in deciding what data are pertinent to the problem he is considering. Thus the economist interested in studying the nature of inflation may look at changes in wage rates and labor productivity; or he may look at changes in the money supply—and which set of variables he regards of primary importance may hinge on the theory he studied in graduate school.[13] But without a theory to direct his search the student of inflation will be lost in a jungle of price indices. Indeed, the question of how such economic phenomena as price movements should be measured is partly a theoretical issue. Theory not only suggests which variables are relevant; theory hopefully serves to tie empirical observations together. Facts may be pearls of wisdom, but just as a string is required to organize a jumble of pearls into a beautiful necklace, a theory is required to organize our observations if they are to contribute to economic understanding.[14] Facts concern the world as it is, not as it should be; more than facts are required to guide the policymaker in formulating economic policy.

The economist is embarrassed by an overabundance of theories, particularly of business cycle phenomena. How should one decide which theory to employ? The teacher and the textbook writer as well as the research economist must decide how they will resolve this issue. And the

[13] And what theory he studied may hinge on which graduate school he attended. For a discussion of whether a "Chicago School" of economics exists, see the papers by H. Laurence Miller, Jr., M. Bronfenbrenner, and G. Stigler in the *Journal of Political Economy*, February 1962, pp. 62–75.

[14] The distinction between theory and fact has been stressed repeatedly by the opponents of evolution. Thus the California State Board of Education voted unanimously to recommend that Darwin's theory of evolution no longer be taught as "fact," but only as "theory" (*San Francisco Chronicle*, May 10, 1969, p. 1). But to distinguish observed facts from theory is not to say that one is superior to the other; they are complementary inputs in the production of knowledge.

student must look with jaundiced eye at whatever theory he is confronted with.

It is tempting to make such choices by recourse to rhetoric instead of to reason. Thus one measure of the revolutionary impact of Keynes' *General Theory of Employment, Interest and Money*[15] is provided by the fact that expressions such as "Keynesian theory," "Keynesian system," and so forth are now used by writers clearly lacking the patience required to understand Lord Keynes' argument. Consider the following statement from "A Manifesto by the Bay Area Collective of Socialist Economists (BACSE)."[16]

"The corporate ruling class has adopted Keynesian and neo-Keynesian economics as major instruments of national and international economic planning. The corporate owners and managers engage economists on technical studies of the most pressing ruling class problems. . . ."

And from the opposite extreme, the Veritas Foundation has declared:[17]

". . . the Keynesian system—if it can be called a system—is the primary economics system being taught at Harvard. . . . Keynesian economics is a misnomer. It is not economics. It is a leftwing political theory. . . . Fabians, Communists and Keynesians all unite in accusing the very businessmen who are supporting them of conspiring to enslave the people and destroy liberty."

The fact that Keynesian theory is now more than three decades old—and presumably 30 years out of date—does not deter extremists on both left and right from appropriating the phrase "Keynesian theory" for their own purposes. And, in the process of reducing the concept to a tired cliche, they have denuded it of meaning.

How *should* one decide which theory to employ? A host of competing criteria exists.

1. *Logical consistency.* Surely a theory must be logically consistent instead of subject to internal contradiction.

2. *Validity.* How well does the theory square with the facts? Are its assumptions valid? Is it useful for predicting future economic developments?[18] Can it be used effectively to predict the consequences of alternative policies designed to control the pace of economic activity?

[15] Harcourt, Brace and Co., 1936.

[16] As quoted in the *Union for Radical Political Economics (URPE) Newsletter*, Summer 1969, p. 9.

[17] *Keynes at Harvard, Economic Deception as a Political Credo*, New York: Veritas Foundation, 1960, pp. 2–3.

[18] Predicting the future may be one way to test a theory, but it is not always a legal activity. Thus Pennsylvania law specifies that anyone who pretends, "for gain or lucre," to tell the future is committing a misdemeanor and is subject to a hefty fine and jail sentence (*Pittsburgh Press*, March 16, 1969, p. 2).

3. *Simplicity*. Teacher and researcher join students in desiring that the theory be as simple as possible. Indeed, the *Principle of Occam's Razor* demands that when confronted with the task of choosing between two competing theories, equally admissible in terms of other criteria, the choice should obviously be resolved in favor òf the simpler theory. Note, however, that the computer revolution has served to reduce many of yesteryear's intractable problems to simple issues easily resolved through the application of simulation techniques.

These idealistic criteria constitute a demanding set of standards. It may well be that given the present stage of development of economic science, too much is being required. Let us consider certain issues that have been raised about the problem of empirical verification in the continuing undercurrent of discussion of economic methodology. Samuelson, in *Foundations of Economic Analysis*,[19] emphasized a quarter of a century ago that at the very least economic theory should be based on operational propositions.

"By a meaningful theorem I mean simply a hypothesis about empirical data which could conceivably be refuted, if only under ideal conditions. A meaningful theorem may be false. It may be valid but of trivial importance. Its validity may be indeterminate, and particularly difficult or impossible to determine. . . . But it is meaningful because under ideal circumstances an experiment could be devised whereby one could hope to refute the hypothesis.

". . . only the smallest fraction of economic writings, theoretical and applied, has been concerned with the derivation of *operationally meaningful* theorems. In part at least this has been the result of the bad methodological preconceptions that economic laws deduced from *a priori* assumptions possessed rigor and validity independently of any empirical human behavior."

Samuelson may have been correct in suggesting that the criterion of operationalism suffices to exclude from our consideration a wide range of economic theories. But Friedman is more restrictive; in his paper on "The Methodology of Positive Economics" he argues that we should judge a theory by its ability to predict, although he would explicitly *exclude* its assumptions from empirical scrutiny.[20]

". . . theory is to be judged by its predictive power for the class of phenomena which it is intended to 'explain.' Only factual evidence can show whether it is 'right' or 'wrong' or, better, tentatively 'accepted' as valid or 'rejected' . . . the only relevant test of the *validity* of a hypothesis is comparison of its predictions with experience. The hypothesis is rejected if its predictions are contradicted ('frequently'

[19] *Foundations of Economic Analysis*, Harvard University Press, 1947, pp. 3, 4.

[20] In his *Essays in Positive Economics*, University of Chicago Press, 1953, pp. 8–9, 15. Copyright 1953 by the University of Chicago, all rights reserved.

or more often than predictions from an alternative hypothesis); it is accepted if its predictions are not contradicted; great confidence is attached to it if it has survived many opportunities for contradiction. . . . [T]he relevant question to ask about the 'assumptions' of a theory is not whether they are descriptively 'realistic,' for they never are, but whether they are sufficiently good approximations for the purpose at hand. And this question can be answered only by seeing whether the theory works, which means whether it yields sufficiently accurate predictions. . . ."

In contrast, it has been argued by Lionel Robbins that:[21]

". . . the propositions of economic theory . . . are all assumptions involving in some way simple and indisputable facts of experience. . . . We do not need controlled experiments to establish their validity: they are so much the stuff of our everyday experience that they have only to be stated to be recognized as obvious. . . ."

Friedman's argument is just the reverse of Robbins'; Friedman would exempt the assumptions of the theory from empirical scrutiny because they are *necessarily false*; the world is so complex that it is incapable of being accurately captured by any set of assumptions. For pragmatic reasons Friedman focuses on the validity of the theory's predictions. But in a critique of Friedman's argument, Samuelson pointed out that if the theoretician employed the minimal set of assumptions giving rise to the predictions, his predictions will be correct if and only if its assumptions are also true. For a tightly formulated theory, unencumbered by gratuitous assumptions, the distinction emphasized by both Robbins and Friedman becomes meaningless.[22]

At this point it is hard to disagree with T. C. Koopmans, who complained in a review of Friedman's methodological argument:[23]

"One is led to conclude that economics as a scientific discipline is still somewhat up in the air."

Koopmans went on to explain:

"We . . . [are] led to the realization that neither are . . . the postulates of economic theory entirely self-evident, nor are the implications of various sets of postulates readily tested by observation. The difficulties of verification seem in large part due to the virtual impossibility of experiments under conditions approaching those of real life, and to the presence of many factors simultaneously influencing actual

---

[21] *An Essay on the Nature and Significance of Economic Science*, Macmillan, London, 1946 (2nd ed.) pp. 78–80.

[22] Samuelson presented his comments at a session of the 1962 meetings of the American Economic Association. His argument, as well as interesting statements by Fritz Machlup, Andreas G. Papandreou, Ernest Nagel, Sherman Krupp, G. C. Archibald and Herbert Simon are published in the May, 1962 issue of the *American Economic Review*.

[23] In *Three Essays on the State of Economic Science*, New York: McGraw-Hill, 1957, pp. 140–142.

economic developments. In such a situation, we have to exploit all the evidence we can secure, direct and indirect."

Koopmans suggests the following methodological strategy.

"Considerations of this order suggest that we look upon economic theory as a sequence of conceptional *models* that seek to express in simplified form different aspects of an always more complicated reality. At first these aspects are formalized as much as feasible in isolation, then in combinations of increasing realism. Each model is defined by a set of postulates, of which the implications are developed to the extent deemed worthwhile in relation to the aspects of reality expressed by the postulates. The study of the simpler models is protected from the reproach of unreality by the consideration that these models may be prototypes of more realistic, but also more complicated, subsequent models."

Of course, this argument leaves unanswered the question of how to measure "closeness to reality." No one would argue that increased complexity in itself necessarily yields greater realism. And judgment is called for when increased validity with regard to certain features of a model can be achieved only at the expense of abstracting further from reality at other points of the argument.

*1.3 THE PLAN OF THIS BOOK

There are important pedagogical benefits to be gained by following Koopmans in viewing economics in terms of a sequence of models, and this procedure has been followed in organizing this volume. Initially, a considerable price will be paid for simplicity as our attention is focused on models that at best are applicable to a very narrow range of phenomena and at worse constitute little more than gross caricatures of reality. Thus we start in Part I with the problem of unemployed resources and develop a simple multiplier model that purports only to explain the level of output, given the magnitude of both government spending and investment. The functions of monetary policy are neglected. And nothing is said about price movements or the balance of payments. Obviously, deriving policy implications from such a model is a dubious practice. But as our knowledge cumulates, we will progress through a sequence of more general models of increasing validity and applicability. In Part II money will come into its own, initially in the form of a crude quantity theory diametrically opposed to the multiplier concept. But as the argument evolves it will be possible to form a synthesis involving key elements of the multiplier analysis and the quantity theory. Part III analyzes inflation by building on the earlier framework. Part IV introduces certain dynamic complications essential for a. understanding of the business cycle. Finally, growth models capable of ex plaining long-run economic trends are analyzed in Part V.

*1.4 A GUIDE FOR THE READER

The chapters in this book are divided into sections, and the sections in turn are often subdivided. Core sections of the text are marked by asterisks, both in the table of contents and in the text; and a dagger denotes optional mathematical material. For ease of reference, sections, tables, and figures are numbered consecutively throughout each chapter; thus, "Section 3.6" is the sixth section of the third chapter, and "Table 3.5" the fifth table of the third chapter. For equations, however, a slightly more detailed scheme proves convenient. Equations are numbered consecutively within each chapter section; thus, "Equation 4.2.3" is the third equation in Section two of the fourth chapter; however, "Equation 2.3" is used to indicate the same equation when the chapter designation can be suppressed without creating confusion.

The symbols used in the text are defined carefully when first used, and many are listed in the index for ease of reference. The attempt to use a convenient notation has been tempered by a desire to conform to custom. An example will illustrate the problems inherent in any effort at developing a consistent notation. According to custom, the symbol "I" denotes investment spending. But that means we need another letter for imports, and custom suggests the use of M. Since this is the second letter of *im*ports, it seems reasonable to use the second letter of e*x*ports, X, to denote that concept. This is fine until one considers money, for it would be confusing to use an M for both money and imports. We cannot use m because the lowercase symbol will be used up in Chapter 3 as a coefficient in the equation explaining how imports are determined. So we use boldface: **M** denotes the money supply. But in the spirit of a continued effort to give equal weight to monetary and fiscal policy we must then also use **G** instead of G to denote government spending.

Certain notational conventions that are followed fairly consistently will be enumerated here for easy reference, although the reader may wish to skip over these complications until they are encountered in the text.

Superscripts n and r distinguish nominal from real values. Superscripts are used to distinguish values expressed in money terms from those that have been adjusted for inflation—the details of this procedure are explained in Chapter 11, Section 3. Thus Y^n is the value of gross national product, while Y^r is the figure adjusted for price change (e.g., the value of output measured in 1957 prices).

Subscript t dates variables. In static analysis, as when looking at the ultimate effect of a policy change, it is not necessary to explicitly date variables. But when attention focuses on *dynamic* questions, as when asking how *rapidly* the system responds to a policy change, it is necessary to date variables with subscripts. Thus, the level of GNP in a particular year, say

1968, is denoted Y_{1968}; more generally, Y_t indicates the level of GNP in year t.

Δ *denotes change.* Instead of writing the change in GNP as $Y_t - Y_{t-1}$, we use a Δ; that is,

$$\Delta Y_t = Y_t - Y_{t-1}$$

Again,

$$\frac{\Delta Y_t}{Y_{t-1}} = (Y_t - Y_{t-1})/Y_{t-1}$$

is the rate of change.

The · over a variable also denotes change. Slightly less cumbersome than the ΔY is $\dot{Y}$. It is customarily used when time is measured continuously instead of in weeks or years; that is,

$$\dot{Y} = \frac{dY}{dt}$$

Again, $\dot{Y}/Y$ denotes the rate of change.

$\bar{R}^2$, σ^2, ϵ. These statistical concepts are *not* essential for reading the body of the text. However, the interested reader will find definitions of these and related concepts in Appendix 4.A.

log, lg, e. These concepts are defined in Appendix 2.C.

REFERENCES

1. Each of these books is authored by a former Chairman of the President's Council of Economic Advisors.

   Arthur F. Burns, *Prosperity Without Inflation*, Fordham University Press, 1957.
   W. W. Heller, *New Dimensions in Political Economy*, Harvard University Press, 1966.
   A. M. Okun, *The Political Economy of Prosperity*, W. W. Norton, 1970.
   Herbert Stein, *Fiscal Revolution in America*, Chicago University Press, 1969.

2. The next three items involve questions of methodology. The Koopmans-Vining exchange of 1947 concerned the fundamental two-way linkage between empirical and theoretical research. The book by T. S. Kuhn analyzes the nature of advancement in the physical sciences, but the approach may be equally applicable in the social sciences, economics in particular. The Lovell article analyzes statistical data on the growth of economic literature; it uses citation evidence in demonstrating that major contributions in economics are customarily made by authors in the early stages of their careers; the citation habits of economists provide a means for estimating the relative quality of specific research contributions, the journals in which they appear, their authors, and graduate training programs.

   T. C. Koopmans, "Measurement Without Theory," *Review of Economics and Statistics*, August 1947, and subsequent exchange with Vining, all reprinted in *Readings in Business Cycles* (R. A. Gordon and L. Klein, eds., for American Economic Association), Richard D. Irwin, Inc., 1965.
   T. S. Kuhn, *The Structure of Scientific Revolutions*, University of Chicago Press, revised edition, 1970.
   Michael C. Lovell, "The Production of Economic Literature, An Interpretation," *Journal of Economic Literature*, March 1973.

KEY CONCEPTS

Employment Act of 1946.

Council of Economic Advisers.

Joint Economic Committee.

Economic Report of the President.

operationally meaningful theorem.

Occam's razor.

self-evident postulates.

predictive accuracy.

unemployment and the elementary theory of income determination

the unemployment gap

*2.1 MEASURING UNEMPLOYMENT

Unemployed resources constitute a recurring macroeconomic problem. In boom times unemployment may not appear to be the most pressing of social problems. But studying it in depth helps prepare the way for the subsequent analysis of inflation, the business cycle, and growth.

Perhaps the best single index of the extent to which slack does or does not exist in our economy is provided by a consideration of statistics on unemployment. Data on the utilization of the labor force in the United States are presented in Table 2.1. The *civilian labor force*, which includes all able-bodied persons over 16 years of age who are either working or looking for work, constitutes approximately 60% of the total population. The data since 1940 have been estimated from a monthly personal interview survey; currently, approximately 40,000 households are interviewed each month.[1] Note that the percentage of the civilian labor force without jobs has ranged from a peak of 25% in the 1933 trough of the Great Depression to a minimum of only 1.2% during World War II.[2]

*2.2 THE SOCIAL COSTS OF UNEMPLOYMENT

Clearly, unemployment has at times constituted a social problem of the first order that has marred the success story of the American economy. And the aggregate figures of Table 2.1 mask the fact that unemployment discriminates. The data in Table 2.2 reveal that unemployment hits hardest at women, at nonwhites, and at teenage citizens just entering the labor force. For white workers 1968 was a boom year—their unemployment rate

---

[1] This is several times larger than the samples used in public opinion surveys. A cluster sampling procedure is used involving some 449 geographic areas in all 50 states and the District of Columbia. For a discussion of the effects of sampling error on the precision of the unemployment estimates, see the appendix to this chapter.

[2] These are annual averages; in May 1953, at the height of the Korean War boom, only 2.5% of the labor force was unemployed.

Table 2.1 UNEMPLOYMENT DATA, 1929-1972 (IN THOUSANDS)

Year	Total Non-institutional Population	Total Labor Force		Civilian Labor Force						Not in Labor Force
					Employed			Unemployed		
		Number	Percent of Population	Total	Total	Agri-culture	Nonagri-cultural Industries	Number	Percent of Labor Force	
Persons 14 Years of Age and Over										
1929	(a)	49,440	(a)	49,180	47,630	10,450	37,180	1,550	3.2	(a)
1930	(a)	50,080	(a)	49,820	45,480	10,340	35,140	4,340	8.7	(a)
1931	(a)	50,680	(a)	50,420	42,400	10,290	32,110	8,020	15.9	(a)
1932	(a)	51,250	(a)	51,000	38,940	10,170	28,770	12,060	23.6	(a)
1933	(a)	51,840	(a)	51,590	38,760	10,090	28,670	12,830	24.9	(a)
1934	(a)	52,490	(a)	52,230	40,890	9,900	30,990	11,340	21.7	(a)
1935	(a)	53,140	(a)	52,870	42,260	10,110	32,150	10,610	20.1	(a)
1936	(a)	53,740	(a)	53,440	44,410	10,000	34,410	9,030	16.9	(a)
1937	(a)	54,320	(a)	54,000	46,300	9,820	36,480	7,700	14.3	(a)
1938	(a)	54,950	(a)	54,610	44,220	9,690	34,530	10,390	19.0	(a)
1939	(a)	55,600	(a)	55,230	45,750	9,610	36,140	9,480	17.2	(a)
1940	100,380	56,180	56.0	55,640	47,520	9,540	37,980	8,120	14.6	44,200
1941	101,520	57,530	56.7	55,910	50,350	9,100	41,250	5,560	9.9	43,990
1942	102,610	60,380	58.8	56,410	53,750	9,250	44,500	2,660	4.7	42,230
1943	103,660	64,560	62.3	55,540	54,470	9,080	45,390	1,070	1.9	39,100
1944	104,630	66,040	63.1	54,630	53,960	8,950	45,010	670	1.2	38,590
1945	105,530	65,300	61.9	53,860	52,820	8,580	44,240	1,040	1.9	40,230
1946	106,520	60,970	57.2	57,520	55,250	8,320	46,930	2,270	3.9	45,550
1947	107,608	61,758	57.4	60,168	57,812	8,256	49,557	2,356	3.9	45,850

Persons 16 Years of Age and Over

Year										
1947	103,418	60,941	58.9	59,350	57,039	7,891	49,148	2,311	3.9	42,477
1948	104,527	62,080	59.4	60,621	58,344	7,629	50,713	2,276	3.8	42,447
1949	105,611	62,903	59.6	61,286	57,649	7,656	49,990	3,637	5.9	42,708
1950	106,645	63,858	59.9	62,208	58,920	7,160	51,760	3,288	5.3	42,787
1951	107,721	65,117	60.4	62,017	59,962	6,726	53,239	2,055	3.3	42,604
1952	108,823	65,730	60.4	62,138	60,254	6,501	53,753	1,883	3.0	43,093
1953	110,601	66,560	60.2	63,015	61,181	6,261	54,922	1,834	2.9	44,041
1954	111,671	66,993	60.0	63,643	60,110	6,206	53,903	3,532	5.5	44,678
1955	112,732	68,072	60.4	65,023	62,171	6,449	55,724	2,852	4.4	44,660
1956	113,811	69,409	61.0	66,552	63,802	6,283	57,517	2,750	4.1	44,402
1957	115,065	69,729	60.6	66,929	64,071	5,947	58,123	2,859	4.3	45,336
1958	116,363	70,275	60.4	67,639	63,036	5,586	57,450	4,602	6.8	46,088
1959	117,881	70,921	60.2	68,369	64,630	5,565	59,065	3,740	5.5	46,960
1960	119,759	72,142	60.2	69,628	65,778	5,458	60,318	3,852	5.5	47,617
1961	121,343	73,031	60.2	70,459	65,746	5,200	60,546	4,714	6.7	48,312
1962	122,981	73,442	59.7	70,614	66,702	4,944	61,759	3,911	5.5	49,539
1963	125,154	74,571	59.6	71,833	67,762	4,687	63,076	4,070	5.7	50,583
1964	127,224	75,830	59.6	73,091	69,305	4,523	64,782	3,786	5.2	51,394
1965	129,236	77,178	59.7	74,455	71,088	4,361	66,726	3,366	4.5	52,058
1966	131,180	78,893	60.1	75,770	72,895	3,979	68,915	2,875	3.8	52,288
1967	133,319	80,793	60.6	77,347	74,372	3,844	70,527	2,975	3.8	52,527
1968	135,562	82,272	60.7	78,737	75,920	3,817	72,103	2,817	3.6	53,291
1969	137,841	84,240	61.1	80,734	77,902	3,606	74,296	2,832	3.5	53,602
1970	140,182	85,903	61.3	82,715	78,627	3,462	75,165	4,088	4.9	54,280
1971	142,596	86,929	61.0	84,113	79,120	3,387	75,732	4,993	5.9	55,666
1972	145,775	88,991	61.0	86,542	81,702	3,472	78,230	4,840	5.6	56,785

Source. *Employment and Earnings,* March 1973.

Note. Figures for periods prior to January 1972 are not strictly comparable with current data because of the introduction of 1970 Census data into the estimation procedures. For example, the civilian labor force and employment totals were increased by more than 300,000 as a result of the census adjustment.

a Not available.

Table 2.2   SELECTED UNEMPLOYMENT RATES (PERCENT)

Year	By Sex and Age				By Color		By Selected Groups					
	All Workers	Both Sexes 16–19 Years	Men 20 Years and Over	Women 20 Years and Over	White	Negro and Other Races	Experienced Wage and Salary Workers	Household Heads	Married Men[a]	Full-time Workers[b]	Blue-collar Workers[c]	Labor Force Time Lost[d]
1948	3.8	9.2	3.2	3.6	3.5	5.9	4.3	—	—	—	4.2	—
1949	5.9	13.4	5.4	5.3	5.6	8.9	6.8	—	3.5	5.4	8.0	—
1950	5.3	12.2	4.7	5.1	4.9	9.0	6.0	—	4.6	5.0	7.2	—
1951	3.3	8.2	2.5	4.0	3.1	5.3	3.7	—	1.5	2.6	3.9	—
1952	3.0	8.5	2.4	3.2	2.8	5.4	3.3	—	1.4	2.5	3.6	—
1953	2.9	7.6	2.5	2.9	2.7	4.5	3.2	—	1.7	—	3.4	—
1954	5.5	12.6	4.9	5.5	5.0	9.9	6.2	—	4.0	5.2	7.2	—
1955	4.4	11.0	3.8	4.4	3.9	8.7	4.8	—	2.8	3.8	5.8	—
1956	4.1	11.1	3.4	4.2	3.6	8.3	4.4	—	2.6	3.7	5.1	5.1

1957	4.3	11.6	3.5	4.1	3.8	7.9	4.6	—	2.8	4.0	6.2	5.3
1958	6.8	15.9	6.2	6.1	6.1	12.6	7.2	—	5.1	7.2	10.2	8.1
1959	5.5	14.6	4.7	5.2	4.8	10.7	5.7	—	3.6	—	7.6	6.6
1960	5.5	14.7	4.7	5.1	4.9	10.2	5.7	—	3.7	—	7.8	6.7
1961	6.7	16.8	5.7	6.3	6.0	12.4	6.8	—	4.6	6.7	9.2	8.0
1962	5.5	14.7	4.6	5.4	4.9	10.9	5.6	—	3.6	—	7.4	6.7
1963	5.7	17.2	4.5	5.4	5.0	10.8	5.5	3.7	3.4	5.5	7.3	6.4
1964	5.2	16.2	3.9	5.2	4.6	9.6	5.0	3.2	2.8	4.9	6.3	5.8
1965	4.5	14.8	3.2	4.5	4.1	8.1	4.3	2.7	2.4	4.2	5.3	5.0
1966	3.8	12.8	2.5	3.8	3.4	7.3	3.5	2.2	1.9	3.5	4.2	4.2
1967	3.8	12.8	2.3	4.2	3.4	7.4	3.6	2.1	1.8	3.4	4.4	4.2
1968	3.6	12.7	2.2	3.8	3.2	6.7	3.4	1.9	1.6	3.1	4.1	4.0
1969	3.5	12.2	2.1	3.7	3.1	6.4	3.3	1.8	1.5	3.1	3.9	3.9
1970	4.9	15.2	3.5	4.8	4.5	8.2	4.8	2.9	2.6	4.5	6.2	5.3
1971	5.9	16.9	4.4	5.7	5.4	9.9	5.7	3.6	3.2	5.5	7.4	6.4
1972	5.6	16.2	4.0	5.4	5.0	10.0	5.3	3.3	2.8	5.1	6.5	6.0

Source: Economic Report of the President

a Married men living with their wives. Data for 1949 and 1951–1954 are for April; 1950, for March.

b Data for 1949–1961 are for May.

c Includes craftsmen, operatives, and nonfarm laborers. Data for 1948–1957 are based on data for January, April, July, and October.

d Man-hours lost by the unemployed and persons on part-time for economic reasons as a percent of potentially available labor force man-hours.

was down to 3.2% of the labor force; but the black teenager living in the urban ghetto suffered from an unemployment rate of 30.4%—worse than white Americans experienced in the depths of the Great Depression of the 1930s.[3] Note that in both boom and depression the black worker is roughly twice as likely to be unemployed as the white. If anything, the data suggest that there may have been a tendency for nonwhite unemployment to increase relative to white unemployment over the last 20 years.

The unemployment rate does not adequately reflect the social costs inflicted by slack times. As can be seen from the data in the last column of Table 2.2, the loss in working time is considerably larger than the unemployment rate; when times are slack many employers distribute the impact among their work force by reducing hours worked by shortening shifts and placing workers on part time. And, of course, in slack times machines as well as workers are idle. While conceptual difficulties make it impossible to measure precisely how much slack exists in manufacturing, Table 2.3 indicates that the extent to which capacity is utilized fluctuates considerably over the course of the business cycle.[4]

*2.3 THE TARGET UNEMPLOYMENT RATE

Many economists have argued that 4% constitutes a reasonable unemployment target for the United States. After all, even a healthy economy

---

[3] The figures on unemployment, particularly for nonwhites, are distorted by the survey "*undercount.*" In spite of the best efforts of the Census Bureau, a fraction of the population is inevitably missed by the enumerators. It has been estimated that the Current Population Survey misses about 13% of the nonwhite population of working age, but only 2% of whites. It was estimated that in 1967 the effect of the "undercount" was to yield a 3.8% unemployment rate instead of 4% for all workers, an error of only 0.2 percentage points; but for all nonwhite workers the true unemployment rate was 8.2% instead of the measured level of 7.3%—that is, an understatement of 0.9 percentage points. For a discussion of the effects of the undercount on unemployment estimates, see *Social and Economic Conditions of Negros in the United States*, Current Population Reports, Series P-23, No. 24 (October 1967), Bureau of Labor Statistics and U.S. Census Bureau, p. 38. For the 1970 Census, Jacob S. Siegel reports that the population undercount ranged from 9.9% for black males to 1.4% for white females; "Estimates of Coverage of the Population by Sex, Race and Age in the 1970 Census," paper presented at the 1973 annual meeting of the Population Association of America.

[4] The data on capacity reported on the table are compiled by the Federal Reserve Board. Their procedure, described in the November 1966 *Federal Reserve Bulletin*, uses data from the McGraw-Hill survey in which firms are asked to rate the extent to which their capacity is being utilized. For a discussion of the McGraw-Hill index and various other measures of excess capacity, see *Measure of Productive Capacity*, Hearings, Subcommittee of Economic Statistics of the Joint Economic Committee, U.S. Government Printing Office, 1962.

Table 2.3   MANUFACTURING OUTPUT, CAPACITY, AND UTILIZATION

Period	Output	Capacity	Utilization Rate (% of Capacity)		
			Total	Primary Processing	Advanced Processing
	1967 Output = 100		*Percent*		
1948	41.5	44.8	92.7	98.1	89.8
1949	39.1	47.3	82.7	83.8	82.1
1950	45.4	49.4	91.9	97.8	88.8
1951	49.3	51.8	95.1	100.1	92.5
1952	50.9	54.9	92.8	91.2	93.7
1953	55.4	58.1	95.5	94.3	96.1
1954	51.4	61.2	84.1	82.9	84.7
1955	58.1	64.4	90.0	93.7	87.7
1956	60.3	68.3	88.2	90.7	86.9
1957	61.1	74.8	84.5	85.2	84.1
1958	56.9	75.7	75.1	75.2	75.0
1959	64.0	78.6	81.4	82.7	80.7
1960	65.3	81.6	80.1	79.4	80.3
1961	65.6	84.5	77.6	78.2	77.3
1962	71.3	87.7	81.4	81.8	81.1
1963	75.7	91.2	83.0	84.0	82.5
1964	81.1	94.8	85.5	88.0	84.2
1965	89.0	100.0	89.0	91.1	87.8
1966	98.1	106.7	91.9	92.1	91.8
1967	99.9	113.7	87.9	85.7	89.1
1968	105.6	120.5	87.7	86.8	88.1
1969	110.4	127.7	86.5	88.5	85.4
1970	105.3	134.6	78.3	81.5	76.5
1971	105.2	140.3	75.0	79.3	72.7
1972	113.0	145.6	77.6	83.5	74.5

Source. Economic Report of the President.

may be expected to experience unemployment as a result of seasonal fluctuations in the demand for labor, particularly in agriculture and construction. And workers in a dynamic economy must adapt to shifting demand and technological advance. Adjustment may involve learning new skills and possibly moving to areas experiencing expansion. For all but the most fortunate, such adjustments may involve a period of transitional unemployment. One indication of the fact that the economy is in a continued state of adjustment is that unfilled job openings may exist simultaneously with substantial unemployment.

The 4% figure, it is often suggested, constitutes a reasonable allowance for such "frictional" factors as well as for the effects of seasonal fluctuations and, if an attempt is made to push unemployment below this target, problems of "overemployment," of inflation, may confront us. It is clear from Table 2.1 that if 4% is regarded as a level of unemployment that should be tolerated, then most of the period between the Korean War and the Viet Nam conflict was characterized by excessive slack in the economy.

Is the 4% target reasonable? In light of our experience in World War II it certainly appears to be a modest objective. Remember, however, that those were years of rapid inflation, of "over-full employment." Nonetheless, the international comparisons of unemployment rates for various countries presented in Figure 2.1 suggest that the 4% target constitutes a modest objective.[5]

After the election of President Kennedy in 1960, a 4% level of unemployment was promulgated by his Council of Economic Advisors as an interim target. By expanding the demand for the nation's output through a comprehensive program of tax reductions the unemployment rate was to be cut to 4% without inflation. In formulating such a policy it is necessary to know how changes in tax rates affect gross national product; it is also necessary to evaluate how alternative policy measures (e.g., increasing government spending or expanding the money supply) affect the demand for the nation's output. But before considering these issues, a prior question demands attention. If the economy is suffering from excess unemployment,

---

[5] While the majority of the countries on the chart experienced more inflation than the United States, both Canada and Germany suffered less from rising prices over the 12-year period recorded on the graph. The data on the graph were presented by Constance Sorrentino in "Unemployment in Nine Industrialized Countries," *Monthly Labor Review*, June 1972. It must be kept in mind in making international comparisons that the unemployment rate is sensitive to certain questions of definition. Is a worker who is laid off with instructions to return to work within 30 days unemployed? Is an individual who has a new job starting within a month also unemployed? Yes, according to the current definition of unemployment. But if these questions were given a negative answer, and if students attending school but starting a job in the following week were classified as not-in-the-labor-force instead of employed, the unemployment figures for the recession year 1954 would be 5% instead of the official 5.6% figure. The figures prepared by Sorrentino were carefully adjusted in order that they would be comparable with official United States data. For example, the figures for Germany and Great Britain are derived from data on registered unemployed as a percent of employed wage and salary workers plus the unemployed. In 1970 the published unemployment rate for Germany was 0.7% and for England 2.6%, but the figures as adjusted by Sorrentino are 0.5% and 4.0%. Furthermore, unemployment data for the United States refer to the over 16 population; the plotted figures are adjusted to coincide as closely as possible with the age at which compulsory schooling ends in each country.

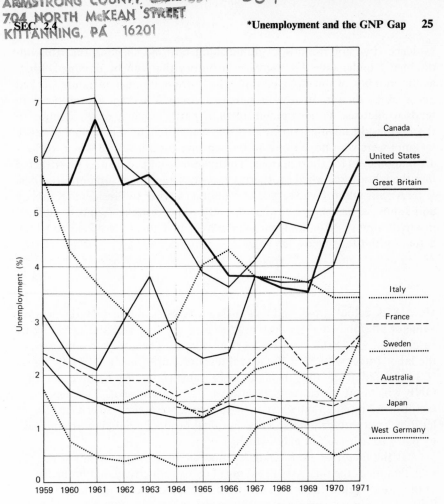

Fig. 2.1 *Unemployment rates in nine countries, 1959–1971.*

how much of an increase in output must be generated in order to cut the unemployment rate to 4%? An answer to this question will also provide a measure of the potential output lost as a result of delays experienced in achieving the desired reduction in unemployment.

*2.4   UNEMPLOYMENT AND THE GNP GAP

It is tempting to argue that when unemployment is at 6%, the gross output of the economy might be increased by 2% by putting these wasted resources to work and reducing the unemployment rate to 4%. Historical evidence (but not the law of diminishing returns) suggests that this undoubtedly understates the increase in output that can be obtained. First, as the number of unemployed falls, the average number of hours worked per week by the typical worker increases. Second, average output per man tends to increase as unemployment falls, partly because of a reduction in the on-the-job unemployment that was generated in the period of slack by employers who hope to avoid the rehiring costs involved when workers are laid off even for short periods. Third, additional people may be attracted into the labor force when prosperity generates additional job opportunities.

Arthur Okun,[6] who served as economic adviser to Presidents Kennedy and Johnson, has suggested that the following formula should be utilized in attempting to estimate from unemployment figures the extent to which actual output falls below capacity.

$$\frac{Y^c - Y}{Y} = 3.2 \left(\frac{L - E}{L} - 0.04 \right) \qquad (4.1)$$

Here Y is actual gross national product (GNP), defined as the market value of all goods and services produced in the economy during the year. In contrast, Y^c is the capacity level of output. The L denotes the size of the labor force, while E is the actual level of employment. The 0.04 figure is subtracted from the unemployment rate, $(L - E)/L$, in order that GNP will be at its capacity level at 4% unemployment. The expansion factor of 3.2 implies that when unemployment is 6% (i.e., exceeds the target level by 2 percentage points), gross national product would have to increase by 6.4% to achieve full employment.[7]

Is the factor of 3.2 in Okun's equation an appropriate allowance for such factors as the increases in average labor productivity and in the length of the work week that can be expected as unemployment falls closer to 4%? Some quite simple computations suggest that Okun's coefficient is not unreasonable. In the first year of recovery from the 1958 recession, real GNP increased by 6.4% while employment increased by only 2.5%, a ratio of 2.6; similar computations made for the first year of recovery from the 1949 and 1954 recessions suggest expansion factors of 3.6 and 2.3, respectively. Okun himself utilized a more sophisticated approach in estimating the expansion coefficient of 3.2 for his equation.

The gap between potential and actual GNP, as initially estimated by Arthur Okun for the Council of Economic Advisers, is reproduced in Figure 2.2 from the 1962 *Economic Report of the President*. In reading

---

[6] "Potential GNP: Its Measurement and Significance," *Proceedings*, American Statistical Association, 1962.

[7] Okun's equation is easily modified to estimate lost output when "full employment" is defined at a different unemployment rate, say 5% or 3%; see Exercise 2.1b.

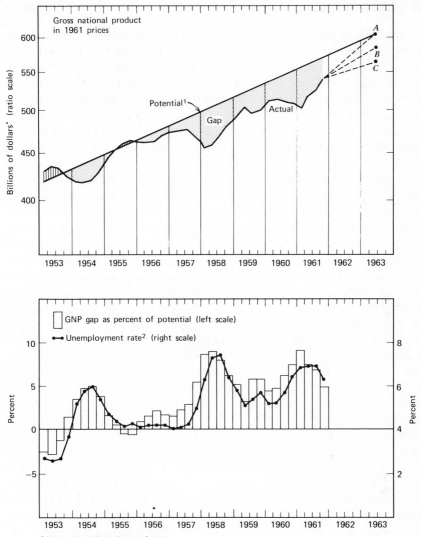

*Seasonally adjusted annual rates.
[1] 3½% trend line through middle of 1955.
[2] Unemployment as percent of civilian labor force; seasonally adjusted.

Note: A, B and C represent GNP in middle of 1963 assuming unemployment
    rate of 4%, 5%, and 6%, respectively.

Fig. 2.2 *Gross national product, actual and potential, and the*
unemployment rate, 1953–1961. (Source. 1962 Economic Report of the President, *p. 52.*)

Figure 2.2 note that there are three statistical details that can be deceptive to the uninitiated. First, in the upper left-hand corner of the graph the reader is advised that GNP is being measured in *"1961 prices."* This means that in every year shown on the graph 1961 prices were used in measuring the value of final product. Serious distortion would have been introduced by inflation if *"current dollar"* GNP figures had been used. For example, with current dollar GNP, 1953 output is measured at 1953 prices, while *real* 1953 GNP is measured with 1961 prices; obviously, a comparison of current instead of constant dollar figures would confound the rise in output with price changes over the decade. The second statistical complication involves the use of quarterly GNP figures at *annual rates*. This means that the point plotted for each quarter indicates four times the actual output in the three-month period. Thus the fact that all four points for 1956 have a height indicating output of about $450 billion does not mean that roughly that amount was produced in each of the four quarters and that the output of goods and services amounted to almost $1.8 trillion for the entire year; quite the contrary, quarterly data at annual rates must be averaged in computing GNP for the entire year.[8] The third statistical complication is hinted at by the words "ratio scale" in labeling the scale of the top panel of the graph, a statement that accounts for the fact that the lines are not evenly spaced on the vertical axis. The scale is squeezed more and more as one approaches the top so that any straight line drawn on the graph will yield a constant *rate* of growth. Regular graph paper might be misleading, since a straight line would yield constant dollar *increments* of growth, but lower *rates* of growth at higher levels of GNP. An alternative to using the ratio scale is to plot the logarithm of potential and actual GNP on regular graph paper.[9]

The estimate of potential GNP plotted on Figure 2.2 was derived with a simplification of the procedure originally suggested by Okun. Specifically, Okun found that essentially the same estimate of potential GNP as derived by Equation 4.1 can be obtained by simply fitting a trend line through mid-1955 GNP with a slope of 3.5%. When this trend line purporting to represent potential GNP was first published in the 1962 *Economic Report of the President*, it constituted an indictment of the current economic situation in that it indicated a substantial gap between actual and potential economic output. It was also a prediction as to the line that actual GNP would have to cross before unemployment would be reduced to 4%.

That Okun accurately predicted the path of potential output that GNP would have to cross in order to reduce unemployment to 4% is sug-

---

[8] Even on a 15-minute drive we report our speed in miles per hour.

[9] For a more complete explanation of logarithmic scales, see Appendix 2.C.

gested by Figure 2.3, which updates the original estimates.[10] Observe that
unemployment did not fall to 4% until actual output crossed the potential
GNP line toward the end of 1965. Furthermore, the two lines touched in
the latter part of 1967, when unemployment creeped up to 4%. They also
crossed in 1969 when unemployment once again began to soar to 4% and
beyond. While the 1962 estimates of potential GNP stand up well in the
light of subsequent developments, the chart reveals that substantial output
was foregone before the economy was restored to full employment.

Needless to say, Okun's estimate of the gap generated heated controversy and was subjected to sharp criticism by Arthur Burns,[11] who had
served as Chairman of the Council of Economic Advisers during the
Eisenhower Administration. More complicated procedures have been developed for estimating the potential output of the economy. Robert Solow[12]
suggested a technique that takes into account the magnitude of the capital
stock. Ronald Soligo[13] has added several further complications in explicitly
taking into account the lags involved in the adjustment process. The estimates of potential GNP are quite sensitive to the procedure employed.
For example, in the recession year 1958 when unemployment was 6.8%,
Soligo's more involved computations suggested that the gap was less than
half of the 9% gap between potential and actual GNP suggested by Okun's
procedure.

It is clear that while unemployment can be measured with some precision, the problem of specifying the appropriate target rate of measured
unemployment that should be regarded as an appropriate policy objective
constitutes an issue open to debate. The answer hinges partly on the extent

[10] The estimate of potential GNP reported in Figure 2.3 is reproduced from *Business
Conditions Digest*, which publishes the graph each month. They use a 3.5% trend line inter-
secting actual GNP in the middle of 1955 through the fourth quarter of 1962; from 1962–
1964 through 1965–1974 they use a 3.75% trend; from 1965–1974 through 1969–1974 the
trend is 4% and from 1969–1974 the trend growth is 4.3%. Since the potential line appears
to be almost straight, these changes do not materially influence the potential GNP estimate.
The estimates after 1968 are not official Council of Economic Adviser figures, which ceased
regular publication of the series.

[11] Burns criticized the Council's "New Stagnation Theory" in an address delivered
at the University of Chicago in April 1961; the speech was published in the *Morgan Guar-
anty Survey*, May 1961. Subsequently, the matter was debated by Burns and the Council
before the Joint Economic Committee. The whole discussion is reproduced in *Business
Fluctuations, Growth and Economic Stabilization*, a book of readings edited by John J.
Clark and Morris Cohen, Random House, 1963, pp. 492–525.

[12] "Technical Progress, Capital Formation, and Economic Growth," *American Economic Review*, May 1962.

[13] "The Short-Run Relationship Between Employment and Output," *Yale Economic
Essays*, Spring 1966.

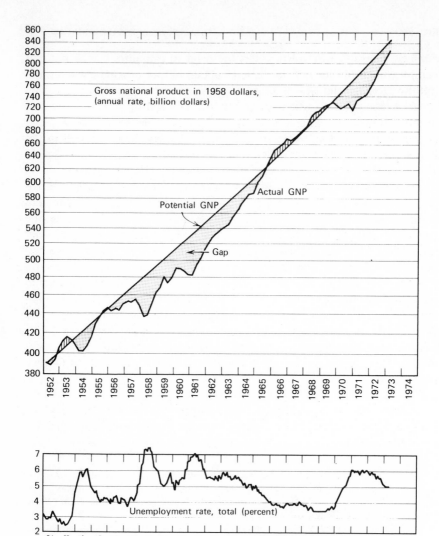

Fig. 2.3 *Actual and potential GNP and the unemployment rate.*

to which measures to push the economy toward full employment will also tend to generate inflation; this, and problems of over-full employment will be considered in later chapters. But the task of diagnosis is further complicated by the obvious difficulties involved in translating a full-employment objective into an estimate of the extent to which the effective demand for the nation's output must be stimulated. In addition to the problem of diagnosing the extent of the gap between potential and actual output, it will be necessary to understand the way in which government spending, tax legislation, and monetary policy influence the level of economic activity.

REFERENCES

1. The Okun reference contains his original presentation of the relationship that has become known as "Okun's law." Levy reviews a variety of alternative estimates of the gap between potential and actual output.

    Arthur M. Okun, "Potential GNP: Its Measurement and Significance," *Proceedings of the Business and Economics Statistics Section of the American Statistical Association*, 1962.

    Michael Levy, "Potential GNP: Concepts and Measurement," Chapter 5 of *Fiscal Policy, Cycles and Growth*, National Industrial Conference Board, 1963.

2. Denison, Juster, and Nordhaus-Tobin are all concerned with the distinction between the growth in economic output as measured by the GNP accounts and the growth in welfare.

    Edward F. Denison, "Welfare Measurement and the GNP, *Survey of Current Business*, January 1971.

    F. Thomas Juster, "On the Measurement of Economic and Social Performance," in *50th Annual Report*, National Bureau of Economic Research, 1970, pp. 8–25.

    William Nordhaus and James Tobin, "Is Growth Obsolete?," *Economic Growth*, Fiftieth Anniversary Colloquium V, National Bureau of Economic Research, 1972.

3. The following three items discuss different facets of the unemployment problem.

    Joseph A. Hickey, "A Report on State Unemployment Insurance Laws," *Monthly Labor Review*, January 1972, pp. 40–50.

    David A. Shannon, *The Great Depression*, Prentice-Hall, 1960.

    Constance Sorrentino, "Unemployment in Nine Industrialized Countries," *Monthly Labor Review*, June 1972, pp. 29–33.

KEY CONCEPTS

labor force versus the unemployment rate

frictional unemployment versus full employment

seasonal unemployment

capacity utilization rate

GNP gap

Okun's law

census undercount

potential GNP

EXERCISES

2.1 a. If unemployment is 6%, approximately what percentage of the nation's capacity is not being utilized?

b. How would you modify Okun's law (Equation 2.4.1) if you wished to determine the level of capacity output corresponding to a 3.5% unemployment rate?

2.2 Consider the following editorial, that appeared on September 15, 1965 in the *Pittsburgh Press*:

"Each month Bureau of Census agents interview . . . about one in 1800 of the country's households on their employment status. Each person 14 or over who claims to be seeking work, whether or not he or she needs a job or has ever held one, becomes statistical evidence as it works out of nearly 2,000 unemployed.

"The resulting figures, as released by BLS, usually give a seemingly shocking view of unemployment in the midst of plenty. Currently they show 3,500,000 unemployed—4.5 percent of the labor force—despite a prolonged boom. What they do not show is that only a small fraction of these should be classified as jobless in the sense of really needing a job."

Write an essay evaluating this statement.

2.3 Explain the implications of a *negative* GNP gap.

2.4 Estimate the economic cost to the United States economy of the Great Depression of the 1930s. [*Hints.* You might find it helpful to use Okun's law. For example, Equation 2.4.1 might be used to determine the level of potential output in each year of the depression (but it would be surprising if the parameters that Okun estimated for the 1960s held without modification for the pre-World War II period). Alternatively, plotting a potential output trend line similar to Figure 2.2 might help in estimating potential output in the Great Depression. One major data source is the *Economic Report of the President*; other possible data sources are listed in Appendix 2.A, "Guide to Sources of Economic Data." And flip ahead to Table 3.1 for GNP data.]

2.5 How closely related during the business cycle are black and white unemployment conditions in the United States? [*Hints.* One possible strategy would be to plot one dot for each year on a graph with the white unemployment rate on the horizontal axis and the black unemployment rate on the ordinate. (Figure 3.2 illustrates the technique.) Does a straight line fit your scatterplot fairly well? How valid is the statement that black unemployment usually runs at twice the white unemployment rate?]

2.6 Try graphing a slight variant of Okun's Law to GNP and unemployment data.

$$\frac{Y_{t+1} - Y_t}{Y_t} = a + b(U_{t+1} - U_t)$$

Here Y_t is this year's GNP, Y_{t+1} next year's GNP, and U_t the current unemployment rate. (*Hints.* You can plot the rate of change in GNP on the vertical axis and the change in unemployment on the horizontal axis. The slope of your line is the estimate of b; the line's intercept is the estimate of a. The unemployment data are on Table 2.1; you will find GNP data on Table 3.1.) If you substitute 4% for U_{t+1} your equation will yield a prediction of how high GNP would have to rise in order to attain that unemployment rate. This suggests that we might write:

$$\frac{Y_{t+1}^p - Y_t}{Y_t} = a + b(4\% - U_t)$$

Thus output must grow at rate a if unemployment is to be constant. (Why would you expect a to be positive?) How do your estimates of a and b compare with the coefficients in Okun's law?

APPENDIX 2.A GUIDE TO SOURCES OF ECONOMIC DATA

Government officials were handicapped in the 1930s by the lack of precise information concerning the seriousness of the Great Depression. Detailed estimates of unemployment were not available prior to the establishment of the Census Bureau's Current Population Survey in 1941. At the time no one knew the precise size of the labor force or the exact magnitude of the unemployment rate, although economic historians now have quite detailed information. The *Federal Reserve Bulletin* did publish monthly data on the state of the economy; for example, the March 1933 issue had about six pages of data on industrial production, construction activity, factory employment, freight carloadings, the balance of payments, and department store sales. But antirecession policy was not guided by detailed figures concerning the magnitude of gross national product. National income figures were not being compiled regularly on a systematic basis.

The precise diagnosis of economic conditions requires reliable economic intelligence. Equally important, an inadequate data base hampers the attempts of scholars to learn more about how economic policies can alleviate economic maladjustment. Fortunately, the art of compiling accurate and up-to-date information on the state of the economy has been revolutionized within the last quarter of a century. Indeed, just learning to find one's way through the overwhelming supply of alternative data sources has become a problem. One must also learn to appreciate the limitations of various types of data.

An ideal compendium of economic data would satisfy a number of competing requirements. It would be up to date, which means it must be published at least monthly. But it would also contain historical series in order that current developments may be judged in perspective. It would include graphs of major series in order that trends and cyclical movements can be tracked visually. It would contain a depth of detail in areas that are likely to attract the interest of the specialized user. Furthermore, it would contain detailed descriptions and definitions in order that the data will be properly interpreted by the user. But the ideal data source would also be compact so that the reader will not be lost in a maze of detail. Obviously, no single source can satisfy all these requirements, and the first problem faced by anyone desiring to learn about the state of the economy is to determine which particular data sources will best meet ones personal requirements. Here is an annotated list.

Economic Indicators. This 30-page monthly publication of the Joint Economic Committee, Congress of the United States, summarizes in convenient graphical and tabular form the most widely used economic time series. From time to time a *Supplement to Economic Indicators* is published; this booklet presents important material describing the various data series as well as historical time series.

Economic Report of the President. This annual publication is one of the most useful sources of data on the general state of the economy. Included are the national income accounts, employment conditions, price and wage data, financial statistics, and information on the balance of payments.

Survey of Current Business. Perhaps the most complete monthly source of basic economic data, this Department of Commerce publication also presents objective discussion of current economic developments. It presents detailed national income and price information; it includes industry data on shipments, employment, orders, inventories, and price movements. *Business Statistics* is a biennial supplement presenting historical statistics and detailed descriptions of the individual series. In addition, a weekly supplement provides for immediate release of weekly and monthly data that become available subsequent to the latest monthly issue of the *Survey of Current Business.*

Federal Reserve Bulletin. The Board of Governors of the Federal Reserve System publishes this fundamental source of data on banking and monetary developments each month. Articles analyzing current monetary developments appear regularly.

Business Conditions Digest. This monthly publication the Bureau of the Census presents graphs of about 150 economic indicators that are thought to be particularly useful in judging current economic trends.

Monthly Labor Review. This basic source of data on labor conditions and price movements is published monthly by the Department of Labor. *Employment and Earnings* gives more detailed information on employment.

International Financial Statistics. The International Monetary Fund publishes monthly data on economic conditions in most of the countries of the world, including balance of payment details.

Statistical Abstract of the United States. This annual publication of social statistics presents detailed data on topics ranging from measures of air pollution in various cities to the number of degrees conferred annually in zoology. It contains an alphabetical listing by subject of primary sources of statistical information on the United States. It is supplemented by *Historical Statistics of the United States, Colonial Times to 1957.*

A more detailed description of United States statistical data sources is provided by the excellent volume on *Government Statistics for Business Use,* edited by Philip M. Hauser and William R. Leonard.[14] For a more general discussion see Ralph L. Andreano, Evan I. Farber, and Sabron Reynolds, *The Student Economist's Handbook, A Guide to Sources*[15] or Leonard S. Silk and M. Louise Curley, *A Primer on Business Forecasting.*[16]

APPENDIX 2.B   ON ERRORS OF MEASUREMENT

In the laboratory it may be possible to measure certain phenomena with extreme precision but, in every field of research, there are variables that cannot be

[14] John Wiley, 2nd edition, 1956.
[15] Schenkman Publishers, 1967.
[16] Random House, 1970.

measured with the desired degree of accuracy. It is important to recognize the extent to which errors of measurement contaminate economic data.[17] We will briefly discuss measurement errors encountered in the national income accounts and in unemployment estimates.

2.B.1 REVISIONS OF THE GNP ACCOUNTS

In judging economic conditions it is extremely important to have fresh data. For this reason national income accountants release preliminary estimates of gross national product at the earliest possible date. The data are subjected to successive revisions as additional evidence accumulates from tax returns, periodic censuses, and other sources. While the revisions may not be large relative to the magnitude of GNP, they are of such magnitude as to suggest that the preliminary figures should be viewed with caution.[18] This is revealed by the data in Table 2.B.1, which reports successive revisions for four recent business recessions. Thus the third row of the table reveals that in February 1950 the readers of the *Survey of Current Business* were informed that 1949 output of $257.4 billion was off some $5 billion from the output of $262.4 billion that had been achieved in 1948. In the July 1950 issue readers would learn that the recent recession had not been nearly as severe as these preliminary figures had suggested, and more recent Department of Commerce estimates suggest that the decline was only about $1 billion, or one fifth of the original estimate. Inspection of the data on the table suggests that there appears to be a systematic tendency for the preliminary figures to overstate the intensity of business recessions. Perhaps this bias in the preliminary data serves to generate undue pessimism during the critical postrecession recovery stage of the business cycle.[19] Fortunately, when statistical procedures are used with preliminary data in estimating economic relationships, the results are usually quite close to recomputed estimates obtained later when revised GNP series become available.[20]

The fact that many economic time series, not just the GNP accounts, are subject to revision means that care is required whenever one is interested in obtaining an economic time series covering a number of years. For example, if you desire data on unfilled orders in manufacturing on a monthly basis from 1955 to date,

[17] The classic work on this topic is Oscar Morgenstern, *On the Accuracy of Economic Observations*, Princeton University Press, 1950.

[18] Arnold Zellner has subjected the problem to statistical analysis in "A Statistical Analysis of Provisional Estimates of Gross National Product and its Components, of Selected National Income Components, and Personal Saving," *Journal of the American Statistical Association*, 53, pp. 54–65, March 1958. For a more recent study see Rosanne Cole, *Errors in Provisional Estimates of Gross National Product*, National Bureau of Economic Research, 1969.

[19] The bias is not apparent in the annual GNP accounts for the 1960–1961 recessions, since that "downturn" does not show up in terms of an actual decline in annual GNP; the increase in GNP from 1960 to 1961 ranges from 15.282 to 16.9, depending on which issue of the *Survey of Current Business* one chooses to inspect.

[20] See the interesting study of F. T. Denton and E. H. Oksanen, "Multi-Country Analysis of Effects of Data Revisions on an Econometric Model," *Journal of the American Statistical Association*, June 1972, pp. 286–291.

Table 2.B.1 REVISIONS OF GROSS NATIONAL PRODUCT DATA (BILLIONS OF CURRENT DOLLARS)

Date of Downturn	Source: Survey of Current Business, (Date and Page)	Gross National Product		
		Peak	Trough	Change
1948–1949	2/1949	254.9		
	7/1949	262.434		
	2/1950, p. 8	262.4	257.4	−5.0
	7/1950, p. 9	259.071	255.578	−3.493
	2/1952, p. 9		257.3	
	7/1952, p. 13	259.045	258.229	−0.816
	7/1954, p. 5	257.325	257.301	−0.024
	7/1958, p. 5	259.426	258.054	−1.362
	8/1965, p. 25	257.562	256.484	−1.078
1953–1954	2/1954	367.2		
	4/1954	364.857		
	2/1955, p. 14	364.9	357.2	−7.7
	7/1955, p. 9	364.520	360.474	−4.046
	7/1956, p. 11	363.218	360.654	−2.564
	7/1957, p. 9	363.218	361.167	−2.051
	7/1958, p. 5	365.385	363.122	−2.273
	8/1965, p. 25	364.593	364.841	−0.258
1957–1958	2/1958, p. 8	434.4		
	7/1958, p. 5	440.328		
	2/1959, p. 12	440.3	437.7	−2.6
	7/1959, p. 7	442.502	441.702	−0.8
	7/1960, p. 8	442.769	444.224	+1.455
	7/1961, p. 6	442.769	444.546	+1.777
	8/1965, p. 25	441.134	447.334	+6.200

you should start with the current issue of the *Survey of Current Business* and go to earlier issues for less recent dates not reported in the current issue. And by carefully reading footnotes you may discover that the revised figures are reported for the period of interest to you in a special section of an issue of the *Survey of Current Business*. As you work further back, you would find it convenient to pick the earlier figures from one of the supplements to the *Survey of Current Business* (e.g., *Income and Output* would have the figures on orders for the period 1957–1960). You should be careful to note changes in classification and coverage and whether the data have been subjected to adjustment that filters out typical seasonal movements. In addition, the footnotes in the supplements to the *Survey of Current Business* should be checked carefully for background information on how the data are collected and classified.

2.B.2　THE STATISTICAL DISCREPANCY

Occasionally there exists more than one way of measuring the same economic variable, and this presents an opportunity for a statistical discrepancy—the magnitude of the discrepancy provides an indication of the extent of measurement error. For example, we know conceptually that precisely the same figure should be obtained by either adding together the incomes earned from participating in the production process or by summing the market value of all goods and services produced in the economy during the same period—provided that certain complications arising from such factors as indirect taxes are appropriately taken into account. But this accounting identity is not realized in practice because certain components of the national income accounts cannot be measured precisely. The gap between the two conceptually identical figures is reported as the "statistical discrepancy" in the national income accounts. The figure is usually small in magnitude relative to GNP, ranging from − $6.4 billion in 1970 to $3.9 billion in 1945. But the discrepancy can be large relative to *changes* in output; for example, GNP is estimated to have increased from $986.3 billion to $989.7 billion from the third to the fourth quarter of 1970; but this coincided with a change in the statistical discrepancy from − $4.0 billion to − $1.0 billion, which accounts for practically the entire $3.4 billion output change.

2.B.3　SAMPLING ERROR IN THE UNEMPLOYMENT ESTIMATES

Because the Census Bureau interviews only a fraction of households each month for the Current Population Survey, sampling errors are to be expected in the unemployment figures. Fortunately, the scientific procedures employed in designing the survey enable statisticians to estimate the magnitude of this problem. The standard error for consecutive month-to-month changes in unemployment is 80,000. This means that in a month in which a complete and accurate census would have revealed no change in unemployment, the chances are 1 out of 3 that the survey would suggest a change, positive or negative, of more than 80,000; but the chance of the survey suggesting a change of 160,000 or more in either direction is only 1 in 20 in any month in which actual unemployment is unchanged. Thus the change in unemployment from July to August 1964 of 159,000 would not be considered by statisticians to be significant at the 5% level. For a more detailed discussion of sampling procedures, see any recent issue of *Employment and Earnings*, a publication of the Bureau of Labor Statistics.

While it is possible every 10 years to compare the sample survey estimates with the complete count of unemployed provided by the decennial census of population, the census estimates are generally thought to be *less* accurate than the survey because of enumerator error arising from the fact that the temporary personnel hired for conducting the census are not as well equipped by training and experience for the interviewing task. On the basis of a careful evaluation of estimation procedures, a specially appointed impartial President's Committee to Appraise Employment and Unemployment concluded that "the survey tends to underestimate by a small percentage the number of unemployed persons. In this it appears to share, though to a lesser degree, the tendency of the population census to under-count the unemployed."[21]

2.B.4 REGIONAL UNEMPLOYMENT ESTIMATES

A geographic breakdown of the unemployment figure is useful for anyone interested in the regional incidence of unemployment. Indeed, the information is required for the administration of a variety of governmental programs. For ex-ample, the amount of unemployment in a region was the principal criterion for the allocation of funds to different areas under the Area Redevelopment Act of 1961 and the Manpower Development and Training Act of 1962. Unfortunately, the Current Population Survey does not yield publishable information for individual states and cities.

The Bureau of Employment Security does provide monthly estimates on un-employment for individual states and regions on the basis of data for insured un-employment. Although an attempt is made to adjust the figures for the presence of unemployed workers not covered by the insurance provisions, this is not an easy task, since the conditions of eligibility differ from state to state. Joseph C. Ullman checked the figures for April 1960 by comparison with decennial census of popula-tion figures.[22] His computations revealed sizable discrepancies, as may be seen from Table 2.B.2. Thus the Bureau of Employment Security overestimated the number of unemployed in New Jersey in the spring of 1960 by 33.8%. It underestimated New Mexico unemployment by more than 50%. Some discrepancy is to be expected because of the differences in definition; for example, workers idled by bad weather or on unpaid vacation are considered employed by the Census Bureau, while they are regarded as unemployed by the Bureau of Employment Security. But the erratic nature of the discrepancies reported on the table indicates that the error is not a systematic bias explicable in terms of variations in terminology. Fortunately, the estimation procedure has benefited from continued refinement and improvement.

2.B.5 ON DEFINING UNEMPLOYMENT

The line of demarcation that conceptually segregates the employed from the unemployed is a ticklish one to draw. For example, should the Census Bureau classify as employed or as unemployed a worker who has been laid off from his job with instructions to return to work within 30 days? At one time such a worker would have been counted among the employed by the compilers of labor force data, but under the revised definitions adopted in January 1957, such a person is considered unemployed. Similarly, an idle worker waiting to start a new job within 30 days had previously been classified as employed; under the new definitions he is regarded as unemployed. However, a person waiting to start a new business or a new farm in 30 days is classified as employed under both the old and new defini-tions. How about the student who is scheduled to start a new job at the end of the

---

[21] *Measuring Employment and Unemployment*, President's Committee to Appraise Employment and Unemployment Statistics, U. S. Government Printing Office, 1962, p. 158.

[22] "How Accurate are Estimates of State and Local Unemployment?" *Industrial and Labor Relations Review*, *16*, April 1963.

Table 2.B.2 ALTERNATIVE ESTIMATES OF STATE AND CITY UNEMPLOYMENT FOR APRIL 1960

Geographic Region	Discrepancy[a]
New Mexico	+56.7%
Michigan	−4.6
West Virginia	−18.2
Pennsylvania	−21.5
New Jersey	−33.8
Detroit	+17.7
Meriden, Connecticut	−53.3
Cleveland	+10.6
Pittsburgh	−5.5

[a] The discrepancy is the excess of the Census Bureau estimate of unemployment in April 1960 over the Bureau of Employment Security estimate for the same date.

Table 2.B.3 EFFECT OF DEFINITIONAL CHANGES ON MEASURED UNEMPLOYMENT

Year	Unemployment Rate (Percent)		
	Old Definitions	New Definitions	Difference
1947	3.6	3.9	0.3
1948	3.4	3.8	0.4
1949	5.5	5.9	0.4
1950	5.0	5.3	0.3
1951	3.0	3.3	0.3
1952	2.7	3.1	0.4
1953	2.5	2.9	0.4
1954	5.0	5.6	0.6
1955	4.0	4.4	0.4
1956	3.8	4.2	0.4
1957	4.0	4.3	0.3

Source. Economic Report of the President, 1960, p. 175.

Note. Effective January 1957, persons on layoff with definite instructions to return to work within 30 days of layoff and persons waiting to start new wage and salary jobs within the following 30 days are classified as unemployed. Such persons had previously been classified as employed (with a job but not at work). The combined total of the groups changing classification has averaged about 200,000 to 300,000 a month. The small number of persons in school during the survey week and waiting to start new businesses or start new farms within 30 days continue to be classified as employed.

semester? Prior to 1957 he was considered employed, but he is now excluded from the labor force.

Such definitional issues sound picayune, but they would constitute a serious problem if it were true that the unemployment rate were quite sensitive to minor changes in definition. Fortunately, the effect is not large, as Table 2.B.3 indicates. Although the revision in estimates cause a minor increase in the level of unemployment, the effect is small, and it does not seriously distort the fluctuations in the series.[23]

APPENDIX 2.C SEMILOGARITHMIC (RATIO) CHARTS, GEOMETRIC GROWTH, AND COMPOUND INTEREST—A SURVEY

2.C.1 ARITHMETIC VERSUS GEOMETRIC GROWTH

The distinction between arithmetic and geometric growth is illustrated in Figure 2.C.1. Arithmetic growth involves a constant increment being added each period, as with the steps on a ladder or a ramp of constant slope. With geometric growth the increment is proportional to the size of the phenomenon. Money left on deposit in your savings bank grows geometrically.

If we let the subscript t indicate the date of the variable, the process of arithmetic growth is described by the following equation.

$$Y_t = Y_{t-1} + k \tag{1.1}$$

For example, with $t = 1971$, we have

$$Y_{1971} = Y_{1970} + k$$

and again, setting $t = 1972$, we find

$$Y_{1972} = Y_{1971} + k$$

Substitution yields

$$Y_{1972} = (Y_{1970} + k) + k = Y_{1970} + 2k$$

And in general, for *any year t*

$$Y_t = Y_{1970} + (t - 1970)k \tag{1.2}$$

While the increment (k) is constant with arithmetic growth, with geometric growth the increase is proportional to the size of the phenomenon. If we had de-

---

[23] The wording of the questionnaire has been changed from time to time. For example, more detailed questioning concerning reasons for nonparticipation in the work force has been undertaken beginning in 1969. Hopefully, the effect on the aggregate unemployment rate is minor. See Paul O. Flaim, "New Data on Persons Not in the Labor Force," *Employment and Earnings*, December 1969, pp. 4–8.

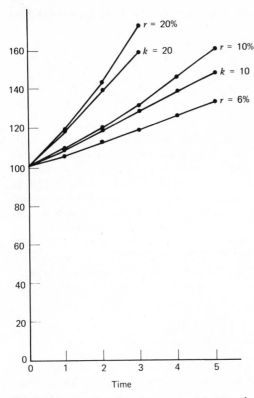

Fig. 2.C.1 *Arithmetic versus geometric growth.*

posited a principal of $100 in our savings bank on December 31, 1970, at 6% per annum interest we would have at the end of 1971

$$\$100 + 0.06 \times \$100 = \$106$$

And if we had left the $106 on deposit we would have at the end of 1972

$$\$106 + 0.06 \times \$106 = \$112.36$$

The interest earned in the second period of $6.36 is larger than that of the first period because we earn interest on the interest left on deposit. Note that

$$\$112.36 = 1.06 \times \$106 = (1.06 \times 1.06 \times \$100) = (1.06)^2 \, \$100$$

And if we leave the money on deposit we will have at the end of year t

$$(1.06)^{t-1970} \times \$100$$

More generally, at the end of year t we would have

$$Y_t = (1 + r)Y_{t-1} \tag{1.3}$$

$$= (1 + r)^{(t-1970)} Y_{1970} \tag{1.4}$$

if we had placed Y_{1970} on deposit at annual interest rate r. From Equation 1.3 we have

$$Y_t - Y_{t-1} = rY_{t-1}$$

and so

$$\frac{Y_t - Y_{t-1}}{Y_{t-1}} = r$$

when growth is geometric.

　　While some banks pay "6% per annum" interest compounded annually, others compound interest twice a year.[24] Thus, at the end of six months, the principal plus accumulated interest on a $100 deposit is $103; interest is credited on this sum for the second half of the year, yielding $1.03 \times \$103 = \$106.09$. That is, money compounded semiannually at 6% earns the equivalent of funds deposited at 6.09% interest compounded once a year. Other banks preserve a still more competitive edge by compounding quarterly: at the end of the first three months a total of $101.50 is put to work to become $103.0225 at the end of six months, $104.5678 after nine months and a total of $106.1363 by the end of the year. When interest is compounded monthly, a sum of $106.1516 is accumulated each year. In general, if a deposit of Y_t earning interest at annual rate r is compounded k times a year, the resulting sum after one year is

$$Y_{t+1} = \left(1 + \frac{r}{k}\right)^k Y_t \qquad (1.5)$$

This equation could be used to compound funds daily or hourly. Indeed, funds can be compounded *continuously*. As explained later in this appendix, a fund growing at 6% per annum compounded continuously grows at the same rate as funds earning 6.18% per annum compounded annually.

2.C.2   EXPONENTS AND LOGARITHMS

　　Multiplication is harder than addition, but logarithms enable us to convert the former problem into the latter. To see how, it is first necessary to recall the *Law of Exponents*:

$$B^m \cdot B^n = B^{m+n} \qquad (2.1)$$

a.   Four Examples

1. If $1 placed on deposit by mother for m years is inherited by her son Nathan, who leaves it on deposit for n more years, the total amount at the end of the entire $m + n$ years is $\$1 \cdot (1 + r)^{(m+n)}$.
2. $100 = 10 \times 10 = 10^2$ and $1000 = 10 \times 100 = 10^1 \times 10^2 = 10^3$.
3. $B^{-1} = 1/B$, and so with $m = 1$ and $n = -1$ the law of exponents states the obvious fact that $B/B = B^{(1-1)} = B^0 = 1$.

---

[24] Banking regulations have prescribed the maximum annual rate of interest that can be paid on deposits, but not the frequency at which it is compounded.

4. If a sum of money placed on deposit in 1970 earns interest at 6% compounded k times per year, by year t we will have accumulated (see Equation 1.5):

$$Y_t = \left(1 + \frac{0.06}{k}\right)^{k(t-1970)} Y_{1970} \tag{2.2}$$

The *logarithm* of a number X to the base B is defined as the power to which B has to be raised to equal X. Thus $B^{\log_B X} = X$ by definition! That this is indeed a convenient concept is illustrated by the law of exponents. Because $B^{\log_B X} = X$ and $B^{\log_B Y} = Y$, $XY = B^{\log_B X + \log_B Y}$, and we have from Equation 2.1 the important fact:

$$\log_B(XY) = \log_B X + \log_B Y \tag{2.3}$$

For example, if $X = 100$ and $Y = 10$ and we choose $B = 10$, then $\log_{10} X = 2$ and $\log_{10} Y = 1$ and $\log(XY) = \log X + \log Y = 3$; that is, $XY = 10^3 = 1000$. That is obvious, but when the Quantity Theory of Money is introduced in Chapter 5, Section 2, it will be convenient to note that the proposition that

$$\mathbf{M}v = pY$$

(here $\mathbf{M}$ is the money supply, v its velocity of circulation, p the price level, and Y real output) can also be written as[25]

$$\log \mathbf{M} + \log v = \log p + \log Y$$

2.C.3 GEOMETRIC GROWTH AND SEMILOGARITHMIC CHARTS

Consider initial sum Y_0 growing at compound interest at rate r. After two periods we have $Y_2 = (1 + r)(1 + r)Y_0$. More generally, after t periods we have

$$\log Y_t = t\log(1 + r) + \log Y_0 \tag{3.1}$$

When this relationship is plotted with time on the horizontal axis we have a straight line with *intercept* $\log Y_0$ and *slope* $\log(1 + r)$. This means that if we plot the logs of a variety of variables all growing at the same rate (e.g., money on deposit in a number of savings accounts) the lines will all have the same slope; however, their intercepts will differ unless they all have the same initial value. To sum up, when the logarithm of any fund growing at a constant rate is plotted against time, we will obtain a straight line; the steeper the line, the faster the rate of growth. And Equation 3.1 holds regardless of the base of the logarithms that one is employing.

Instead of looking up the logarithms of each item and plotting them on standard graph paper, one can save considerable effort by using semilogarithmic paper. The original values can be plotted directly on the semilogarithmic paper because the scale has been squeezed appropriately so that precisely the same line is obtained. This is illustrated by the examples in Figure 2.C.2. Note that the arithmetic growth

---

[25] The statement holds regardless of the base B; however, when the base is not specified it is usually assumed that we are talking about logarithms to the base 10, the so-called "common" logarithms.

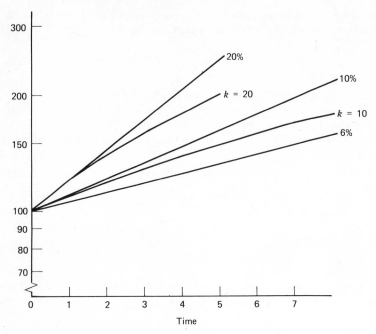

Fig. 2.C.2   *Semilogarithmic scale.*

lines bend down, while those displaying constant geometric growth are straight. For examples of semilogarithmic graphs, see Figures 2.2 and 2.3.

2.C.4   NATURAL LOGARITHMS AND THE CONTINUOUS COMPOUNDING OF INTEREST

Equation 2.2 revealed how a sum of money grows at annual interest rate r when the bank compounds the accumulated interest k times a year. But suppose that instead of compounding interest quarterly, weekly, or hourly, the bank continuously compounds the funds? It turns out that

$$\lim_{k \to \infty} \left(1 + \frac{r}{k}\right)^{kt} = e^{rt} \tag{4.1}$$

where e equals approximately 2.71828. Thus, if Y_{1970} is compounded continuously at rate r, we have at the end of period t:

$$Y_t = \lim_{k \to \infty} \left(1 + \frac{r}{k}\right)^{k(t-1970)} Y_{1970} = Y_{1970} e^{r(t-1970)} \tag{4.2}$$

Using logarithms to any base B:

$$\log_B Y_t = \log_B Y_{1970} + r(t - 1970)\log_B e$$

The most convenient base for the logarithms, as John Napier (1550–1617) recognized long ago, is obtained by setting $B = e$, since then $\log_B e = 1$ and this last equation reduces to

$$\log_e Y_t = \log_e Y_{1970} + r(t - 1970)$$

Many natural phenomena are conveniently described as growing at a continuously compounded rate; for example, the height of a tree may best be described as a continuous function of time. This also holds for many economic phenomenon. The fact that GNP is only measured at discrete points of time does not mean that it is inconvenient to consider its growth as being compounded continuously. It is customary to abbreviate $\log_e$ as ln, and we have as the general proposition that a magnitude growing at rate r, continuously compounded, is

$$\ln Y(t) = \ln Y(0) + rt \tag{4.3}$$

where $Y(0)$ is its magnitude at initial date 0. Finally, note that $\ln e^{rt} = rt$ *by definition*, consequently

$$Y(t) = Y(0)e^{rt} \tag{4.4}$$

elementary multiplier theory

*3.1 INTRODUCTION

Developed in the Great Depression of the 1930s, multiplier analysis is particularly helpful when widespread unemployment reveals, in accordance with Okun's law, that the economy is operating well below capacity levels. Multiplier theory provides an elementary explanation of how changes in the level of government spending and tax policy can be used to stimulate the pace of economic activity.

The basic variables of the multiplier model are:

Y gross national product.
C consumption spending.
Y_d disposable income.
I gross investment.
X exports.
M imports.
G government spending on goods and services.

Gross national product is the market value of all goods and services produced in the economy.[1] Disposable income constitutes the flow of after-tax purchasing power received by consumers, while consumption is the amount they choose to spend on goods and services. These first three variables are *endogenous* and are to be determined by the model. In contrast, the last four variables of this model are regarded as *exogenous* and will not be explained by the system. Investment constitutes the sum of residential construction, new plant and equipment spending, and the change in business inventories. Government spending, the control variable, is to be manipulated in an attempt to stabilize output. The multiplier explains the affects

---

[1] Only "final product" is counted; for example, while the value of the loaf of bread sold by the baker is included in GNP, the flour used by the baker in making the bread is not counted. However, any increase in the baker's inventory of flour on hand would be included.

of changes in **G**, the control variable, on *Y* and *C*, assuming that changes in **G** do not affect the other exogenous variables.

The basic building blocks of the multiplier model are introduced in the next section of this chapter. Then, in Section 3, a numerical example illustrates the way in which an increase in government spending can induce a much larger increase in output; this is the essence of the multiplier concept. Section 4 uses a simple graphical device in examining the affects on *Y* of tax cuts and changes in **G**. Then a variety of spending and tax multipliers are developed algebraically. Finally, a more detailed analysis of tax policy is presented in Section 6. The reader is forewarned that the multiplier model abstracts from monetary complications and price changes. But studying the multiplier process will provide a basic framework to be elaborated on in later chapters when the time comes to study the process of inflation, balance of payments equilibrium, and the sources of economic growth.

*3.2 AN IDENTITY AND TWO BEHAVIORAL EQUATIONS

The flow of goods and services available during the year is GNP plus imports from foreign countries, and the uses of this supply may be classified into the categories of consumption, investment, exports, and government spending; that is,

$$Y + M = C + I + G + X$$

Subtracting imports from both sides yields the fundamental national income accounting identity:

$$Y = C + I + G + X - M \qquad (2.1)$$

This expression holds because national income accountants exercise care in defining the individual components of GNP, but certain of their definitions do not conform to popular usage.

G (government) denotes spending by federal, state, and local governments on goods and services. Wages earned by government employees count, but *transfer payments* received by veterans, by the unemployed, and by those who have retired or are on welfare are excluded, since they are not payments for current productive services.

I (gross investment) is not the purchase of stocks and bonds from a broker. Instead, it is the construction of new houses, the building of factories, and the installation of new machinery that put men and materials to work. Investment is defined by the national income accountant as the part of current output that is set aside to contribute to the production of future instead of current satisfaction. *Gross investment* is an overstatement of this contribution to the nation's physical stock of productive capital, since it is computed without appropriate deductions for the wear and tear on existing plant and equipment. In contrast, *net investment* deducts an allowance for capital consumption (depreciation). In figuring the amount of investment it does not matter whether the new factory building or house is financed through a hefty mortgage from the bank or from funds accumulated over the years. Regardless of how it is financed, the entire cost of the factory building or new house is included in *I*.

C (consumption) or more precisely "personal consumption expenditures," includes spending for such nondurables as food and clothing plus funds spent on such durables as washing machines and automobiles. It cannot include the cost of buying a new home, which is already in *I*. And it excludes consumer interest payments. But the costs of a variety of services are included. Medical treatment, haircuts, and rental payments for a house or apartment are all part of *C*.

As always, accounting definitions must be tempered in the light of practical problems of measurement. For example, the expense of attaining a college education might be classified as investment, but the national income accountant considers such additions to the stock of *human capital* as current consumption spending; neither the national income accountant nor the tax assessor deducts depreciation on human capital in computing income.

Some tedious complications are created by the decision to count all residential construction as investment. Rental payments are counted as part of consumption spending, since they are made in return for the services provided by the house or apartment. And the landlord's income includes the rental payments, less appropriate allowances for depreciation, mortgage interest, property taxes, and so forth. And depreciation must also be subtracted each year from gross investment in order to obtain the proper figure for net investment. But how should the national income accountant adjust his books if the apartment dweller should build a new house? The entire purchase price of the house certainly is investment spending, not current consumption. But the services provided by the new house over the years should be included in consumption spending, just as if it were being rented. The national income accountant makes the appropriate adjustments by entering all the transactions as though the owner-occupant were his own landlord. The accountant perpetuates the fiction that the owner is simultaneously his own landlord by including the *rental value of owner-occupied housing* as a component of consumption spending. The deprecia-

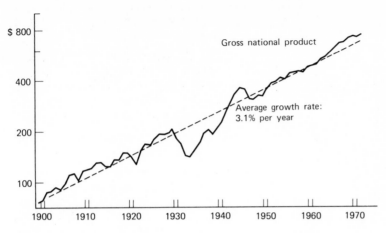

Fig. 3.1   *Gross national product, 1900–1972 (billions of 1958 dollars).*

tion on the house is subtracted in moving from gross to net investment. And *inputed rental income* is added to the consumer-landlord's income.[2]

Table 3.1 reveals the historical movements of GNP and its components. Note that $X - M$, the surplus in the balance of trade, is entered in the column labeled "Net Exports of Goods and Services." The figures recorded on the first half of Table 3.1 are in current dollars; for example, GNP for 1929 is measured in 1929 prices, and GNP for 1972 is measured in 1972 prices. However, such figures are of limited usefulness because, with inflation, current dollars are a rubber yardstick for measuring the nation's output. It is useful to be able to determine how much of the tenfold increase in current dollar GNP is due to an expansion in output of goods and services and how much should be attributed to changing prices. This issue is clarified by using prices for a particular year. Inspecting the figures measured in 1958 dollars (i.e., prices in 1958) reveals that the output of goods and services increased about fourfold from 1929 to 1972. The growth in real GNP since 1900 is plotted on Figure 3.1.

The basic multiplier model will explain the determination of Y, C, and Y_d—given the magnitude of the exogenous variables I, G, and $X - M$.

---

[2] While, in principle, the same investment-rental fiction should be applied to automobiles and other durable consumption goods, the national income accountant finds the procedure too complicated and instead treats such items as if they were consumed at date of purchase. But, in statistical studies of consumer behavior, many econometricians often find it useful to treat all consumer durables in the same way that the national income accountant handles residential construction.

Table 3.1a GROSS NATIONAL PRODUCT, 1929–1972 (BILLIONS OF DOLLARS)

Year	Total Gross National Product	Personal Consumption Expenditures	Gross Private Domestic Investment	Net Exports of Goods and Services	Government Purchases of Goods and Services		Federal			State and Local	Disposable Income
					Total	Total	National Defense	Other		
1929	103.1	77.2	16.2	1.1	8.5	1.3	1.3		7.2	83.3
1930	90.4	69.9	10.3	1.0	9.2	1.4	1.4		7.8	74.5
1931	75.8	60.5	5.6	.5	9.2	1.5	1.5		7.7	64.0
1932	58.0	48.6	1.0	.4	8.1	1.5	1.5		6.6	48.7
1933	55.6	45.8	1.4	.4	8.0	2.0	2.0		6.0	45.5
1934	65.1	51.3	3.3	.6	9.8	3.0	3.0		6.8	52.4
1935	72.2	55.7	6.4	.1	10.0	2.9	2.9		7.1	58.5
1936	82.5	61.9	8.5	.1	12.0	4.9	4.9		7.0	66.3
1937	90.4	66.5	11.8	.3	11.9	4.7	4.7		7.2	71.2
1938	84.7	63.9	6.5	1.3	13.0	5.4	5.4		7.6	65.5
1939	90.5	66.8	9.3	1.1	13.3	5.1	1.2	3.9	8.2	70.3
1940	99.7	70.8	13.1	1.7	14.0	6.0	2.2	3.8	8.0	75.7
1941	124.5	80.6	17.9	1.3	24.8	16.9	13.8	3.1	7.9	92.7
1942	157.9	88.5	9.8	.0	59.6	51.9	49.4	2.5	7.7	116.9
1943	191.6	99.3	5.7	-2.0	88.6	81.1	79.7	1.4	7.4	133.5
1944	210.1	108.3	7.1	-1.8	96.5	89.0	87.4	1.6	7.5	146.3
1945	211.9	119.7	10.6	-.6	82.3	74.2	73.5	.7	8.1	150.2
1946	208.5	143.4	30.6	7.5	27.0	17.2	14.7	2.5	9.8	160.0

Year										
1947	231.3	160.7	34.0	11.5	25.1	12.5	9.1	3.5	12.6	169.8
1948	257.6	173.6	46.0	6.4	31.6	16.5	10.7	5.8	15.0	189.1
1949	256.5	176.8	35.7	6.1	37.8	20.1	13.3	6.8	17.7	188.6
1950	284.8	191.0	54.1	1.8	37.9	18.4	14.1	4.3	19.5	206.9
1951	328.4	206.3	59.3	3.7	59.1	37.7	33.6	4.1	21.5	226.6
1952	345.5	216.7	51.9	2.2	74.7	51.8	45.9	5.9	22.9	238.3
1953	364.6	230.0	52.6	.4	81.6	57.0	48.7	8.4	24.6	252.6
1954	364.8	236.5	51.7	1.8	74.8	47.4	41.2	6.2	27.4	257.4
1955	398.0	254.4	67.4	2.0	74.2	44.1	38.6	5.5	30.1	275.3
1956	419.2	266.7	70.0	4.0	78.6	45.6	40.3	5.3	33.0	293.2
1957	441.1	281.4	67.9	5.7	86.1	49.5	44.2	5.3	36.6	308.5
1958	447.3	290.1	60.9	2.2	94.2	53.6	45.9	7.7	40.6	318.8
1959	483.7	311.2	75.3	.1	97.0	53.7	46.0	7.6	43.3	337.3
1960	503.7	325.2	74.8	4.0	99.6	53.5	44.9	8.6	46.1	350.0
1961	520.1	335.2	71.7	5.6	107.6	57.4	47.8	9.6	50.2	364.4
1962	560.3	355.1	83.0	5.1	117.1	63.4	51.6	11.8	53.7	385.3
1963	590.5	375.0	87.1	5.9	122.5	64.2	50.8	13.5	58.2	404.6
1964	632.4	401.2	94.0	8.5	128.7	65.2	50.0	15.2	63.5	438.1
1965	684.9	432.8	108.1	6.9	137.0	66.9	50.1	16.8	70.1	473.2
1966	749.9	466.3	121.4	5.3	156.8	77.8	60.7	17.1	79.0	511.9
1967	793.9	492.1	116.6	5.2	180.1	90.7	72.4	18.4	89.4	546.3
1968	864.2	536.2	126.0	2.5	199.6	98.8	78.3	20.5	100.8	591.0
1969	930.3	579.5	139.0	1.9	210.0	98.8	78.4	20.4	111.2	634.4
1970	976.4	616.8	137.1	3.6	219.0	96.5	75.1	21.5	122.5	689.5
1971	1,050.4	664.9	152.0	.7	232.8	97.8	71.4	26.3	135.0	744.4
1972	1,152.1	721.1	180.2	-4.1	254.9	105.9	76.2	29.7	148.9	795.1

Source. Economic Report of the President.

Table 3.1b GROSS NATIONAL PRODUCT,

Year	Total Gross National Product	Personal Consumption Expenditures Total	Durable Goods	Nondurable Goods	Services	Gross Private Domestic Investment Total	Fixed Investment Total	Nonresidential Total	Structures	Producers' Durable Equipment	Residential Structures	Change in Business Inventories
1929	203.6	139.6	16.3	69.3	54.0	40.4	36.9	26.5	13.9	12.6	10.4	3.5
1930	183.5	130.4	12.9	65.9	51.5	27.4	28.0	21.7	11.8	9.9	6.3	−.6
1931	169.3	126.1	11.2	65.6	49.4	16.8	19.2	14.1	7.5	6.6	5.1	−2.4
1932	144.2	114.8	8.4	60.4	45.9	4.7	10.9	8.2	4.4	3.8	2.7	−6.2
1933	141.5	112.8	8.3	58.6	46.0	5.3	9.7	7.6	3.3	4.3	2.1	−4.3
1934	154.3	113.1	9.4	62.5	46.1	9.4	12.1	9.2	3.6	5.6	2.9	−2.7
1935	169.5	125.5	11.7	65.9	47.9	18.0	15.6	11.5	4.0	7.5	4.0	2.4
1936	193.0	138.4	14.5	73.4	50.5	24.0	20.9	15.8	5.4	10.3	5.1	3.1
1937	203.2	143.1	15.1	76.0	52.0	29.9	24.5	18.8	7.1	11.8	5.6	5.5
1938	192.9	140.2	12.2	77.1	50.9	17.0	19.4	13.7	5.6	8.1	5.7	−2.4
1939	209.4	148.2	14.5	81.2	52.5	24.7	23.5	15.3	5.9	9.4	8.2	1.2
1940	227.2	155.7	16.7	84.6	54.4	33.0	28.1	18.9	6.8	12.1	9.2	4.9
1941	263.7	165.4	19.1	89.9	56.3	41.6	32.0	22.2	8.1	14.2	9.8	9.6
1942	297.8	161.4	11.7	91.3	58.5	21.4	17.3	12.5	4.6	7.9	4.9	4.0
1943	337.1	165.8	10.2	93.7	61.8	12.7	12.9	10.0	2.9	7.2	2.9	−.2
1944	361.3	171.4	9.4	97.3	64.7	14.0	15.9	13.4	3.8	9.6	2.5	−1.9
1945	355.2	183.0	10.6	104.7	67.7	19.6	22.6	19.8	5.7	14.1	2.8	−2.9
1946	312.6	203.5	20.5	110.8	72.1	52.3	42.3	30.2	12.5	17.7	12.1	10.0
1947	309.9	206.3	24.7	108.3	73.4	51.5	51.7	36.2	11.6	24.6	15.4	−.2
1948	323.7	210.8	26.3	108.7	75.8	60.4	51.7	34.0	12.3	25.7	17.9	4.6
1949	324.1	216.5	28.4	110.5	77.6	48.0	51.9	34.5	11.9	22.6	17.4	−3.9
1950	355.3	230.5	34.7	114.0	81.8	69.3	61.0	37.5	12.7	24.8	23.5	8.3
1951	383.4	232.8	31.5	116.5	84.8	70.0	59.0	39.6	14.1	25.5	19.5	10.9
1952	395.1	239.4	30.8	120.8	87.8	60.5	57.2	38.3	13.7	24.6	18.9	3.3
1953	412.8	250.8	35.3	124.4	91.1	61.2	60.2	40.7	14.9	25.8	19.6	.9
1954	407.0	255.7	35.4	125.5	94.8	59.4	61.4	39.6	15.2	24.5	21.7	−2.0
1955	438.0	274.2	43.2	131.7	93.3	75.4	69.0	43.9	16.2	27.7	25.1	6.4
1956	446.1	281.4	41.0	136.2	104.1	74.3	69.5	47.3	18.5	28.8	22.2	4.8
1957	452.5	289.2	41.5	138.7	108.0	68.8	67.6	47.4	18.2	29.1	20.2	1.2
1958	447.3	290.1	37.9	140.2	112.0	60.9	62.4	41.6	16.6	25.0	20.8	−1.5
1959	475.9	307.3	43.7	146.8	116.8	73.6	68.8	44.1	16.2	27.9	24.7	4.8
1960	487.7	316.1	44.9	149.6	121.6	72.4	68.9	47.1	17.4	29.6	21.9	3.5
1961	497.2	322.5	43.9	153.0	125.6	69.0	67.0	45.5	17.4	28.1	21.6	2.0
1962	529.8	338.4	49.2	158.2	131.1	79.4	73.4	49.7	17.9	31.7	23.8	6.0
1963	551.0	353.3	53.7	162.2	137.4	82.5	76.7	51.9	17.9	34.0	24.8	5.8
1964	581.1	373.7	59.0	170.3	144.4	87.8	81.9	57.8	19.1	38.7	24.2	5.8
1965	617.8	397.7	66.6	178.6	152.5	99.2	90.1	66.3	22.3	44.0	23.8	9.0
1966	658.1	418.1	71.7	187.0	159.4	109.3	95.4	74.1	24.0	50.1	21.3	13.9
1967	675.2	430.1	72.9	190.2	167.0	101.2	93.5	73.2	22.6	50.6	20.4	7.7
1968	706.6	452.7	81.3	197.1	174.4	105.2	98.8	75.6	23.4	52.2	23.2	6.4
1969	725.6	469.1	85.6	201.3	182.2	110.5	103.8	80.1	24.3	55.8	23.7	6.7
1970	722.1	477.0	83.1	207.0	186.8	104.0	99.9	77.6	23.6	54.0	22.3	4.1
1971	741.7	495.4	92.1	211.1	192.2	108.6	105.9	76.8	22.8	54.0	29.1	2.6
1972	789.7	524.8	103.1	220.5	201.2	123.8	119.3	84.3	22.9	61.3	35.0	4.5

Source. Economic Report of the President

54

Net Exports of Goods and Services			Government Purchases of Goods and Services				
Net Exports	Exports	Imports	Total	Federal	State and Local	Disposable Income	Year
1.5	11.8	10.3	22.0	3.5	18.5	150.6	1929
1.4	10.4	9.0	24.3	4.0	20.2	139.0	1930
.9	8.9	7.9	25.4	4.3	21.1	133.7	1931
.6	7.1	6.6	24.2	4.6	19.6	115.1	1932
.0	7.1	7.1	23.3	6.0	17.3	112.2	1933
.3	7.3	7.1	26.6	8.0	18.6	120.4	1934
−1.0	7.7	8.7	27.0	7.9	19.2	131.8	1935
−1.2	8.2	9.3	31.8	12.2	19.6	148.4	1936
−.7	9.8	10.5	30.8	11.5	19.4	153.1	1937
1.9	9.9	8.0	33.9	13.3	20.6	143.6	1938
1.3	10.0	8.7	35.2	12.5	22.7	155.9	1939
2.1	11.0	8.9	36.4	15.0	21.4	166.3	1940
.4	11.2	10.8	56.3	36.2	20.1	190.3	1941
−2.1	7.8	9.9	117.1	98.9	18.3	213.4	1942
−5.9	6.8	12.6	164.4	147.8	16.6	222.8	1943
−5.8	7.6	13.4	181.7	165.4	16.3	231.6	1944
−3.8	10.2	13.9	155.4	139.7	16.7	229.7	1945
8.4	19.6	11.2	48.4	30.1	18.4	227.0	1946
12.3	22.6	10.3	39.9	19.1	20.8	218.0	1947
6.1	18.1	12.0	46.3	23.7	22.7	229.8	1948
6.4	18.1	11.7	53.3	27.6	25.7	230.8	1949
2.7	16.3	13.6	52.8	25.3	27.5	249.6	1950
5.3	19.3	14.1	75.4	47.4	27.9	255.7	1951
3.0	18.2	15.2	92.1	63.8	28.4	263.3	1952
1.1	17.8	16.7	99.8	70.0	29.7	275.4	1953
3.0	18.8	15.8	88.9	56.8	32.1	278.3	1954
3.2	20.9	17.7	85.2	50.7	34.4	296.7	1955
5.0	24.2	19.1	85.3	49.7	35.6	309.3	1956
6.2	26.2	19.9	89.3	51.7	37.6	315.8	1957
2.2	23.1	20.9	94.2	53.6	40.6	318.8	1958
.3	23.8	23.5	94.7	52.5	42.2	333.0	1959
4.3	27.3	23.0	94.9	51.4	43.5	340.2	1960
5.1	28.0	22.9	100.5	54.6	45.9	350.7	1961
4.5	30.0	25.5	107.5	60.0	47.5	357.3	1962
5.6	32.1	26.6	109.6	59.5	50.1	381.3	1963
8.3	36.5	28.2	111.2	58.1	53.2	407.9	1964
6.2	37.4	31.2	114.7	57.9	56.8	435.0	1965
4.2	40.2	36.1	126.5	65.4	61.1	458.9	1966
3.6	42.1	38.5	140.2	74.7	65.5	477.5	1967
1.0	45.7	44.7	147.7	78.1	69.6	499.0	1968
.2	48.4	48.3	145.9	73.5	72.4	513.6	1969
2.2	52.2	50.0	139.0	64.7	74.3	533.2	1970
.1	52.6	52.5	137.6	60.8	76.8	554.7	1971
−1.8	56.9	58.7	142.9	61.6	81.3	578.7	1972

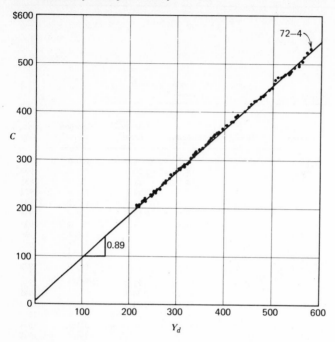

Fig. 3.2 *Consumption on disposable income (quarterly data at annual rates, billions of 1958 dollars. 1947–1972).*

The model includes two behavioral equations in addition to the national income accounting identity. The first concerns the relationship between disposable income and consumption spending. Each dot on Figure 3.2 indicates a particular quarter's disposable income and consumption. For example, the point labeled 72-4 has coordinates ⟨578.7, 538.6⟩, because disposable income was $578.7 billion in that quarter while consumption was $538.6 billion. The quite precise relationship between consumption spending and disposable income revealed by the graph suggests a linear equation of the form

$$C = c_0 + c_1 Y_d \tag{2.2}$$

Presumably c_1, the *marginal propensity to consume*, is positive but less than unity, since it is reasonable to assume that people will spend only a fraction of any increase in income.[3] The second behavioral equation explains disposable income in terms of GNP. Figure 3.3 suggests that it may

---

[3] The way in which such other variables as wealth influence consumption will be discussed in a later chapter.

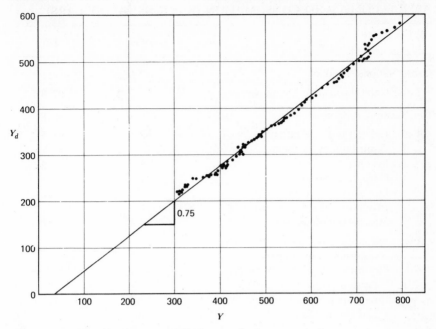

Fig. 3.3 *Disposable income on GNP (quarterly data at annual rates, billions of 1958 dollars, 1947–1972).*

not be too inappropriate to summarize this relationship in terms of a second linear equation:

$$Y_d = d_0 + d_1 Y \tag{2.3}$$

Equation 2.3 purports to explain the substantial gap between gross national produce and disposable income. The gap amounted to $286.9 billion in 1970, for while total GNP was $976.4 only $689.5 billion filtered down to consumers as disposable income. Table 3.2 briefly summarizes the major accounting factors contributing to the discrepancy, and it is necessary to digress for a moment in order to consider the various factors involved.[4] First, of course, we have to subtract capital consumption allowances (depreciation) from GNP to get to net national product. While this is a sizable factor, it is clear from the table that the major leakage between

---

[4] Most elementary textbooks summarize the principles of national income accounting (e.g., Paul A. Samuelson, *Economics: An Introductory Analysis*), but for more detailed discussions see Ruggles and Ruggles, *National Income Accounts and Income Analysis*. The Department of Commerce publishes detailed data on United States national income in July issues of the *Survey of Current Business*; back data appear in a survey supplement, *The National Income and Products Accounts of the United States, 1929–1965*.

Table 3.2 RELATIONSHIP OF GROSS NATIONAL PRODUCT, DISPOS-
ABLE INCOME, AND CONSUMPTION (BILLIONS OF DOLLARS)

	1965	1970
Gross National Product	684.9	977.1
Less: Capital consumption allowances	59.8	87.3
Net National Product	625.1	889.8
Less: Indirect business taxes	62.5	93.5
Contributions for Social Security	29.6	57.7
Personal taxes	65.7	116.6
Corporate profits taxes	31.3	34.8
Undistributed corporate profits	26.7	14.6
Inventory valuation adjustment	−1.7	−4.7
Statistical discrepancy	−3.1	−6.4
Plus: Subsidies less current surplus of government enterprise	1.3	1.7
Government transfer payments to persons	37.2	75.1
Interest paid by government (net) and consumers	20.5	31.0
Disposable Personal Income	473.2	691.7
Personal consumption expenditure	432.8	617.6
Interest paid by consumers	11.3	16.8
Personal transfer payments to foreigners	0.7	1.1
Personal Saving	28.4	56.2
Addendum		
Corporate Profits and Inventory Valuation Adjustment	76.1	69.2
Less: Inventory valuation adjustment	−1.7	−4.7
Corporate Profits Before Taxes	77.8	74.0
Less: Corporate taxes	31.3	34.8
Dividends	19.8	24.7
Undistributed profits	26.7	14.6

Source. Survey of Current Business.
Note. (Corporate profits *plus* inventory valuation adjustment *less* dividends) *equals* (corporate profits taxes *plus* undistributed profits *plus* inventory valuation adjustment).

GNP and disposable income arises from tax payments: indirect business (sales and excise) taxes, personal (income) taxes, and social security contributions appear as separate entries on the table. On the other hand, the government contributes to the income stream through transfer payments (e.g., old age, health insurance, unemployment, and veterans benefits). Government subsidies to farms and business add to disposable income, although any surplus of government enterprise (minus the loss of the Post Office) is netted out.

Certain subtle points concerning the accounting relationship presented in Table 3.2 deserve some discussion. First, note that both the taxes paid by corporations and undistributed corporate profits are among the items substracted out in moving from GNP to disposable income. In voting on the dividend rate a corporation's directors will usually retain with the firm a portion of profits to be reinvested for future expansion. Neither retained earnings nor corporate taxes filter down to the consumer. See the bottom of Table 3.2 for the relevant figures. Second, observe that interest payments by government and by consumers are added in getting to disposable personal income. Because interest paid by the government to the public constitutes a source of funds available for spending, it rightfully belongs in the lender's disposable income; but national income accountants exclude government interest payments from GNP because they are largely the consequence of debt incurred in wartime instead of a part of the value of goods and services currently being produced by the nation. A similar argument is applied to interest payments by consumers: the recipients of these interest payments regard them as income, but they are not part of GNP. That is, consumer interest payments are part of disposable income, but they are left out in adding up the market value of all goods and services produced by the economy.[5]

It is clear that disposable income Equation 2.3 suppresses important detail concerning government tax structure and corporate dividend policy. Certainly, it constitutes a grossly simplified picture of the determinants of disposable income; after all, changes in tax legislation, such as the 1954 and 1964 tax cuts, undoubtedly shift the relationship between disposable income and GNP. In the construction of econometric models to be used for predictive purposes it is necessary to introduce a variety of equations explaining the behavior of the various accounting factors entering into

---

[5] The alternative of including consumer interest payments within GNP instead of adding it on in moving from GNP to disposable income was at one time used by the national income accountants. When interest payments by consumers are included as part of GNP, it is also necessary to include them in consumption spending in order that Equation 2.1 will still hold; clearly, the national income accountant has only a limited number of degrees of freedom in deciding how to define such concepts as GNP and consumption.

Table 3.2. As a first approximation, however, Equation 2.3 will suffice in the construction of our simplified model of income determination.

The coefficients of the equations may be estimated from the straight lines on the two graphs. Thus c_0 in the intercept of the line on Figure 3.2, and c_1 is that line's slope. In the same way, d_0 is the intercept and d_1 the slope of the line on Figure 3.3. As an alternative to plotting the straight lines by eye on the graphs, they may be estimated by a statistical procedure known as "least squares." Application of the procedure (described in Appendix 4.1) to the post-World War II quarterly data yields rough estimates of the magnitude of the parameters of the two behavioral equations.

$$c_0 = \$9.94 \text{ billion}$$
$$c_1 = 0.89$$
$$d_0 = -\$24 \text{ billion}$$
$$d_1 = 0.75$$

That is,

$$C = 9.94 + 0.89 Y_d \tag{2.2'}$$
$$Y_d = -24 + 0.75 Y \tag{2.3'}$$

About three fourths of a dollar increase in Y filters down to the consumer as disposable income. About 90% of the increase in disposable income is consumed. While these estimates are obviously approximate, they will suffice for illustrative purposes.[6]

The flowchart presented in Figure 3.4 reveals schematically how the pieces of the model fit together. First, four variables (indicated by circles) feed into Equation 2.1 (indicated by a box) to yield GNP. Second, we have a *feedback loop* consisting of the effects of GNP on disposable income, through Equation 2.3, plus the effect of disposable income, in turn, on consumption spending, Equation 2.2. The presence of the feedback loop means that the three equations must be solved simultaneously in order to determine the magnitude of consumption, disposable income, and GNP. And Okun's law may be appended in order to determine unemployment.

*3.3 ROUNDS OF INDUCED EXPENDITURE—THE KAHN MULTIPLIER

As a first step in understanding how this interdependent system operates, let us trace through the successive effects of a $1 increase in govern-

---

[6] In order to eliminate the effects of price changes, the regressions were run with constant dollar GNP data measured in 1958 dollars. The details of these regressions, and a brief summary of econometric studies of the consumption relationship, will be presented in the next chapter.

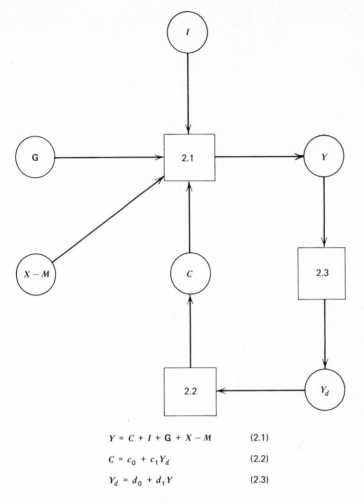

$$Y = C + I + G + X - M \qquad (2.1)$$

$$C = c_0 + c_1 Y_d \qquad (2.2)$$

$$Y_d = d_0 + d_1 Y \qquad (2.3)$$

Fig. 3.4 *The elementary multiplier flow chart.*

ment spending. The first column of Table 3.3 shows the immediate contribution of the increase in government spending to GNP. Further down the
first column we find that (as with Equation 2.3) the $1 increase in GNP
causes a $0.75 rise in disposable income. The bottom entry in the first
column is the effect of this change in disposable income on consumption;
that is, from Equation 2.2, consumption changes by 0.89 times the change
in disposable income, or by 0.6675. Of course, this is not the end of the
story, since this *induced* increase in consumption constitutes an increase in
the demand for the nation's output; the induced consumption feeds back

Table 3.3 SUCCESSIVE ROUNDS OF THE MULTIPLIER PROCESS

$(c_1 = 0.89; d_1 = 0.75)$

Change in	Round 1	Round 2	Round 3	Round 4	...	Sum over All Rounds
Government spending	1					$=1$
GNP	1 $+$	0.6675 $+$	0.4456 $+$	0.2974 $+$	...	$=3.01$
Disposable income	0.75	0.5006	0.3342	0.2231	...	$=2.26$
Consumption	0.6675	0.4456	0.2974	0.1985	...	$=2.01$

to contribute to a further rise in GNP which, in turn, generates a further increment in disposable income and hence additional consumption, as shown in the second column of the table. The additional increment to consumption gives rise to a third round, and so on. Each round may be regarded as the period of time required for consumers to adjust to a new level of disposable income, but the details of the lags involved are a "dynamic" issue best deferred to a later chapter.

How much of an increase in GNP will ultimately be generated may be determined from the formula for summing a geometric series.[7] We have as the sum of the GNP row:

$$1 + 0.6675 + (0.6675)^2 + (0.6675)^3 + \cdots = \frac{1}{1 - 0.6675} = 3.01$$

The ultimate change in disposable income must be simply $0.75 \times 3.01 = 2.26$, since in each round the entry in the disposable income row is 0.75 of the corresponding element in the row immediately above it; similarly, the consumption changes sum to 2.01 because in every round the change in consumption is 0.89 of the corresponding increase in disposable income.

Considering the successive rounds of spending stimulated by the increase in government spending reveals a fundamental truth: an increment in government spending can cause a much larger increase in output because the resulting increase in disposable income induces increased consumption spending. This is the essence of the multiplier process. The concept was carefully enunciated by Richard F. Kahn in a paper published in Britain's *Economic Journal* in 1931,[8] and the concept became the cornerstone of "Keynesian" theory. But only very timid doses of the government spending medicine were tried during the Great Depression of the 1930s; not until

---

[7] Let

$$S_n = 1 + \beta + \beta^2 + \beta^3 + \ldots + \beta^n$$

the sum of the first n power of β. On multiplying through by β we have

$$\beta S_n = \beta + \beta^2 + \beta^3 + \ldots + \beta^n + \beta^{n+1}$$

Subtraction yields

$$S_n - \beta S_n = (1 - \beta)S_n = 1 - \beta^{n+1}$$

Hence

$$S_n = (1 - \beta^{n+1})/(1 - \beta)$$

and in the limit, as

$$n \to \infty, \ S_n \to S = 1/(1 - \beta)$$

provided that

$$-1 < \beta < 1$$

[8] Richard F. Kahn, "The Relation of Home Investment to Unemployment," *Economic Journal*, June 1931, pp. 175–198.

World War II did government spending rise to the level required for full employment.

*3.4 GRAPHICAL ANALYSIS OF THE MULTIPLIER

A graph provides an alternative way of understanding this multiplier process. Figure 3.5 reveals how endogenous variables Y, Y_d, and C are determined by the exogenous variables and the parameters of the model. Disposable income is plotted on the abscissa and various categories of expenditures on the ordinate. The heavy line, the consumption function, reveals the magnitude of consumer spending as a function of disposable

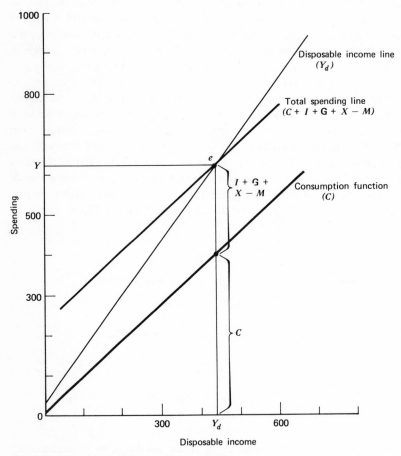

Fig. 3.5 *Graphical analysis of the multiplier.*

income, in accordance with Equation 2.2. The *total spending line* adds total exogenous spending, $G + I + X - M$, to consumption. Since it has been drawn for $G = 125$, $I = 90$, and $X - M = 0$, each point on this line is precisely 215 units above the consumption function. If we knew the level of disposable income, we could now determine GNP, since it would be the height of the point on the total spending line immediately above the specified value of disposable income. But disposable income is endogenous and must be determined.

Another behavior relation, the *disposable income line*, is needed to solve the system. The disposable income line comes from Equation 2.3′. That is, we borrow the straight line from Figure 3.3. However, it is much steeper than the line on Figure 3.3 because the axes are reversed; that is, Y instead of Y_d is plotted on the ordinate. The equation for the disposable income line on Figure 3.5 is

$$Y = -\frac{d_0}{d_1} + \frac{1}{d_1} Y_d = 32 + 1.33 Y_d$$

Thus the intercept of the disposable income line is 32 and its slope is 1.33.

Point e at the intersection of the disposable income line and the total spending line reveals the solution of the system. Consumers are on the consumption function and e is on the disposable income line. Furthermore, Y does equal the sum of its components, as required by Equation 2.1. For the specified values of G, I, $X - M$, and the parameter estimates utilized in plotting the curve, we have $Y_d = 436$, $C = 398$, and $Y = 612$.[9]

The effect of an increase in government spending (G) can be analyzed graphically by drawing a higher total spending line, as illustrated on Figure 3.6. The total spending line shifts upward by ΔG because the gap between output and consumption—$Y - C = G + I + X - M$ by Equation 2.1— is larger than before. Point e' on the graph reveals that output has expanded by much more than ΔG, the change in government spending. This multiplier effect comes about because of the induced increase in consumption (ΔC) that is generated by the expansion in disposable income.

The effects of tax adjustments may also be determined graphically. We will see that a cut in personal income taxes will shift the disposable income line instead of the total spending line. If GNP were to remain at Y the level of disposable income would increase as a result of the cut in taxes— more funds would filter down to the consumer instead of being taxed away

---

[9] This may be called the "equilibrium solution" in that the basic behavioral equations of the model are satisfied. But it is not like the demand-supply equilibrium of price theory; in particular, it would be a coincidence if point e corresponded to a full-employment equality of the supply of labor with the demand.

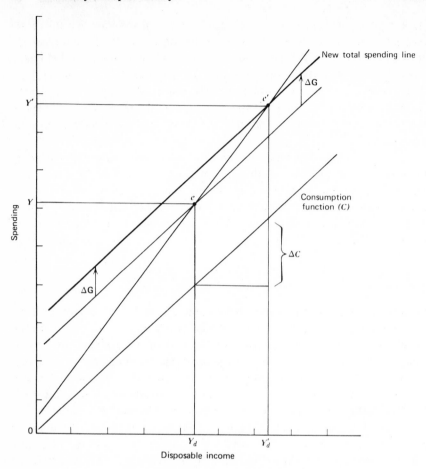

Fig. 3.6 *Multiplier effects of increased government spending. The increase* ΔG *in government spending shifts the total spending line up. At* e′ *output is* Y′ *instead of* Y. *Disposable income has risen from* Y_d *to* $Y_d′$ *and consumption has increased by* ΔC.

by the government; the arrow connecting point *e* to *x* on Figure 3.7 indicates the shift that would take place if output were to remain constant. But at any level of GNP disposable income will be increased as a result of the reduction in the personal income tax. Thus every point on the disposable income line shifts, as illustrated on the graph. It is easily seen graphically that the tax cut, because it induces additional consumption spending, may be used to stimulate the level of economic activity.

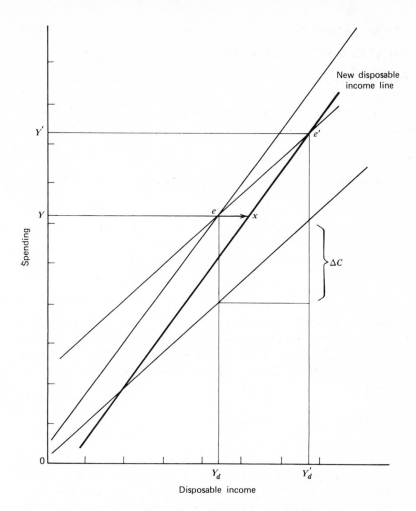

Fig. 3.7 *Effects of a personal income tax cut. A cut in personal income taxes means that, at any given level of output, disposable income must be bigger than before. This means that the disposable income line shifts to the right. As a result, disposable income increases from Y_d to Y_d', consumption increases by ΔC, and output rises to Y'.*

*3.5 A FAMILY OF MULTIPLIERS

While the graph provides insight into how the process works, a more precise understanding of the effects of various policy actions may be gained by solving the system explicitly. Substituting Equation 2.2 into Equation 2.3 yields

$$C = c_0 + c_1 d_0 + c_1 d_1 Y \tag{5.1}$$

Substitution of Equation 5.1 into the national income accounting identity, Equation 2.1, yields

$$Y = c_0 + c_1 d_0 + c_1 d_1 Y + I + G + X - M$$

Hence,

$$Y = \frac{1}{1 - c_1 d_1} (c_0 + c_1 d_0 + I + G + X - M) \tag{5.2}$$

To determine the multiplier affects on an increase in government spending from G to G^*, note first that once the economy has adjusted to the increased government demand, the new level of output (call it Y^*) must be of such magnitude as to satisfy the above equation. That is, after the change, we must again have:

$$Y^* = \frac{1}{1 - c_1 d_1} (c_0 + c_1 d_0 + I + G^* + X - M)$$

Since we are inquiring about the effects of an increase in government spending, *given* the magnitude of the other exogenous variables, we do not put asterisks on I or $X - M$. The second and final step is to subtract 5.2 from this after-change equation. When we execute the subtraction, a number of items cancel out, and we are left with the following equation for the change in output.

$$Y^* - Y = \frac{1}{1 - c_1 d_1} (G^* - G) \tag{5.3}$$

If we let ΔY denote $Y^* - Y$ and ΔG the change in government spending, we have as our first multiplier

m1: $\dfrac{\Delta Y}{\Delta G} = \dfrac{1}{1 - c_1 d_1} = 3.01$

The numerical estimate, which is at best only approximate, was calculated from the least-squares parameter estimates mentioned earlier.

Of course, the above argument is trivial for anyone who has had even a rudimentary introduction to calculus, because m1 is just the first derivative of Equation 5.2 with respect to **G**.[10] Here are some other multipliers.

m2: $\qquad \dfrac{\Delta Y_d}{\Delta G} = \dfrac{\Delta Y_d}{\Delta Y} \cdot \dfrac{\Delta Y}{\Delta G} = \dfrac{d_1}{1 - c_1 d_1} = 2.26$

m3: $\qquad \dfrac{\Delta C}{\Delta G} = \dfrac{c_1 d_1}{1 - c_1 d_1} = \dfrac{1}{1 - c_1 d_1} - 1 = 2.01$

m4: $\qquad \dfrac{\Delta Y}{\Delta I} = \dfrac{1}{1 - c_1 d_1} = 3.01$

m5: $\qquad \dfrac{\Delta Y}{\Delta c_0} = \dfrac{1}{1 - c_1 d_1} = 3.01$

m6: $\qquad \dfrac{\Delta Y}{\Delta d_0} = \dfrac{c_1}{1 - c_1 d_1} = 2.68$

m7: $\qquad \dfrac{\Delta Y_d}{\Delta d_0} = 1 + d_1 \dfrac{\Delta Y}{\Delta d_0} = \dfrac{1}{1 - c_1 d_1} = 3.01$

m8: $\qquad \dfrac{\Delta Y_d}{\Delta c_0} = \dfrac{\Delta Y_d}{\Delta Y} \cdot \dfrac{\Delta Y}{\Delta c_0} = \dfrac{d_1}{1 - c_1 d_1} = 2.26$

m9: $\qquad \dfrac{\Delta C}{\Delta d_0} = \dfrac{c_1}{1 - c_1 d_1} = 2.68$

m10: $\qquad \dfrac{\Delta C}{\Delta c_0} = \dfrac{\Delta C}{\Delta Y_d} \cdot \dfrac{\Delta Y_d}{\Delta c_0} + 1 = \dfrac{c_1 d_1}{1 - c_1 d_1} + 1 = \dfrac{1}{1 - c_1 d_1} = 3.01$

We will be considering various applications of these multipliers.

a. Effects of Increased Government Spending

The effects on GNP, disposable income, and consumption of a change in government spending are revealed by the first three multipliers. The magnitudes of these multipliers, calculated from the parameter estimates reported earlier, are in agreement with those worked out on Table 3.3 by summing the total induced effects of an increase in government spending. The fourth multiplier agrees in magnitude with the first since, with this simple model, an autonomous increase in private investment spending has a stimulative effect equivalent to that of an equal increase in government spending.

[10] The linear nature of the model means that *multipliers* obtained by differentiation are valid for finite instead of just infinitesimal changes.

As an application of multiplier analysis, consider the economic effects of defense mobilization occasioned by the conflict in Viet Nam. From the first quarter of 1965 to the end of 1966 our GNP grew from $660.8 to $759.3 billion, and the unemployment rate dropped from 4.8 to 3.7%. To what extent was the increase in GNP caused by the growth in defense expenditures during this period from $48.2 to $65.5 billion? In principle, at least, the multiplier $\Delta Y/\Delta G = 3.01$ can be utilized to obtain an approximate answer to this question. Specifically, we seek an estimate of the value that GNP would have assumed in the fourth quarter of 1966 if government spending had not changed from the first quarter of that year (G_{66-1}); let $\tilde{Y}_{66-4}$ denote this hypothetical value of GNP. We compute

$$Y_{66-4} - \tilde{Y}_{66-4} = \Delta Y/\Delta G \ (G_{66-4} - G_{66-1})$$

$$= 3.0 \ (65.5 - 48.2)$$

$$= \$52.0 \text{ billion}$$

This is no more than a crude estimate of the impact of rising government spending. The Joint Economic Committee was provided with a more precise estimate by Professor Daniel B. Suits of the University of Michigan. His figures, obtained with a complex simultaneous equation model of the economy, are reported in Table 3.4.[11] The same table reveals the extent of unemployment that would have occurred, in the absence of Viet Nam, *if* measures were not taken to offset the tendency toward recession.

b. Effects of a Tax Cut

Consider next the effect of a change in the personal income tax structure. For simplicity, suppose that a change in tax legislation—perhaps an increase in the personal exemption—has the effect of reducing by $1 billion the amount of tax revenue that will be collected at each level of GNP. A tax *cut* means that the intercept of the disposable income function, d_0, of Equation 2.3, is *increased*; at any given level of GNP, disposable income will be $1 billion higher.[12] Multiplier m·6 suggests that GNP will be increased by $2.68 billion as a result of the tax cut. Thus the cut in personal taxes stimulates the economy, but by a lesser amount than an equal in-

---

[11] Professor Suits' statement appears in "Economic Effect of Viet Nam Spending," Hearings before the Joint Economic Committee, Congress of the United States, April 26, 1967, pp. 157–159. For a more detailed study see L. R. Klein and K. Mori, "The Impact of Disarmament on Aggregate Economic Activity: An Econometric Analysis," *Adjustment of the U.S. Economy to Reductions in Military Spending*, ed. by B. Udis (Washington, D.C., U.S. Arms Control and Disarmament Agency), 1970, pp. 93–120.

[12] In a later chapter we will see that the Council of Economic Advisers thought that the 1964 personal income tax cut would be of this "lump-sum" form. A tax may also influence the magnitude of d_1. See Exercise 3.9.

Table 3.4 IMPACT OF VIET NAM EXPENDITURE ON GROSS NATIONAL PRODUCT AND UNEMPLOYMENT (ESTIMATED BY DANIEL SUITS)

Year and Quarter	1965				1966			
	I	II	III	IV	I	II	III	IV
Defense expenditure[a]	48.2	49.1	50.7	52.5	54.6	57.1	62.0	65.5
Gross national product[a]								
Actual historical experience	660.8	672.9	686.5	704.4	721.2	732.3	745.3	759.3
Estimated effect of Viet Nam		2.7	6.0	9.3	13.3	18.5	26.6	31.8
GNP without Viet Nam expenditure	660.8	670.2	680.5	695.1	707.9	713.8	718.7	727.5
Unemployment rate[b]								
Actual historical experience	4.8	4.7	4.5	4.2	3.8	3.8	3.8	3.7
Estimated rate in absence of Viet Nam expenditures	4.8	5.0	5.1	5.1	5.1	5.6	6.2	7.7

[a] Billions of current dollars.
[b] Percent of civilian labor force.

crease in government spending. Because a part of the increase in disposable income achieved by the tax cut is saved instead of spent on consumption, the expansionary effect of the tax cut is smaller.

While the elementary multiplier is a useful approximation, it is obviously too simple for analyzing the precise effects of an actual tax cut. For example, the tax cut of 1964 involved reductions in the corporate profit tax as well as personal income tax rates. Arthur Okun, of the President's Council of Economic Advisers, considered a number of complications to this basic model in analyzing the stimulus provided to the economy by the 1964 tax reduction. In particular, the relationship between GNP and disposable income was broken up into a number of separate equations. Furthermore, a more complicated consumption function, involving other variables in addition to disposable income, was employed. An attempt was also made to estimate the effects of the tax cut on investment spending. The estimates derived by Okun, if not the details of his model, are of interest. The change in tax legislation reduced federal income tax liabilities by $6.7 billion in 1964 and $11.5 billion in 1965. And the tax burden on corporations was reduced by $1.8 billion in 1964 and $3.0 billion in 1965. Okun estimates that instead of the rapid growth in GNP of more than $10 billion a quarter in 1964 and the first half of 1965, our economy would have had an increase of only $6.3 billion per quarter without the tax cut. Thus Okun attributes almost 40% of the growth of this six-quarter period to the tax cut.[13] A little over half of this increment would have been generated if investment had been unaffected by the tax cut. It must be emphasized that these are rough estimates; thus Gregory C. Chow,[14] utilizing a more sophisticated econometric model, estimated that only 1/10 of the increase in GNP in 1964 should be attributed to the tax cut.

c. The Balanced-Budget Multiplier

Suppose that government spending and taxes both increase by $1 billion. If the government's budget was initially balanced, such a policy would not create a deficit; or, if the government were initially running in the red, the policy would not increase the deficit. However, our intuition is wrong if it suggests that the expansionary effect of the increase in government spending would be precisely offset by the higher tax take. That a simultaneous increase in government spending and taxes will stimulate the

[13] Okun originally presented his paper, "Measuring the Impact of the 1964 Tax Cut," at the 1965 meetings of the American Statistical Association. It was published in *Perspectives on Economic Growth*, edited by Walter Heller, Random House, 1968.

[14] Multiplier, Accelerator, and Liquidity Preference in the Determination of National Income in the United States," *Review of Economics and Statistics*, February 1967, pp. 1–15.

economy may be seen by subtracting multiplier m6 from multiplier m1;[15] that is,

$$\frac{\Delta Y}{\Delta G} - \frac{\Delta Y}{\Delta d_0} = \frac{1}{1 - c_1 d_1} - \frac{c_1}{1 - c_1 d_1} = \frac{1 - c_1}{1 - c_1 d_1} = 0.33 \qquad (5.4)$$

This is the *balanced-budget multiplier*. While positive, it is considerably less than unity. Note that the balanced-budget multiplier would be exactly one if d_1, the slope of the disposable income line, were unity. But this would require that such leakages between GNP and disposable income as retained earnings would have to be completely insensitive to changes in the level of output.

d. The Paradox of Thrift

The effects of a shift in consumer spending habits may be evaluated with the aid of the fifth multiplier. Suppose that consumers decide to save more. To be more precise, suppose their preferences between today's versus tomorrow's consumption change so that they will save, collectively, $1 billion more at whatever their disposable income turns out to be. This means that the intercept c_0 of the consumption function (Equation 2.2) is reduced by $1 billion.[16] Since multiplier m5 is identical to m1, this has the same effect as a reduction in government spending of $1 billion; GNP falls by $3.01 billion. This effect is also shown in Figure 3.8; the change in saving habits shifts the consumption function, and hence the total spending line, downward by $1 billion. Further thought suggests that the actual change in GNP can be determined with multiplier m5: Δc_0 is minus $1 billion, and so $\Delta Y = -\$3.01$. Multiplier m8 reveals that the decline in disposable income is $\Delta Y_d = -\$2.26$. Thus, in addition to the planned $1 billion cut in

---

[15] That this analysis is correct may be seen by noting that after the policy change the new level of income Y^* has to satisfy Equation 5.2; that is,

$$Y^* = \frac{1}{1 - c_1 d_1} [c_0 + c_1(d_0 - \Delta T) + I + (G + \Delta G) + X - M]$$

with the change in taxes, ΔT, equal to the increase in government spending, ΔG; subtracting this after-change equation from Equation 5.2 reveals

$$\Delta Y = Y^* - Y = \frac{1}{1 - c_1 d_1} (-c_1 \Delta T + \Delta G) = \left(\frac{1 - c_1}{1 - c_1 d_1}\right) \Delta G \quad \text{if} \quad \Delta G = \Delta T$$

The analysis becomes more involved if it is assumed, for greater realism, that tax revenue is influenced by the level of economic activity; then a change in tax rates may influence d_1 and the change in tax revenue will depend on the change in income.

[16] To simplify the graph, the case of a parallel downward shift (a decrease in intercept c_0) is illustrated. In this instance the marginal propensity is unchanged by the decision to save more (the slope is unaffected), but at each level of income more is saved (the average propensity to consume is smaller than before).

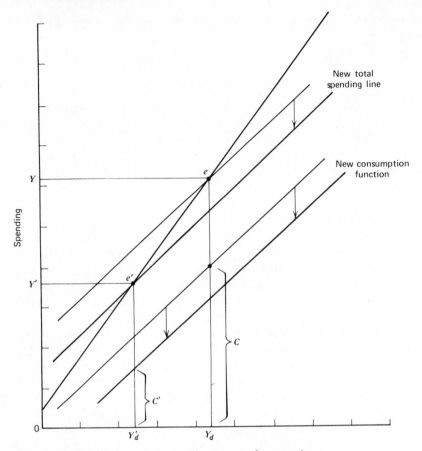

Fig. 3.8 *The paradox of thrift. The increased propensity to save means that at any given level of disposable income consumption must be less. Hence the consumption function shifts downward. Since* G, I, *and* X − M *are constant, the total spending line shifts down by the same amount. As a result, the equilibrium output is* e' *instead of* e. *Thus output and disposable income as well as consumption decline as a result of the decision to save more.*

consumption, there is an induced drop of $2.01 in consumption as a result of the decline in disposable income, or a total fall of $3.01. Personal saving, the excess of disposable income over consumption, has risen by only $ .75; that is, $\Delta S = \Delta Y_d - \Delta C = -\$2.26 - (-\$3.01) = +\$ .75$. To sum up, the planned rise in saving is not fully realized because the greater thrift leads to a fall in income. Ben Franklin was wrong in saying that "a penny saved is a penny earned"! This *paradox of thrift* arises because the reduction in effective demand occasioned by the collective decision of consumers to save more reduces disposable income as well as consumption.[17]

The paradox of thrift has two morals. First, it illustrates the *fallacy of composition*: the combined effects of individual decisions may work out, once all the interrelationships are taken into account, quite differently from what might be concluded by considering only the individual's decision in isolation. Second, it suggests that care is required in interpreting the government spending multiplier. To the extent that an increase in government spending means that the state will provide services that individuals would otherwise have purchased for themselves, the expansionary effect may be considerably less than the first multiplier suggests. For example, the increase in GNP generated by higher government spending occasioned by a medicare program might be partially offset if individuals are induced to curtail private medical expenditures and save more. On the other hand, other categories of government spending may not compete with private spending. After all, increased military expenditures may have a neutral effect on consumption habits, while an expanded highway construction program may induce a complementary increase in car and gasoline purchases.

e. A Simplification

For certain purposes it is essential to emphasize the distinction between disposable income and GNP. But when concern centers on the effects of changes in government spending instead of on tax policy, it may be more convenient to suppress the disposable income concept. To do this we rewrite Equation 5.1 as

$$C = \mathbf{c}_0 + \mathbf{c}_1 Y \tag{5.1'}$$

where

$$\mathbf{c}_0 = c_0 + c_1 d_0$$

and

$$\mathbf{c}_1 = c_1 d_1$$

Then Equation 5.2 can be written as

$$Y = \frac{1}{1 - \mathbf{c}_1} (\mathbf{c}_0 + I + G + X - M) \tag{5.2'}$$

---

[17] In more complex models there may be an actual decline in saving as a result of greater thrift! This can happen if investment spending depends on the level of output instead of being exogenous. See also Exercise 3.6.

Furthermore, the spending multipliers simplify:

$$\frac{\Delta Y}{\Delta G} = \frac{\Delta Y}{\Delta I} = \frac{\Delta Y}{\Delta X} = \frac{-\Delta Y}{\Delta M} = \frac{1}{1 - c_1} \tag{5.5}$$

When necessary, to avoid confusion, c_1 may be referred to as the *marginal propensity to consume out of GNP*, while c_1 is the *marginal propensity to consume out of disposable income.*

It is often useful to define (gross) saving as the part of output that is not consumed:

$$S = Y - C = Y - (c_0 - c_1 Y) = -c_0 + (1 - c_1) Y$$
$$= -c_0 + s Y \tag{5.6}$$

where

$$s = 1 - c_1$$

We call **s** the *marginal propensity to save* out of GNP. This is the useful concept, since the multiplier is simply

$$\frac{\Delta Y}{\Delta G} = \frac{1}{s} \tag{5.7}$$

the reciprocal of the marginal propensity to save.

3.6   EVALUATING TAX POLICY: THE FULL-EMPLOYMENT BUDGET

Sizable errors occur in predicting the deficit in the government's budget when changes in output are not anticipated. And, in recession, tax revenues fall off because personal income and corporate profits shrink, while rising unemployment benefits add to the government's deficit. The full-employment budget is an estimate of what the government's surplus or deficit would have been, given expenditure programs and tax rates, *if* the economy were operating at full employment. The full-employment budget is designed to segregate the effects of changes in the government's tax and spending policy from the effect of changes in the pace of economic activity.

During both Democratic and Republican administrations the concept of the full-employment budget has been used in persuading Congress and the public that sizable deficits in the federal budget should be tolerated. Subject to appropriate qualifications, the concept provides a useful tool for evaluating fiscal policy. Consider, for example, the 1971 deficit of $21.7 billion. The Council of Economic Advisers estimated that a $1 billion surplus would have been realized if the economy had been operating at full employment. In 1972 cuts in excise taxes and a variety of other types of tax relief marked a shift by the government toward a more expansionary fiscal policy. As a result, the full-employment budget had a deficit of $4 billion instead of a surplus. But the actual deficit fell from $21.7 billion to about $18.5 billion, because the economy moved closer to full employment.[18] Thus the two budgets moved in opposite directions.

a. Graphical Analysis

The full-employment budget concept is clarified in Figure 3.9. Line G is horizontal, reflecting the assumption that government spending on goods and services is independent of the level of output. But total government spending, indicated by line G_{exp}, is downward sloping because transfer payments fall off when the economy expands. The positively sloped T line reflects the tendency for a rise in output to generate additional tax revenue. To the right of x, tax revenues exceed government expenditures; there is a deficit to the left. Since Y_c, capacity output, lies to the right of x, a full-employment surplus is indicated on the graph. But, since actual output Y falls substantially short of Y_c, there will be a deficit on the government's books.

A change in tax policy shifts the T line as indicated on the right panel on the graph. In this instance a reduction in tax rates has created a deficit in the full-employment budget. But, if output expands from Y to Y', there will be no increase in the realized deficit. And, if expansionary policies or exogenous forces should cause output to exceed Y', the government's books will show an actual decline in the deficit.

Although the full-employment budget concept has its uses, it does not summarize fully the amount of stimulus that the government's fiscal policy is providing the economy. On the upper panel of Figure 3.10 the same full-employment budget surplus is realized as in the left panel of Figure 3.9. But because an adjustment in tax rates has made the T line much steeper than before, much more stimulus is provided to the economy whenever it is operating at less than full employment. In this instance, the actual budget may give a more accurate measure of fiscal policy than is provided by the full-employment budget. In the second panel a change in the composition of government expenditure, an increase in spending coupled with a decrease in transfer payments, has provided additional fiscal stimulus. But this shift is not revealed by the full-employment budget,

---

[18] The Council analyzed the full-employment budget in the 1973 *Economic Report of the President*, pp. 40–42. The figures quoted here are for the calendar year deficit as measured for the GNP accounts; the 1972 figures are not corrected for personal income tax overwithholding of about $9 billion.

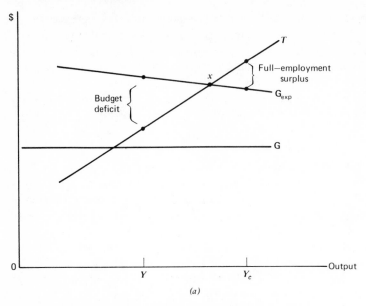

Fig. 3.9   *The full-employment budget. (a) If the economy operates at capacity it will realize a full-employment surplus, since the* T *line is above the* G_{exp} *at capacity output* Y_c, *indicating that tax revenue exceeds government spending. But, if actual output is* Y, *the government's books will reveal that the*

and it will show up on the government's books only to the extent that the rise in output causes an increase in revenue.

b.   Algebraic Analysis of the GNP—Disposable Income Gap

A more precise understanding of how changes in fiscal policy influence GNP requires a tedious look at the determinants of the disposable income line (Equation 2.3). The major factors linking GNP and disposable income, which were listed in Table 3.2, may be summarized as follows: start with GNP (Y), add on transfer payments (T_r), and then subtract off depreciation (D), excise taxes (T_e), corporate retained earnings (R_c), and the corporate profit taxes (T_c); this yields personal income (Y_p). Finally, subtract personal income taxes (T_p) from personal income to obtain disposable income (Y_d). More concisely,

$$Y_p = Y + T_r - (D + T_e + R_c + T_c) \qquad (6.1)$$

$$Y_d = Y_p - T_p \qquad (6.2)$$

A simple set of assumptions will be used to explain how each term in these

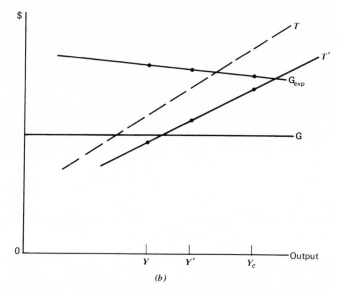

government is running a substantial deficit. (b) A tax cut shifts the tax revenue line down to T'. *Now there is a full-employment deficit since, even if the economy were to operate at capacity, expenditures would exceed revenue. But, if output should expand from* Y *to* Y', *the realized deficit will be the same as before the tax cut.*

equations is generated. First, suppose that depreciation and corporate profits are explained by output.

$$D = dY \tag{6.3}$$

$$\Pi = \pi_0 + \pi_1 Y \tag{6.4}$$

It is also reasonable to assume

$$\mathbf{T}_r = \mathbf{t}_0{}^r + \mathbf{t}_1{}^r Y \tag{6.5}$$

$$T_e = t^e Y \tag{6.6}$$

$$T_c = t^c \Pi \tag{6.7}$$

$$T_p = t_0{}^p + t_1{}^p Y_p \tag{6.8}$$

$$R_c = \rho(\Pi - T_c) \tag{6.9}$$

Here $\mathbf{t}_0{}^r$ and $\mathbf{t}_1{}^r$ reflect welfare policy, the various t's are parameters determined by tax rates; $t_0{}^p$ reflects the personal income tax exemption; ρ is the

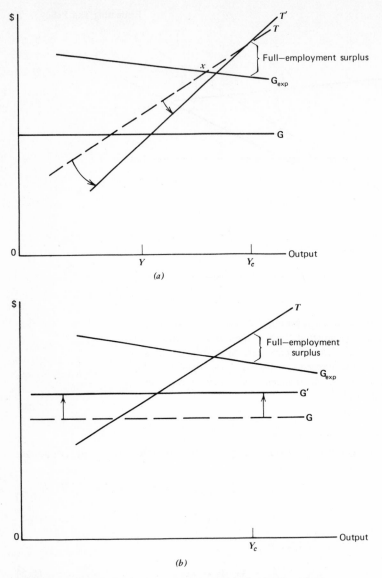

Fig. 3.10 *Imprecise budget measures of fiscal stimulus. (a) A change in tax rates could twist the* T *line so as to provide fiscal stimulus without changing the full-employment surplus. (b) An increase in the proportion of government expenditure devoted to the purchase of goods and services instead of to transfer payments would provide fiscal stimulus without changing the government deficit, at any level of output, or the full-employment surplus.*

80

corporate profit retention factor. Substituting into Equation 6.1 yields:

$$Y_p = Y + \mathbf{t}_0{}^r + \mathbf{t}_1{}^r Y - dY - t^e Y - [\rho(1 - t^c) + t^c](\pi_0 + \pi_1 Y)$$

$$= \{\mathbf{t}_0{}^r - [\rho(1 - t^c) + t^c]\pi_0\}$$

$$+ \{1 + \mathbf{t}_1{}^r - d - t^e - [\rho(1 - t^c) + t^c]\pi_1\} Y \qquad (6.10)$$

From Equation 6.2 we now have

$$Y_d = -t_0{}^p + (1 - t_1{}^p)\{\mathbf{t}_0{}^r - [\rho(1 - t^c) + t^c]\pi_0\}$$

$$+ (1 - t_1{}^p)\{1 + \mathbf{t}_1{}^r - d - t^e - [\rho(1 - t^c) + t^c]\pi_1\} Y \qquad (6.11)$$

This equation reduces to disposable income Equation 2.3 by defining

$$d_0 \equiv -t_0{}^p + (1 - t_1{}^p)\{\mathbf{t}_0{}^r - [\rho(1 - t^c) + t^c]\pi_0\}$$

and

$$d_1 \equiv (1 - t_1{}^p)\{1 + \mathbf{t}_1{}^r - d - t^e - [\rho(1 - t^c) + t^c]\pi_1\}$$

With these coefficients the effect of a change in corporate dividend payout practices or in tax rates can be evaluated in two steps. First, the effect of the change on the coefficients d_0 and d_1 is determined. Second, the multipliers developed earlier in this chapter can be used to find out how the change in the coefficients of the disposable income equation influence the level of output. For example, an increase in the personal income tax exemption ($t_0{}^p$) causes a corresponding change in d_0, the intercept of the disposable income function. From multiplier m6 we find that output rises by 2.68 x $\Delta t_0{}^p$. A change in t_1, on the other hand, will cause both the intercept and the slope of the disposable income function to shift, but the effect can be determined on Figure 3.5 or by using Equation 5.2 to solve for the new Y.

A decrease in d_1, Equation 5.2 reveals, lowers the level of GNP. Indeed, it makes all the multipliers smaller. This happens because a reduction in d_1 reduces the amount of GNP that filters down to consumers as disposable income. From Equation 6.11 it is clear that an increase in tax rates, a reduction in transfer payment coefficient $t_1{}^r$, or an increased tendency for corporations to retain earnings would all tend to depress the economy in precisely this way. It is sometimes said that an economy with high marginal tax rates suffers from "*fiscal drag*," a tendency for the stimulus of increased autonomous spending, **G** or **I**, to be diluted by leakages into tax revenue instead of contributing through a larger multiplier to the achievement of full employment.

One final point should be noted about the disposable income line. It should not be regarded as a particularly stable relationship since, as Equation 6.11 reveals, it will be subject to shift as a result of changes in tax regulations, adjustments in the dividend policy of corporations, and modifications in the procedures that business firms use to calculate depreciation. Thus it is surprising that the relationship in Figure 3.3, although not as stable as the consumption function, nonetheless exhibits a fair degree of regularity.

*3.7 A CAVEAT

Multiplier analysis gives simple answers to complex policy questions. But it should be clear that it constitutes no more than a partial exploration of the effects of changes in saving habits, government spending, and tax policy. In particular, it is necessary to relax the assumption that private investment spending and imports are exogenous. It is also necessary to evaluate the extent to which monetary policy provides an alternative instrument for achieving the full-employment objective. These issues will be analyzed in the next chapter. In addition, it will be necessary to consider the problem of price stability. Later we will focus on questions of economic dynamics. How *should* changes in government spending, tax structure, and monetary policy be timed if they are to contribute to the elimination of economic fluctuations? What types of policies will best contribute to the attainment of long-run growth objectives? It will also be necessary to disaggregate the model so that the effects of changes in the composition of government spending may be explored.

REFERENCES

1. Okun and Klein have both evaluated the effects of the 1964 tax cut on employment and output. Since Okun served on the President's Council of Economic Advisers at the time of the tax reduction, his analysis cannot be assumed to be completely impartial.

   Lawrence R. Klein, "Econometric Analysis of the Tax Cut of 1964," in *The Brookings Model: Some Further Results*, Rand-McNally, 1969.

   Arthur M. Okun, "Measuring the Impact of the 1964 Tax Reduction," in *Perspectives on Economic Growth* (Walter Heller, ed.), Random House, 1968.

2. A careful estimate of the balanced budget multiplier based on the Wharton econometric model appears in the following.

   Michael K. Evans, "Reconstruction and Estimation of the Balanced Budget Multiplier," *Review of Economics and Statistics*, February 1969, pp. 14–26.

3. The following contributions are all concerned with input-output analysis, a generalization of the multiplier concept discussed in the appendix to this chapter. Almon uses input-output procedures in an attempt to predict how output in each industry will change over time. Leontief et al. explain how disarmament might influence the demand for output—industry by industry and region by region. The remaining items are concerned with the proof of a remarkable theorem.

   Clopper Almon, Jr., *The American Economy to 1975*, Harper and Row, 1967.

   Wassily Leontief, Alison Morgan, Karen Polenski, David Simpson, and Edward Tower, "The Economic Impact, Industrial and Regional, of an Arms Cut," *Review of Economics and Statistics*, August 1965.

   Paul A. Samuelson, "Abstract of a Theorem Concerning Substitutability in Open Leontief Models"; Tjalling C. Koopmans, "Alternative Proof of the Substitution Theorem for Leontief Models in the Case of Three Industries"; Kenneth J. Arrow, "Alternative Proof of the Substitution Theorem for Leontief Models in the General Case," all in *Activity Analysis of Production and Allocation*, Cowles Commission Monograph Number 13, 1951. For a graphical analysis of this problem see Koopmans, *Three Essays on the State of Economic Science*, McGraw-Hill, 1957, pp. 101–105.

KEY CONCEPTS

disposable income

investment

transfer payments

corporate retained earnings (undistributed profits)

total spending line

disposable income line
exogenous versus endogenous variables
$\Delta Y/\Delta c_0$ versus $\Delta C/\Delta G$
balanced budget multiplier

EXERCISES

3.1   Determine, with the multipliers presented in this chapter, how a \$7 billion increase in private investment spending, other things being equal, would influence GNP, disposable income, and consumption spending.

3.2   The latest data plotted on Figures 3.2 and 3.3 are for 1972. Update these figures by obtaining the most recent data published. Do the new points lie along the same line? (*Hint.* Appropriate sources are listed in Appendix 2.A.)

3.3   Update Table 3.2 with the most recent data available.

3.4   Verify the formulas presented in the text for the following multipliers.

$$\text{m4: } \frac{\Delta Y}{\Delta I}, \quad \text{m5: } \frac{\Delta Y}{\Delta c_0}, \quad \text{m6: } \frac{\Delta Y}{\Delta d_0}, \quad \text{m2: } \frac{\Delta Y_d}{\Delta G}, \quad \text{m3: } \frac{\Delta C}{\Delta G}$$

[*Hint.* The derivation of m1 from Equation 5.2 was carefully spelled out in the text. In deriving m4 you can follow the same subtraction procedure, but use I^* instead of G^* in the after-change equation (and c_0^* for m5, etc.). To check the formula for m2, note that the first equality is obvious because the two ΔY's cancel out; then observe that $\Delta Y_d/\Delta Y = d_1$ and that $\Delta Y/\Delta G$ is m1. If you have a working knowledge of calculus simply differentiate.]

3.5   Quarterly data for 1947–1964 yield the following consumption and disposable income equations.

$$C = 2.48 + 0.91 Y_d + e$$

$$Y_d = -2.38 + 0.70 Y + e$$

Recompute multipliers $\Delta Y/\Delta G$, $\Delta Y/\Delta c_0$, and $\Delta C/\Delta G$.
Do these multipliers, based on evidence through 1964, differ substantially from those in the text, which were estimated with 1947–1972 data?

3.6   Determine, for the model presented in this chapter, whether personal savings ($Y_d - C$) could ever decrease as a result of a decision to save more, for *any* reasonable values of the models parameters ($0 < c_1 < 1$) and ($0 < d_1 < 1$).

3.7　Evaluate the following statement from the President's 1972 Budget message:

"[In a] full employment budget . . . spending does not exceed the revenues the economy could generate under the existing tax system at a time of full-employment. . . . The full-employment budget idea is in the nature of a self-fulfilling prophecy: By operating as if we were at full employment, we will help to bring about that full employment."

3.8　In January 1959, when unemployment was 6%, the budget submitted to Congress called for \$77 billion of government expenditure. It was expected that tax revenues through the year would be just sufficient to balance the budget. In Hearings before the Joint Economic Committee Maurice H. Stans, Director of the Budget Bureau, was asked by Representative Reuss of Wisconsin whether it might not be more appropriate from the point of view of the needs of the economy to have "a balanced budget of \$79 billion obtained by adding \$2 billion of the most imperative needs and repairing the gap by plugging \$2 billion worth of tax loopholes." Stans replied by stating that he would "find it extremely difficult offhand to weigh the effect on the employment level of the country of a \$2 billion increase in expenditures and a \$2 billion increase in the tax take." Representative Reuss then requested a memorandum from Stans on the issue.

Prepare a not-too-technical memorandum answering the question raised by Representative Reuss.

3.9　Find out how a change in d_1 from 0.75 to 0.80 would influence (a) multiplier m1, and (b) the level of output, given the magnitude of government spending and other exogenous variables of the model.

3.10　Suppose that corporations decide to cut the corporate profit retention coefficient (ρ of Equation 6.9) in half. Explain how this will change the link between GNP and disposable income. Then show how it would affect the level of economic activity, given investment spending and the other exogenous variables of the model. What would happen if investment was reduced by the amount of the cut in retained earnings?

3.11　Determine how well Equation 6.9 predicts corporate retained earnings. (*Hint.* Obtain back data from an appropriate source, as indicated in Appendix 2.A. Then plot a graph similar to Figure 3.2, but with retained earnings on the vertical axis and corporate profits on the horizontal axis. Fit a line by eye to the data in order to estimate the coefficient of Equation 6.9.) Save your data for Exercise 4.7 at the end of the next chapter.

3.12 Suppose that imports, instead of being exogenous, are endogenously determined by the following equation.

$$M = m_0 + m_1 Y$$

    a. How will this elaboration change the equations for the following multipliers?

        m1: $\dfrac{\Delta Y}{\Delta G}$

        m2: $\dfrac{\Delta Y_d}{\Delta G}$

        m5: $\dfrac{\Delta Y}{\Delta c_0}$

        m6: $\dfrac{\Delta Y}{\Delta d_0}$

    b. How will the modification affect the balanced budget multiplier?

    c. Draw a scatter plot of the United States imports against gross national product, perhaps using annual data from 1950–1970; fit a line to the data points and estimate m_0 and m_1.

3.13 A "reduced form" equation explains an endogenous variable in terms of exogenous variables. An example is provided by Equation 5.2, which explained GNP in terms of $I + G + X - M$. The reduced form equation was derived from the two underlying structural equations of the model, the consumption function and the disposable income equation, along with the GNP accounting identity. A reduced form equation facilitates the direct computation of the values of an endogenous variable from information on the magnitude of the exogenous variables.

    a. Since there are three endogenous variables for the model, there must be three reduced form equations. Derive the two remaining reduced form equations, similar to Equation 5.2, but with one explaining disposable income and the other explaining consumption behavior. (*Hint.* Instead of starting from scratch, substitute Equation 5.2 into Equation 2.3 in order to have the reduced form equation explaining Y_d; subtract $Y - C = I + G + X - M$ from both sides of Equation 5.2 to get the consumption reduced form equation.)

    b. The coefficients of the reduced form equations may be calculated indirectly from estimates of the structural parameters of the behavioral equations. In this way we estimated $1/(1 - c_1 d_1) = 3.01$ in the course of solving for m1. Find the other reduced form coefficients in the same way.

c. An alternative procedure for determining the reduced form coefficients is to estimate them directly from the data (e.g., by plotting Y against $I + G + X - M$). The following estimates were obtained in this way.

$$Y = -23.06 + 2.93\,(I + G + X - M) + e$$
$$Y_d = -37.12 + 2.17\,(I + G + X - M) + e$$
$$C = -23.06 + 1.93\,(I + G + X - M) + e$$

Do these alternative estimates suggest that the multiplier effects of changes in government spending are larger or smaller than those calculated in Section 3.5?

d. Can you solve backward from the three reduced form equations to find alternative estimates of the parameters of the underlying behavioral equations and the other multipliers of the model?[19]

3.14 The 20 periods of data on the following table were generated by the attached Fortran computer program on the Wesleyan University DEC 10. Observe that in period 3 government spending took a step increase from 125 to 135. You can trace through on the table the subsequent changes in GNP and related variables.

a. Write out the equations of the model used by the computer. You can estimate the consumption function and other behavioral equations from the data. Alternatively, you may be able to determine the consumption function by reading the computer program.[20]

[19] Should multiplier estimates be derived from structural equations (as in the text) or from the reduced form directly (as in this exercise)? The two procedures may yield different estimates. Which estimation procedure is preferred constitutes a tricky statistical issue discussed in econometric textbooks. See, for example, J. Johnston, *Econometric Methods*, McGraw-Hill, 1960, 2nd ed., 1972, or Ronald J. Wonnacott and Thomas H. Wonnacott, *Econometrics*, John Wiley, 1970.

[20] Unless you have been blessed with an exposure to FORTRAN you may have difficulty in reading the computer program, but the following hints help: an asterisk means "times" to the computer; furthermore, the computer perverts the meaning of an equal sign by interpreting = as an instruction to set the variable on the left of the equality equal to the value of the expression on the right. For example, one line says that retained earnings (REARN) are to be set equal to 5% of GNP. The comment lines provide further hints as to how to read the program. The IF instruction says to raise government spending by 10 in the third period (IF $I \neq 3$ the computer goes to 101 directly instead of executing instruction 99).

```
SIMULATION OF A MULTIPLIER MODEL FOR 20 PERIODS

QTR   GNP    INVS    CON     TAX     REAN    YD      GOVT

  0                                          435,2
  1   612,3   90,0   397,3   146,5   30,6   435,2   125,0
  2   612,3   90,0   397,3   146,5   30,6   435,2   125,0
  3   622,3   90,0   397,3   148,5   31,1   442,7   135,0
  4   628,9   90,0   403,9   149,8   31,4   447,7   135,0
  5   633,4   90,0   408,4   150,7   31,7   451,1   135,0
  6   636,4   90,0   411,4   151,3   31,8   453,3   135,0
  7   638,4   90,0   413,4   151,7   31,9   454,8   135,0
  8   639,7   90,0   414,7   151,9   32,0   455,8   135,0
  9   640,6   90,0   415,6   152,1   32,0   456,4   135,0
 10   641,2   90,0   416,2   152,2   32,1   456,9   135,0
 11   641,6   90,0   416,6   152,3   32,1   457,2   135,0
 12   641,8   90,0   416,8   152,4   32,1   457,4   135,0
 13   642,0   90,0   417,0   152,4   32,1   457,5   135,0
 14   642,1   90,0   417,1   152,4   32,1   457,6   135,0
 15   642,2   90,0   417,2   152,4   32,1   457,6   135,0
 16   642,2   90,0   417,2   152,4   32,1   457,7   135,0
 17   642,3   90,0   417,3   152,5   32,1   457,7   135,0
 18   642,3   90,0   417,3   152,5   32,1   457,7   135,0
 19   642,3   90,0   417,3   152,5   32,1   457,7   135,0
 20   642,3   90,0   417,3   152,5   32,1   457,7   135,0
```

```
COMMENT: THIS PROGRAM SIMULATES THE MULTIPLIER MODEL FOR 20 PERIODS
         REAL INVS
         YD=435.2
         GOV=125
         INVS=90
         TAXR=0.20
         WRITE(5,35) YD
35       FORMAT(' SIMULATION OF A MULTIPLIER MODEL FOR 20 PERIODS'//
         1' QTR    GNP     INVS    CON     TAX     REAN    YD      GOVT',//
         2'   0',35X,F7.1)
COMMENT: THE DO COMMAND REPEATS 20 TIMES ALL INSTRUCTIONS THROUGH 300
         DO 300 I=1,20
         CON =9.94 + 0.89*YD
         IF(I-3) 101,99,101
99       GOV=GOV+10
101      GNP=CON+INVS+GOV
         TAX=24+TAXR*GNP
         REARN = 0.05*GNP
         YD=GNP-TAX-REARN
         WRITE(5,201)  I,GNP,INVS,CON,TAX,REARN,YD,GOV
201      FORMAT(1H ,I3,7F7,1)
300      CONTINUE
COMMENT: THIS ENDS THE ITH ITERATION
         END
```

b. Explain how the behavior of the system would be modified if the change in government spending had been accompanied by tax legislation increasing the intercept of the tax function from 24 to 34.[21]

[21] If you know FORTRAN you may be able to modify the computer program in order to determine the effects of a tax cut.

APPENDIX 3.A   MULTISECTOR MULTIPLIERS

3.A.1   INTRODUCTION

The simple multiplier concept neglects complications created by international trade. It also fails to take into account obvious difficulties involved in working with such national income accounting aggregates as GNP and government spending without regard to the composition of output and final demand. The concept of the matrix multiplier is addressed to this problem. First, we consider the foreign trade multiplier. Then the same analytic framework will be used in developing an interindustry model of the economy. Furthermore, certain empirical input-output applications of the interindustry model will be summarized.

3.A.2   THE FOREIGN TRADE MULTIPLIER

Consider a hypothetical world composed of only two countries: country 1 might be the United States and country 2 the United Kingdom. We will analyze the consequences of an increase in government expenditures in the United States on the level of output in the United Kingdom.

Let C_1 denote consumption in the United States, and suppose that

$$C_1 = 0.9 Y_1 \tag{2.1}$$

In addition, assume that M_1, imports by the United States from the United Kingdom, are

$$M_1 = 0.1 Y_1 \tag{2.2}$$

We let G_1 denote United States government spending and I_1 United States private investment spending. Effective demand in the United States is

$$Y_1 = C_1 + G_1 + I_1 + X_1 - M_1 \tag{2.3}$$

X_1 denotes the exports of the United States.

For the United Kingdom, the other country in our two-country world, we have similar equations.

$$C_2 = 0.9 Y_2 \tag{2.1'}$$

$$M_2 = 0.2 Y_2 \tag{2.2'}$$

$$Y_2 = C_2 + G_2 + I_2 + X_2 - M_2 \tag{2.3'}$$

Since there are only two countries, United Kingdom imports *are* United States exports; $X_1 = M_2$; also, $X_2 = M_1$.

It is easy to verify that the following hypothetical data satisfy these eight equations.

	Y	$=$	C	$+ I$	$+ G$	$+ X$	$- M$
United States	225	=	202.5	+ 10	+ 10	+ 25	− 22.5
United Kingdom	125	=	112.5	+ 7	+ 8	+ 22.5	− 25

Note that the export surplus of the United States of 2.5 is matched by a corresponding deficit in the United Kingdom balance of trade. But how will the accounts be affected if United States government spending increases to 20?

To determine how changes in the exogenous variables—each country's investment and government spending—influence the level of economic activity and the balance of trade, we substitute Equations 2.1, 2.2, and 2.2′ into Equation 2.3, and Equations 2.1′, 2.2′, and 2.2 into Equation 2.3′. We now have two simultaneous equations.

$$\text{United States} \qquad Y_1 = 0.9Y_1 + G_1 + I_1 + 0.2Y_2 - 0.1Y_1$$
$$\text{United Kingdom} \quad Y_2 = 0.9Y_2 + G_2 + I_2 + 0.1Y_1 - 0.2Y_2$$
$$(2.4)$$

Note that the level of economic activity in the United States is influenced by the United Kingdom's imports, which in turn are influenced by government spending in the United Kingdom and her exports to the United States. This is illustrated schematically by the flowchart in Figure 3.A.1. Solving the two simultaneous equations yields:

$$\text{United States} \qquad Y_1 = 7.5(I_1 + G_1) + 5(I_2 + G_2)$$
$$\text{United Kingdom} \quad Y_2 = 2.5(I_1 + G_1) + 5(I_2 + G_2)$$
$$(2.5)$$

So there are four multipliers; each country's output is influenced by investment and government spending both at home and abroad. An increase in G_1 has three times as big an impact on Y_1 as it does on Y_2; but an increase in G_2 influences output equally in both countries. These differences arise even though both countries have the same marginal propensity to consume out of GNP; the critical difference is in the marginal propensities to import. When effective demand in country 2 increases, a sizable portion of expenditures leaks into country 1; for this reason, the second country has smaller multipliers. To illustrate, if G_1 increases by 10, Y_1 will increase by 75 to 300 and Y_2 will increase by 25. The revised National Income Accounts, determined with the aid of the simultaneous equations, reflect the induced increase in consumption and imports.

$$Y = C + I + G + X - M$$

| United States | $300 = 270 + 10 + 20 + 30 - 30$ |
| United Kingdom | $150 = 135 + 7 + 8 + 30 - 30$ |

Note that the United States enjoys higher output but no longer experiences a surplus in the balance of trade.

Under what circumstances will equilibrium be achieved in the balance of trade? From Equations 2.2 and 2.2′ we note that $M_1 = M_2$ implies that $0.1Y_1 = 0.2Y_2$; that is, United States output must be twice United Kingdom output ($Y_1 = 2Y_2$) if imports are to equal exports. Whether equilibrium will be achieved in the balance of trade depends on the level of government expenditures and investment in both countries, since from Equation 2.5 we find that $Y_1 = 2Y_2$ yields

$$Y_1 = 7.5(I_1 + G_1) + 5(I_2 + G_2) = 2Y_2 = 5(I_1 + G_1) + 10(I_2 + G_2)$$

or

$$I_1 + G_1 = 2(I_2 + G_2)$$

as the condition for exports to equal imports. Unfortunately, we can hope to achieve equilibrium in both the balance of trade and full employment simultane-

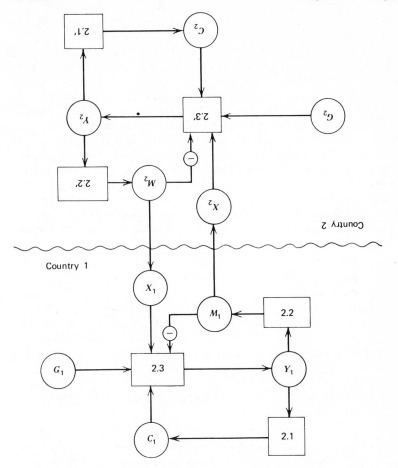

Fig. 3.A.1 *Foreign trade multiplier flowchart. Foreign trade links countries 1 and 2, because country 1 imports are the exports of country 2 and country 2 imports are the exports of country 1.*

ously only if the capacity output in country one happens to be twice that of country two. Thus, in terms of the hypothetical data considered earlier, if the capacity output of the United States is 225 and that of the United Kingdom is 125, full employment will involve a United Kingdom deficit of 2.5. Of course, earnings from foreign investments may pay for an excess of imports over exports in order to achieve equilibrium in the balance of payments while both economies operate at capacity. And, in Chapter 9, we will see that central banks may manipulate monetary controls to induce capital movements that will help reconcile the full employment objective with balance of payments equilibrium. But eventually it may be necessary to change the propensities of the two countries to import through adjustments in relative prices; price adjustments may be achieved by inflation or deflation or, less painfully, by currency devaluation. Alternatively, tariffs, quotas, export subsidies, and foreign exchange rationing may be resorted to in an effort to reconcile full employment with international financial stability.

The foreign trade multiplier concept is rather involved; later in this appendix we will see that it becomes still more complicated when more countries are considered. But it is an important concept because sizable errors in estimating the multiplier can develop when countries are erroneously treated in isolation. For example, suppose that foreign trade complications were neglected entirely in determining the multiplier effect of increased government spending. Since both countries have the same marginal propensity to consume, we would have estimated $\Delta Y/\Delta G = 1/(1 - 0.9) = 10$ for each country, and this is much too large. Sizable errors in estimating the multiplier would be made if imports alone were treated as exogenous, the feedback interaction of exports being neglected; specifically, we would erroneously estimate

$$\frac{\Delta Y_1}{\Delta G_1} = \frac{1}{(1 - 0.9 + 0.1)} = 5$$

and

$$\frac{\Delta Y_2}{\Delta G_2} = \frac{1}{(1 - 0.9 + 0.2)} = 3\tfrac{1}{3}$$

The true multiplier is underestimated when the feedback of effective demand through the other country is neglected.

3.A.3 INPUT-OUTPUT ANALYSIS—A TWO-INDUSTRY EXAMPLE

Elementary multiplier analysis relates changes in aggregate GNP to changes in government spending. But how would the effects of a reduction in government spending, such as might be occasioned by disarmament, be distributed among different sectors of the economy? Which industries would be hardest hit? What geographical regions of the country are most sensitive to changes in government spending? Input-output analysis, a procedure pioneered by Professor Leontief of Harvard University, is designed to answer this type of question.

In one application Leontief and his collaborators at the Harvard Economic Research Project utilized a model involving 60 sectors and 19 geographical regions in estimating the impact that a $6.3 billion (20%) reduction in military spending would have had on the American economy in 1958.[22] They projected that a $7.6 billion increase in nonmilitary expenditure would be required to prevent a reduction in total employment. But even with the offsetting expansion preventing any change in the overall level of employment, those industries and geographical regions particularly sensitive to cuts in defense spending would suffer: For example, they pro-

---

[22] Wassily Leontief, Alison Morgan, Karen Polenske, David Simpson, and Edward Tower, "The Economic Impact—Industrial and Regional—of an Arms Cut," *Review of Economics and Statistics*, August 1965, pp. 217–241.

Table 3.A.1 INTERINDUSTRY TRANSACTIONS (ALL FIGURES IN TONS)

			Final Bill of Goods	
Uses:	Coal	Steel	(Consumption + Government)	Total Output
Sources				
Coal[a]	1800	250	200	2250
Steel[b]	225	875	150	1250

[a] The first row of the table reveals that 1800 tons of coals were used in the production of coal, 250 in the production of steel, and 200 were used by consumers and the government.

[b] The second row indicates how the 1250 tons of steel output were allocated among alternative uses.

jected a 16.05% reduction in aircraft output, a 15.42% cut in ordinance, a 13.26% cut in research and development, and a 5.4% cut in electronics equipment. But motor vehicles would be up by 1.21%, apparel by 1.66%, tobacco by 1.76%, and so on. California was the region most sensitive to the arms cut, experiencing an employment reduction of 1.85%; on the other hand, New York would benefit slightly as a result of the offsetting civilian expenditure; Minnesota, North Dakota, and South Dakota would benefit the most, with a gain of 1.54% in employment.

How input-output analysis works may be explained with a simple numerical example of a hypothetical economy producing only two commodities, coal and steel. Suppose that the relevant technology is summarized by Table 3.A.1, where the information has been gathered in the course of collecting data for a census of manufacturers.[23]

Input-output analysis is designed to forecast the effects of a change in the final bill of goods—consumption plus private investment plus government spending—on the output of each industry. For example, we can ask how the total output of coal and steel will shift if final demand for coal changes to 190 and final demand for steel rises to 180. The question asked differs in several respects from traditional multiplier analysis: (1) consumption as well as investment plus government spending is treated as exogenous; (2) information concerning the composition instead of just the total dollar value of government spending is provided; and (3) we wish to forecast the *gross* output of each industry, including goods used up in the course of producing other commodities instead of just the market value of final product excluding interindustry transactions.

Input-output analysis provides an answer to questions of this type by making a heroic assumption. It is assumed that the recipe for the production of each good involves fixed proportions. For example, Table 3.A.1 revealed that 225 tons of steel

[23] The data are obviously not realistic; the numbers were picked in a way that simplifies subsequent computation.

Table 3.A.2 DIRECT REQUIREMENTS PER TON OF GROSS OUTPUT

	Coal	Steel
Coal	0.8 (1800/2250)	0.2 (250/1250)
Steel	0.1 (225/2250)	0.7 (875/1250)

Note. For the composition of inputs to an industry read the column for that industry.

Table 3.A.3 TOTAL REQUIREMENTS (DIRECT PLUS INDIRECT) PER TON OF DELIVERY OF FINAL DEMAND

	Coal	Steel
Coal	7.5	5
Steel	2.5	5

Note. Each entry represents the output required, directly and indirectly, from the industry named at the beginning of the row for each ton delivered to final demand of the industry named at the head of the column.

were used in the production of 2250 tons of coal; so it will be assumed that $225/2250 = 0.1$ ton of steel is required per ton of coal output. The four "input-output" coefficients in Table 3.A.2 summarize the technology for producing coal and steel derived from the census data under the assumption of fixed proportions and constant returns to scale. Inspection of the table reveals that production of 2000 tons of coals will directly require 200 tons of steel; but this is not the full amount, since coal is required in the production of the steel used to produce the coal. In order to determine the total requirements, direct and indirect, we must consider the following two simultaneous equations.

$$0.8C + 0.2S + Y_c = C$$
$$0.1C + 0.7S + Y_s = S \tag{3.1}$$

Here C and S are gross outputs of coal and steel, while Y_c and Y_s denote final demand for these two commodities. Solution of these two simultaneous equations yields:[24]

$$C = 7.5Y_c + 5Y_s$$
$$S = 2.5Y_c + 5Y_s \tag{3.2}$$

Table 3.A.3 presents in tabular form the multipliers relating gross output to final demand for each industry. It is now possible to predict how the demands on each

---

[24] The figures in Table 3.A.1 were artfully chosen to make the two simultaneous equations constituting Equation 3.1 equivalent to the foreign trade Equation 2.4; for this reason the multipliers of Equation 3.2 are identical to the foreign trade multipliers derived earlier (see Equation 2.5).

Table 3.A.1′ PREDICTED INTERINDUSTRY TRANSACTIONS

Uses:	Coal	Steel	Final Bill of Goods	Total Output
Sources				
Coal	1,680	260	160	2,100
Steel	210	910	180	1,300

industry will be affected by changes in the final bill of goods. Suppose, for example, that final demand of Y_c = 160 and Y_s = 180 are forecast for next year. Equation 3.2 yields the estimated gross output of each industry; furthermore, the input requirements can be obtained with the aid of the coefficients in Table 3.A.2. The predictions for the revised, final bill of goods are summarized in Table 3.A.1′. Comparison with the initial set of interindustry transactions recorded on Table 3.A.1 reveals how the shift in the composition of final demand has influenced output of both commodities.

3.A.4 INPUT-OUTPUT APPLICATIONS

Input-output tables have been estimated for a very large number of countries, including the United States. In planning for defense mobilization the input-output approach facilitates the advance identification of critical sectors of the economy that are likely to encounter capacity ceilings. In addition to its obvious planning applications in controlled economies, input-output has been invoked to derive detailed forecasts of future developments in the American economy. For example, in Clopper Almon's 1966 book, *The American Economy to 1975*, he published for 90 industries a set of "mutually consistent forecasts of what consumers will buy, how much they will invest, what exports, imports and government purchases will be, how technology will change, how much each industry will sell to each other industry, how labor productivity will increase, and how many people will be employed."[25] And in the comparative analysis of the structure of different economies, inspection of input-output tables can provide great insight.[26]

Part of an 84 x 84 sector table recording interindustry transactions for the United States economy in 1963 is presented in Table 3.A.1*.[27] The entries receive exactly the same interpretation as the hypothetical data reported on corresponding 2 x 2 Table 3.A.1. However, the input-output statisticians find it easier to measure

[25] Clopper Almon, Jr., *The American Economy to 1975*, Harper & Row, 1966, p. ix.

[26] A variety of input-output applications are summarized by Hollis B. Chenery and Paul G. Clark in *Interindustry Economics*, John Wiley, 1959.

[27] The full 84 x 84 sector tables, estimated from the 1963 Census of Manufactures, is published in the November 1969, *Survey of Current Business*. The Department of Commerce will also provide a more detailed 370 sector table, but with 136,900 entries it is almost unmanageable except on an electronic computer; the census releases the larger tables on magnetic tape for computer applications at cost.

Table 3.A.1* INTERINDUSTRY TRANSACTIONS UNITED STATES ECONOMY, 1963 (IN MILLIONS OF DOLLARS AT PRODUCERS' PRICES)

For the Distribution of Output of an Industry, Read the Row for that Industry

For the Composition of Inputs to an Industry, Read the Column for that Industry

Industry Number	Industry	1 Livestock and Livestock Products	2 Other Agricultural Products	3 Forestry and Fishery Products	4 Agricultural, Forestry and Fishery Services	5 Iron and Ferroalloy Ores Mining	6 Nonferrous Metal Ores Mining	7 Coal Mining	8 Crude Petroleum and Natural Gas	9 Stone and Clay Mining and Quarrying	10 Chemical and Fertilizer Mineral Mining	Intermediate Outputs, Total	Total Final Demand	Total
1	Livestock and livestock products	4,750	1,819	117	192	—	—	—	—	—	—	24,492	2,193	26,684
2	Other agricultural products	7,897	769	117	550	—	—	—	—	—	—	20,901	6,365	27,266
3	Forestry and fishery products	—	—	35	—	—	—	—	—	—	—	1,411	340	1,751
4	Agricultural, forestry and fishery services	445	1,053	74	—	—	—	—	—	—	—	1,762	9	1,772
5	Iron and ferroalloy ores mining	—	—	—	—	55	1	(a)	(a)	(a)	1	1,357	72	1,429
6	Nonferrous metal ores mining	—	—	—	—	25	263	(a)	(a)	5	(a)	1,279	239	1,519
7	Coal mining	6	1	—	—	5	1	410	—	5	1	2,117	520	2,637
8	Crude petroleum and natural gas	—	—	—	—	—	(a)	1	297	17	5	12,237	27	12,265
9	Stone and clay mining and quarrying	1	85	—	(a)	5	(a)	1	—	—	—	1,938	26	2,024
10	Chemical and fertilizer mineral mining	—	35	—	—	—	6	(a)	—	1	31	609	88	696
11	New construction	—	—	—	—	—	—	—	—	—	—	—	65,519	65,519
12	Maintenance and repair construction	200	367	—	—	1	7	14	379	11	3	14,871	4,924	19,791
13	Ordnance and accessories	—	—	—	—	—	—	—	—	—	—	648	5,654	6,302
14	Food and kindred products	3,554	2	44	34	—	(a)	—	—	(a)	(a)	21,306	52,957	74,263
15	Tobacco manufactures	—	—	—	—	—	—	—	—	—	—	1,950	5,474	7,425
16	Broad and narrow fabrics, yarn and thread mills	—	9	—	—	(a)	(a)	—	—	—	(a)	12,141	990	13,131
17	Miscellaneous textile goods and floor coverings	9	29	62	41	(a)	(a)	(a)	2	(a)	—	2,471	1,197	3,668
18	Apparel	17	43	1	—	—	(a)	—	—	—	—	3,974	14,655	18,029
19	Miscellaneous fabricated textile products	—	—	—	—	—	—	—	—	—	—	1,541	1,634	3,174
20	Lumber and wood products, except containers	2	2	—	—	2	10	17	(a)	(a)	(a)	10,152	502	10,654

a Less than $500,000

all units in terms of their dollar value at producer's prices (which excludes excise taxes and transport costs) instead of in physical units. To illustrate, the first entry of row 12 indicates that the livestock sector purchased $200 million of maintenance and repair construction in 1963. In Table 3.A.2* the figures are normalized; here the first entry in row 12 of 0.0075 indicates that every million dollars of livestock output requires $7500 worth of maintenance and repair construction. This is only the direct requirement and does not take into account the demand generated indirectly for other sectors whose outputs are used in the production of livestock. Finally, Table 3.A.3* reveals that $28,030 of maintenance construction, directly and indirectly, is required per million dollars of livestock output; the 0.028030 entry is but one of 7056 multipliers on the full 84 x 84 table. Apart from possible planning applications, these tables are of interest to business firms; for example, a company may try to identify potential markets by comparing its own customer mix with the distribution of sales for all firms in its industry.

Input-output analysis relies on the assumption that the recipe for producing each commodity is independent of the scale of output and unaffected by changes in the composition of the final bill of goods. Surely these assumptions are unrealistic (in cooking for an army one doesn't simply multiply the recipe for a bachelor by the number of troops). Profit-maximizing firms can be expected to substitute one input for another when relative prices change as a result of shifts in the composition of demand. But the critical question is not whether the assumptions are accurate; the crux of the matter concerns the accuracy with which the input-output procedure can predict the effects of shifts in the composition of final demand.

The prediction issue is still shrouded in controversy.[28] The customary test uses an input-output matrix derived from census year data to predict the composition of outputs in another year, the input-output predictions being compared with those derived from an alternative "naive" projective procedure. One naive alternative presumes that the output of each industry will change by the same percentage as GNP; a second "final-demand-blowup" procedure assumes that each industry's output changes by the same percentage as the final demand for its product. The record is mixed relative to the naive alternatives and the accuracy of the input-output projections clearly deteriorates when the projection year is not close to the census year or when a small input-output table is employed. It has been argued that when the final bill of goods changes little, as between the peacetime years used for testing purposes, we would expect roughly the same projections from input-output analysis and the naive blowup procedures. But even if input-output does not have a decisive margin of superiority in comparing normal years, it can still do much better than the naive alternatives when looking at the effects of drastic changes in the composition of demand, such as would occur in a period of defense mobiliza-

[28] In the *Structure of the American Economy, 1919–1939*, Leontief reported favorable results that were subsequently questioned by Carl Christ in "A Review of Input-Output Analysis," *Input-Output Analysis, An Appraisal*, National Bureau of Economic Research, 1955. The evidence was also discussed by Robert Dorfman, "The Nature and Significance of Input-Output Analysis," *Review of Economics and Statistics*, 1954; see also T. C. Koopmans, *Three Essays in the State of Economic Science*, McGraw-Hill, 1957, and Hollis Chenery and P. Clark, *Interindustry Economics*, Wiley, 1959.

Table 3.A.2* DIRECT REQUIREMENTS PER DOLLAR OF GROSS OUTPUT, 1963 (PRODUCERS' PRICES)

Industry Number	For the Composition of Inputs to an Industry, Read the Column for that Industry	Livestock and Livestock Products 1	Other Agricultural Products 2	Forestry and Fishery Products 3	Agricultural, Forestry and Fishery Services 4	Iron and Ferroalloy Ores Mining 5	Nonferrous Metal Ores Mining 6	Coal Mining 7	Crude Petroleum and Natural Gas 8	Stone and Clay Mining and Quarrying 9
1	Livestock and livestock products	0.17800	0.06673	0.06687	0.10823	—	—	—	—	—
2	Other agricultural products	0.29596	0.02819	0.06665	0.31040	—	—	—	—	—
3	Forestry and fishery products	—	—	0.01992	—	—	—	—	—	—
4	Agricultural, forestry and fishery services	0.01667	0.03863	0.04243	—	—	—	—	—	0.00002
5	Iron and ferroalloy ores mining	—	—	—	—	0.03816	0.00089	0.00004	—	—
6	Nonferrous metal ores mining	0.00021	—	—	—	0.01782	0.17332	0.00010	0.00002	0.00225
7	Coal mining	—	0.00002	—	—	0.00861	0.00090	0.15561	(a)	0.00227
8	Crude petroleum and natural gas	0.00006	—	—	—	—	—	—	0.02418	—
9	Stone and clay mining and quarrying	—	0.00311	—	(a)	0.00339	0.00029	0.00026	—	0.00860
10	Chemical and fertilizer mineral mining	—	0.00129	—	—	—	0.00408	0.00001	—	0.00072
11	New construction	—	—	—	—	—	—	—	—	—
12	Maintenance and repair construction	0.00750	0.01344	—	—	0.00060	0.00491	0.00549	0.03093	0.00543
13	Ordnance and accessories	—	—	—	—	—	—	—	—	—
14	Food and kindred products	0.13319	0.00008	0.02529	0.01933	—	—	—	—	—
15	Tobacco manufactures	—	—	—	—	—	—	—	—	0.00007
16	Broad and narrow fabrics, yarn and thread mills	0.00035	0.00034	0.03536	0.02296	0.00001	0.00019	—	—	—
17	Miscellaneous textile goods and floor coverings	—	0.00106	—	—	(a)	0.00010	(a)	0.00017	0.00006
18	Apparel	—	—	—	—	—	0.00001	—	—	—
19	Miscellaneous fabricated textile products	0.00065	0.00158	0.00072	—	—	—	—	—	—
20	Lumber and wood products, except containers	0.00008	0.00008	—	—	0.00169	0.00651	0.00636	0.00001	0.00002

a Less than 0.00001

Table 3.A.3* TOTAL REQUIREMENTS (DIRECT AND INDIRECT) PER DOLLAR TO DELIVERY OF FINAL DEMAND, 1963 (PRODUCERS' PRICES)

Industry Number	Each Entry Represents the Output Required, Directly and Indirectly, from the Industry Named at the Beginning of the Row for Each Dollar of Delivery to Final Demand by the Industry Named at the Head of the Column	Livestock and Livestock Products	Other Agricultural Products	Forestry and Fishery Products	Agricultural Forestry and Fishery Services	Iron and Ferroalloy Ores Mining	Non-ferrous Metal Ores Mining	Coal Mining	Crude Petroleum and Natural Gas	Stone and Clay Mining and Quarrying
		1	2	3	4	5	6	7	8	9
1	Livestock and livestock products	1.31963	0.10112	0.11907	0.18536	0.00291	0.00268	0.00239	0.00483	0.00253
2	Other agricultural products	0.43481	1.07832	0.12999	0.39019	0.00381	0.00314	0.00285	0.00639	0.00286
3	Forestry and fishery products	0.00141	0.00073	1.02000	0.00130	0.00048	0.00134	0.00124	0.00033	0.00038
4	Agricultural, forestry and fishery services	0.03898	0.04347	0.05041	1.01832	0.00028	0.00029	0.00027	0.00042	0.00021
5	Iron and ferroalloy ores mining	0.00074	0.00090	0.00111	0.00153	1.04173	0.00375	0.00242	0.00063	0.00233
6	Nonferrous metal ores mining	0.00063	0.00091	0.00083	0.00143	0.02314	1.21088	0.00113	0.00051	0.00395
7	Coal mining	0.00182	0.00156	0.00120	0.00187	0.00653	0.00433	1.18698	0.00113	0.00630
8	Crude petroleum and natural gas	0.01799	0.02576	0.01660	0.01405	0.01088	0.01089	0.01162	1.03246	0.02066
9	Stone and clay mining and quarrying	0.00245	0.00460	0.00107	0.00225	0.00447	0.00135	0.00120	0.00112	1.01508
10	Chemical and Fertilizer mineral mining	0.00180	0.00373	0.00081	0.00174	0.00090	0.00701	0.00090	0.00050	0.00202
11	New construction	—	—	—	—	—	—	—	—	—
12	Maintenance and repair construction	0.02803	0.02957	0.00964	0.01835	0.01685	0.01670	0.01643	0.05321	0.01650
13	Ordnance and accessories	0.00008	0.00007	0.00009	0.00015	0.00012	0.00016	0.00023	0.00011	0.00026
14	Food and kindred products	0.21689	0.02195	0.05810	0.06081	0.00409	0.00560	0.00466	0.00484	0.00550
15	Tobacco manufactures	0.00021	0.00020	0.00042	0.00043	0.00019	0.00029	0.00026	0.00027	0.00040
16	Broad and narrow fabrics, yarn and thread mills	0.00313	0.00340	0.01341	0.00975	0.00084	0.00152	0.00139	0.00068	0.00279
17	Miscellaneous textile goods and floor coverings	0.00290	0.00326	0.04164	0.02729	0.00062	0.00095	0.00119	0.00055	0.00239
18	Apparel	0.00064	0.00047	0.00091	0.00099	0.00035	0.00048	0.00047	0.00034	0.00064
19	Miscellaneous fabricated textile products	0.00228	0.00227	0.00261	0.00195	0.00019	0.00026	0.00028	0.00015	0.00056
20	Lumber and wood products, except containers	0.00485	0.00562	0.00319	0.01094	0.00468	0.01367	0.01318	0.00365	0.00326

tion. Still, it may also be true that a clearer margin of superiority is required to justify the great expense involved in marshalling data for input-output projections. Be that as it may, part of the contribution of input-output analysis has been in serving as a stepping-stone to more complicated but more realistic "process analysis" models that allow for input substitution.

†3.A.5 MATRIX ANALYSIS

Readers familiar with matrix notation will find that the two equation examples used to illustrate the foreign-trade multiplier and input-output analysis may be easily generalized to encompass additional sectors. Thus the two equation coal and steel input-output system may be written:

$$\begin{bmatrix} 0.8 & 0.2 \\ 0.1 & 0.7 \end{bmatrix} \begin{bmatrix} C \\ S \end{bmatrix} + \begin{bmatrix} Y_C \\ Y_S \end{bmatrix} = \begin{bmatrix} C \\ S \end{bmatrix} \qquad (3.1\text{m})$$

As a first step in solving this equation, we subtract the matrix product on the left from both sides, yielding:

$$\begin{bmatrix} Y_C \\ Y_S \end{bmatrix} = \begin{bmatrix} C \\ S \end{bmatrix} - \begin{bmatrix} 0.8 & 0.2 \\ 0.1 & 0.7 \end{bmatrix} \begin{bmatrix} C \\ S \end{bmatrix} = \begin{bmatrix} 1 - 0.8 & - 0.2 \\ - 0.1 & 1 - 0.7 \end{bmatrix} \begin{bmatrix} C \\ S \end{bmatrix}$$

Premultiplication of this equation by the inverse of the 2 x 2 matrix on the far right yields:[29]

$$\begin{bmatrix} 7.5 & 0.5 \\ 2.5 & 0.5 \end{bmatrix} \begin{bmatrix} Y_C \\ Y_S \end{bmatrix} = \begin{bmatrix} C \\ S \end{bmatrix} \qquad (3.2\text{m})$$

And this is the system of two simultaneous equations constituting solution set 3.2. The coefficients of the inverse were reported as the "direct plus indirect requirements" of Table 3.A.3.

Consider an economy of n sectors, each producing a single commodity. Let X_i denote the gross output of commodity i, X_{ij} the output of good i used as inputs by sector j, and Y_i the final demand for commodity i (output of good i utilized other than in the productive process—consumption, government, investment, and exports-imports). Since Y_i is a residual category, we have gross outputs

$$X_i = \sum_j X_{ij} + Y_i \qquad (i = 1, \dots, n) \qquad (5.1)$$

Furthermore, if we define $a_{ij} = X_{ij}/X_j$, the amount of good i used per unit of commodity j produced, we also have $X_i = \sum_j a_{ij}X_j$ or, in matrix notation,

$$X = AX + Y \qquad (5.2)$$

where $X = \text{col}(X_i)$, $Y = \text{col}(Y_i)$, and $A = [a_{ij}]$. Thus, for the two-industry example, A is the 2 x 2 matrix on the left of equation 3.1m and the a_{ij} coefficients are

---

[29] The reader can verify that the square matrix in Equation 3.2m is the inverse of the 2 x 2 matrix at the right of the immediately preceding equation.

those reported on Table 3.A.2 presenting the "direct requirements per unit of output." As before, we subtract AX from both sides, obtaining

$$Y = X - AX = (I - A)X$$

This states that the sum of the direct input requirements plus final demand must be met by gross outputs. Premultiplying by $(I - A)^{-1}$, provided it exists, yields as the n sector analog of Equation 3.2m the solution vector:

$$X = (I - A)^{-1}Y \tag{5.3}$$

If the a_{ij} are insensitive to changes in Y, we can compute the vector X of gross output generated by any vector Y of final demands. Equation 5.3 is the generalization of the multiplier concept to n sectors.

a. Price Implications

The price implications of input-output analysis also deserve consideration and will prove useful when the time comes to study wage-push and cost-push inflation. Let p_i denote the price of the ith commodity. The cost of the input from sector i required to produce a unit of commodity j is then $p_i a_{ij}$. The total cost of all purchased inputs utilized in the production of a unit of commodity j is $\sum_i p_i a_{ij}$.

Also, let w be the wage rate and L_j the amount of labor used in producing one unit of commodity j; then wL_j is the labor cost. Finally, let m_j denote the gross profit margin per unit of output received by the producers of the jth commodity—the excess of the price of j over its input and labor cost—for example, net profits, taxes, depreciation allowances; that is:

$$m_j = p_j - \sum_i p_i a_{ij} - wL_j \qquad (j = 1, \ldots n)$$

In matrix notation we may write

$$P = PA + wL + M$$

where $P = \text{row}(p_i)$, $M = \text{row}(m_j)$, and $L = \text{row}(L_j)$, and we have

$$P = (M + wL)(I - A)^{-1} \tag{5.4}$$

an equation that would be useful for predicting the effect on different prices of changes in markups resulting from wage changes only if the a_{ij} were insensitive to price movements. Note that

$$GNP = PY = (M + wL)(I - A)^{-1}Y = (M + wL)X \tag{5.5}$$

The first equality says that GNP is the sum of sector final demands evaluated at market price; the last equality, which follows from Equation 5.3, says that GNP is the sum of value added.

b. Viable Solutions, a Theorem

Under what circumstances will the matrix A be nonsingular so that the inhomogeneous system of simultaneous Equation 5.2 will turn out to be solvable? And is there any reason to expect that the solution vector will involve only nonnegative "outputs?" Clearly, it would be disastrous to invest the great amount of effort involved in estimating an empirical input-output matrix if it turned out that the system yielded no solution; it would be equally unfortunate if the system ended up predicting negative outputs for certain sectors; for example, the steel process operating in reverse by generating coke and pig iron from steel—disposal of scrap is not that simple. Fortunately, it can be shown that neither of these incongruities can arise with empirically estimated input-output matrices.

First we must introduce a definition.

Definition: A nonnegative square matrix A is *productive* if there exist vectors

$$X > 0 \text{ and } Y > 0 \text{ such that } X - AX = Y.$$

Clearly, census year data collected in an empirical input-output study will yield vectors of gross outputs and final demand satisfying this condition.

Lemma: If the square matrix $A \geq 0$ is productive, then $\displaystyle\lim_{t \to \infty} A^t = 0$.

Proof: Since A is productive, we have $x_i - y_i = \sum_j a_{ij} x_j$ for $i = 1$ to n, with $x_i, y_i > 0$.

Define $\lambda_i = (x_i - y_i)/x_i$ and we have $0 \leq \lambda_i < 1$ and $\lambda_i x_i = \sum_j a_{ij} x_j$.

Furthermore, if $\lambda = \max_i \lambda_i$, it follows that $0 \leq \lambda < 1$ and $\lambda X \geq AX$.

Consequently, *if* $A^t X \leq \lambda^t X$, then $A^{t+1} X = A(A^t X) < A\lambda^t X = \lambda^t A X \leq \lambda^{t+1} X$. So, by induction, we have for all positive integers t, $\lambda^t X \geq A^t X$.

Now $A \geq 0$ and $X > 0$ imply $A^t X \geq 0$. Consequently,

$$\lim_{t \to \infty} \lambda^t X \geq \lim_{t \to \infty} A^t X \geq 0$$

Therefore, since $\lambda^t \to 0$, $A^t \to 0$, as was to be shown.

Theorem: If $A \geq 0$ is productive, then $|I - A| \neq 0$ and $(I - A)^{-1} = I + A + A^2 + A^3 + \ldots \geq 0$.

Proof: Let $S_n = I + A + A^2 + \ldots + A^n$. Then $AS_n = A + A^2 + \ldots + A^{n+1}$ and $(I - A)S_n = I - A^{n+1}$.

If follows immediately from the lemma that $(I - A) \displaystyle\lim_{n \to \infty} S_n = I$.

Hence, $\displaystyle\lim_{n \to \infty} S_n = I + A + A^2 + \ldots$, a nonnegative matrix, is the inverse of $I - A$.

Corollary: $X = (I + A + A^2 + \ldots)Y$.

The iterative procedure suggested by this theorem constitutes a simple but not necessarily efficient technique for inverting large input-output matrices.

c. Material balance in planned economies

Professor Michael Montias has argued that insight into the process by which Soviet-type planned economies achieve "material balance" between the availabilities and needs of each commodity can be gained by studying certain implications of the theorem.[30] Material balance is achieved by a production plan when the scheduled output of each sector is enough to meet the sum of final demand for its output plus all the input requirements for its product from other sectors of the economy; this condition is summarized by Equation 5.2. In principle, the solution vector of sector outputs X required to produce final demand Y could be calculated by inverting an input-output matrix, as shown by Equation 5.3. But, in the absence of estimates of the input-output matrix and large-scale electronic computers, it may be possible for central planners to adopt administrative procedures yielding a good approximation to the solution. Suppose planners prepare a preliminary estimate, a vector X^*, of the output requirements involved, both directly and indirectly, in the production of the vector Y of scheduled final demand requirements. Each industrial ministry may then be asked to estimate the various inputs it would require to meet its industries preliminary output target. When these estimates are summed over all industries the planners will obtain an estimate of AX^*, the goods required to produce X^*. Adding the vector of final demand to this estimate of indirect input requirements yields

$$X^1 = Y + AX^* \qquad (5.6)$$

But unless the preliminary estimate X^* was quite precise, the preliminary output target may deviate substantially from X^1, the materials required to produce that target plus final demand; that is, the preliminary output targets X^* may not yield material balance. But the administrative bureaucracy may repeat the process by interrogating the industrial ministries about the inputs needed to meet revised output targets X^1; summing these estimates along with final demand yields as a second approximation

$$X^2 = Y + AX^1 \qquad (5.7)$$

Hopefully, estimated material requirements X^2 will now lie reasonably close to output targets X^1; if not, the interrogation procedure can be repeated, and on the nth interrogation we will have

$$X^n = Y + AX^{n-1} \qquad (5.8)$$

That these successive rounds of administrative effort may eventually converge on a vector of outputs achieving "materials balance" is made clear once the result of the nth iteration is expressed as:

$$X^n = Y + A(Y + AX^{n-2}) = (I + A)Y + AX^{n-2} = \ldots$$

$$= (I + A + A^2 + \ldots + A^n)Y + A^n X^* \qquad (5.9)$$

Subtracting the value of $X = (I - A)^{-1}Y$ as expressed in the corollary yields the

---

[30] "Planning with Material Balances in Soviet-Type Economies," *American Economic Review*, December 1959. A Soviet input-output matrix for 1966 is discussed by Vladimir G. Treml, Barry L. Kostinsky, and Dimitri M. Gallik in "Interindustry Structure in the Soviet Economy: 1959 and 1966," in *Soviet Economic Prospects for the Seventies*, Joint Economic Committee, 1973.

gap between the outputs projected on the nth iteration and those required to achieve exact material balance:

$$X^n - X = A^n X^* - (A^{n+1} + A^{n+1+2} + \ldots)Y = A^n[X^* - (I - A)^{-1}Y] \quad (5.10)$$

Since $A^n \to 0$, the material imbalance must ultimately be eliminated if sufficient rounds of preliminary trial balances are attempted by the planners. While the energies of the *Gosplan* are not inexhaustible, it may be hoped that the gap between planned outputs X^{n-1} and material requirements X^n will become negligible after only a few iterations. As is clear from Equation 5.10, this is likely to happen if X^* was a close initial guess or A has certain properties (e.g., mostly zeros above the diagonal) so that A^n approaches 0 rapidly.

consumption

*4.1 INTRODUCTION

The assumption that consumer spending is linearly related to disposable income is a first approximation convenient for pedagogical purposes. But how does it square with the facts? It turns out that considerable elaboration is required in refining the hypothesis to the point where it yields accurate predictions.

Imagine, if you will, that a quarter of a century ago you had been charged with the responsibility of predicting what civilian consumption spending would be at the end of World War II. Figure 4.1 displays the data available at the time for estimating the relationship between consumption and income. The consumption function obtained by fitting a straight line to the data for the prewar period was relatively flat, the marginal propensity to consume being only 0.79.[1] Thus the available evidence suggested that the multiplier was small and that without substantial government or private investment spending widespread unemployment would prevail at war's end. Fortunately, the dismal predictions proved wrong, partly because consumption spending after World War II was much higher than the prewar experience had given us any right to expect. In the immediate postwar period consumer spending may have been stimulated by an effort to make up for the purchases postponed during wartime because of shortages and rationing; and the wherewithal for spending was provided by the war bonds and savings accounts accumulated during the war.[2] But in the light of subsequent developments, consumer spending immediately after World War II was not spectacularly large relative to the level of current disposable income. This may be seen from examining the scatter of points in Figure 4.2: The errors made by those who predicted that the period of postwar reconversion would be characterized by widespread unemployment came about largely because the consumption function estimated from prewar

---

[1] A variety of "least-squares" estimates of the marginal propensity to consume are discussed in Appendix 4.B. The evidence suggests that from 1929-1940 the estimated marginal propensity to consume was 0.792. And if the war years are included, data over the period yield an MPC of 0.499.

[2] For a further discussion of the errors made at the close of World War II see Lawrence R. Klein, "A Post-Mortem on Transition Predictions of National Product," *Journal of Political Economy*, August 1946.

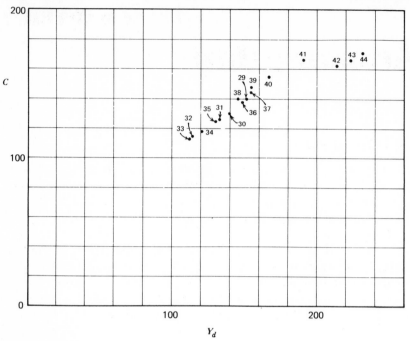

Fig. 4.1 *Consumption on disposable income, 1929–1944*
(*billions of 1958 dollars*).

data was much too flat. Over the longer historical period recorded in Figure
4.2 the line with a slope of 0.91 fits the data quite well. Indeed, Table 4.1
reveals that if the ratio of consumption to disposable income was below
average in 1946, it was above average in 1947. Over the 40-year period the
ratio exhibits no discernible secular trend. That the ratio of consumption
to income would be trendless after World War II may have been predict-
able, because research published by Simon Kuznets in the 1940s showed
that the ratio of consumption to income had remained remarkably stable
since the Civil War.[3] But the short-run departures of the 1930s combined
with the distortions of the war were of such magnitude as to substantially
influence the pace of economic activity. An adequate theory should explain
both the long-run stability of the consumption income ratio and the short-
run deviations from it.

Because of the obvious shortcomings of the elementary hypothesis
that aggregate consumption is a linear function of income, econometricians

---

[3] Kuznets used data for overlapping decades in *National Product Since 1869*, National Bureau of Economic Research, 1946.

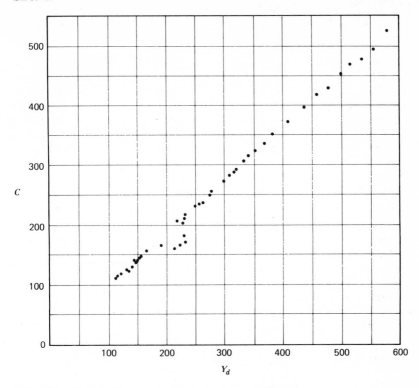

Fig. 4.2 *Consumption on disposable income, 1929–1972* (*billions of 1958 dollars*).

devoted a vast amount of effort, particularly in the two decades following World War II, to the task of refining our knowledge of the determinants of consumer behavior. Introspection provides preliminary insight as to how other variables, in addition to current disposable income, may influence consumption. It seems reasonable to suppose that how much one wants to spend is influenced by one's customary standard of living, which may be approximated statistically by data on consumption spending in prior years. Desired consumption may also be influenced by a wish to emulate spending habits of friends and neighbors. How much one can afford to spend today depends in part on how much has been saved or borrowed in prior years as well as current income. How much one will decide to spend is obviously influenced by anticipations about future income prospects and long-run obligations. Certain of these considerations have entered into a variety of competing theories that have been developed by economists interested in explaining consumption behavior. It will be necessary for us to consider several alternative explanations that were advanced by economists in an

Table 4.1 CONSUMPTION AND DISPOSABLE INCOME: 1929–1972
(BILLIONS OF 1958 DOLLARS)

Year	Y_d	C	C/Y_d
1929	$150.6	$139.6	0.93
1930	139.0	130.4	0.94
1931	133.7	126.1	0.94
1932	115.1	114.8	1.00
1933	112.2	112.8	1.01
1934	120.4	118.1	0.98
1935	131.8	125.5	0.95
1936	148.4	138.4	0.93
1937	153.1	143.1	0.93
1938	143.6	140.2	0.98
1939	155.9	148.2	0.95
1940	166.3	155.7	0.94
1941	190.3	165.4	0.87
1942	213.4	161.4	0.76
1943	222.8	165.8	0.74
1944	231.6	171.4	0.74
1945	229.7	183.0	0.80
1946	227.0	203.5	0.90
1947	218.0	206.3	0.95
1948	229.8	210.8	0.92
1949	230.8	216.5	0.94
1950	249.6	230.5	0.92
1951	255.7	232.8	0.91
1952	263.3	239.4	0.91
1953	275.4	250.8	0.91
1954	278.3	255.7	0.92
1955	296.7	274.2	0.92
1956	309.3	281.4	0.91
1957	315.8	288.2	0.91
1958	318.8	290.1	0.91
1959	333.0	307.3	0.92
1960	340.2	316.1	0.93
1961	350.7	322.5	0.92
1962	367.3	338.4	0.92
1963	381.3	353.3	0.93
1964	407.9	373.7	0.92
1965	435.0	397.7	0.91
1966	458.9	418.1	0.91
1967	477.5	430.1	0.90
1968	499.0	452.3	0.91
1969	511.5	467.7	0.91
1970	533.2	477.0	0.89
1971	554.7	495.4	0.89
1972	578.7	524.8	0.91

Source. Economic Report of the President.

attempt to explain the fluctuations taking place in the consumption ratio, particularly in recession. While certain subtleties of the argument may at times seem picayune, the variations on the basic consumption function hypothesis to be considered in this chapter deserve close attention because of their interesting implications for economic policy. First, the argument of those egalitarians who assert that income redistribution is required in order to stimulate consumption and avoid stagnation requires careful scrutiny. Second, the "life-cycle hypothesis" will be found to have a number of provocative implications; in particular, this theory suggests that the response of consumers to tax adjustment is critically dependent on whether the change is regarded as a temporary measure or a permanent change. Third, it will be necessary to investigate how changes in the reward for thrift—the interest rate—influence savings and consumption. It will also be necessary to look at several alternative explanations of the time lag of the response of consumption to fluctuations in income.

*4.2 CONSUMPTION AND THE DISTRIBUTION OF INCOME

"Tax the Rich" has long been a rallying cry of those who argue that the American economy stagnates because of an inherent tendency toward underconsumption. Particularly in the 1930s an attempt was made to establish a scientific argument in favor of progressive taxation. And a related argument was advanced in the 1960s when the Kennedy Administration's tax cut proposal was a subject of heated congressional debate. The Consumer Advisory Council argued that low-income tax payers should receive a bigger share of the pending tax cut than the Administration had proposed.[4]

"The major tax cuts should come in the taxes of the small taxpayer; it is the low income consumers who are most likely to spend the additional money which a tax cut would permit them to retain."

The act Congress finally passed gave much larger percentage increases in disposable income to those in upper-income brackets. Would a greater stimulus to aggregate economic activity have been achieved if tax relief had been granted primarily to lower-income groups?[5]

Empirical evidence obtained by polling a sample of families about their income and consumption habits has been relied on by those arguing that redistributing income to the poor serves to stimulate the economy. Table 4.2 summarizes in convenient tabular form the relationship between

---

[4] *New York Times*, October 9, 1963, p. 17.

[5] A negative answer to this question does not imply that income should never be redistributed to the poor. It only means that the redistribution must be justified on egalitarian principles instead of as a means of stimulating the economy in times of unemployment.

Table 4.2 EXPENDITURES AND SAVING OF FAMILIES BY INCOME CLASS: 1935–1936 (NONFARM)

Row	Family Income Class	Average Disposable Income	Average Consumption	Average Saving	Consumption as Percent of Income	Marginal Propensity to Consume (%)
a	Under $500	292	493	−201	168.8	70.5
b	500–1,000	730	802	−72	109.9	88.3
c	1,000–1,500	1,176	1,196	−20	101.7	87.4
d	1,500–2,000	1,636	1,598	38	97.7	80.2
e	2,000–3,000	2,292	2,124	168	92.7	72.6
f	3,000–4,000	3,243	2,814	429	86.8	67.7
g	4,000–5,000	4,207	3,467	740	82.4	62.0
h	5,000–10,000	6,598	4,950	1,648	75.0	45.7
i	10,000 and over	22,259	12,109	10,150	54.4	

Source. Dorothy S. Brady, "Family Saving, 1888 to 1950," in *A Study of Saving in the United States*, Vol. 3, by Raymond W. Goldsmith, Dorothy S. Brady, and Horst Mendershausen, Princeton, N.J.: Princeton University Press, 1956, p. 183.

household income and consumption as revealed by a budget study conducted in the 1930s. For example, row *f* reveals that the average income received by those in the $3000 to $4000 bracket was $3243 and that, on the average, families in this bracket consumed $2814 and saved the residual of $429. The same data are plotted in Figure 4.3, each letter corresponding to a row of data on the table. The curve connecting the points on the graph is dubbed the *propensity to consume.*

The income redistribution argument runs as follows: suppose a tax of $100 is imposed on a Fat-Cat in the $5000 to $10,000 bracket and given to his Poor-Cousin in the $1000 to $1500 bracket. The Fat-Cat will move from point *h* toward point *g*; since the *slope* of the consumption schedule (the marginal propensity to consume) is about 0.62 in this region, his consumption may be expected to decline by about $62. On the other hand, when Poor-Cousin received the $100 transferred by the government, he will tend to move from point *c* toward point *d*. Since the *slope* of the consumption schedule (the marginal propensity to consume) is about 0.874 in this income region, his consumption will tend to increase by about $87.40.

Thus the net effect of the redistribution is an increase in total consumption spending of about $25—*given* the current level of aggregate dis-

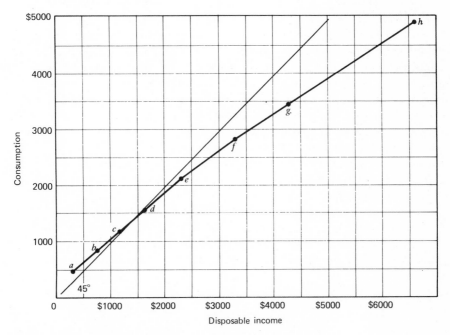

Fig. 4.3   *The propensity to consume, 1935–1936, family budget data.* (Data Source. *See Table 5.2.*)

posable income. But the increased consumption constitutes an increase in effective demand; as a result, output rises and this, in turn, induces a concomitant rise in disposable income and another round of increased consumption. Specifically, multiplier m5 of Chapter 3 is applicable: GNP increases by $1/(1 - c_1 d_1)$ times the magnitude of the upward shift in the intercept of the aggregate consumption function.[6] If we were correct in estimating this multiplier to be 3.01 in Chapter 3, the ultimate effect of redistributing $100 from Fat-Cat to Poor-Cousin is to raise aggregate output by $3.01 \times \$25 = \$75.25$. Of course, the more extensive the effort toward income redistribution, the greater will be the tendency for aggregate consumption to rise. Alternatively, if Congress and the Administration are willing to run a budget deficit, then an even stronger stimulus could be achieved by cutting taxes while increasing government transfer payments. But the magnitude of the stimulus, inspection of Figure 4.3 suggests, will be larger when government transfer payments and tax relief are given to the poor instead of to the rich.

It must be noted immediately that even if the argument is valid, it constitutes a case for redistributing income to the poor only when an economy suffers from stagnation. In a period of open inflation when the economy suffers from excess demand the same logic implies that taxes should be levied primarily on lower-income groups in order to maximize the cut in consumption spending. Of course, an alternative to taxing the poor in periods of excess demand would be to cut government spending or raise a larger sum from taxes on the rich. But it is also true that alternatives to income redistribution in times of slack exist. The redistribution of income may conceivably be more acceptable than higher government spending for those influential politicians who are particularly adverse to budget deficits. But the concept of the balanced budget multiplier suggests an alternative fiscal strategy for combating recession that does not involve an increase in the government deficit. And it would seem unlikely that legislators who are adverse to combating unemployment by simultaneously raising taxes and government spending would be happy with a program for stimulating the economy by redistributing income to the poor.

Those who argue for redistribution in order to stimulate the economy often couch their argument in terms of the empirical generalization that the rich consume a smaller portion of their income than the poor. That this is an inaccurate statement of the condition required for redistribution

[6] In contrast, the multiplier effect of a change in the *slope* of the aggregate consumption function, obtained by differentiating Equation 5.2 of Chapter 3, is

$$\frac{dY}{dc_1} = \frac{d_0 + d_1 Y}{1 - c_1 d_1}$$

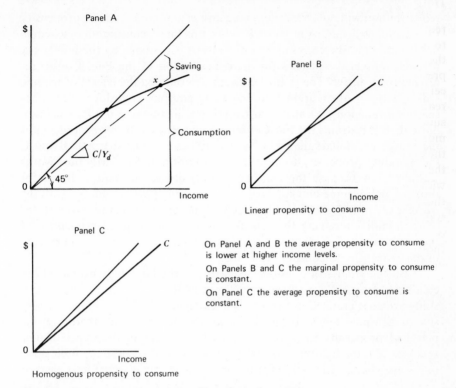

Fig. 4.4 *Propensities to consume: Hypothetical examples.*

to have its anticipated effect is illustrated by Figure 4.4. On Panel A we have a curve rising from the origin in a similar fashion to the consumption schedule plotted on Figure 4.3 with data from the 1935–1936 budget survey. Saving, the excess of income over consumption, is indicated at each income level by the gap between the 45° line and the consumption line. The *consumption ratio* C/Y_d (or *average propensity to consume*) at any point x may be read directly off the graph, since it is the slope of the line (radius vector) connecting the origin to point x (the "rise" is C, the "run" is Y_d, and the slope is "rise over run" or C/Y_d).[7] Note that on both Panels A and B the average propensity to consume falls as income rises, while on Panel C the average propensity to consume is constant. Nonetheless,

---

[7] For example, when $C = c_0 + c_1 Y_d$, the marginal propensity to consume is c_1, while the average propensity to consume is $C/Y_d = c_0/Y_d + c_1$. Therefore only the average propensity to consume changes with disposable income when the consumption function is linear.

redistribution will not influence aggregate consumption when the propensity to consume is linear, as in Panel B. With this linear consumption schedule the reduction in the consumption of Fat-Cat occasioned by the higher tax precisely offsets the increase in the consumption of the Poor-Cousin receiving the transfer. The critical concept determining the effects of income redistribution is the marginal propensity to consume (the slope of the consumption function), because redistribution will stimulate the Poor-Cousin more than it restrains the Fat-Cat only if he spends a higher proportion of the *transferred* dollars than Fat-Cat would have. On both Panels B and C the marginal propensity to consume is a constant. Redistribution works with Panel A because the marginal propensity to consume is lower for those in high-income brackets. And how big an impact is achieved with the transfer of funds depends on how much the marginal propensity to consume of the families receiving the transfer exceeds the marginal propensity of those who are taxed—that is, the effect is larger the greater the curvature of the propensity to consume schedule.

Budget studies of consumer behavior in the United States have been conducted frequently over the better part of the last century. The budget study evidence graphed in Figure 4.5 does suggest that the average propensity to consume tends to fall at higher income levels. Furthermore, the marginal propensity to consume is usually smaller in the upper-income brackets. But the fact that the marginal propensity to consume often shifts in a somewhat erratic fashion from one income group to the next casts at

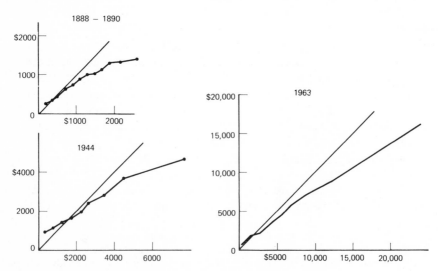

Fig. 4.5 *Propensities to consume: Historical budget study evidence.* (Source. *See Table 4.2.*)

least some doubt on the proposition that income redistribution, whether justified or not on equalitarian principles, is a reliable strategy for stimulating economic activity. And if the marginal propensity to consume drops as income rises, why has the ratio of aggregate consumption to aggregate income remained stable in the United States for so many years?

Doubt about the efficacy of the income-redistribution panacea arises when one considers the following conundrum. While every spendthrift eventually learns that the credulity of creditors is limited and that consumption spending must eventually be brought into line with income, budget studies generally suggest that at sufficiently low income levels, people spend more than they make. This apparent contradiction is explained by the fact that families in the same income bracket spend widely different amounts on consumption. As Table 4.3 reveals, in every income bracket there exist both savers and dissavers, but only in the lower bracket does dissaving predominate. The permanently poor obviously do not perpetually spend more than their disposable income; those with temporarily low incomes can. For example, senior citizens spending accumulated wealth during their retirement years can consume in excess of any current income. Furthermore, both the businessman suffering a short-run reversal in market conditions and the worker experiencing a temporary run of unemployment are likely to spend in excess of current income. Such factors as these must be introduced in order to explain the variations of individual consumption behavior within each income bracket.

Many economists specializing in the consumption area have concluded that consumption spending is proportional to income, properly measured. The proportionality hypothesis accounts for the long-run stability of the ratio of aggregate consumption to aggregate income. The "life-cycle hypothesis" of Modigliani-Brumberg and the "permanent income" theory of Friedman both emphasize that there is no difficulty in reconciling the evidence provided by budget studies with the proportionality hypothesis once the theory of the consumer is enriched sufficiently to explain individual behavior. These arguments will receive close attention, because Panel C of Figure 4.4 revealed that the proportionality hypothesis implies that income redistribution will not influence aggregate consumption spending. This conclusion need not be disconcerting to the liberal who favors redistribution for humanitarian reasons. Although it implies that taxing the rich and subsidizing the poor is not a cure for depression, it also means that in times of excess demand, regressive taxes hitting hardest at the poor do not constitute a particularly potent procedure for curtailing spending in order to stem inflationary pressures. And it demolishes the argument that an unequal distribution of income is necessary to generate the savings required for rapid economic growth.

Table 4.3 SAVING BY INCOME BRACKETS, 1963 (PERCENTAGE DISTRIBUTION OF CONSUMER UNITS)

1963 Disposable Income	Saving of								No Saving or Dissaving	Dissaving of				
	$25,000 and over	$10,000–24,999	$5,000–9,999	$2,500–4,999	$1,000–2,499	$500–999	$100–499	$1–99	$1–99	$1–99	$100–499	$500–999	$1,000–4,000	$5,000 and over
0–$2,999	—	—	*	1	5	8	16	12	22	7	14	8	6	1
$3,000–4,499	*	2	1	5	16	21	17	7	3	4	9	7	6	1
$5,000–7,499	*	1	1	10	31	19	17	3	2	4	4	3	5	3
$7,500–9,999	*	3	5	24	33	11	7	2	1	1	2	3	5	3
$10,000–14,999	1	6	13	25	23	8	6	2	*	3	2	3	5	3
$15,000–24,999	4	8	25	24	17	4	3	1	*	*	*	*	7	3
$25,000–49,999	23	23	21	3	7	*	1	*	*	*	*	1	2	20
$50,000 and over	32	13	1	1	25	1	*	*	*	*	*	*	2	24
All units	*	2	3	10	19	14	14	6	7	4	7	5	6	2

Source. Dorothy S. Projector, *Survey of Changes in Family Finance*, Board of Governors of the Federal Reserve System, November 1968, p. 106.

4.3 THE LIFE-CYCLE HYPOTHESIS

How income fluctuates with age, given educational attainment, is suggested by Figure 4.6. The estimates are derived from survey data for a particular year, 1967. Thus the figure of about $11,000 plotted for the average 30-year-old college educated American is the average income earned in 1967 by all sampled individuals in that age category. Obviously, this is not how much a typical 20-year old should expect to make at age 30 if he graduates from college. He must worry about how his inherent abilities and career choice influence his prospects. He must also recognize that in projecting 10 years into the future appropriate adjustments must be made for inflation and for the general upward trend in living standards generated by technological advance and capital accumulation. Such adjustments twist the income profile, for the growth forces will have longer to operate and will generate a higher upward shift the further ahead in age one projects. But the graph does provide a reasonably close first approximation, suggesting that an individual should anticipate sizable changes in his income over his

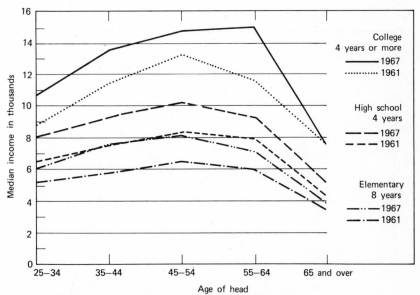

Fig. 4.6 *Income profiles. Median income in 1967 and 1961 of families in the United States with heads 25 years and over, by educational attainment and age of head (in 1967 dollars).* (Source. Current Population Reports, *U.S. Department of Commerce, Series P-60, Number 59, April 18, 1969.*)

entire life cycle. And, of course, a rational consumer will also recognize that his consumption requirements will be fluctuating.

In determining how various complicating factors might influence consumption spending, it is helpful to consider how a hypothetical consumer might behave. To be specific, suppose that our rational consumer is 30. For simplicity, suppose that he thinks he can forecast the future with certainty; in particular, he expects to die at age 73. Furthermore, if we suppose that the interest rate is zero, we can neglect the effect of interest earnings on asset accumulation. On the top panel of Figure 4.7 we have plotted

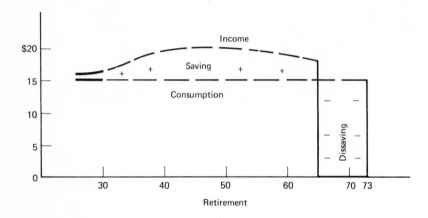

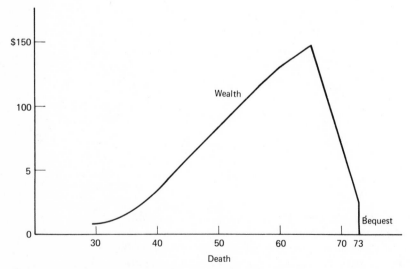

Fig. 4.7 *Hypothetical consumption-saving life cycle.*

data on the hypothetical consumer's income; the first part of the curve records historical behavior, while the dashed extension beyond the age of 30 indicates how he expects his income profile to fluctuate over the remainder of his life span. Also plotted on the graph are the hypothetical consumer's consumption history and a projected path of his planned future consumption spending. Note that he plans to continue saving over the remainder of his working years so that he can dissave during retirement. A wealth plan is implied by the consumption-income plan, since wealth changes in direct response to saving and dissaving; in other words, given our consumer's wealth at the beginning of his 30th year, it is possible to plot how his wealth changes with time on the basis of the data on the top panel. As indicated in the bottom panel, his life plan implies a small bequest.

The consumption plan of the hypothetical consumer was undoubtedly influenced by his earning history and his savings behavior prior to his current age of 30. Had he earned less in prior years, he would probably have less wealth at age 30, he might have a less optimistic outlook about income prospects in the future, and he might be accustomed to a lower standard of living. Clearly, past as well as current income influences today's consumption spending.

The hypothetical consumer's anticipations about the future are reflected in his consumption plan. Let us consider a few examples suggesting how his plan might be revised in response to changing expectations about the future.

1. Suppose a medical checkup suggests that his health has improved to the point where his life expectancy is lengthened appreciably. It seems reasonable to suppose that our rational consumer is likely to cut current and future consumption somewhat in order to provide for a longer period of retirement.

2. Suppose our consumer experiences a sudden reduction in wealth—a capital loss—as a result of fire, robbery, or stock market reversal. He might conceivably try to make up the entire loss promptly by cutting current consumption drastically, or he might continue merrily along his planned consumption path and find himself short in his old age; it seems more likely that an unexpected change in wealth will be prorated over the entire life span in order to moderate the impact on current consumption.

3. How a change in current income will influence his behavior depends on whether it is regarded as a temporary reduction or a permanent change. If an unexpected reduction in this year's income is regarded as a temporary reversal it seems likely that he will prorate the loss over a number of years, as with the capital loss. But if he anticipates that the cut constitutes a permanent reduction in his disposable income throughout

the remainder of his earning years, he must recognize that a much greater loss in total revenue is involved, and it seems likely that he will revise both his current and his future consumption drastically. Not only does the response to a change in current income depend on whether the change is regarded as temporary or permanent; it also depends on age. The marginal propensity to consume out of a permanent change in income will be smaller for an older worker because he has fewer earning years remaining until retirement; a much greater proportion of his future consumption is to be financed by current wealth instead of by future earnings. On the other hand, the marginal propensity to consume out of a temporary change in income is likely to be larger for older than for younger workers because it must be prorated over a shorter remaining life span.

Economists who have stressed the distinction between transitory versus permanent changes in income argue that only a distorted picture of consumer behavior is provided by cross-sectional studies of family behavior. According to life-cycle theory, the substantial variations in savings by families receiving the same current income, such as Table 4.3 revealed may, in large measure, reflect differences in past income and divergent anticipations about the future. Unfortunately, information on income anticipations is hard to come by. The available evidence is compatible with the hypothesis that in the long run each consumer wishes to spend a fixed proportion of average income.

It must be admitted that the life-cycle hypothesis, particularly the simplified version presented here, suffers from a number of quite serious limitations. First of all, it involves a variety of variables that are difficult to measure; in particular, anticipated future income is virtually unobservable.[8] While it may be tempting to relegate responsibility for resolving these issues to the statisticians, the data problem means that the theory is very difficult to test. Certainly, the data problem is of such severity as to increase the attractiveness of alternative explanations of consumption behavior that do not rely to such an extent on unobservable variables. Second, the theory assumes an unreasonable degree of rationality and clairvoyance. Introspection suggests that few consumers attempt to look far into the future with much precision, and their shortsightedness may arise because they recognize the folly involved in mimicking a soothsayer. Equally serious is the fact that few consumers are in a position to borrow sizable sums except at increasing rates of interest; restrictions on the availability of credit may

---

[8] An ingenious technique for circumventing the problem of unobserved expectations was developed by Harold W. Watts, "Long-Run Income Expectations and Consumer Saving," *Studies in Household Economic Behavior* by Thomas F. Dernburg, Richard Rosett, and Harold Watts, Yale University Press, 1958.

prevent a young family from consuming as much as a rational plan might otherwise recommend. Fortunately, many of these complications have been taken care of by a number of sophisticated studies. In a later section of this chapter the effects of interest rates on savings and consumption will be investigated. First, however, it will be of some interest to observe how the life-cycle hypothesis explains certain observed characteristics of aggregate consumption behavior.

An interesting macroeconomic implication of the life-cycle hypothesis of consumer behavior concerns the effect of the rate of population growth on the aggregate ratio of savings to income. The Great Depression of the 1930s has been attributed by some to the decline in the rate of population growth and the concomitant reduction in demand for new housing, schools, and so forth. But the life-cycle hypothesis implies that a low rate of population growth need not generate a tendency toward underinvestment and underconsumption; savings may drop as well. To see why, consider first the case of zero population growth. With zero growth the fraction of the population living in retirement will be equal to the proportion of his lifetime that the average wage earner expects to spend in retirement; the saving of those in their earning years will be precisely offset by those in retirement, except in so far as the representative citizen desires to leave his children a larger bequest than he himself inherited. In contrast, with positive population growth, the average age of the population is reduced and so the proportion of families saving for retirement increases. And the more rapid the rate of population growth, the larger the aggregate savings rate, because the proportion of savers rises relative to the fraction of dissaving retirees.[9] Thus the savings required for the houses, schools, and factories needed to accommodate an expanding population may be generated automatically, even if no member of the population is planning either net saving or dissaving on balance over his entire life span. Conversely, the boogy of economic stagnation is deflated by this argument; a decline in population growth reduces aggregate saving and helps to insure an adequate level of consumption. Finally, Modigliani and Brumberg[10] argue that empirical support for the life-cycle hypothesis is provided by the fact that the observed rate of saving for the American economy is roughly what one should expect, given the long-run rate of population growth, the customary retirement age, and observed life expectancy.

The life-cycle hypothesis helps to explain why changes in fiscal policy are not always effective. For example, some skeptics have asked why, if

[9] See Exercise 4.4.

[10] This argument was developed in detail in 1953 by Modigliani and Brumberg in an unpublished paper, "Utility Analysis and Aggregate Consumption Functions." For further discussion see M. J. Farrell, "The New Theories of the Consumption Function," *Economic Journal*, December 1959.

the Kennedy-Johnson tax cut really served to stimulate a stagnant economy in 1964, the 10% income tax surcharge imposed in the middle of 1968 failed to stem the inflationary pressure generated by Viet Nam. It was less a matter of a prescription of the wrong magnitude than a question of subtle differences in the type of medicine being applied. The 1964 tax cut was publicized as a permanent change in tax structure, while the 1968 surtax was only a temporary change in current tax take. Because the Kennedy-Johnson tax cut was thought to be a permanent change, it induced an upward shift in the representative consumer's disposable income profile, as illustrated in the top panel of Figure 4.8. However, a temporary change causes only a pip in the disposable income profile, as illustrated on the bottom panel. The effect of the transitory change occasioned by a temporary tax adjustment is prorated over the remaining life span of the representative consumer. In contrast, the change in current income of the permanent tax shift does not have to be prorated, because it is accompanied by a sizable change in anticipated future income. An obvious moral of this argument is that while it may be possible on rare occasion to use changes in the personal income tax to stabilize the economy, its effectiveness as a countercyclical device will gradually fade as it becomes generally recognized that the shifts in tax rates are temporary instead of permanent adjustments.

4.4   CONSUMPTION AND THE RATE OF INTEREST

Since the rate of interest is the reward for thrift, it seems obvious that an increase in the interest rate would serve to encourage saving; indeed, this argument was generally accepted as beyond dispute by most if not all economists prior to the 1930s. And since income minus saving equals consumption by definition, this line of reasoning implies that consumption will be stimulated, given Y_d, if the rate of interest is reduced. More formally, if the functional relationship determining saving is denoted by $S(Y_d, r)$, the consumption function must take the form

$$C(Y_d, r) = Y_d - S(Y_d, r)$$

Obviously, the change in consumption as a result of adjustments in the interest rate is of equal magnitude but of opposite sign from the response of saving. That is, in terms of the calculus

$$\frac{\partial C(Y_d, r)}{\partial r} = -\frac{\partial S(Y_d, r)}{\partial r}$$

A tight monetary policy must lower consumption, other things being equal, if saving increases when the monetary authorities raise the rate of interest.

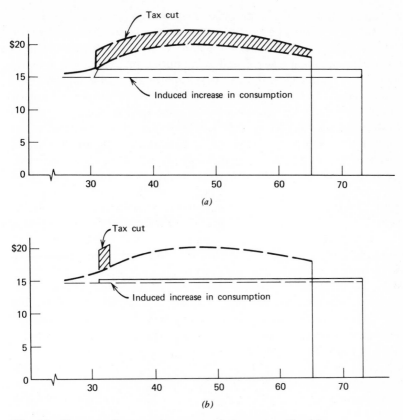

Fig. 4.8 *Tax cut effects on the consumer's income profile.* (*a*)
*A permanent tax cut, because it is assumed to raise disposable
income over the remainder of his working years, may induce a
substantial increase in current consumption.* (*b*) *A temporary
tax cut does not add much to the consumer's* lifetime *income.
And because its effect may be prorated over the entire life span,
it will not have much of an impact on current consumption.*

Conversely, a reduction in the rate of interest, if it discourages saving, will
increase consumption and help to stimulate a depressed economy. And the
multiplier process will tend to reinforce the impact of interest rate adjustments.[11] Indeed, members of the classical school of economists argued that
full employment is assured if only the monetary authorities allow the interest rate to adjust to the "natural rate" at which consumption and investment spending expand enough to equate total effective demand with
capacity output.

[11] See Exercise 4.5.

But under certain circumstances it may not be irrational for a consumer to save less when the rate of interest rises. For example, a higher rate of interest means that a worker has to set fewer dollars aside each month to achieve a given level of well-being during his retirement, because at a higher rate of interest his wealth will compound more rapidly. And new parents saving to send their infant daughter to college need put aside fewer dollars each year for tuition when interest rates are high.

In order to visualize more clearly how the rate of interest may affect consumption, consider as a grossly simplified example a hypothetical individual who knows with certainty that his wages will be $20 today and $20 tomorrow and that he will die tomorrow night! This morbid example is sufficiently artificial to enable us to plot his possible consumption choices on a graph. In Figure 4.9 we will compare his behavior when the rate of interest is 25% with his behavior when the interest rate is zero. Point *a* denotes the fact that by saving nothing today the hypothetical consumer can spend the same amount, $20, each day. However, he might consume $30 today by borrowing (dissaving $10) today; but with a zero rate of interest he would have only $10 for tomorrow, which yields point *b*. These two points are on the "budget line," labeled *r* = 0, which denotes the entire set of possible choices that will exhaust total earnings. How the possibilities open to our doomed consumer change if the rate of interest increases to 25% is illustrated on the second panel of the figure. The thrifty individual who was initially at point *c* can obviously do better because, if he continues to consume only $10 today, his $10 of saving will grow to $12.50 by tomorrow; thus he might consume $32.50 tomorrow, which is

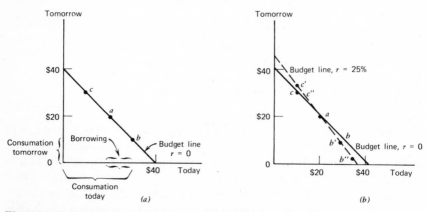

Fig. 4.9   *Consumption and the rate of interest.* (*a*) *Borrowing permits the individual to consume more today and less tomorrow, as at point* b. (*b*) *Both the borrower and the saver* may *save more when the rate of interest increases to 25%.*

point c'. But it certainly is reasonable for him to decide to consume more on *both* days, as at point c''. Thus our thrifty consumer's current consumption might increase as a result of the rise in the rate of interest. However, the borrower can no longer choose point b, and he might decrease consumption on both days by moving to b'. But he might conceivably prefer point b'' to any of the other choices available to him on the steeper budget line corresponding to a 25% rate of interest, and this involves an increase in current consumption spending.

Almost anything appears possible in theory[12] and, since the hypothesis that individuals maximize utility does not rule out the possibility that a rise in interest rates might increase current consumption, the issue can only be resolved empirically. Much of the empirical evidence suggests that the effect is negligible, and it is often argued that the effects of interest rates on consumption spending can be safely neglected in practice. One recent study does suggest that, if anything, higher rates of interest discourage thrift to a moderate extent;[13] that is, *higher* interest rates may actually stimulate current consumption spending.

4.5 INERTIA AND EXPECTATIONS: DISTRIBUTED LAG ANALYSIS OF CONSUMPTION

Introspection, the cross-sectional evidence provided by surveys of household behavior, and microeconomic theory all suggest that consump-

---

[12] On the other hand, there are certain types of behavior that seem irrational; for example, consider an individual who consumed at c when the rate of interest was zero and at b' when the rate of interest was 25%. His behavior when the rate of interest was zero suggests that he prefers c to b, and b is clearly better than b'; this means that c should be chosen over b'. Since c'' is better than c (because it involves having more on both days) c'' must be preferred to b or b'. Why then does this individual select b' instead of c'' when the interest rate is 25%? For further discussion of the effects of interest rate changes on consumption based on the use of indifference curves, see Donald Bear, "The Relationship of Savings to the Rate of Interest, Real Income, and Expected Future Prices," *Review of Economics and Statistics*, February 1961.

[13] See Warren Weber, "The Effect of Interest Rates on Aggregate Consumption," *American Economic Review*, September 1970, pp. 591–600. Weber's approach was to work in terms of a multiperiod model obtained by including interest rate effects within the life-cycle model; thus he synthesized the two-period approach illustrated in this section with the longer planning horizon developed by Modigliani and Brumberg. As Weber explains, however, he followed such writers as Modigliani and Ando (see Section 4.6) in including only depreciation instead of the full price of consumers' durables in his concept of consumption; his evidence may arise from a tendency for higher interest rates to induce the substitution of nondurable consumer items for durables; thus it is still conceivable that in terms of the Commerce Department definition (capital expenditure on durables plus nondurables) aggregate consumption may fall when interest rates increase.

tion is a highly complex phenomenon. Nonetheless, a very simple elaboration on the elementary hypothesis that consumption is a linear function of income is helpful in explaining how aggregate consumption is determined. The elaboration will lead to a very simple dynamic model. Because time is important, it is necessary to date the variables. It will be supposed that current consumption depends linearly on both disposable income and consumption of the recent past.[14]

$$C_t = \beta_0 + \beta_1 Y_{dt} + \beta_2 C_{t-1} + \epsilon_t \qquad (5.1)$$

Here the subscript t denotes the current period and $t-1$ denotes the preceding period. For example, suppose we have quarterly (three month) observations and wish to explain consumption for the second quarter (April, May, and June) of 1975; the equation says that consumption depends on the level of disposable income in that *same* quarter and the level of consumption for the preceding quarter (January, February, and March) of 1975.

The coefficients of this more complicated consumption function cannot be estimated by plotting data on a *two*-dimensional graph; but this complication does not faze the electronic computer. When the "method of least-squares," described in the appendix, was applied to the 104 quarterly observations from 1947–1972 for the United States economy, the computer generated the following estimated relationship.

$$C_t = 2.36 + 0.30 Y_d + 0.68 C_{t-1} + e_t \qquad (5.2)$$

This equation suggests that a $1 billion increase in disposable income would raise aggregate consumption by about $.3 billion. In contrast, when we leave out lagged consumption (i.e., force $\beta_2 = 0$), the best data fit is provided by the following estimated relationship.

$$C_t = 9.94 + 0.89 Y_{dt} + e_t \qquad (5.3)$$

Is the marginal propensity to consume out of disposable income 0.30 or 0.89? The discussion of the multiplier in Chapter 3 indicates that this is a question of vital importance. And it turns out that the answer hinges on whether one is asking about the short- or long-run effects of income change.

How distributed lag determined consumption responds to an increase in disposable income is illustrated by a hypothetical example reported in Table 4.4 and plotted in Figure 4.10. In order to focus more closely on the consumption response, disposable income is assumed to be exogenous for the moment. Specifically, disposable income is initially 1000, but it steps up to 1100 in period 3. For periods 1 to 10 the level of consumption has

---

[14] The ϵ_t at the end of the equation is a random disturbance, a complication explained in the appendix to this chapter. While ϵ_t is not observed directly, an estimate of it could be obtained by calculating e_t in the next equation.

Table 4.4 DISTRIBUTED LAG CONSUMPTION
RESPONSE TO A CHANGE IN DISPOSABLE
INCOME

Time	Y_d	C
0	—	944.88
1	1000	944.88
2	1000	944.88
3	1100	974.88
4	1100	995.28
5	1100	1009.15
6	1100	1018.58
7	1100	1024.99
8	1100	1029.36
9	1100	1032.32
.10	1100	1034.34
∞	1100	1038.63

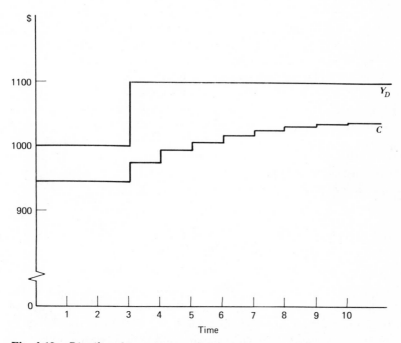

Fig. 4.10 *Distributed lag response of consumption to a change
in disposable income.*

been determined with Equation 5.2. To determine consumption in period 1 with Equation 5.2, we had to know the level of consumption in the preceding period; it was supposed as an historical fact—an "initial condition"—that consumption had been 944.88 in Period 0. We solved

$$C_1 = 2.36 + 0.30\,Y_{d_1} + 0.68C_0$$
$$= 2.36 + 0.30 \times 1000 + 0.68 \times 944.88 = 944.88$$

Thus there is *no* change in consumption from period 1 to period 2. But for period 3 we have an increase in consumption because of the step in disposable income.

$$C_3 = 2.36 + 0.30 \times 1100 + 0.68 \times 944.88 = 974.88$$

This is not the end of the story; in period 4 we have more consumption, even with no further change in disposable income, because C_{t-1} is now 974.88 instead of 944.88.

$$C_4 = 2.36 + 0.3 \times 1100 + 0.68 \times 974.88 = 995.28$$

That the subsequent entries reported on Table 4.4 and plotted on the graph all obey Equation 5.2 may be readily verified. Note that consumption remains at its initial level of 944.88 until disturbed by a 10-unit increase in disposable income; then it rises in a series of steps of gradually decreasing magnitude; after 10 periods consumption has risen by 89.46 units. At least for these particular estimates of the parameters of the model *and* for the specified initial condition, the step increase of 100 in disposable income has led to a sizable cumulative expansion of consumption.

How large is the ultimate change in consumption? What determines how rapidly the system adjusts in response to a disturbance? To answer these two questions we consider a simple two equation model that turns out to be intimately related to Equation 5.1. First, suppose that there is associated with each level of disposable income a target or equilibrium level of income toward which consumption spending adjusts.

$$C_t^e = \gamma_0 + \gamma_1 Y_{d_t} \qquad (5.4)$$

Second, assume that because of habit and inertia consumers only partially adjust each period toward this equilibrium target.

$$C_t - C_{t-1} = \delta(C_t^e - C_{t-1}) \qquad (5.5)$$

For example, if $\delta = 1/3$, consumers only adjust their consumption one third of the way toward its equilibrium level in each period. Substituting Equation 5.4 into Equation 5.5 yields an equation explaining the change in consumption in terms of disposable income and lagged consumption.

$$C_t - C_{t-1} = \delta\gamma_0 + \delta\gamma_1 Y_{d_t} - \delta C_{t-1} \qquad (5.6)$$

Finally, adding C_{t-1} to both sides of this last equation reveals

$$C_t = \delta\gamma_0 + \delta\gamma_1 Y_{d_t} + (1 - \delta)C_{t-1} \qquad (5.7)$$

This equation is of the same form as Equation 5.1, but with $\beta_0 = \delta\gamma_0$, $\beta_1 = \delta\gamma_1$, and $\beta_2 = 1 - \delta$. The speed of adjustment, δ, depends only on the coefficient of lagged consumption; the long-run incremental effect of a change in disposable income on consumption depends on the ratio $\beta_1/\delta = \gamma_1$. Equation 5.2 suggested that the order of magnitude of these parameters is $\beta_0 = 2.36$, $\beta_1 = 0.30$, and $\beta_2 = 0.68$. Thus we must have $\delta = (1 - \beta_2) = 0.32$, $\gamma_0 = \beta_0/(1 - \beta_2) = 7.38$, and $\gamma_1 - \beta_1/\delta = \beta_1/(1 - \beta_2) = 0.94$. The system tends to adjust 32% of the way toward equilibrium in each time period. And substituting the parameter estimates into Equation 5.4 yields as the equation for equilibrium consumption

$$C_t^e = 7.38 + 0.94 Y_{dt} \tag{5.8}$$

Interestingly, this equilibrium equation is fairly close to the estimates of Equation 5.3, which neglected the influence of consumption inertia. Of course, equilibrium consumption cannot be observed directly by the national income accountant, although Equation 5.8 can be used to estimate how it has fluctuated historically. In conclusion, it is useful to distinguish between the short- and long-run marginal propensity to consume. The initial impact of an increase in disposable income is the coefficient $\beta_1 = 0.30$ of Equation 5.1; this is the short-run marginal propensity to consume. The long-run marginal propensity to consume, $\gamma_1 = 0.94$, reveals the ultimate effect that a change in disposable income has on consumption—once consumers have adjusted to it.

While Equation 5.1 constitutes a convenient way of incorporating habit and inertia into the consumption function, it can be given a quite different interpretation in terms of expectations about the future, where expectations are in turn generated by historical experience. Suppose that "expected" or "permanent" disposable income is generated by the following expression.

$$Y_t^p = (1 - \lambda)(Y_{dt} + \lambda Y_{dt-1} + \lambda^2 Y_{dt-2} + \ldots)$$

$$= (1 - \lambda) \sum_{i=0}^{\infty} \lambda^i Y_{dt-i}, \qquad 0 < \lambda < 1 \tag{5.9}$$

This equation says that nothing is forgotten, that the entire history enters into the determination of Y_t^p, but that more weight is attached to recent experience.[15] Now suppose that consumption is linearly related to Y_t^p.

$$C_t = \gamma_0 + \gamma_1 Y_t^p \tag{5.10}$$

[15] The $(1 - \lambda)$ term in the equation makes Y_t^p a proper average of the income terms *if* there is no systematic trend. In particular, if disposable income were constant throughout recorded history, it would be only reasonable to have Y_t^p assume the same value. To verify that $Y_{dt-i} = Y_d$ for all i insures that $Y_d = Y_t^p$, it is only necessary to recall from the formula for the sum of a geometric series that $\sum_{i=1}^{\infty} \lambda^i Y_d = Y_d \sum_{i=1}^{\infty} \lambda^i = Y_d[1/(1 - \lambda)]$.

To solve the system, let us exploit the tricky but interesting fact that the lagged values of disposable income enter Equation 5.9 in an artful fashion that allows the following manipulations. First, Equation 5.9 holds for all t, including $t - 1$.

$$Y_{t-1}^p = (1 - \lambda)(Y_{dt-1} + \lambda Y_{dt-2} + \ldots)$$

And when this expression is multiplied by λ it can be substituted for practically everything on the right-hand side of Equation 5.9.

$$Y_t^p = (1 - \lambda)Y_{dt} + \lambda Y_{t-1}^p \qquad (5.11)$$

Now Equation 5.10 held for period $t - 1$, and it can be used to eliminate Y_{t-1}^p from Equation 5.11.

$$Y_t^p = (1 - \lambda)Y_{dt} + \lambda\left(\frac{C_{t-1} - \gamma_0}{\gamma_1}\right)$$

Substituting this last expression into Equation 5.10 finally yields

$$C_t = (1 - \lambda)\gamma_0 + (1 - \lambda)\gamma_1 Y_{dt} + \lambda C_{t-1} \qquad (5.12)$$

Although the expectations scenario employed in generating Equation 5.12 is forward looking while the argument underlying Equation 5.7 relies on habit and inertia, the resulting dynamic consumption functions are for all intents and purposes the same, but with $\lambda = 1 - \delta$.

Both the delayed adjustment argument and the simplified "permanent" income concept developed here serve to explain why consumption may fall by considerably less than disposable income during recession. Since consumption tends to approach an equilibrium level that is linearly related to disposable income, the model is capable of generating the observed long-run constancy of the consumption/income ratio if γ_0, the intercept, is small. Nothing has been said about the influence of the rate of interest and other variables, with the exception of disposable income, but these may be easily incorporated by modifying the expression for equilibrium consumption. For example, if Equation 5.4 is replaced with

$$C^e = \gamma_0 + \gamma_1 Y_{dt} - \gamma_2 r_t \qquad (5.4')$$

where r_t is the rate of interest, substitution into Equation 5.5 yields

$$C_t = \delta\gamma_0 + \delta\gamma_1 Y_{dt} - \delta\gamma r_t + (1 - \delta)C_{t-1} \qquad (5.7')$$

Although the distributed lag model is capable of explaining many essential features of observed consumption behavior, it possesses one characteristic that is rather unrealistic. Equation 5.5 is perfectly symmetrical with respect to positive and negative deviations from equilibrium; this symmetry implies that it is as easy to adjust consumption down in recession as it is to adjust up to new levels in periods of boom. An alternative model, developed by T. M. Brown[16] and Franco Modigliani,[17] stresses the highest previous peak level of consumption, C_{t-1}^m, instead of last period's consumption

$$C_t = \beta_0 + \beta_1 Y_{d_t} + \beta_2 C_{t-1}^m$$

where

$$C_{t-1}^m = \max_{\tau < t} |C_\tau|$$

During booms, when $C_{t-1}^m = C_{t-1}$, the behavior of the model is indistinguishable from that of the distributed lag model; but in recession the accustomed standard of consumption, as represented by C_{t-1}, keeps consumption from falling off as rapidly as it would with either the elementary function (Equation 5.3) or the distributed lag model.[18] A closely related alternative, developed by James S. Duesenberry, uses highest previous peak disposable income rather than peak consumption.[19] In terms of goodness of fit, evidence presented in Appendix 4.B suggests that lagged consumption does marginally better, but it is a very close race and all models do very well at predicting short-run movements in consumption.

4.6 WEALTH, INCOME, AND CONSUMPTION

That the consumer's accumulated wealth as well as his current income should influence how much he can afford to spend is an obvious truism whose importance is emphasized by the life-cycle hypothesis of consumer behavior. Why not use wealth instead of lagged consumption to buttress disposable income in empirical attempts at explaining current consumption behavior?

$$C_t = \rho_0 + \rho_1 Y_{d_t} + \rho_2 W_{t-1} \tag{6.1}$$

Here W_{t-1} is the stock of wealth available at the beginning of period t.

The wealth model has been subjected to intensive study by Ando and Modigliani in empirical tests of the life-cycle hypothesis.[20] The simplest

[16] "Habit Persistence and Lags in Consumer Behavior," *Econometrica*, July 1952.

[17] "Fluctuations in the Saving-Income Ratio: A Problem in Economic Forecasting," in *Studies in Income and Wealth*, National Bureau of Economic Research, Vol. 11, 1949.

[18] See Exercise 4.6.

[19] *Income, Saving and the Theory of Consumer Behavior*, Harvard University Press, 1952.

[20] "The 'Life Cycle' Hypothesis of Saving," *American Economic Review*, March 1963, pp. 55–84.

equation they tested explained consumption in terms of after-tax labor income and wealth with annual United States data from 1929–1959, excluding the war years.

$$C_t^* = 8.1 + 0.75Y_t^* + 0.042W_{t-1}^*$$

The equation suggests that the marginal propensity to consume out of income is much larger than the marginal propensity to consume out of wealth. Why becomes apparent once the precise definitions of the variables used by Ando and Modigliani are clarified. First, C_t^* is not customary consumption spending as measured by national income accountants. Instead of assuming that durable goods are consumed in year of purchase, Ando and Modigliani recognize that they are an investment; only the services provided by durable goods during the current year (as estimated by depreciation) are included with nondurables in C_t^*.[21] Furthermore, Y_t^* is labor income net of taxes; it excludes dividends, rental income, interest, and other forms of property income. Finally, W_{t-1}^* is the value of nonhuman wealth at the end of period $t - 1$. For example, a student adding to his future earning capacity by going to college may be said to add to his "human wealth" and hence his future income; but such investment does not contribute to nonhuman wealth. Now Y_t^* can be regarded as a rough index of the return on human capital; if human capital itself could be measured and substituted for Y_t^*, its coefficient might be of the same order of magnitude as the coefficient for physical wealth. Alternatively, if nonlabor income were included in the equation instead of wealth, it might be expected to have a coefficient of the same order of magnitude as labor income. Thus the discrepancy between the labor income and wealth marginal propensities in Equation 6.1 does not necessarily arise from a tendency of capitalists to consume a smaller proportion of income than workers.

While the wealth model appears to be totally different from the distributed lag approach, initial appearances in this case are somewhat de-

---

[21] As explained in Chapter 3, Section 2, houses alone are treated in this way in constructing the United States national income accounts; more precisely, the "estimated rental on owner occupied houses" is added to consumption, and the purchase of a new house is an act of investment. This practice insures that the way in which houses are handled in the accounts depends on whether one is looking at a society in which houses are largely rented or largely owned by those who occupy them. For most purposes, the tedious and somewhat tenuous procedures required to estimate the "owner rental" on such goods as automobiles and can openers excuses the treatment of these items as though they were consumed on date of purchase, but for refined estimation of sophisticated consumption function concepts such details may be critical. Note that Y_t^* is a flow of purchasing power, while W_{t-1}^* is a stock; thus, with quarterly instead of annual data, Y_t^* and C_t^* would be of approximately $\frac{1}{4}$ their annual magnitude, while W_{t-1}^* would be unaffected.

ceptive. To see why, suppose as a first approximation that changes in the representative consumer's wealth result only from saving.[22]

$$W_t - W_{t-1} = Y_{dt} - C_t \tag{6.2}$$

Now Equation 6.1 also holds for period $t - 1$.

$$C_{t-1} = \rho_0 + \rho_1 Y_{dt-1} + \rho_2 W_{t-2}$$

Subtracting this expression from Equation 6.1 gives

$$C_t - C_{t-1} = \rho_1(Y_{dt} - Y_{dt-1}) + \rho_2(W_{t-1} - W_{t-2}) \tag{6.3}$$

Eliminating the change in wealth with Equation 6.2 yields

$$C_t - C_{t-1} = \rho_1(Y_{dt} - Y_{dt-1}) + \rho_2(Y_{dt-1} - C_{t-1})$$

But this last equation simplifies to a slightly complicated version of the distributed lag model.

$$C_t = \rho_1 Y_{dt} + (\rho_2 - \rho_1)Y_{dt-1} + (1 - \rho_2)C_{t-1} \tag{6.4}$$

Empirical evidence in Appendix 4.B suggests that this equation fits the quarterly data quite well with ρ_1 equal to about 0.46 and ρ_2 equal to about 0.24. If it should have turned out that $\rho_1 = \rho_2$, the lagged level of disposable income would have dropped out, leaving the elementary distributed lag relationship, Equation 5.1, but with $\beta_0 = 0$. Since this did not happen, the evidence suggests that the wealth model constitutes an improvement over the simpler distributed lag approach.

An interesting implication of the wealth model has to do with the level of savings in a mature economy. The simple proposition that consumption depends only on income, with a marginal propensity to consume less than unity, implies that a high level of effective demand can only be maintained with a high level of private investment or government spending; it suggests that if opportunities for profitable investment are eventually used up, the mature economy will be characterized by underinvestment and underconsumption—unless government spending or tax policy fills the gap. But the wealth consumption function denies the boogy of economic stagnation; it is easily shown that consumption function 6.1 implies that if any given level of disposable income is maintained long enough, consump-

---

[22] An individual may also augment his wealth through gifts, but this is offset by the reduction in the wealth of the donor in the process of aggregation unless the gift is from abroad. Accountants concerned with estimating the balance of payments and national income have to worry about immigrant remittances and gifts that are ignored in Equation 6.2. Of more importance are capital gains and losses due to the reevaluation of assets; this can be a substantial factor in periods of inflation and when the stock market is subject to volatile fluctuations.

tion will ultimately rise to meet it. To verify this implication, observe with the aid of Equations 6.2 and 6.3 that $Y_{d_t} = Y_{d_{t-1}}$ implies

$$C_t - C_{t-1} = \rho_2(W_{t-1} - W_{t-2}) = \rho_2(Y_{d_{t-1}} - C_{t-1})$$

Thus ρ_2 is the fraction of the gap eliminated each period as C_t approaches Y_{d_t}. The distributed lag consumption function yields this same result only for a particular set of parameter values; specifically, $\beta_0 = 0$ and $\beta_2 = 1 - \beta_1$ implies that $\gamma_0 = 0$ and $\gamma_1 = 1$ and equilibrium consumption equals income (see Equation 5.10).

4.7   LIQUID ASSETS AND THE "WEALTH" EFFECT OF PRICE AND INTEREST RATE CHANGES

A country's central bank attempts to stabilize the economy by manipulating the type of financial assets held by the public and the interest rate (precisely how is explained in Chapter 10). Monetary policy would have an immediate impact on consumer spending if the interest rate belonged directly in the consumption function, a possibility already discussed in Section 4.4. But monetary policy may also indirectly influence consumption spending through its effect on wealth.

Several investigators have found it fruitful to focus sharp attention on particular components of total wealth instead of looking only at the aggregate. The argument turns on some rather subtle but important points of considerable significance in determining the effectiveness of monetary policy. As will be made clear in Chapter 10, the Federal Reserve System has the power to increase the money supply and influence the *composition* of total wealth holdings. The effectiveness of monetary weapons as a means for influencing the pace of economic activity depends partly on how sensitive consumption is to changes in the composition of wealth. Certain types of wealth are more easily liquidated than others. Given two consumers with equal income and wealth, the one who has his assets tied up in a house instead of as ready cash or money in the bank may be expected to spend less in the immediate future; it is difficult to convert the house into cash— it is said to be "less liquid" in that time is required to obtain funds through a second mortgage or by selling it.[23] The most liquid of assets is money, defined as the sum of currency plus demand deposits (checking accounts); in some empirical studies of consumption money is the *only* form of wealth included. But funds held in a savings account are only slightly less liquid

---

[23] Anybody selling a house learns that a delay must be anticipated in finding the right buyer unless one is so eager to part with it that one is willing to settle considerably below market value.

in practice, since no more than a slight delay is involved in converting them into money. Government notes and bonds maturing within one year are usually classified as liquid assets for statistical purposes. In his studies elaborating on the distributed lag consumption function, Arnold Zellner included a liquid assets variable instead of just money or total wealth. Although changes in liquid assets may be a useful indicator of future consumer behavior, this variable may be more of a signal than a cause of consumption. For example, a consumer planning sizable expenditures on consumer durables may convert assets into liquid form in advance; the decision to buy is what causes the increase in liquid holdings instead of the reverse.[24] Patinkin included money as one variable and other forms of wealth as a second. Although Patinkin's coefficient of money was larger than that for other liquid assets, he concluded that the observed difference might be attributed to sampling and measurement error instead of to a true liquidity influence.[25]

There is another partition of the wealth variable that proves to be of considerable importance in analyzing consumption behavior. Many assets and liabilities have their value expressed in "nominal units"; that is, money itself, mortgages and consumer installment debts, government bonds and savings deposits all involve obligations expressed in dollar units. Consumers with money invested in the stock market may be expected to increase their consumption when a boom in stock market prices increases wealth; conversely, they may curtail spending when stock prices fall in a bear market. But the holder of assets of fixed nominal value is immune from the vicissitudes of the stock market. However, the purchasing power of his nominal assets will decline during periods of rising prices. If W_n denotes the dollar value of that part of wealth whose value is expressed in nominal units, and p is the price level, we have W_n/p as the purchasing power of nominal wealth. Let $W_{\bar{n}}$ denote the other forms of wealth whose dollar value tends to change in proportion to the pace of inflation, for example, houses and other durable goods and corporate stocks. Then total wealth in real terms is

$$W = W_{\bar{n}} + \frac{W_n}{p} \tag{7.1}$$

It is clear that at a higher price level, other things being equal, a consumer with positive nominal wealth will find that he has lost as a result of rising

---

[24] Also, a consumer experiencing an unexpected increment of income receipts may hold them in liquid form temporarily. For additional discussion see A. Zellner, D. S. Huang, and L. C. Chau, "Further Analysis of the Shortrun Consumption Function with Emphasis on the Role of Liquid Assets," *Econometrica*, July 1965.

[25] Don Patinkin, *Money Interest and Prices*, 2nd edition, New York: Harper & Row, 1965, Note M, pp. 651–664.

prices; conversely, a lower price level will mean an increase in the purchasing power of wealth. Now the effect of price induced changes in wealth on consumption is dubbed the "*wealth effect.*" In evaluating its potency it is important to note that the assets of one person are likely to be someone else's liabilities. When Presidential Candidate William Jennings Bryan asked whether our country should be "crucified on a Cross of Gold," the silver-tongued orator was attempting to exploit the fact that inflation would make it easier for farmers to pay off their mortgages; but this would be at the expense of the Eastern money lenders.[26] The wealth effect of lenders and creditors may more or less cancel out, but not entirely; the fact that the general public is a net lender to the government means that the dollar value of nominal assets exceeds the nominal value of liabilities owed by one citizen to another. It is the debt of the government—currency and coin, government bonds—that provides the fulcrum by which the wealth effect of price changes has its impact on consumption spending. When prices rise, the value of the outstanding government debt is decreased, discouraging consumption; conversely, when prices fall, the value of outstanding government debt is enlarged, stimulating consumption spending.

There is another point about the wealth variable that deserves consideration in evaluating the effects of monetary policy. As mentioned in Section 4.4, the rate of interest may not belong directly in the consumption function. However, a rise in the interest rate may operate indirectly, by causing a decline in wealth. For example, the market value of a piece of rental property depends on the present value of the stream of future rental receipts and, given the monthly rental, the present value will be lower the higher the rate of interest that has to be used for discounting. Or, to put it another way, when the rate of interest is high, the increased attractiveness of placing money in a savings account, buying bonds, or making loans means that the demand for real property, such as apartment houses, will be reduced. Thus a rise in the rate of interest, by causing a reduction in wealth, can lead to a reduction in consumption spending.

*4.8 POLICY IMPLICATIONS

An adequate theory of the consumption function must explain both the long-run stability of the consumption/income ratio and its short-term fluctuations. It should also reconcile the survey evidence suggesting a

---

[26] Since World War II many homeowners have benefited substantially from inflation. Anyone with a large mortgage on his investment is "leveraged," since the mortgage obligation declines in real terms as the price level rises. Of course, the gain of the homeowner may be offset by the loss of his banker or, more precisely, by his banker's depositors.

tendency for higher-income groups to have a smaller marginal propensity to consume with the historical tendency for the consumption/income ratio to be stable, notwithstanding the continued growth in per capita income realized in the United States. The consumption theories reviewed in this chapter meet these objectives by adding dynamic complications—wealth or lagged values of consumption or income. Since a variety of theories all yield quite good fits when used in describing historical experience, it is more interesting to look at their policy implications than to quibble over their relative merits. The theories all yield a much smaller short-run propensity to consume than is provided by the simple hypothesis that consumption is linearly related to income. Therefore the short-run multiplier effects of changes in government spending are much smaller than our elementary multiplier estimates suggested. However, the theories do yield a large long-run marginal propensity to consume and a powerful multiplier once income changes are adjusted to, either through the accumulation of wealth, the revision of expectations, and/or the overcoming of habit and inertia.

Each theory adds a certain amount of insight into our understanding of how fiscal and monetary policy influence economic developments. Thus the life-cycle hypothesis emphasizes that adjustments in tax policy that are regarded by the public as temporary will not have much effect. This means that "surtaxes" and "war taxes" may have little impact. It also means that fiscal weapons will gradually lose potency if Congress changes tax rates frequently in an attempt to stabilize the economy.[27] More optimistic are the life-cycle theory's conclusions on the issue of secular stagnation. The proponents of the life-cycle hypothesis argue that the aggregate savings ratio adjusts in response to changes in the rate of population growth to allow for needed capital accumulation in an expanding economy and to avoid the perils of underconsumption if we approach zero-population growth. The wealth hypothesis, too, has a built-in mechanism for avoiding underconsumption, since the long-run proportion of income consumed approaches unity, given time for the level of wealth to adjust, through saving, to changes in income. The discussion also indicated that monetary as well as fiscal policy can influence consumption spending. The evidence is not conclusive but, while it appears that the rate of interest probably has little or no direct effect on consumer spending, changes in liquid assets and the effects on wealth of interest rate fluctuations may be significant.

---

[27] During the early 1960s it was suggested that Congress should give the President the prerogative of adjusting the personal income tax rates when unemployment is excessive. At times it has been suggested that a formula for automatically adjusting the tax rate in response to changes in unemployment should be built into the tax laws. But quite apart from Constitutional objections raised by certain Congressmen, if consumers do not respond abruptly to changes in disposable income, these measures would be ineffective.

REFERENCES

1. Here are a number of fundamental contributions to our understanding of consumption behavior. The work of Keynes is must reading.

J. M. Keynes, *General Theory of Employment, Interest and Money*, Harcourt Brace, 1936, Chapters 8, 9, and 10.

Albert Ando and E. Cary Brown, "Personal Income Taxes and Consumption Following the 1964 Tax Reduction" in *Studies in Economic Stabilization* (edited by Albert Ando, E. Cary Brown, and Friedlaender), The Brookings Institution, 1968.

Franco Modigliani and Albert Ando, "The 'Life Cycle' Hypothesis of Saving: Aggregate Implications and Tests," *American Economic Review*, March 1963.

James S. Duesenberry, *Income, Saving and the Theory of Consumer Behavior*, Harvard University Press, 1949.

Janet A. Fisher, "Income, Spending, and Saving Patterns of Consumer Units in Age Groups," in *Studies in Income and Wealth*, Vol. 15, National Bureau of Economic Research, 1952.

Milton Friedman, *A Theory of the Consumption Function*, Princeton University Press, 1957.

Zvi Griliches, G. S. Maddala, Robert Lucas, and Neil Wallace, "Notes on Esimated Aggregate Consumption Functions," *Econometrica*, July 1962.

H. Lubell, "Effects of Redistribution of Income on Consumer Expenditures," *American Economic Review*, March 1947.

Franco Modigliani, "Monetary Policy and Consumption" in *Consumer Spending and Monetary Policy: The Linkages*, Monetary Conference Series No. 5, Federal Reserve Bank of Boston, June 1971.

James O'Leary, "Consumption as a Factor in Postwar Employment," *American Economic Review*, May 1945.

James Tobin, "Relative Income, Absolute Income and Saving," in *Money, Trade and Economic Growth: Essays in Honor of J. H. Williams*, Macmillan, 1951.

James Tobin and Walter Dolde, "Wealth, Liquidity and Consumption," in *Consumer Spending and Monetary Policy: The Linkages*, Monetary Conference Series No. 5, Federal Reserve Bank of Boston, June 1971.

2. The following references contain excellent expository material summarizing the literature on consumption. Because other chapters in the first three books analyze the empirical literature on investment spending and other important macroeconomic phenomenon, the interested student may find them useful supplements to materials presented in later chapters of this textbook. Malinvaud, however, discusses advanced econometric techniques in his textbook.

M. Farrell, "The New Theories of the Consumption Function," *Economic Journal*, December 1959.

J. L. Bridge, *Applied Econometrics*, North-Holland, 1971.

Michael K. Evans, *Macroeconomic Activity*, Harper and Row, 1969.

E. Malinvaud, "The Consumption Function, Discussion of an Econometric Problem," Chapter 3 of *Statistical Methods of Econometrics*, North-Holland, 1970.

KEY CONCEPTS

marginal versus average propensity to consume

permanent versus transitory income

life-cycle hypothesis

dissaving

distributed lag

wealth

liquid assets

durable goods

EXERCISES

4.1 Suppose that consumption of a typical family is determined by the following equation.

$$C = 1000 + 0.6Y_d$$

a. What is the marginal propensity to consume?

b. What will be the average propensity to consume of a family with disposable income of $10,000? What is it if the family's income is $20,000?

c. Will redistribution of income from the rich to the poor increase aggregate consumption spending (assuming the consumption of each individual family is correctly described by this equation)?

4.2 Evaluate critically the following statement: "Since empirical evidence establishes that people in high income brackets spend a smaller proportion of their disposable income than the poor, it is appropriate to tax the poor in times of inflation and the rich in times of excess capacity."

4.3 Explain, in terms of a variety of alternative theories of the consumption function, the factors determining the extent to which aggregate consumption spending can be influenced by tax and monetary policy.

4.4 Growth and the savings rate: In Never-Never-Land everyone has the same life cycle. Everyone works from 20 to 60 and then spends the years 60 to 80 in retirement. The interest rate is zero and no one leaves a bequest, but everyone saves one third of his annual income of $3 during each working year in order that he can maintain a constant standard of living over the entire life cycle by consuming $2 worth of goods each year. As the data on the table indicate, the population of Never-Never-Land has been doubling every 20 years; specifically, the

1950 Census revealed that there were 100 people in retirement, 200 in the 40 to 60 generation, and 400 in the 20 to 40 generation.

| | Population by Age | | | Aggregate | Aggregate | |
Year	20–40	40–60	60–80	Income	Consumption	C/Y
1950	400	200	100	$1800	$1400	7/9
1970	800	400	200	3600	—	—
1990	800	—	400	—	4000	—
2010	800	800	800	4800	—	—

a. Population and income figures for 1970 appear on the table. Compute aggregate consumption spending and the consumption ratio (C/Y) for 1970.

b. As a result of the discovery of a pill, each couple has, on the average, two children. The 1990 census reveals that there are 400 in retirement, 800 in the 40 to 60 generation and 800 in the 20 to 40 generation. Determine the proportion of income saved.

c. The census for year 2010 reveals that there are 800 people in each generation; zero population growth (ZPG) has been achieved! Determine the savings ratio in Never-Never-Land.

4.5 Suppose that consumption was determined by the following equation

$$C = c_0 + c_1 Y_d - c_2 r$$

where r is the rate of interest. You are to determine how the multiplier analysis of Chapter 3 must be modified.

a. Show how Equation 3.5.1, explaining consumption as a function of GNP, must be modified.

b. Revise Equation 3.5.2, which explained GNP as a function of investment, government spending, and the foreign trade balance.

c. Now find the equation for multiplier m1: $\Delta Y/\Delta G$; is there any change? Why or why not?

d. Determine the effect of an increase in the rate of interest on Y. Why is your expression related to the formula for the multiplier?

4.6 Suppose that consumer spending is determined by the following Duesenberry consumption function.

$$C_t = 9.5 + 0.73 Y_{d_t} + 0.16 Y_{t-1}^m$$

Here Y_{t-1}^m is the highest previous peak level of disposable income.

a. What is the immediate effect of a $1000 increase in disposable income? How large is the longer-run effect of an increase in disposable income to a new historic high?

b. Explain how Table 4.4 will be modified when this equation (instead of the lag model) explains consumption behavior.

c. If disposable income first increases to a historic high and then reverts to its original level, will consumption also fall back to its former level?

d. What does this imply about the efficacy of tax changes for combating a problem of excess demand as contrasted with their efficacy in combating unemployment?

4.7 Other variables, not just consumption, respond with a lag to changing economic conditions. Harvard Professor John Lintner says the analysis may be applied to dividends.[28] Suppose, for example, that the Board of Directors of a corporation aim at a long-run dividend payout ratio target

$$\text{Div}^e = d_1 \Pi^n$$

Here Div^e is the equilibrium level of dividends, Π^n is after tax profit, and d_1 is the equilibrium payout ratio. However, the stockholders, many of whom are retired, prefer a reasonably steady income stream from their investments. So dividends are adjusted only partially to the target each year:

$$\text{Div}_t - \text{Div}_{t-1} = \delta(\text{Div}_t^e - \text{Div}_{t-1})$$

Although Div^e is unobservable, we can estimate

$$\text{Div}_t = 0.92\,\text{Div}_{t-1} + 0.05\Pi_t^n$$

Derive estimates of δ and d_1.

4.8 (Calculus) To see how a change in the rate of interest might affect the behavior of a utility maximizing consumer, consider the following two-period problem. Suppose a consumer's utility function takes the simple product form

$$U = C_1 C_2 \qquad (1)$$

Furthermore, his saving today is $Y_1 - C_1$, and he will earn interest of $r(Y_1 - C_1)$ by tomorrow. Thus his dissaving tomorrow must be

$$C_2 - Y_2 = (1 + r)(Y_1 - C_1) \qquad (2)$$

if he is to exhaust his resources by tomorrow night.

a. Under the hypothesis that the consumer maximizes (1) subject to (2), find C_1 as a function of r and wealth, where we define wealth as the present value of his lifetime earnings

$$W = Y_1 + \frac{Y_2}{1 + r}. \qquad (3)$$

b. Now compare $\partial C_1/\partial r$ with $\partial C_1/\partial W$.

c. Would the answers to Exercises 1a and 1b change if the utility function took the following form? Why or why not?

$$U = \sqrt{C_1 C_2}$$

[28] John Lintner, "Distribution of Incomes of Corporations Among Dividends, Retained Earnings, and Taxes," *American Economic Review*, May 1956.

APPENDIX 4.A   THE METHOD OF LEAST-SQUARES

4.A.1   INTRODUCTION

A simple procedure for estimating such parameters as the marginal propensity to consume is to simply plot observations of consumption and income on a graph, such as Figure 4.2. Of course, the accuracy of this procedure is limited by the degree of precision that the draftsman is able to achieve; furthermore, there may be room for differences of opinion as to precisely what constitutes the line of best fit. But the graphical procedure is hardly feasible once it is conceded that more than one variable plays a causative role. If one admits the possibility that *both* income and wealth simultaneously influence consumption, the problem takes on an added dimension; clearly, the graphical procedure becomes intractable with three or more dimensions. The method of least-squares constitutes a computational procedure for handling this problem. Prior to the development of the electronic computer, the computations had to be performed laboriously on the desk calculator. But it is now a trivial matter to apply the method of least-squares to economic data on the computer, since there are a variety of "canned programs" that make this a menial activity. Unfortunately, the method of least-squares is misused more often than it is correctly employed, because considerable effort is required in order to learn the precise circumstances in which the procedure is appropriate; that is, it is easier to learn how to apply the method of least-squares on the computer than it is to understand it.

This appendix is not a "how-to manual";[29] instead, it constitutes a minimal introduction to the problem of interpreting least-squares estimates. We will discuss first some simple descriptive statistics that might be used to summarize certain characteristics of a sample; then we will turn to the more difficult problem of trying to make inferences about a population through the application of the method of least-squares to sample data. For example, we may find that the method of least-squares constitutes a convenient way to describe the historical relationship between aggregate consumption and income; but we are more likely to want to use the method in making inferences about the properties of the consumption function.

†4.A.2   DESCRIPTIVE STATISTICS

Suppose, as a concrete example, that we have data on consumption spending and income; for example, we might have *time-series* data covering a number of years as provided by the national income accountant, or we might have data in the form of *cross-sectional* observations on both consumption and income for a number of individuals in a particular year. In what follows y_t and x_t can be interpreted as observation t for consumption and income, respectively.[30] Suppose there are n observations in all.

---

[29] For an introduction, see Thomas H. Wonnacott and Ronald J. Wonnacott, *Introductory Statistics*, John Wiley, 1969, or Edward J. Kane, *Economic Statistics and Econometrics*, Harper & Row, 1968; for a slightly more advanced treatment, try Jack Johnston's *Econometric Methods*, McGraw-Hill, 1972.

[30] We use this alternative to the notation employed earlier in discussing consumption and income in order to abide by the statistical convention that y denote the dependent and x the explanatory variable.

In analyzing the data we can plot points on a graph, one point for each observation (year or individual), with y_t on the ordinate and x_t on the abscissa, as in Figure 4.2. As everyone knows, a straight line can be drawn that will fit the n consumption-income points quite closely; but, of course, most of the points will not lie precisely on the line. More formally, we can say that in this graphical exercise we have tried to approximate the data with an equation.

$$\hat{y} = a + bx \tag{2.1}$$

What is a "good fit"? Given from our graph the numbers a and b (intercept and slope) we could find out the error made by the line in approximating a particular observation (say observation t) by computing e_t from

$$y_t = a + bx_t + e_t \qquad t = 1, \ldots, n \tag{2.2}$$

Obviously, there may be room for debate as to which straight line (values of a and b) provide the "best" fit to the set of data points. The customary method of least-squares uses a particular definition of good fit;[31] specifically, it picks the coefficients so as to minimize

$$\sum e_t^2 = e_1^2 + e_2^2 + \ldots + e_n^2 \tag{2.3}$$

It is a simple exercise in the calculus to find formulas for a and b that minimize the sum of the squared deviations.

To take an example, application of the method of least-squares to quarterly data for the United States economy from 1947 to 1972 yields the following *regression equation*.

$$y_t = 9.935 + 0.8862x_t + e_t \qquad \bar{R}^2 = 0.998$$
$$(1.356) \quad (0.0036) \qquad \bar{S}_e = 3.927$$
$$d = 0.72 \tag{2.4}$$
$$df = 102$$

The *explanatory variable* (x_t) is disposable income; the *dependent variable* (y_t) is consumption. We have as the intercept $a = 9.935$ and as the slope $b = 0.8862$. (In addition we have some other numbers that we will discuss later.) About the same *regression coefficients* might have been read off the graph; the computer comes into its own when there are more explanatory variables, say wealth as well as income, because the computer is happy to execute multiple regressions of the form[32]

$$y_t = a + b_1 x_{1t} + b_2 x_{2t} + \ldots b_k x_{kt} + e_t$$

In addition to knowing the slope of the line that best describes the relationship observed between consumption and income, it is also useful to have an index

---

[31] This is only one possible criterion. If we tried the easier procedure of just minimizing $\sum e_t$, we would be embarrassed to find an infinite variety of lines for which the sum of the deviations is zero. We could, however, minimize $\sum |e_t|$, by disregarding signs in adding the deviations; estimators derived in this way are called "mean absolute deviation" or MAD estimators.

[32] What happens to the e_t when the number of explanatory variables $k = n - 1$? Why does the computer have troubles when $k > n - 1$? If y_t were a constant, what would happen?

summarizing in a single number how close the points lie to the line. One obvious measure of goodness of fit, suggested by Equation 2.3, is the sum of the squared deviations; since it was the thing we tried to minimize in fitting the line, it is obviously a reasonable measure of how well the line does in approximating the data points.[33] But an obvious drawback in just computing the sum of the squared deviations is that the number will grow as we accumulate more data; it makes more sense to use as the measure of goodness of fit the average squared deviation, the *variance* of the error

$$S_e^2 = \frac{\sum e_t^2}{n}$$

or its square root

$$S_e = \sqrt{\frac{\sum e_t^2}{n}} \tag{2.5}$$

the *standard error of estimate*. It is more usual, however, to report these statistics modified by having as the denominator $n - k - 1$, where k is the number of explanatory variables; that is,

$$\bar{S}_e = \sqrt{\frac{\sum e_t^2}{(n - k - 1)}} \tag{2.6}$$

is the standard error of the estimate adjusted for degrees of freedom (df).[34]

The correlation coefficient is a second yardstick for measuring goodness of fit. It is "unit free"; that is, its magnitude is insensitive to our decision to measure things in pennies or in billions of dollars. It is defined as

$$R = \sqrt{1 - \frac{S_e^2}{S_y^2}} \tag{2.7}$$

where

$$S_y^2 = \frac{\sum (y_t - \bar{y})^2}{n}$$

is the variance of the dependent variable; $\bar{y} = \sum y / n$. Usually the computer will report the correlation coefficient adjusted for degrees of freedom.

$$\bar{R} = \sqrt{1 - \frac{\bar{S}_e^2}{\bar{S}_y^2}} \tag{2.8}$$

[33] One alternative measure would be the sum of the deviations, but it can be proved that this is necessarily zero! Another is the sum of the absolute values of the deviations, obtained by treating all errors as though they were of positive sign. But obviously, anyone who fits a line by the method of least-squares suffers from schizophrenia if he then uses the average absolute deviation to measure goodness of fit; he should have used the line that minimizes the average absolute deviation (finding it is a problem in linear programming).

[34] The student of elementary statistics knows that S_e^2 is a "maximum likelihood" estimator while $\bar{S}_e^2$ is an "unbiased" estimator. It is important if n is small to know whether adjustment has been made for degrees of freedom or not; but the subtle reasons for using one measure instead of the other are less critical.

where

$$\bar{S}_y = \sqrt{\frac{\sum (y - \bar{y})^2}{(n - 1)}}$$

For our illustrative example, Equation 2.4, $\bar{R}^2$ ("r-square") instead of $\bar{R}$ is reported, as is customary. Since $\bar{R}^2$ (and hence $\bar{R}$) is close to unity, an exceptionally good fit has been obtained. If the equation was a perfect fit, we would have all the $e_t \equiv 0$, so that $\bar{S}_e = 0$ as well and $\bar{R} = 1$. The reader can easily verify that $R = \bar{R} = 1$ only if all the points lie precisely on the line. Note, too, that in the worst possible case, in which the explanatory variables are of no help in explaining y_t, the computer will obtain the best possible fit by setting $a = \bar{y}$ and all the $b, = 0$; then $S_e{}^2 = S_y{}^2$ and so $R = 0$.[35]

It is time to relax with a lesson on how to lie with statistics. If we subtract Equation 2.2 from the identity $x_t = x_t$, we have

$$x_t - y_t = -a + (1 - b)x_t - e_t \qquad (2.9)$$

Remember that x_t is income and y_t is consumption spending; so it is obviously reasonable to define $x_t - y_t$ as *savings*, since it is the excess of income over consumption. If we let

$$y'_t = x_t - y_t, \qquad a' = -a, \qquad e'_t = -e_t \quad \text{and} \quad b' = (1 - b)$$

we may write as our equation for savings:

$$y'_t = a' + b'x_t + e'_t. \qquad (2.10)$$

When we ran this regression with the savings series computed form the same data used for Equation 2.4, we obtained from our computer:

$$
\begin{aligned}
y'_t = -9.935 + 0.1138 X'_t + e_t & \qquad \bar{R}^2 = \quad 0.908 \\
(1.356) \quad\ (0.0036) & \qquad \bar{S}_e = \quad 3.927 \\
& \qquad d = \quad 0.718 \\
& \qquad df = 102 \qquad (2.11)
\end{aligned}
$$

The intercept of the savings function is $a' = -9.935$, which is $-a$; also $b' = 0.1138 = (1 - b)$, as expected. Furthermore, $e_t = -e'_t$ implies that the standard errors of the estimates for both regressions should be identical, and they are. But $\bar{R}^2$ is *smaller* for the savings regression than it is for the consumption regression. The naive investigator who regards a high $\bar{R}^2$ as the *sine qua non* of a successful statistical investigation is likely to conclude that the consumption function is "better" than the savings function, when they are obviously just opposite sides of the same relationship. Inspection of the equation defining the correlation coefficient will reveal that the discrepancy between the two $\bar{R}^2$'s arises because consumption has a bigger variance than saving.[36]

[35] Is $\bar{R} < 0$ a possibility?

[36] A similar anomaly has arisen in certain empirical studies: the longer the period over which the data are collected, pre- as well as post-World War II, for example, the bigger is $\bar{S}_y$ as a simple consequence of secular growth; consequently R may be expected to be larger as well.

†4.A.3 STATISTICAL INFERENCE

It has been hard to resist the temptation to call the slope coefficient $b =$ 0.8862 of Equation 2.4 the marginal propensity to consume, but a moment's reflection will suggest that at best it can be only an estimate of that parameter. After all, we would expect to get a different estimate if we reran the regression with quarterly data over the period 1947–1968, or even again over the same 1947 to 1972 period with revised data subject to fewer measurement errors. Furthermore, the consumption function may shift with the passage of time as a result of changes in wealth and other variables—or to put it another way, more than one explanatory variable may be required. But there are circumstances in which the method of least squares constitutes a useful estimation procedure.

a. The Model

In elementary economic theory one may postulate

$$y = \alpha + \beta x \tag{3.1}$$

as an exact relationship; but when considering problems of estimation it is important to admit that nature may be random, to add a stochastic disturbance ϵ, and write

$$y_t = \alpha + \beta x_t + \epsilon_t \tag{3.2}$$

This expression would be vacuous if we did not place a restriction on the random variable ϵ_t; otherwise, ϵ_t, like the "Skinner's constant" of freshman calculus,[37] could be just the difference between the right answer and the prediction of Equation 3.1. We will suppose that ϵ_t has zero expected value and write $E(\epsilon_t) = 0$; that is, while ϵ_t is sometimes positive and sometimes negative, on the average it is zero. The random variable ϵ_t might arise from measurement error; it also may be interpreted as representing the effects of variables omitted from the equations in the interest of simplicity. How does ϵ_t differ from the e_t of Equation 2.3? They will be identical if the regression coefficients happen to equal α and β; more generally, the e_t will be reasonable estimates of the ϵ_t if the method of least-squares has provided reasonable estimates of α and β. But when will this happen?

b. Estimation

Under certain circumstances least-squares constitutes an *unbiased* estimation procedure; that is, $E(b) = \beta$, so that there is no systematic tendency to either over- or underestimate the true value of the parameter. This will happen if, in addition to $E(\epsilon_t) = 0$, we can also assume that ϵ_t is distributed *independently* of the explanatory variables, the x_t; in a loose molar sense, this means that the correlation between ϵ and x_t must be zero. This condition would be satisfied if the variable x is unrelated to other variables that are omitted from Equation 3.2; it may also be satisfied if there are random errors in measuring y_t. But it will be violated if there are random errors in measuring x_t. We will say that the desired independence property is a part

---

[37] "Skinner's constant" is the number added to one's own answer in order that it will agree with the answer printed in the back of the textbook.

of the *maintained hypothesis* and, unfortunately, there is no empirical way of checking its validity.[38]

There are often a number of different unbiased procedures for estimating a parameter from a sample of data; it seems reasonable to use an unbiased estimate that is likely to lie close to β. Under rather general circumstances the least-squares constitutes the best linear unbiased procedure. Specifically, suppose we also can assume, as part of the maintained hypothesis, that the ϵ_t have constant variance (homoscedasticity). Suppose, further, that for any $t \neq t'$, ϵ_t, and ϵ'_t are independently distributed so that knowledge of ϵ'_t does not help to predict ϵ. Then the variance of b will be smaller than that of any other estimate that can be calculated linearly.

c. **Hypothesis Testing**

We have now recognized that at best the method of least-squares provides *sample estimates* $(a, b$ and $\bar{S}^2)$ of *unknown parameters* $(\alpha, \beta,$ and $\sigma_\epsilon^2)$. Is it likely that we would have obtained from our sample an estimate $b = 0.8862$ if, in fact, $\beta = 0$, income having no effect on consumption spending? Or, to put it another way, is the sample evidence compatible with the hypothesis that $\beta = 0$? The numbers in parentheses below the regression coefficients of Equation 2.4 provide a means for answering this question; these are the standard errors $\bar{S}_a = 1.356$ and $\bar{S}_b = 0.0036$. Under certain circumstances[39] the following probability statement is true.

$$P(-t_{0.025,n'} < \frac{\beta - b}{\bar{S}_b} < t_{0.025,n'}) = 0.95 \tag{3.3}$$

The valued $t_{0.025,n'}$ is determined from a table of the "t-distribution," with $n' = n - 2$ "degrees of freedom." For our 26 years of quarterly data we have $n = 104$, $n' = 102$, and the standard published tables reveal that $t_{0.025,102} = 1.99$. If, in fact, $\beta = 0$, $P(-2 < b/\bar{S}_b < 2) = 0.95$; clearly, if β were zero, we would be very unlikely to have obtained a sample ratio as large as

$$\frac{b}{S_b} = \frac{0.8862}{0.0036} = 246$$

Therefore we say that β is significant at the 5% level.

The computer is a wonderful beast that will grind out statistics even when certain aspects of the maintained hypothesis are not satisfied. Fortunately, it did compute $d = 0.72$, the Durbin-Watson statistic. This is a danger signal much like the light on the instrument panel on the jet liners that glows when any of the other instruments are not working—at least it glows when it is not burnt out. The Durbin-Watson statistic glows by deviating substantially from two, and the value of $d = 0.72$ suggests we are in trouble; specifically, this low d means that the ϵ_t are not independently distributed; that is, knowledge of the value of ϵ_{t-1} helps in predicting ϵ_t. No longer is the least-squares the best linear estimation procedure; furthermore,

---

[38] In particular, the residuals e_t obtained when the method of least-squares is applied to a data sample are of necessity uncorrelated with the explanatory variables.

[39] We must have, as part of our maintained hypothesis, that ϵ is normally distributed; see also the next paragraph.

the hypothesis testing procedure is not strictly valid. Unfortunately, the Durbin-Watson warning signal does not always light up even when the independence condition is violated; in particular, it does not warn appropriately when the regression model involves a lagged dependent variable; for example,

$$y_t = \alpha + \beta_1 x_t + \beta_2 y_{t-1} + \epsilon \tag{3.4}$$

We must look at J. Johnston's *Econometric Methods* or some other text to find out what to do.

APPENDIX 4.B   SOME CONSUMPTION FUNCTION ESTIMATES

A variety of consumption functions were considered in Chapter 4. Here are three alternatives to the simple regression of consumption on disposable income, all based on deflated quarterly observations for 1946–1972. First, consider the effect of including last quarter's consumption in the regression

$$C_t = 2.361 + 0.2959 Y_{d_t} + 0.6755 C_{t-1} + e_t \qquad \bar{R}^2 = 0.999$$
$$ (1.229) \quad (0.0582) \qquad (0.0666) \qquad\qquad \bar{S}^e = 2.783$$
$$d = 1.77 \tag{1}$$

The lagged consumption term is highly significant, since it is more than 10 times its standard error. Also, the standard error of the estimate $(\bar{S}_e)$ is considerably smaller than that of Equation A2.4, implying that a much tighter fit is achieved when C_{t-1} is included. The next two regressions have previous peak consumption (C_{t-1}^m) and previous peak income $(Y_{d_{t-1}}^m)$ as explanatory variables.

$$C_t = 1.974 + 0.3492 Y_{d_t} + 0.6168 C_{t-1}^m + e_t \qquad \bar{R}^2 = 0.999$$
$$ (1.446) \quad (0.0653) \qquad (0.0749) \qquad\qquad \bar{S}_e = 3.0611$$
$$d = 1.17 \tag{2}$$

$$C_t = 9.459 + 0.7282 Y_{d_t} + 0.1607 Y_{t-1}^m + e_t \qquad \bar{R}^2 = 0.998$$
$$ (1.420) \quad (0.1104) \qquad (0.1124) \qquad\qquad \bar{S}_e = 3.925$$
$$d = 0.586 \tag{3}$$

Evidently, previous peak consumption is stronger than previous peak income, but neither equation achieves as tight a fit as the lagged consumption regression. Finally, consider the following regression, which includes both lagged consumption and lagged disposable income.

$$C_t = 1.807 + 0.4552 Y_{d_t} - 0.2386 Y_{d_{t-1}} + 0.7623 C_{t-1} + e \qquad \bar{R}^2 = 0.999$$
$$ (1.207) \quad (0.0806) \qquad (0.0862) \qquad\quad (0.0717) \qquad\qquad \bar{S}_e = 2.695$$
$$d = 2.14 \tag{4}$$

This is Equation 4.6.4, which was derived through a simplification of the wealth hypothesis. As can be seen from that equation, the estimated coefficients of Y_d and C_{t-1} suggest that $\rho_1 = 0.455$ and $\rho_2 = 0.238$; the difference $\rho_2 - \rho_1 = 0.217$

should supposedly equal the coefficient of lagged disposable income, and it comes fairly close.[40] Note that the intercept is almost as small as its standard error, implying that it is insignificant at the 5% level. Since this equation has the smallest $\bar{S}_e$, it is reasonable to conclude that this simplified wealth approach dominates the other models considered here. But it is a close race; all the $\bar{R}^2$ round off to the same figure.

Here is a disposable income regression, also based on quarterly deflated data and covering the same time span.

$$Y_{d_t} = -24.77 + 0.7519\text{GNP}_t + e_t \qquad \bar{R}^2 = 0.993$$
$$\phantom{Y_{d_t} = } (3.424) \quad (0.0064) \qquad\qquad \bar{S}_e = 9.2930$$
$$d = 0.134 \qquad\qquad (5)$$

The graphs in Chapter 3 had suggested that this equation would not fit the data as tightly as the consumption function, and it is not surprising on comparing it with Equation A2.4 to find that it has a smaller $\bar{R}^2$ and a larger $\bar{S}_e$.

Regressions were also run on annual data, which are readily available for the pre-World War II period. A comparison of the following results reveals that the estimates of the elementary consumption function are quite sensitive to the period covered.

Period of Regression		
1929–1940	$C_t = 22.58 + 0.792 Y_{d_t} + e_t$ (5.33) (0.038)	$\bar{R}^2 = 0.975$ $\bar{S}_e = 2.148$ $d = 0.905$
1929–1945	$C_t = 62.54 + 0.499 Y_{d_t} + e_t$ (6.48) (0.039)	$\bar{R}^2 = 0.911$ $\bar{S}_e = 6.262$ $d = 0.795$
1929–1972	$C_t = 1.54 + 0.901 Y_{d_t} + e_t$ (4.17) (0.013)	$\bar{R}^2 = 0.911$ $\bar{S}_e = 11.59$ $d = 0.365$
1929–1940, 1946–1972 (excluding war years)	$C_t = 9.078 + 0.888 Y_{d_t} + e_t$ (1.22) (0.004)	$\bar{R}^2 = 0.999$ $\bar{S}_e = 3.229$ $d = 1.55$

[40] If the equation immediately preceding Equation 6.4 had been used, the coefficients would have been forced to be consistent. Equation 6.4 would have an intercept if Equation 6.1 had been modified to include a trend term:

$$C_t = \rho_0 + \rho_1 Y_{d_t} + \rho_2 W_{t-1} + \rho_3 t$$

PART II

money and the pace of economic activity

money and
the economy:
an overview

*5.1 WHAT MONEY IS

Money is traditionally described as a medium of exchange, a unit of account, and a store of value. As a medium of exchange it facilitates the execution of business transactions without resorting to inefficient barter. And money does function as the most important unit of account in describing a man's economic worth or the financial position of a business firm. While the miser who hides coins in his mattress is obviously eccentric, most of us find it convenient to carry currency in our pocket even in an age that has been said to mark the transition into a credit card economy. But in spite of the importance of these three roles, money could be taken more or less for granted in the study of macroeconomics if these were the only functions it served. The quantity of money in circulation demands our attention because of the key role it performs in influencing the pace of economic activity and the price level. To understand what money is, why people hold it, and what determines its supply is to begin to appreciate how the Federal Reserve System influences the financial community and the entire economic environment. The monetary theorists who assert that the money supply has a stronger influence than either government spending or tax policy also argue that studying the quantity theory of money instead of the multiplier will provide the most direct explanation of business fluctuations and inflation.

In day-to-day language the term money is sometimes used interchangeably with income. But the economist stresses the fact that income is a *flow*, while *money* is a stock. Thus, in describing gross national product, we talk about the output of the economy over a specified period, usually a year. In contrast money is the size of a stock of a particular type of wealth on a particular date. But what should be included in the money stock? This question does not admit an unambiguous answer. As Table 5.1 indicates, a whole spectrum of monies and near monies exists. Depending on which of three definitions is employed, the money supply in December

Table 5.1 THE MONETARY SPECTRUM (BILLIONS OF DOLLARS)

Year and Month	Overall Measures			Components and Related Items						
	M_1 (Currency plus Demand Deposits)	M_2 (M_1 plus Time Deposits at Commercial Banks Other Than Large CD's)	M_3 (M_2 plus Deposits at Nonbank Thrift Institutions)	Deposits at Commercial Banks		Time and Savings[c]			Deposits at Nonbank Thrift Institutions[e]	U.S. Government Demand Deposits (Unadjusted[f])
				Currency[a]	Demand[b]	Total	Large CD's[d]	Other		
1947: December	113.1	—	—	26.4	86.7	35.4	—	—	—	1.0
1948: December	111.5	—	—	25.8	85.8	36.0	—	—	—	1.8
1949: December	111.2	—	—	25.1	86.0	36.4	—	—	—	2.8
1950: December	116.2	—	—	25.0	91.2	36.7	—	—	—	2.4
1951: December	122.7	—	—	26.1	96.5	38.2	—	—	—	2.7
1952: December	127.4	—	—	27.3	100.1	41.1	—	—	—	4.9
1953: December	128.8	—	—	27.7	101.1	44.5	—	—	—	3.8
1954: December	132.3	—	—	27.4	104.9	48.3	—	—	—	5.0
1955: December	135.2	—	—	27.8	107.4	50.0	—	—	—	3.4
1956: December	136.9	—	—	28.2	108.7	51.9	—	—	—	3.4
1957: December	135.9	—	—	28.3	107.6	57.4	—	—	—	3.5
1958: December	141.1	—	—	28.6	112.6	65.4	—	—	—	3.9
1959: December	142.6	—	—	28.9	113.7	67.4	—	—	—	4.9

Year										
1960: December	141.7	—	—	28.9	112.8	72.9	—	—	—	4.7
1961: December	146.0	—	—	29.6	116.5	82.7	—	—	—	4.9
1962: December	148.1	—	—	30.6	117.6	97.8	—	—	—	5.6
1963: December	153.6	—	—	32.5	121.1	112.2	—	—	—	5.1
1964: December	160.5	273.8	422.9	34.2	126.3	126.6	13.3	113.3	149.2	5.5
1965: December	168.0	298.1	459.4	36.3	131.7	146.8	16.7	130.1	161.3	4.6
1966: December	171.7	314.0	481.3	38.3	133.4	158.1	15.9	142.2	167.4	3.4
1967: December	183.1	345.7	528.8	40.4	142.7	183.4	20.8	162.6	183.1	5.0
1968: December	197.4	378.0	572.6	43.4	154.0	204.2	23.6	180.6	194.6	5.0
1969: December	203.7	386.8	588.3	46.0	157.7	194.1	11.0	183.2	201.5	5.6
1970: December	214.8	418.2	633.9	49.0	165.8	228.9	25.5	203.4	215.7	7.3
1971: December	228.2	464.7	718.1	52.5	175.7	269.9	33.4	236.4	253.4	6.7
1972: December	246.9	514.5	810.2	56.9	190.0	311.2	43.7	267.6	295.8	7.2

Source. Economic Report of the President.

a Currency outside the Treasury, the Federal Reserve System, and the vaults of all commercial banks.

b Demand deposits other than those due to domestic commercial banks and the U.S. Government, less cash items in process of collection and Federal Reserve float, plus foreign demand balances at Federal Reserve Banks.

c Time and savings deposits other than those due to domestic commercial banks and the U.S. Government. Effective June 1966, excludes balances accumulated for payment of personal loans (about $1.1 billion).

d Negotiable time certificates of deposit issued in denominations of $100,000 or more by large weekly reporting commercial banks.

e Average of the beginning- and end-of-month deposits of mutual savings banks and savings and loan shares.

f Deposits at all commercial banks.

1970, ranged from $214.8 to $633.9 billion! Currency as well as coin obviously counts as money. And, since checks, because of their convenience and safety, are used much more frequently than currency and coin in effecting payment, it seems reasonable to include demand deposits—the funds the public has on deposit in checking accounts—as part of the money supply. The smallest money supply concept, denoted M_1, is the sum of demand deposits plus currency and coin. But when needed for effecting payment, both time and savings deposits at commercial banks can be readily converted into cash or redeposited in one's checking account; they are so close to money that for many purposes it is convenient to include them in the money supply, which is money supply concept M_2. Funds deposited at a savings bank may also be converted into cash without difficulty; this adds another $215.7 billion in calculating money supply concept M_3. Other forms of near-money are presented in Table 5.2.

No one figure is the "correct" definition of money; there is obviously room for debate concerning the relative merits of these and alternative definitions of the money supply but, when an economist talks of money, it is customarily assumed that he is referring to M_1, unless otherwise specified. And, as the footnotes on Table 5.1 indicate, any definition must be somewhat arbitrary; it is partially accounting convenience, for example, that explains why federal but not state and local government demand deposits are excluded in computing M_1. Fortunately, a precise definition is not required in much theoretical discussion. And, in empirical work, results are often unaffected or insensitive to the choice of M_1, M_2, or M_3.

*5.2 THE QUANTITY THEORY OF MONEY

The quantity theory of money, which predates Adam Smith and his *Wealth of Nations*, constitutes the simplest explanation as to how the money stock influences the economy. The quantity theory as championed in the United States by Irving Fisher in the 1920s took the form

$$Mv = pT \tag{2.1}$$

In this equation T is the volume of transactions to be executed with money during the year, p is a measure of the general price level, and v the velocity of circulation. Thus pT is the dollar value of transactions to be executed in the economy, and M is the stock of money used over and over again in executing these transactions; transactions velocity v is the number of times that the average unit of money changes hands during the year. The volume of transactions is much larger than GNP, because it is usually interpreted

Table 5.2 PRIVATE LIQUID ASSET HOLDINGS, NONFINANCIAL INVESTORS (AVERAGES OF DAILY FIGURES; BILLIONS OF DOLLARS)

Year and Month	Total Liquid Assets	Currency and Deposits			Time Deposits		U.S. Government Securities		Negotiable Certificates of Deposit	Commercial Paper
		Total	Currency	Demand Deposits	Commercial Banks	Non-bank Thrift Institutions	Savings Bonds	Short-Term Marketable Securities		
1965: December	557.7	447.4	35.3	115.5	125.2	170.4	49.5	38.2	15.5	7.1
1966: December	588.2	469.6	38.3	117.3	136.8	177.3	50.1	43.3	15.0	10.2
1967: December	637.5	516.0	40.4	125.2	156.2	194.2	51.0	39.5	19.5	11.5
1968: December	692.1	559.7	43.4	135.2	174.2	206.8	51.4	44.2	22.6	14.2
1969: December	719.2	576.3	46.0	138.1	177.1	215.2	51.1	61.9	9.1	20.9
1970: December	766.8	623.4	49.0	144.8	198.5	231.1	51.3	49.4	23.2	19.5
1971: December	850.2	710.0	52.5	153.5	232.4	271.7	53.7	38.6	30.1	17.7
1972: December	961.4	803.3	56.8	166.9	262.3	317.3	56.9	42.6	39.9	18.6

Source. Economic Report of the President.

as including intermediate transactions that are netted out as "double counting" in computing final product; also, T includes financial transactions in securities and sales of secondhand goods. An alternative version of the quantity equation replaces T with real gross national product.

$$\mathbf{M}v_y = pY \tag{2.2}$$

Here v_y is the "income velocity of money." Furthermore, English economists Pigou and Marshall and other members of the Cambridge University school of quantity theorists advocated the "cash balance" approach.

$$\mathbf{M} = kpY \tag{2.3}$$

Here k, the reciprocal of income velocity, denotes the proportion of income that the public desires to hold as money. Which equation is employed is not all that critical, although a disadvantage of Equation 2.1 is that T, in contrast to GNP, is not directly observable.[1]

What distinguishes one group of quantity theorists from another is not the form of the equation they choose to employ so much as the assumptions that are invoked about the determinants of velocity. The naive quantity theory treats v_y as a constant, subject perhaps to historical variation, but not affected by variations in $\mathbf{M}$, Y, or p. When velocity is regarded as a fixed parameter, the quantity theory implies that an increase in $\mathbf{M}$ must manifest itself in an increase in money GNP. How the increase will be divided between inflation versus an increase in real output is not answered by the quantity equation itself. If, as is often argued, the level of output (Y) in the longer run is uninfluenced by monetary factors, an increase in $\mathbf{M}$ must ultimately lead to a proportional increase in the price level; this implies that the real value of the money supply, $\mathbf{M}/p$, cannot be influenced by the monetary authorities in the long run. Quantity theorists emphasize that in the *short* run $\mathbf{M}$ certainly can influence real output; indeed, $\mathbf{M}$ is assigned a prominent role in causing fluctuations in economic activity. And several quantity theorists, most notably Milton Friedman of Chicago, Edward S. Shaw of Stanford, and Alan Meltzer of Carnegie-Mellon, have argued that the business cycle is *caused* by the mistakes made by the Federal Reserve System in controlling the money supply!

How individual components of the quantity equation have behaved since 1929 is revealed in Figure 5.1. The heavy black line indicates the path of our current dollar GNP (Y^n). In terms of the left-hand side of quantity Equation 2.2, Y^n factors into $\mathbf{M}$ and income velocity; these two component

[1] Data on the value of payments made by checks—bank debits—is sometimes used in approximating T.

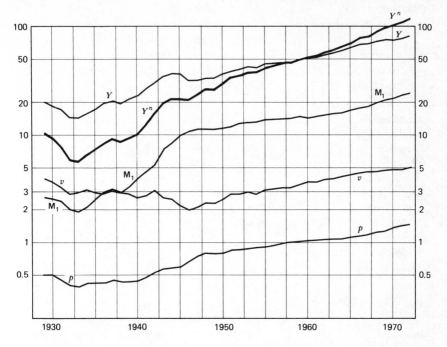

Symbols:
 Y^n — Gross national product
 Y — Real GNP (1957 prices)
 M_1 — Money supply (currency + demand deposits)
 v — Income velocity of money (Y^n/M)
 p — GNP implicit price deflator (Y^n/Y, 1957=1)
(The first three variables are measured in $10 billion units)

Fig. 5.1 *Components of the quantity theory—United States, 1929–1972 (logarithmic scale).*

series appear about halfway down the graph.[2] In terms of the right-hand side of the equation, money GNP may be factored into real GNP and price; these two series are also plotted on the graph. The graph reveals that ve-locity, measured by the ratio pY/M, has not exhibited the pronounced upward secular trend that characterizes the other series. Instead, it has been subject to erratic year-to-year fluctuations. And the fluctuations from

[2] Since the chart is semilogarithmic, we can exploit the proposition that

$$\log M + \log v = \log p + \log Y = \log Y^n$$

Measuring vertically with a ruler on the graph adds the logs; therefore, the height of the p curve plus the height of the Y line equals the arithmetic height of the Y^n curve, provided that when measuring distances with a ruler note is taken of the fact that $\log 1 = 0$. See Appendix 2.C.2 for a review of logarithms.

Table 5.3 INCOME VELOCITY OF MONEY, INTERNATIONAL COMPARISONS

	1950	1955	1960	1965	1970
United States	2.46	2.87	3.47	3.92	4.37
United Kingdom	2.33	3.18	3.85	4.51	5.21
Industrial Europe					
Austria	4.10	4.52	4.78	4.81	5.32
Belgium		2.36	2.56	2.64	3.04
Denmark	3.30	3.99	4.04	4.06	4.16
France	3.23	2.88	3.18	2.78	3.50
Germany	5.82	6.21	6.47	6.37	6.66
Italy	*	3.33	2.98	2.55	1.85
Netherlands	2.74	3.10	3.74	4.00	4.38
Norway	3.12	3.62	4.21	4.80	4.72
Sweden	5.39	6.51	6.51	7.38	9.53
Switzerland	1.72	1.97	1.89	2.01	1.89
Canada	4.16	5.23	5.94	5.79	5.93
Japan	*	3.69	3.74	3.10	3.33
Finland	7.79	9.22	10.58	12.39	11.00
Greece	12.16	8.99	6.64	5.36	4.39
Ireland	3.04	3.37	3.17	3.27	3.93
Portugal	1.70	1.64	1.58	1.72	1.97
Spain	*	3.12	3.03	3.02	3.07
Turkey	9.20	7.97	9.31	9.00	8.27
Yugoslavia					4.22
Australia	2.92	3.25	3.53	5.03	5.46
New Zealand	2.93	3.22	3.55	4.87	6.39
South Africa	2.96	4.15	5.32	5.40	5.47
Israel	2.50	5.33	5.02	5.54	5.52
Latin America					
Argentina	2.74	2.80	5.63	7.27	*
Bolivia	9.20	27.29	10.71	7.61	*
Brazil	3.95	4.49	3.99	4.07	4.86
Chile	5.27	11.30	10.83	9.62	9.17
Columbia	8.07	6.93	6.71	6.51	*
Costa Rica	6.61	6.24	6.44	6.61	5.71
Dominican Republic	9.55	7.37	7.14	7.66	*
Ecuador	7.94	9.26	8.16	8.07	6.61
El Salvador	*	*	6.99	7.97	8.10
Guatemala	10.95	9.37	9.49	9.32	10.52
Honduras	11.70	10.27	11.67	9.85	8.47

(Continued)

Table 5.3   (Çontinued)

	1950	1955	1960	1965	1970
Mexico	6.59	8.19	8.99	8.15	8.72
Nicaragua	*	8.11	9.95	7.84	10.16
Panama	10.75	10.12	9.88	11.89	9.29
Paraguay	6.16	10.04	12.91	11.36	10.32
Peru	8.07	8.27	8.67	9.50	*
Uruguay	*	5.70	5.67	4.98	.6.80
Venezuela	7.51	7.41	7.18	8.06	6.72

Source. *International Financial Statistics*, 1972 Supplement.
Note. An * indicates data unavailable.

one year to the next in money GNP appear to be related to variations in velocity as well as in **M**. In particular, both income velocity and the money supply dropped dramatically in the Great Depression of the 1930s. Variations in the velocity of money for a number of countries over the last 20 years are recorded on Table 5.3.

Modern quantity theorists, except for occasional lapses when writing for popular consumption, are careful to stress that the hypothesis of a constant income velocity is no more than a gross caricature of their position. Rather, the velocity of money is influenced by a variety of variables, particularly the rate of interest, the rate of price change, and wealth. But once the quantity theory is complicated in this way it becomes a theory of why people hold money—a theory of the "demand for money" or "liquidity preference." The demand for money, like the demand for wheat or any other commodity, may depend upon its price; it also depends upon the types of services it can perform for its user and the price of money substitutes; and how much money people will want to hold may also hinge on their income and their wealth. All this is common sense, but it will be necessary for us to explore in detail what constitutes the price of holding money and how a variety of factors influence demand. Certain of these issues are explored in subsequent sections of this chapter; but most of the complications arising from changes in the price level will be delayed until Part III, which focuses on the determinants of the price level and the sources of inflation.

*5.3 THE TRANSACTIONS DEMAND FOR MONEY

Holding money is expensive. When the rate of interest paid on savings accounts is 5% per annum, anyone who manages to reduce the average size of his holdings of currency and demand deposits by $100 can end up $5 ahead at the end of the year. And still higher yields might be expected by converting ones money into other forms of wealth, for example, by purchasing government bonds or investing in the stock market. The yield that would be earned by holding alternative forms of wealth is the opportunity cost of holding money. But, in spite of the obvious costs, households and business firms hold money balances for a variety of reasons. First, it is of use as a medium of exchange; we do not pay all our bills on payday, and we need currency and coin for executing a variety of transactions every day. This motive for holding money is stressed by the Fisher version of the quantity theory. The consumer determines his demand for money by balancing the convenience it yields against the costs of holding it.

How a number of factors influence the amount of money a typical consumer might want to hold is illustrated on Figure 5.2. Suppose that the hypothetical consumer is paid the sum of $500 on the first of each month, and suppose that he spends the same amount of money every day. Then the sawteeth reveal the day-to-day fluctuations in the individual's cash holdings. His holding for transactions purposes of $500 at the beginning of each month are run down to zero by the subsequent payday; thus his holdings for transactions average half his paycheck, or $500/2 = $250. The income velocity of circulation of his money balances is simply the ratio of annual money income to average money holdings, or a rate of $6000/$250 = 24 per annum.

The middle panel illustrates how the hypothetical consumer might respond if his monthly paycheck is raised to $600. Total money balances will now average out to $600/2 = $300. In this instance, total money holdings have risen in proportion to the rise in income; income velocity is unchanged.

How our hypothetical individual might respond if his employer converted to a semimonthly payment schedule is shown on the bottom panel; now that he is paid $300 twice a month, the saw has much finer teeth. And his holdings for transactions purposes are cut in half, even though his annual income is still $7200. Specifically, his money holdings are now $300/2 = $150. Now his income velocity is $7200/$150 = 48 per annum. This crude argument suggests that a change in a society's *habits of payment*, such as a change in the length of the pay period, might be expected to have a dramatic influence on the amount of money an individual would want to hold and the velocity at which it circulates. But for the economy as a whole such changes may be partially offsetting; to the extent that such shifts do not cancel out they are likely to cause small shifts in velocity from one year to the next that, hopefully, can be predicted by extrapolating from past trends.

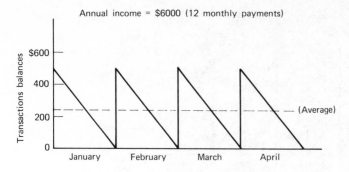

Annual income = $6000 (12 monthly payments)

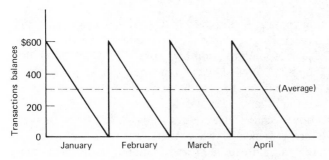

Annual income = $7200 (12 monthly payments)

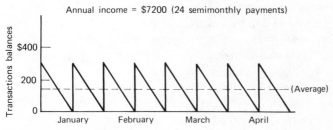

Annual income = $7200 (24 semimonthly payments)

Fig. 5.2 *Transactions balances.*

The argument illustrated in Figure 5.2 suggests that the demand for money may be roughly proportional to income. But how will a change in the cost of holding money, the rate of interest, affect demand? When the carrying costs incurred by holding money increase, we can expect that efforts will be made to economize on money holdings. At higher rates of interest large money holders (corporations and financial institutions in particular) take steps to cut down on the magnitude of idle deposits. It may become worthwhile to allocate administrative talent to the task of reducing

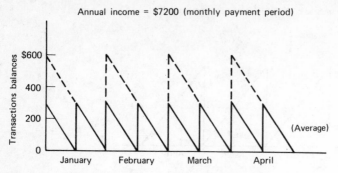

Fig. 5.3 *Interest rate and transactions balances.*

the size of transactions balances. Figure 5.3 illustrates one way in which economies may be achieved.[3] The sawteeth reproduced from the middle panel of Figure 5.2 correspond to monthly cash receipts of $600. But suppose the rise in the rate of interest leads to the following effort to reduce idle cash balances. Only half of the funds received on the first of each month is held as cash; the other half is placed in interest earning assets for 15 days. The transaction balances that are drawn down to zero at the middle of each month are replenished when the investment matures. The smaller sawteeth on the graph illustrate how total money holdings fluctuate under this plan (they are identical to those generated in the bottom panel of Figure 5.2 when cash payments were made semimonthly). Thus velocity has risen from 24 to 48 as a result of the decision to economize on cash balances. And how much interest will be earned? The small trapezoids on the graph indicate the amount invested; $300 is held in interest-earning assets during the first half of each month; thus, if r denotes the rate of interest, total interest income is $r \times \$150$; that is, it is the rate of interest times $\frac{1}{4}$ of payday receipts. This is not all gain, however, because transactions costs are incurred in arranging the investment; for the private citizen this may be simply the inconvenience of making two trips each month to the savings bank; for a corporation it involves bookkeeping expenses, brokerage fees, and similar charges. Indeed, the interest rate must be rather high in order to warrant the complications involved by the whole proce-

[3] How the optimal quantity of money to hold is related to the rate of interest and income has been analyzed by Tobin and Baumol. The argument is related to the "square-root rule" of inventory behavior; that is, the optimal stock may rise with the square of income instead of in proportion to it. See W. J. Baumol, "The Transactions Demand for Cash: An Inventory Theoretic Approach," *Quarterly Journal of Economics*, 1952; James Tobin, "The Interest Elasticity of the Transactions Demand for Cash," *Review of Economics and Statistics*, 1956; Thomson M. Whitin, *The Theory of Inventory Management*, Princeton University Press, 1953.

dure. But, if the interest rate rises sufficiently, it may be worthwhile to achieve still further economy by making several short-term investments within each payment period. Thus, the higher the interest rate, the lower the transactions demand for money, and the faster the velocity of circulation.

*5.4 PRECAUTIONARY AND SPECULATIVE BALANCES

There are other reasons for holding money, quite apart from the transactions motive, that may influence the proportion of his wealth that an individual will choose to hold in money of one form or another. For example, it is a wise precaution to guard against unforeseen events by holding extra cash instead of planning to spend one's last nickel just before payday. Not only does the holding of extra cash provide protection against adverse developments, such as a car breakdown while on a trip; it may also enable one to take advantage of unanticipated bargains and other opportunities. Furthermore, money may at times of uncertainty constitute a particularly attractive investment outlet, because it provides its holder with protection against the capital losses that unfavorable market conditions inflict on the stock market speculator, the bond holder, and the real estate investor. Thus, in the absence of perfect foresight, there are precautionary and speculative reasons for holding money over and above its utility in the execution of transactions. In order to understand how uncertainty influences the demand for money it is necessary to consider other assets that compete with money as reservoirs for storing wealth.

Precautionary balances in excess of transactions requirements constitute a type of insurance against surprise, and the cost of holding money balances is the premium paid for this type of protection. Precautionary balances may be held in savings accounts instead of as cash or demand deposits, in which case they are part of M_3 but not M_1 (see Table 5.1 for the precise definition of these alternative concepts of money and near money).[4] It is reasonable to assume that the demand for precautionary balances, like the transactions demand, is negatively related to the interest rate. And we will see that speculative balances display this same tendency.

As alternatives to currency and demand deposits there exists a variety of other assets in which wealth may be held. For the typical citizen the savings account is attractive, and it is included in the more generic definition of money. And Series E Government Bonds may be an attractive alterna-

---

[4] In the *General Theory*, p. 195, Keynes mentions savings deposits; he also refers readers to Chapter 3 of his earlier work, the *Treatise on Money* (Macmillan, 1930), where he elaborated on the importance of savings and time deposits.

tive yielding a modest but safe return. For the wealthier investor and the corporation with more cash than currently required for transactions purposes, the stock market and the government bond market command careful consideration.

Various types of securities issued by the United States government are recorded in Table 5.4. Who holds the public debt is revealed by Table 5.5. How the yields earned by investors on various types of government securities have fluctuated historically is recorded on Table 5.6 and plotted in Figure 5.4. Note that only a rather small proportion of the government's debt is held by private individuals. Also, the government literally owes part

Table 5.4 TYPES OF SECURITIES ISSUED BY THE UNITED STATES GOVERNMENT (BILLIONS OF DOLLARS)

| | | Interest-Bearing Public Debt | | | | | | |
| | | Marketable Public Issues by Maturity Class | | | Nonmarketable Public Issues | | | Matured Public Debt and Debt Bearing No Interest |
End of Year	Total Public Debt Securities	Within 1 Year	1 to 10 Years	10 Years and Over	U.S. Savings Bonds and Notes	Foreign and International	Other	Special Issues	
1946	259.1	54.8	61.7	60.1	49.8	—	6.7	24.6	1.5
1947	256.9	49.6	56.1	60.0	52.1	—	7.4	29.0	2.7
1948	252.8	44.6	55.1	57.7	55.1	—	6.3	31.7	2.2
1949	257.1	49.4	51.8	53.9	56.7	—	9.3	33.9	2.1
1950	256.7	49.4	50.5	52.5	58.0	—	10.1	33.7	2.4
1951	259.4	47.1	56.7	38.8	57.6	—	20.9	35.9	2.3
1952	267.4	57.7	62.2	28.7	57.9	—	19.6	39.1	2.1
1953	275.2	73.9	50.4	30.3	57.7	—	19.3	41.2	2.3
1954	278.7	62.8	64.7	30.2	57.7	—	17.7	42.6	3.0
1955	280.8	61.7	68.6	32.9	57.9	—	12.7	43.9	3.0
1956	276.6	68.6	58.9	32.9	56.3	—	11.9	45.6	2.4
1957	274.9	75.3	56.9	32.0	52.5	—	10.4	45.8	2.0
1958	282.9	72.6	71.0	32.0	51.2	—	9.2	44.8	2.1
1959	290.8	79.9	83.7	24.6	48.2	—	7.8	43.5	3.1
1960	290.2	75.3	89.5	24.2	47.2	—	6.3	44.3	3.4
1961	296.2	85.9	84.7	25.4	47.5	0.5	5.3	43.5	3.5
1962	303.5	87.3	95.6	20.1	47.5	0.7	4.6	43.4	4.3
1963	309.3	89.4	94.2	24.0	48.8	1.3	3.8	43.7	4.1
1964	317.9	88.5	100.4	23.6	49.7	1.8	3.5	46.1	4.4
1965	320.9	93.4	95.6	25.6	50.3	2.4	2.9	46.3	4.4
1966	329.3	105.2	87.5	25.4	50.8	1.5	2.7	52.0	4.3
1967	344.7	104.4	97.0	25.1	51.7	3.2	2.6	57.2	3.5
1968	358.0	108.6	103.4	24.8	52.3	4.4	2.6	59.1	2.9
1969	368.2	118.1	93.3	24.4	52.2	4.7	2.5	71.0	2.0
1970	389.2	123.4	104.9	19.4	52.5	6.5	2.4	78.1	1.9
1971	424.1	119.1	123.0	19.9	54.9	17.4	2.4	85.7	1.8
1972	449.3	130.4	117.7	21.4	58.1	21.3	2.4	95.9	2.0

Source. Economic Report of the President.

Table 5.5 WHO HOLDS THE PUBLIC DEBT (PAR VALUES, BILLIONS OF DOLLARS)

				Total Public Debt Securities						
					Held by Private Investors					
End of Year	Total	Held by Government Accounts	Held by Federal Reserve Banks	Total	Commercial Banks	Mutual Savings Banks and Insurance Companies	Other Corporations	State and Local Governments	Individuals	Miscellaneous Investors
1946	259.1	27.4	23.3	208.3	74.5	36.7	15.3	6.3	64.1	11.4
1947	256.9	30.8	22.6	203.6	68.7	35.9	14.1	7.3	65.7	11.9
1948	252.8	33.7	23.3	195.8	62.4	32.7	14.8	7.9	65.5	12.5
1949	257.1	35.9	18.9	202.4	66.8	31.5	16.8	8.1	66.3	12.9
1950	256.7	36.0	20.8	199.9	61.8	29.6	19.7	8.8	66.3	13.6
1951	259.4	39.3	23.8	196.3	61.5	26.2	20.7	9.6	64.6	13.7
1952	267.4	42.9	24.7	199.8	63.4	25.5	19.9	11.1	65.2	14.7
1953	275.2	45.4	25.9	203.8	63.7	25.1	21.5	12.7	64.8	16.1
1954	278.7	46.7	24.9	207.1	69.1	24.1	19.1	14.4	63.5	16.9
1955	280.8	49.0	24.8	207.0	62.0	23.1	23.2	15.4	65.0	18.3
1956	276.6	51.2	24.9	200.5	59.5	21.2	18.7	16.3	65.9	18.9
1957	274.9	52.8	24.2	197.9	59.5	20.1	17.7	16.6	64.9	19.1
1958	282.9	52.1	26.3	204.5	67.5	19.8	18.1	16.5	63.7	18.9
1959	290.8	51.4	26.6	212.7	60.3	19.4	21.4	18.0	69.4	24.3
1960	290.2	52.8	27.4	210.0	62.1	18.1	18.7	18.7	66.1	26.5
1961	296.2	52.5	28.9	214.8	67.2	17.4	18.5	19.0	65.9	25.9
1962	303.5	53.2	30.8	219.5	67.1	17.4	18.6	20.1	88.0	30.2
1963	309.3	55.3	33.6	220.5	64.2	16.8	18.7	21.1	68.2	31.6
1964	317.9	58.4	37.0	222.5	63.9	16.5	18.2	21.2	69.8	33.0
1965	320.9	59.7	40.8	220.5	60.7	15.6	15.8	22.9	72.1	33.4
1966	329.3	65.8	44.3	219.2	57.4	14.1	14.9	24.3	74.6	33.9
1967	344.7	73.1	49.1	222.4	63.8	12.7	12.2	21.1	74.0	35.7
1968	358.0	75.6	52.9	228.5	86.0	11.6	14.2	24.4	75.8	36.7
1969	368.2	89.0	57.2	222.0	56.8	10.0	11.7	25.9	81.4	36.2
1970	389.2	97.1	62.1	229.9	62.7	9.8	9.4	25.2	81.9	41.0
1971	424.1	106.0	70.2	247.9	65.3	9.3	12.4	25.0	74.0	61.9
1972	449.3	116.9	89.9	262.5	63.3	8.8	12.7	28.8	74.9	74.0

Source. Economic Report of the President.

of the total debt to itself; this strange fact arises because several government agencies, notably the Social Security Administration, place in government securities the funds that have accumulated for paying future obligations (e.g., old age and survivor benefits).

The United States Savings Bond, with which we are all familiar, is not the dominant type of security issued by the United States government. Series E Savings Bonds are issued in the name of the holder; they cannot be sold but, if desired, they can be redeemed in accordance with a fixed maturity schedule at a post office or through most banks. In contrast, Treasury bills and marketable government bonds do not bear the name of

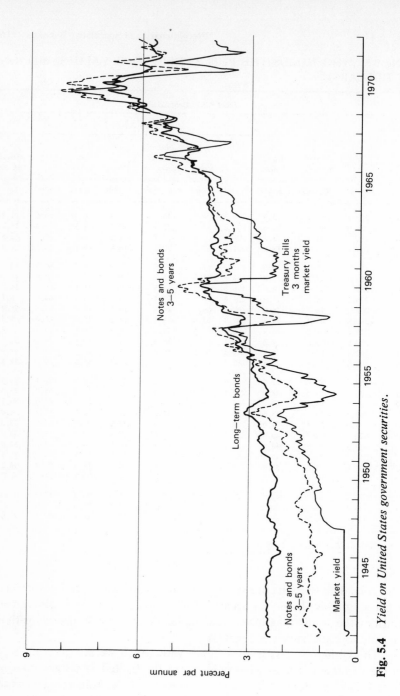

Fig. 5.4 *Yield on United States government securities.*

168

Table 5.6 BOND YIELDS AND INTEREST RATES 1929–1970 (PERCENT PER ANNUM)

Year	U.S. Government Securities				Corporate Bonds (Moody's)		High-Grade Municipal Bonds (Standard & Poor's)	Average Rate on Short-Term Bank Loans to Business—Selected Cities	Prime Commercial Paper, 4–5 Months	Federal Reserve Bank Discount Rate	FHA New Home Mortgage Yields[e]
	3-Month Treasury Bills[a]	9–12 Month Issues[b]	3–5 Year Issues[c]	Tax-able Bonds[d]	Aaa	Baa					
1929	(f)	—	—	—	4.73	5.90	4.27	(g)	5.85	5.17	—
1930	(f)	—	—	—	4.55	5.90	4.07	(g)	3.59	3.04	—
1931	1.402	—	—	—	4.58	7.62	4.01	(g)	2.64	2.12	—
1932	0.879	—	—	—	5.01	9.30	4.65	(g)	2.73	2.82	—
1933	0.515	—	2.66	—	4.49	7.76	4.71	(g)	1.73	2.56	—
1934	0.256	—	2.12	—	4.00	6.32	4.03	(g)	1.02	1.54	—
1935	0.137	—	1.29	—	3.60	5.75	3.40	(g)	0.75	1.50	—
1936	0.143	—	1.11	—	3.24	4.77	3.07	(g)	0.75	1.50	—
1937	0.447	—	1.40	—	3.26	5.03	3.10	(g)	0.94	1.33	—
1938	0.053	—	0.83	—	3.19	5.80	2.91	(g)	0.81	1.00	—
1939	0.023	—	0.59	—	3.01	4.96	2.76	2.1	0.59	1.00	—
1940	0.014	—	0.50	—	2.84	4.75	2.50	2.1	0.56	1.00	—
1941	0.103	—	0.73	—	2.77	4.33	2.10	2.0	0.53	1.00	—
1942	0.326	—	1.46	2.46	2.83	4.28	2.36	2.2	0.66	[h]1.00	—
1943	0.373	0.75	1.34	2.47	2.73	3.91	2.06	2.6	0.69	[h]1.00	—
1944	0.375	0.79	1.33	2.48	2.72	3.61	1.86	2.4	0.73	[h]1.00	—

(Continued)

Table 5.6 *(Continued)*

Year	U.S. Government Securities				Corporate Bonds (Moody's)		High-Grade Municipal Bonds (Standard & Poor's)	Average Rate on Short-Term Bank Loans to Business—Selected Cities	Prime Commercial Paper, 4-5 Months	Federal Reserve Bank Discount Rate	FHA New Home Mortgage Yields[e]
	3-Month Treasury Bills[a]	9-12 Month Issues[b]	3-5 Year Issues[c]	Taxable Bonds[d]	Aaa	Baa					
1945	0.375	0.81	1.18	2.37	2.62	3.29	1.67	2.2	0.75	h1.00	—
1946	0.375	0.82	1.16	2.19	2.53	3.05	1.64	2.1	0.81	h1.00	—
1947	0.594	0.88	1.32	2.25	2.61	3.24	2.01	2.1	1.03	1.00	—
1948	1.040	1.14	1.62	2.44	2.82	3.47	2.40	2.5	1.44	1.34	—
1949	1.102	1.14	1.43	2.31	2.66	3.42	2.21	2.68	1.49	1.50	4.34
1950	1.218	1.26	1.50	2.32	2.62	3.24	1.98	2.69	1.45	1.59	4.17
1951	1.552	1.73	1.93	2.57	2.86	3.41	2.00	3.11	2.16	1.75	4.21
1952	1.766	1.81	2.13	2.68	2.96	3.52	2.19	3.49	2.33	1.75	4.29
1953	1.931	2.07	2.56	2.94	3.20	3.74	2.72	3.69	2.52	1.99	4.61
1954	0.953	0.92	1.82	2.55	2.90	3.51	2.37	3.61	1.56	1.60	4.62
1955	1.753	1.89	2.50	2.84	3.06	3.53	2.53	3.70	2.18	1.89	4.64
1956	2.658	2.83	3.12	3.08	3.36	3.88	2.93	4.20	3.31	2.77	4.79
1957	3.257	3.53	3.62	3.47	3.89	4.71	3.60	4.62	3.81	3.12	5.42
1958	1.839	2.09	2.90	3.43	3.79	4.73	3.56	4.34	2.46	2.15	5.49
1959	3.405	4.11	4.33	4.03	4.38	5.05	3.95	i5.00	3.97	3.36	5.71
1960	2.928	3.55	3.99	4.02	4.41	5.19	3.73	5.16	3.85	3.53	6.18
1961	2.378	2.91	3.60	3.90	4.35	5.08	3.46	4.97	2.97	3.00	5.80

1962	2.778	3.02	3.57	3.95	4.33	5.02	3.18	5.00	3.25	3.00	5.61
1963	3.157	3.28	3.72	4.00	4.26	4.86	3.23	5.01	3.55	3.23	5.47
1964	3.549	3.76	4.06	4.15	4.40	4.83	3.22	4.99	3.97	3.55	5.45
1965	3.954	4.09	4.22	4.21	4.49	4.87	3.27	5.06	4.38	4.04	5.46
1966	4.881	5.17	5.16	4.65	5.13	5.67	3.82	6.00	5.55	4.50	6.29
1967	4.321	4.84	5.07	4.85	5.51	6.23	3.98	[i]6.00	5.10	4.19	6.55
1968	5.339	5.62	5.59	5.26	6.18	6.94	4.51	6.68	5.90	5.17	7.13
1969	6.677	7.06	6.85	6.12	7.03	7.81	5.81	8.21	7.83	5.87	8.19
1970	6.458	6.90	7.37	6.58	8.04	9.11	6.51	8.48	7.72	5.95	9.05
1971	4.348	4.75	5.77	5.74	7.39	8.56	5.70	6.32	5.11	4.88	7.78
1972	4.071	4.86	5.85	5.64	7.21	8.16	5.27	5.90	4.69	4.50	7.53

Source. Economic Report of the President.

[a] Rate on new issues within period. Issues were tax exempt prior to March 1, 1941, and fully taxable thereafter. For the period 1934–1937, series includes issues with maturities of more than 3 months.

[b] Certificates of indebtedness and selected note and bond issues (fully taxable).

[c] Selected note and bond issues. Issues were partially tax exempt prior to 1941, and fully taxable thereafter.

[d] First issued in 1941. Series includes bonds that are neither due nor callable before a given number of years as follows: April 1953 to date, 10 years; April 1952–March 1953, 12 years; October 1941–March 1952, 15 years.

[e] Data for first of the month, based on the maximum permissible interest rate (8% beginning December 2, 1970). Through July 1961, computed on 25-year mortgages paid in 12 years and thereafter, 30-year mortgages prepaid in 15 years.

[f] Treasury bills were first issued in December 1929 and were issued irregularly in 1930.

[g] Not available on same basis as for 1939 and subsequent years.

[h] From October 30, 1942, to April 24, 1946, a preferential rate of 0.50% was in effect for advances secured by government securities maturing in 1 year or less.

[i] Beginning 1959, series revised to exclude loans to nonbank financial institutions.

[j] Beginning February 1967, series revised to incorporae changes in coverage, in the sample of reporting banks, and in the reporting period (shifted to the middle month of the quarter).

171

the holder and are freely transferable in the government bond market; provided one has the required funds (many bonds are sold only in denominations of $10,000 or more) they may be purchased or sold through a stockbroker or a bank. Treasury bills are a short-term security constituting a promise by the government to pay a specified sum, $5000 say, on maturity date, usually three or six months from date of issue; they are issued by the United States Treasury at periodic auctions at a discount below their maturity value; the purchaser is rewarded for lending his funds to the government when he receives the full face value of his bills on maturity. And if it should turn out that the funds are needed prior to maturity, the bill may be sold to another investor at a price determined by supply and demand conditions, the market clearing price being quoted daily on the financial pages of major newspapers and the *Wall Street Journal*.

Marketable government bonds are issued for a much longer period than Treasury bills; some of the government's outstanding bonds will not mature until 1998! Dated coupons affixed to the bond entitle its holder to periodic interest payments. For example, twice each year the holder of a $10,000 4% bond clips off the coupon entitling him to a payment of $200 ($200 = 4% of $10,000/2); he will also receive $10,000 cash if he holds the bond to maturity. And if he needs funds prior to maturity, he can liquidate his investment promptly by selling the security at the market clearing price in the government bond market.

While the holder of transferable government bonds must guard against theft, an activity that has at times attracted the attention of organized crime, this is not the chief risk that must be considered in deciding whether to enter the government bond market. Although there is no more risk of the government defaulting on its debt than on its currency outstanding, the price of government securities prior to maturity is subject to all the vicissitudes of the marketplace. That prices may swing quite markedly is suggested by the data on Table 5.7. On one date recorded on the table, November 1, 1961, the 4% government bonds maturing in 1980 sold precisely at par. But the price swung from a historic high of 103.18 in May 1961 to a historic low of 71.04 in 1969. A $10,000 bond purchased on December 31, 1959 would have cost $9368.68.[5] With phenomenal foresight it might have been sold on May 12, 1961 for $10,356.19, a capital gain of $987.51 supplementing the coupon payments. But if the 4% bond had been held for 10 years it would have brought only $7243.80, or a capital loss of $2124.88.

The yield column on the table indicates how the rate of return earned by holding the bond until maturity has fluctuated. When purchased at par, as on November 30, 1961, the rate of return on the $10,000 was precisely

---

[5] Prices are customarily quoted to $\frac{1}{32}$ per $100. Thus the December 31, 1959, price is $93\frac{22}{32}$ per $100 of par value, or $9368.68 for a $10,000 bond.

Table 5.7   PRICE AND YIELD OF 4% UNITED STATES
GOVERNMENT BOND MATURING FEBRUARY 15, 1980
(ISSUE DATE JANUARY 23, 1959

Date	Market Price[a]	Yield to Maturity (in %)
December 31, 1970	83.08	6.46
December 31, 1969	72.14	8.03
December 29, 1969	71.04	(Historic high)
December 31, 1968	83.08	6.01
December 31, 1967	85.02	5.67
December 30, 1966	94.00	4.61
December 31, 1965	94.08	4.56
December 31, 1964	97.28	4.19
December 31, 1963	98.08	4.15
December 31, 1962	101.00	3.92
November 30, 1961	100.00	4.00
May 12, 1961	103.18	(Historic low)
December 30, 1960	102.16	3.81
December 31, 1959	93.22	4.48

Source. U.S. Treasury Bulletin.

[a] Price decimals are 32nds.

4%. When the bond sold at a premium, as in May 1961, the yield to maturity was below the coupon rate; more money had to be spent on the bond than would be required to buy an asset yielding a return calculated at 4%. Conversely, when selling below par, as in 1969, less money had to be put up than would have been required to buy an asset valued with a 4% return; indeed, the yield was more than twice the coupon rate. There is an inverse relationship between bond price and bond yield. The formula relating yield to current price, given the maturity date of the security and its coupon rate, is rather involved:[6] bond tables can be used to compute the effective yield obtainable on a bond offered in the marketplace. Fortunately, the financial

[6] Consider a bond with face value B and coupon rate r maturing n periods in the future. Its coupons have a value of $C = rB$. The yield is that rate of discount that serves to equate the maturity value of B together with its stream of coupons worth C with current market price; that is, let the yield on the bond be y and define for notational convenience the discount factor $\beta = 1/(1 + y)$; then the current price of the bond is

$$P = B\beta^n + C(\beta + \beta^2 + \ldots + \beta^n) = B\left[\beta^n + r\left(\frac{\beta - \beta^{n+1}}{1 - \beta}\right)\right]$$

Note that when the bond sells at par (i.e., $P = B$) we must have $y = r$.

press publishes daily for its reader's convenience the yields on government bonds of various maturities and coupon rates.

For one particular type of security, British Consols, the relationship between yield and market value is easily calculated. In contradistinction to the United States Treasury note, British Consols pay a coupon return but *never* mature. Thus a 4% British Consol of £10,000 denomination constitutes a promise to pay the bearer and his heirs £400 each year for ever more! If the 4% Consol should sell at a $33\frac{1}{3}$% discount, or £6666$\frac{2}{3}$, its purchaser would have acquired possession of an infinite stream of future payments, each payment equal to 6% of his initial investment; the yield would be 6%. And if investors will only hold assets with yields of 8%, the value of the Consol has to fall to £5000, a 50% discount on its face value. The inverse relationship existing between yield and price for any bond takes a particularly simple form for British Consols; the yield for Consols is simply the annual interest earned (£400 on a 4% Consol of £10,000 denomination) divided by the current market price.[7]

A security's yield only tells the investor what his rate of return will be if he holds the security to maturity—or forever, in the case of Consols. The yield can be calculated with precision each day without any need to guess how the price of the bond will fluctuate prior to maturity. But any type of transferable security—government bond or corporate security—offers the buyer the hope of a capital gain and the fear of a capital loss. Thus the yield of 6.01% that could be obtained at the end of 1968 by purchasing the 4% government bond maturing in 1980 may have appeared attractive at the time. But, in retrospect, the substantial fall in price during the next year implied a capital loss much in excess of the coupon yield. It would have been far better to have held money—currency under one's mattress or demand deposits. Even the investor wishing to loan out funds until 1980 would have done better to have postponed his purchase, holding cash for a year, instead of buying bonds at the end of 1968.

The demand for speculative money balances arises from the fear of capital loss. How much in the way of money balances will be held for speculative reasons depends on the assessment of market prospects. Security investors are inclined to increase the proportion of their portfolio held in idle money stocks when they expect a price decline. How the optimal composition of an investment portfolio responds to shifting expectations about future market conditions is a complicated topic, discussed in the appendix of this chapter. And how expectations shift in response to external factors (e.g. war and presidential heart attacks) is beyond the scope of this textbook.

[7] Consols are of obvious advantage to the British Treasury, because they save the trouble and costs involved in turning over the government debt as securities mature. But the simple relationship between yield and market price means that if they did not exist they might have to be invented for pedagogical purposes.

But as a rough approximation it seems reasonable to presume that when security prices are high relative to their customary historical levels, investors are particularly likely to fear capital losses and hold speculative money balances; since high security prices mean low yields, this argument implies that the demand for money balances will be large when the yield offered in the security market is low. Conversely, when yields are exceptionally high (i.e., bond prices are depressed) and investors expect a reversal toward more normal conditions, the demand for speculative money balances falls off. Thus the demand for speculative as well as transactions balances is negatively related to the interest rate.

*5.5 THREE PERSPECTIVES ON THE DEMAND FOR MONEY—DERIVATION OF THE *LM* CURVE

In light of the discussion of the transactions and speculative motives for holding money it is reasonable to specify that the quantity of money that the public desires to hold is influenced by *both* the level of economic activity and rate of interest.[8]

$$\mathbf{M}_d = L(\dot{Y}, r) \tag{5.1}$$

Each panel in Figure 5.5 plots the demand for money from a different perspective. The first panel is a standard downward sloping demand curve showing how the demand for money varies with its "price," where the price of money is the interest that is foregone by holding money instead of some alternative interest yielding asset. Two reasons explain why the demand curve is downward sloping. First, when the interest rate is high, efforts are made to economize on money balances. Second, the strength of the speculative and precautionary motives is tempered when the interest rate increases. As with any demand curve, the money demand curve must be drawn for a specific level of income. A higher level of income shifts the demand curve upward, more money being held at any given rate of interest. The second panel of the graph focuses more directly on the relationship between income and the demand for money, suppressing the interest rate dimension. The positive slope of the Engel's curve indicates the normal situation in which an increase in income stimulates demand. The third panel in Figure 5.5 focuses on the combinations of income and the interest

---

[8] Both the level of prices and the rate of price change are abstracted from in Equation 5.1. If the demand for money is proportional to income, so that $L(Y,r)/Y = L(1,r)$, we may define $k(r) = L(Y,r)/Y$ and rewrite Equation 5.1 as $\mathbf{M}_d = Yk(r)$; then $\mathbf{M}_d{}^n = p\mathbf{M}_d = pYk(r) = Y^n k(r)$. Note that $k(r)$, the reciprocal of velocity, is independent of real income Y when the demand for money is proportional to income; it is in precisely this situation that the real and nominal demand for money functions are identical.

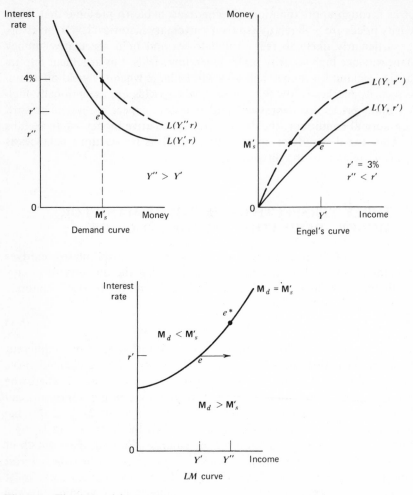

Fig. 5.5 *The demand for money.*

rate at which the public would be content holding a specific quantity of money. In accordance with custom it is called the *"LM* curve," because it shows the circumstances under which the public's desire for "liquidity"— its demand for money—will equal the supply. Above the *LM* curve the interest rate is so high, relative to income, that the demand for money falls short of the supply; below the *LM* curve there is excess demand. The *LM* curve must have a positive slope. To see why, consider point *e* on the bottom panel; an expansion of income with no change in the interest rate (indicated by the arrow) would cause a rise in the demand for money; in order to constrain the demand for money to the given supply the rate of interest must rise to offset the increased transaction demand generated by the increase in income; at e^* the demand for money is again equated with the fixed supply.

The demand curve plotted on the first panel of Figure 5.5 becomes infinitely elastic as the rate of interest falls toward 2%, a reflection of the Keynesian notion of the *liquidity trap* below which the rate of interest cannot be driven no matter how the monetary authorities manipulate the supply curve for money. The quantity of money demanded approaches infinity at low rates of interest if the speculative motive becomes insatiable. This allegedly happens as the long-term rate of interest falls, because the price of bonds rises to exceptionally high levels, further increases become doubtful, and capital losses appear more and more likely; in such circumstances, investors become willing to hold a larger and larger proportion of their wealth as money (recall Section 5.4) instead of running the risk of impending capital losses. Whether the liquidity-trap floor to the rate of interest in fact exists is an empirical matter still open to debate; evidence on the matter is presented in Appendix 5.A. But, in any case, the phenomenon has not been of much importance historically; as Keynes himself suggested, the monetary authorities may never have expanded the money supply to the point where the liquidity trap comes into play.[9]

The effects of a change in the supply of money are examined in Figure 5.6. It is assumed, pending the more elaborate discussion of central banking policy in Chapter 10, that the quantity of money in circulation, denoted by M'_s, is an exogenous quantity independent of both income and the rate of interest. Then the supply curve, as indicated in the first panel of Figure 5.6, must be vertical. However, in the second panel, where money is plotted on the ordinate, the horizontal line indicates the money supply. Point e (each panel) indicates one possible equilibrium where the quantity of money equals the supply; that is, with output Y' and the rate of interest r', we have:

$$M'_s = M'_d = L(Y', r') \qquad (5.2)$$

At equilibrium, output and the interest rate will have adjusted so that the public is content holding the quantity of money created by the banking system. Now consider the implications of an increase in the money supply. As the first panel reveals, the rate of interest must fall to r'' if the demand for money is to equal the supply *and* output remains unchanged; e', on each panel, denotes the new equilibrium point *if* income does not change.[10]

---

[9] *General Theory of Employment Interest and Money*, p. 207.

[10] In elementary price theory, when one is looking at individual markets in isolation, precisely this mode of adjustment is assumed; any change in income resulting from the shift in supply of "wheat," for example, is presumed to be negligible, and price falls until demand and supply are equated. But the money market cannot be analyzed under the assumption that Y is constant.

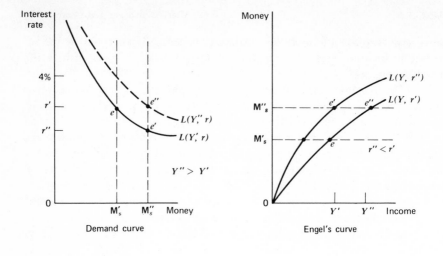

Demand curve

Engel's curve

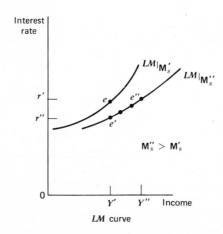

LM curve

Fig. 5.6 *An expanded money supply. An increase in the money supply may lead to a reduction in the rate of interest and a movement to* e′. *Alternatively, the increase in the money supply may be accommodated by a rise in income to* Y″ *and a movement to* e″. *But both income and the rate of interest may change, as indicated by the points on the new* LM *curve in the bottom panel.*

178

It is also conceivable that the increased supply of money can be accommodated without any change in the rate of interest, provided that output changes appropriately to Y'', since at e'' the demand for money again equals the increased supply. But we would adjust to an increase in the money supply by moving along the Engel's curve only if the rate of interest remained constant.

In practice, both interest rates and income may change when the quantity of money increases, as indicated by the shift in the LM curve in the bottom panel of Figure 5.6. Thus knowledge about the demand for money (Equation 5.1) does not suffice to reveal precisely how the economy will adjust to a change in the money supply.

The LM curve could be used to predict the level of economic activity if the rate of interest were known. But by itself the LM curve does not suffice to determine either the rate of interest or the level of output. Furthermore, velocity—the ratio of income to money—cannot be determined. While the study of the demand for money provides essential information for understanding how variations in the money supply affect the pace of economic activity, additional equations are required in order to have a determinate system.

*5.6 THE ROLE OF MONEY: AN AGENDA

The next several chapters develop an analytic framework constituting a synthesis of multiplier analysis with the quantity theory of money. In contrast to the elementary theory of the multiplier, investment spending will no longer be treated as an exogenous variable; Chapter 6 analyzes how such variables as the rate of interest influence the pace of capital accumulation. And, in contradiction to the elementary version of the quantity theory, income velocity can no longer be regarded as a constant; instead, it becomes an endogenous variable to be determined in the course of solving for the level of economic activity and the market rate of interest. After the basic argument is developed, the problems of coordinating monetary and fiscal policy in a fashion that will best contribute to equilibrium in the balance of payments are explored. In Chapter 10 we will discuss the techniques by which the central bank influences money market conditions in general and the quantity of money in circulation in particular. However, the complications arising from changes in the price level must be postponed, because the problem of measuring the rate of inflation, of explaining how it comes about, and of showing how various policy measures affect it is of such importance as to warrant several chapters in Part IV.

REFERENCES

1. Here are two fundamental studies of the quantity theory of money.

   Irving Fisher, *The Purchasing Power of Money*, Macmillan, 1926.
   Milton Friedman, "The Quantity Theory of Money: A Restatement," in *Studies in the Quantity Theory of Money*, ed. Milton Friedman, Chicago University Press, 1958.

2. The theory of the demand for money under uncertainty was developed in a fundamental paper by James Tobin; a simplified textbook exposition appears in William F. Sharp.

   James Tobin, "Liquidity Preference as Behavior Towards Risk," *Review of Economic Studies*, February 1958.
   William F. Sharpe, *Portfolio Theory and Capital Markets*, McGraw-Hill, 1970.

3. Alfred Cowles, the patron saint of econometrics in its formative years, founded the Cowles Commission, first at the University of Colorado and then at the University of Chicago. In 1955 much of the faculty of the Cowles Commission transferred to Yale University, becoming the Cowles Foundation for Research in Economics. Alfred Cowles was an early expositor of the proposition that the purchase of a representative market basket of securities, possibly selected at random, would on the average yield at least as high a return as that achieved by professional portfolio managers and mutual fund consultants. The literature on the random-walk hypothesis is reviewed by Eugene F. Fama.

   Alfred Cowles, "Stock Market Forecasting," *Econometrica*, July–October 1944.
   Eugene F. Fama, "The Behavior of Stock-Market Prices," *Journal of Business*, January 1965.

4. A variety of institutional changes, such as the development of credit cards and computers, will influence the demand for money and the potency of monetary policy.

   Donald D. Hester, "Monetary Policy in the 'Checkless' Economy," *Journal of Finance*, May 1972.

KEY CONCEPTS

M_1 versus M_2

quantity theory

income velocity of money

transactions demand

speculative balances

liquidity trap

bond yields

capital gains

EXERCISES

5.1 In 1970 the quantity of money in circulation in the United States was $214.8 billion; furthermore, real gross national produce was $722.1 billion, measured in 1958 prices, and the price index (GNP deflator) stood at 135.23% (1958 = 100). What was the income velocity of money? If the money supply had been only $193.3 billion, but velocity was unaffected, what would have been the level of current dollar gross national produce (pY)?

5.2 Suppose that the demand for money function is of the additive form

$$\mathbf{M}_d = \frac{1}{2} Y + \frac{20}{r}$$

where r, the rate of interest, is measured in percent per annum. For example, if the rate of interest is $r = 5\%$ and $Y = 1000$, we have $20/r = 400$ and $\mathbf{M}_d = 900$.

a. What quantity of money will be demanded if $Y = 1000$ and $r = 2\%$? What will be the income velocity of money?

b. What quantity of money will be demanded if $Y = 2000$ and $r = 4\%$? What is velocity?

c. Plot the *LM* curve for this demand equation, given that $\mathbf{M}_s = 1500$.

d. Explain how the *LM* curve will shift if the money supply increases to 2500.

(*Suggestion*: Save your graph of the *LM* curve for Exercise 8.1.)

5.3 Suppose the demand for money function is of multiplicative form

$$\mathbf{M}_d = \left(\frac{1}{2} + \frac{1}{50r}\right) Y$$

a. What quantity of money will be demanded if $Y = 1000$ and $r = 5\%$? What is the income velocity?

b. Plot the *LM* curve for $\mathbf{M}_s = 1500$.

c. How will the *LM* curve shift if $\mathbf{M}_s$ increases to 2500?

d. Contrast the multiplicative demand function form of this question with the additive form of the demand function in Exercise 5.2. Does the distinction appear critical or immaterial?

5.4 Consider the following demand function for money.

$$M_d = \frac{1}{2} Y + \left(\frac{20}{r - 1.5\%} \right)$$

    a. Explain the essential difference between this equation and the one introduced in Exercise 5.2.

    b. Explain how the demand for money equation introduced in Exercise 5.3 may be modified in order to incorporate a liquidity trap.

APPENDIX 5.A   THE DEMAND FOR MONEY, AN EMPIRICAL ILLUSTRATION

The demand for money (liquidity preference) has been the subject of many empirical studies. To illustrate, let us consider a simple functional form used by Howard Pifer.[11]

$$\mathbf{M}_d = \rho_0(r - \rho)^{-\lambda_1}W^{\lambda_2}Y_n^{\lambda_3} \tag{1}$$

Here $\mathbf{M}_d$ is the sum of demand deposits plus currency, W is wealth, and Y_n is *money* national income ($Y_n = pY$); r is the yield on corporate bonds 20 years to maturity. The demand for money will increase with either wealth or income, provided λ_2 and λ_3 are positive. And an increase in the rate of interest will reduce the demand for money, provided that λ_1 is positive and $r > \rho$. The demand for money approaches infinity as r falls toward ρ, the liquidity trap floor to the rate of interest. Manipulation of this equation yields an expression relating nominal income to money, the rate of interest, and wealth.

$$Y_n = \mathbf{M}_d^{1/\lambda_3}(r - \rho)^{\lambda_1/\lambda_3}W^{-\lambda_2/\lambda_3}\rho_0^{-1/\lambda_3} \tag{2}$$

The *LM* curve of Figure 5.6 shows this relationship between nominal income and r, given money and W. And Pifer's demand for money equation can also be manipulated to obtain an expression for the ratio of income to money—income velocity of Equation 2.2.

$$v_y = (r - \rho)^{\lambda_1}W^{-\lambda_2}\frac{Y_n^{(1-\lambda_3)}}{\rho_0}$$

On the basis of annual data covering the period 1900 to 1958, Pifer tentatively advanced the following parameter estimates.

$$\rho = 2\%, \quad \lambda_1 = 0.27, \quad \lambda_2 = 0.68, \quad \text{and} \quad \lambda_3 = 0.31$$

It is not surprising to find that the demand for money is an increasing function of both income and wealth. While the transactions motive suggests that income is important, the speculative and precautionary motives explain the presence of wealth. Pifer's parameter estimates suggest that if, in a period of steady economic expansion, income and wealth are both growing at the same rate, 5% for example, then the demand for money will be expanding equally rapidly, unless the rate of interest changes. This follows because Pifer finds that $\lambda_2 + \lambda_3 \doteq 1$; that is, the

---

[11] Howard W. Pifer, "A Nonlinear Maximum Likelihood Estimate of the Liquidity Trap," *Econometrica*, April 1969, pp. 324–332. Pifer's functional form is quite different from that used by Keynes. In his *General Theory of Employment Interest and Money* Keynes wrote (pp. 195–198) the demand for money equation as the sum of two components: $M = L_1(Y) + L_2(r)$. The first term in the sum indicated transactions and contingency balances, while the second stood for speculative balances. But Keynes also stressed that the partition was only for expository convenience, that the individual's demand for money results from a single decision, and that money forms a single pool of liquidity instead of being held in separate watertight compartments to satisfy specific motives. For constructive comments on Pifer's estimates, see Robert Eisner, "Non-Linear Estimates of the Liquidity Trap," *Econometrica*, September 1971.

demand for money is homogeneous of degree one in income plus wealth.[12] In the short run, however, when depression or recession interrupts the growth process, income falls off much more rapidly than wealth. Then, Equation A.1 suggests, the demand for money will decline by only a fraction of the fall in income, because velocity will also be declining. Conversely, in periods of exceptional boom, income rises more rapidly than wealth and velocity will increase unless the rate of interest also rises.

The estimate of λ_1 (the exponent of the term $r - \rho$) implies that at higher rates of interest the demand for money falls off while velocity increases. And ρ (the liquidity trap floor) is estimated to be 2%.

Equation A.1 fits the historical data quite well. And the corresponding expression, Equation A.2, does serve to explain much of the fluctuation in velocity. Nonetheless, it is only one of a variety of models that have been developed in explaining the determinants of the demand for money. A more elaborate study might consider a variety of interest rates instead of just the long-term corporate bond rate. And other investigators have studied more generic concepts of money and attempted to explain how the demand for saving deposits fluctuate over the cycle. This latter elaboration, which involves using M_3 instead of M_1 as the dependent variable, is of some importance; Keynes was inclined to link the speculative motive and the liquidity trap to savings deposits instead of M_1. In Appendix 5.B the influence of uncertainty on the demand for different types of liquid assets is discussed in more detail. But the Pifer model explains how, in terms of Equation A.2, the velocity of money fluctuates in response to changes in income, wealth, and the rate of interest.

APPENDIX 5.B   PORTFOLIO SELECTION AND THE DEMAND FOR MONEY

5.B.1   RISK AND RETURN

An individual endowed with both the funds to invest in financial markets and the conceit to regard himself as having perfect forecasting ability might well place all his funds in the particular security that he is convinced will have the highest yield (gross of capital gains). While it might be argued that a clairvoyant eccentric might diversify his portfolio of assets because of a desire for paper of a variety of colors in his safe deposit box, it is difficult to explain, without appeal to bizarre examples, why an investor who believes he lives in a world of certainty would fail to place all his eggs in one basket. In particular, in the absence of uncertainty, an investor would not hold money in excess of that required for executing transactions.

---

[12] Suppose that W and Y both increase by 5%; then

$$[1.05W]^{\lambda_2} \cdot [1.05Y]^{\lambda_3} = 1.05^{\lambda_2+\lambda_3}W^{\lambda_2}Y^{\lambda_3}$$

Here $\lambda_2 + \lambda_3 = 1$. Hence, if r remains constant, the demand for money will also grow by 5%.

Modern portfolio analysis rests on the foundations provided by the theory of decision making under *uncertainty*. The investor is not assumed to anticipate with certainty the exact price at which he will be able to sell a security at the end of his investment period. Instead, the investor recognizes that a number of alternative outcomes are conceivable. He may hold some shares of uranium stock in the faint hope that a lucky strike will reward him richly for his gamble. And, for security, the investor may also place part of his funds in American Telephone and Telegraph or even deposit part of his wealth in his savings bank.

Many amateur investors, recognizing their limited knowledge, buy shares in mutual funds. How well the professional managers of a mutual fund's investment portfolio carry out their responsibilities may be measured by comparing the historical performance of their fund with other funds and with general movements of the market. For example, investors in the Johnston Mutual Fund suffered a fall in net asset value of 7.3% in 1970 when the Dow Jones average of representative stocks rose by 4.8%; but, in 1972, investors in the Johnston Fund realized a gain of 23.6%, well above the Dow Jones' rise of 14.6%. However, risk as well as return must be considered in evaluating market performance. The dots in Figure 5.B.1 record the risk and return experience of a large number of mutual funds. Of course, risk and return are rather nebulous concepts, and we will define them more precisely in a moment. The point to note now is that the more ambitious "growth"

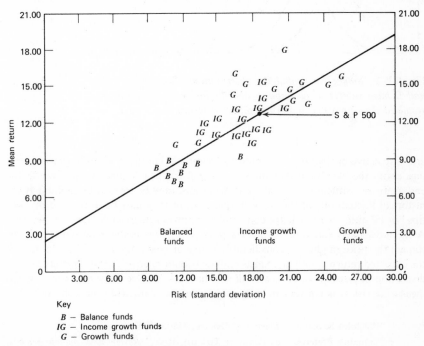

Key

B — Balance funds
IG — Income growth funds
G — Growth funds

Fig. 5.B.1   *Risk-return tradeoff, 1953–1969.*

funds generally did better in terms of average return than more conservative "balanced" funds, but at the expense of greater risk. And, unfortunately, some *inefficient* funds managed to combine a relatively low return with considerable risk for their shareholders. Obviously, an investor comparing a variety of investment opportunities all involving the same risk will want to buy into the opportunity offering the highest expected return.

In presenting a simplified account of the modern theory of portfolio selection as pioneered by Harry Markowitz[13] and James Tobin,[14] we will focus on the implication of that theory for the determination of the demand for money. We will see that an efficient portfolio may involve the holding of idle funds in excess of the cash balances required for transaction purposes.

†5.B.2 EFFICIENT PORTFOLIOS: A NUMERICAL EXAMPLE

For illustrative purposes consider an investor who is choosing between two investment opportunities. Each of the securities has a current price of $1. As Figure 5.B.2 illustrates, the future price of the security is not known with certainty. These

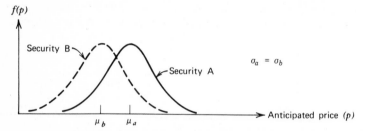

Fig. 5.B.2 *Subjective probability distributions. Securities A and B have subjective probability distributions with identical standard deviations ($\sigma_a = \sigma_b$) but different means ($\mu_a \neq \mu_b$).*

are "subjective probability distributions" summarizing the investor's personal feelings about the likelihood that the security will have each conceivable price at the end of the investment period; these distributions may be formed by looking at the historical fluctuations of the stock in question, or they may be influenced by "hot tips" or by intimate knowledge concerning the prospects of each firm. For Security A the most likely outcome involves a price of μ_a; this is the expected return, although the price might rise considerably above or below this price. For Security B the expected return is only μ_b. Since both distributions involve the same spread (or dispersion of possible values), we will say that they involve the same "risk." When measuring risk it is convenient to borrow from the statistician the concept of the

---

[13] "Portfolio Selection," *Journal of Finance*, March 1952.

[14] "Liquidity Preference as Behavior Towards Risk," *Review of Economic Studies*, February 1958.

distribution's standard error (σ) and, for the case illustrated, $\sigma_a = \sigma_b$.[15] Obviously, if out investor has only \$1 to invest and, if he were constrained to choose between placing all his funds in the first or all in the second asset, he would choose the first; it offers a higher expected return with the same risk. A portfolio consisting of nothing but Security B is inefficient, because it is dominated by a portfolio of the same risk consisting of Security A.

We will find that a rich variety of efficient portfolios do include Security B. In order to see this, we must remember from elementary statistics that if λ is the proportion of his dollar that our investor spends on Security A while he invests $1 - \lambda$ dollars in Security B, then

$$\mu = \lambda\mu_a + (1 - \lambda)\mu_b \tag{2.1}$$

The risk involved (the standard deviation of the composite portfolio) is harder to calculate. If Securities A and B are in closely related sectors of the economy their prices may be expected to move together; for example, in a bad auto year, Ford and General Motors stocks are likely to fall together; this is illustrated by the scatter in the right panel of Figure 5.B.3. In this situation a mixed portfolio will not offer

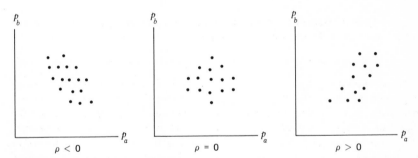

Fig. 5.B.3 *Correlation of returns.*

greatly increased safety. On the other hand, certain types of assets may tend to move in opposite directions; what is good contract news for one aerospace firm may be bad news for its competitor. In this situation, illustrated in the left panel, purchase of a mixed portfolio may yield a substantial reduction in risk. But it is also possible for the good fortunes of one company to be uncorrelated with those of the other, yielding the random scatter in the center panel of the figure. The correlation coefficient ρ is negative on the left, zero in the middle, and positive on

---

[15] Admittedly, the standard deviation is only one measure of dispersion; its appropriateness as a particularly convenient measure of risk is discussed in the next section of this appendix. The standard deviation concept was briefly discussed in Appendix 4.A.

Table 5.B.1   PORTFOLIO MEAN AND STANDARD DEVIATION

λ	μ	σ
1	3	4
$\frac{3}{4}$	2.75	3.1622
$\frac{2}{3}$	2.63	2.976
$\frac{1}{2}$	2.5	2.8285
$\frac{1}{3}$	2.33	2.976
$\frac{1}{4}$	2.25	3.1622
0	2	4

Based on data for two hypothetical stocks:

Security A: $\mu_a = 3$ $\sigma_a = \sigma_b = 4$

Security B: $\mu_b = 2$ $\rho_{ab} = 0$

λ = proportion of $1 invested in Security A.

$1 - \lambda$ = proportion of $1 invested in Security B.

the right.[16] How it enters into the determination of the standard deviation of a mixed portfolio is revealed by the following equation.

$$\sigma = \sqrt{\lambda^2\sigma_a{}^2 + (1 - \lambda)^2\sigma_b{}^2 + 2\lambda(1 - \lambda)\rho\sigma_a\sigma_b} \qquad (2.2)$$

Now suppose that $\mu_a = 3$, $\mu_b = 2$, $\sigma_a = \sigma_b = 4$, and $\rho = 0$. Then a number of the combinations of risk and return may be obtained by investing $1 in a composite portfolio, as revealed in Table 5.B.1.[17] The points on the table all lie on the curve connecting points A and B on the left panel of Figure 5.B.4. It is apparent that if the investor's opportunities are restricted to the purchase of a mixture of these two assets, he will have to choose one of the points on the curve connecting point A with coordinates $\langle 4, 3 \rangle$ and B with coordinates $\langle 4, 2 \rangle$; that is his opportunity set. It is also clear that only the points on that segment of the curve from point $\langle 2.83, 2.5 \rangle$ to $\langle 4, 3 \rangle$ are efficient; investing more than $\frac{1}{2}$ of one's funds in Security B is inefficient, since a higher return can be obtained with no increase in risk.

Let us now see how the risk-expected return opportunities are expanded once the investor is allowed to invest part of his dollar of wealth in money. The risk of holding money, at least if we abstract from the possibility of inflation, is zero; our

[16] The covariance of the two assets is

$$\sigma_{ab} \equiv E[(P_a - \mu_a)(P_b - \mu_b)]$$

the "normalized covariance" or correlation coefficient is $\rho = \sigma_{ab}/\sigma_a\sigma_b$.

[17] The reader can easily verify that for the two particular assets now being considered, Equation 2.1 reduces to $\mu = 2 + \lambda$ and

$$\sigma = 4\sqrt{\lambda^2 + (1 - \lambda)^2} = 4\sqrt{2\lambda^2 - 2\lambda + 1} = 4\sqrt{2\mu^2 - 10\mu + 13}, \qquad (2 \le \mu \le 3)$$

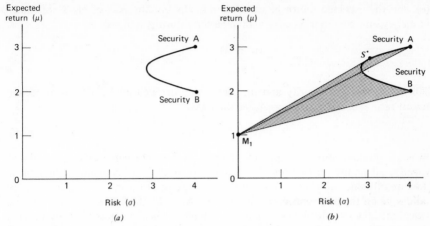

Fig. 5.B.4 *Feasible risk-return portfolios. (a) Point A indicates a portfolio consisting entirely of security A; point B denotes a portfolio containing only security B. The curve reveals other combinations of risk and return obtained by holding a mixed portfolio. By holding some of security B it is possible to reduce risk by sacrificing expected return. (b) M_1 indicates that perfect safety can be obtained by holding only money. The line segment connecting A with M_1 indicates the mix of risk and return obtainable with a portfolio consisting only of security A and money. The shaded area indicates all possible mixes of risk and return obtainable by holding the three assets. The curve connecting M_1, S^*, and A is the efficiency frontier revealing the maximum obtainable return, given the degree of risk the investor is willing to bear.*

investor would have an expected return of $1 with zero risk if he elected to hold only money instead of investing in either Security A or B. This is point M_1 with coordinates $\langle 0,1 \rangle$ in the second panel of the graph. In order to see how the existence of money expands the opportunities available to our investor, consider first the effects of holding a mixture of money and a security with expected value μ_s and risk σ_s. If he invests λ cents in the security and holds $1 - \lambda$ cents in cash, his expected return will be

$$\mu = \lambda\mu_s + (1 - \lambda) = 1 + \lambda(\mu_s - 1) \tag{2.3}$$

as may be readily determined by referring to Equation 2.1. Similarly, as with Equation 2.2, we find that the risk is

$$\sigma = \sqrt{\lambda^2\sigma_s^2 + (1 - \lambda)^2 0^2} = \lambda\sigma_s \tag{2.4}$$

With the aid of Equation 2.4 we eliminate λ from Equation 2.2, obtaining the following linear relationship between the level of risk that our investor elects to assume

(σ), and the expected return he can obtain (μ) by holding part of his \$1 of funds in money and part in a security with expected return μ_s and risk σ_s.

$$\mu = 1 + \frac{(\mu_s - 1)}{\sigma_s}\, \sigma, \qquad 0 \leq \sigma \leq \sigma_s \qquad (2.5)$$

This holds for any security and, in particular, for Security B, with an expected return of $\mu = 2$ and a risk $\sigma = 4$; we then have

$$\mu = 1 + 0.25\sigma \qquad (2.6)$$

which is the line connecting point B and M_1 in the right panel of Figure 5.B.4.[18] Clearly, all points on this line are dominated by those obtainable by holding a mixture of money and Security A with expected return of 3 and $\sigma = 4$; these possibilities lie on the line connecting point A and M_1. The shaded region of the graph constitutes the expanded opportunity set obtained when the possibility of holding money is introduced. In particular, if our investor holds a composite mixture of $\frac{2}{3}$ of Security A to $\frac{1}{3}$ of Security B, he can obtain any point on the line connecting point S^*, with coordinates 2.5 and $2\frac{2}{3}$ and M_1. In fact, this line constitutes the set of all *efficient* portfolios involving the holding of some money. If an investor holds money as well as securities (given the nature of his subjective expectations with regard to the future prices of the assets), he will hold the assets in a mixture of two units of Security A to one unit of Security B. That this must be the case follows from the fact that the line from M_1 to S^* is tangent to the curve connecting A and B.

This example illustrates that a rational investor may find a place in his investment portfolio for money, even though it has zero expected return; money allows him to take a more conservative market position. This is the liquidity motive for holding money; it can lead to holding funds much in excess of what would be needed for transaction purposes in the absence of uncertainty. Of course, currency and demand deposits are not the only zero risk asset; deposits in a savings account yielding a 5 % annual return may be just as secure as demand deposits; then point M would have coordinates $\langle 0, 1.05 \rangle$. Thus the liquidity preference motive may be particularly pertinent in explaining more generic concepts of money, such as M_3, which includes savings deposits. The theory provides a useful framework for analyzing the effects of changing market prospects on portfolio composition. Given the indifference map describing the investor's preferences with regard to choices between risk and return, his response to changes in expected return can be deter-

---

[18] If the returns on the two assets are perfectly correlated, the efficiency frontier will again be a straight line. To see this, remember that $\rho = \sigma_{ab}/\sigma_a\sigma_b = 1$ implies that $\sigma_{ab} = \sigma_a\sigma_b$. Substituting into equation 2.2 yields

$$\sigma^2 = \lambda^2\sigma_a{}^2 + (1 - \lambda)^2\sigma_b{}^2 + 2\lambda(1 - \lambda)\sigma_a\sigma_b = [\lambda\sigma_a + (1 - \lambda)\sigma_b]^2$$

or

$$\sigma = \lambda\sigma_a + (1 - \lambda)\sigma_b$$

Hence $\lambda = (\sigma - \sigma_b)/(\sigma_a - \sigma_b)$, which when substituted into Equation 2.1 yields μ as a linear function of σ; that is, we have a linear efficiency frontier.

mined. And the same mode of analysis can be employed in exploring the effects of alternative tax policies on the willingness of investors to carry risky assets in their portfolios.[19]

†5.B.3 RISK: QUADRATIC UTILITY AND VARIANCE

The argument concerning the presence of money in the investor's portfolio relied on the use of the standard deviation of his subjective probability distribution as an appropriate measure of risk. But why the standard deviation instead of the semi-interquartile range, expected absolute deviation, or what have you? Two alternative arguments that have been advanced in the portfolio-selection literature to motivate the choice of σ as the appropriate measure of risk.

The first argument relies on the fact that *if* the probability distribution of expected change in security prices is multivariate normal, the distribution of W, being normal, will be completely characterized by its first two moments. This means that however complicated the utility function explaining the investor's preferences with regard to alternative distributions of expected returns, it can be reduced under conditions of normality to a function of μ_w and σ_w. For example, the investor's preferences may involve the third moment of the distribution of expected returns, since this is a measure of skewness, and it might well be argued that an investor choosing between two portfolios with the same μ and σ might prefer the one with the smaller probability of extreme losses. But, under the normality assumption, the only opportunities offered by the market involve a zero third moment, and so his degree of aversion to skewness is irrelevant in describing his behavior. While the assumption of normality is convenient, it can only be regarded as a useful approximation—after all, the value of a share cannot become negative.

The second argument for the selection of the variance as the appropriate measure of risk, to which we now turn, places restrictions on the investor's utility of wealth function instead of on the subjective probability distribution of anticipated returns. Under conditions of uncertainty with regard to future values of the various assets that he may buy for his portfolio, our investor, who is "rational" in that his behavior conforms to the axioms of Von Neumann and Morgenstern, will *maximize his expected utility*.[20] Suppose, for purposes of simplicity, that his utility function describing the satisfaction that he will obtain from realizing wealth W can be reasonably well approximated by the simple quadratic form

$$U = \alpha + \beta W - \gamma W^2 \qquad (3.1)$$

---

[19] See Susan J. Lepper, "Effects of Alternative Tax Structures on Individuals' Holdings of Financial Assets," *Yale Economic Essays*, Spring 1964, and M. K. Richter, "Cardinal Utility, Portfolio Selection and Taxation," *Review of Economic Studies*, June 1960.

[20] The classic reference is the pioneering contribution of John von Neumann and Oskar Morgenstern, *Theory of Games and Economic Behavior*, Princeton University Press, 1947; for an excellent textbook exposition, see Duncan Luce and Howard Raiffa, *Games and Decisions*, John Wiley, 1967, or W. Baumol, *Economic Theory and Operations Analysis*, Chapter 22, 2nd ed., Prentice Hall, 1965. von Neumann made major contributions to physics as well as economics; his daughter served on President Nixon's Council of Economic Advisers.

then expected utility

$$E(U) = \alpha + \beta E(W) - \gamma E(W^2) \tag{3.2}$$

$$= \alpha + \beta \mu_w - \gamma(\sigma_w^2 + \mu_w^2) \tag{3.3}$$

so only the mean and variance of W are involved in maximizing expected utility.[21] Of course, an investor attempting to maximize expected utility is subject to the restraint imposed by his limited resources. His problem is to maximize Equation 3.3, subject to his budget constraint. And, if his utility function has the convenient quadratic form, he will be completely oblivious in selecting his portfolio to questions of skewness, and so on (e.g., $E(W^3)$).[22]

---

[21] $E(W^2) = \mu_w^2 + \sigma_w^2$ is a useful proposition used in elementary statistics to facilitate the computation of the variance. To prove the proposition, observe that

$$E(W^2) = E\{[(W - \mu_w) + \mu_w]^2\} = E[(W - \mu_w)^2 + 2E(W - \mu_w)\mu_w + \mu_w^2]$$

The first term on the right-hand side is the variance; the second term vanishes because $E(W) = \mu_w$ by definition.

[22] It should be conceded that while it proves convenient and instructive to develop a theory of portfolio selection based on a quadratic utility function, it must also be observed that at best that utility function can only be regarded as an approximation valid within only a limited range. For one thing, if β and γ are both positive, as it is reasonable to assume, the utility of wealth reaches a maximum at the point where

$$\frac{\partial U}{\partial W} = \beta - 2\gamma W = 0$$

that is, $W^* = \beta/2\gamma$. Increases in wealth beyond W^* reduce utility, and it will eventually become negative! On the other hand, if $\gamma < 0$, implying that our investor is a "risk lover" who would select the more risky of two portfolios with the same expected return, his utility is unbounded; such utility functions are customarily ruled out in the analysis of decision making under uncertainty because they admit Daniel Bernoulli's (1700–1782) St. Petersburg paradox. So if we are to use Equation 3.1 as our utility function, we must also assume that the market returns that the investor regards as conceivable is confined over a limited range within which Equation 3.1 constitutes a reasonable approximation of utility. The complications created if changes in stock prices have infinite variance have received intensive study in recent years; see, for example, Eugene F. Fama, "The Behavior of Stock-Market Prices," *Journal of Business*, January 1965.

investment and the rate of interest

*6.1 THE DECISION TO INVEST

The entrepreneur's decision to invest is a decision to enlarge the capital stock of plant, inventories, and equipment available for the production process. How much he invests will be affected by the extent of his optimism about future sales volume and by the price of plant and equipment required for expansion. Because the investor also considers the interest rate that must be paid on the funds tied up in the investment project, the volume of investment spending can be influenced by the central bank. Similar conditions govern the pace of residential construction. But the decision to invest is critical not only for the individual decision-making unit. Because investment spending is a very unstable component of GNP, fluctuations in the overall level of economic activity will be explained largely by variations in the rate of investment spending over the course of the business cycle (Table 6.1).

*6.2 THE ACCELERATOR

It is a convenient simplification to partition the investment decision into two components. First, what is the optimal capital stock that the entrepreneur would like to have, given his expectation about future market conditions and the cost of borrowed funds? Second, how rapidly will the entrepreneur attempt to adjust the capital stock he has initially on hand toward this desired level? Thus we might first postulate that the desired capital stock is simply

$$K_t^d = k_0 + k_1 Y_t - k_2 r_t \qquad (2.1)$$

under the assumption that current output Y_t is an appropriate index of expectations concerning sales and that r_t, the rate of interest, constitutes an adequate measure of the cost of funds. In Figure 6.1 the relationship between the desired capital stock and output is plotted, given the rate of interest. As for the question of timing, it is necessary to recognize that a

Table 6.1 GROSS PRIVATE DOMESTIC INVESTMENT (BILLIONS OF DOLLARS)

Year	Total Gross Private Domestic Investment	Fixed Investment Total	Nonresidential Total	Structures Total	Structures Non-farm	Producers' Durable Equipment Total	Producers' Durable Equipment Non-farm	Residential Structures Total	Residential Structures Non-farm	Residential Structures Farm	Change in Business Inventories Total	Change in Business Inventories Non-Farm
1929	16.2	14.5	10.6	5.0	4.8	5.6	4.9	4.0	3.8	0.2	1.7	1.8
1930	10.3	10.6	8.3	4.0	3.9	4.3	3.7	2.3	2.2	0.1	−0.4	−0.1
1931	5.6	6.8	5.0	2.3	2.3	2.7	2.4	1.7	1.6	0.1	−1.1	−1.6
1932	1.0	3.4	2.7	1.2	1.2	1.5	1.3	0.7	0.7	0.0	−2.5	−2.6
1933	1.4	3.0	2.4	0.9	0.9	1.5	1.3	0.6	0.5	0.0	−1.6	−1.4
1934	3.3	4.1	3.2	1.0	1.0	2.2	1.8	0.9	0.8	0.1	−0.7	0.2
1935	6.4	5.3	4.1	1.2	1.2	2.9	2.4	1.2	1.1	0.1	1.1	0.4
1936	8.5	7.2	5.6	1.6	1.6	4.0	3.3	1.6	1.5	0.1	1.3	2.1
1937	11.8	9.2	7.3	2.4	2.4	4.9	4.1	1.9	1.8	0.1	2.5	1.7
1938	6.5	7.4	5.4	1.9	1.8	3.5	2.9	2.0	1.9	0.1	−0.9	−1.0
1939	9.3	8.9	5.9	2.0	1.9	4.0	3.4	2.9	2.8	0.1	0.4	0.3
1940	13.1	11.0	7.5	2.3	2.2	5.3	4.6	3.4	3.2	0.2	2.2	1.9
1941	17.9	13.4	9.5	2.9	2.8	6.6	5.6	3.9	3.7	0.2	4.5	4.0
1942	9.8	8.1	6.0	1.9	1.8	4.1	3.5	2.1	1.9	0.2	1.8	0.7
1943	5.7	6.4	5.0	1.3	1.2	3.7	3.2	1.4	1.2	0.2	−0.6	−0.6
1944	7.1	8.1	6.8	1.8	1.7	5.0	4.2	1.3	1.1	0.1	−1.0	−0.6
1945	10.6	11.6	10.1	2.8	2.7	7.3	6.3	1.5	1.4	0.1	−1.0	−0.6

Year												
1946	6.4	6.4	0.5	6.7	7.2	9.2	10.2	6.1	6.8	17.0	24.2	30.6
1947	1.3	-0.5	0.7	10.4	11.1	14.0	15.9	6.7	7.5	23.4	34.4	34.0
1948	3.0	4.7	0.9	13.6	14.4	15.5	18.1	8.0	8.8	26.9	41.3	46.0
1949	-2.2	-3.1	0.8	12.8	13.7	13.7	16.6	7.7	8.5	25.1	38.8	35.7
1950	6.0	6.8	0.8	18.6	19.4	15.7	18.7	8.5	9.2	27.9	47.3	54.1
1951	9.1	10.3	0.8	16.4	17.2	17.7	20.7	10.4	11.2	31.8	49.0	59.3
1952	2.1	3.1	0.8	16.4	17.2	17.6	20.2	10.5	11.4	31.6	48.8	51.9
1953	1.1	0.4	0.8	17.2	18.0	18.6	21.5	11.9	12.7	34.2	52.1	52.6
1954	-2.1	-1.5	0.7	19.0	19.7	18.0	20.6	12.3	13.1	33.6	53.3	51.7
1955	5.5	6.0	0.6	22.7	23.3	21.2	23.8	13.6	14.3	38.1	61.4	67.4
1956	5.1	4.7	0.7	20.9	21.6	24.2	26.5	16.5	17.2	43.7	65.3	70.0
1957	0.8	1.3	0.7	19.5	20.2	25.9	23.4	17.2	18.0	46.4	66.5	67.9
1958	-2.3	-1.5	0.6	20.1	20.8	22.0	25.0	15.8	16.6	41.6	62.4	60.9
1959	4.8	4.3	0.5	24.8	25.5	25.4	28.4	15.9	16.7	45.1	70.5	75.3
1960	3.3	3.6	0.6	22.2	22.8	27.7	30.3	17.4	18.1	48.4	71.3	74.8
1961	1.7	2.0	0.6	22.0	22.6	25.8	23.6	17.7	18.4	47.0	69.7	71.7
1962	5.3	6.0	0.6	24.8	25.3	29.5	32.5	18.5	19.2	51.7	77.0	83.0
1963	5.1	5.9	0.6	26.4	27.0	31.2	34.8	18.8	19.5	54.3	81.3	87.1
1964	6.4	5.8	0.5	26.6	27.1	36.3	39.9	20.5	21.2	61.1	88.2	94.0
1965	8.6	9.6	0.5	26.7	27.2	41.6	45.8	24.9	25.5	71.3	98.5	108.1
1966	15.0	14.8	0.5	24.5	25.0	48.4	53.1	27.8	28.5	81.6	106.6	121.4
1967	7.5	8.2	0.6	24.5	25.1	50.0	55.3	27.3	28.0	83.3	108.4	116.6
1968	6.9	7.1	0.5	29.5	30.1	53.6	58.5	29.6	30.3	88.8	118.9	126.0
1969	7.7	7.8	0.6	32.0	32.6	59.2	64.3	33.5	34.2	98.5	131.1	139.0
1970	4.8	4.9	0.5	30.7	31.2	59.2	64.9	35.2	36.0	100.9	132.2	137.1
1971	2.4	3.6	0.6	42.0	42.6	60.9	67.4	37.5	38.4	105.8	148.3	152.0
1972	5.5	5.8	0.7	53.2	53.9	70.3	78.2	41.4	42.2	120.4	174.3	180.2

Source. Economic Report of the President.

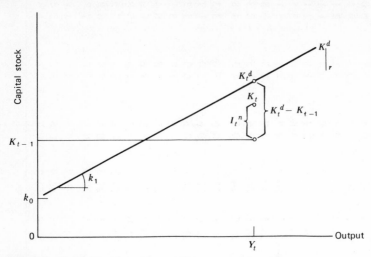

Fig. 6.1 *Capital stock and output. Investment partially adjusts the capital stock toward the desired level, given the rate of interest and output.*

considerable period is required in the design and construction of factory buildings. Ordering and arranging installation of new machines is also a time-consuming process. These factors suggest that in the short run there will be only a partial adjustment of the capital stock inherited from the preceding period (K_{t-1}) toward the desired level; that is, investment net of depreciation may be simply

$$I_t^n = \delta(K_t^d - K_{t-1}) \qquad 0 < \delta \le 1 \qquad (2.2)$$

On the graph, positive investment is indicated, since the inherited capital stock is less than that desired at output Y_t.[1]

If we suppose that depreciation, D_t, is proportional to the magnitude of the initial capital stock ($D_t = dK_{t-1}$) then, since gross investment is defined as $I_t = I_t^n + D_t$, we have

$$I_t = \delta K_t^d + (d - \delta)K_{t-1} \qquad (2.3)$$

---

[1] This partial adjustment mechanism is similar to the role of inertia and expectations in explaining consumption in Chapter 4, Section 5. The substitution procedure is sometimes referred to as the "Koyck distributed lag," after L. M. Koyck, who pioneered its application in *Distributed Lags and Investment Behavior*, North Holland, 1954. Shirley Almon developed a more involved procedure in "The Distributed Lag Between Capital Appropriations and Expenditures, *Econometrica*, 1965.

Substituting from Equation 2.1 now yields as the equation for gross investment

$$I_t = \delta(k_0 + k_1 Y_1 - k_2 r_t) + (d - \delta)K_{t-1} \qquad (2.4)$$

Thus higher levels of economic activity, by enlarging the desired capital stock, induce additional investment spending. On the other hand, an increase in the rate of interest discourages investment activity. At the end of the current period the capital stock will have changed from K_{t-1} to

$$K_t = K_{t-1} + I_t^n = \delta(k_0 + k_1 Y_t - k_2 r_t) + (1 - \delta)K_{t-1} \qquad (2.5)$$

The presence of the lagged capital stock in Equation 2.4 means that the investment process is *dynamic*. With the passage of time the capital stock changes in accordance with Equation 2.5, unless net investment happens to be zero, and this change in the magnitude of the capital stock will, in turn, influence investment spending in the next period, even if Y_t and r_t remain constant.

Complicated as it is, this flexible accelerator model of investment behavior neglects some important factors. For example, it might be more appropriate to replace actual with anticipated output and augment the model with an additional equation explaining the process by which entrepreneural expectations about future sales are generated.[2] But complexity is not always a blessing, and for certain purposes it is useful to consider special simplifications of this model of investment behavior. One of these simplifications, the crude accelerator model, has been found particularly helpful in studying the business cycle. According to the crude accelerator, net investment is proportional to the change in output.

$$I_t^n = k_1(Y_t - Y_{t-1}) \qquad (2.6)$$

The crude accelerator is obtained by assuming that the capital stock is adjusted instantaneously to its desired level ($\delta = 1$) and that the desired

---

[2] This factor is often thought to be important in explaining inventory investment. It has been argued that Equation 2.2 neglects another complication that may be quite critical in a period of economic depression. While Equation 2.2 suggests that substantial negative investment might take place if output were to decline precipitously, the aggregate capital stock, can, in fact, be liquidated no more rapidly than it depreciates; thus the rate of depreciation is said by Hicks and Leontief to provide a floor, for gross fixed investment cannot be negative and net investment must be no less than depreciation; that is, gross investment is the maximum of zero and the figure obtained from Equation 2.2; we must also have the rate of change of the capital stock constrained by the condition $I^n/K_{t-1} \geq -d$, the depreciation rate. How this complicates the business cycle will be examined in exercise 3, Chapter 16. Hicks advanced his argument for the one-way accelerator in his *Contribution to the Theory of the Trade Cycle*, Oxford, Clarendon Press, 1949; Leontief used the one-way accelerator in a multisector dynamic model, *Studies in the Structure of the American Economy*, New York: Oxford University Press, 1953.

capital stock is insensitive to the rate of interest ($k_2 = 0$).[3] On the other hand, an alternative simplification is convenient when analyzing the short-run effects of monetary policy. This second simplification has investment spending depending only on the rate of interest, which may be legitimate for a period of analysis sufficiently short to permit changes in the capital stock and the expectations of entrepreneurs about future business conditions to be regarded as negligible.[4]

*6.3 THE COST OF FUNDS AND THE MARGINAL EFFICIENCY OF INVESTMENT

The effect of changes in the cost of funds required for investment deserves closer scrutiny, because the role of the rate of interest as a determinant of investment spending constitutes a critical issue in the evaluation of monetary policy. In order to analyze this problem in greater depth, consider a representative firm with (1) given expectations about future market conditions, (2) a given stock of existing capital, and (3) a number of alternative investment opportunities open for consideration. Suppose that one of the investment projects being considered by the firm involves the acquisition of a machine that has an initial cost P and an expected life of T years. Let Q_t denote the dollar return expected t years hence, net of the costs of raw materials, labor, and other operating costs. Let S be the scrap value of the machine. Then the yield on this investment, called the "marginal efficiency of investment," may be obtained by solving the following equation for i.

$$P = \frac{Q_1}{(1 + i)} + \frac{Q_2}{(1 + i)^2} + \cdots + \frac{Q_T + S}{(1 + i)^t} = \sum_{t=1}^{T} \frac{Q_t}{(1 + i)^t} + \frac{S}{(1 + i)^T} \quad (3.1)$$

Thus the marginal efficiency of an investment project is defined as the rate of return that equates the present value of the stream of net receipts to be obtained from undertaking the project with the initial expenditure required for the project. Presumably, there are likely to be a number of alternative investment projects available for consideration at any point of time, and each may involve a different initial expenditure. The firm may rank these projects, regarding that with the highest marginal efficiency as most de-

---

[3] Note that $\delta = 1$ implies, from Equation 2.2 and the first equality of Equation 2.5, that $K_t = K_t^d$ for all t, including $t - 1$. Replacing K_{t-1} in Equation 2.2 with last period's desired capital stock then yields Equation 2.6, if $k_2 = 0$.

[4] Precisely this assumption was invoked by Keynes, *The General Theory of Employment, Interest and Money*, New York: Harcourt Brace & World, 1936. Subsequently, many other writers have invoked the same assumption; see, for example, Lloyd A. Metzler, "Wealth, Savings and the Rate of Interest," *Journal of Political Economy*, April 1951.

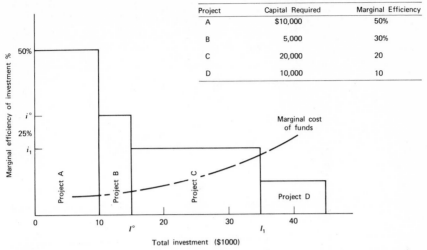

Project	Capital Required	Marginal Efficiency
A	$10,000	50%
B	5,000	30%
C	20,000	20
D	10,000	10

Fig. 6.2 *The marginal efficiency of investment schedule.*

sirable.[5] The result of this ranking yields the downward sloping step function graphed in Figure 6.2. If the firm is only willing to undertake projects with a marginal efficiency of i_0 or greater, it will execute projects A and B; this involves a total investment expenditure of I_0. If the firm is willing to undertake projects with a lower marginal efficiency, say i_1, a total of I_1 in investment expenditures will take place. Thus, given the firm's expectations about the future, everything depends on the cost of funds for investment projects.

The cost of funds to the firm is determined partly by its credit history, but it is also sensitive to the amount of investment actually undertaken. It may be possible to finance at least part of the expansion internally from retained earning. That is, it may be possible to plow back into the firm the accumulation of profits in excess of taxes and dividend payout. As Table 6.2 reveals, the flow of internal funds fluctuates a fair amount from one

[5] If the manager of the firm is wise, he will worry about whether the various projects are complementary or competitive in nature, so that their marginal efficiency of investment is not independent of the decision on other projects. He will also consider the length of the payback period of various projects if he is concerned about having ample funds in the future in the event that new investment opportunities become available. He will take uncertainty into account, possibly by subtracting a risk allowance from the magnitude of i obtained on solving Equation 3.1. And, if he is a mathematical worrywart, he may lose sleep over the question of whether Equation 3.1 has a unique nonnegative real i as a solution. Such are the issues that receive attention in the literature on capital budgeting. See, for example, William J. Baumol, "Capital Budgeting," Chapter 19 of *Economic Theory and Operations Analysis*, Prentice Hall, 1972.

Table 6.2 SOURCES AND USES OF FUNDS (NONFARM, NONFINANCIAL, CORPORATE BUSINESS) (BILLIONS OF DOLLARS)

	Sources							Uses			Discrepancy (Uses Less Sources)
			External								
				Credit Market Funds							
Period	Total	Internal[a]	Total	Total	Long Term[b]	Short Term[c]	Other	Total	Purchase of Physical Assets[d]	Increase in Financial Assets	
1946	18.3	7.8	10.5	6.8	3.5	3.3	3.7	16.5	17.9	-1.4	-1.8
1947	28.1	12.6	15.5	8.7	5.6	3.1	6.8	25.5	17.2	8.3	-2.5
1948	29.0	18.7	10.4	6.3	6.4	-0.1	4.0	25.3	20.3	5.1	-3.7
1949	20.4	19.1	1.3	3.1	5.1	-1.9	-1.8	18.8	15.3	3.5	-1.6
1950	41.8	17.9	23.8	7.2	3.9	3.3	16.7	40.5	24.1	16.4	-1.3
1951	37.6	19.9	17.6	10.0	5.9	4.1	7.7	37.2	29.9	7.3	-0.4
1952	29.4	21.2	8.2	8.7	7.9	0.8	-0.5	29.0	24.4	4.6	-0.3
1953	29.3	21.1	8.2·	5.7	6.0	-0.3	2.5	26.9	24.6	2.2	-2.4
1954	29.6	23.3	6.3	6.1	6.7	-0.6	0.2	26.5	21.6	4.8	-3.2
1955	53.4	29.2	24.3	10.4	6.6	3.8	13.8	48.0	31.5	16.5	-5.4

Year										
1956	46.5	28.9	17.6	12.7	7.5	5.2	4.8	39.9	35.9	4.0	−6.6
1957	39.4	30.6	8.8	12.0	10.4	1.6	−3.1	38.9	34.7	4.2	−0.5
1958	46.5	29.5	17.0	10.2	10.7	−0.4	6.8	37.9	27.3	10.6	−8.6
1959	57.3	35.0	22.3	11.9	8.2	3.7	10.4	51.2	36.9	14.2	−6.1
1960	48.2	34.4	13.8	11.4	7.6	3.8	2.4	41.6	39.0	2.6	−6.6
1961	55.1	35.6	19.5	12.5	11.1	1.5	7.0	49.1	36.7	12.5	−5.9
1962	62.6	41.8	20.7	12.4	9.7	2.7	8.4	55.1	44.0	11.1	−7.5
1963	67.5	43.9	23.6	12.3	8.5	3.8	11.4	59.7	45.6	14.2	−7.8
1964	74.4	50.5	23.9	14.6	9.0	5.7	9.3	65.5	52.1	13.4	−9.0
1965	94.4	56.6	37.8	20.6	9.3	11.3	17.2	83.0	62.8	20.2	−11.4
1966	100.2	61.2	39.1	25.2	15.6	9.5	13.9	89.7	77.1	12.6	−10.6
1967	98.7	61.5	37.3	29.7	21.5	8.2	7.6	88.8	72.0	16.8	−9.9
1968	109.8	61.7	48.1	30.7	17.9	12.9	17.4	99.5	76.2	23.3	−10.3
1969	117.6	60.8	56.9	40.3	21.2	19.1	16.6	105.2	84.0	21.1	−12.5
1970	102.5	59.1	43.4	39.8	32.3	7.5	3.6	95.5	84.6	10.9	−6.9
1971	126.7	67.1	59.6	48.5	44.0	4.6	11.0	106.9	85.2	21.7	−19.8

Source. Economic Report of the President.

[a] Undistributed profits (after inventory valuation adjustment) and capital consumption allowances.

[b] Stocks, bonds, and mortgages.

[c] Bank loans, commercial paper, finance company loans, bankers' acceptances, and government loans.

[d] Plant and equipment, residential structures, and inventory investment.

year to the next, but not nearly as much as funds raised externally by borrowing from banks or by issuing bonds and stocks. The opportunity cost of internal financing is relatively low when the best alternative to utilizing these funds for investment purposes is to purchase low-yielding bonds or Treasury Bills. If investment in excess of the funds available from retained earnings is to be undertaken, the firm can resort to borrowing; this will involve a higher cost, and the interest rate at which the firm will be able to borrow funds will rise if large amounts of capital are being obtained in this way, because banks become concerned and demand a higher yield. Finally, the firm may consider the issuance of equities, although the firm's managers may be reluctant to obtain funds by issuing additional shares if this involves a dilution of control; furthermore, flotation costs and the possible reduction in the value of existing shares will have to receive careful consideration. All these factors mean that the cost of funds will increase for the firm as it becomes more and more ambitious about expansion. Thus the marginal cost of funds must be plotted as an increasing function of investment in Figure 6.2.

Given the cost of funds and the marginal efficiency of investment schedule, investment of I_1 will be undertaken by the hypothetical firm of Figure 6.2. The marginal cost of funds is i_1. It is clear from the preceding discussion, however, that the cost of funds does not correspond to a particular rate quoted in the money market, such as the prime rate or the yield on Treasury Bills. The cost of funds will be influenced by the availability of internal funds, the debt/equity position of the firm, and whether the stock market is currently favorable to new issues.

6.4 EMPIRICAL EVIDENCE

As viewed by the individual firm, the extent to which funds are available from internal sources and the extent to which banks impose covenants as a condition for making loans may be much more important than the rate of interest charged on borrowed funds. Indeed, in their pioneering survey, J. E. Meade and P. W. S. Andrews found that businessmen place very little emphasis on the interest rate as a determinant of their investment spending.[6] This does not mean, however, that aggregate investment spending for the entire economy will be insensitive to the level of interest rates. It may be true that individual firms find that their investment behavior is governed largely by changes in sales instead of by the rate of interest. But the random gains in sales volume of one firm may be partially offset by reductions in the sales volume of other firms and, to the extent that the first firm's investment is offset by disinvestment by other firms, aggregate

[6] Summary of "Replies to Questions on Effects of Interest Rates," *Oxford Economic Papers*, October 1938.

investment spending may be unaffected. However, the effects of monetary factors are highly synchronized. When credit markets tighten, all firms simultaneously find that the cost of credit has increased; when credit eases, all firms simultaneously find that they can borrow cheaply. Because it affects all firms simultaneously, the monetary factor may add up to a much more pronounced effect on the aggregate than the examination of data for individual firms or interview studies would suggest.

Empirical studies of aggregate investment behavior have not yielded decisive evidence as to the importance of monetary factors. The issue is still a matter of debate. Part of the difficulty arises from the problem of measuring interest costs precisely. A multitude of interest rates are quoted in the marketplace; to some extent the econometric results are sensitive to the particular rate selected as the determinant of investment spending. The problem is complicated by the fact that changes in the terms on which firms can borrow may be inadequately reflected in the quoted rate. For example, when money becomes tight, a firm may find that its banker is no longer willing to continue lending at the *prime rate*; instead, the loan will be made only if the borrower agrees to pay a premium rate ordinarily charged riskier customers. Sometimes the borrower will be allowed the prime rate, but the effective cost of funds is raised by requiring the firm to carry a larger average level of demand deposits at the bank.

A second source of the difficulty encountered in empirical studies may have arisen from the form in which the interest rate has been introduced into the investment equation. Dale Jorgenson has argued,[7] on the basis of an appeal to profit maximizing considerations, that the equation for the desired capital stock should have a form quite different from that of Equation 2.1. With some simplification, his analysis can be explained as follows. Jorgenson considers a firm with a Cobb-Douglas production function; that is, output Y depends on labor, L, and capital, K.[8]

$$Y = aK^{\lambda}L^{(1-\lambda)} \qquad (4.1)$$

It can be shown that profit maximization under competitive conditions requires that each firm must adjust its capital stock to the point at which its marginal product is equal to the cost of funds;[9] that is,

$$\frac{\partial Y}{\partial K} = \lambda aK^{\lambda-1}L^{1-\lambda} = \lambda \frac{Y}{K} = r \qquad (4.2)$$

---

[7] "Capital Theory and Investment Behavior," *American Economic Review*, May 1963.

[8] The Cobb-Douglas production function is discussed in detail in the appendix to Chapter 12. The reader may wish to verify at this point that the function exhibits constant returns to scale; that is, if the quantity of labor and capital employed are doubled, output will also double.

[9] This microeconomic argument, which is discussed at length in courses in price theory, will be developed in greater detail in Appendix 12.A.

Since the adjustment process is time consuming, it is the equilibrium or desired capital stock (K^e) that is determined by the last equality.

$$K^e = \lambda \frac{Y}{r} \qquad (4.3)$$

Substituting this desired capital stock expression into Equation 2.3 yields, as an alternate to Equation 2.4,

$$I = \delta\lambda \frac{Y}{r} + (d - \delta)K_{t-1} \qquad (4.4)$$

In his empirical work, Jorgenson used a sophisticated measure of the cost of capital complicated by the effect of tax considerations instead of a simple interest rate variable; his investment equation was further complicated by the use of a more involved adjustment mechanism than Equation 2.2. While his work is still subject to controversy,[10] it has served to stimulate additional studies pointing the way to a precise estimate of the extent to which investment spending is affected by changes in the structure of interest rates.

*6.5 REGULATING THE PACE OF INVESTMENT

The debate over the precise form of the equation explaining the response of investment spending to changes in income and the rate of interest is no mere academic quarrel. The effectiveness of monetary policy as a means of stabilizing economic activity hinges largely on the timing and magnitude of the response of investment spending to changes in the rate of interest. But monetary policy is not the only means by which the government influences the pace of investment spending.

Some sectors of the economy are much more sensitive than others to changes in the rate of interest. Residential construction is particularly sensitive because of the way in which this industry is regulated by a number of state and federal agencies. Many states have usury laws establishing the maximum rate that a lender can charge for mortgage funds. Also, the Federal Housing Authority (FHA) and the Veterans Administration (VA) will insure housing loans only when the rate of interest conforms to their regulations. When the Federal Reserve System raises the structure of in-

---

[10] One theoretical difficulty arises from the fact that with constant returns to scale, the optimal size of the firm is indeterminant under competitive conditions; Jorgenson treats output as exogenous instead of a variable subject to control by the firm. Also, his analysis rests on the simplifying assumption that current output constitutes an appropriate index of anticipations with regard to future demand conditions.

terest rates in order to slow an excessive boom, potential home purchasers often find that the mortgage market has dried up. Instead of granting mortgage loans at rates below the market in conformity with the interest ceiling, lenders are inclined to funnel their funds into other types of loans in unregulated markets so that their funds can earn their full potential. Thus the attempt to insure that the homeowner can borrow at a reasonable rate of interest may mean that he cannot borrow at all. And, as a result, the home construction and lumber industries are particularly vulnerable in periods of tight money.

Tax policy can also be varied in an attempt to influence private investment spending. Consider, for example, the schedules used by the Internal Revenue Service in computing depreciation. In 1962, 1971, and on a number of other occasions the regulations have been relaxed to allow accountants greater scope in computing business profits. Under revised guidelines the Internal Revenue Service allows businesses greater scope for accelerating the pace at which they depreciate capital assets. When firms are allowed to depreciate their assets over a shorter period than their true rate of economic decay, net profits are understated because the depreciation cost is a deductible item. Profits look smaller on the firms' books, at least for tax purposes. But with a reduced tax burden, profits after taxes, when properly measured, are larger than they would otherwise be. Obviously, this makes new investment projects look more worthwhile. And the firm has more funds available internally for investment because its tax burden has been reduced.[11]

The investment tax credit, initially introduced under President Kennedy in 1962, is another device for encouraging private investment spending. The investment tax credit allows the firm to deduct a certain percentage of its current investment spending from its tax bill. For example, when an investment tax credit of 7% is allowed, the firm gets back $70 on every $1000 of new investment spending. Because part of the funds required for the investment are provided by the government through the taxbreak, the effect is similar to a reduction in the interest rate. In principle, the investment tax credit percentage can be manipulated in order to stabilize the economy. But this adds an additional note of uncertainty to the investment decision. Furthermore, the response by business firms to the investment

---

[11] Must there be an eventual day of reckoning when the firm's machine has been depreciated down to zero? In principle, yes, but at the very least the tax burden has been shifted into the future, so its discounted present value is less. Furthermore, the firm may find it worthwhile to sell its depreciated machine on the second-hand market, reaping a capital gain, since the book value of the machine was understated. By starting the process all over again with a new machine, the firm ends up having to pay only the reduced capital gains tax rate instead of the full burden. The same accelerated depreciation technique has been used to encourage apartment developments.

tax credit may be slow, just as it is to interest changes, because time will be required to draw up new plans for expansion. But quite apart from such difficulties, a serious forecasting problem has been incurred. Toward the end of 1966 the investment tax credit was suspended, much to the consternation of business firms that had been drawing up blueprints for expansion with the hope of obtaining the subsidy. The tax was suspended because the economy seemed to be overheating. But by early 1967 the economy definitely appeared to be moving into a slump. In an embarrassing reversal of policy the investment tax credit was reinstated in March, only five months after it had been suspended. The investment subsidy was repealed by the Nixon Administration in April 1969. But it was restored in December 1971 and retained even in the face of widespread inflation and excessive boom.

REFERENCES

1. The empirical literature on investment behavior has been carefully surveyed by Michael K. Evans.

   Michael K. Evans, *Macro-Economic Activity: Theory, Forecasting and Control*, Harper & Row, 1969.

2. A brief summary of the literature on capital budgeting is presented by William Baumol.

   William J. Baumol, *Economic Theory and Operations Analysis*, 3rd ed., Prentice-Hall, 1972, Ch. 19.

3. Investment behavior has been subjected to intensive empirical study. Here is a sample of the literature.

   W. H. Locke Anderson, *Corporate Finance and Fixed Investment*, Harvard Business School, 1964.

   Charles W. Bischoff, "Business Investment in the 1970's: A Comparison of Models," in *Brookings Papers on Economic Activity*, Vol. 1, 1971.

   Frank DeLeeuw, "The Demand for Capital Goods by Manufacturers: A Study of Quarterly Times Series," *Econometrica*, July 1962.

   Robert Eisner, "A Permanent Income Theory for Investment," *American Economic Review*, June 1967.

   Robert Eisner and Robert H. Strotz, "Determinants of Business Investment," in *Impacts of Monetary Policy* (Commission on Money and Credit), Prentice-Hall, 1963.

   Robert Ferber (ed.), *Determinants of Investment Behavior*, National Bureau of Economic Research, 1967.

   Trygve Haavelmo, *A Study in the Theory of Investment*, University of Chicago Press, 1960.

   Dale W. Jorgenson, "Capital Theory and Investment Behavior," *American Economic Review*, May 1963.

   Michael C. Lovell, "Determinants of Inventory Investment," in *Models of Income Determination* (edited by Irwin Friend), Princeton University Press, 1964.

   R. W. Resek, "Investment by Manufacturing Firms: A Quarterly Time-Series Analysis of Industry Data," *Review of Economics and Statistics*, August 1966.

KEY CONCEPTS

accelerator

capital stock

desired capital stock

marginal efficiency of investment

retained earnings

investment tax credit

accelerated depreciation

EXERCISES

6.1 Consider the accelerator model introduced by Equations 6.2.1 through
6.2.4. Assume that $k_0 = 500$, $k_1 = 0.8$, $k_2 = 8000$, and $\delta = 0.6$.
Thus, if the rate of interest is 5% and output is 1000 in year 0, the
equilibrium capital stock will be:

$$K_0^e = 500 + 0.8 \times 1000 - 8000 \times 0.05 = 900$$

    a. If the actual capital stock in year 0 is at 900 (the equilibrium level),
how much net investment will take place if $r = 5\%$ and $Y = 1000$
in year 1?

    b. Suppose that in period 2 we still have $r = 5\%$, but output increases
to $Y = 1100$. What is the new equilibrium capital stock? How
much net investment will take place in period 2?

    c. Analyze the process by which the capital stock will adjust to its
new equilibrium level if, for ever more, $Y = 1100$ and $r = 5\%$.

    d. If output had remained at 1000 but the rate of interest had changed
to 4%, how would your answers to parts b and c have been
affected?

    (*Hint.* Compare this model with the distributed lag analysis of con-
sumption, particularly Table 4.4.)

6.2 Data are provided on the following table for four investment projects
under consideration at the Fly-By-Knight Aircraft Company.

	Machine A	*Machine B*	*Machine C*	*Machine D*
Price of machine	$1000	$1000	$2000	$5000
Life of machine	2 years	2 years	2 years	Forever
Dollar return, first year	$500	$550	$1200	$300
Dollar return, second year	$500	$605	$1440	$300
Scrap value	0	0	0	0

    a. Which project is worth undertaking even if funds cost 15% per
annum?

    b. Which project would not be worth undertaking unless the rate of
interest were zero?

    c. Determine the marginal efficiency of investment for each project.
(*Hint.* Use Equation 6.3.1, trying $i = 0$, 6%, 10%, 20%.)

d. Plot on a graph the marginal efficiency of investment schedule for this firm.

6.3 Suppose that the firm considered in Exercise 6.2 has $5000 of retained earnings; it can either invest these funds in machinery or use them to buy short-term government securities yielding 5%. Furthermore, it can borrow at 9% from its bank, up to limit of $2000. Finally, it can issue bonds paying 10%.

a. Plot the cost of funds schedule for this firm on the same graph used in 6.2d.

b. Which investment projects should the firm undertake?

c. How should this analysis be modified in order to take into account uncertainty and other "real world" complications?

investment, the multiplier, and stagnation: the IS schedule

*7.1 THE INTEREST RATE AND THE DETERMINATION OF OUTPUT

How must the simple multiplier model be modified in order to take into account the endogenous nature of the process of capital accumulation? In answering this question we will find that the rate of interest can be used as an additional policy variable influencing the level of GNP. It will also prove useful to make imports as well as private investment spending endogenous because, while this constitutes only a minor complication, it will facilitate an examination of the effects of fiscal and interest rate policy on the balance of payments as well as on GNP and employment.

The level of government spending, the interest rate, and exports will now constitute the exogenous variables of our model. The equations of the system, listed in Figure 7.1, have all received attention in earlier chapters. Specifically, we have from Chapter 3 national income accounting identity 3.2.1 and the disposable income equation 3.2.3. Furthermore, we will employ consumption function 4.6.1, which includes the initial level of wealth as well as disposable income. Investment equation 6.2.4 explains that category of spending in terms of the current level of output, the rate of interest, and the inherited capital stock. Also, imports are determined by the level of aggregate economic activity.

$$M = m_0 + m_1 Y \tag{1.1}$$

At higher levels of output more raw materials will be needed and consumers will have more to spend on foreign as well as domestic goods and services. The interdependent nature of this five-equation system may be appreciated by examining Figure 7.1. In contrast to the schematic picture of the simple multiplier model provided by Figure 3.4, we now have three feedback loops. First, there is the feedback of GNP on disposable income and consumption.

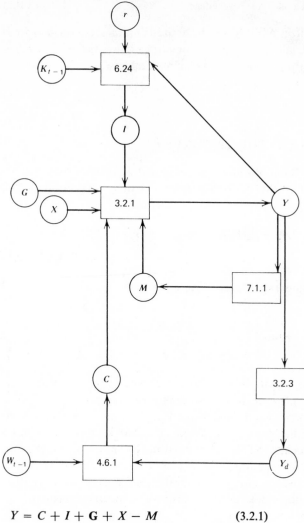

$$Y = C + I + \mathbf{G} + X - M \qquad (3.2.1)$$
$$C = c_0 + c_1 Y_d + c_2 W_{t-1} \qquad (4.6.1)$$
$$Y_d = d_0 + d_1 Y \qquad (3.2.3)$$
$$I = \delta(k_0 + k_1 Y - k_2 r) + (d - \delta)K_{t-1} \qquad (6.2.4)$$
$$M = m_0 + m_1 Y \qquad (7.1.1)$$

Fig. 7.1 *The interest rate and the determination of output: Flowchart of a five-equation model.*

Second, there is the effect of GNP on the desired capital stock, which feeds back to GNP through added investment spending. Third, there is the negative feedback of GNP on imports, which limits effective demand for domestic output.

*7.2 DERIVATION OF THE *IS* CURVE

To solve the system of simultaneous equations, substitute the behavioral equations into the national income identity (Equation 3.2.1), obtaining

$$Y = c_0 + c_1 d_0 + c_1 d_1 Y + c_2 W_{t-1} + \delta(k_0 + k_1 Y - k_2 r)$$
$$+ (d - \delta)K_{t-1} + X - m_0 - m_1 Y + G \quad (2.1)$$

This yields the fundamental reduced form equation[1]

$$Y = \frac{1}{1 - c_1 d_1 - \delta k_1 + m_1} [c_0 + c_1 d_0 + c_2 W_{t-1} + \delta k_0 - \delta k_2 r$$
$$+ (d - \delta)K_{t-1} - m_0 + X + G] \quad (2.2)$$

The pace of economic activity is determined by three exogenous variables: the rate of interest (r), government spending (G), and exports (X)—and two historically given predetermined variables: the initial level of wealth (W_{t-1}) and the inherited capital stock (K_{t-1}).[2] That is, given the initial wealth and capital stock, GNP is determined in the short run by the rate of interest, government spending, and export volume. And once output has been determined the remaining structural equations can be solved for the four remaining endogenous variables: disposable income, consumption, investment, and imports.

How output responds to changes in the interest rate is illustrated by the "*IS* curve" plotted on Figure 7.2; this relationship was obtained from Equation 2.2 for fixed values of G, X, W_{t-1}, and K_{t-1}. A reduction in the rate of interest, by lowering the cost of funds, encourages investment spending and induces a multiple expansion in GNP, as illustrated on the

---

[1] A "reduced form equation" (see Exercise 3.12) uses only exogenous and lagged (predetermined) variables in explaining the magnitude of an endogenous variable; in this instance, output is the endogenous variable, and none of the variables on the right are endogenous (at least within the context of the current model).

[2] The equation is analogous to Equation 3.2.5. Indeed, it reduces to that expression if $c_2 = d = \delta = m_0 = m_1 = 0$.

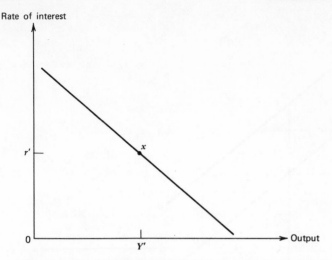

Fig. 7.2 *The* IS *curve. For specified rate of interest output can be determined with the* IS *curve.*

graph. How sensitive output is to changes in the rate of interest may be determined from Equation 2.2.[3]

$$\frac{\Delta Y}{\Delta r} = \frac{-\delta k_2}{1 - c_1 d_1 - \delta k_1 + m_1} \tag{2.3}$$

Because the *IS* curve is customarily plotted with output measured on the abscissa and the rate of interest on the ordinate, its slope is the reciprocal of the right-hand side of Equation 2.3. The larger δ and k_2, the greater the sensitivity of output to changes in the rate of interest; but the parameters entering into the denominator of Equation 2.3 also influence the responsiveness of output to shifts in monetary policy.

An increase in government spending shifts the *IS* schedule to the right, as illustrated by the new *IS* curve in Figure 7.3. But even if the monetary authorities take whatever steps are necessary to prevent the interest rate from changing (so that we move from Y' to Y'' in Figure 7.3), the elementary multiplier presented in Chapter 3 will no longer reveal the precise change in output. Induced changes in investment and imports caused by expanding output must now be taken into account. The full multiplier

---

[3] Just as when we were deriving the multiplier in Chapter 3, Equation 2.3 can be obtained by first obtaining an after-change version of Equation 2.2 showing the new level of output Y^* corresponding to the new interest rate r^*; subtracting the old equation from the after-change equation gives Equation 2.3. But the easy way is to differentiate Equation 2.2 with respect to r.

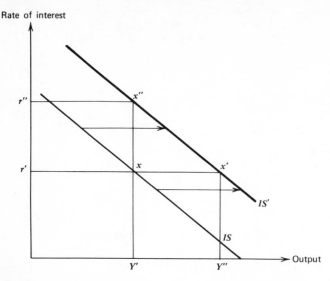

Fig. 7.3 *Shifts of the* IS *curve. An increase in government spending, a cut in taxes, or enlarged exports shifts the* IS *curve to the right. If the rate of interest remains constant, output expands to* Y″. *But, if the rate of interest were to rise to* r″, *output would not change.*

effect of an increase in government spending, obtained from Equation 2.2, is

$$\frac{\Delta Y}{\Delta G} = \frac{1}{1 - c_1 d_1 - \delta k_1 + m_1} \tag{2.4}$$

This will be larger than multiplier m1 of Chapter 3, Section 5 if $\delta k_1 > m_1$; that is, if current investment spending is more sensitive than imports to changes in GNP. It must be emphasized that Equations 2.3 and 2.4 are both *impact multipliers* because they reveal only the short-run effects of government policy. Subsequent developments depend on how the capital stock changes with the passage of time. An analysis of the longer-run effects of changes in G and r is postponed until the discussion of business cycles.

In summary, note that the distance between points x and x' in Figure 7.3 is not just the increase in government spending. Instead, it is the multiplier of Equation 2.4 times the change in government spending. Why does an increase in **G** cause such a large shift? First, points x and x' both involve the same rate of interest. Second, inspection of Equation 2.2 reveals that a change in government spending times the multiplier gives the change in income if the rate of interest is constant. Thus the magnitude of the shift, measured horizontally, is the government spending multiplier, as specified by Equation 2.4, times the change ΔG.

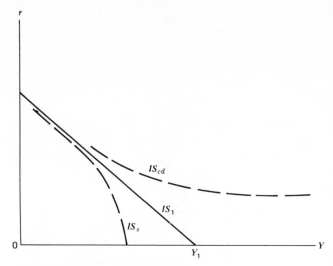

Fig. 7.4   *Alternative* IS *schedules.*

*7.3 THE STAGNATION THESIS

Can full employment be achieved by lowering the interest rate sufficiently, or is it necessary to rely on expansionary fiscal policy? The answer
hinges on the sensitivity of investment spending to the rate of interest, as
summarized in the shape of the *IS* curve. Figure 7.4 suggests three possibilities. If the *IS* curve is linear, as Equation 2.2 implies, there exists for
given G a maximum level of income that can be generated; after all, the
interest rate cannot be reduced below zero.[4] With IS_1 on Figure 7.4, point

---

[4] If the interest rate were negative, it would pay to borrow funds and hold them in
cash, for this would yield a return without any risk to the investor. Silvio Gesell (1862–
1930) suggested that a negative interest rate could be achieved through "stamped money."
Currency would retain its value only if affixed with stamps that would have to be purchased
each month at the post office; Gesell suggested a charge for stamps amounting to 5.4%
per month. In discussing this scheme, John Maynard Keynes (*General Theory*, pp. 353–358)
pointed out that the stamping provision might lead to the substitution of bank demand
deposits, jewelry, and precious metals as alternatives to currency as a store of liquidity.
Precisely the opposite of stamped money is involved in a policy recommendation advanced
by many modern economists, who argue that the interest loss incurred from holding the
medium of exchange instead of bonds and other interest-earning assets leads to an econo-
mizing of cash balances that is not warranted in that no true cost is involved in increasing
the supply of the medium of exchange; it is argued that increased economic efficiency would
be achieved if banks were permitted to pay interest on deposits, since this would induce
individuals and business firms to enlarge their cash holdings. For an analysis of this argument, which presumes that full employment is maintained, see Edgar L. Feige and Michael
Parkin, "The Optimal Quantity of Money, Bonds, Commodity Inventories and Capital,"
American Economic Review, June 1971.

Y_1 indicates the maximum level of GNP that can be obtained without resort to an expansionary fiscal policy. The situation will be more serious if the curve bends downward, as with IS_s. In the 1930s many economists, members of the "stagnation school," argued that investment spending was quite insensitive to interest rates. Even after World War II, Professor Alvin Hansen[5] was arguing at Harvard:

"... under certain circumstances ... in advanced industrial countries, rich in the accumulated volume of capital formation ... it may be difficult to open investment outlets of any considerable magnitude by merely lowering the rate of interest. In this circumstance investment outlets would have to await an upward shift in the marginal efficiency schedule, caused for example by technological innovations, the invention of new processes and new products, public development of regional resources, public investment in urban redevelopment, public lending and guaranteeing operations stimulating private investment in housing and rural electrification, etc.... Of course, a devastating war, such as the Second World War, will for a time make even rich countries capital-poor.... It is easy to overcome any tendency toward secular stagnation if we fight a war every 10 or 15 years; but this is not a tolerable method of solving the ... problem."

It can be argued, on the other hand, that a vast array of investment projects exist that become profitable as the interest rate approaches zero; the relevant payoff period becomes longer and the discount factor smaller. Professor Paul Samuelson explained:[6]

"As long as there is a single hilly railroad track left, it would pay at a zero rate of interest ... in a world of perfect certainty ... to make it level. Why? Because in enough years, the savings in fuel would pay for the cost."

An optimistic view about the effectiveness of interest rate policy as a weapon for stimulating the economy is illustrated by curve IS_{cd} in Figure 7.3. An IS curve of this form may be obtained by utilizing the Jorgenson investment equation (Equation 6.4.4), which was derived from the Cobb-Douglas production function. Utilizing this alternative investment equation instead of Equation 6.2.4, yields

$$Y = \frac{1}{1 - c_1 d_1 + m_1 - \delta\lambda/r} [c_0 + c_1 d_0 + c_2 W_{t-1} + (d - \delta)K_{t-1} - m_0 + X + G] \quad (2.3')$$

Effective demand can be stimulated indefinitely by a sufficient reduction

[5] *Monetary Theory and Fiscal Policy*, New York: McGraw Hill, 1949, p. 78.

[6] *Economics*, New York: McGraw Hill, 1973, p. 603.

in the rate of interest.[7] With this alternative equation for effective demand, the magnitude of the multiplier depends on the rate of interest.[8] It can be objected, however, that in deriving the investment equation underlying Equation 2.3′ we abstracted from the real world problem of uncertainty.[9] If investors demand a "risk premium," over and above the rate of interest, before they will be induced to undertake investment activity, the *IS* curve may be considerably lower than IS_{ed} in Figure 7.3. More than a reduction in interest rates may be required to achieve full employment.

---

[7] More precisely, the value of the multiplier approaches infinity as the rate of interest falls toward $\delta\lambda/(1 - c_1 d_1 + m_1)$. The expansion of Y makes it inconceivable that the central bank could push r below this critical value.

[8] As the rate of interest approaches closer and closer to $r_0 = \delta\lambda/(1 - db + m_1)$ the multiplier and GNP increase without limit. Since negative GNP does not make sense, neither do rates of interest below r_0; of course, the situation would be reversed in the hypothetical case in which K_{t-1} were so large as to make the expression in brackets of Equation 2.3′ negative.

[9] That is, Samuelson's use of the qualifying phrase "perfect certainty" in the hilly railroad track quotation is critical.

KEY CONCEPTS

IS curve

impact multiplier

stagnation thesis

EXERCISES

7.1 Consider the following simplified model.

$$I = 125 - 1000r \qquad Y_d = \frac{5}{6} Y$$

$$C = \frac{9}{10} Y_d \qquad Y = C + I + G$$

a. Derive the equation for the *IS* curve [i.e., *Y* as a function of exogenous government spending (**G**) and the rate of interest (*r*)]. Then determine the level of output when **G** = 300 and *r* = 10%. Check your answer by computing *C* and *I*.

b. If the rate of interest changes to *r* = 9%, what will happen to investment, consumption, and output?

c. Is it true that $\Delta Y/\Delta r = -1000 \, (\Delta Y/\Delta G)$? Why?

d. Plot the *IS* curve on a graph for **G** = 300. Show how it will shift if government spending increases to **G** = 350. (*Suggestion.* Save your graph of the *IS* curves for Exercise 8.1.)

7.2 Suppose that aggregate saving is defined as $S = Y - C - G - (X - M)$. Show that at the level of income specified by reduced form Equation 2.2 aggregate saving is equal to investment ($S = I$). (*Hint.* Use the national income accounting identity.) This explains why Equation 2.2 is referred to as the *IS* curve.

7.3 Consider one minor complication in the equations used in Exercise 7.1. Specifically, suppose that

$$C = \frac{9}{10} Y_d - 50r$$

while all the other equations are the same as before.

a. How will this influence the *IS* curve? How will it alter the level of output when **G** = 300 and *r* = 10%?

b. What happens to investment, consumption, and output if the rate of interest changes to *r* = 9%. Find the formula for $\Delta Y/\Delta r$.

c. Do you think that the introduction of the rate of interest into the consumption function constitutes a major modification of the *IS* model? Why or why not?

7.4 Consider the following six-equation dynamic model.

$$C_t = \frac{9}{10} Y_{dt} \qquad\qquad Y_{dt} = \frac{5}{6} Y_t$$

$$Y_t = C_t + I_t + G_t \qquad\qquad K_t = K_{t-1} + I_t$$

$$K_t^d = 2000 + \frac{1}{4} Y_t - 10{,}000 r_t$$

$$I_t = \frac{1}{2} (K_t^d - K_{t-1})$$

a. Suppose that $G_1 = 3000$, $r_1 = 10\%$, and $K_0 = 4000$. Determine the level of output for period 1; find K_1.

b. Determine the *IS* schedule for period 1, given that $G_1 = 3000$ and $K_0 = 4000$.

c. Suppose that in period 2 government spending remains at \$3000, but the rate of interest falls to 4%. What will happen to output in period 2? How large a gap will develop between the actual and desired capital stock?

d. Trace through the process by which the economy adjusts over time to the discrepancy between the actual and desired capital stock mentioned in part c. If G remains at 3000 and r remains at 4%, will the long-run level of output and the capital stock differ from the level you found in part a?

e. Explain the distinction between the short- and long-run effects of changes in the interest rate.

7.5 The FORTRAN computer program presented in Exercise 3.14 had investment spending exogenous. The computer program may be modified to reflect the endogenous nature of investment spending with the following instructions, *provided* they are inserted in the right place.

```
R = 5
KLAG = 1500
KD = 2000 + 0.25*GNP-100*R
INVS = 0.5*(KD-KLAG)
KLAG = K
```

a. Modify the computer program in order to determine the dynamic implications of having investment endogenously determined.

b. Investigate the way in which the model behaves when r instead of G changes in period 3.

monetary policy and the determination of GNP

*8.1 ALTERNATIVE CONTROL STRATEGIES

At certain periods of its history, most notably during World War II, the Federal Reserve System has concentrated its energies on maintaining a particular pattern of interest rates. Figure 5.4 reveals that the pattern of interest rates was remarkably stable in World War II and beyond. Long-term rates were stable in the early 1960s. (See also Table 5.6.) During episodes when it is appropriate to regard the interest rate as exogenous, the level of economic activity can be determined from the *IS* curve, given government spending. And once Y has been determined, the way in which the quantity of money must have been manipulated by the central bank in order to preserve the desired rate of interest can be determined from demand for money equation 5.5.1.[1] At other times, however, central bankers have not focused their attention primarily on the rate of interest. Let us see what happens when the money supply is exogenous.

*8.2 THE *IS-LM* APPARATUS

A schematic view of the seven-equation *IS-LM* model is presented in Figure 8.1. In this model the interest rate is one of the endogenously determined variables; the money supply and government expenditure are exogenously determined control variables; wealth, the initial capital stock, and exports are also exogenous or predetermined instead of explained by the model. This model does not attempt to explain the price level, a task that is deferred until Part III.

[1] The process resembles in certain respects the strategy employed by the Department of Agriculture in maintaining the price of wheat; just as the total supply of wheat is adjusted to maintain its price (a specified fraction of "parity"), so the quantity of money can be manipulated to maintain the desired interest rate. Details of the process by which the Fed controls the money supply are explained in Chapter 10.

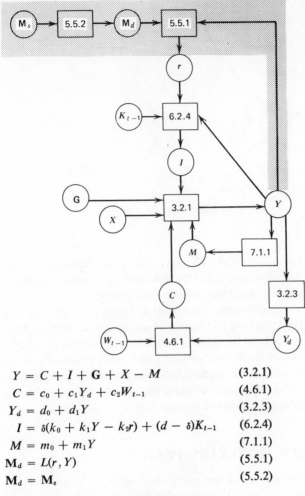

$$Y = C + I + \mathbf{G} + X - M \qquad (3.2.1)$$
$$C = c_0 + c_1 Y_d + c_2 W_{t-1} \qquad (4.6.1)$$
$$Y_d = d_0 + d_1 Y \qquad (3.2.3)$$
$$I = \delta(k_0 + k_1 Y - k_2 r) + (d - \delta)K_{t-1} \qquad (6.2.4)$$
$$M = m_0 + m_1 Y \qquad (7.1.1)$$
$$\mathbf{M}_d = L(r, Y) \qquad (5.5.1)$$
$$\mathbf{M}_d = \mathbf{M}_s \qquad (5.5.2)$$

Fig. 8.1 *Flowchart of the* IS-LM *apparatus.*

The flowchart resembles Figure 7.2, which explained the equations underlying the *IS* curve. But an additional feedback loop involving the determination of the equilibrium rate of interest has been added. More precisely, the lower part of the flowchart reproduces the *IS* apparatus; the shaded part is the *LM* relationship. Both Y and r are on the line of demarcation, since they participate in both halves of the story by entering into the *IS* apparatus and by influencing the demand for money.

The model is solved by plotting the *IS* and *LM* curves on the same graph. This has been done in Figure 8.2. At every point on the *LM* curve the demand for money is equal to the supply; that is, the money market is

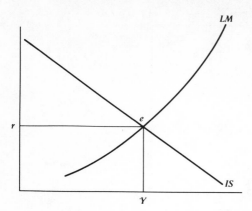

Fig. 8.2   *The* IS-LM *graph.*

in equilibrium. At every point on the *IS* curve the "real" equations of the system are satisfied—the consumption function, the investment equation, the import equation and the national income accounting identity; that is, the goods market is in equilibrium. Therefore, at point *e*, where the two curves intersect, all the equations of the model are satisfied, and we have determined simultaneously both the equilibrium levels of the rate of interest and output. With the aid of these two variables, the other equations of the system may be solved to yield consumption, investment spending, disposable income, and imports. And, of course, velocity can also be calculated as an end product by computing the ratio of income to the money supply.

*8.3 FISCAL VERSUS MONETARY POLICY

How do policy changes affect the equilibrium level of income? First, consider an increase in government spending. If the rate of interest were to remain constant at *r*, GNP would increase by the change in government spending times the multiplier to *Y'*; indeed, every point on the *IS* curve is shifted to the right by the multiplier times the change in government spending; see the first panel of Figure 8.3. But if the money supply is constant, the full effect of the multiplier cannot be realized. As GNP expands, the demand for money will increase above the fixed supply unless offset by a rise in the interest rate. This explains the upward slope of the *LM* curve. Thus the new equilibrium must be at point *e''*, where the new *IS* curve crosses the *LM* curve. Output expands only to *Y''*; the full multiplier effect of the increase in government spending is not fully realized, since it is offset partially by the fall in private investment spending that results when the interest rate goes up.

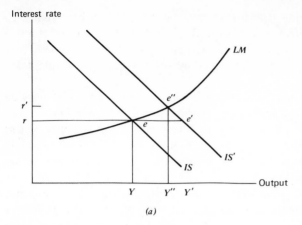

(a)

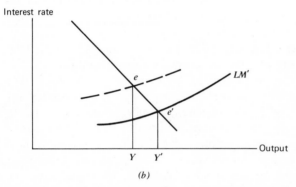

(b)

Fig. 8.3 *Fiscal versus monetary policy. (a) An increase in government spending shifts the IS curve to the right, but because the interest rate rises and snubs investment spending, output expands only to Y''. (b) An increase in the money supply shifts the LM curve to the right; at the new equilibrium, the rate of interest is lower while private investment and output have increased.*

Now consider the effect of an increase in the money supply, given the level of government spending and tax policy. As illustrated in the second panel of Figure 8.3, the increase in the money supply shifts the *LM* curve to the right, since at any rate of interest the public will be willing to hold the enlarged quantity of money only if income rises. It is evident from the graph that the new equilibrium must be at point *e′*, but why? The process by which the economy adjusts to the injection of new money can be clarified by tracing around the flowchart circuits of Figure 8.1; the increase in the stock of money tends to lower the rate of interest and stimulate investment spending; the higher investment spending contributes to total GNP, and the effect is reinforced by the additional consumption induced by the multiplier loop; the expansion process is only partially damped by the tendency of rising income to stimulate the demand for imports and money.

How big a stimulus an increase in the money supply will provide depends partly on the parameters of the investment function and the demand for money equation. Whether monetary policy will be more or less effective than fiscal policy as a means of influencing the level of economic activity is still a matter of heated professional debate, but several extreme positions warrant attention.

On the one hand, there are those who follow Keynes in arguing that investment spending may be insensitive to the rate of interest, particularly in recession. Obviously, if a reduction in the rate of interest does not stimulate private investment spending, an increase in the money supply will not provide much stimulus to a depressed economy. The situation is illustrated in the first panel of Figure 8.4, where the *IS* curve is almost vertical. That the *IS* curve must have this unfortunate property if investment is insensitive to the rate of interest can be verified by inspecting Equation 7.2.2. It is clear that even if the Federal Reserve System succeeds in lowering the rate of interest from r to r' by shifting the *LM* curve to the right with an increase in the money supply, the economy will not be stimulated if investment spending remains constant. Note however, that in precisely these conditions an increase in government spending, for public works or what have you, will come close to exerting its full multiplier stimulus on the economy, as illustrated in the bottom panel of Figure 8.4; the rise in output equals the magnitude of the shift of the *IS* curve, the multiplier times the increase in government spending, since even if the money supply is kept constant, so that the rate of interest rises as Y expands, private investment will not be choked off if investment spending is insensitive to changes in the interest rate.

The Keynesian school buttressed its argument concerning the impotency of monetary policy as a means of stimulating a depressed economy by arguing that at low rates of interest the public's appetite for money may be virtually insatiable. The horizontal *LM* curve on the graph, reproduced from Figure 5.6, reflects this pathological situation. It is clear from Figure 8.5 that if the economy is in the liquidity trap, monetary policy will be an ineffectual weapon for combating unemployment. Even if the central bank succeeds in expanding the money supply, shifting the system to *LM'*, the economy will not move out of recession; since the rate of interest does not fall, private investment is not stimulated. Because the slope of the *IS* curve does not matter when the economy is in the liquidity trap, the economy

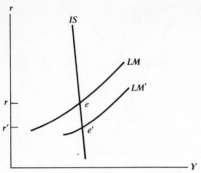

Effect of increase in money supply on output is negligable

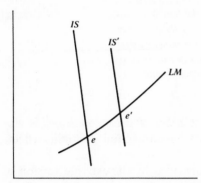

An increase in *G* has its full multiplier effect

Fig. 8.4 *Investment insensitive to the rate of interest.*

stagnates regardless of how sensitive investment spending is to the rate of interest.

If a depressed economy suffers from the liquidity trap, the problem of restoring full employment is far from insurmountable, since precisely this condition insures that fiscal policy will be fully effective. As seen in the second panel of the graph, the full multiplier effect of an increase in government spending will be realized regardless of the slope of the *IS* curve. Thanks to the liquidity trap, the rise in output generated by the shift in the *IS* curve does not tend to raise the rate of interest, and private investment spending is not choked off.

To sum up the argument of those who are pessimistic about the effectiveness of monetary policy as an antidepression weapon, increases in the money supply will stimulate a depressed economy only if the interest elasticity of demand for money is not infinite *and* the volume of investment

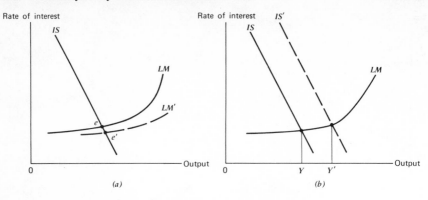

Fig. 8.5 *The liquidity trap. (a) Because the fall in the rate of interest is negligible when the economy is in the liquidity trap, an increase in the money supply fails to stimulate the economy. (b) The full multiplier effect of an increase in government spending is realized when the economy is in the liquidity trap because the rate of interest does not rise to choke off investment spending.*

is sensitive to the rate of interest. And if *either* of these conditions is violated, government spending and tax cuts have their full multiplier effects on the level of economic activity.

One rebuttal to this argument is provided by the extreme version of the quantity theory of money. Suppose that the demand for money is proportional to the level of income, but completely insensitive to the rate of interest, as illustrated in Figure 8.6. Since the *LM* curve is a vertical straight line, the level of income is completely determined by the money supply (provided that the *IS* curve is not also vertical).[2] Now an increase in the money supply will stimulate the economy, even if investment spending is rather insensitive to the rate of interest. But while monetary policy will be effective, fiscal policy will not. An increase in government spending or a tax cut will shove the *IS* curve to the right but, if the monetary authorities fail to act, the *LM* curve remains fixed, and the new equilibrium is e''. Increased government spending or a tax cut serves only to raise the rate of interest by whatever amount is required to achieve an offsetting reduction in private investment spending.

The two opposing positions just enumerated are extreme viewpoints, and considerable empirical effort has been devoted to their resolution. The debate came to a head in the early 1960s, when Friedman and Meiselman argued, in a provocative paper, that the simple quantity theory assertion

---

[2] If both the *IS* and *LM* curve were vertical the system would have no solution unless, by coincidence, they happen to be superimposed on each other; and, if they were superimposed, the interest rate would be indeterminate.

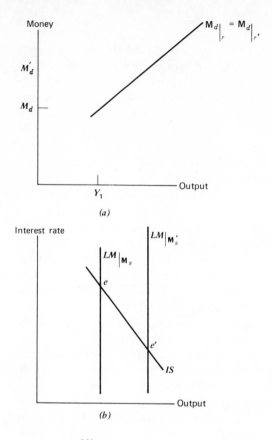

(a)

(b)

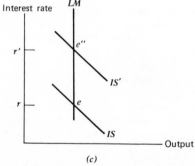

(c)

Fig. 8.6 *The crude quantity theory.* (*a*) *According to the crude version of the quantity theory, the demand for money is proportional to income and insensitive to the rate of interest.* (*b*) *If the demand for money is insensitive to the rate of interest the* LM *curve is vertical, and an increase in the money supply has a dramatic impact on output.* (*c*) *Shifts in the* IS *curve influence only the interest rate but not output when the* LM *curve is vertical.*

that the level of economic activity is determined by the money supply constitutes a more stable empirical relationship than the simple "Keynesian" theory that the level of output is determined by the multiplier times the sum of government plus investment spending.[3] In essence, the controversy involved the question of whether one would do better to assume that the LM curve is vertical or to assume that the IS curve has this property. (Figure 8.6 versus Figures 8.4 and 8.5). In rebuttal, Ando and Modigliani argued that the historical record, properly interpreted, supported the "Keynesian" instead of the quantity theory position.[4] The debate was prolonged and acrimonious, but concensus was not forthcoming, partly because the relative success of the two models seemed to depend on which years happened to be covered or omitted in the statistical analysis. Further difficulties are created by a question concerning the direction of causality; can movements in the money supply be at least partly a reflection of changes in output instead of an exogenous driving force?

The controversy concerning the potency of monetary and fiscal techniques continues, but the mode of analysis has shifted from a comparison of the simple quantity and multiplier alternatives to a debate about the relative merits of sophisticated econometric models capable of explaining the price level, unemployment, and the money supply simultaneously; this type of model will be discussed in Chapter 17.[5] For many economists the Friedman-Meiselman debate appears in retrospect to have been equivalent to arguing whether the left or the right leg is stronger when the important point was to recognize that both are needed in walking. The issue is not whether we should hop along on either the monetary or the fiscal foot; instead, it is a problem of properly coordinating monetary and fiscal

[3] Milton Friedman and David Meiselman, "The Relative Stability of Monetary Velocity and the Investment Multiplier in the United States, 1897–1958," in *Stabilization Policies* (Commission on Money and Credit), Prentice-Hall, 1963, pp. 165–268.

[4] Albert Ando and Franco Modigliani, "The Relative Stability of Monetary Velocity and the Investment Multiplier"; Michael De Prano and Thomas Mayer, "Tests of the Relative Importance of Autonomous Expenditures and Money"; and Milton Friedman and David Mieselman, "Reply to Ando and Modigliani and to De Prano and Mayer," all in *American Economic Review*, 1965, pp. 693–792. See also Donald D. Hester, "Keynes and the Quantity Theory: A Comment on the Friedman-Meiselman CMC Paper," and Milton Friedman and David Meiselman, "Reply to Donald Hester," *Review of Economics and Statistics*, 1964, pp. 364–377.

[5] Ando and Modigliani, op. cit., p. 693, did say that the purpose of their paper was "above all . . . to make it clear why the Friedman and Meiselman game of testing a one-equation one-variable model in search of the highest correlation, fascinating as it might be, cannot be expected to throw any light on such basic issues as how our economic system works, or how it can be more effectively stabilized." Their point was that since neither extreme simplification was close to the truth, more sophisticated simultaneous equation estimation procedures are required; simple least-squares is an inadequate guide for determining the relative potency of monetary and fiscal policy.

policy. Neither the simple quantity theory nor the simply multiplier are adequate for this task. More sophisticated empirical research on the demand for money and the determinants of investment behavior establish that *both* are sensitive to the rate of interest; therefore, neither the *LM* nor the *IS* curves is vertical, and both monetary and fiscal policy have a role to play in the determination of the pace of economic activity. But while the *IS-LM* apparatus provides a synthesis of monetary and fiscal viewpoints facilitating an analysis of how fiscal and monetary policy can be coordinated, it is necessary to consider foreign trade complications and to move on to a more sophisticated analytical framework in which price movements can be taken explicitly into account.

REFERENCES

1. The *IS-LM* apparatus was originally developed by Sir J. R. Hicks.

   J. R. Hicks, "Mr. Keynes and the Classics," *Econometrica*, April 1937.

2. Reading the following items will reveal the heated nature of professional controversy concerning the proper scope of monetary policy.

   Edward S. Shaw, "Money Supply and Stable Economic Growth," in *United States Monetary Policy*, The American Assembly, 1959.

   Friedman and Meiselman, "The Relative Stability of Income Velocity and the Investment Multiplier," in Commission on Money and Credit, *Stabilization Policies*, Prentice-Hall, 1963.

   Albert Ando and Franco Modigliani, "The Relative Stability of Monetary Velocity and the Investment Multiplier," *American Economic Review*, September 1965.

   Nicholas Kaldor, "The New Monetarism," *Lloyd's Bank Review*, July 1970; also "Comment" by Milton Friedman and "Reply" by Kaldor in the October 1970 issue.

   William Poole, "Optimal Choice of Monetary Policy Instruments in a Simple Stochastic Macro Model," *Quarterly Journal of Economics*, May 1970.

   James Tobin, "Money and Income: Post Hoc Ergo Propter Hoc?," with a comment by Milton Friedman, in *Quarterly Journal of Economics*, May 1970.

KEY CONCEPTS

"crude" quantity theory

"Keynesian" theory

fiscal versus monetary policy

money market equilibrium

EXERCISES

8.1 Suppose that government spending is $G = 300$ and the money supply is $M_s = 1500$.

   a. You are to find the level of output and the rate of interest graphically, using the assumptions concerning the demand for money equation of Exercise 5.2 and the behavioral equations of Exercise 7.1. (*Hint.* Superimpose the *LM* curve of Exercise 5.2.c on the graph of the *IS* curve you obtained in Exercise 7.1.a.)

b. Suppose that government spending declines to $G = 250$. Show how this will change the IS curve, equilibrium output, and the interest rate. What happens to investment spending?

8.2 Suppose that the equation for the demand for money is $M_d = Y$, but the other equations are the same (i.e., they are those specified in Exercise 7.1). Draw the new LM curve for $M_s = 1500$ and explain what happens to C, Y, and I if government spending changes from 300 to 250.

8.3 Use the IS-LM apparatus to analyze the effect on aggregate output of a \$2 billion increase in government spending financed by a \$2 billion increase in tax revenue, assuming that the Fed keeps the money supply constant. (*Hint.* Consider Exercise 3.8.)

8.4 Explain any errors in the following statement: "enlarging the money supply will be more expansionary if (a) the marginal efficiency of investment schedule is elastic, (b) the marginal propensity to consume is small, (c) the volume of investment spending is sensitive to the level of economic activity as well as the rate of interest, (d) higher rates of interest lead to more saving at any given level of income, (e) the economy is in a liquidity trap."

balance of payments equilibrium and full employment

9.1 THE BALANCE OF PAYMENTS

Central bankers have to maintain the value of their country's currency in the foreign exchange market as well as worry about domestic economic conditions. On occasion monetary authorities have found themselves confronted with a very difficult choice in discharging these responsibilities. At the very time when economic recession suggests a low interest rate policy, balance of payments considerations may dictate that the central bank adopt a tight monetary policy in order to protect the currency. For example, when England was forced in 1931 to abandon the gold standard, the shock to confidence led to the withdrawal of considerable gold from the United States by speculators who thought that the dollar would be next to fall. Although the United States was suffering from widespread unemployment and experiencing an unprecedented wave of bank failures, the Federal Reserve System reverted to tight money. Motivated partly by fear that the Bank of France would withdraw large deposits that she held in the United States, the Federal Reserve System doubled the "rediscount rate" it charged on loans to member banks. The dollar was temporarily saved, but at a cost of additional bank failures and heightened unemployment.[1] And the United States' experience is not an isolated example, since at various times in the 1930s every major country, in the midst of widespread unemployment, was induced to raise interest rates and contract bank credit in order to preserve the gold price of its currency.

A nation's international trade transactions—exports and imports, foreign loans and investments, gifts, and foreign aid—are recorded on the

---

[1] For a discussion of this episode, see E. A. Goldenweiser, *American Monetary Policy*, McGraw-Hill, 1951. The loss of gold by the United States was around half a billion dollars; while this constituted only a small fraction of our $4 billion in gold reserves, most of the Federal Reserve System's holdings of gold were tied up as collateral; that is, the Fed was legally required to hold gold equal to 40% of her note issue plus 60% of her discounts and advances. The Glass-Steagall Act of 1932 relaxed these collateral requirements, thus permitting the Fed to pursue a looser monetary policy.

balance of payment's accounts. A deficit is revealed when a country's earnings from abroad fall short of requirements, so that resort must be made either to reserves (e.g., gold) or to special loans (e.g., borrowings from the International Monetary Fund or foreign governments and central banks).

Movements of the United States balance of payments over the last 50 years are summarized in Figure 9.1. As suggested by the chart, the precise dollar magnitude of the surplus or deficit depends on which accounting definitions are employed. But regardless of definition, the recent dollar crisis involves a deficit that drops off the bottom of the page. More detail concerning various factors entering into the balance of payments is provided by Table 9.1. In particular, the extreme right-hand column indicates that our gold reserves have dropped in half over the last quarter century. How this has come about is an involved story, but much of it is revealed by the table. Starting with the left-hand columns, observe that while the United States has customarily exported more than enough goods to pay for imports, this tradition has recently been violated because imports have risen more rapidly than exports. The earnings on funds Americans have invested overseas have been a positive factor helping to pay for imports. But in recent years we have been paying for substantial military expenses. When these factors, the expenditures of tourists, and various other items are taken into account, the net effect in 1972 was a $4,913 million deficit in the Balance on Goods and Services column. Capital movements must also be taken into account in evaluating the international position of the dollar since, when an American buys securities issued by a foreign government or purchases shares in an overseas corporation, he must convert his dollar into foreign currency; conversely, dollars are purchased by foreigners who decide to invest their funds in the United States. When these net capital movements are taken into account, the deficit is $13,093 million or $11,632

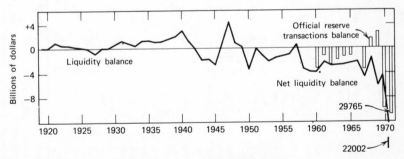

Fig. 9.1   *The United States Balance of Payments, 1920–1971.*
(Source. *Board of Governors, Federal Reserve System.*)

Table 9.1 THE UNITED STATES BALANCE OF PAYMENTS, 1946–1972 (MILLIONS OF DOLLARS)

Year	Merchandise[a,b]			Military Transactions			Net Investment Income		Net Travel and Transportation Expenditures	Other Services, Net	Balance on Goods and Services[a]	Remittances, Pensions, and Other Unilateral Transfers[a]	Balance on Current Account
	Exports	Imports	Net Balance	Direct Expenditures	Sales	Net Balance	Private[c]	U.S. Government					
1946	11,764	−5,067	6,697	−493	(h)	−493	750	6	733	114	7,807	−2,922	4,885
1947	16,097	−5,973	10,124	−455	(h)	−455	997	50	946	−45	11,617	−2,625	8,992
1948	13,265	−7,557	5,708	−799	(h)	−799	1,177	85	374	−27	6,518	−4,525	1,993
1949	12,213	−6,874	5,339	−621	(h)	−621	1,200	73	230	−3	6,218	−5,638	580
1950	10,203	−9,081	1,122	−576	(h)	−576	1,382	78	−120	6	1,892	−4,017	−2,125
1951	14,243	−11,176	3,067	−1,270	(h)	−1,270	1,569	151	298	2	3,817	−3,515	302
1952	13,419	−10,838	2,611	−2,054	(b)	−2,054	1,535	140	83	41	2,356	−2,531	−175
1953	12,412	−10,975	1,437	−2,615	192	−2,423	1,566	166	−238	24	532	−2,481	−1,949
1954	12,929	−10,353	2,576	−2,642	182	−2,460	1,899	213	−269	0	1,959	−2,280	−321
1955	14,424	−11,527	2,897	−2,901	200	−2,701	2,117	180	−297	−43	2,153	−2,498	−345
1956	17,556	−12,803	4,753	−2,949	161	−2,788	2,454	40	−361	47	4,145	−2,423	1,722
1957	19,552	−13,291	6,271	−3,216	375	−2,841	2,584	4	−189	72	5,901	−2,345	3,556
1958	16,414	−12,952	3,462	−3,465	300	−3,185	2,416	168	−633	78	2,356	−2,361	−5
1959	16,458	−15,310	1,148	−3,107	302	−2,805	2,658	68	−821	62	310	−2,448	−2,138
1960	19,650	−14,744	4,906	−3,087	335	−2,752	2,825	16	−964	77	4,107	−2,292	1,815
1961	20,107	−14,519	5,588	−2,998	402	−2,596	3,451	103	−978	30	5,599	−2,513	3,086
1962	20,779	−16,218	4,561	−3,105	656	−2,449	3,920	132	−1,155	115	5,126	−2,631	2,495
1963	22,252	−17,011	5,241	−2,961	657	−2,304	4,056	97	−1,312	178	5,957	−2,742	3,215
1964	25,478	−18,647	6,831	−2,830	747	−2,133	4,872	3	−1,149	142	8,568	−2,754	5,814
1965	26,438	−21,496	4,942	−2,952	830	−2,122	5,274	21	−1,318	301	7,098	−2,835	4,263
1966	29,287	−25,463	3,824	−3,764	829	−2,935	5,331	44	−1,380	286	5,170	−2,890	2,280
1967	30,638	−26,821	3,817	−4,378	1,240	−3,138	5,847	40	−1,763	334	5,136	−3,081	2,055
1968	33,576	−32,904	612	−4,535	1,392	−3,143	6,157	63	−1,565	302	2,425	−2,909	−484
1969	36,417	−35,796	621	−4,856	1,512	−3,344	5,820	155	−1,784	442	1,911	−2,946	−1,035
1970	41,963	−39,799	2,164	−4,852	1,478	−3,374	6,376	−115	−2,061	574	3,563	−3,208	356
1971	42,770	−45,459	−2,689	−4,816	1,922	−2,894	8,962	−967	−2,432	748	727	−3,574	−2,847
1972	47,391	−54,355	−6,964	−4,716	1,153	−3,563	9,211	−1,803	−2,589	795	−4,913	−3,737	−8,651

Source. Economic Report of the President.

a Excludes military grants.

b Adjusted from Census data for differences in timing and coverage.

c Includes fees and royalties from U.S. direct investments abroad or from foreign direct investments in the United States.

d Excludes liabilities to foreign official reserve agencies.

e Private foreigners exclude the International Monetary Fund (IMF), but include other international and regional organizations.

234

Table 9.1 *(continued)*

Year	Long-Term Capital Flows, Net — U.S. Government[d]	Long-Term Capital Flows, Net — Private[e]	Balance on Current Account and Long-Term Capital	Nonliquid Short-Term Private Capital Flows, Net	Allocations of Special Drawing Rights	Errors and Omissions, Net	Net Liquidity Balance	Liquid Private Capital Flows, Net[e]	Official Reserve Transactions Balance	Changes in Liabilities to Foreign Official Agencies, Net[f]	Changes in U.S. Official Reserve Assets, Net[g]	U.S. Official Reserve Assets, Net (End of Period)	Gold Stock
1946	—	—	—	-253	—	155	—	—	—	—	-623	20,706	20,706
1947	—	—	—	-236	—	861	—	—	—	—	-3,315	24,021	22,868
1948	—	—	—	-131	—	1,115	—	—	—	—	-1,736	25,758	24,699
1949	—	—	—	158	—	717	—	—	—	—	-266	26,024	24,563
1950	—	—	—	75	—	-124	—	—	—	—	1,752	24,265	22,820
1951	—	—	—	-227	—	354	—	—	—	—	-33	24,299	22,873
1952	—	—	—	-41	—	497	—	—	—	—	-419	24,714	23,252
1953	—	—	—	183	—	220	—	—	—	—	1,256	23,458	22,091
1954	—	—	—	-556	—	60	—	—	—	—	480	22,978	21,793
1955	—	—	—	-328	—	371	—	—	—	—	182	22,797	21,753
1956	—	—	—	-479	—	390	—	—	—	—	-869	23,666	22,058
1957	—	—	—	-174	—	1,012	—	—	—	—	-1,165	24,832	22,837
1958	—	—	—	-145	—	361	—	—	—	—	2,292	22,540	20,582
1959	—	—	—	-89	—	260	—	—	—	—	1,035	21,504	19,507
1960	-889	-2,100	-1,174	-1,405	—	-1,098	-3,676	273	-3,403	1,258	2,145	19,359	17,804
1961	-901	-2,181	4	-1,200	—	-1,064	-2,251	903	-1,348	742	606	18,753	16,947
1962	-892	-2,607	-1,003	-657	—	-1,206	-2,864	214	-2,650	1,117	1,533	17,220	16,057
1963	-1,150	-3,357	-1,292	-968	—	-456	-2,713	779	-1,934	1,557	377	16,843	15,596
1964	-1,349	-4,470	-4	-1,642	—	-1,048	-2,696	1,162	-1,534	1,363	171	16,672	15,471
1965	-1,532	-4,577	-1,846	-154	—	-476	-2,477	1,183	-1,289	67	1,222	15,450	13,966
1966	-1,469	-2,555	-1,744	-104	—	-302	-2,151	2,370	219	-787	568	14,882	13,235
1967	-2,424	-2,912	-3,280	-522	—	-881	-4,683	1,285	-3,418	3,366	52	14,830	12,065
1968	-2,159	1,198	-1,444	230	—	-399	-1,610	3,251	1,641	-761	-880	15,710	10,892
1969	-1,926	-50	-3,011	-640	—	-2,470	-6,122	8,824	2,702	-1,515	-1,187	16,964	11,859
1970	-2,018	-1,398	-3,059	-482	867	-1,174	-3,851	-5,988	-9,839	7,362	2,477	14,487	11,072
1971	-2,378	-4,079	-9,304	-2,386	717	-11,031	-22,002	-7,763	-29,765	27,417	2,348	12,167	10,206
1972	-959	-632	-10,243	-611	-710	-2,951	-13,093	1,461	-11,632	11,441	191	13,150	10,487

[f] Includes liabilities to foreign official agencies reported by U.S. Government and U.S. banks and U.S. liabilities to the IMF arising from reversible gold sales to, and gold deposits with, the United States.

[g] Official reserve assets include gold, special drawing rights, convertible currencies, and the U.S. gold tranche position in the IMF.

[h] Not available separately.

235

million, depending on whether one looks at the Net Liquidity Balance or the Official Reserve Transaction Balance. The accounting technicalities explaining the $1,461 million gap between these two alternative definitions of the deficit are not critical;[2] the important point is that the deficit has to be met either by running down reserves—gold, primarily—or by borrowing from foreign central banks and governments or the International Monetary Fund.

The deficit in the United States balance of payments persisted because the dollar was being supported at an artificially high price. Advocates of currency devaluation argue that the dollar should have been allowed to find its own value as dictated by the forces of supply and demand. A lower exchange rate will encourage exports, since foreigners will be able to buy United States goods at lower prices. And it will discourage imports, since foreign goods will cost Americans more. Furthermore, the increase in the foreign trade balance, $X - M$ in the GNP accounts, will stimulate the domestic economy. Of course, devaluation has its costs; the higher price of imports will obviously contribute to inflation. And, if the economy is already at full employment, the increase in $X - M$ may add a further contribution to rising prices. Obviously, monetary and fiscal policy are likely to need revision when a country revalues its currency.

Historically, in other countries no less than in the United States, governments have been reluctant to adjust the official value of their nation's currency even when confronted with sizable deficits in the balance of payments. Instead, a number of defensive strategies have been substituted for devaluation. Protective tariffs can be imposed in order to reduce imports; subsidies can be given to exporters to encourage them to ship more goods abroad; and in order to induce favorable capital movements, a tight monetary policy can be imposed. High interest rates will encourage investors to keep their funds at home instead of investing in foreign financial markets, and high interest rates encourage foreigners to place their funds in United States securities. Further assistance may be given to the balance of payments if high interest rates induce a cutback in the purchase of new plants and equipment, houses and inventory—the investment component of GNP. This will be beneficial to the domestic economy if inflation is a problem. But all too frequently an unfortunate side effect of adopting a tight money policy in order to protect the balance of payments has been a substantial rise in unemployment. A fundamental issue concerns the question of whether the two policy measures—monetary and fiscal policy—can be co-

[2] The precise magnitude of the deficit in the balance of payments depends on which accounting definition is employed. The question of how the deficit should be defined has been a subject of much discussion. See, for example, Richard N. Cooper, "The Balance of Payments in Review," *Journal of Political Economy*, August 1966.

ordinated in order to achieve simultaneously the twin objectives of full employment and equilibrium in the balance of payments.[3]

9.2 ANALYSIS

Suppressing certain accounting details, let us define the balance of payments as the excess of exports over the sum of imports plus capital outflows. Letting $BofP(Y, r)$ denote the balance of payments, we have

$$BofP(Y, r) = X - M(Y) + C(r) \qquad (2.1)$$

Here $C(r)$ indicates the dependence of foreign capital flows—international lending—on the rate of interest. Exports are exogenous, but imports are assumed to be an increasing function of the level of economic activity. Capital movements, denoted $C(r)$, hinge critically on the structure of interest rates. Given the level of interest rates in foreign countries, capital will tend to flow into the United States when interest rates are high, since foreign investments will be relatively less attractive. Conversely, capital will flow out of the United States when low interest rates at home make foreign investment opportunities relatively more attractive. If the rate of interest available domestically is higher than that which can be earned abroad, funds will tend to flow into our economy, helping our balance of payments. Thus we have $dC/dr > 0$, and we may write:

$$\frac{\partial BofP}{\partial r} > 0, \qquad \frac{\partial BofP}{\partial Y} < 0 \qquad (2.2)$$

That is, high interest rates tend to generate a surplus in the balance of payments by attracting foreign funds to the United States, but an increase in Y tends to generate a deficit, because it means that additional income is available for importing goods from abroad—the greater the marginal propensity to import (coefficient m_1, in Equation 7.1.1), the greater the tendency for the economy to generate a deficit in the balance of payments as it moves toward full employment.

---

[3] Conceptually a "control problem" may not admit a unique solution when there are more control instruments than "targets"—that is, there may be a variety of alternative mixes of interest rates, tax policy, and levels of government spending that will yield full employment—this involves only one target and three instruments. Conversely, there may be no solution if there are fewer instruments than targets; for example, if only the interest rate can be manipulated in an attempt to achieve full employment and balance of payments equilibrium simultaneously. But even if the level of government spending is constrained, possibly by military considerations, there will remain *two* instruments—tax policy and the interest rate—that can be manipulated in an effort to achieve *two* targets—full employment and balance of payments equilibrium.

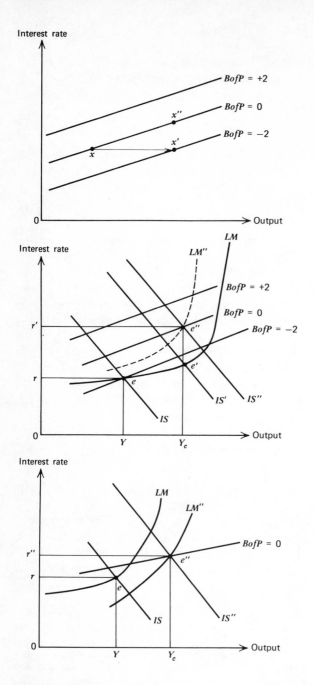

Fig. 9.2 *The balance of payments, full employment, and the rate of interest.*

In the top panel of Figure 9.2 a number of *BofP* curves have been plotted; every point on any given *BofP* curve yields the same figure for the balance of payments. Thus, curve *BofP* = 0 indicates those combinations of interest rates and GNP that yield equilibrium in the balance of payments. All combinations below this line lead to a deficit; in particular, the points on the line *BofP* = −2 yield a deficit of $2 billion. Similarly, points on the line *BofP* = 0 imply equilibrium; and the *BofP* = 2 line yields a surplus of $2 billion. In conformity with the inequalities of Equation 2.2, an increase in Y, given r, tends to generate a deficit; furthermore, an increase in r, given Y, will help to create a surplus. That these two offsetting effects explain why, as a matter of mathematical necessity, the balance of payments line must have a positive slope may be seen from the graph:[4] a rise in income moves us east, from x to x', and the deficit worsens but, if the rate of interest then rises, we move north toward x'' and the balance of payments improves; let point x'' mark the spot where these two effects exactly offset each other, so that it involves the same deficit as x; since it must obviously be northeast of x, the *BofP* line connecting x and x'' must have a positive slope.

Now suppose that the economy is initially at point e in the second panel of Figure 9.2; observe that we have a balance of payments deficit of −2 and a level of output of Y, well below the full employment GNP of Y_c. If steps are taken to shift the *IS* curve over to the right to *IS'*, by increasing government spending or cutting taxes, full employment would be achieved at point e', but at the expense of an increase in the balance of payments deficit. A different policy mix is required. Specifically, the interest rate must be raised to r'; this requires a cutback in the money supply in order to shift the *LM* curve to the left. This restrictive monetary policy must be coupled with a simultaneous application of more vigorous fiscal medicine, either a tax cut or increased government spending, in order to move the *IS* curve over to *IS''*. At equilibrium point e'' the full-employment level of GNP is achieved without a deficit in the balance of payments.

Several complications are involved in coordinating monetary and fiscal policy in a way that will reconcile balance of payments equilibrium with full employment. If the monetary adjustments required to move the *LM* curve to point e'' are not matched by an appropriate shift in the *IS* curve, we may end up northwest of e with a reduced balance of payments deficit

[4] Since

$$dBofP = \frac{\partial BofP}{\partial r}\, dr + \frac{\partial BofP}{\partial Y}\, dY$$

the fact that $dBofP = 0$ on any *BofP* line implies that its slope must be

$$\frac{dr}{dY} = -\frac{\partial BofP}{\partial Y} \Big/ \frac{\partial BofP}{\partial dr} > 0$$

but increased unemployment; or with excessive money we might find our-
selves at some point on the *IS* curve to the southeast of *e″* with a problem
of overfull employment and a payments deficit. The appropriate way in
which the money supply should be adjusted is not obvious. When a country
suffering from a balance of payments deficit and unemployment, as at
point *e*, has the *LM* curve indicated in the second panel of the graph, the
money supply must contract at the same time that the *IS* curve shifts to
the right as a result of expansionist fiscal measures. However, a different
situation is shown in the bottom panel of the graph; here the *LM* curve is
much steeper, because the demand for money is less sensitive to the rate of
interest and an expansion of the money supply is required to reconcile the
objective of full employment with equilibrium in the balance of payments.
The critical difference in the required direction of money supply adjustment
arises because the *LM* curve in the bottom panel is steeper than the *BofP* line,
so that it cuts above instead of below point *e″*. That is, as income rises, the
rate of interest goes up so fast, given the money supply, that the balance of
payments improves.

9.3   THEORY AND PRACTICE

In theory balance of payments considerations do not provide an insurmountable obstacle to the attainment of full employment. But, in practice, the appropriate mix of monetary and fiscal policy is too frequently not
achieved. For one thing, the pool of international capital responsive to
interest rates is not inexhaustible, and a country experiencing continued
deficits may have to raise its interest rates higher and higher if it is to continue to attract funds from abroad. But even in the short run serious difficulties arise, partly because of an incomplete understanding of the principles involved and partly because of political obstacles. The countries that
resorted to restrictive monetary policy in the 1930s in order to protect the
balance of payments should have applied a more expansionary fiscal policy
simultaneously. And it is unfortunate that the vicious competition for international reserves caused many countries to raise their interest rates simultaneously. Since it is the level of the domestic interest rate relative to those
prevailing in other countries that governs the flow of international capital,
the attempts to improve the balance of payments by resorting to tight money
largely cancelled out, while unemployment became more and more serious.
Let us consider certain other strategies for dealing with balance of payments
deficits.

a.   The Gold Standard

That the balance of payments might automatically tend to adjust itself
to equilibrium is a fascinating proposition that has intrigued economists

ever since David Hume (1711–1776) advanced his notion of a "self-equili-brating specie flow mechanism" in the eighteenth century. According to the theory of the gold standard, each central bank was supposed to follow specific "Rules of the Game"; a country experiencing a balance of pay-ments surplus should expand its money supply, and a country with a deficit should reduce the quantity of money in circulation. Indeed, this would tend to happen automatically, since the accumulation of gold in the surplus country would add to the reserves of the banking system; conversely, the banks in the country losing gold would find their reserves reduced. Accord-ing to Hume, prices would rise in the surplus country with an expanding money supply and fall in the deficit country in response to the contracting supply of money. The rising prices in the surplus country would make its exports less competitive on world markets and encourage imports. Con-versely, the fall in the deficit country's price level would make it easier to compete in world markets. Thus the price changes, induced by the gold movement, would tend to equilibrate the balance of payments auto-matically. This was the mechanism; but in practice it did not work in exactly that way.

Adherence to the gold standard did tend to correct the deficit in the balance of payments, but it turned out that the adjustment process in-volved changes in the level of employment more than changes in prices. Consider Figure 9.3, where the country is experiencing a deficit in the balance of payments. If the deficit leads to a decrease in the money supply the *LM* curve moves to the left. The rising interest rate helps meet the deficit directly by attracting an equilibrating flow of short-term capital from abroad. But it also reduces domestic investment spending, thus inducing a recession and a curtailment of imports. And, if the central bank continues to contract the money supply in response to the deficit in the balance of

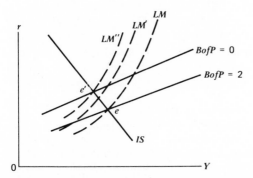

Fig. 9.3 *A self-correcting deficit. If the money supply con-tracts in response to the deficit, the shift in the* LM *curve will contribute to a rise in the interest rate, a reduction of income, and the elimination of the deficit, as at* e'.

payments, the LM curve will continue to shift until the deficit has been eliminated. Under the gold standard the central bank focused its attention on the balance of payments instead of on domestic economic conditions. However, adherence to the gold standard need not have precluded full employment, since at least in theory an appropriate mix of tax and spending policy might have moved the IS curve so that it would cross the $BofP = 0$ line at the capacity level of output.

b. Operation Twist

In the early 1960s political difficulties delaying the passage of the Kennedy Administration's tax cut meant that fiscal policy was not sufficiently expansive. An attempt was made through "Operation Twist" to make monetary policy do double duty. Short-term interest rates were allowed to rise, while long-term rates were kept stable. The effect was revealed in Figure 5.4, where we saw that from the middle of 1960 through 1965 the yield on three-month Treasury Bills rose steadily, while the return on long-term government bonds (maturing in 10 years or more) and corporate bonds remained stable.[5] Operation Twist was motivated by the theory that short-term interest rates are the relevant factor influencing international capital movements, while the long-term rate influences the contribution of domestic private investment spending to GNP. By preventing the long-term rate from rising, private investment spending would not be discouraged; by raising the short-term rate, the balance of payments would be improved. That the policy did not go far enough is clear, since high unemployment persisted while a variety of distorting restrictions were imposed in a further effort to buttress the value of the dollar.

c. Currency Devaluation

Devaluation of a country's currency tends to improve the balance of trade. By making foreign goods expensive, devaluation discourages imports; making goods shipped overseas less expensive on foreign markets encourages exports. A fall in the exchange rate is good news in Detroit, because it raises the price of imported cars and encourages foreigners to buy our product. Currency devaluation should lower the rate of interest required, at any given level of output, for balance of payments equilibrium.[6]

[5] Additional data on interest rates appear in Table 5.6.

[6] Exceptions are possible, since devaluation influences the terms of trade, and it is conceivable that devaluation will worsen the balance of payments. Thus, if German demand for United States goods is inelastic, the reduction in price brought about by devaluation of the dollar will lead to a reduction in the number of marks spent by Germans for United States exports—we will be exporting more goods for fewer marks. But even if foreign demand for American exports is inelastic, the United States balance of payments may still improve, given income, if devaluation leads to a sufficient cut in United States imports.

Thus the $BofP = 0$ line in Figure 9.4 shifts downward when the currency is devalued. The adjustment in the balance of trade also has a multiplier effect, shifting the IS curve to the right. This is obvious once one recalls that the equation for the IS curve is

$$Y = \left(\frac{1}{1 - c_1 d_1 - \delta k_1 + m_1}\right) [c_0 + c_1 d_0 + c_2 W_{t-1}$$
$$+ \delta(k_0 - k_2 r) + (d - \delta)K_{t-1} - m_0 + X + G] \quad (7.2.2)$$

Since currency devaluation both encourages exports and decreases imports (raises X and lowers m_0 and/or m_1), it tends to increase the level of effective demand generated at any specific interest rate. As the graph suggests, devaluing the country's currency can contribute to full employment and a surplus in the balance of payments; but the opposite effects are experienced by trading partners, who may retaliate.

The final effects of devaluation depend on what happens to the money supply and the price level. If the LM curve remains in the position indicated in Figure 9.4, the economy will simultaneously eliminate the balance of payments deficit and experience an increase in output as it moves to e_1. Provided the economy was not already operating close to full employment, the expansionary stimulus will be welcomed. But if the expansionary movement adds to inflationary pressure in an economy already experiencing full employment, the devaluating country may eventually find that its goods are once again priced out of the market. When a fully employed country

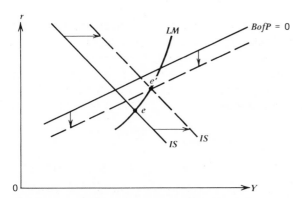

Fig. 9.4 *Currency devaluation. By stimulating exports and discouraging imports, currency devaluation shifts the* BofP *line downward. Simultaneously, the stimulus to exports causes an expansionary shift in the* IS *schedule. With the indicated* LM *curve the economy moves from* e *to* e', *the deficit being eliminated while output expands.*

devalues, it must simultaneously adopt contractionary monetary or fiscal measures if it is to avoid inflation.

During the Great Depression of the 1930s a chain reaction of currency devaluations was generated as country after country attempted to export its unemployment problems. But, if two countries devalue equally in terms of gold, the relative value of their currencies returns to the former ratio. Thus competitive devaluations offset each other. To insure that international financial markets would not be subject to the distortive effect of competitive rounds of currency devaluations after World War II, the Charter of the International Monetary Fund, drawn up at Bretton Woods in 1944, contained a rigid code of rules restricting each country's freedom to adjust the value of its currency. Unemployment was no excuse for devaluation. And a temporary deficit did not justify devaluation either. Only a country experiencing a "fundamental disequilibrium" in its balance of payments should devalue. And, when devaluation came, it was to be a drastic, once and for all adjustment.

d. Flexible Exchange Rates

Instead of pegging its currency to gold, why shouldn't the central bank allow the exchange rate to be freely determined by supply and demand? In the absence of government intervention and speculative currency movements the balance of payments would always be in equilibrium regardless of the level of output and the interest rate. That is, the foreign exchange rate would be free to adjust so that regardless of r:

$$BofP = X - M + C(r) = 0 \qquad (3.1)$$

How much the foreign exchange rate would have to fluctuate in order to preserve equilibrium in the balance of payments would depend on a variety of factors, including the elasticity of our demand for imports.

Condition 3.1 has implications for the IS curve, for we now have $C(r) = -(X - M)$; therefore we may derive the IS curve with $C(r)$ substituted for $X - M$. It turns out that Equation 7.2.2 must be replaced with

$$Y = \left(\frac{1}{1 - c_2 d_1 - \delta k_1} \right) [c_0 + c_1 d_0 + c_2 W_{t-1}$$
$$+ \delta(k_0 - k_2 r) + (d - \delta)K_{t-1} - C(r) + G] \qquad (3.2)$$

This revised equation deviates from the IS curve under pegged exchange rates (Equation 7.2.2)[7] in two critical respects. First, the multiplier is larger, because m_1 (the marginal propensity to import) no longer appears in its denominator. With fixed exchange rates part of the multiplier effect of an expansionary policy leaks abroad in the form of increased imports.

---

[7] The old IS curve is reproduced in part c of this section.

With floating exchange rates the tendency to import more will cause the value of our currency to fall so that the balance of payments will remain in equilibrium; this depreciation stimulates exports and retards imports so as to contribute to effective demand. In addition to a larger multiplier, flexible exchange rates also make the *IS* curve flatter; that is, effective demand is more sensitive to the rate of interest. With flexible exchange rates a rise in the rate of interest not only chokes off domestic investment spending on new plants and equipment; it also attracts foreign capital from abroad. The inflow of foreign capital involves an increased demand for the dollar, causing it to appreciate in value, discouraging exports and encouraging imports. The fall in $(X - M)$ depresses effective demand.

How fiscal policy works under flexible exchange rates is illustrated in Figure 9.5. A solid *IS* curve is plotted from Equation 3.2; for comparison purposes a steeper dotted *IS* curve reflecting the alternative situation of fixed exchange rates also appears on the graph. A rise in government spending, which has a relatively large multiplier under flexible exchange rates, generates the *IS'* curve and an expansion in output from *e* to *e'*. Since the fall in the value of the dollar has kept the tendency toward boom from being dissipated abroad in rising imports, the expansionary effect is stronger than with fixed exchange rates.

Things need not work out in exactly this way, however. If the demand for money had been much less sensitive to the rate of interest the *LM* curve

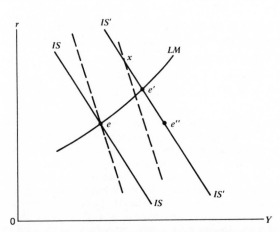

Fig. 9.5 *The multiplier process with flexible exchange rates. An increase in government spending shifts the* IS *curve to* IS', *leading to equilibrium at* e'. *The dotted lines indicate that with fixed exchange rate the* IS *curve is steeper and the multiplier is smaller.*

would have been more nearly vertical. If it should rise above intersection point x the expansion in output resulting from the increase in government spending would have been smaller with flexible than with fixed exchange rates. In this case the rise in interest rates would be sharp enough to induce such an inflow of capital as to more than offset the rise in imports generated at higher output levels. That is, the currency would appreciate.

The effects of an expansionary policy work out more forcefully if the monetary authorities are unwilling or unable to tolerate the continued movements of international capital that occur when $C(r) \neq 0$. If the money supply, instead of being exogenous, continually adjusts so as to stabilize the interest rate the LM curve must shift so that the full multiplier effect of changes in fiscal policy will be realized at point e'' in Figure 9.5. But the uninhibited tendency for imports to rise with income means that an increase in government spending will necessarily cause a fall in the exchange rate.

Critics of floating exchange rates express concern for the inconvenience and uncertainty imposed on traders and tourists when the exchange rate is not pegged at a specific value; proponents of flexible rates reply that in other markets buyers and sellers experience day-to-day fluctuations in price in return for the benefits of economic efficiency; furthermore, the uncertainty can be minimized through the operation of forward markets in foreign exchange.[8] It has also objected that wide swings in the exchange rate might be generated by speculators; but the proponents of flexible exchange rates argue that speculators play a constructive stabilizing role, because their profits depend on buying when the price is low and selling when it is high.[9]

The debate continues, but several steps in the direction of freer exchange rates have been effected. The International Monetary Fund, established at the end of World War II, had prescribed that each member country must preserve its currency within 1% of par value, the par value itself being subject to adjustment only when it was established that the country

[8] For example, on July 26, 1973, the price of the German mark closed at 42.78¢, up from 31.48 ¾¢ a year earlier; these are spot prices quoted for immediate delivery. But on the same date that the spot price was determined by supply and demand to be 42.78¢, the price for marks to be delivered 90 days hence was determined by the free market to be 43.13¢. Thus someone planning a trip to Germany could avoid uncertainty by purchasing marks for delivery three months hence at a price determined in the marketplace today. Of course, an alternative way of obtaining certainty is to simply buy the marks today and hold them for three months, but this would involve foregone interest earning. Prices of the pound sterling and other major currencies for delivery three months hence have been quoted in the financial press for generations. In 1972 the International Monetary Market was established by the Chicago Mercantile Exchange to facilitate forward trading in a wider variety of foreign currencies.

[9] But Michael Farrell argues that this need not be so in "Profitable Speculation," *Economica*, May 1966.

was suffering from a "fundamental disequilibrium" in the balance of payments; short-run imbalances were to be met by borrowing from other countries or from the International Monetary Fund itself. Late in 1971 the major industrial countries of the world, concurrently with a realignment of exchange rates, agreed to widen the spread to $2\frac{1}{4}\%$ above or below parity, thus allowing a wider band within which the rate would be free to fluctuate. A more far-reaching proposal would have announced a creeping exchange rate that would be allowed to change gradually by a certain percentage each year. The creeping rate, a compromise between the old rigidities under the International Monetary Fund and freely floating flexible exchange rates, would avoid wide swings while allowing the exchange rate to gradually move upward or downward in response to market forces. Perhaps the adoption of such a scheme would have protected the dollar from the succession of devaluations experienced in the early 1970s. By early 1973 the system of rigid exchange rates had become untenable, and official foreign exchange markets were temporarily closed in the face of widespread speculation against the dollar. Subsequently, the dollar was freed, its value being allowed to "float" in the market place, but subject to official central bank intervention.

REFERENCES

Robert A. Mundell, "Capital Mobility and Stabilization Policy Under Fixed and Flexible Exchange Rates," *Canadian Journal of Economics and Political Science*, November 1963.

Milton Friedman, "The Case for Flexible Exchange Rates," reprinted from *Essays in Positive Economics*, University of Chicago Press, 1953, in *Readings in International Economics*, Richard Caves and H. G. Johnson, eds., Irwin, 1968.

Sidney S. Alexander, "Effects of Devaluation on a Trade Balance," *IMF Staff Papers*, April 1952.

KEY CONCEPTS

balance of payments equilibrium

exchange rate

currency devaluation

BofP(Y,r) line

gold standard

International Monetary Fund (IMF)

operation twist

forward markets

international capital movements versus *I*

EXERCISES

9.1 Indicate how each of the following items contributes to the United States balance of payments by placing a plus $(+)$ in front of items that make a positive contribution and a minus $(-)$ in front of items that contribute to the deficit.

  $+$ exports

  $-$ imports

    overseas military expenditures

    sale of fighter planes to Argentina

    travel by Americans in Spain

    purchase of United States government bonds by a German citizen

    dividends earned by an American on Swiss corporate stock

    purchase of shares in Texas Gulf by Canada Development Corporation

9.2 Suppose that a central bank, in accordance with the gold standard, contracts the money supply whenever it loses gold; conversely, when gold flows in from foreign countries, it expands the money supply. Explain, using the *IS-LM* apparatus, how this policy can help to equilibrate the balance of payments.

9.3 Show, using the *IS-LM* apparatus, the precise circumstances in which an increase in government spending, given the money supply, can lead simultaneously to an increase in output and an improvement in the balance of payments.

CHAPTER 10
on monetary policy

*10.1 THE LENDER OF LAST RESORT

A central bank is the bankers' bank: among other services the central bank's customers are provided with a ready source of credit, a depository for funds, and facilities for the interbank clearing of checks. But, in the course of providing a variety of banking services, it also serves as a regulator of credit markets and the money supply. A central bank may have gradually assumed its responsibilities through a process of evolution. For example, the Bank of England was established by Parliament in 1694, but not as a central bank. Instead, her special charter specified that she was to loan a substantial sum to the financially embarrassed crown; in return, she was granted a virtual monopoly on the issue of notes, and her owners received the protection of limited liability. Initially, the Bank of England was not too secure and, during episodes of general financial panic, holders of her notes, doubting her ability to survive, rushed to convert their holdings into gold. But, by the middle of the eighteenth century, the Bank of England had established a reputation for safety that enabled her to serve as "lender of last resort," the first step in becoming a central bank. Thus, in the financial crisis of 1763, she was actively lending funds to financial houses that were in difficulty. The "lender of last resort" fights fires in times of crisis and may earn a healthy financial return by charging a penalty interest rate for accommodation. But at a higher stage of evolution a central bank assumes preventive responsibilities. A central bank should manage its financial affairs with an eye to the task of preventing crises, even when this means a sacrifice of opportunities for commercial profit. More than a century before her nationalization in 1946, the "Old Lady of Threadneedle Street" had assumed the responsibility of serving as England's central bank.[1]

The act creating the Federal Reserve System, signed into law by Woodrow Wilson in December 1913, was hardly the product of inspiration

---

[1] For a discussion of early banking history in England, see John Clapham, *The Bank of England, A History*, Macmillan, 1945; R. G. Hawtrey, *The Art of Central Banking*, Longman Green, 1932; and M. C. Lovell, "The Role of the Bank of England as Lender of Lest Resort in the Crises of the Eighteenth Century," *Explorations in Entrepreneurial History*, October 1957.

guided by the successes and failures of the distinguished central banks of Europe. Quite the contrary, the many contradictory features of the Federal Reserve Act reveal it as the product of acrimonious debate and legislative compromise. The chaotic failure of a host of banks in the Panic of 1907 had provided the impetus for legislative reform. Many could agree that the United States had existed for too long without a central bank, but the architects could not agree on the form the edifice should take. The Aldrich Commission's plan to create a National Reserve Association to serve as the central bank was rejected in favor of a federated system. Congress attempted to insure against domination by banking interests through a number of provisions, in particular the requirement that half of the directors of each regional bank, instead of being experienced bankers, were to be representatives of business, industry, and agriculture—but throughout most of its history neither the regional banks nor their directors have played the decisive role anticipated for them. The system of 12 regional central banks specified in the final compromise served to allay the fears of those who worried that a single bank would inevitably fall under the influence of eastern financial interests—but, in practice, the extreme fluidity of money markets enabled the New York Federal Reserve Bank to dominate the system during the 1920s under the decisive leadership of Governor Benjamin Strong.

The compromise establishing the Fed provided for an "elastic currency" whose supply would respond in semiautomatic fashion to the public's desire for liquidity. In practice the ability of the Federal Reserve Banks to fulfill their responsibilities was severely limited by stringent requirements for gold reserves backing their note issue and deposit liabilities. And, with the onset of the Great Depression, bank failures became epidemic. When Roosevelt took office, some 8000 banks were insolvent. The wave of bank failures forced immediate action.

On March 6, 1933, the newly inaugurated President of the United States issued the following proclamation.

". . . I, Franklin D. Roosevelt, President of the United States of America . . . do hereby proclaim . . . that . . . there shall be maintained and observed . . . a bank holiday, and that all banking transactions shall be suspended. During such holiday . . . no . . . banking institution . . . shall pay out, export, earmark, or permit the withdrawal of transfer in any manner or by any device whatsoever, of any gold or silver coin or bullion or currency; nor shall any such banking institution or branch pay out deposits, make loans or discounts, deal in foreign exchange, transfer credits from the United States to any place abroad. or transact any other banking business whatsoever. . . ."

This drastic step was *not* authorized by the Federal Reserve Act of 1913; the only legal authority for the bank holiday was provided through a liberal interpretation of wartime powers under Trading with the Enemy legislation. But, if the country was not at war, it was nonetheless in peril. The depression-bred decline in business meant that many borrowers were unable to meet their obligations to the banks. When the banks foreclosed on delinquent loans, they found that the assets pledged with them as collateral were often inadequate because of precipitous declines in security prices and real-estate values. When concerned depositors attempted simultaneously to withdraw their funds in cash, many banks were unable to honor their requests. Their demand deposits were no longer money.

A hastily called Congress passed emergency banking laws; banks began to reopen within a week; with the public's confidence restored, currency flowed back into the banks. In part the legislation strengthened the powers of the Federal Reserve System to make loans to member banks in accordance with its responsibilities as lender of last resort. But the most important step was the establishment of the Federal Deposit Insurance Corporation. Since 1933 depositors have not had to fear bank insolvency, because their deposits are insured by an agency of the United States Government.[2] The banks are now subject to regulation and inspection by the Federal Deposit Insurance Corporation. When, as still happens on occasion, a bank does fail, its depositors are guaranteed prompt access to their funds. Bank panics, which for centuries had rocked the financial centers of the world with distressing frequency, were abolished. While the average citizen may at times worry about the international solvency of the dollar and the evaporation of its purchasing power through inflation, bank failures are no longer a serious concern. While the Federal Reserve System still exercises supervisory powers over the banking practices of member banks, the major thrust of monetary policy concerns the general economic health of the nation instead of the solvency of the banking system.

*10.2 RESERVE REQUIREMENTS, THE DISCOUNT RATE, AND OPEN MARKET OPERATIONS

The invention of fractional reserve banking anticipated the industrial revolution. In the absence of panic, cash on reserve to meet day-to-day withdrawals need be only a fraction of total deposits. Banking is profitable because it is possible for each banker to loan out at interest all but a fraction of funds placed on deposit. Since cash reserves earn no interest, holding them involves a sacrifice by the bank of interest income and, in the absence of regulation, the size of reserves would be determined by a desire

---

[2] Initially the insurance covered only the first $5000 in each account; the ceiling has now been raised to $20,000.

to balance the urge for the profit to be gained by loaning out deposited funds against the desire for a prudent allowance for safety as prescribed by the customs of sound banking.

Today the Federal Reserve System prescribes a minimum level of reserves that each member bank must hold; each nonmember bank is subject to the regulations prescribed by the state issuing its charter. No longer do reserves function primarily as protection for deposits. Instead, the reserves of the banking system provide the fulcrum by which the Federal Reserve System influences the nation's monetary climate. As Table 10.1 indicates, less than half of the commercial banks in the country belong to the Federal Reserve System; but the member banks dominate the system; they are larger on the average and account for over 80% of all demand deposits.

The legal reserves of each member bank are defined as the sum of currency and coin in vault plus the demand deposits it has on account at the Fed; let R denote this sum, which constitutes an asset on the member bank's balance sheet. The member banks are required to hold reserves proportional to deposits.

$$R_r = \rho_d DD + \rho_t TD \tag{2.1}$$

Table 10.1   THE BANKING SYSTEM

December 31, 1969

			Deposits (in Millions of Dollars)				
			Interbank		U.S. Govern-	Other Demand	
Type of Bank	Number of Banks	Total	Demand	Time	ment	Other	Time
1969 Federal Reserve member banks							
Reserve city	178	201,876	21,689	525	2,443	101,820	74,399
Country banks	5,691	148,007	3,152	84	1,671	67,930	75,170
All member banks	5,869	349,883	24,841	609	4,114	169,750	149,569
Nonmember banks	7,792	85,949	1,333	126	940	39,120	44,430
All commercial banks	13,661	435,577	27,174	735	5,054	208,870	193,744
All commercial banks							
December 31, 1941	14,278	71,283	–10,982–		–44,349–		15,952
December 31, 1947	14,181	144,103	12,792	240	1,343	94,367	35,360
December 31, 1966	13,767	352,287	19,770	967	4,992	167,751	158,806
December 31, 1972	13,927	616,037	33,854	4,194	10,875	252,223	314,891

Source. Federal Reserve Bulletin.

Here R_r denotes required reserves, DD is demand deposits, and TD is time deposits. Required reserve ratios ρ_d and ρ_t denote the proportion of reserves that each member bank must hold behind its demand deposits and time deposits, respectively. For example, if the Fed prescribes $\rho_d = 15\%$ and $\rho_t = 5\%$, a commercial bank with \$40 million of demand deposits and \$60 million of time deposits must have legal reserves of at least

$$R_r = \$9 \text{ million} = 15\% \times \$40 \text{ million} + 5\% \times 60 \text{ million}$$

Data on the behavior of required reserves are reported in Table 10.2. As indicated in the table, the member banks are free to accumulate excess reserves; let R_e denote this surplus.

$$R_e = R - R_r \tag{2.2}$$

For example, we see in Table 10.2 that all the member banks combined had excess reserves of \$200 million at the end of 1972. This was the excess of \$31,351 million in reserves—deposits at the Fed plus cash in vault—over the required reserves of \$31,151 million. Obviously, a member bank can avoid a reserve deficiency only if

$$R \geq R_r = \rho_d DD + \rho_t TD \tag{2.3}$$

The Federal Reserve system has authority to vary the magnitude of the coefficients within a range prescribed by Congress. As Table 10.3 reveals larger banks are customarily required to keep a larger proportion of reserves than "country banks." Member banks must adjust their activities so as to keep their reserves from falling below the required level.[3]

There are three powerful techniques by which the Federal Reserve System influences member bank behavior. The Fed can curb the banking system's power to lend funds and create demand deposits by raising ρ_d and ρ_t, since this increases the reserves that the member banks need to support their demand and time deposits. As Equation 2.3 indicates, raising the reserve coefficients, given R, places a squeeze on excess reserves. While this is a powerful technique, changes in the required reserve ratios are made infrequently. Much more important are two other methods by which the Fed influences R, the aggregate reserves of the banking system. Member banks can borrow from the central bank—after all, the central bank is the "banker's bank." By raising the "discount rate," the rate of interest charged the member banks for borrowed funds, the Fed can discourage member

---

[3] Although this requirement need not be satisfied on a day-to-day basis, it must be met on the average over a two-week period for country banks and over a shorter period for reserve city banks; otherwise, the bank allowing a reserve deficiency to develop is subject to fine.

Table 10.2   FEDERAL RESERVE BANK CREDIT AND MEMBER BANK RESERVES (AVERAGES OF DAILY FIGURES, MILLIONS OF DOLLARS)

| Year and Month | Reserve Bank Credit Outstanding | | | | Member Bank Reserves[a] | | | Member Bank Free Reserves (Excess Reserves Less Borrowings) |
	Total	U.S. Government Securities	Member Bank Borrowings	All Other, Mainly Float	Total	Required	Excess	
1929: December	1,643	446	801	396	2,395	2,347	48	−753
1930: December	1,273	644	337	292	2,415	2,342	73	−264
1931: December	1,950	777	763	410	2,069	2,010	60	−703
1932: December	2,192	1,854	281	57	2,435	1,909	526	245
1933: December	2,669	2,432	95	142	2,588	1,822	766	671
1934: December	2,472	2,430	10	32	4,037	2,290	1,748	1,738
1935: December	2,494	2,430	6	58	5,716	2,733	2,933	2,977
1936: December	2,498	2,434	7	57	6,665	4,619	2,046	2,039
1937: December	2,628	2,565	16	47	6,879	5,808	1,071	1,055
1938: December	2,618	2,564	7	47	8,745	5,520	3,226	3,219
1939: December	2,612	2,510	3	99	11,473	6,462	5,011	5,008
1940: December	2,305	2,188	3	114	14,049	7,403	6,646	6,643
1941: December	2,404	2,219	5	180	12,812	9,422	3,390	3,385
1942: December	6,035	5,549	4	482	13,152	10,776	2,376	2,372
1943: December	11,914	11,166	90	658	12,749	11,701	1,048	958
1944: December	19,612	18,693	265	654	14,188	12,834	1,234	1,019
1945: December	24,744	23,708	334	702	15,027	14,536	1,491	1,157
1946: December	24,746	23,767	157	822	16,517	15,617	900	743
1947: December	22,858	21,905	224	729	17,261	16,275	986	762
1948: December	23,978	23,002	134	842	19,990	19,193	797	663
1949: December	19,012	18,287	118	607	16,291	15,488	803	685
1950: December	21,606	20,345	142	1,119	17,391	16,364	1,027	885
1951: December	25,446	23,409	657	1,380	20,310	19,484	826	169
1952: December	27,299	24,400	1,593	1,306	21,180	20,457	723	−870
1953: December	27,107	25,639	441	1,027	19,920	19,227	693	252
1954: December	26,317	24,917	246	1,154	19,279	18,576	703	457
1955: December	26,853	24,602	839	1,412	19,240	18,646	594	−245
1956: December	27,156	24,765	688	1,703	19,535	18,883	652	−36
1957: December	26,186	23,982	710	1,494	19,420	18,843	577	−133
1958: December	28,412	26,312	557	1,543	18,899	18,383	515	−41
1959: December	29,435	27,036	906	1,493	18,932	18,450	482	−424
1960: December	29,060	27,248	87	1,725	19,283	18,527	756	669
1961: December	31,217	29,098	149	1,970	20,118	19,550	568	419
1962: December	33,218	30,546	304	2,368	20,040	19,468	572	268
1963: December	36,610	33,729	327	2,554	20,746	20,210	536	209
1964: December	39,873	37,126	243	2,504	21,609	21,198	411	168
1965: December	43,853	40,885	454	2,514	22,719	22,267	452	−2
1966: December	46,864	43,760	557	2,547	23,830	23,438	392	−165
1967: December	51,268	48,891	238	2,139	25,260	24,915	345	107
1968: December	56,610	52,529	765	3,316	27,221	26,766	455	−310
1969: December	64,100	57,500	1,086	5,514	28,031	27,774	257	−829
1970: December	66,708	61,688	321	4,699	29,265	28,993	272	−49
1971: December	74,255	69,158	107	4,990	31,329	31,164	165	58
1972: December	76,845	71,094	1,050	4,701	31,351	31,151	200	−850

Source. Economic Report of the President.

a Beginning December 1959 total reserves held include vault cash.

255

Table 10.3   REQUIRED RESERVE RATIOS

	Demand[a]	Savings[b]
Legal limits set by Congress		
Reserve city banks[c]	$10\% \leq \rho_d \leq 22\%$	$3\% \leq \rho_t \leq 14\%$
Country banks	$7\% \leq \rho_d \leq 14\%$	$3\% \leq \rho_t \leq 10\%$
Required ratio, June 30, 1974[d]		
Volume of demand deposits		
0–$2 million	8.0%	3%
$2–$10 million	10.5	3
$10–$100 million	12.5	3
$100–$400 million	13.5	3
over $400 million	18	3

Source. Federal Reserve Bulletin.

[a] Demand deposits subject to reserve requirements are gross demand deposits minus cash items in process of collection and demand balances due from domestic banks.

[b] Time deposits, other than savings, of over $5 million are subject to a 5% reserve requirement.

[c] The criterion for classifying commercial banks as reserve city banks has changed from time to time. Currently, banks with demand deposits of more than $400 million are classified as reserve city banks.

[d] The graduated requirement schedule is progressive, and the table reveals the marginal ratio applicable to successive increments of deposits. Thus a bank with $5 million of demand deposits must keep reserves of $475,000. (0.08 × 2 = $160,000 behind the first $2 million of deposits and an additional 0.105 × $3 = $315,000 behind the remaining $3 million of deposits.)

bank borrowing, thus limiting R. Raising the discount rate also has an "announcement effect," because it constitutes a signal to the stock market and the business community that the Fed is tightening up. Conversely, lowering the discount rate indicates that the Fed is relaxing its constraints and that credit is becoming easier to obtain. Although it was anticipated in drafting the Federal Reserve Act that variations in the discount rate would be the major source of control, it has turned out that "open market operations" are much more decisive: when the Fed buys government securities on the open market it adds reserves to the banking system; when it sells securities, it reduces R. The way in which member bank borrowing and the Fed's holdings of government securities have fluctuated over the years is indicated in Table 10.2. But a deeper understanding of how these techniques work requires a survey of how a variety of financial transactions influence the balance sheets of the member banks.

10.3 BANK TRANSACTIONS AND RESERVE POSTURE

The reserves of each commercial bank are determined largely by the skill with which it competes for deposits and the decisions it makes concerning the extension of loans and the purchase of securities. But the competition for deposits is constrained by the central bank, because it controls the environment within which the member banks operate. The way in which a variety of transactions affect a member bank's balance sheet must be considered so that it will be possible to appreciate how the Federal Reserve System influences the behavior of the banking system.

a. Loans

There are many ways in which a bank finding itself with excess reserves can put them to work. One possibility is to loan funds to its customers. The *T-account* reveals how the balance sheet of a hypothetical bank would change when a $10,000 loan is extended to a local manufacturer.

T-Account: First Hypothetical Bank of Middletown

(Changes in assets)	(Changes in liabilities and net worth)
Δ Loans outstanding +$10,000	Δ Demand Deposits +$10,000

(a1)

The manufacturer now has a $10,000 obligation to the bank, an increase in his liabilities. However, the customer's obligation is an *asset* for the bank; therefore, it appears on the left-hand side of the bank's T-account in accordance with standard accounting practice. Note that the customer has received the loan in the form of an increase in his checking account deposit, a liability of the bank that must be entered on the right-hand side of the T-account. Observe that the T-account reports only these two *changes* in the bank's balance sheet; items that are unchanged on the balance sheet are suppressed. Since assets always equal the sum of liabilities plus net worth, a bookkeeping error would be indicated if the two sides of the T-account did not sum to the same figure. But, in addition to this bookkeeping requirement, there are certain restrictions that must be satisfied when the bank extends a loan. For one thing, the bank must have adequate assurance concerning the security of the loan. But the essential point is that the increase in demand deposits of $10,000 means that the bank's required reserves have gone up by $\rho_d \times \$10,000$; for example, if the bank is required to keep reserves equal to 15%, required reserves will have gone up by $1500 as a result of the bank's decision to extend credit to its customer.

b. Check Clearing

It is not likely that a bank's customer would borrow $10,000 in order to leave the funds idle in his checking account. How will the accountant's books be affected if the borrowing manufacturer writes a $10,000 check to pay a bill to its Boston supplier? Suppose the supplier deposits the check in his checking account at the Second Boston Hypothetical Bank. Obviously, that bank does not desire simply to hold the check; instead, it may clear it through the Federal Reserve System. Specifically, the Boston Bank presents the check to the Fed, which "pays" for it by adding $10,000 to the amount of the Boston bank's deposit at the Fed. The Fed forwards the check to the First Hypothetical Bank of Middletown, deducting $10,000 from that bank's deposits. Finally, the Middletown bank deducts the $10,000 from its customer's account. How the balance sheets of the three financial institutions are affected by the check-clearing process is summarized in the following three T-accounts.

First Hypothetical Bank of Middletown

Δ Deposit at the Fed	− $10,000	Δ Demand deposits	− $10,000

(b1)

Second Boston Hypothetical Bank and Trust Co.

Δ Deposits at the Fed	+ $10,000	Δ Demand deposits	+ $10,000

(b2)

Federal Reserve Bank

	Member bank deposits	
	First Hypothetical Bank of Middletown	− $10,000
	Second Hypothetical Bank of Boston	+ $10,000

(b3)

As the T-accounts indicate, the check-clearing process has served to increase both the reserve assets and the demand deposit liabilities of the bank in which the check is deposited; it has had the opposite effect on the bank on which the check was drawn. And, again, inspection of the three T-accounts reveals that the sum of the changes in assets equals the sum of the changes in liabilities. The reserves of the bank receiving the deposit are up by the full $10,000; its required reserves increase by $\rho_d \times \$10,000 =$ $1500. Conversely, the bank on which the check is drawn has a $10,000 decline in its reserves. While the Middletown Bank has experienced a reserve drain, the Boston bank is likely to find itself with a reserve surplus.

But, for the entire banking system, there has been no change as a result of the check-clearing process in either reserve requirements or the funds available to meet them.[4]

To recapitulate, consider the combined effect of the decision to make the loan (step a) plus the resultant check-clearing process when the borrowed funds are spent (step b). The lending bank has had an increase in loans outstanding offset by an equal reduction in its deposit at the Fed. Furthermore, the Boston bank has experienced an increase in its reserve deposits at the Fed that just equals its increased liabilities to depositors. If the Middletown bank initially had excess reserves of $10,000, it is now "loaned up," but it has converted idle funds into an interest earning asset. However, the Boston bank has an increase of $10,000 in both its demand deposits and its reserves on deposit at the Fed. Since required reserves have gone up by only $\rho_d \times \$10,000 = \$1500$, it has increased its required reserves by less than the increase in its reserve capacity. If it was initially loaned up, it now has excess reserves, and it may decide to lend them out.

c. Currency Drain

At certain times of the year, particularly near Christmas, the banking system experiences an increased desire on the part of the public for currency. Suppose that a customer of the Second Boston Hypothetical Bank desires to convert part of his demand deposit, say $500, into cash. The effect of the withdrawal, revealed on the T-account, is to reduce the currency in the bank's vault and its demand deposit liability by $500.

Second Boston Hypothetical Bank and Trust Co.

Δ Cash in vault	− $500	Δ Demand deposits	− $500

(c1)

The money supply is unchanged, but the bank's reserves are reduced by $500. The bank could replenish its vault holdings of cash from the Fed, paying for them with a reduction in the magnitude of its Fed deposit. But regardless of whether it chooses to replenish its cash holdings or not, the bank's required reserves have fallen only by $\rho_d \times \$500 = \$75$, while its reserves have fallen by $500; thus the net effect is a $425 reduction in excess reserves—and, if reserves were not initially in excess, the bank is now faced with a reserve deficiency.

---

[4] Checks do not have to clear through the Federal Reserve System; if the Middletown Bank had a deposit with the Boston bank the transaction might be handled directly. And even when there is no direct correspondent relationship between two banks, checks may be cleared through a private "clearinghouse" created by an association of banks in the same geographical area instead of through the Fed.

d. Federal Funds Market

Banks can borrow from each other. Instead of lending out surplus funds to its own customers, the First Hypothetical Bank of Middletown may arrange to loan funds to another bank. The loans are customarily made in the Federal Funds Market on a daily basis. The potential borrower is identified through the efforts of a middleman broker who makes the Federal Funds Market, usually Garvin, Bantel and Co. of New York City. The rate of interest is the market clearing rate determined by the interacting forces of supply and demand; it is published daily in major newspapers. The transfer of funds is executed as a courtesy to the banking community by the Federal Reserve System. The effect on the balance sheets is illustrated in the following T-accounts.

Hypothetical Bank of Middletown

Δ Deposits at the Fed	$-\$100,000$		
Loans outstanding			
Δ Hypothetical Bank of California	$+\$100,000$		

(d1)

Hypothetical Bank of California

Δ Deposits at the Fed	$+\$100,000$	Accounts payable	
		Δ Hypothetical Bank of Middletown	$+\$100,000$

(d2)

The transaction in the Federal Funds Market has served to transfer surplus reserves from one bank to another; it has not affected either the money supply or the total reserves of the banking system.

e. Buying Government Securities

Suppose that the bank buys a $100,000 bond issued by the federal government, and that the federal government places the funds it receives in an account at the Federal Reserve Bank.

Hypothetical Bank of Middletown

Δ Deposit at the Fed	$-\$100,000$		
Δ Government securities	$+\$100,000$		

(e1)

And at the Fed the balance sheet changes as follows.

Federal Reserve Bank

	Member bank deposits	
	Δ Hypothetical Bank of Middletown	−$100,000
	Δ U.S. government deposits	+$100,000

(e2)

If, instead, the bonds had been bought by a customer of the bank, possibly an insurance firm or a rich citizen, the bank's balance sheet would have changed as follows:

Hypothetical Bank of Middletown

Δ Deposit at the Fed	−$100,000	Δ Demand deposits	−$100,000

(e3)

Instead of having an increase in government securities (an asset) to offset the reduction in reserves, the bank experiences a decrease in its demand deposits. Either way, the bond purchase has reduced the reserves of the banking system but, in the latter case, there has been a reduction in the money supply.

f. Government Expenditures

What happens when the federal government uses deposits at the Fed to pay for items it purchases from the public? Suppose that the recipient of a $100,000 government check deposits it in his checking account and that his bank, in turn, gains a deposit at the Fed. The net result on the balance sheet of the commercial bank is an increase in both reserves and demand deposits.

Hypothetical Bank of Middletown

Δ Deposits at Fed	+$100,000	Δ Demand deposits	+$100,000

(f1)

And at the Fed:

Federal Reserve Bank

	Δ U.S. Government deposits	−$100,000
	Member bank deposits	
	Δ Hypothetical Bank of Middletown	+$100,000

(f2)

Because demand deposits are up, the bank's required reserves have increased, but by less than its reserve assets.

What has been the combined impact of government spending plus the borrowing to pay for it? If the funds were borrowed from the commercial banks the net effect may be obtained by consolidating T-accounts e1 and f1: the changes in deposits at the Fed cancel out; there is no net change in reserves; however, there are increases in demand deposits and in bank holdings of government bonds. Thus the demand deposit increase has not been matched by any increase in reserves; if the banking system did not initially have excess reserves there will now be a reserve deficiency. In contrast, if the funds had been borrowed from the public, the increased deposits of the recipients of government funds would be precisely offset by the decrease in the deposits of the citizens buying the government bonds.[5]

g. Open Market Operations

Suppose that the Fed buys government securities formerly held by a commercial bank? The Fed pays the bank for the securities by crediting to its account a sum equal to the market value of the securities it purchases. As the T-account indicates, the open market purchase by the Federal Reserve System converts the securities held by the commercial bank into reserves.

Hypothetical Bank of Middletown

Δ Government bonds	− $100,000	
Δ Deposits at the Fed	+ $100,000	

(g1)

The sale of government bonds to the Fed by the Hypothetical Bank of Middletown has eased its reserve position. If it was initially loaned up, it now has excess reserves that it can put to work by making loans to its customers. If the bank initially had a reserve deficiency, the problem has been remedied without having to cut back on its lending operations. Thus the decision of the Fed to add government securities to its portfolio has been expansionary. Conversely, when the Fed sells government securities on the open market—and at a low enough price there will always be a willing buyer—the reserves of the member banks are reduced, and they

---

[5] The United States Treasury also maintains sizable demand deposits at commercial banks. The commercial banks favored with these deposits are required to keep reserves behind them, as with a private account. However, deposits of the United States government are usually not counted as part of the money supply. Therefore, if the United States Treasury allows these accounts to be run down in paying its obligations there will be an increase in the money supply but no change in required reserves.

may have to take offsetting contractionary steps to avoid a reserve deficiency.

10.4 THE MONEY SUPPLY EXPANSION COEFFICIENT

At the time the Federal Reserve Act was passed, the monetary impact of open-market purchases was not fully appreciated. Indeed, in the early 1920s the Federal Reserve Banks were purchasing government securities because they needed the interest income to cover their current operating expenses. And, prior to the creation of the Federal Open Market Committee in 1923, there was no coordination of the open-market purchases of the 12 Federal Reserve Banks. The money managers did not fully appreciate the mechanics of central banking![6]

Suppose the Federal Reserve System purchases $100,000 of government bonds from a member bank. The immediate effect on the T-account of the bank selling the securities to the Fed was described in part g of Section 10.3; there it was shown that the reserves of the banking system would increase by $100,000. But this is only the first step in a chain reaction. It seems reasonable to suppose that the commercial bank will put its $100,000 of new reserves to work by making a loan to one of its customers (part a of Section 10.3). The check-clearing process (part b of Section 10.3) will transfer both reserves and the deposit liability to other banks. Although the loan will result in an increase in demand deposits equal to the full value of the securities purchased by the Fed in the open market, reserve requirements go up by only a fraction of the increase in demand deposits; there are still excess reserves in the system. The banks holding the idle excess reserves are likely to loan them out, creating still more demand deposits, and the process continues. If member banks are unwilling to hold excess reserves, several dollars of new money must be created for each dollar of reserves generated through the open-market purchase of government securities.

As a very rough rule-of-thumb approximation, it may be said that the change in the money supply will equal the reciprocal of the required reserve ratio times the increase in member bank reserves brought about by the open-market operation. Thus, if banks are required to keep reserves of 20% behind their demand deposit liabilities, the $100,000 increase in reserves would support a $500,000 = 1/0.20 × $100,000 increase in the money supply; but, if the required reserve ratio were 15%, a $666,666 = 1/0.15 × $100,000 increase in the money supply would be generated.

---

[6] See "Reflections on the Early Development of Open Market Policy," by W. Randolph Burgess in the New York Federal Reserve Bank's *Monthly Review*, November 1964; he was there.

This *reciprocal rule* provides a useful but very rough estimate of the increase in the money supply resulting from an open-market operation. We must look more closely at the factors determining how great an increase in the money supply can be generated by open-market operation.

It is convenient to simplify the analysis by neglecting entirely the nonmember banks and suppressing the distinction between reserve city and country members; that is, all banks are assumed to be subject to the same reserve requirement. Furthermore, suppose initially that banks choose not to change the size of their excess reserves. Since required reserves will be affected by the public's decision to hold part of the increase in the total money supply in currency instead of in demand or time deposits, we must make some assumption about the behavior of the money-holding public. The easiest hypothesis to advance is to suppose that the public desires to hold each of the various types of money in some fixed proportion to the total money supply; that is, suppose that

$$C = \sigma_c \mathbf{M}_1$$

$$DD = \sigma_d \mathbf{M}_1$$

$$TD = \sigma_t \mathbf{M}_1 \tag{4.1}$$

Since $C + DD = \mathbf{M}_1$ by definition, we must have $\sigma_c + \sigma_d = 1$.

Simple algebraic manipulation will reveal the effect of a change in reserves on the money supply. Substituting Equation 4.1 into Equation 2.3 yields

$$R \geq R - R_e = R_r = \rho_d DD + \rho_t TD = (\rho_d \sigma_d + \rho_t \sigma_t)M_1 \tag{4.2}$$

Multiplying through by

$$\mu_1 = \frac{1}{\rho_d \sigma_d + \rho_t \sigma_t} \tag{4.3}$$

yields

$$\mathbf{M}_1 = \mu_1 R_r = \mu_1(R - R_e) \leq \mu_1 R \tag{4.4}$$

Here μ_1 is the coefficient of expansion of the banking system.[7] Furthermore, $\mathbf{M}_1 + TD = (1 + \sigma_t)\mathbf{M}_1 = \mathbf{M}_2$ by definition, implying that

$$\mathbf{M}_2 = \mu_2 R_r = \mu_2(R - R_c) \leq \mu_2 R \tag{4.5}$$

where

$$\mu_2 = (1 + \sigma_t)\mu_1 = \frac{1 + \sigma_t}{\rho_d \sigma_d + \rho_t \sigma_t} \tag{4.6}$$

---

[7] Sometimes this concept is referred to as the "money multiplier." If $\sigma_d = 1$, this reduces to the reciprocal rule; that is, $\mu_1 = 1/\rho_d$.

A simple numerical example may be helpful. Suppose that $\rho_d = 15\%$ and $\rho_t = 3\%$ are the required reserve ratios imposed on the banking system by the Fed. Suppose also that the public desires to hold 20% of M_1 as currency and 150% of M_1 as time deposits; that is, $\sigma_c = (1 - \sigma_d) = 20\%$ and $\sigma_t = 150\%$. Substituting into Equation 4.4 yields as the coefficient of expansion of the money supply

$$\mu_1 = \frac{1}{\rho_d\sigma_d + \rho_t\sigma_t} = \frac{1}{0.15 \times 0.8 + 0.03 \times 1.5} \doteq 6$$

Consequently, the effect of $100,000 increase in reserves is

$$\Delta M_1 \doteq 6 \times \Delta R = 6 \times \$100,000 = \$600,000$$

Because $\sigma_d = 80\%$, the change in demand deposits is $\sigma_d\Delta M_1 \doteq \$480,000$. Furthermore, time deposits expand by $900,000; therefore $\Delta M_2 \doteq \$1,500,000$. As a check on the computations, note that the additional reserves required to support the increase in demand and time deposits is $0.15 \times \$480,000 + 0.03 \times \$900,000 \doteq \$100,000$. What has been achieved—and how? The bank receiving the initial increase in reserves lent out the funds (T-account example a of Section 10.3); this generated an increase in the money supply, but even after the borrower spent the funds (example b) there were additional excess reserves left in the banking system, and this permitted further loans and an additional increase in the money supply. If banks have used lending to businesses and consumers as the primary outlet for their excess reserves, $1,380,000 of credit will have been extended by the banks in creating the new demand and time deposits.

These computations illustrate how a $100,000 increase in reserves might be expected to influence the money supply. But the computations are likely to exaggerate the ultimate effect of the purchase by the Fed of $100,000 of bonds on the open market, even granting the restrictive set of assumptions on which the calculations are based. The effect of the open-market operation is exaggerated, because the public's decision to hold part of the enlarged money stock in currency causes a cash drain on the commercial banking system (T-account transaction c), and this partially offsets the initial $100,000 increase in reserves generated by the open-market operation. Of course, the Fed might loan the currency and coin to the member banks, but unless additional accommodation of some sort is extended, the effect of the currency drain means that Equation 4.3 exaggerates the effect of an open-market operation on the money supply.

The effect of the currency drain is readily taken into account by modifying the money supply expansion coefficient to encompass the "monetary base" (B), the sum of reserves of the banks plus currency held by the public.

$$B = R + C$$

Only the composition, R versus C, instead of the size of the monetary base is influenced by a decision of the public to increase its holdings of currency. To obtain a revised coefficient of expansion of the money supply in terms of the monetary base, we first add $C = \sigma_c \mathbf{M}_1$ to both sides of Equation 4.2.

$$B = R + C \geq B - R_e = R_r + C = (\sigma_c + \rho_d\sigma_d + \rho_t\sigma_t)\mathbf{M}_1 \quad (4.7)$$

Consequently, we may write

$$\mathbf{M}_1 = \mu_1{}^B(B - R_e) \leq \mu_1{}^B B \quad\quad\quad (4.8)$$

where

$$\mu_1{}^B = \frac{1}{\sigma_c + \rho_d\sigma_d + \rho_t\sigma_t} = \frac{1}{\sigma_c + 1/\mu_1} \quad (4.9)$$

As before, we have, for a more generic concept of the money supply,

$$\mathbf{M}_2 = \mu_2{}^B(B - R_e) \leq \mu_2{}^B B \quad\quad\quad (4.10)$$

where

$$\mu_2{}^B = (1 + \sigma_t)\mu_1{}^B \quad\quad\quad\quad (4.11)$$

In terms of the numerical example,

$$\mu_1{}^B = \frac{1}{0.2 + 0.15 \times 0.8 + 0.03 \times 1.5} = 2\frac{3}{4}$$

and the effect of the \$100,000 open-market purchase of government securities is $\Delta\mathbf{M}_1 = \$275,000$; hence $\Delta DD = \$220,000$; $\Delta C = \$55,000$, and $\Delta TD = \$412,500$. Since $\Delta C = \$55,000$ is a reserve drain, an increase in reserves of only \$45,000 is generated by the Fed's purchase on the open market of \$100,000 worth of government securities.

The coefficient of expansion of the money supply, whether expressed in terms of reserves or the monetary base, does not provide an adequate explanation of how the money supply is determined. For one thing, it is necessary to examine carefully the circumstances in which the banks may allow at least a part of an open-market operation to spill over into idle excess reserves. For another, the underlying coefficients, σ_c and σ_t for example, may be expected to change when the interest rate fluctuates. Until these and certain other complications are taken into account, the coefficient of expansion of the money supply is little more than a tautology, although it does reveal how several factors interact in determining the amount of additional money a given increase in the reserve base is capable of supporting.

10.5 EXCESS RESERVES, INTEREST RATES, AND THE MONEY SUPPLY

That banks have at certain times held sizable excess reserves was revealed by the last column of Table 10.2. There it will be observed that in 1935 the reserves of member banks were more than twice the magnitude required to back their deposit liabilities! A powerful stimulus might have been provided to the economy if some scheme had been devised to induce the member banks to put their idle reserves to work. But when banks are already sitting on excess reserves of such magnitude it seems all too likely that a sizable proportion of any increase in reserves that the Fed might achieve through open-market operations would be kept idle instead of being loaned out. When business is generally bleak and numerous firms are facing insolvency, even old customers who have been reliable in the past must be looked on with suspicion by the careful banker. And interest rates below a fraction of a percent on prime commercial paper are not a rewarding proposition. In the Great Depression government securities were providing such low yields to their holder that they offered only a marginal improvement over idle excess reserves. A bank with excess reserves may invest them in three-month Treasury Bills without risk of default. But, in 1940, the Treasury Bill rate was only 0.14%, and a bank that converted $100,000 of excess reserves into three-month Treasury Bills (essentially transaction e of Section 10.4) would have gained only $35 after three months. It has been said that in such circumstances the efforts of central bankers at stimulating the economy through open-market operations are likely to be no more effective than "pushing on a string."

If the extremely low interest rates of the 1930s were exceptional so, also, were the tight money conditions characterizing the economy in the late 1960s and early 1970s. Thus, in January 1970, the Treasury Bill rate rose to 7.91%, and banks could obtain 8.86% on short-term business loans. With such opportunities the banks watched their reserve position with care. And, by February 1970, the member banks were in debt to the Fed by more than $1 billion. The demand of banks for excess reserves, like the public's demand for speculative money balances, may be explained by the structure of interest rates.

How the money supply is related to the rate of interest, given the monetary base (reserves plus currency in circulation), is illustrated in Figure 10.1. In the left-hand panel the excess reserves that the banks are willing to hold decrease as the rate of interest rises. On the second panel the dotted vertical $M_s{}^P$ line indicates the *potential money supply* that the banking system is capable of creating in the absence of excess reserves; from Equation 4.8 we have $M_s{}^P = \mu_1{}^B B$. The upward-rising money supply curve is derived from the excess-reserve demand function of the left-hand panel

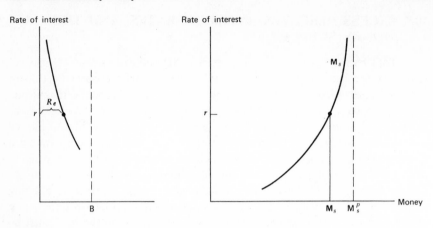

Fig. 10.1   *Excess reserves and the money supply. At rate of interest* r *banks hold excess reserves* R$_e$. *Therefore,* M$_s$^{P} (*the full potential money supply that the monetary base will support*) *is not realized.*

with the aid of Equation 4.8; the positive slope of the money supply curve reflects the fact that banks are less willing to tolerate excess reserves when the return from loaning funds increases.[8]

In Figure 10.2 the rate of interest and the quantity of money in circulation are determined by the interaction of demand and supply, given the level of output and the size of the monetary base. The M$_s$ curve is reproduced from the right-hand panel of Figure 10.1. The effect of a shift in the demand function for money, such as might be generated by an increase in Y, given the base, is illustrated on the upper panel of Figure 10.2. Since the base remains constant, the money supply increases slightly as the money market moves to e_1 in adapting to the increased demand for money. Note that the increase in the interest rate is less than would have occurred if the money supply were completely insensitive to the rate of interest. The *LM* curve concept, developed in Chapter 5, is easily modified to take these complications into account. It is only necessary to note that the *LM* curve corresponding to a given monetary base is flatter than the bottom panel of Figure 5.6 suggested because the increase in the de-

---

[8] A slight modification of the graph would take care of the possibility that the public will economize on cash holdings at higher rates of interest. This means that σ_e is a function of the rate of interest; by Equation 3.3, μ_1 will depend on the rate of interest also. At higher rates of interest the public's reduced holdings of currency mean that the banks will have larger reserves, given the base. Therefore, multiplying $R - R_e$ by $\mu_1{}^B$ gives an M$_s$ curve that is more responsive to r than the one on Figure 10.1.

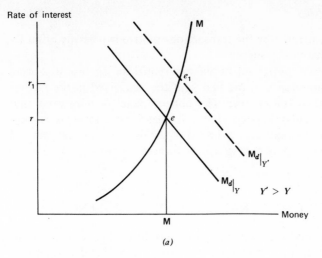

(a)

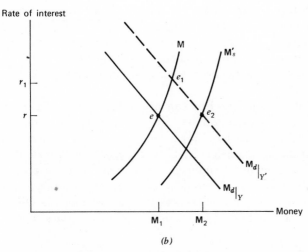

(b)

Fig. 10.2 *The demand and supply of money. (a) An increase in the demand for money, possibly generated by an increase in Y, causes the interest rate to rise and the money supply to expand, as indicated by e₁, even though the monetary base (reserves + currency) remains constant. (b) The tendency of the interest rate to rise could be partially or completely offset if the Fed shifts the supply curve of money to the right by increasing the monetary base.*

mand for money generated by the transactions motive is partially offset by the expansion of the money supply.[9]

The adjustments portrayed in the top panel of Figure 10.2 were based on the presumption that the Fed kept the base fixed in the face of the increased demand for money. The bottom panel demonstrates that the rate of interest could be kept constant if the base were allowed to expand sufficiently. With a less vigorous expansion of the base the interest rate will rise somewhat, the economy ending up somewhere between e_1 and e_2.

*10.6 EVALUATING CENTRAL BANK PERFORMANCE

How well the Federal Reserve System has succeeded in handling its responsibilities is a question providing a persistent topic for debate in academic circles and before congressional committees. Some evidence concerning the behavior of several "monetary indicators" over the last 20 years is presented in Figure 10.3. In addition, the unemployment rate shows how close to full employment the economy was operating, while the P's and T's at the top of the chart indicate the occurrence of business cycle peaks and troughs.

In defense of its actions the Fed can argue that it has effectively "leaned against the wind" of expansionary forces. The tightening of money market conditions, as indicated by rising interest rates, has discouraged private investment spending and helped stabilize the economy. Admittedly, such actions have not completely snubbed the upswing, but the central bank should not be expected to shoulder complete responsibility for stabilizing the economy. And in downswings the interest rate has fallen, encouraging investment spending. The movements of interest rates suggest

[9] More formally, the LM curve may be defined as the loci of all points satisfying

$$\mathbf{M}_d = L(Y, r) = \mathbf{M}_s = \mu_1{}^B[B - R_e(r)]$$

Since the equality between demand and supply holds for all r and Y, we must have

$$d\mathbf{M}_d = \frac{\partial L}{\partial Y} dY + \frac{\partial L}{\partial r} dr = -\mu_1{}^B \frac{dR_e}{dr} dr$$

or

$$\frac{\partial L}{\partial Y} dY = -\left(\mu_1{}^B \frac{dR_e}{dr} + \frac{\partial L}{\partial r}\right) dr$$

Hence

$$\frac{dr}{dY} = -\frac{\partial L}{\partial Y} \bigg/ \left(\mu_1{}^B \frac{dR_e}{dr} + \frac{\partial L}{\partial r}\right)$$

This expression is necessarily positive, since excess reserves and the demand for money are negatively related to the rate of interest.

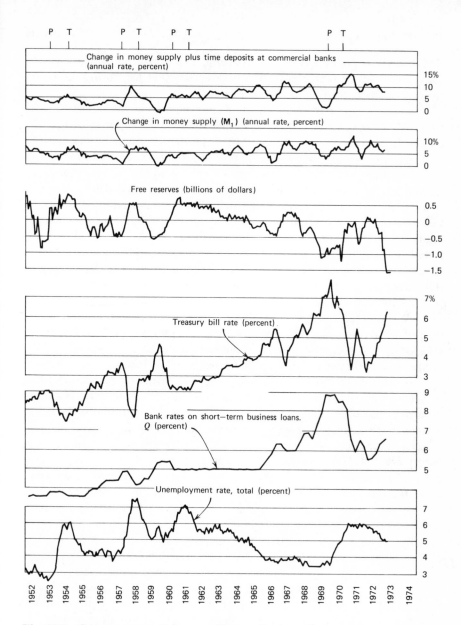

Fig. 10.3 *Some monetary indicators.* (Source. Business Conditions Digest.)

that monetary policy has been stabilizing, if somewhat tardily, although some have argued that it is rising interest costs that help bring the boom to a close and contribute to the recession.

Critics of the Fed focus on the rate of change in the money supply, either M_1 or M_2. There is a definite tendency for the rate of growth of the money supply to slow down in advance of turndowns in economic activity—although not every slowdown in the rate of growth of money has been followed by a contraction in economic activity. And the perverse tendency for the money supply to contract in recession has persisted over a longer time span, as Figure 5.1 revealed. According to the quantity theory, the Fed's behavior has been destabilizing. Members of the "Chicago School" argue that the economy would have been more stable if the Fed had followed the simple rule of having the money supply expand at a constant rate, say the long-run $3\frac{1}{2}\%$ trend rate of economic growth. According to this view, economic stability can be achieved by replacing discretionary policy with a mechanistic rule.

A simplified example will illustrate why a look at the interest rate instead of at the money supply can lead to opposing evaluations of the effectiveness of monetary policy. Suppose that the central bank allows the monetary base to expand during the upswings of the business cycle, but not by enough to keep interest rates from rising. In terms of the bottom panel of Figure 10.2 the economy moves to a point intermediate between e_1 and e_2 in response to the rise in the demand for money generated by the transactions motive. Interest rates have gone up and excess reserves of the commercial banks are down, but the reserves of the banks and the money supply have increased. Has the central bank moved in the right direction or has it behaved perversely? What kind of report card the central bank will receive when the record is appraised will depend partly on the criteria employed.

Whether "monetary policy" is interpreted to mean money supply or the interest cost incurred in holding money assets may have appeared initially to be purely a matter of semantics, but this indicator problem obviously has a profound impact on what type of appraisal the Fed receives when her historical performance is evaluated. And both "interest rate structure" and "money supply" are, in themselves, concepts capable of different interpretations. There is room for controversy concerning the appropriate rate of interest to look at—the discount rate paid by member bank's rediscounting at the Fed, the Federal Fund market rate paid by member banks in borrowing reserves from each other, the Treasury Bill rate, or the yield on longer-term government securities. And the quantity theory yields a more damning appraisal when M_1 instead of M_2 is used in evaluating the Fed's performance. These ambiguities make a difference in evaluating the historical record. When an effort is made to formulate rules to govern central bank behavior, they become even more critical; a rule that M_1 should expand at a constant rate might mean that M_2 would fluctuate erratically, while having M_2 expand at a constant rate might mean that M_1 would not.

The task of evaluating the way in which alternative types of monetary policy will, in fact, contribute to economic stability must be tabled until problems of inflation and the business cycle are examined in Parts III and IV. But it is interesting to ask at this juncture *why* the money supply expanded in booms and contracted in recessions. At various stages in its history the Fed has been governed by divergent conceptions concerning the appropriate role of monetary policy. But regardless of what theory has happened to be in vogue, the Fed has responded to increases in the demand for money by allowing at least a partial expansion in the reserves of the banking system. A few brief episodes from the Fed's history will indicate why its behavior has been more consistent than the theories that have guided the policy makers.

a. The Real-Bills Doctrine

The architects of the Fed were enamored with the real-bills doctrine, a proposition implying that the Federal Reserve Banks should respond in semiautomatic fashion to changing economic conditions. According to this doctrine, the central bank would automatically supply the appropriate quantity of money if it stood willing to advance loans to the member banks through the rediscounting of "eligible commercial paper." Before we can appreciate this proposition, we must work through the sequence of financial transactions that give rise to the rediscounting of commercial paper at the Fed.

When a merchant purchases supplies, he often does not pay until the end of a specified period, say 60 or 90 days; instead he signs a "bill" acknowledging his indebtedness to the supplier. And the supplier, in turn, if he is in need of cash, may sell the bill to a bank at a discount from its face value. The bank may hold the bill to maturity, at which point it receives its face value; alternatively, the commercial bank may replenish its funds by rediscounting the bill at the Federal Reserve Bank. Rediscounting replenishes the reserves of the commercial banks; the interest charged by the Fed for this service is called the *discount rate*. One result of this involved sequence in transactions is the advancement of credit to the merchant, who need not pay for his supplies until they are sold. But how about the aggregate economy? The act of rediscounting serves to increase the reserves of the banking system, since it is equivalent in its effect on the bank's balance sheet to the purchase by the Fed of government bonds (transaction g of Section 3). Thus the ultimate effect of the merchant's purchase may be an expansion of the money supply.

This entire process was thought by the advocates of the real-bill's doctrine to be self-regulating in that it would supply the appropriate amount of credit to the economy so long as the Federal Reserve Banks stood ready to discount only *eligible commercial paper*; that is, the bills should arise from the "genuine needs of trade"—the merchant's inventory instead of stock market or commodity speculation.

When the central bank adheres to the real-bills doctrine, the reserves of the banking system will expand in a business boom, as illustrated by the bottom panel of Figure 10.2, because the accelerated pace of business activity will generate more bills eligible for discounting. The real-bills doctrine influenced the behavior of the Fed during its early history. But nowadays the discounting process is quite different. When member banks borrow from the Fed, which they are reluctant to do except when market interest rates are very high, they generally secure their loans with government securities instead of with other types of collateral, including eligible commercial paper.

b. Financing War

During World War II a sizable portion of United States military expenditures was financed by selling government bonds. The Treasury was interested in minimizing the costs of servicing the debt; that is, it wanted to borrow at a low rate of interest. But the rapid expansion in output generated by war spending shifted the demand for money to the right. The Fed purchased large quantities of government securities in order to keep their price up (i.e., keep the interest rate down). As Figure 5.4 illustrated, the Fed preserved a remarkably stable pattern of interest rates throughout the war. Precise estimates of the relevant demand curves were not needed to achieve this, because it was only necessary to buy government securities whenever their price began to fall. But the open-market operations increased the reserves of the banking system (transaction e of Section 2), and this contributed to an excessive expansion of the money supply.

c. Ratification of the 1964 Tax Cut

When Kennedy was elected President in 1960, he inherited from the preceding administration the Chairman of the Federal Reserve Board, William McChesney Martin. Martin felt that unemployment was so high as to make it unwise to raise the structure of interest rates in order to attract funds from abroad; he also thought the balance of payments situation was too serious to allow drastic steps to loosen money and stimulate the economy. Short-term interest rates were maintained within a fairly narrow band, although long-term government securities were purchased in an attempt to lower the long-term rate of interest to encourage private domestic investment—this was "Operation Twist."[10] Later, when the tax cut gradually moved

---

[10] Additional data on interest rate movements during this period appear in Table 5.6 and Figure 5.4.

the sluggish economy toward full employment, the money supply expanded in response. If it had not, much of the effect of the tax cut would have been dissipated in rising interest rates and curtailed investment; that is, the Fed ratified the recovery by enlarging the money supply instead of by snubbing the expansion by allowing interest rates to rise (point e_2 instead of e_1 in the bottom panel of Figure 10.2). Once again the money supply expanded concurrently with growing output. Again the money supply was influenced by endogenous forces. This influence of output on money can be readily visualized with a slight modification of the *IS-LM* flowchart (Figure 8.1). All that is needed is to add a line linking M_s (in the upper left-hand corner) to Y. But the existence of this additional feedback loop means that it is quite difficult to disentangle empirically the effects of changing output on the money supply from the effects of the changing money supply on output. Until these two interacting forces are successfully disentangled, controversy will persist concerning the monetarists' assertion that the economy would be more stable if the Fed abandoned discretionary monetary policy by severing the $Y \rightarrow M_s$ feedback loop in order to make the money supply grow at a constant rate, year in an year out, regardless of the current level of unemployment and the pace of inflation.

REFERENCES

1. A highly readable description of how the banking system of the United States is regulated is available free of charge.

    The Federal Reserve System: Purposes and Functions, Board of Governors, Federal Reserve System, Washington, D.C.

2. The way in which power is in practice exercised within the Federal Reserve System has been explored by a political scientist.

    Michael Reagan, "The Political Structure of the Federal Reserve System," American Political Science Review, March 1961.

3. The proposition that discretionary policy should be abandoned is stated with great force in the two following papers.

    Milton Friedman, "A Monetary and Fiscal Framework for Economic Stability," American Economic Review, June 1948.
    Henry C. Simons, "Rules versus Authorities in Monetary Policy," Journal of Political Economy, February 1936.

4. The Joint Economic Committee occasionally invites the Chairman of the Federal Reserve Board to testify concerning the conduct of monetary policy. In November 1973, Arthur F. Burns responded in writing to questions raised by Senator William Proxmire concerning the role of the money supply. The letter was published in the November 1973 Federal Reserve Bulletin.

KEY CONCEPTS

lender of last resort

"elastic currency"

Federal Deposit Insurance Corporation (FDIC)

excess reserves

free reserves

T-accounts

assets and liabilities

Federal Funds market

open-market operations

money supply expansion coefficient

currency drain

monetary base

Real-bills doctrine

commercial paper

EXERCISES

10.1 In many introductory economics textbooks students learn that if the commercial banks are required to keep reserves of 20% behind demand deposits, every $1 increase in reserves will lead to a $5 increase in the money supply. In contrast, the argument of this chapter has suggested:

$$\Delta M_1 = \mu_1 \Delta R$$

provided $\Delta R_e = 0$,
where

$$\mu_1 = \frac{1}{\rho_d \sigma_d + \rho_t \sigma_t} \qquad (4.3)$$

is the money supply expansion coefficient.

Write an essay, suitable for publication on the financial page of the *Wall Street Journal*, explaining clearly and concisely the factors entering into Equation 4.3. In your essay you should explain why Equation 4.3 may exaggerate the effects on the money supply of an open-market purchase of $1 in government securities.

10.2 The purchase by the Fed of $1 in government securities on the open market might, according to Section 10.4, lead to a $2.75 increase in the money supply. Investigate, for each of the following three possible changes, how the magnitude of $\mu_1{}^B$ would be affected, everything else unchanged, if

a. ρ_d were 0.20 instead of 0.15.

b. σ_d were 0.9 instead of 0.8 (and $\sigma_c = 0.1$ instead of 0.2).

c. σ_t were 0.75 instead of 1.5.

10.3 Consider the evidence presented in Figure 10.3, but covering up the P's and T's at the top of the page and the unemployment rate data at the bottom of the page.

a. On the basis of the movements of the two money supply series, M_1 and M_2, try to predict (without peeking) the periods of business slump and excessive boom. Do the fluctuations in the rate of change in M_1 and M_2 appear to be more or less stable in the first half of the period covered by the table or in the second half?

b. There are several "monetary indicators" plotted on Figure 10.3— the rate of change in M_1 and M_2, the level of free reserves, the Treasury Bill rate. Looking at each series individually, can you distinguish the periods in which the Fed was pursuing a "tight," "neutral," or "loose" monetary policy? What additional information would you like to have in order to characterize the type of policy being pursued by the central bank?

10.4   a. Determine, step by step, using T-accounts, how the following sequence of events would change the reserve position of the commercial banking system.

  (1) The Treasury of the United States sells $5 billion of government securities to commercial banks.

  (2) The $5 billion is spent on an antiballistic missile system.

  (3) The Fed purchases $2 billion in government securities from the commercial banking system.

  b. The banks make or call loans as appropriate in response to their changed reserved position. Show what happens to the money supply and loans outstanding. (Specify carefully any assumptions you find it convenient to invoke in the course of your analysis.)

  c. Why might the United States Treasury be inclined to encourage the Fed to take step 3 above? Under present conditions, would you judge the above sequence of transactions as constituting an appropriate procedure for financing an ABM system? Why or why not?

10.5 Suppose that the income velocity of money is constant. For example, suppose that the demand function for money is of the form $M_d = 1/2\,Y$. Explain why this does not imply that the LM curve is vertical *if* the banking system's holdings of excess reserves depend on the rate of interest.

monetary policy and the price level

CHAPTER 11
inflation and deflation

*11.1 WHAT IT IS

As everyone knows, inflation is a general tendency for prices to rise. Figure 11.1 reveals that the American economy has been plagued with inflationary episodes ever since the Revolutionary War; and this is so whether one looks at the index of wholesale commodity prices or the prices paid by consumers for goods and services.[1] But the United States has also suffered from periods of precipitous decline in the general price level so that the overall trend in prices displays a modest rate of growth, not even doubling in the last century. Viewed in historical perspective, price movements were moderate in the decades after World War II. We had a considerable amount of inflation, but nothing comparable to the inflations associated with the War of 1812, the Civil War, or the two World Wars. And the data in Table 11.1 and on Figure 11.2 reveal that relative to most countries the United States economy has been more or less immune from the dread specter of hyperinflation. In the early 1970's many blamed the United States inflation on a perverse mixture of ineptitude and mendacity in the White House. But inflation in the 1970's is a worldwide phenomenon. If no president in recent times can claim to have won the battle against inflation, some solace is offered by the fact that the majority of countries have done much worse than the United States.

The most extreme inflations usually occur during war or in its immediate aftermath. For example, in the first year of the Korean War, the retail price level in Pusan, South Korea's capital, increased to eight times its prewar level; during the second year prices doubled; by the end of the war the price index had risen from 100 to 2167! While Viet Nam also suffered from inflation, it was more successfully controlled than in Korea, the price index rising from 100 in 1963 to 900 by the end of 1972.[2] A classic

---

[1] Measuring changes in the general price level, particularly over long periods, is a tricky business; some of the complications are discussed later in this chapter. The index of consumer prices plotted on the table was constructed by the Bureau of Labor Statistics by splicing a number of series: 1800–1851, index of prices paid by Vermont Farmers for Family Living; 1851–1890, Consumer Price Index by Ethel D. Hoover; 1890–1912, Cost of Living Index constructed by Albert Rees.

[2] A comparison of the two inflations is provided by G. E. Makinen, "Economic Stabilization in Wartime: A Comparative Case Study of Korea and Vietnam," *Journal of Political Economy*, November–December 1971.

Table 11.1 INFLATION: AN INTERNATIONAL COMPARISON

	Cost of Living (1963 = 100)			Average Annual Percentage Rate of Price Change	
	1948	*1960*	*1970*	*37–64*	*48–64*
Argentina	3.0	56.0	380.0		
Australia	—	97.3	124.1	4.7	5.2
Austria	36.8	89.9	128.5	8.7	6.3
Belgium	82.3	95.6	128.7	6.2	1.5
Bolivia	0.6	88.4	151.0	32.1	38.4
Brazil	4.0	27.0	1,048.0	23.0	27.5
Canada	72.9	96.2	126.0	3.0	2.1
Ceylon	85.0	95.1	127.0	4.2	1.2
Chile	1.0	57.0	598.0	25.1	31.2
Colombia	27.5	68.0	196.6	10.1	9.5
Costa Rica	64.3	91.5	116.3	4.8	2.9
Denmark	58.0	84.8	149.9	4.3	3.7
Dominican Republic	86.3	87.8	106.6	—	1.1
Ecuador	75.7	88.2	134.6	—	2.0
El Salvador	58.0	101.1	107.9	3.9	3.0
Finland	48.0	90.0	145.0	12.3	6.1
France	39.2	88.3	131.2	15.2	6.2
Germany	—	92.2	120.5	2.7	1.8
Greece	44.1	95.7	117.5	—	5.3
Guatemala	78.5	98.3	106.7	4.0	1.5
Honduras	—	94.5	117.6	—	2.4
Iceland	31.0	76.0	228.0	9.8	8.2
India	72.0	93.0	169.0	5.9	2.7
Iran	53.0	95.9	113.9	11.1	4.3
Iraq	115.8	94.1	116.8	7.0	−1.0
Ireland	61.7	91.1	145.0	4.6	3.5
Israel	27.6	80.3	138.0	10.5	8.9
Italy	65.0	87.1	128.2	17.8	3.1
Japan	47.6	82.5	145.6	21.1	5.0
Korea	0.4	72.4	248.9	—	43.9
Mexico	40.4	96.6	125.7	8.8	5.6
Netherlands	63.0	93.0	140.2	5.0	3.6
New Zealand	56.4	93.8	135.9	3.8	3.9
Norway	55.1	90.3	140.2	4.5	4.2
Pakistan	—	96.9	135.6	—	1.9
Panama	106.1	98.2	111.3	2.6	−0.1
Peru	30.4	82.6	206.3	10.1	8.5

(*Continued*)

Table 11.1 Continued

| | Cost of Living (1963 = 100) | | | Average Annual Percentage Rate of Price Change | |
	1948	1960	1970	37–64	48–64
Phillipines	85.4	88.1	148.4	6.5	1.5
Portugal	83.2	94.0	145.6	3.2	1.5
South Africa	62.6	95.5	125.4	3.6	3.1
Spain	43.4	86.3	155.2	9.8	5.7
Sweden	57.0	91.0	135.0	4.2	3.9
Switzerland	80.9	90.9	126.3	2.8	1.5
Thailand	59.5	95.5	116.7	12.8	3.9
Turkey	34.0	87.7	155.6	9.3	7.1
United Kingdom	57.7	91.0	135.3	4.5	3.7
United States	77.8	96.6	126.8	3.0	1.6
Uruguay	13.0	61.0	2313.0	12.2	16.2
Venezuela	77.8	102.0	112.4	—	1.6

Source. International Financial Statistics.

Ratio scale (1957–1959 = 100)

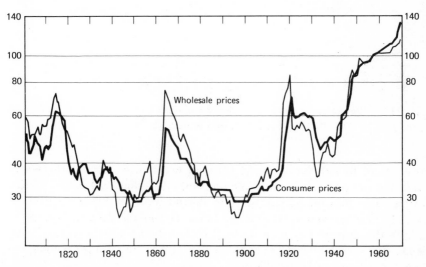

Fig. 11.1 *The dance of the dollar, 1800–1970.* (Source. *Bureau of Labor Statistics*.)

Ratio scales

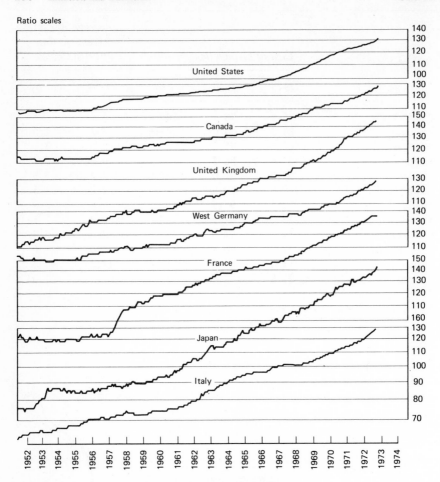

Fig. 11.2 *The consumer price index, international comparisons (1967 = 100).* (Source. Business Conditions Digest.)

example of hyperinflation is the German experience after World War I when the price level rose to 10 million times its initial level in 16 months. In the same postwar period prices in Poland went up 700 times over, in Austria 70 times, and in Hungary 44 times. During the Russian hyperinflation in the early 1920s, the price level rose to 10,000 times its initial level. And after World War II the currencies of Greece and Hungary collapsed in extreme bouts of hyperinflation.[3]

[3] The figures are reported by Philip Cagan in "The Monetary Dynamics of Hyperinflation," *Studies in the Quantity Theory of Money* (Milton Friedman, ed.), University of Chicago Press, 1956, p. 26. The Greece and Hungary inflation involved an increase in prices of 4.70×10^8 and 3.81×10^{27}.

Inflations are not a purely capitalistic phenomena. Quite the contrary, the Soviet Union has experienced several inflationary episodes. When repulsing the German invasion during World War II, prices rose dramatically. And the Soviet Union experienced serious price and wage inflation in the 1930s under the forced draft of accelerated industrialization. The inflation was not planned; it resulted partly from acute labor shortages; and in part it was accelerated by shortages of consumer goods that developed when planned production targets proved too optimistic.[4] And in China inflation is an institution that has survived the revolution. During the final stages of Chiang Kai-shek's regime, China experienced serious bouts of inflation; and under Communism, periods of price stability have been mixed with episodes of rapidly rising prices.[5]

*11.2 LIVING WITH INFLATION—AND WHO GETS HURT

If governments cannot control inflation the public must learn to live with it, however painful that may be. Not everyone suffers from inflation, and how much anyone loses depends partly on whether he has successfully anticipated the rate of price change and taken appropriate steps to deal with it. Judging from the *Survey of Consumer Finances*, conducted annually at the University of Michigan, consumers in the United States find learning to live with inflation a particularly difficult lesson. The *Surveys* usually indicate a general anticipation of price stability, but starting in late 1969 a majority of respondents expected 5% or more inflation during the subsequent 12 months. But only a minority of households—27% in 1969— think that they can do anything to protect themselves from inflation; of those who think something can be done, most suggest that buying less and postponing purchases offers the best protection. Only about 12% indicated that they had recently made a purchase because they thought the item would cost more later. This is understandable. It is hard to protect oneself by buying far in advance of need if most of the inflation is being generated by rising prices for food and services while most consumer durable prices are relatively stable. One cannot purchase medical treatment in advance of need, no matter how certain one is that its cost will continue to soar in the future. Only 7% of the respondents to the 1969 survey reported that they would invest in the stock market as a means of protecting their savings from inflation. But, in retrospect, their pessimism was justified, because the minority who, fearing inflation, turned to the stock market in the late

[4] See Franklyn D. Holzman, "Soviet Inflationary Pressures, 1928–1957; Causes and Cures," *Quarterly Journal of Economics*, May 1960.

[5] An interesting description of the Chinese experience is provided by Colin D. Campbell and Gordon C. Tullock, "Hyperinflation in China, 1937–49," *Journal of Political Economy*, June 1954, pp. 236–45.

1960s found that while their concern for rising prices was justified, they would have probably done better putting their funds in the savings bank instead of buying into a bear market.

The longer inflation continues and the more rapidly prices rise, the more time and effort the public will devote to escaping the losses it would otherwise inflict. In extreme cases, when money has become a totally unreliable store of value, resort has frequently been made to barter, in spite of its obvious inconveniences. How much hardship inflation really causes is still a matter of debate. In summing up his lengthy 1937 study of the German hyperinflation, Bresciani-Turroni reported:[6]

"[I]nflation, by imposing a restriction on consumption on many classes of society, allows a part of the productive energies of the country to be employed in the manufacture of new instruments of production. But [in Germany] a large part of the new fixed capital was later revealed as useless. . . . Inflation . . . exercised an increasingly disadvantageous influence, disorganizing and limiting production. It annihilated thrift; it made reform of the national budget impossible for years . . . it destroyed incalculable moral and intellectual values. It provoked a serious revolution in social classes, a few people accumulating wealth and forming a class of usurpers of national property, whilst millions of individuals were thrown into poverty . . . it poisoned the German people by spreading among all classes the spirit of speculation and diverting them from proper and regular work, and it was the cause of incessant political and moral disturbance. It is indeed easy to understand why the record of the sad years 1919–23 always weighs like a nightmare on the German people."

In contrast, Pedersen and Laursen argued in a more recent study that the German experience has been misinterpreted. They assert, on the basis of an intensive reevaluation of the evidence, that inflation does not have such devastating effects on production and human welfare as has generally been supposed. They conclude:[7]

"If control of wages is not possible, inflation should be tolerated, because the sacrifice of employment opportunities necessary to curb it would reduce production more than would inflation."

Pedersen and Laursen protest that a misreading of history had disastrous consequences during the worldwide depression on the 1930s.[8]

". . . the spectre of the German hyper-inflation . . . served as an obstacle to the pursuance of expansionary [economic] policies all over the world. . . ."

---

[6] Constantino Bresciani-Turroni, *The Economics of Inflation: A Study of Currency Depreciation in Post-War Germany*, London: George Allen & Unwin, 1937, pp. 403–404.

[7] J. Pedersen and K. Laursen, *German Inflation 1918–1923*, Amsterdam, North Holland, 1964, pp. 126–127.

[8] Ibid., p. 11.

The controversy concerning the appropriate reading of the lessons to be learned from prior bouts with inflation persists. How seriously inflation distorts production and the distribution of income and wealth is still a subject of heated debate among professional economists. But it is recognized that a variety of institutional adjustments serve to mitigate the hardships that would otherwise be wrought by inflation even if citizens acting individually are not too successful at protecting themselves. Let us see how the economy adjusts to the inflationary presence.

Rising prices need not hurt the worker if money wages rise in step with the increasing cost of living. In normal times few workers divide their weekly take-home pay by the consumer price index to see whether their real wage has fallen; workers are more inclined to regard the increase in their money wage as a just reward to which they are more than entitled instead of as compensation for rising prices. But, during periods of persistent inflation, union leaders will quote the price statistics when negotiating labor contracts at the bargaining table. While labor is inclined to argue that wage increases lag price increases, their employers assert that the price increases have been caused by higher wages. The resulting compromise may include an explicit cost of living wage adjustment. In appraising its adequacy, the critical figure to look at is the *real wage*.

$$w^r = \frac{w^n}{p} \tag{2.1}$$

Here w^n denotes the money wage and p is the cost of living. Workers, for generations, have enjoyed a secular upward trend in real wages as a result of improvement in productivity generated by technological advance and capital accumulation, but professional economists still debate whether major changes in the real wage can be attributed to inflation.

Escalator wage clauses provide that the worker's wage will be automatically adjusted to keep pace with changes in the cost of living. The escalator wage clause insures that the real wage will not be eroded by inflation during the life of the labor contract; it allows the worker to shift the burden of uncertainty about inflation to his employer. Unions in this country have been inclined to push for escalator clauses in wage contracts only during periods when the inflation has persisted long enough to become an obvious threat—and this in itself involves a lag. Once the inflationary episode passes, the provision is often dropped from the contract in favor of other benefits. But, in countries experiencing hyperinflation, it is customary to tie wages of both union and unorganized workers to the price level. For example, in the post-World War I hyperinflation in Germany, wages were set on the basis of a forecast of what the price index would rise to during the week following payday. And during the hyperinflation in Nationalist China the wages of government workers were computed by multiplying their 1937 money wage by the cost-of-living index on payday.[9] As an alternative, wages have sometimes been stated in terms of a foreign currency of more stable purchasing power. Thus, in the last stages of the German inflation, the current exchange rate of the dollar on the Berlin money market was used as the numeraire in computing wage rates.

Inflation is particularly painful for those who depend on fixed incomes. Since a fixed pension can evaporate as a result of inflation during the retirement years, those whose pensions provide for the escalation of benefits in line with changes in current salary scales are particularly fortunate. The pension plans of civil servants and veterans sometimes contain such provisions. Even in the absence of escalator provisions, veterans and social security recipients often find during inflationary episodes that they have sufficient political clout to effect benefit increases without an inordinate lag. Welfare payments also tend to be adjusted upward when their purchasing power is dissipated by inflation. The data in Table 11.2, while rudimentary, do indicate that inflation has not been disastrous for social security and public assistance recipients. It is the retiree living off a fixed private pension plan who is most likely to suffer from inflation.

Those who have lent money at fixed rates of interest—by putting their funds in a savings bank, buying corporate or government bonds, or making mortgage loans—lose from unanticipated inflation, since the dollar payments they are legally entitled to will buy less in the future. Conversely, those who have borrowed money gain. For example, anyone who in 1950 had either the good fortune or the foresight to purchase a house with a 25-year mortgage found that his monthly payment did not increase, even though its purchasing power dropped to half the initial value over the life of the mortgage (property-tax payments undoubtedly increased)—and the fortunate buyer also finds that he can enjoy a substantial capital gain whenever he decides to sell the house since, in all likelihood, it is now priced considerably above what he paid for it. Clearly, it pays to buy instead of rent when prices are rising. However, during periods of deflation, those who borrow suffer. Witness the sad experience during the protracted deflation following the Civil War of Midwestern farmers who bought property and machinery on mortgage and had to grow more and more wheat to meet the payments. If inflation is the bane of some and a boon for others, the tables are reversed in deflation, because with declining prices the borrower is apt to lose and the lender gain.

The stock market and real estate become particularly attractive investments when inflation is anticipated. And, if many anticipate inflation, there will be a tendency to bid up the price of such assets relative to alter-

---

[9] See Campbell and Tullock, op. cit., p. 241, passim, for information on how the Chinese adapted to hyperinflation.

Table 11.2 SOME DISTRIBUTIONAL ASPECTS OF INFLATION

	1950	1955	1960	1965	1970	Percent Gain 1950–1970
Average monthly benefit, Social Security						
Retired workers						
Current dollars	$43.86	$61.90	$73.04	$83.92	$118.10	169.4
1970 dollars	69.74	91.69	98.70	104.71	118.10	69.3
Widowed mothers						
Current dollars	34.24	45.91	59.29	65.45	86.51	152.7
1970 dollars	54.45	68.01	79.03	81.66	86.51	58.9
State unemployment insurance						
Average weekly benefit for total unemployment						
Current dollars	20.76	—	32.87	37.19	50.31	142.3
1970 dollars	33.01	—	43.81	46.40	50.31	52.4
As percent of average weekly wage	34.4%	—	35.2%	50.3%	37.5%	9.0
Public assistance						
Aid to dependent children, per family						
Current dollars	71.	86.	105.	137.	187.	163.4
1970 dollars	113.	128.	140.	171.	187.	65.5
Aid to totally, permanently disabled						
Current dollars	44.	49.	55.	67.	97.	120.5
1970 dollars	70.	73.	74.	83.	97.	38.6

Source. Statistical Abstract of the United States.

native investments, such as bonds, which offer a fixed dollar return of principle and interest that can evaporate when prices rise rapidly. Indeed, if
the inflation is sufficiently rapid, it may become profitable to borrow in
order to buy assets that one would not have considered purchasing in more
normal times. The increased demand for borrowed funds will lead to a
higher rate of interest. This explains the spectacularly high interest rates
often paid during periods of rapid inflation. For example, borrowers in
Nationalist China after World War II were willing to pay banks as much
as 2% a day for borrowed funds. This was the *nominal* or *money rate of
interest*; the *real interest rate*, taking into account the rapid pace of inflation, was not exceptional.

The crucial distinction between nominal and real interest rates needs
clarification, and a simple example may help. Suppose one is obligated to
pay back $112 on a one-year bank loan of $100; then the (nominal) rate
of interest is 12%. But if the asset purchased with the borrowed funds rises
in value to $110 in the interim, the actual costs of borrowing the money
instead of postponing the purchase will be only 2%; conversely, if the price
of the asset falls to $90, the cost of not postponing the purchase is 22%.
Whether or not the purchase was a wise decision thus depends on what
happens to prices. In distinguishing the money rate of interest that appears
on legal lending documents from the real rate of interest paid by the borrower, it is convenient to write

$$r^n = r + \left(\frac{\dot{p}}{p}\right)^e \qquad (2.2)$$

Here r^n is the nominal rate of interest, $(\dot{p}/p)^e$ is the anticipated rate of price
change, and r is the real rate of interest. Thus the investor who pays 12%
for borrowing money and expects the price level to go up by 10% envisions
himself as paying a real rate of only 2%. It is this anticipated or *ex ante*
real rate that governs behavior. In retrospect, of course, one can calculate
an *ex post* real rate on the basis of the actual price change.

When rapid inflation is generally anticipated, we should expect loans
to be made at a high rate of interest. Indeed, this is part of the process of
adjusting to inflation, since it eliminates the exceptional gains of the borrower and the pain to the lender that would otherwise be generated by
inflation. Where usury restrictions impose a legal ceiling on interest rates,
the adjustment process is frustrated, and the real interest rate may even
become negative if assets are expected to appreciate more rapidly than the
cost of borrowing funds; precisely this situation has arisen from time to
time in many South American countries. Obviously, every one wants to
borrow, and banks must ration available funds to favored clients when the
interest-rate ceiling prevents the market mechanism from allocating loan-
able funds; this situation is more conducive to bribery than to economic

Table 11.3   THE *EX POST* REAL RATE OF INTEREST IN THE 1930s

Year	Investment Good Prices		Prime Commercial Paper		Corporate Bond Rate	
	Level (1958 = 100)	Rate of Change	Money	Real	Money	Real
1929	39.4	—	5.85%	—	4.73%	—
1930	37.9	−3.81%	3.59	7.40%	4.55	8.36%
1931	35.2	−7.12	2.64	9.76	5.58	12.70
1932	31.6	−10.23	2.73	12.96	5.01	15.24
1933	30.6	−3.17	1.73	4.90	4.49	7.16
1934	33.7	10.13	1.02	−9.11	4.00	−6.13
1935	34.3	1.78	0.75	−1.03	3.60	1.82
1936	34.6	0.87	0.75	−0.12	3.24	2.37
1937	37.8	9.25	0.94	−8.31	3.26	−5.99
1938	38.2	1.06	0.81	−0.25	3.19	2.13
1939	37.7	−1.31	0.59	2.90	3.01	4.32

Source. Investment good prices is the implicit price deflator for gross private domestic investment. The price deflator and the money interest rates are from the *Economic Report of the President*; the real rates are computed with Equation 2.2 for an investor who correctly anticipates the rate of price change.

efficiency. In the United States banking regulations have limited the rate of interest that can be paid on savings accounts; as a result, savings institutions often compete by offering "gifts" for new deposits; the ceiling also means that small savers, who are more likely than the wealthy to rely on savings accounts for storing their savings, suffer an added penalty during inflationary episodes.[10]

During the Great Depression interest rates on borrowed funds fell drastically, but prices were falling also. Table 11.3 provides an estimate of what happened to the real rate of interest. Instead of falling, the relevant rate for those contemplating investment increased from 1929 to 1933! Of course, the "real" rates recorded on the table are *ex post* rates revealing what the actual cost of borrowing funds turned out to be. Only a clair-

---

[10] In the absence of such restrictions many savings and loan associations would find themselves in financial trouble. Savings banks are financial intermediaries in the business of raising funds on a short-term basis, as from savings accounts, and then lending them, as for home mortgages. The interest they receive on a mortgage loan may be at a low rate determined years ago and, if banks have to pay higher rates to acquire short-term funds to cover these loans, it will be only a matter of time before they experience bankruptcy. Of course, banks find it profitable to support restrictions on interest payments to depositors because savings are the input they use in the production of mortgage loans.

voyant investor could profit fully from the wide fluctuations in the *ex post* rate of interest. In practice, investors must do the best they can at predicting price movements on the basis of past experience when they attempt to determine the true cost of borrowing funds for investment purposes. The investor makes his decision in advance and, if he anticipates no change in prices, he need look only at the nominal rate quoted to him by his banker.

The financially astute may be able to avoid much of the pain of inflation by investing in stocks or real estate, but the small saver planning for retirement may not have the requisite expertise. And we have seen that in the United States the small saver depositing his funds in a savings account has been rewarded with a regulated rate of interest kept unreasonably low in periods of inflation. Since government bonds constitute a promise by the government to pay a specific sum of money at a particular future date, the holder of such securities bears the burden of uncertainty concerning the future course of prices. From time to time governments have issued *constant purchasing power bonds* with indebtedness expressed in terms of the price index. In this way the saver is guaranteed a fixed amount of purchasing power at maturity. Price index linked bonds were used after World War I in Germany; since World War II, they have been issued in China, Finland, Israel, Austria, France, and Sweden. But not in the United States. Some have opposed price index linked bonds on the grounds that it would be immoral for the government to concede in this way that it will not be able to stabilize the purchasing power of the dollar. But there might well be a ready market for securities that enables the lender to escape the uncertainty of inflation.[11]

11.3 MEASURING INFLATION

At wage negotiation time the presence of a variety of price indices, some suggesting more and some less inflation, means that debate over the appropriate procedure for measuring inflation persists even when the need for fairly compensating for rising prices has been agreed on. And government officials confronted with the task of reviewing how well their administration has fared in achieving price stability find that the question of whether the pace of inflation has accelerated or slowed in recent months may de-

---

[11] In 1925 the Rand Kardex Company issued 30-year bonds with both interest payments and principle tied to the wholesale price index, but this was a unique experience. M. C. Lovell and Robert Vogel have suggested that in the absence of purchasing power bonds, brokers might provide the saver with equivalent protection by extending future markets to encompass a composite market-basket commodity measured in terms of the consumer price index; see "A CPI-Futures Market," *Journal of Political Economy*, July/August, 1973.

pend on whether they emphasize the wholesale price index, the consumer price index with or without the food component, or call attention to the latest pip in the implicit price deflator. Inflation is not an entirely unambiguous concept amenable to exact measurement.

Movements in the consumer price index (CPI) and the GNP implicit price deflator (IPD) are plotted in Figure 11.3. Alternative measures of inflation move more or less together, although they start at different points because they do not all have the same base year; that is, the implicit price deflator is calculated so that it equals 100 in 1958, while the consumer and wholesale indices are both normalized to equal 100 in 1967 (Table 11.4). But at times the indices do not all indicate the same rate of inflation; in particular, during much of the 1960s, the CPI showed continuing inflation, while the WPI suggested that prices were relatively stable (Table 11.5). These discrepancies deserve explanation, and the sources of such gaps will become apparent in the process of explaining how the various indices are constructed.

The consumer price index measures the changing cost of buying at retail a representative "market basket" purchased by the typical family. Included in the market basket are the services of doctors and auto mechanics, the cost of renting an apartment, food, clothing, and other commodities. In contrast, the wholesale price index is designed to measure average changes in the prices of commodities sold in primary markets. The relative importance of commodities in the WPI market basket—their "weight" in the index—depends on the total sales volume of the item. The WPI concerns all commodities produced and imported for sale in commercial transactions, but it excludes services. Thus steel has a relatively heavy weight in the WPI index, but increases in its price show up only indirectly in the CPI as they enter into the cost of automobiles, refrigerators, and so forth. Instead of using prices paid by consumers at retail, the WPI measures prices of commodities f.o.b. at their production or central marketing point and net of applicable discounts and excise taxes. Both the CPI and WPI suffer from deficiencies in coverage. Since the WPI omits services, it can suggest price stability in periods in which the rising cost of such services as medical care cause substantial increases in the cost of living. On the other hand, the CPI also suffers from sins of omission, since it neglects changes in the costs to investors of constructing apartment buildings, factories, machinery, and so forth.

A useful compromise is provided by a third type of index, the national income accountant's implicit price index (IPD). The IPD is a useful by-product obtained in calculating movements in real national product; since data collected for the CPI and the WPI are used in calculating real GNP, the IPI relies on the same basic data collected for the other two series. But it is calculated in a way that gives due weight to the changing cost of

Table 11.4 ALTERNATIVE MEASURES OF INFLATION (1967 = 100)

Year	Consumer Prices (1967 = 100) All Items	Food	Wholesale Prices (1967 = 100) All Commodities	Farm Products	Implicit Price Deflator (1958 = 100) GNP	Personal Consumption
1929	51.3	48.3	49.1	64.1	50.64	55.3
1930	50.0	45.9	44.6	54.2	49.26	53.6
1931	45.6	37.8	37.6	39.7	44.78	47.9
1932	40.9	31.5	33.6	29.5	40.25	42.3
1933	38.8	30.6	34.0	31.4	39.29	40.6
1934	40.1	34.1	38.6	40.0	42.46	43.5
1935	41.1	36.5	41.3	48.1	42.62	44.4
1936	41.5	36.9	41.7	49.5	42.73	44.7
1937	43.0	38.4	44.5	52.9	44.50	46.5
1938	42.2	35.6	40.5	42.0	43.83	45.6
1939	41.6	34.6	39.8	40.0	43.23	45.1
1940	42.0	35.2	40.5	41.4	43.87	45.5
1941	44.1	38.4	45.1	50.3	47.22	48.7
1942	48.8	45.1	50.9	64.8	53.03	54.8
1943	51.8	50.3	53.3	75.0	56.83	59.9
1944	52.7	49.6	53.6	75.5	58.16	63.2
1945	53.9	50.7	54.6	78.5	59.66	65.4
1946	58.6	58.1	62.3	90.9	66.70	70.5
1947	66.9	70.6	75.5	109.4	74.64	77.9
1948	72.1	76.6	82.8	117.5	79.57	82.3
1949	71.4	73.5	78.7	101.6	79.12	81.7
1950	72.1	74.5	81.8	106.7	80.16	82.9
1951	77.8	82.8	91.1	124.2	85.64	88.6
1952	79.5	84.3	88.6	117.2	87.45	90.5
1953	80.1	83.0	87.4	106.2	88.33	91.7
1954	80.5	82.8	87.6	104.7	89.63	92.5
1955	80.2	81.6	87.8	98.2	90.85	92.8
1956	81.4	82.2	90.7	96.9	93.99	94.8
1957	84.3	84.9	93.3	99.5	97.49	97.7
1958	86.6	88.5	94.6	103.9	100.00	100.0
1959	87.3	87.1	94.8	97.5	101.55	101.3
1960	88.7	88.0	94.9	97.2	103.29	102.9
1961	89.6	89.1	94.5	96.3	104.62	103.9
1962	90.6	89.9	94.8	98.0	105.78	104.9
1963	91.7	91.2	94.5	96.0	107.17	106.1

(*Continued*)

Table 11.4   (*Continued*)

Year	Consumer Prices (1967 = 100)		Wholesale Prices (1967 = 100)		Implicit Price Deflator (1958 = 100)	
	All Items	Food	All Commodities	Farm Products	GNP	Personal Consumption
1964	92.9	92.4	94.7	94.6	108.85	107.4
1965	94.5	94.4	95.6	93.7	110.86	108.8
1966	97.2	99.1	99.8	105.9	113.95	111.5
1967	100.0	100.0	100.0	100.0	117.59	114.4
1968	104.2	103.6	102.5	102.5	122.30	118.4
1969	109.8	108.9	106.5	109.1	128.20	123.5
1970	116.3	114.9	110.4	111.0	135.23	129.3
1971	121.3	118.4	113.9	112.9	141.61	134.2
1972	125.3	123.5	119.1	125.0	145.83	137.4

Source. Economic Report of the President.

both services and investment goods. The IPD is obtained by comparing the level of current dollar GNP—the market value of all goods and services—with the constant dollar GNP—the value of all goods and services measured in terms of prices prevailing in the base year (usually 1958). For example, current dollar GNP in 1970 was $974.1 billion—measured in 1970 (current year) prices; but measured in terms of 1958 prices only $720.0 billion worth of goods and services were produced in 1970. For 1970 the GNP deflator, with 1958 base, is $974.1/$720.0 = 135.3%. More generally, the implicit GNP price deflator recorded in Figure 11.2 is simply

$$\text{IPD}_t(1958 = 100) = \frac{\text{Current dollar GNP in year } t}{\text{GNP in year } t \text{ measured in 1958 prices}} \quad (3.1)$$

The same formula is used for calculating implicit price deflators for government spending, consumption, investment, and certain subcomponents of the GNP accounts; however, the IPD is not available in the detailed commodity breakdowns provided by both the WPI and the CPI.

None of these indices constitutes an ideal measure of inflation. But some limitations are more serious than others. While the indices are subject to sampling error, it turns out in studying recent United States inflations that this is not a serious factor because the Bureau of Labor Statistics uses very large samples. Prior to 1947 some 900 items were priced for the WPI, and the sample has now been increased to about 2450 commodities. For

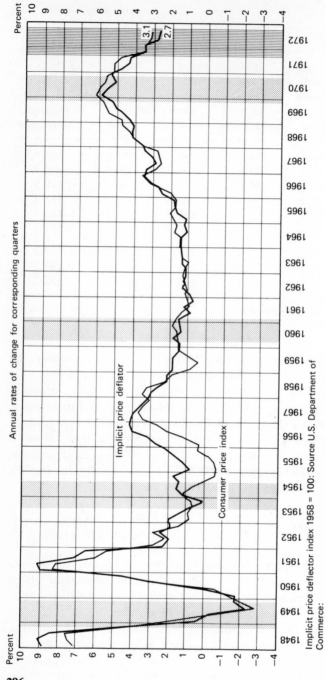

Annual rates of change for corresponding quarters

Implicit price deflator index 1958 = 100: Source U.S. Department of Commerce:

Consumer price index 1967 = 100: source U.S. Department of Labor:

The first four shaded areas represent periods of business recessions as defined by the National Bureau of Economic Research.

The last shaded area represents the wage–price–control period.

Fig. 11.3 *Alternative measures of price fluctuations.*

Table 11.5   THE PACE OF INFLATION, 1948–1972

	Wholesale Prices		Consumer Prices		Implicit Price Deflator	
Year	All	Farm Products	All	Food	Total Private	Private Non-farm
1948	1.5	−6.8	2.7	−0.8	6.7	6.8
1949	−6.1	−8.9	−1.8	−3.7	−1.0	0.8
1950	14.7	17.0	5.8	9.6	1.0	1.1
1951	1.2	3.5	5.9	7.4	7.3	6.5
1952	−3.4	−8.2	0.9	−1.1	1.9	2.6
1953	0.5	−2.3	0.6	−1.3	0.7	1.8
1954	−0.6	−2.6	−0.5	−1.6	1.2	1.7
1955	1.6	−6.4	0.4	−0.9	0.9	1.3
1956	4.5	6.0	2.9	3.1	3.2	3.4
1957	2.0	4.2	3.0	2.8	3.6	3.7
1958	0.5	−0.2	1.8	2.2	2.1	1.7
1959	−0.3	−4.4	1.5	−0.8	1.4	1.8
1960	0.5	3.9	1.5	3.1	1.4	1.4
1961	−0.2	−0.6	0.7	−0.9	0.9	0.9
1962	0.0	0.6	1.2	1.5	0.9	0.9
1963	−0.1	−2.1	1.6	1.9	1.0	1.2
1964	0.4	0.0	1.2	1.4	1.2	1.3
1965	3.4	9.5	1.9	3.4	1.7	1.4
1966	1.7	0.2	3.4	3.9	2.5	2.2
1967	1.0	−1.8	3.0	1.2	2.9	3.3
1968	2.8	3.5	4.7	4.3	3.6	3.5
1969	4.8	7.5	6.1	7.2	4.5	4.5
1970	2.2	−1.4	5.5	2.2	4.8	5.0
1971	4.0	6.0	3.4	4.3	4.3	4.3
1972	6.5	14.4	3.4	4.7	2.6	2.1

Source. *Economic Report of the President.*

the CPI approximately 400 different items are priced in 56 different geographical areas. This is more than sufficient; statisticians estimate that the CPI sample is of such size as to insure that recorded changes of more than one tenth of a percentage point reflect actual changes in the cost of living instead of sampling error.[12] A caveat concerning sampling error is in order

[12] The standard error for annual changes is 0.06; there is only a 5% probability that a change larger than 0.12 will be observed if, in fact, prices have been stable. The standard error, and hence the confidence interval, is smaller for quarterly and monthly changes.

when looking at fluctuations in minor components of the price indices, but no problem is involved in measuring the overall movement of the price level.

A serious problem is created by the introduction of new products and changes in quality. Color television is an expensive consumer durable that obviously belongs in the CPI; 20 years ago it was unavailable at any price—its price was infinite. As with most new consumer durables, during the years following its introduction, the price of color television sets declined considerably. If it had been included very early in the CPI this downward trend might have introduced a negative bias into the CPI—thus timing is important. Quality change is an even more difficult problem; if the rise in the price of an item reflects an improvement in quality it should not be interpreted as inflationary. For cars ingenuity is required in attempting to take into account changes in warranty provisions, horsepower, size, and so forth.[13] And while almost everyone will agree that the quality of medical care has been subject to continued improvement, how can the statistician determine if the improvement in quality has more than offset the spiraling increase in treatment cost? The patient-day cost of hospital treatment has skyrocketed, but the length of time a patient will spend in the hospital for obstetrical purposes or an appendectomy has declined considerably within the last generation. And the house call is a service that the patient can no longer purchase from a busy physician. These are the problems that cause the price statistician to lose sleep.

That the quality improvement factor may lead to a substantial exaggeration of the seriousness of inflation is suggested by a simple test proposed by Professor Richard Ruggles of Yale University. Ruggles suggests that one consider the choice between spending a hypothetical gift of $100 in this year's Sears Roebuck catalog or the alternative of spending the same number of dollars in a 20-year old catalog. When confronted with the choice, most choose the current catalog, implying that the quality improvements and new items now available more than offset the apparent rise in prices; that is, there has been no inflation. Of course, such a test neglects services, style changes, and the greater variety of goods now offered by leading mail-order houses.

---

[13] From 1954 to 1960 the price of new cars, unadjusted for quality change, increased by 34%; the Bureau of Labor statistics attributed 23% to product improvement and regarded 11% as inflationary. But a study by Professor Zvi Griliches suggests that with proper allowance for quality improvement the price of new cars actually dropped by 27% over this period. Subsequently, the Bureau of Labor Statistics has improved its procedures and reported that the automobile manufacturers have become more helpful in providing information facilitating the evaluation of quality changes. For a discussion of this and more general problems of measuring style, see Franklin Fisher, Z. Griliches, and C. Kaysen, "The Costs of Automobile Model Changes Since 1949," *Journal of Political Economy*, October 1962.

Quality improvement biases are not limited to the CPI. The whole-sale price index for machinery and equipment is obviously subject to distortion through quality improvement. The implicit price index is subject to additional distortion because it is assumed in measuring the product of the government and most of the service sector that output per man-hour never changes; in practice the introduction of office machinery and electronic computers had greatly improved productivity, and this has partially offset increases in hourly pay.[14] Indices of construction cost, both residential and industrial, have been computed on the basis of wage rates and material costs without allowance for changes in output per man-hour that have resulted from the development of off-the-site fabrication of components, the introduction of the backhoe for excavation work, and so forth.

Another measurement problem arises from discrepancies between quoted and actual prices. This is very serious in periods of wartime rationing when black-market transactions are ignored in the official price indices. But even in normal circumstances it may be a continuing problem of more than negligible magnitude, judging by the investigation of George Stigler and James Kindahl.[15] In contrast to the Bureau of Labor Statistics, they constructed price indices based on what customers reported *paying* for commodities instead of the prices that producers said they charged. While the Stigler-Kindahl index moved with the general trend in the official index most of the time, their index showed a different picture in periods of slack. Stigler and Kindahl suggest that sellers do not revise price quotations downward when market conditions soften, even though rebates, a relaxation of payment terms, adjustments in delivery times, and the substitution of higher-quality merchandise may mean that the effective price paid by the buyer has fallen considerably; such a tendency is likely to be exaggerated in periods when the threat of government price controls or wage-price "guideposts" make it likely that producers will have difficulty in raising price quotations once demand for their product picks up. To the extent that price indices are sticky downward, they will not reveal promptly the extent to which anti-inflationary measures are effective.

Factors causing price indices to overstate the pace of inflation also result in a corresponding tendency to underestimate real GNP. For example, if the price index for the auto sector overstates the extent of price rise because quality improvement is neglected, the estimated value of auto output obtained by deflating auto sales by the index will be too small (the simple alternative of counting the number of cars produced would neglect

[14] The early development of electronic computers was spurred largely by the overwhelming problems encountered in processing census returns by hand.

[15] George J. Stigler and James K. Kindahl, *The Behavior of Industrial Prices*, National Bureau of Economic Research, 1970.

entirely quality improvement and changes in size). Note from Equation 3.1 that if real output is underestimated by the GNP accountant, the resulting rise in the IPD will be too high. Obviously, the issue of quality improvement must concern anyone interested in measuring the rate of growth of the economy.

Fortunately, the problem of improving our measures of price change has received continuing attention from academic researchers, the Joint Economic Committee, and governmental agencies.[16] Considerable progress has been made in measuring quality improvement. And, in any case, the tendency for price indices to exaggerate the seriousness of inflation because of inadequacies in measuring quality improvements in certain commodities may be offset at least partially by other factors. Because the GNP accounts neglect the effects of air pollution, they provide an exaggerated picture of improved well-being. In much the same way, such factors as increased population density as well as air pollution may provide an offsetting downward bias if the consumer price index is interpreted as a measure of the *cost of living.*

*11.4 TYPES OF INFLATION; REMEDIES AND PANACEAS

There are numerous types of inflation and at least an equal number of remedies. The first step in treatment is diagnosis and, in preparation for more detailed analysis in subsequent chapters, we must briefly survey the various types of inflation and the associated remedies. We will find that while no one advocates inflation, its prevalence is not to be explained entirely in terms of ineptitude on the part of central bankers and fiscal authorities. Sometimes inflation appears to be the lesser evil. Sometimes the remedies are worse than the disease. Sometimes the task of fighting inflation is given a low priority. Let us consider some examples.

a. Wage-Push and Cost-Push Inflation

The consumer blames the butcher and the grocer for rising prices, the retailer blames the manufacturer, and the manufacturer blames the rising costs of raw materials and labor. In countries heavily dependent on imports, currency devaluation can have a substantial cost-push impact. And, in every country, rounds of price increases can follow the negotiation of key labor contracts. But labor union leaders are quick to claim that the price increases are larger than required to meet the increased wages bill

---

[16] See, in particular, the statement by Dr. Arthur M. Ross, Commissioner of Labor Statistics, before the Joint Economic Committee, Hearings on *Government Price Statistics* in May 1966.

and that management has picked the moment of contract settlement as a particularly opportune time from a public relations viewpoint for announcing price increases that had been planned all along. *Cost-push* and *wage-push* explanations of inflation abound whenever prices are rising; and while it is true, without question, that the exercise of restraint by producers and workers can do much to moderate the pace of price advance, it is difficult to find inflations that are purely wage-push or cost-push in origin.

b. Wage and Price Controls

The wage- and cost-push diagnoses suggest wage and price controls as an immediate corollary. And, when price controls are adopted in an attempt to repress inflation, shortages inevitably result unless the economy was already afflicted with considerable excess capacity and unemployment.[17] And the shortages frequently lead to the adoption of formal rationing procedures in the hope that the gap between supply and demand can be equitably apportioned. In the absence of major war, somewhat less formal controls are often imposed; the "incomes policy" adopted by many European countries and the "wage-price guideposts" promulgated early in the Kennedy Administration were attempts to focus the spotlight of public opinion on those industries following "inflationary" pricing strategies. Price controls and rationing may be tolerated for a while; indeed, during World War II they received much patriotic support in many countries, including the United States. But the longer controls are imposed, the more frustrating the shortages and the more prevalent the blackmarket. After World War II, Congress was reluctant to continue the extensive network of direct controls that President Truman thought he needed to prevent inflation. The lifting of restrictions was followed by a period of intense inflation; the net effect of controls had been to postpone instead of eliminate inflation.

One cost of controls involves the great administrative and enforcement expense. During World War II about 60,000 people, hardly a negligible fraction of the work force, were employed in the price control program. And, during the Korean War, when controls were not nearly as extensive, about 15,000 government employees were assigned to price regulation jobs.[18] But the manpower involved is not the major resource expense incurred when a program of price controls is adopted. Price controls

---

[17] Simple supply and demand analysis suggests that the imposition of price controls on competitive markets inevitably leads to a gap between supply and demand. However, if the demand curve facing the firm is downward sloping, price controls can induce profit-maximizing monopolists to increase output.

[18] President Nixon's Economic Stabilization Program in 1972 used about 3000 Internal Revenue Service personnel; partly for this reason it was judged by many to be a "cosmetic" public relations effect instead of a serious attempt at regulation.

rigidify the economy; in times of all out defense mobilization they may prevent the shift in relative prices required to bid resources away from the civilian sector. Indeed, the process of inflation can make a positive contribution to the task of shifting resources from civilian to military use. In principle, the increase in the relative wages required to induce workers to move to the shipyards, the defense plant, and United Aircraft might be achieved without a rise in the average money wage rate by imposing a reduction of money wages in industries producing civilian goods. But it is always difficult to impose a reduction in money wages, particularly when labor markets are tight. It may be much less damaging to worker morale and production incentives to pay premium wages for defense workers and achieve the required reduction in the real wage through inflation.

In peacetime, too, the forces leading to inflation may gain so much momentum that controls receive serious consideration. Professor Arthur F. Burns, Chairman of the Board of Governors of the Federal Reserve System, argued before the Senate Committee on Banking and Housing and Urban Affairs in January 1973:

"The performance of the American economy in recent years, as well as that of other industrialized nations, has persuaded me that there is a need for legislation permitting some direct controls over wages and prices. I do not think that resort to such controls will be required all, or even much, of the time. However, the structure of our economy—in particular, the power of many corporations and trade unions to exact rewards that exceed what could be achieved under conditions of competition—does expose us to upward pressure on costs and prices that may be cumulative and self-reinforcing. In dealing with the immediate inflationary problem, it would not be safe to rely exclusively on the Government's management of aggregate demand policies."

It is generally recognized that wage and price controls may contain the inflation for short periods, but they tend to deteriorate in effectiveness as the public gradually learns how to circumvent them, as their distortive effects on resource allocation becomes obvious, and as it becomes more and more apparent that the inflation may not be cost-push in origin after all.

c. Demand-Pull Inflation and the Inflationary Gap

Particularly in times of war or forced industrialization, an excess of aggregate demand over available supply will generate irresistible inflationary pressure. This situation, sometimes referred to as "too much money chasing too few goods," is illustrated in Figure 11.4. Here all the GNP accounting concepts are measured in real terms—constant prices of a particular year—so that the analysis will not be distorted by a change in the price level. Initially the economy is in full-employment equilibrium at a capacity output Y_c. But a step-up in the level of government spending of ΔG, perhaps due to war, means that equilibrium could only be achieved at output Y_e,

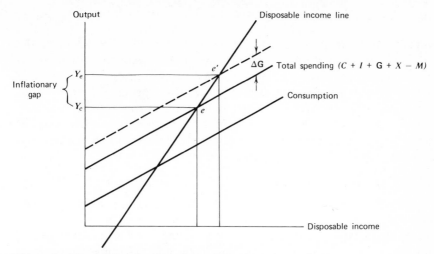

Fig. 11.4 *The inflationary gap. By pushing the economy beyond the capacity level of output* (Y_c), *an injection of additional
government spending generates an inflationary gap* ($Y_e - Y_c$).

well beyond the capacity level. Prices rise in an attempt to ration the short
supply of goods. Inflationary pressure would be eliminated if capacity
could be increased from Y_c to Y_e. And, as a first approximation, it may be
assumed that the rate of price change is proportional to this "inflationary
gap" between equilibrium and capacity output, the distance $Y_e - Y_c$.[19]
Thus the greater government spending, the greater the gap and the more
rapid the inflation.

Inflationary gap analysis implies that the way to stop inflation is to
restrict effective demand. Rationing is only one weapon that can be used
to achieve this objective. During World War II every effort was made to
encourage saving instead of consumption; the public was urged to buy
war bonds to be sure that Uncle Sam would have the money to buy the
weapons our boys needed in Iwo Jima! Although many recognized that
the government could borrow from the Fed or even print money in order
to buy weapons, the bond drives did induce the public to make sizable
purchases. That such measures did indeed help to eliminate the inflationary
gap is suggested by Figure 4.2, where it may be observed that consumption
fell far below the level that the consumption function predicted.

During periods of less than all out mobilization, as with the Korean
and Viet Nam conflicts, it may be possible to finance military expenditures
entirely with higher taxes. This, in itself, is likely to arouse domestic oppo-

[19] This is only one of a variety of related definitions of the inflationary gap; alternative concepts will be introduced in later chapters.

sition to the war effort and weaken work incentives. Furthermore, the balanced budget multiplier concept suggests that excessive demand—an inflationary gap—may be generated unless taxes are raised by more than enough to match the higher level of government spending; a government surplus would be required to prevent an inflationary gap. If the government runs a deficit instead, the same economic costs are involved, but they will not be so apparent to the public, particularly if the inflation is interpreted as being wage- or cost-push in origin.

d. Monetary Policy

That an excessive injection of money by the central bank can generate inflation is suggested by the quantity theory of money. But to assert that money frequently contributes to inflation is not to offer an alternative to the demand-pull explanation. An inflationary gap may be generated even in the absence of an increase in government spending if the central bank creates too much money, since an inappropriate reduction in the rate of interest may generate an excessive increase in private investment spending. That all this must be so will become clear with the aid of the *IS-LM* apparatus, which provides a convenient framework for appraising the role of monetary factors in inflation.

The *IS-LM* approach treats the level of investment as an endogenous variable; and it determines the conditions under which the public will be willing to hold the existing stock of money. In Figure 11.5 all variables will be measured in constant dollars. In particular, the *LM* curve must correspond to those combinations of the rate of interest and real output at which the public will be willing to hold the existing money supply, where the money supply itself is measured in real terms—$M_s = M^n/p$, demand deposits plus the number of dollar bills the central bank has created divided by an appropriate price index.

Suppose an initial full-employment equilibrium is disturbed by an increase in the money supply. The immediate effect, illustrated in the graph, will be to push the *LM* curve out to the right, as explained in Chapter 5.5. But because the economy is already operating at capacity, an inflation gap—most conveniently measured by the distance $Y_e - Y_c$—means rising prices. And the inflationary gap will be self-correcting if the central bank restrains itself from injecting additional new money into the system. Given the nominal money supply, M_s^n, rising prices reduce its purchasing power; M_s must fall. This pushes the *LM* curve back to the left toward its original position. Indeed, it can be argued that prices will continue to rise and the real money supply will continue to contract until the inflationary gap is eliminated—hence the *LM* curve must ultimately return to its original position. The increase in the money supply causes prices to rise for a period; eventually the price index will level out, but on a higher plateau

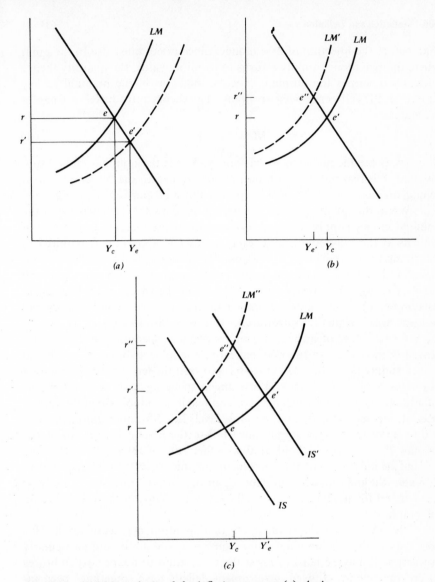

Fig. 11.5 IS-LM *analysis of the inflationary gap.* (a) *An increase in the money supply shifts the* LM *curve, generating an inflationary gap of* $Y_e - Y_c$, *but the resulting inflation serves to reduce the real value of the money supply, moving the* LM *curve back toward its original position.* (b) *A reduction in the money supply reduces the level of effective demand, creating unemployment.* (c) *An increase in government spending that pushes the equilibrium level of output beyond capacity causes inflation, but rising prices induce a leftward shift of the* LM *curve that gradually eliminates the inflationary pressure.*

than before the injection of new money. Since prices must rise to the point where the *real* money supply returns to its initial value, the quantity theory correctly describes the ultimate effect of increases in the nominal money supply on the fully employed economy. The theory introduced in Chapter 5.2 states

$$\mathbf{M}_s^n v_y = p Y \tag{4.1}$$

where v_y is the income velocity of money, $\mathbf{M}_s^n$ is the nominal money supply, and Y is real output; with output constrained to the full-employment ceiling, an increase in $\mathbf{M}_s^n$ must be matched by a proportionate change in p.

While the quantity theory accurately predicts that an increase in the nominal money supply will lead to a proportionate increase in p if output remains at the full-employment level, the *IS-LM* apparatus is required to determine how a reduction in the quantity of money will influence output, prices, and velocity. This deflationary process is illustrated on the righthand panel of Figure 11.4. The bottom panel shows the effects of an increase in government spending, a case already considered when the inflationary gap concept was originally introduced. But the *IS-LM* apparatus reveals the ultimate effect of an increase in government spending on a fully employed economy, given the nominal money supply; as prices rise, the real money supply falls, the *LM* curve shifts toward the left, and the rising rate of interest serves to restrict real investment spending so as to eliminate the inflationary gap; in this instance, the end result is an increase in the rate of interest, income velocity, and the price level. Equilibrium requires that the real value of the money supply must fall to the point where it equals the amount the public will hold at this higher rate of interest, r''; thus the amount of inflation and the corresponding change in velocity required to eliminate the inflationary gap depends in part on the interest elasticity of the demand for money, which is reflected in the slope of the *LM* curve on the graph.

The *IS-LM* apparatus suggests that inflation may cure itself. This does require that the nominal money supply be stabilized, and particularly in wartime it may be hard to resist the temptation to finance expenditures by creating money. Indeed, government deficits have sometimes been increased by efforts to reduce the hardships of inflation; for example, during the Korean War, the government of South Korea tried to keep down the price of necessities such as rice with government subsidy payments, but the effort only stimulated more inflation because the subsidy was financed by printing money.

e. Monetary Conversion

Letting inflation cure itself may be preferable in the longer run to repressing inflation through wage and price controls. But instead of letting prices rise it may be more expeditious to reduce drastically the quantity of money in circulation. Monetary conversion is a dramatic procedure for dealing with a drastically swollen money supply. In June 1948 citizens of West Germany were suddenly informed that they must register all their holdings of the German Reichmark immediately. Half of the currency they deposited was promptly converted into the new Deutsche mark at the rate of one new Deutsch mark for 10 old Reichmarks; for the other half they received only a receipt, as these funds were placed in blocked bank accounts and could not be withdrawn; all undeclared currency became worthless.[20] Demand deposits were also converted at the 10 to 1 ratio. In this way the money supply of Western Germany was reduced from about 150 billion Reichmarks to 12 billion Deutsche marks. Here is a monetary experiment that dwarfs the most violent changes in the money supply ever attempted by central banks in normal times!

This drastic move was required because the increase in the German money supply from 35 billion Reichmarks in 1936 to 200 in 1945 had been accompanied by a drop in production to half its prewar level. Prior to the war the velocity of money—v in the quantity equation $M_s^n v_y = pY$—had been about 1.7. At the close of the war velocity had been pushed down to about 0.12, because price controls had repressed the inflationary implications of a rising money supply coupled with reduced output. Although controls had kept prices from rising much, the German currency was nonetheless discredited; while everybody had currency in their pockets, there were few goods in the marketplace. The chief motive for holding a job was to obtain a ration card. An enormous amount of manpower was devoted to barter and foraging for food instead of to productive activity. Simply removing controls would have precipitated a severe inflation. If, in the absence of price controls, velocity had returned to its old value, the price index would have risen to about 13 or 14 times prewar levels.

By 1948 reform was long overdue, and ample precedent was provided by the Belgium experience with currency conversion in 1944. But in Germany reform was delayed partly because of the Morgenthau plan. Henry Morgenthau, the influential Secretary of the United States Treasury, had argued that Germany must be converted into an agrarian state so that she would never again become a threat to world peace. Initially, American occupation policy had been to do nothing that would encourage the rebuilding of Germany into a self-supporting economy. And, when this policy was reversed, additional delay followed because of an unsuccessful attempt to negotiate an all-German reform involving the Soviet Sector. The June 1948 reform was executed unilaterally. Since West Germany possessed

---

[20] Because the old currency continued to circulate in East Germany, some undeclared currency found its way into Russian-occupied territory, where it added to inflationary pressure.

about $\frac{2}{3}$ of the German population it was reasonable to guess that at pre-war levels of production the appropriate money supply would be about $\frac{2}{3}$ of the 35 billion Reichmarks circulating throughout Germany before the war, or $23\frac{1}{3}$ billion. But production had dropped in half and, according to the quantity theory, this implied that a further cutback in the money supply to about $11\frac{2}{3}$ billion was required.

In the absence of more precise data, the quantity theory estimate of a money supply of 12 billion Deutsche marks seems like a reasonable target for the architects of the German monetary reform to have aimed at. And, in the aftermath of war, the quantity theory turned out to be the best one-eyed monster in the valley of the blind; the reform worked! The pressure on price controls relaxed, inflationary expectations were broken, and hoarded goods returned to the shops. Industrial production rose by 50% within six months. A good share of the miracle of German recovery has been attributed to this successful application of the quantity theory.

Some 24 monetary conversions were executed in Europe after World War II; the same technique was employed repeatedly in South Korea, Vietnam, and numerous other Asian countries. The conversions fared with mixed success. In terms of the *IS-LM* apparatus, monetary reform serves to shift the *LM* curve of Figure 11.5 over to the left without rising prices. When applied repeatedly, conversion will be anticipated by the public, and their efforts to dispose of currency holdings in advance of con-version will only add to inflationary pressures. And monetary conversion cannot work if the government does not resist the temptation to finance additional expenditures through renewed expansion of the money supply. Indeed, the money supply expanded fairly rapidly in Germany after the 1948 reform, but this was the consequence of intensive bank lending to finance business activities instead of government deficits. And it should be noted that currency conversion works many of the same hardships as inflation itself; the holder of money balances is taxed either way. Of course, if the conversion catches a black marketeer concealing his illegal trans-actions by carrying large amounts of cash, so much the better. And when drastic surgery is required, currency conversion dramatically adjusts the money supply in order to eliminate inflationary pressures. In contrast, just letting prices rise might generate adverse expectations of still more inflation and disrupt the efficiency with which markets operate during the longer time required in transition to equilibrium.[21]

[21] In times of armed conflict it might be possible to disrupt the enemy's economy by flooding it with currency. It is said that in World War II the Germans planned to flood the British economy with counterfeit currency. And according to *Newsweek* (January 1, 1973, p. 7) the outlawed Irish Republican Army was planning to flood Londonderry and Belfast with counterfeit £1 and £5 notes. This type of economic warfare would have consequences just the opposite of those of monetary reform.

*11.5 STUDYING INFLATION

In surveying the topic of inflation it was convenient to resort to such descriptive concepts as "cost-push" and "demand-pull" inflation. But, in subsequent chapters, an alternative dichotomy in terms of the distinction between static and dynamic concepts proves more fruitful. Static analysis is concerned with the factors determining how much of a change in the price level will ultimately be generated by a disturbance. Thus, in terms of the top panel of Figure 11.6, static analysis tries to explain why more inflation occurred in Case A than in Case B. Dynamic analysis focuses on questions of timing. Dynamic analysis should explain why prices rose more rapidly in Case B than in Case A, as illustrated in the bottom panel of Figure 11.5. In Chapter 12 we use static analysis in studying the determinants of aggregate demand and supply and investigating the circumstances

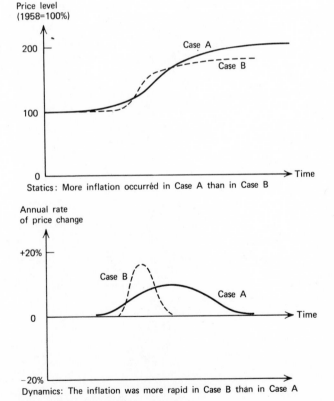

Fig. 11.6 *Statics versus dynamics.*

under which wage and price rigidities may prevent the attainment of full employment. We will look at the full-employment world of flexible money wages analyzed by classical economists. We will compare their model with the Keynesian system, in which wages do not decline even in the face of widespread unemployment. In Chapter 13 the dynamic process determining the rate of price change is subjected to analysis. In particular, we will look at the "Phillips curve" link between the rate of unemployment and the speed of inflation. We will also investigate the circumstances under which the continued injection of new money may allow a government to finance spending by "forced saving" instead of by taxation.

REFERENCES

1. A comprehensive survey of the theory of inflation was presented by M. Bronfenbrenner and F. D. Holzman.

   M. Bronfenbrenner and F. D. Holzman, "Survey of Inflation Theory," *American Economic Review*, September 1963.

2. An exciting account of how the abrupt changes in the money supply achieved by monetary reforms influenced price movements in post-World War II Europe is provided by John Gurley.

   John Gurley, "Excess Liquidity and European Monetary Reform," *American Economic Review*, March 1953.

3. The following papers discuss various distributional aspects of inflation.

   Albert Ando and G. L. Bach, "The Redistributional Effects of Inflation," *Review of Economics and Statistics*, February 1957.

   Andrew Brimmer, "Inflation and Income Distribution in the United States," *Review of Economics and Statistics*, February 1971.

   Seymour E. Harris, "The Incidence of Inflation: Or Who Gets Hurt?"; H. S. Houthakker, "Protection Against Inflation"; and Alfred H. Conrad, "The Share of Wages and Salaries in Manufacturing Income, 1947–56," in Joint Economic Committee, 86th Congress, 1st Session, November 26, 1959, *Study of Employment, Growth, and Price Levels.*

   William D. Nordhaus, "The Effects of Inflation on the Distribution of Economic Welfare," *Journal of Money, Credit, and Banking*, 1973.

   James Tobin and Leonard Ross, "Living with Inflation: A Liberal Perspective on the Eve of Nixon's New Economic Policy," *New York Review of Books*, May 6, 1971.

KEY CONCEPTS

hyperinflation

repressed inflation

money wage versus the real wage

nominal versus real rate of interest

inflationary gap

demand pull versus cost push inflation

implicit price deflator

wholesale versus consumer price index

EXERCISES

11.1 The projections reported on the following table were initially published in the 1970 *Economic Report of the President*, p. 79.

GROSS NATIONAL PRODUCT, 1969 AND PROJECTIONS FOR
1970–1975 (BILLIONS OF DOLLARS, 1969 PRICES)

Year	1970	1971	1972	1973	1974	1975
Potential output	944	980	1042	1103	1150	1200

The potential output series estimated what "the economy would be capable of producing when operating at an unemployment rate of about 3.8%." It was estimated that potential output would rise by about 4.3% in real terms.

Since the figures are reported in 1969 prices, they are not directly comparable to either current dollar or 1958 dollar GNP data. Convert the figures so that they can be compared with actual GNP figures, either 1958 or current dollars.

11.2 The following editorial statement appeared in the Pittsburgh Press on August 5, 1966.

"The gross national product (statistical measure of all the goods and services produced in the nation) reached a record high in current dollars of 732 billion dollars (at an annual rate) in the second quarter of 1966. But in terms of 1958 dollars, as computed by the Federal Reserve Board, these goods and services were worth only 644 billion dollars. In short, in eight years inflation has cost us nearly 90 billion dollars."

a. How much did the GNP implicit price deflator rise during this eight-year period?

b. What are the major problems involved in trying to measure the rate at which prices are rising? What are the strengths and weaknesses of the GNP deflator, the wholesale price index, and the cost of living index as yardsticks for measuring movements in the general level of prices?

c. Explain any weaknesses in the method utilized by the *Press* for analyzing the costs to our economy of inflation.

11.3 Prepare a rough estimate of what happened to the (*ex post*) real rate of interest on new homes from 1965 on.

APPENDIX 11.A   INDEX NUMBERS

11.A.1   INTRODUCTION

The cost of living data compiled by the Bureau of Labor Statistics is only one example of a wide variety of indices used in analyzing economic developments. The industrial production index, published in the *Federal Reserve Bulletin*, provides a monthly indicator of movements in manufacturing output. The Dow Jones Industrial Average, first compiled in 1896, and the Standard and Poor 500 are only two of many stock market indicators watched daily by investors. And, in addition to measuring changing magnitudes over time, indices may also be constructed to compare the cost of living in different regions of the country and to facilitate international comparisons of output levels. Several of the problems involved in constructing summary measures of the rate of inflation were mentioned in Chapter 11, Section 3. In this appendix a variety of difficulties encountered in attempting to summarize divergent movements over a variety of commodities in a single "index number" are considered in greater detail.

11.A.2   A PRODUCTION INDEX

For illustrative purposes we will consider data for only two commodities in a hypothetical economy. But we will develop a notation that will permit us to generalize the analysis over an arbitrary number of commodities (more than 2200 items are considered in the construction of the WPI). Consider the data in Table 11.A.1.

Table 11.A.1   HYPOTHETICAL PRICE AND QUANTITY DATA

	1970		1971	
Commodity	Price	Quantity	Price	Quantity
1 apples	$.70	200	$1	150
2 pears	$.85	200	$1	100

Let the symbol p_{it} denote the price of the ith commodity for time period t and let q_{it} denote the corresponding quantity; thus p_{10} indicates the $.70 price of the first commodity (apples) in 1970 (we suppress 197) and q_{21} is the output of 100 pears in 1971. Now how can we construct an index of fruit production? We know that we are not supposed to "add apples and pears," otherwise it would be tempting to conclude that output had fallen from 400 to 250 (for similar commodities such an approach might not be too bad, but it would be more difficult in comparing the output of a multitude of commodities, ranging from TV sets to coal and textbooks). The alternative approach is to "weight" the output of each commodity by its price. The *value of output* in 1970 is

$$0.70 \times 200 + 0.85 \times 200 = p_{10}q_{10} + p_{20}q_{20} = \$310 \qquad (2.1)$$

And the value of output in 1971 is

$$1.00 \times 150 + 1.00 \times 100 = p_{11}q_{11} + p_{21}q_{21} = \$250 \tag{2.2}$$

However, it is hardly reasonable to say that the index of 1971 output (relative to 1970) is $250/310 = 80.6\%$, since the output of the first commodity is only 75% of its former level and the second has dropped by 50%! The 80.6% figure is obviously distorted by the rising trend in prices.

One appropriate strategy is to recognize that the dollar bill constitutes a "rubber yardstick" and use the same prices in evaluating both period's output. The value of 1971 output evaluated in terms of 1970 prices is

$$0.70 \times 150 + 0.85 \times 100 = p_{10}q_{11} + p_{20}q_{21} = \$190 \tag{2.3}$$

Comparing this figure, the value of 1971 output in 1970 prices, with the value of 1970 output given in Equation 2.1, suggests that output in 1971 was at $190/310 = 61.3\%$ of its 1970 level. This figure seems reasonable, but an alternative approach that is equally legitimate exists. Instead of using 1970 prices in evaluating output in the two periods, why not use 1971 prices? Now 1970 output evaluated in 1971 prices is

$$1.00 \times 200 + 1.00 \times 200 = p_{11}q_{10} + p_{21}q_{20} = \$400 \tag{2.4}$$

Comparing this figure with the 1971 output evaluated in 1971 prices (Equation 2.2 above) yields $250/\$400 = 62.5\%$, a figure that differs only slightly from the 61.3% figure computed with the alternative 1970 price weights.

Before investigating how serious such "*index number problems*" turn out to be in practice, it will be useful to summarize the argument in terms of summation notation; this will provide us with formulas appropriate when dealing with any arbitrary number of commodities. Remembering that p_{it} and q_{it} denote the price and quantity of the ith commodity at date t, we may write

$$\sum_i p_{it}q_{it'} = p_{1t}q_{1t'} + p_{2t}q_{2t'} + \ldots + p_{nt}q_{nt'} \tag{2.5}$$

to denote the value of output produced in t' evaluated in year t prices (the i under the summation sign, which indicates that the sum is over the i commodities instead of over the t subscript, may be omitted when there is no danger of confusion). It is easily verified that in terms of this notation we have for our hypothetical data

$$\sum_i p_{i0}q_{i0} = \$310; \qquad \sum_i p_{i1}q_{i1} = \$250$$

$$\sum_i p_{i0}q_{i1} = \$190; \qquad \sum_i p_{i1}q_{i0} = \$400$$

The first of the two production indices, sometimes called a *Laspeyres* index, is given by the formula

$$Q_L(t) = \frac{\sum p_{i0}q_{it}}{\sum p_{i0}q_{i0}} \tag{2.6}$$

This index measures the change in overall *production* in year t relative to output in year 0 (the base year). For our example, the Laspeyres index was

$$Q_L(1971) = \frac{\$190}{\$310} = 61.3\%$$

For an alternative output index based on the more recent price weights, the *Paasche* quality index, we have the formula

$$Q_p(t) = \frac{\sum p_{it}q_{it}}{\sum p_{it}q_{i0}} \tag{2.7}$$

And for our example the Paasche index was

$$Q_p(1971) = \frac{\$250}{\$400} = 62.5\%$$

Although the choice between alternative price weights in practice often has no larger effect than that indicated by this numerical example, sizable discrepancies may be encountered at times. Consider the problem of comparing the Gross National Product of the Soviet Union with that of the United States. Detailed data compiled by Morris Bornstein for 1955 are presented in Table 11.A.2. It is indeed disconcerting to find that in 1955 the Soviet Union's GNP is either 26.8% or 53.4% as large as that of the United States, depending on whether the ruble or dollar prices are used in making the comparison. That is, the Soviet economy does better relative to the United States in terms of those items that have the highest price in our capitalistic economy. One way of reconciling this index number problem is to take an average. Alfred Marshall (1842–1924) suggested the arithmetic average, which

Table 11.A.2 INDEX NUMBER COMPARISONS OF THE GROSS NATIONAL PRODUCTS OF THE UNITED STATES AND RUSSIA FOR 1955

	Ruble Comparison (*Billions*)	*Dollar Comparison* (*Billions*)
Soviet GNP	1285.8	212.4
United States GNP	4802.1	397.5
Indices	$\frac{1285.8}{4802.1} = 26.8\%$	$\frac{212.4}{397.5} = 53.4\%$
Arithmetic average (Alfred Marshall)$(26.8\% + 53.4\%)/2 = 40.1\%$		
Geometric average (Irving Fisher) $\sqrt{26.8\% \cdot 53.4\%} = 37.8\%$		

Source. Morris Bornstein, "A Comparison of Soviet & United States National Product," in *Comparisons of the United States and Soviet Economies*, Joint Economic Committee, 86th Congress, 1st Session, U.S. Government Printing Office, 1960, p. 385.

in this comparison yields a figure of 40.1%. But Irving Fisher (1867–1947) recommended as an "ideal index" the use of the geometric average which, in this case, yields 37.8%. Although the figures are now in the same ball park, the remaining gap, even between the two averages, is disconcertingly large.[22]

11.A.3   PRICE INDICES

The problems involved in constructing price indices parallel in a number of respects those encountered in constructing quantity indices. To find out how much prices have increased, we must weigh those of each commodity appropriately, but what weights should be used? In terms of our hypothetical data on Table 11.A.1 there are two obvious candidates, either 1970 or 1971 quantity weights. That is, we can compare the cost of buying the 1970 "market basket" in 1970 with its cost in 1971; from Equation 2.4 we note that the basket cost $400 in 1970 instead of the $310 that Equation 2.1 reveals as its actual price in 1970; hence the Laspeyres price index is $400/$310 $=$ 129.0%. The general formula for the Laspeyres price index is

$$P_L(t) = \frac{\sum p_{i1}q_{i0}}{\sum p_{i0}q_{i0}}$$

But we can construct a Paasche price index by noting that the output of 1971 would have cost, according to Equation 2.3, only $190 in 1970 instead of its actual 1971 cost of $250; thus the alternative index is $250/$190 $=$ 131.6%. The formula for this Paasche price index is

$$P_p(t) = \frac{\sum p_{i1}q_{i1}}{\sum p_{i0}q_{i1}}$$

In this instance the two indices are practically identical.

How this index number problem affects actual measures of inflation is indicated on Table 11.A.3. Here the rate of change in the implicit GNP deflator for the United States economy is compared with a second GNP deflator based on 1967 quantity weights. That is, the first column uses the current composition of GNP in weighting prices, while the second column used the 1967 GNP composition. In magnitude, the differences are at times substantial. But note that both indices usually move in the same direction. The peak in the implicit GNP deflator occurred in the fourth quarter of 1970 while that of the 1967 fixed weight deflator occurred in the next quarter. While at the time policymakers were obviously anxious to know as soon as possible that the inflation had peaked, a one quarter discrepancy may, in retrospect, not appear all that important. The changes in the composition of output from one year to the next is not enough to cause major problems in measuring short-run fluctuations in the rate of inflation. The choice between using the CPI, the WPI, or the IPI is much more critical than the index-number weighting problem.

---

[22] Since it can be shown mathematically that the geometric average is necessarily lower than the arithmetic average (unless both indices are the same), Fisher's approach must necessarily give a better estimate of the United States strength relative to that of the Soviet Union, at least when the United States output appears in the denominator.

Table 11.A.3 INFLATION MEASURED WITH
ALTERNATIVE OUTPUT WEIGHTS

	Implicit GNP Deflator	Fixed 1967 Weights
1969–1	4.22	4.55
2	5.49	4.90
3	6.13	6.71
4	5.48	5.43
1970–1	6.55	5.99
2	4.30	5.13
3	4.04	3.68
4	6.46	5.51
1971–1	5.90	7.04
2	4.36	4.73
3	2.88	3.53
4	1.50	2.50

Source. "Alternative Measures of Price Change for GNP,
1969–1971, *Survey of Current Business,* August 1972,
pp. 33–35.

aggregate demand and supply

*12.1 OVERVIEW OF A SEQUENCE OF MODELS

Since the supply and demand apparatus is used to explain the price and output of individual commodities, why can't the same approach be used to explain how the aggregate price level and total output for the entire economy are determined? Indeed, if price in each market is determined so as to equate demand and supply, how can there ever be excess supply in the aggregate? Can it not be argued that unemployment is simply the *sine quo non* of too high a wage rate? In this chapter we will develop an aggregate supply and demand apparatus appropriate for the analysis of these issues. Demand and supply will be equated by adjustments in the price level, just as in microanalysis. But the apparatus will not constitute an alternative to the multiplier and *IS-LM* models; instead, we will elaborate on our earlier effort. The resulting synthesis of micro- and macroeconomics will be used to analyze wage inflation, technological unemployment, and the effect of monopolistic imperfections on the level of aggregate output.

The building blocks to be used in constructing the aggregate demand and supply schedules are enumerated on Table 12.1. As indicated in the table, a sequence of models of increasing complexity can be assembled by the successive addition of equations. As we progress through the sequence of models, previously exogenous variables are explained by new equations, and certain new variables are introduced. Thus the three equations of the elementary model of the multiplier (with foreign trade complications suppressed) become the *IS* model once the assumption of exogenous investment is replaced with an equation determining that variable. Again, the *IS-LM* apparatus is obtained by making the rate of interest endogenous and adding the demand for money as an additional endogenous variable; two more equations are now required to explain the two additional endogenous variables, and we have the real money supply as a new exogenous variables. The aggregate demand and supply model, to be developed in Sections 2, 3, and 4 of this chapter, will require five new equations. And the classical model, to be described in Section 6, will require two more. Left for later chapters are dynamic models incorporating the rate of price change and the effects of capital accumulation.

Table 12.1 A SEQUENCE OF MODELS

I. Elementary Multiplier

Exogenous variables: $\mathbf{G}$, I

Three equations for three endogenous variables:

I.1	$Y = C + I + G$	GNP identity
I.2	$C = c_0 + c_1 Y_d$	Consumption function
I.3	$Y_d = d_0 + d_1 Y$	Disposable income relationship

II. *IS* Curve

Exogenous variables: r, $\mathbf{G}$

Predetermined variable: $\bar{K}$

One additional endogenous variable and equation:

II.1	$I(r, Y, \bar{K})$	Investment depends on the interest rate, output, and the inherited capital stock.

III. *IS-LM* Model

Exogenous variables: $\mathbf{M}_s$, $\mathbf{G}$

Two additional endogenous variables and equations:

III.1	$\mathbf{M}_d(r, Y)$	Demand for money (liquidity preference) depends on the rate of interest and the level of economic activity.
III.2	$\mathbf{M}_s = \mathbf{M}_d$	Demand for money equals the supply.

IV. Aggregate Demand and Supply (p denotes the price level, the superscript n denotes nominal values; all other variables are measured in real terms)

Exogenous variables: w^n, $\mathbf{M}_s{}^n$, $\mathbf{G}$

Five additional endogenous variables and equations:

IV.1	$Q(N, \bar{K})$	Output is related by the aggregate production function to employment and the initial capital stock.
IV.2	$p\mathbf{M}_s = \mathbf{M}_s{}^n$	The price level times the real money supply equals the nominal money supply.
IV.3	$\dfrac{\partial Q}{\partial N} = w$	The marginal product of labor equals the wage rate.
IV.4	$w = \dfrac{\bar{w}^n}{p}$	The real wage equals the nominal wage divided by the price level.
IV.5	$Q = Y$	Output equals gross national product.

V. "Classical" Full-Employment Model

Exogenous variables: $\mathbf{M}_s{}^n$, G

Two additional endogenous variables and equations:

V.1	$N_s(w)$	Labor supply is a function of the real wage.
V.2	$N = L(w)$	Demand for labor equals the supply.

12.2 AGGREGATE DEMAND AND PRICES

The aggregate demand schedule summarizes a relationship that is all but explicit in the *IS-LM* model. That model contained no specific mention of the price level, and all of its variables are best regarded as being expressed in real instead of nominal terms. But the model did suffice to determine how aggregate demand responds to changes in the real money supply, given the other exogenous and predetermined variables. We are now going to treat the *nominal* instead of the real money supply as exogenous, because the Fed determines the dollar value of currency in circulation and demand deposits; we have by definition

$$\mathbf{M}_s = \frac{\mathbf{M}_s{}^n}{p} \tag{2.1}$$

If we were given p as well as the nominal money supply we could determine the real money supply and then use the *IS-LM* apparatus to determine such other variables as Y, just as in Chapter 8.2. Furthermore, given $\mathbf{M}_s{}^n$, an increase in the price level reduces the real value of the money supply; and with a lower value of $\mathbf{M}_s$ output as determined by the *IS-LM* apparatus is reduced. Thus the aggregate demand schedule on Figure 12.1 is downward sloping, which is in conformity with the law of demand of microeconomic theory.

The precise slope of the aggregate demand curve will depend on the sensitivity of Y to changes in the real money supply. If the demand for money is quite insensitive to the rate of interest while investment spending

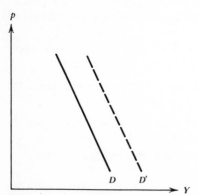

Fig. 12.1   *The aggregate demand schedule. An expansion in* $\mathbf{M}_s{}^n$ *or* **G** *shifts the aggregate demand schedule to the right by the amount predicted by the* IS-LM *apparatus; but what happens to output and the price level cannot be determined without an aggregate supply schedule.*

is responsive to changes in the cost of funds, only a moderate change in the real money supply will be required to stimulate Y substantially. Precisely in these circumstances, then, aggregate demand will be quite elastic with respect to the price level. On the other hand, the aggregate demand schedule would be inelastic if the economy were in the liquidity trap, because any reduction in the price level, while increasing the real money supply, would not lead to a reduction in the interest rate; therefore the increased investment required for higher output would not be forthcoming.

Changes in either fiscal or monetary policy shift the aggregate demand curve. For example, an increase in government spending shifts each point on the aggregate demand schedule to the right. The rightward shift caused by the rise in government spending is less than the multiplier analysis would suggest, because the increase in output causes the interest rate to rise, given the price level and the nominal money supply, and the higher rate of interest discourages private investment spending. An increase in the nominal money supply, given the price level, will increase aggregate demand by lowering the rate of interest and stimulating private investment spending; thus monetary policy also shifts the aggregate demand schedule. But the ultimate effects of monetary and fiscal policy cannot be determined once p is no longer assumed to be exogenous. In order to determine output and prices simultaneously, it is necessary to construct an aggregate supply schedule.

12.3 OUTPUT AND THE REAL WAGE

An analysis of the relationship between output and the real wage must precede the derivation of the aggregate supply schedule. This argument relies on the supposition that the behavior of the aggregate economy can be captured in terms of a "representative firm" maximizing profits under competitive conditions. It will first be demonstrated that under competition a profit-maximizing firm will adjust employment to equate the marginal product of labor with the real wage. The exposition is eased by allowing for only two inputs, capital and labor. Furthermore, we will be restricting our attention to the short run, the supply of capital (machinery, factory buildings, etc.) being regarded as fixed. Let $Q = Q(N, \overline{K})$ denote the production function revealing the technological possibilities open to the firm;[1] specifically, the function yields the level of output (Q) produced as a function of man-hours of employment (N), and the fixed supply of capital ($\overline{K}$). Figure 12.2a indicates this short-run relationship between output and employment. The *slope* of this total product curve, dubbed the

[1] For simplicity we neglect raw materials, and so forth; see Exercise 12.9.

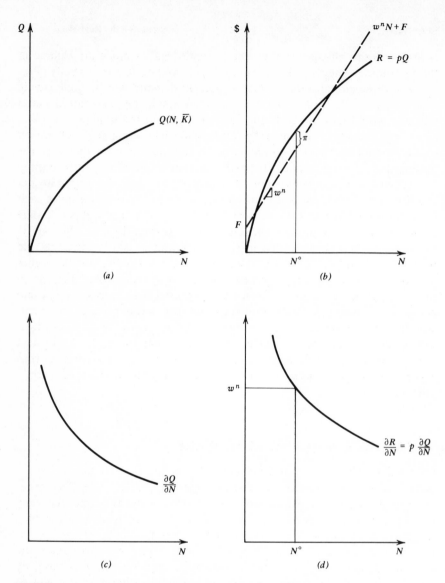

Fig. 12.2 *Employment and the money wage.* (*a*) *Total product curve.* (*b*) *Profit maximization.* (*c*) *Marginal product of labor.* (*d*) *Employment and the money wage.*

"marginal productivity of labor," is plotted in Figure 12.2c. Observe that the total product curve becomes flatter (the marginal productivity of labor declines) at higher levels of employment in conformity with the law of diminishing returns; this means that as more and more workers are employed, given $\overline{K}$, the incremental gains in aggregate output fall off.

Technological factors do not suffice to determine how much will be produced by the profit-maximizing firm. The competitive price at which output can be sold (p) and the money wage rate (w^n) must also be known by the representative entrepreneur before he can decide on the level of output. With this information the entrepreneur will note that total revenue is $R(N, \overline{K}) = pQ(N, \overline{K})$; furthermore, total labor costs are $w^n N$. Therefore, the profits of the firm are

$$\pi(N, \overline{K}) \equiv R(N, \overline{K}) - w^n N - F \qquad (3.1)$$

Here F denotes fixed costs. In Figure 12.2b, where total revenue and total costs are plotted as functions of employment, it is clear that profits are maximized at employment level N^0; there π, the excess of total revenue over total costs, is as large as possible. Now it can be shown by the rules of elementary calculus that the first derivative of profits must equal zero when this *optimal* amount of labor is combined with the fixed quantity of capital; consequently

$$w^n = \frac{\partial R(N^0, \overline{K})}{\partial N^0} = p \frac{\partial Q(N^0, \overline{K})}{\partial N^0} \qquad (3.2)$$

That this condition must be satisfied at the optimal level of employment can easily be verified graphically instead of with calculus. Inspection of Figure 12.2b and d reveals that the *slope* of the total revenue curve, $\partial R(N^0, \overline{K})/\partial N^0 = p[\partial Q(N^0, \overline{K})/\partial N^0]$, cannot be greater than the *slope* of the total cost curve (w^n) at the optimal level of employment—otherwise, it would obviously pay to hire more workers, since revenue would rise more than costs. Similarly, the slope of the total revenue curve cannot be less than the money wage rate—otherwise, it would pay to lay off workers. Thus, equality 3.2 is a necessary condition for profit maximization under competitive conditions. If we now divide through by p, the price level, we obtain the fundamental equation

$$\frac{w^n}{p} = w = \frac{\partial Q(N, \overline{K})}{\partial N} \qquad (3.3)$$

Here w denotes the *real* wage and $\partial Q(N, \overline{K})/\partial N$ is the marginal product of labor.

The fact that any firm maximizing profits under competitive conditions must adjust output and employment so as to equate the marginal

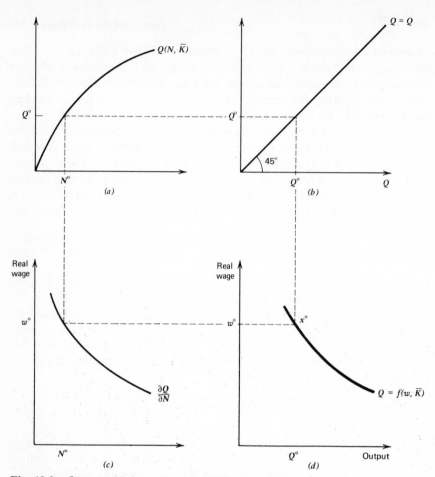

Fig. 12.3 *Output and the real wage. (a) Total product curve.*
(b) $Q \equiv Q$ *identity. (c) Employment and the real wage. (d)*
Output and the real wage.

productivity of labor with the real wage is of fundamental importance.[2] It means that given the real wage rate, the production function will dictate both employment and output, at least over periods short enough to allow the supply of capital to be regarded as fixed. This is made clear in Figure 12.3, where the two left-hand panels have been reproduced from the preceding figure. From Figure 12.3c we find for any specified real wage w^0 the corresponding number of workers N^0 that will be employed as prescribed

---

[2] Since this condition holds for *any* given K, it must also be satisfied when capital is adjusted to the optimal long-run level.

324

by profit maximizing condition 3.3. Moving north on the graph, we find from the total product curve the level of output that will be produced by the N^0 workers hired when the real wage is w^0. We wish to record this link between output and the real wage in Figure 12.3d. To do so we first move east from Figure 12.3a to the 45° line in Figure 12.3b and then drop down to record as point x^0 the profit-maximizing level of output for real wage w^0. To repeat, for any specified real wage, we found the profit-maximizing level of employment in Figure 12.3c; next we moved north to obtain the resulting output from the production function recorded in Figure 12.3a; then we moved east to the 45° line and dropped down to record in the southeast panel the point relating output to the real wage. Each point on the curve $Q = f(w, \overline{K})$ of Figure 12.3d was generated in this way. This curve indicates the profit-maximizing level of output as a function of the real wage, given the capital stock $\overline{K}$.

12.4 RIGID MONEY WAGES AND AGGREGATE SUPPLY

A rather startling implication follows from the short-run relationship we have derived between output and the real wage rate under the assumption that firms maximize profits in a competitive environment.

Given the state of technology and the stock of capital, the level of employment and output can expand only if workers are induced to accept a cut in real wages.

This result might be interpreted as supporting an argument often advanced by management in periods of slack demand. The employer faced with a serious loss of sales volume is inclined to lament that if only his workers would accept a cut in their money wages, it would enable his firm to avoid a layoff and maintain production; the reduction in wages would permit his firm to lower price in order to acquire a larger share of the market. How successful this approach will be for the individual firm hinges only in part on the elasticity of demand for its product; if demand has fallen off generally and workers throughout the industry accept lower wages in order to facilitate price reductions, the vicious competition can lead to further price reductions in which no producer is able to increase his share of the shrunken market. Of course, the general downward reduction in price may lead to an increase in demand for the industry's output. But won't this be at the expense of a cut in the demand for the output of other industries? And won't other industries in turn be induced to cut wages and lower prices in a vicious downward deflationary spiral?

Where this downward spiral leads constitutes an issue that excited the intellectual curiosity of much of the economics profession, particularly during the Great Depression of the 1930s. In exploring the issue it is helpful to ask two questions. First, if money wages are rigid, will unemployment persist, and under what circumstances? Second, if money wages were flexible, would unemployment be eliminated?

Whether, in fact, money wages should be regarded as flexible or not depends partly on institutional factors, such as the strength of trade unions and the prevalence of minimum wage legislation. But it also hinges on whether one is talking about the short run or the long run. After all, union contracts come up for review periodically; in the interim, money wages rates are usually not subject to adjustment.[3] In support of his hypothesis of rigid money wages, John Maynard Keynes argued:[4]

"Since there is imperfect mobility of labor . . . , any individual or group of individuals, who consent to a reduction of money wages relative to others, will suffer a relative reduction in real wages, which is sufficient justification to resist it. On the other hand it would be impracticable to resist every reduction of real wages, due to a change in the purchasing power of money, which affects all workers alike. . . . Every trade union will put up some resistance to a cut in money wages, however small. But since no trade union would dream of striking on every occasion of a rise in the cost of living . . . they do not raise the obstacle to any increase. In other words, the struggle about money wages primarily affects the distribution of the aggregate real wage between different labor-groups. . . . The effect of combinations on the part of a group of workers is to protect their *relative* real wage. . . ."

The success of union leadership in retaining control of their union may hinge partly on the invidious comparison that the rank and file draws between what their leaders have been able to achieve with what the leaders of other unions have won for their members—so it may be relative performance that counts when a union's leadership is challenged at election time.

Admittedly, the assumption of rigid money wages is quite crude, even for the short run, and it will obviously have to be modified later. But it does permit us to derive at once the aggregate supply curve relating output to the price level. If the money wage rate is fixed at $\bar{w}^n$, the real wage $w = \bar{w}^n/p$ moves inversely with the price level. And, if aggregate supply is a decreasing function of the real wage, it must be an increasing function of price. Thus the aggregate supply function is obtained by substituting $w = \bar{w}^n/p$ into the function $Q = f(w, \bar{K})$ in Figure 12.3d, which gave output as a function of the real wage. Figure 12.4 illustrates graphically how the aggregate supply curve may be derived. The two left-hand panels repeat once more the total and marginal product curves. The rectangular hyperbola

---

[3] Exceptions to this rule arise when labor contracts incorporate escalator wage adjustment clauses that tie the money wage to changes in living costs.

[4] *The General Theory of Employment, Interest and Money*, New York: Harcourt, Brace and Company, 1936, pp. 14–17.

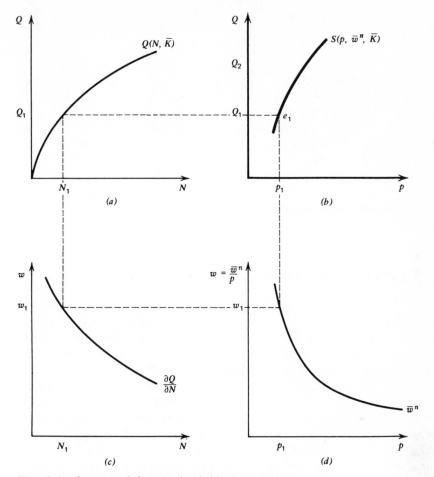

Fig. 12.4 *Output and the price level.* (*a*) *Total product curve.*
(*b*) *Aggregate supply curve.* (*c*) *Employment and the real wage.*
(*d*) *Real wage and the price level* (*given the money wage* $\overline{w}^n$).

constituting the southeast panel recognizes that the product of the real wage times the price level is the fixed money wage, $\overline{w}^n$. Finally, the derived aggregate supply curve appears in the northeast panel, but with price on the abscissa and quantity on the ordinate. To obtain output generated by a particular price level p_1 we start by finding from the southeast panel the corresponding real wage w_1; moving to the left we find the profit-maximizing level of employment N_1 on the southeast panel; moving north we find output Q_1 from the production function, which we record as point e_1 on the aggregate supply curve in Figure 12.4b. Each point on the aggregate supply schedule was derived in this way.

It is worth noting two properties of the aggregate supply curve. First, for any $\rho > 0$, we have

$$S(\rho p, \rho \bar{w}^n, \overline{K}) = S(p, \bar{w}^n, \overline{K})$$

That is, aggregate output will be unchanged when the money wage changes *if* prices rise by precisely the same proportion. This statement's validity is obvious because, if prices and money wages both change by the same proportion, the real wage rate is unaffected. Second, if the production function is homogeneous of degree one, so that a doubling of both labor and capital will double output, then for any $\rho > 0$

$$S(p, \bar{w}^n, \rho \overline{K}) = \rho S(p, \bar{w}^n, \overline{K})$$

Effective supply will increase in proportion to the increase in the stock of capital, other things being equal.[5]

12.5 INTERACTION OF AGGREGATE DEMAND AND SUPPLY

The aggregate supply schedule of Figure 12.4 is confronted with the aggregate demand schedule on the next graph. Observe that price is now plotted on the ordinate and output on the abscissa in accordance with the standard convention of microeconomics. Equilibrium point *e*, where aggregate demand and supply are equated, yields both the price level and output. Once this equilibrium point has been found, it is easy to solve for all the other variables of the model with the equations listed through Part IV, Table 12.1. Thus, given output, the level of employment is found from the production function. Furthermore, the real value of the money supply and the real wage rate are obtained by deflating their nominal values by the price index. Then the rate of interest can be found with the aid of the liquidity preference schedule. Finally, the consumption and investment functions determine the allocation of output between consumption and investment spending.

a. Price-Output Response to M_s^n and G

Either an increase in the nominal money supply or expansionary fiscal policy will serve to shift the aggregate demand schedule to the right, as explained in Section 2. But output does not increase by the full amount of the shift in the aggregate demand schedule, Figure 12.5 reveals, because there is a tendency for prices to rise as we glide up the aggregate supply schedule. Prices rise, given the money wage rate, because the marginal productivity of labor declines when additional manpower is put to work.

---

[5] For an example, see Equation A.4 of the appendix, with $\lambda' = 1 - \lambda$.

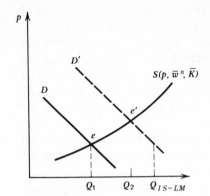

Fig. 12.5 *Aggregate demand and supply. Output and price are determined by the intersection of aggregate demand and supply. By shifting the aggregate demand schedule to the right, an increase in the money supply or an expansionary fiscal policy serves to raise both output and the price level.*

How much prices must rise depends largely on the slope of the aggregate supply schedule, and this, in turn, is influenced by how rapidly the law of diminishing returns sets in.

The increase in output from Q_1 and Q_2 in Figure 12.5, resulting from an increase in government spending, is much smaller than simple multiplier analysis would suggest because of two factors that contribute to a partially offsetting reduction in private investment spending. The analysis in an earlier chapter of the *IS-LM* apparatus revealed that the simple multiplier tended to overstate the expansionary impact of an increase in the level of government spending, given the *real* value of the money supply, since the tendency of expanding output to increase the demand for money must be offset by a rise in the rate of interest, and a rise in the rate of interest discourages investment spending. But to the extent that prices rise as output expands the *IS-LM* apparatus itself will overstate the expansionary effect of an increase in government spending, *given* the nominal money supply. If prices were to remain constant, so that the real as well as the nominal money supply is fixed, output would expand to Q_{IS-LM} in Figure 12.5. But the tendency of rising prices to reduce the real value of the money supply contributes to a further rise in the rate of interest and an additional reduction in investment spending; so output rises only to Q_2. Obviously, how much the *IS-LM* apparatus overstates the impact of an increase in government spending depends partly on the elasticity of the aggregate supply curve.

How large a GNP increase is achieved by a given dose of fiscal medicine depends on the response of the central bank. Suppose, for example, that the monetary authorities expand the nominal money supply instead of letting interest rates rise. Then the rate of interest instead of M_s^n is exogenous. The dose of fiscal medicine will shift the aggregate demand schedule by a larger amount; also, aggregate demand will be inelastic. In this situation, the simple multiplier provides a more accurate measure of the expansionary effect of an increase in government spending. How much inflation is generated by the expansionary fiscal policy will depend on the elasticity of the aggregate supply schedule.

The tendency for prices to rise as output expands in response to an increase in effective demand reduces the purchasing power of the number of dollar bills in circulation; that is, the real value of the money supply falls. It is sometimes argued that this effect constitutes an automatic stabilizer: the decline in the real money supply, by helping to raise interest rates, curtails effective demand during periods of boom; conversely, in recession, the lower price level tends to raise the real value of the money supply. But this argument is hardly complete. For one thing, if the rising prices are anticipated as the economy expands, additional investment spending will be encouraged. Conversely, if falling prices are anticipated as the economy moves toward recession, investors may defer buying new plants and equipment, and this will make the downturn even more severe. Clearly, a more sophisticated *dynamic* model must be developed that will properly distinguish the stabilizing static effects of a lower price level from the destabilizing transitory effects of changing prices; this is the task of Chapter 13.

b. Wage-Push Inflation

How will a change in the money wage rate affect the equilibrium? Suppose, for example, that workers achieve a doubling of the money wage rate. The increase in the money wage only affects the aggregate supply schedule; the money wage does not enter into the determination of aggregate demand. The result may be observed graphically by returning to Figure 12.4. Remember that the assumption of profit maximization establishes the relationship between output and the *real* wage. But a higher *money* wage means that the rectangular hyperbola constituting Figure 12.4d must move northeast; that is, any given real wage can be obtained only with a higher price level. Consequently, the aggregate supply schedule in Figure 12.4b must shift in response to the rise in the money wage. To see how much the aggregate supply curve must shift, recall from the end of Section 12.4 that the level of aggregate supply would be precisely the same as before *if* prices were also to double so as to restore the initial real wage. This means that a doubling of the money wage must shift each point on the aggregate supply curve upward so as to have twice as high a price level

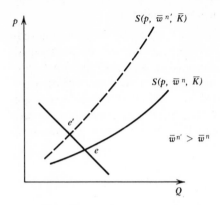

Fig. 12.6 *Wage-push inflation. By shifting the aggregate supply schedule upward, an increase in the money wage rate raises prices and reduces output.*

corresponding to each level of output. As Figure 12.6 illustrates, the resulting shift in equilibrium to point e' involves a reduction in output and an increase in the real wage, since prices have risen less than the money wage rate. The precise amount of output that will be lost hinges on the shape of both the aggregate demand and supply schedules. But it is clear that workers win the wage increase at the expense of higher unemployment. The workers who retain their jobs because of seniority obviously gain; younger workers who are laid off because they lack sufficient seniority obviously lose. The elasticity of the aggregate demand schedule determines whether aggregate labor income increases or not.

The *wage-push* argument provides one explanation as to why we can have serious inflationary episodes during periods of substantial unemployment, but it is subject to several qualifications. For one thing, if we had admitted that the distribution of income constituted an essential determinant of consumption spending, it would be necessary to consider the effects on the aggregate demand schedule of the increase in the money wage rate. It is clear that if the redistributional effects of a wage increase shifts the aggregate demand schedule upward, the inflationary spiral will be augmented. But this is not the more serious qualification of the argument. The inflationary pressure may not be *wage-push* in origin. After all, an increase in the costs of raw materials imported from abroad could also generate upward pressure on the price level. And we will see that cost inflation can also come about when business firms attempt to increase their profit margins.

c. Market Imperfections and Cost-Push Inflation

When firms exercise monopolistic power, the real wage is less than the workers' marginal product, and the second equality of profit-maximizing condition 3.2 no longer holds. Since price is a declining function of the quantity that the firm chooses to market, fewer workers will be hired, and output will be less at any given real wage. How all this affects aggregate supply is indicated in Figure 12.7. The effective relationship between the real wage and employment is indicated by the new curve in the south-

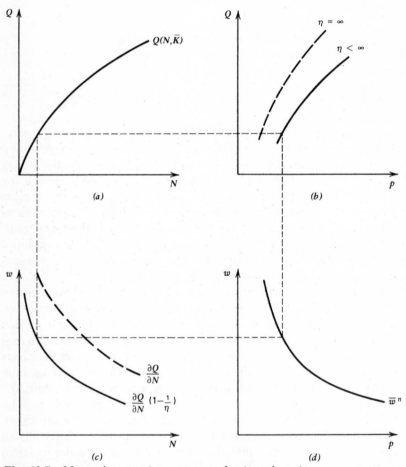

Fig. 12.7 *Monopoly constricts output and raises the price level.* $\eta = (-\partial Q/\partial P)(P/Q)$. (a) *Total product curve.* (b) *Aggregate supply curve.* (c) *Employment and the real wage.* (d) *Real wage and the price level (given the money wage).*

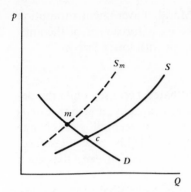

Fig. 12.8 *Imperfect markets influence prices and output. With imperfect markets the aggregate supply schedule is higher than under competition, given the money wage rate. Therefore, output is reduced and prices are higher at equilibrium point* m.

west panel, which is labeled $(\partial Q/\partial N)[1 - (1/\eta)]$. This relationship between the real wage and employment reflects the fact that when the demand curve facing the representative firm is downward sloping, profit maximization requires that Equation 3.3 be modified to read

$$w = \frac{w^n}{p} = \frac{\partial Q}{\partial N}\left(1 - \frac{1}{\eta}\right) \qquad (3.3')$$

where η is the price elasticity of demand;[6] profit-maximizing monopolists do not hire enough workers to equate the marginal product of labor with the real wage. Given the money wage rate, the aggregate supply curve must shift so that less output is forthcoming at each price level. In Figure 12.8 we see that the shift in the aggregate supply has led to less output and

---

[6] To see why this is so, let $p(Q)$ denote the relationship between output and price as perceived by the representative firm. Then revenue is $Qp(Q)$ and profits are $\pi = Qp(Q) - w^nN - F$. Differentiation with respect to N yields as a necessary condition for profit maximization:

$$\frac{\partial \pi}{\partial N} = \frac{\partial Q}{\partial N}p + Q\frac{\partial p}{\partial Q}\frac{\partial Q}{\partial N} - w^n = 0$$

or

$$\frac{w^n}{p} = \frac{\partial Q}{\partial N}\left(1 - \frac{1}{\eta}\right)$$

where

$$\eta = -\frac{\partial Q}{\partial p}\frac{p}{Q}$$

is the price elasticity of demand.

less employment than under competition. Moral: government promotion of competitive conditions through more effective enforcement of the anti-trust laws contributes to an expansion of output with lower prices.

d. Technological Change

Technological change is both loved and hated because, while the development of new productive techniques expands capacity, it also threatens to create technological unemployment. Adaptation to technological change may be facilitated by retraining workers, but new skills may not suffice. A direct stimulus to effective demand may be required if excessive slack in the economy is to be avoided.

The effects of a particularly simple type of technological change are illustrated in Figure 12.9. The top two panels of Figure 12.4 have been modified to reflect a simple additive improvement in the techniques of production that has served to shift the production function to

$$Q^*(N, K) = Q(N, K) + k$$

Here k denotes the increased output made possible by the advancement in technique.[7] We leave out the transitory shift in the aggregate demand schedule that will occur if the implementation of the improved productive techniques requires investment spending. In Figure 12.9a the total product curve has moved directly upward by the factor k, because we are supposing that k more units of output can be produced with any given quantity of labor and capital. With this simple type of technological change the marginal product of labor at any given N and K is unaffected. Therefore Figure 12.9c needs no modification. Furthermore, Figure 12.9d remains the same, because the relationship between the real wage and the price level is unchanged, given the money wage rate. Thus, corresponding to any price level, say p_1, we have the same real wage, the same level of employment, and k more units of output. Therefore the aggregate supply curve must shift by k units, as illustrated in Figure 12.9b.

How the shift in the aggregate supply curve affects economic conditions is revealed by Figure 12.10. Here the new aggregate supply schedule is confronted with a fixed aggregate demand schedule. Since aggregate demand is not infinitely elastic, the level of output expands by less than k. But this means that less labor (the variable input) is needed than before. While output expands and prices fall as a result of technological advance, there is also a reduction in total employment. Of course, the problem of mass technological unemployment may not manifest itself immediately. Investment spending is temporarily stimulated because new construction

---

[7] This is a simple but analytically convenient type of technological change. See Exercise 12.6.

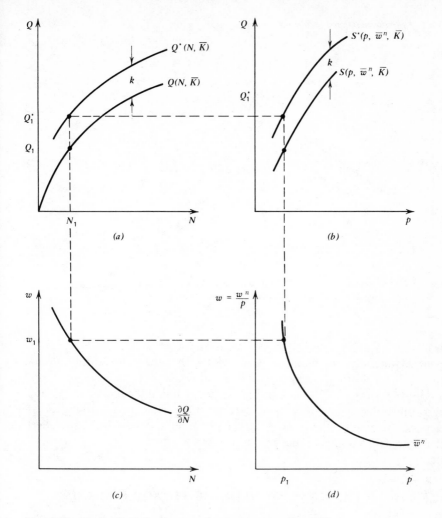

Fig. 12.9 *Technological change and aggregate supply. Additive technological change shifts the total product curve upwards from its position in Figure 12.4. The bottom two panels are unaffected.* (a) *Total product curve.* (b) *Aggregate supply.* (c) *Employment and the real wage.* (d) *Real wage and the price level* (given the money wage).

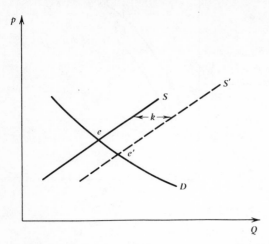

Fig. 12.10   *Technological change, output, and prices. Output expends by less than the shift in aggregate supply.*

or machinery are usually required when introducing technological improvements. Hopefully, the monetary and fiscal authorities will restore full employment by shifting the aggregate demand schedule to the right with appropriate expansionary policies.[8] Failing this, a fall in the money wage rate, by shifting the aggregate supply schedule still further to the right, might increase the equilibrium level of output to the point where the former level of employment opportunities are once more available.

12.6 THE "CLASSICAL WORLD" OF FLEXIBLE MONEY WAGES

The hypothesis that money wages are rigid is a useful assumption to invoke as a first approximation for the short-run analysis of less than full-employment conditions. But something more must be said about the supply of labor—surely the limited size of the work force places an upper bound on the capacity of the economy. It is reasonable to suppose that the available supply of labor is an increasing function of the real wage rate (w), and we will denote the supply of labor by $N_s(w)$.[9] This curve is recorded in Figure

---

[8] We will return to this problem in Chapter 19, where problems of growth under full-employment conditions are analyzed.

[9] The reader is invited to see what happens to the subsequent argument if the supply of labor curve is "backward bending," so that less labor is forthcoming when the real wage rises.

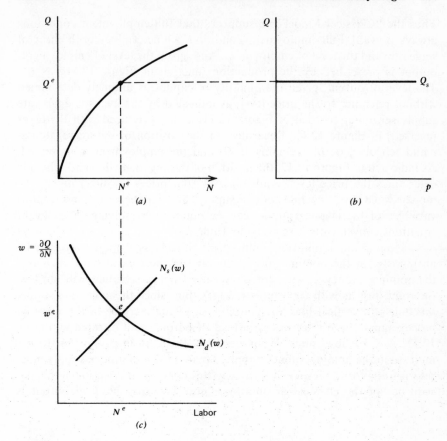

Fig. 12.11 *Employment and the real wage: Classical model.*
(a) Total product curve. (b) Aggregate supply. (c) Demand and
supply for labor.

12.11c. We have already argued that under competitive conditions, profit-maximizing firms will hire workers to the point where the marginal product of labor equals the real wage; hence the demand for labor is revealed by the curve labeled $\partial Q/\partial N$ in the southwest panel of Figure 12.2 and reproduced in Figure 12.11. Thus e indicates the equilibrium solution, w^e is the equilibrium real wage, and N^e is the corresponding level of employment. According to the classical theory, money wages and prices are completely flexible, and the wage rate always adjusts to equate the quantity of labor demanded with the supply.

$$N_d(w) = N_s(w) \tag{5.1}$$

Thus the "Classical Model" presupposes that full-employment conditions always prevail! Full-employment condition 5.1 determines both the real wage rate and the level of employment. And, given the level of employment, output is prescribed by the production function in Figure 12.11a as Q^e. The level of output, given the quantity of capital, is uniquely determined without reference to the price level, as indicated by the inelastic aggregate supply schedule recorded in Figure 12.11b and reproduced with the (axes reversed) in Figure 12.12. Regardless of the position of the aggregate demand schedule, output remains at Q^e and full employment is preserved. As indicated in Figure 12.12, the position of the aggregate demand schedule determines the price level. And, once Q^e and prices are determined, the money wage rate, the real money supply, and all the other endogenous variables of the classical model can be obtained by solving the relevant equations conveniently assembled in Table 12.1.

How is the equilibrium solution of this classical model affected by an increase in the nominal money supply? If the central bank increases the nominal money supply, the aggregate demand schedule will shift to the right, just as with rigid money wages. But, since the aggregate supply schedule is a vertical line, the entire effect of the increase in the nominal money supply is to raise prices instead of output, as illustrated in Figure 12.12. And by how much will prices rise? Precisely in proportion to the increase in the nominal money supply, because the *real* money supply must return to its former level.   To see why this conclusion is an inevitable co-sequence of the classical assumptions, note first that physical output is

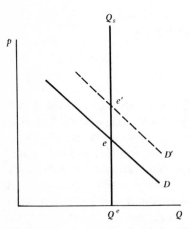

Fig. 12.12 *Aggregate demand and supply: Classical model. An expansionary shift in the aggregate demand schedule causes inflation.*

unchanged. Hence real consumption must be the same as before. Furthermore, government spending on goods and services is regarded as fixed, since we are investigating in isolation the effects of an increase in the money supply. All this implies, by the GNP identity (I.1 of Table 12.1), that real investment spending also remains unchanged. And, from Equation II.1, this means that there can be no change in the rate of interest. Now, if the rate of interest and real income are both unchanged, the demand for real money balances, specified by Equation III.1, must be unaffected also. But the demand for money equals the supply in equilibrium, so the real money supply cannot change. We conclude that in the long-run classical world of completely flexible money wages, the central bank does not influence the *real* money supply.

As an immediate corollary, the quantity theory of money describes the effects of changes in the nominal money supply. Income velocity, which was defined as $v_y \equiv pY^r/M^n$, has to remain constant when M^n changes, since neither Y^r nor M^n/p can be affected by the central bank. Thus the quantity theory of money stands as a *result* of the classical assumption of completely flexible money wages, regardless of the form of the demand function for money, provided we restrict our horizon to changes in M_s^n.

How do changes in fiscal policy affect the classical economy? Suppose, for example, that the pace of government expenditure increases, and that this is financed by a tax increase or in some other "neutral" fashion that leaves the nominal money supply unaffected.[10] This expansionary effect will manifest itself in a shift to the right of the aggregate demand schedule, just as in Figure 12.12. Since we are retaining the assumption of flexible money wages, the expansion in demand, given output, forces the price level to rise. And the rise in prices, given M_s^n, reduces the real money supply; since output is given, the interest rate must rise in order that the public will be content with the reduced supply of monetary purchasing power. But the rising rate of interest dampens investment spending. This upward inflationary spiral continues until investment is reduced by just enough to offset the increase in government spending. In the process the velocity of money must rise, other things being equal since, while p has gone up, neither M_s^n nor real output changes.

Although shifts in aggregate demand do not influence either output or the real wage in the classical world, shifts in either the production function or the supply schedule of labor will affect the entire set of relationships constituting the classical model. For example, if technological advance causes an upward shift of the production function, the aggregate supply

---

[10] Neutrality is here defined as keeping the nominal money supply constant; this may be achieved by raising taxes, but the effect would be the same if the funds are raised by government borrowing with offsetting open-market operations or appropriate adjustments in reserve requirements.

schedule in Figure 12.12 will shift to the right, and prices will fall. But, as prices fall, the increasing real value of the money supply leads to a reduction in the rate of interest and more investment spending; output tends to expand, and the stimulus is strengthened by an induced increase in consumption spending; that is, we slide down the aggregate demand curve. This expansionary process continues until full employment is restored. Similarly, if the supply of labor schedule (recorded in Figure 12.11c) shifts to the right, possibly as a result of an expanding population, employment and output will expand because real wages and prices fall. The shift in aggregate supply does not lead to permanent unemployment if money wages are allowed to fall to the point where effective demand rises to meet the increased output. All this is in accordance with Jean Babtist Say's (1767–1832) dictum that "Production creates its own demand." With flexible money wages "Say's law" holds because prices adjust to the point where the *real* money supply is of precisely the magnitude required for full employment.[11]

12.7 THE GREAT DEBATE

Writing in the depths of the Great Depression, Keynes described in his *General Theory of Employment Interest and Money* a hybrid mating of aggregate demand and supply analysis with the classical model of full employment. Under conditions of less than full employment the assumption of complete money wage rigidity is useful in the short run, since workers will be successful in resisting wage rate reductions. Does this mean that wages would not fall to their full-employment equilibrium value if we were willing to wait long enough? No, but Keynes asserted that "in the long run we are all dead." He argued that the deflationary process is so drawn out and so painful that a deliberate policy of expansion must be undertaken. His aggregate demand and supply model is appropriately used in guiding antidepression policy or, as rougher approximations, the *IS-LM* or the multiplier simplification may be employed. But if the level of employment required to produce the output predicted under the assumption of rigid money wages exceeds the available supply, the assumption of wage rigidity is relaxed by Keynes and the classical model comes into its own as a description of the economics of full employment. Money wages are assumed to be rigid downward. But at full employment and beyond, both wages and prices adjust to insure equilibrium in the labor and product markets.

[11] For a discussion of alternative interpretations of "Say's law," see Oscar Lange's paper, "Say's Law: A Restatement and Criticism," in *Studies in Mathematical Economics and Econometrics* (Lange, McIntyre and Yntema, eds.), University of Chicago Press, 1942

Rate of wage change
(ẇ/w)

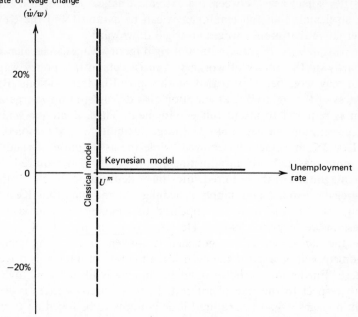

Fig. 12.13   *Money-wage adjustments. In the Keynesian model (solid "L" line) money wages remain rigid when unemployment is above the minimum U^m; at U^m the money wage rate will rise by however much is required to preserve equilibrium between the demand and supply of labor. In the Classical model (dotted line) money wages rise or fall at U^m so as to continuously preserve equilibrium at full employment.*

The critical distinction between the Keynesian and Classical models is summarized in Figure 12.13. As the dotted vertical line illustrates, the Classical model involves the assumption that money wages will adjust rapidly enough to preserve full employment. The solid *"L"* line indicates the Keynesian position, since it shows that money wages are rigid downward. The alternative assumptions are polar extremes, and the truth undoubtedly lies somewhere in between. Average hourly earnings in manufacturing fell from 56¢ in 1929 to 44¢ in 1933, a decline of a little more than 20%; in agriculture money wages fell to 50% of their 1929 value.[12] But while wages were certainly not perfectly rigid, they adjusted at such a slow rate that unemployment had climbed to 25% by 1933. The

---

[12] For wage data, see *Economic Report of the President, 1973*, Appendix C, Table C29.

truth thus lies somewhere between the extreme classical assumption that wages are so flexible that full employment can be assumed and the Keynesian alternative that money wages are rigid downward.

How reasonable is the assumption of rigid money wages? The answer depends partly on the ability of workers to resist cuts in the money wage rate, which may have been buttressed by the spread of trade unions. But the usefulness of the rigid wage assumption also depends on how large an adjustment is required to attain full employment. Thus, if money wages fall at 5% per annum, the assumption of wage flexibility will be reasonable if only a 1 or 2% movement is required, while the assumption of rigidity would be more reasonable if an adjustment of 10 or 20% is required. Of course, the magnitude of the required adjustment depends on the elasticities of the aggregate demand and supply schedules. At the time that Keynes was writing his *General Theory*, it appeared that aggregate demand was quite unresponsive to price changes. He argued that in periods of severe depression the confidence of businessmen is shaken to the point where little investment will be undertaken even when the rate of interest is driven close to zero. Furthermore, the demand for money is likely to be highly elastic with respect to the rate of interest. In these circumstances a very drastic fall in wages would be required if deflation is to be relied on to increase the real money supply to the point where full employment can be achieved. Conceivably, as with the liquidity trap, the curves might not intersect, and no amount of deflation would suffice, so while flexible wages would permit a downward deflationary spiral, prices would be falling proportionately with wages, and there would be no reduction in the real wage and no increase in employment.

In rebuttal to Keynes, Professors Pigou[13] and Haberler[14] argued that deflation may provide a direct stimulus to consumption spending. They argued that wealth as well as current income influences consumption. When prices fall, wealth goes up, because the purchasing power of that part of the government debt owned by the public goes up. The increased wealth stimulates consumption, as explained in Chapter 4, Section 7. This process is known as the *"real-balance"* or *"wealth"* effect. Since the induced consumption helps to make the aggregate demand curve more elastic, even if investment were totally unresponsive, the real-balance effect means that if prices fall far enough, aggregate demand will be stimulated to the point of full employment.

[13] A. C. Pigou, "Economic Progress in a Stable Environment," *Economica*, 1947, as reprinted with revisions in *Readings in Monetary Theory* (Lutz and Mints, eds.), Blakiston Co., 1951.

[14] Gottfried Haberler, *Prosperity and Depression*, 1943 League of Nations Edition, enlarged by Part III, as reprinted by the United Nations, 1952, pp. 498–503.

In a seminal paper clarifying the issues, Don Patinkin[15] argued that the real-balance effect meant that there exists necessarily a price level that would generate full employment if the public expected it to continue indefinitely (i.e., the aggregate demand and supply curves necessarily cross at a point corresponding to full employment). But Patinkin also argued that dynamic complications concerning the structure of expections might make the deflationary process unstable:

"It is quite possible that the original price decline will lead to the expectation of further declines. Then purchasing decisions will be postponed, aggregate demand will fall off, and the amount of unemployment increased still more.... The end result may be a disastrous deflationary spiral, continuing for several years without ever reaching any equilibrium position."

Unfortunately, the way in which the rate of price change influences aggregate demand is neglected by the static aggregate supply and demand apparatus. While a discussion of these dynamic complications must await the next chapter, the important point emphasized by Patinkin is that even when the role of wealth as a determinant of consumption is recognized, deflation is not an appropriate policy for combating depression. Indeed, both Haberler and Pigou stressed the role of the real-balance effect as a rebuttal to the boogy of secular stagnation; they did not advocate price reductions as a feasible remedy for cyclical departures from full employment.

Keynes had argued that since deflation may be a protracted process, its costs must be compared with those that would be incurred with alternative policies aimed at achieving full employment. If unemployment is to be cured by expanding the real money supply it would be better for the central bank to do it, since it is surely easier for the monetary authorities to expand the amount of money in circulation than for the economy to go through the painful and protracted process of negotiating downward revisions in money wages and prices.

In developing this argument Keynes failed to emphasize several factors that complicate the distinction between an expansionary monetary policy and deflation. For one thing, the monetary authorities cannot mobilize the real balance effect; for example, the purchase of government securities by the central bank induces a substitution of member bank deposits for government securities, but this changes only the composition and not the magnitude of the net indebtedness of the government to the public; the net wealth of fixed nominal value held by the public includes the total interest- and noninterest-bearing government debt held outside

---

[15] Don Patinkin, "Price Flexibility and Full Employment," *American Economic Review*, 1948, pp. 543–64, as reprinted with revisions in *Readings in Monetary Theory* (Lutz and Mints, ed.), Blakiston Co., 1951.

the central bank plus the net amount owed by the central bank to member banks.[16] It can also be argued that a fall in the general price level will encourage exports and discourage imports, provided that other countries are not undergoing deflation also. But, of course, an alternative to deflation is currency devaluation and, in any case, in a world of countries all undergoing deflation, the only country that gains in exports relative to imports is the one that manages to deflate faster than her trading partners.

Fortunately, the characteristics of depression that are likely to make deflation and/or monetary expansion weak reeds to rely on constitute precisely the conditions that allow the full multiplier effects of government spending and tax cuts to be realized. Thus, if the liquidity preference schedule is very elastic or investment is insensitive to the rate of interest, so that the aggregate demand schedule is very inelastic, neither deflation nor monetary policy will work effectively, while fiscal weapons will not have their potency dulled by offsetting reductions in private investment spending. And, to the extent that an expansionary fiscal policy involves a government deficit, the resulting increase in the net indebtedness of the government to the public will provide a direct stimulus to consumption by mobilizing the real-balance effect. Thus fiscal policy is likely to constitute a particularly effective weapon for combating depression.

---

[16] It is not to be confused with the money supply—demand deposits plus currency— as Patinkin emphasizes, op. cit., pp. 261–266. Precisely the same conclusion follows if one invokes the legal fiction that the Federal Reserve System is owned by the public instead of being an agent of the government.

REFERENCES

1. The first Modigliani paper provided a clear and concise exposition of the Keynesian model that has been read by successive generations of graduate students. The second Modigliani paper updated the earlier contribution. And Warren Smith has provided us with a convenient graphical summary of the model.

   Franco Modigliani, "Liquidity Preference and the Theory of Interest and Money," *Econometrica*, January 1944.

   ———, "The Monetary Mechanism and Its Interaction with Real Phenomenon," *Review of Economics and Statistics*, February 1963.

   Warren L. Smith, "A Graphical Exposition of the Complete Keynesian System," *Southern Economic Journal*, October 1956.

2. Here is a sampling from the controversy concerning Keynesian and Classical viewpoints.

   A. C. Pigou, "Economic Progress in a Stable Environment," *Economica*, August 1947.

   Don Patinkin, *Money, Interest, and Prices*, Harper & Row, 1965.

   G. C. Archibald and Richard G. Lipsey, "Monetary and Value Theory: A Critique of Lange and Patinkin," *Review of Economic Studies*, October 1958.

   Lloyd A. Metzler, "Wealth, Saving, and the Rate of Interest," *Journal of Political Economy*, April 1951.

KEY CONCEPTS

aggregate demand versus aggregate supply

real versus nominal money supply

total product curve

technological change

rigid money wage rate

Classical model

Say's law

real-balance effect

EXERCISES

12.1 Suppose that in a fully employed economy the Prince prints up 10% more currency and gives it to the people. How will this bonanza influence the equilibrium rate of interest, prices, and the income velocity of money?

12.2 Evaluate the effect of a 10% reduction in money wages on the level of output, employment, and the price level. Make use of aggregate supply and demand functions in your answer.
Next evaluate the following two statements in the light of your analysis.

     a. Unemployment results from monopolistic practices and wage rigidities; if wages and prices were flexible, the *real wage rate* would adjust so as to equate the demand for labor with the supply.

     b. Excess capacity in industry, stockpiles of surplus agricultural commodities, and unemployed labor can all be explained in terms of imperfections that prevent the free operation of the forces of demand and supply. In order to combat widespread unemployment, labor unions should voluntarily agree to an across the board reduction in money wages.

12.3 In the 1966 *Economic Report of the President*, President Johnson stated:

"Millions of workers at the bottom of our wage scale still lack the protection of Federal minimum standards. At the same time, we need to reinforce this protection by raising the minimum wage. . . . In enacting higher minimum wage levels, the Congress should consider carefully their effects on substandard incomes, on cost and price stability, and on the availability of job opportunities for marginal workers."

Utilize the theory of income determination—*IS-LM* apparatus, aggregate demand and supply curves, and so forth—in analyzing the short-run price and employment effects of an increase in the money wage rate. Spell out in detail the essential features of the model. Then show how the effects would vary under the following conditions.

     a. The Fed keeps interest rates instead of the nominal money supply constant.

     b. The demand for money function is of the form $M_d = kY$, instead of being sensitive to the rate of interest. Consider also, the case of the liquidity trap.

     c. The level of investment is exogenous instead of sensitive to the rate of interest and the level of output.

     d. The economy is suffering from substantial unemployment instead of operating at full capacity.

Finally, enumerate what you regard as the major inadequacies of the model that limit its relevance for analyzing the effects of an increase in the minimum wage rate.

12.4 Show that the elasticity of the aggregate demand curve approaches unity (i.e., pQ is the same at every point) if the demand for money is insensitive to the rate of interest but proportional to income.

12.5 The aggregate demand and supply apparatus can be used to show how an increase in government spending will influence the level of economic activity, the rate of interest, investment spending, the real wage, and the level of employment—given the money wage rate and the nominal money supply. Show how the analysis must be modified if the Fed engages in open-market operations to keep the interest rate constant; that is, the nominal money supply instead of the interest rate is endogenously determined and the money wage is still rigid.

12.6 As a result of technological improvement, the production function shifts from $Q(L, K)$ to $Q^* = 1.1Q(L, K)$. That is, any specified combination of labor and capital now yields 10% more output.

  a. Determine how the aggregate supply curve shifts, given that the money-wage remains constant; in particular, at what price level would employment remain the same as before the technological improvement?

  b. Show, using the aggregate demand apparatus, how the technological improvement changes the level of output, employment prices, and the rate of interest—given the money supply, the current level of government spending, and tax policy.

  c. What policy measures, if any, should be adopted to ease the task of adjusting to technological advance?

12.7 Determine the optimal level of output and employment for a firm that sells its product for $4 per unit. The money wage rate is $150 per week and fixed costs are $160 per week. The firms production function is

$$Q = 50\sqrt{NK}$$

Here K is the number of machines, and we suppose that there are 16 available for the production process.

You can find the approximate answer by filling in the blanks in the first six columns of the following table or, for greater precision, you can use calculus.

N	Q	$R = pQ$	wN	$R - wN$	Profits $(R - wN - \$160)$	$\frac{\partial Q}{\partial N}$	$\frac{\partial \pi}{\partial N}$
1	200	$800	$150	$650	$490	100	$250
2	283	——	——	——	——	——	——
4	400	——	——	——	——	——	——
6	489	——	——	——	——	——	——
9	600	——	——	——	——	——	——
16	800	$——	——	——	——	——	——

Calculus option: fill in the last two columns with the marginal product $(\partial Q/\partial N)$ and the marginal profit of labor $[\partial \pi/\partial N = (\partial Q/\partial N)p - w]$.

†12.8 (Calculus)

Suppose that the demand function faced by a monopolist is $p = \alpha Q^{-\eta}$. Find by substituting into Equation 2.1 the expression for profits. Then find by differentiation the relationship between the real wage and the marginal product of labor. Now suppose that the production function is $Q = 2\sqrt{NK}$; what is the relationship between the real wage and output if $K = 1$?

†12.9 (Calculus)

A firm operating in a competitive environment uses a variety of inputs. Specifically, the production function is

$$Q(x_1, x_2, \ldots, x_n), \tag{1}$$

where x_1 is the quantity of the ith input used in the production process. If p_i is the price of the ith input and p is the price of a unit of output, the profits of the firm are

$$\Pi = pQ - \sum_i x_i p_i \tag{2}$$

a. Show that under competition the profit-maximizing firm will equate the marginal product of the ith factor with the ratio p_i/p. Contrast with Equation 12.3.2. (*Hint.* Substitute Equation 1 into Equation 2 and differentiate.)

b. How will the behavior of the firm be modified if the price received by the firm depends on the quantity sold, $p = p(Q)$?

†APPENDIX 12.A PRODUCTION FUNCTIONS

For illustrative purposes let us consider a simple form of the production function that has proved particularly useful in empirical research.

$$Q = AN^\lambda K^{\lambda'} \qquad A > 0, 0 < \lambda < 1; \quad 0 < \lambda' < 1 \qquad (A.1)$$

In a pioneering paper published in 1928 Charles W. Cobb and Paul H. Douglas employed this equation in explaining historically the determination of United States industrial output.[17] Let us use this Cobb-Douglas function as an illustrative example in the explicit derivation of the relationship between wages and real output. To begin, we have upon differentiating

$$\frac{\partial Q}{\partial N} = \lambda A N^{\lambda-1} K^{\lambda'} = w \qquad (A2)$$

where we equate the marginal productivity of labor to the real wage rate under the assumption that profits are being maximized in a competitive environment.

Note that for this particular production function we have, upon substituting Equation A1 into A2, an extremely helpful simplification.

$$\frac{\partial Q}{\partial N} = \lambda \frac{Q}{N} = w$$

When firms maximize profits by equating the marginal product of labor with the wage rate, the average product of labor (e.g., output per man-hour) is

$$\frac{Q}{N} = \frac{w}{\lambda} \qquad (A3)$$

That is, output per man-hour is proportional to the real wage under competitive conditions if the production function is Cobb-Douglas.

To find how output is related to the real wage, substitute $(\lambda/w)Q$ for N in Equation A1.

$$Q = A \left(\frac{\lambda}{w} Q \right)^\lambda K^{\lambda'}$$

Dividing by Q^λ gives us

$$Q^{1-\lambda} = A \left(\frac{\lambda}{w} \right)^\lambda K^{\lambda'}$$

Finally, we raise both sides to the power $1/1 - \lambda$ to obtain

$$Q = A^{(1/1-\lambda)} \left(\frac{\lambda}{w} \right)^{(\lambda/1-\lambda)} K^{(\lambda'/1-\lambda)} = f(w, K) \qquad (A4)$$

[17] "A Theory of Production," *American Economic Review*, 1928. Douglas served in the United States Senate from 1949 to 1967 and, for many years, was the influential Chairman of the Joint Economic Committee.

This is the function plotted, for fixed K, on the southeast panel of Figure 12.3. The aggregate supply schedule of the northeast panel of Figure 12.4 is simply $f(w^n/p, \overline{K})$.

How responsive is output to changes in the real wage rate? To answer this question first write Equation A4 as follows.

$$Q = w^{(-\lambda/1-\lambda)}[A^{(1/1-\lambda)}\lambda^{(\lambda/1-\lambda)}K^{(\lambda'/1-\lambda)}]$$

Differentiation now yields

$$\frac{\partial Q}{\partial w} = -\frac{\lambda}{1-\lambda}w^{(\lambda/1-\lambda)-1}[A^{(1/1-\lambda)}\lambda^{(\lambda/1-\lambda)}K^{(\lambda'/1-\lambda)}]$$

which simplifies to

$$= -\left(\frac{\lambda}{1-\lambda}\right)\frac{Q}{w} < 0 \qquad (A5)$$

Hence, the *elasticity* of output with respect to the real wage is

$$\frac{\partial Q}{\partial w} \cdot \frac{w}{Q} = -\frac{\lambda}{1-\lambda} < 0$$

To obtain the relationship in terms of the *money* wage, we remember that

$$w = \frac{w^n}{p}$$

by definition; furthermore, from elementary calculus, we have

$$\frac{\partial Q}{\partial w^n} = \frac{\partial Q}{\partial w}\frac{\partial w}{\partial w^n} = \frac{\partial Q}{\partial w}\frac{1}{p}$$

Consequently, the *elasticity of aggregate supply* with respect to the money wage rate is again

$$\frac{\partial Q}{\partial w^n} \cdot \frac{w^n}{p} = -\frac{\lambda}{1-\lambda} < 0$$

The Cobb-Douglas production function has an interesting implication with regard to the distribution of income during the process of economic development. From Equation A3 we observe that

$$\frac{w^n N}{pQ} = \lambda \qquad (A6)$$

upon substituting $w^n/p = w$. Now $w^n N$ is total labor income, while the denominator is the value of output. That is, *labor's share*, the fraction of total output received by workers, is equal to λ under competition. The distribution of income is completely determined by the parameter λ if markets are competitive and the production function is Cobb-Douglas.

A slightly more complicated production function admits the possibility of variations in labor's share. Consider the following.

$$Q = \gamma[aK^{-\beta} + bN^{-\beta}]^{-1/\beta} \tag{A.7}$$

The marginal product of labor is

$$\frac{\partial Q}{\partial N} = -\frac{1}{\beta}\gamma[aK^{-\beta} + bN^{-\beta}]^{-(1+\beta)/\beta}(-\beta b)N^{-(\beta+1)} \tag{A8}$$

$$= b\left(\frac{Q}{N}\right)^{1+\beta}$$

Under competitive conditions, when profit-maximizing firms adjust employment so as to equate the real wage with the marginal product of labor, we find that labor's share is

$$\frac{w^n N}{pQ} = b\left(\frac{Q}{N}\right)^{\beta} \tag{A9}$$

As economic development causes a secular rise in output per worker, labor's share of total output will also rise *if* $\beta > 0$. Conversely, the process of capital accumulation and the concomitant rise in output per worker will be accompanied by a fall in labor's share if $\beta < 0$. The limiting case of $\beta = 0$ corresponds to the constant labor share case obtained with the Cobb-Douglas production function. A pioneering empirical study of Arrow, Chenery, Minhas, and Solow suggested that in manufacturing industries $\beta > 0$,[18] but the issue is still a subject of debate.

[18] "Capital-Labor Substitution and Economic Efficiency," *The Review of Economics and Statistics*, August 1961, pp. 225–250. Sometimes Equation A4 is referred to as the SMAC production function, an ancronym obtained by inverting the order of the authors' initials. Robert Solow first called the attention of economists to this functional form in a fundamental theoretical paper, "A Contribution to the Theory of Economic Growth," *Quarterly Journal of Economics*, 1956, pp. 65–94. For a convenient discussion of the mathematical properties of this constant elasticity of substitution production function, see R. G. D. Allen, *Macro-Economic Theory, A Mathematical Treatment*, St. Martins Press, 1968, pp. 52–55.

dynamic aspects of inflation and deflation

*13.1 STATICS AND DYNAMICS

The static analysis of inflation told us how much the price level must rise in order to restore equilibrium; it did not tell us how rapidly the adjustment will take place. The analysis in this chapter focuses on factors determining the *rate* of increase in prices. What type of wage settlements deserve the accolade of "noninflationary" in that they lead to a rate of increase in the money wage rate that is compatible with overall price stability? How rapidly will prices rise as the unemployment rate is lowered through expansionary monetary and fiscal policy? How does the rate of price change influence effective demand? Is it possible to finance government spending by continued injections of new money? All these issues concern dynamic aspects of the inflationary process.

*13.2 WAGE CHANGES, PRODUCTIVITY, AND INFLATION

Labor always wants a larger share of the pie; management naturally is interested in protecting and enlarging the capitalist's share; and government demands a portion. Can this conflict be resolved without inflation? Whenever governments attempt to regulate the pace of inflation, debate focuses on the question of what rate of increase in the money wage is compatible with price stability.

Often it is argued that conflict over how the nation's output is to be distributed can be resolved by defining as "noninflationary" those wage settlements that allow the money wage rate to increase just rapidly enough to preserve labor's share of national income. In applying this definition it must be recognized that the continuing nature of technological progress means that the real income of workers can gradually improve with the passage of time; and this rise in the real wage can be obtained through a secular increase in the money wage rate without an increase in the overall price level.

As a practical matter, application of this principle rests on a comparison of the rate of change in wages with the change in output per worker. If L is the number of hours worked and w^n is the average money wage rate, the product $w^n L$ is labor income; and if Q denotes real output and p is the price level, pQ is the value of output. Then "labor's share" in the nation's income is

$$\lambda \equiv \frac{w^n L}{pQ} = \frac{w^n}{p} \bigg/ \frac{Q}{L} \tag{2.1}$$

That is, the real wage divided by output per worker is labor's share. The data on output per man-hour and related series reported in Table 13.1 indicate erratic, short-run fluctuations over the course of the business cycle; but, in the longer run, over the last 100 years of American history, labor's share has remained quite stable. Labor's share will remain constant, Equation 2.1 indicates, if the real wage and output per worker both change at the same rate. Even if inflation is contained, so that p remains stable, the money wage can rise at the same rate as output per worker. More formally, constancy of labor's share implies

$$\frac{\dot{w}}{w} = \left(\frac{\dot{w}^n}{w^n}\right) - \frac{\dot{p}}{p} = \rho \tag{2.2}$$

where ρ is the rate of change in output per worker, $\dot{w}^n/w^n$ is the rate of change in the money wage rate, and $\dot{p}/p$ is the rate of inflation.[1]

This labor share arithmetic provided the underpinnings for the "guideposts for noninflationary wage and price behavior" promulgated by President Kennedy's Council of Economic Advisors in the 1962 *Economic Report of the President*.[2]

"If hourly labor costs increase at a slower rate than productivity, the share of non-labor incomes will grow or prices will fall, or both. Conversely, if hourly labor costs increase more rapidly than productivity, the share of labor incomes in the total product will increase or prices will rise, or both. It is this relationship among long-run economy wide productivity, wages and prices which makes the rate of productivity change an important benchmark for noninflationary wage and price behavior."

The Kennedy Council advanced two general guides for noninflationary behavior. First, money wages (including fringe benefits) should increase at the trend rate of nationwide productivity increase, where productivity increase is indexed by the rate of growth in output per man-hour. Second,

---

[1] The "$\cdot$" over a variable denotes change; for example, $\dot{w} \equiv dw/dt$. And the rate of change is $\dot{w}/w = (\partial w/\partial t)/w = \partial \log w/\partial t$. Also, $\rho \equiv [\partial(Q/L)/\partial t]/Q/L$, the rate of change in output per worker. Since $\log \lambda = \log w - \log(Q/L)$ we have $\partial \log \lambda/\partial t = \partial \log w/\partial t - \partial \log(Q/L)/\partial t = \dot{w}/w - \rho$.

[2] P. 186.

Table 13.1 OUTPUT PER MAN-HOUR AND RELATED DATA, THE UNITED STATES EXPERIENCE

	Private Nonfarm									
	Output per Man-Hour, etc. (1967 = 100)					Changes in Output per Man-Hour, etc. from Preceding Year (Percent)				
Year	Output[a]	Man-Hours[b]	Output per Man-Hour	Compensation per Man-Hour[c]	Unit Labor Costs	Output[a]	Man-Hours[b]	Output per Man-Hour	Compensation per Man-Hour[c]	Unit Labor Costs
1947	44.5	78.0	57.1	38.3	67.1	—	—	—	—	—
1948	46.5	79.1	58.8	41.8	71.0	4.4	1.3	3.0	9.0	5.8
1949	46.4	76.0	61.1	43.0	70.3	-0.1	-3.9	4.0	2.9	-1.0
1950	51.3	79.0	65.0	45.3	69.7	10.6	4.0	6.3	5.5	-0.8
1951	55.0	82.9	66.3	49.3	74.3	7.0	4.9	2.0	8.7	6.6
1952	56.3	84.1	66.9	52.0	77.6	2.5	1.5	0.9	5.5	4.5
1953	59.1	85.9	68.9	54.9	79.7	5.1	2.1	2.9	5.6	2.6
1954	58.3	82.6	70.5	56.6	80.3	-1.5	-3.8	2.3	3.2	0.9
1955	63.4	86.1	73.6	58.6	79.6	8.8	4.2	4.4	3.5	-0.9
1956	64.7	88.4	73.2	62.0	84.7	2.0	2.6	-0.6	5.8	6.4

Year										
1957	65.7	87.9	74.8	65.5	87.6	1.6	−0.6	2.2	5.7	3.4
1958	64.8	84.5	76.7	68.1	88.7	−1.5	−3.9	2.5	3.8	1.3
1959	69.5	87.6	79.3	71.0	89.5	7.3	3.7	3.4	4.3	0.9
1960	71.1	88.6	80.3	73.9	92.0	2.4	1.1	1.2	4.1	2.8
1961	72.5	87.7	82.7	76.3	92.3	1.9	−1.0	3.0	3.2	0.2
1962	77.6	89.8	86.4	79.3	91.8	7.1	2.5	4.6	4.0	−0.5
1963	80.9	90.9	89.1	82.2	92.3	4.3	1.2	3.1	3.6	0.5
1964	85.9	92.9	92.4	86.1	93.2	6.1	2.3	3.7	4.7	1.0
1965	91.5	96.3	95.1	89.2	93.9	6.6	3.6	2.9	3.7	0.8
1966	97.9	99.5	98.4	94.6	95.2	7.0	3.3	3.5	6.1	2.5
1967	100.0	100.0	100.0	100.0	100.0	2.2	0.5	1.6	5.7	4.0
1968	105.1	102.1	102.9	107.3	104.3	5.1	2.1	2.9	7.3	4.3
1969	108.0	105.1	102.7	114.8	111.8	2.8	2.9	−0.1	7.0	7.2
1970	107.2	103.8	103.4	123.1	119.1	−0.7	−1.3	0.6	7.2	6.6
1971	110.4	103.2	107.1	131.8	123.2	3.0	−0.6	3.6	7.1	3.4
1972	118.8	105.9	112.1	140.3	125.1	7.6	2.7	4.7	6.4	1.6

Source. *Economic Report of the President.*

a Output refers to gross national product in 1958 dollars.

b Hours of all persons in private industry engaged in production, including man-hours of proprietors and unpaid family workers.

c Wages and salaries of employees plus employers' contribution for social insurance and private benefits plans. Also includes an estimate of wages, salaries, and supplemental payments for the self-employed.

prices should fall in industries experiencing greater than average increases. in productivity and rise in industries lagging in productivity advance. These two rules, with certain refinements, were meant to describe "how prices and wage rates *would* behave in a smoothly functioning competitive economy operating near full employment."[3] The guideposts were not submitted to Congress as the basis for wage and price-control legislation. Instead, they were promulgated by President Kennedy and his Council as the touchstone for invoking moral suasion when focusing the force of public opinion on "inflationary" wage and price adjustments in key industries. Thus, in 1962, when the U.S. Steel Corporation issued a surprise announcement that the price of steel would be raised by $6 per ton, the administration declared this adjustment inflationary and mustered sufficient pressure to force a price rollback. The guideposts appeared to work with some success for several years. But, in the late 1960s, when the unemployment rate fell below 4% in the Vietnam War buildup, the inflationary pressure became irresistible and this system of informal controls was discredited.

In 1972 President Nixon's Council of Economic Advisors invoked precisely the same labor share arithmetic that Kennedy's Council had employed 10 years earlier. The Pay Board had presented a $5\frac{1}{2}\%$ permissible pay increase standard in an effort to moderate the pronounced inflation trend. The Council argued:[4]

"If compensation per hour of work rises by $5\frac{1}{2}$ percent per annum, and if output per hour of work rises by 3 percent per annum, labor costs per unit of output will rise by approximately $2\frac{1}{2}$ percent per annum. If prices rise in the same proportion as labor costs, which are the largest element in total costs for the economy as a whole, then prices will also rise by $2\frac{1}{2}$ percent, a rate within the range of the goal set by the Cost of Living Council."

In other words, with a targeted price rise of $2\frac{1}{2}\%$, the $5\frac{1}{2}\%$ permissible increase in the money wage would yield a real wage increase just matching the projected gain in productivity.

This link between wages and output per worker can be supported without reference to the concept of labor's share. A basic tenet of introductory price theory is the proposition, reviewed in Chapter 12, Section 3, that profit-maximizing employers under competitive conditions adjust the level of employment to the point where the *marginal* product of labor is equal to the real wage. This means that price stability requires that the *marginal* product of labor and the money wage move proportionately. While it is unfortunate that the marginal product of labor, in contrast to Q/L, is not readily observable, the two concepts should not be confused. Nonetheless, under certain conditions, changes in the average product of

[3] Op cit., p. 188, italics added.
[4] *1972 Economic Report of the President*, p. 96.

labor provide a useful index of changes in the marginal product, even in the face of technological advance and fluctuations in the ratio of capital to labor. Specifically, the marginal productivity of labor will be proportional to Q/L if a competitive economy's aggregate production function is of the form assumed by Cobb and Douglas in their pioneering econometric investigations of the 1920's.[5] This means that the average productivity of labor, output per worker, provides under certain conditions a useful index of labor's marginal product.

To sum up, there are two distinct arguments as to why labor should be content with real wages rising at the same rate as average productivity. The first argument is that "labor's share" in the nation's income will be held constant if the real wage rises at the same rate as output per worker. The second argument relies on the proposition that in a *competitive* economy with a Cobb-Douglas production function, the real wage will rise at the same rate as output per man-hour; hence a money wage rising at the same rate as productivity is compatible with price stability.

That government restraints on wages and prices will inevitably be violated is an obvious lesson of history. But it is sometimes suggested that if the inflationary tide could only be stemmed in certain "key industries," the rest of the economy would not do so much damage to the goal of overall price stability. Steel, in particular, has been singled out for attention—in World War II, the Korean War, and under the Kennedy-Johnson wage-price guideposts. Since steel is basic in the production of so many commodities, won't any change in its price ripple through the economy? The following proposition helps in evaluating such questions.[6]

"The impact upon the GNP implicit price deflator of an autonomous increase in the gross profit margin of a particular industry may be approximated by dividing GNP into the product of the change in the margin times the level of gross output

---

[5] As indicated in Appendix A of Chapter 12, if $Q = Ae^{\rho t}L^{\lambda}K^{\lambda'}$ (where K is the capital stock and $e^{\rho t}$ allows for the increased output arising from productivity advance), the marginal product of labor is $\partial Q/\partial L = \lambda Q/L$ and labor's share is $pQ/wL = \lambda$.

[6] The validity of this proposition may be established with the aid of certain results developed in Appendix 3.A on input-output analysis. The GNP deflator is simply $p = $ GNP/GNP°, where GNP is the money value of gross national product with the steel price increase and GNP° is its value in the absence of the increase. Matrix equation 3.A.5.5 gave gross national product as a function of industry profit markups and wage rates. Differentiating with respect to the profit markup in the ith industry yields $\partial p/\partial m_i = x_i$, where x_i is the output of industry i. Because the model is linear, $\Delta p = x_i \Delta M_i$, which is the proposition stated in the text. When money wages in the rest of the economy are allowed to rise in order to preserve labor's share, the resulting rise in the implicit price index is about three times as large. For further discussion of these and related propositions, see William Brainard and Michael C. Lovell, "Some Simple Propositions Concerning Cost-Push Inflation," together with the comments of Eckstein and Fromm, in *The American Economic Review*, September 1966. The propositions assume that input-output coefficients remain fixed; if the rise in the price of steel led to the substitution of aluminum and other metals for steel, the rise in p would be smaller because GNP would rise by less.

for that industry, provided that gross profit margins in other sectors and money wage rates are unaffected."

This proposition incorporates the price rises induced by other industries in passing cost increases through to their customers. For an application, consider the 1962 confrontation between President Kennedy and the steel industry, which resulted in the suspension of a planned $6 per ton increase in the price of steel. The proposition suggests that if the steel industry had raised prices by $6 per ton (or 3.8%) it would have raised the general price level as measured by the GNP deflator by only $\frac{1}{10}$ of 1%; that is, since 98.3 million tons of steel were produced in that year and GNP was $553.9 billion,

$$\frac{\Delta p}{p} = \frac{\$6 \times 98.3 \text{ million tons}}{\$553.9 \text{ billion}} = 0.001065 \text{ or } 0.1065\%$$

This $\frac{1}{10}$ of 1% estimate takes into account the price increases of steel using firms when they pass through their cost increases, but it presumes that they won't use the price increase as an excuse for raising their profit markups. The estimated increase is negligible, suggesting that even this most flagrant violation of rules of noninflationary pricing behavior would not have generated much inflation. Evidently, cost-push forces have much effect on the overall level of prices only when inflationary pricing and wage adjustments permeate the economy. And, to be successful, controls must do more than limit inflationary adjustments in a few conspicuous sectors of the economy.

*13.3 THE "PHILLIPS CURVE," AN EMPIRICAL RELATIONSHIP

When the demand for a commodity exceeds supply, we expect its price to rise; how rapidly depends in part on the magnitude of excess demand. A. W. Phillips argued that the same proposition holds for labor services.[7]

"When the demand for labor is high and there are very few unemployed we should expect employers to bid wage rates up quite rapidly, each firm and each industry

[7] A. W. Phillips, "The Relation Between Unemployment and the Rate of Change of Money Wage Rates in the United Kingdom, 1861–1957," *Economica*, November 1958, p. 283. The "Phillips curve" relationship between unemployment and inflation has been intensively studied by a number of investigators. Indeed, in the June 1926 *International Labour Review* there appeared an article on "A Statistical Relation Between Unemployment and Price Changes" by Irving Fisher of Yale University; Fisher claimed only to be providing statistical support for a much discussed relationship; he concluded that fluctuations in employment might be reduced by stabilizing the purchasing power of the dollar. His essay is reprinted in the March–April 1973 *Journal of Political Economy*. Professor A. W. Phillips, who was originally trained as an electrical engineer, has made major contributions in applying control-theory concepts to problems of economic stabilization.

being continually tempted to offer a little above the prevailing rates to attract the most suitable labor from other firms. . . ."

This notion is reflected in the Phillips curve relationship between the rate of inflation and the level of unemployment. Figure 13.1 shows a rough estimate of the Phillips curve relationship for the United States. Given the unemployment rate, both the speed of inflation and the rate of increase in the money wage may be read from the graph, because the two scales on the ordinate reflect the assumption that the rate of growth in the money wage ($\dot{w}^n/w^n$) exceeds the rate of inflation ($\dot{p}/p$) as a result of a $2\frac{1}{2}\%$ secular rise in output per man-hour.

The Phillips curve indicates that the policymaker may be confronted with a bitter choice between high unemployment with price stability or low unemployment plus inflation. At point A on Figure 13.1 the 2.5% increase in the money wage rate just equals the rate of productivity growth, so the price index is stable, but at A unemployment is $5\frac{1}{2}\%$. And at point B, where the unemployment rate is cut to 3%, prices rise at 4.5% per annum and wages at 7%.[8] Much of the controversy concerning the appropriateness of domestic economic policy has arisen because of divergent views concerning the appropriate mix of unemployment and inflation. This is not to say that politicians will admit that they are deliberately taking steps to increase unemployment in order to achieve price stability. Nor is it to say that their political opponents will concede that an all-out effort to reduce aggregate unemployment means that the objective of price stability must be abandoned. But rhetoric aside, a major difference between Republican and Democratic administrations concerns the relative weight given to the conflicting objectives of price stability and full employment. And, if a succession of alternating administrations means that the economy vascillates between an antiinflationary and a full-employment emphasis, the results can be more painful than the Phillips curve of Figure 13.1 suggests. Suppose, for example, that half the time the economy is at point A on Figure 13.1 with $5\frac{1}{2}\%$ unemployment and half the time at point B with 3% unemployment; then the unemployment rate will average out at $4\frac{1}{4}\%$ and the average rate of inflation will be 2.25%. So the alternations in policy average out at point C, which is above the Phillips curve on the line segment connecting A and B and involves more inflation than a steady-at-the helm unemployment rate of $4\frac{1}{4}\%$.

The Phillips curve may be regarded as a relaxation of the assumption invoked by Keynes in the *General Theory* that money wages are flexible

---

[8] Paul A. Samuelson and Robert M. Solow suggested that the United States Phillips curve would pass through points A and B in their paper on "Analytical Aspects of Anti-Inflation Policy," *American Economics Review*, May 1960. Phillips, op cit., thought that $2\frac{1}{2}\%$ unemployment would insure price stability in the United Kingdom; assuming a 2% rate of growth in productivity, he suggested that an unemployment rate of $5\frac{1}{2}\%$ would correspond to a constant money wage rate.

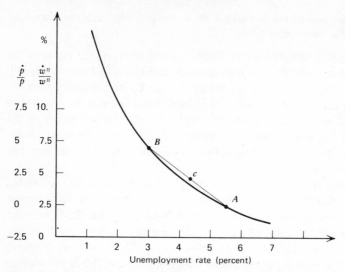

Fig. 13.1   *A United States Phillips curve.* $\dot{p}/p$ *denotes the annual rate of price rise.* $\dot{w}^n/w^n$ *denotes the annual rate of increase in the money wage rate. Point* c, *which is above the Phillips curve, indicates the average rate of inflation if the economy experiences 3% unemployment half the time and 5.5% unemployment the rest of the time.*

upward but rigid downward; that is, an L-shaped Phillips curve; contrast Figure 13.1 with Figure 12.13. The Phillips curve may also be interpreted as a bridge between the "wage-push" and "demand-pull" explanations of inflation, since Figure 13.1 suggests that an upward push on wages is generated by the reduction in unemployment occasioned by an increase in aggregate demand. It is tempting to blame the upward pressure on wages at low unemployment rates on the monopoly power of labor unions. And it is frequently asserted that oligopolistic firms are likely to administer excessive price increases when wage pressure provides an excuse for charging more. Deeper insight into the Phillips curve mechanism is gained by recognizing that in a dynamic world there are always people looking for jobs and jobs looking for workers. The people looking for jobs are counted by the government's monthly survey of unemployment conditions; job vacancies cannot be enumerated so precisely, but they may be roughly indexed by tabulating the help wanted notices in newspaper classified ads.[9]

[9] The National Industrial Conference Board has prepared an index of help wanted ads that stretches back a quarter of a century; the Department of Commerce has recently started a job vacancy survey. Both series are plotted each month in *Business Conditions Digest.*

The unemployed worker may be searching over a range of possibilities, looking for a suitable position utilizing his skills and conveniently located. Simultaneously, employers are looking over many candidates for a good worker with appropriate skills. By accepting a lower wage the unemployed worker can cut short the amount of time spent between jobs. By raising the wage offer the employer may shorten the amount of time lost before his job opening is filled. Whether the end result of such compromises will involve an upward or downward creep in wages depends on the tightness of labor markets. When there are larger numbers of unemployed and the average period of unemployment has lengthened, on the average, workers may be more inclined to accept lower wages. When employers are having trouble filling the orders of their customers, they will be inclined to allow an upward adjustment in wages in order to fill job openings more promptly. Thus the speed with which wages adjust depends on the tightness of the market.

The postulated relationship between wage rates, inflation, and unemployment plotted in Figure 13.1 is not adequate for explaining historical wage-price movements. A wide variety of additional variables has been nominated for inclusion in the Phillips curve relationship. A. W. Phillips himself suggested that the change in unemployment also belongs in the equation; other investigators have argued that the wage negotiation process obviously must be sensitive to changes in the cost of living; and it has also been asserted that workers will be more insistent in negotiating wage increases when profit rates are high. Also, the Phillips curve process involves time in an essential way: firms may not immediately pass cost increases along to their customers, time may be required before workers become cognizant of the extent to which inflation is eating into the purchasing power of their wages, labor contracts came up for renewal at relative infrequent intervals, and unions may play follow-the-leader in contract negotiations.

George L. Perry has suggested the following equation on the basis of quarterly United States data from 1947 to 1960.[10]

$$\frac{\dot{w}^n}{w^n} = -4.3 + 14\,\frac{1}{U_{t-1}} + 0.37\left(\frac{\dot{p}}{p}\right)_{t-1} + 0.42\pi_{t-1}$$
$$+ 0.79(\pi_{t-1} - \pi_{t-2}) + e_t \quad (2.3)$$

Here

$$\frac{\dot{w}^n}{w^n} = \text{annual percentage change in the money wage rate}$$

[10] "Wages and the Guideposts," *American Economic Review*, September 1967, pp. 897–904. See also the comments of Paul S. Anderson, Michael L. Wachter, and Adrian W. Throop, together with Perry's reply in the June 1969 *American Economic Review*.

U_{t-1} = unemployment rate (%), lagged three months

$\left(\dfrac{\dot{p}}{p}\right)_{t-1}$ = annual rate of change in consumer price index, lagged three months (%)

π_t = after-tax profits as a percent of equity[11]

The reciprocal relationship between the rate of money wage increase and the unemployment rate suggests that a policy of deliberately slowing down the economy in order to stop an inflationary spiral runs into diminishing returns; that is, an increase in unemployment from 4% to 5%, other things being equal, will slow the rate of wage increase by 0.8%; a further increase in unemployment to 6% yields only a 0.45% additional reduction in the rate of increase in money wages. But, from another viewpoint, the reciprocal relationship means that successive reductions in unemployment from 5% to 4% and 3% involve accelerating increases in the rate of inflation.

The rate of change of the consumer price index, $(\dot{p}/p)_{t-1}$, may be interpreted as an allowance for catching up with the inflationary spiral. But it may reflect partially an effort to allow for anticipated inflation if expectations in turn are derived by projecting recent experience. Either way, the fact that the estimated coefficient of $\dot{p}/p$ is less than unity implies that increases in the cost of living are not fully reflected in current wage negotiations. However, this does not mean that labor's share is continuously eroded by inflation. To see why, it is necessary to note that higher wages are likely to lead to higher prices, and that higher prices in turn may induce a further increase in money wages. This long-run feedback may be easily taken into account when the forces of competition are of such strength as to keep firms from raising prices enough to reduce labor's share; that is, $\dot{p}/p = (\dot{w}^n/w^n) - \rho$ in accordance with Equation 2.2. Substitution into Perry's equation will lead to an expression explaining the long-run relationship between unemployment and inflation. First, substituting for lagged prices in Perry's short-run Phillips curve yields

$$\frac{\dot{w}^n}{w^n} = -4.3 + 14\,\frac{1}{U_{t-1}} + 0.37\left(\frac{\dot{w}_{t-1}}{w^n_{t-1}} - \rho\right)$$
$$+\ 0.42\pi_{t-1} + 0.79(\pi_{t-1} - \pi_{t-2}) + e_t$$

Now, in the long-run, when we are experiencing a steady inflationary spiral,

$$\frac{\dot{w}_t^{\,n}}{w^n_{\,t}} = \frac{\dot{w}^n_{\,t-1}}{w^n_{\,t-1}}$$

---

[11] Perry reports $R^2 = 0.88$ and a Durbin-Watson statistic of 1.2; all of the t coefficients are substantially in excess of 2.

hence

$$\frac{\dot{w}^n}{w^n} = \frac{1}{1 - 0.37}\left[-4.3 + 14\,\frac{1}{U_{t-1}} - 0.37\rho\right.$$

$$\left. + 0.42\pi_{t-1} + 0.79(\pi_{t-1} - \pi_{t-2}) + e\right]$$

or

$$\frac{\dot{w}^n}{w^n} = -6.8 - 0.55\rho + 23.1\,\frac{1}{U_{t-1}} + 0.67\pi_{t-1}$$

$$+ 1.25(\pi_{t-1} - \pi_{t-2}) + 1.5e \quad (2.4)$$

This is a long-run Phillips curve in that it shows the rate of wage inflation generated when the level of unemployment has persisted long enough for the feedback of higher wages on prices to manifest itself fully. Because $\dot{p}/p = (\dot{w}/w) - \rho$, a long-run expression for the rate of price change could be obtained by subtracting ρ from both sides of Equation 2.4. Feedback effects make both $\dot{p}/p$ and $\dot{w}^n/w^n$ more sensitive in the long run to changes in unemployment than Equation 2.3 implied. This explains why the coefficient of $1/U_{t-1}$ is so much larger in Equation 2.4 than in Equation 2.3. And this is why the long-run curve in Figure 13.2 must be considerably steeper than that of the two short-run curves. And the long-run curve does not shift whenever $\dot{p}_{t-1}/p_{t-1}$ changes.

Dynamic elements in the wage-price unemployment nexus may generate the Phillips curve loop illustrated in Figure 13.2. During the early phase of business cycle expansion, it may be possible to reduce unemployment substantially without much initial inflation by moving along the short-run Phillips curve; once the forces of inflation gain momentum, and the effect of rising prices on wage demands manifests itself, the process accelerates and the short-run Phillips curve shifts upward. The effect will be enhanced if, as Packer and Park have argued, relative wage rates become distorted during the expansionary phase of the cycle, leading workers who feel relatively underpaid to push harder for wage increases.[12] The looping process may explain so called "cost-push" or "wage-push" episodes of rapidly rising prices coupled with substantial unemployment, such as occurred in the mid-1950s and the early 1970s. Indeed, one transitional portion of the unemployment-inflation loop involves rising output and reduced inflation; a second portion involves a politically disastrous rise in unemployment coupled with accelerating inflation.

[12] Arnold H. Packer and Seong H. Park, "Distortions in Relative Wages and Shifts in the Phillips Curve," *Review of Economics and Statistics*, February 1973, pp. 16–22. They present a simulated Phillips curve loop based on empirically estimated equations.

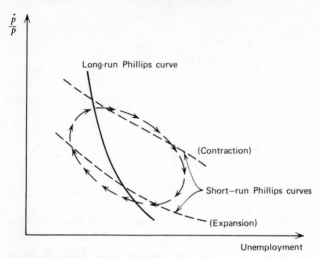

Fig. 13.2   *The clockwise Phillips curve loop. During the expansion the lower short-run Phillips curve is exploited; unemployment is reduced without much inflation. But once the public becomes accustomed to rapidly rising prices, the Phillips curve shifts upward and inflation may persist for a while, even though unemployment is rising.*

The Phillips curve loop in Figure 13.2 revolves clockwise around a negatively sloped long-run relationship, suggesting that even in the long-run there exists some scope for substituting higher rates of inflation for unemployment. While this is compatible with Equation 2.4, the point has been contested by a number of economists who object that in the long run the level of output and employment is insensitive to the speed of inflation; in the short run, union contracts may delay adjustment, the public may not fully anticipate the rate of price rise, and workers may mistakenly accept a wage less than the marginal disutility of work. But the longer the inflationary process continues, the less deception can take place and the pace of inflation will accelerate. According to the accelerationists, any attempt to push the unemployment rate below its "natural" level must generate more and more rapid inflation; the long-run Phillips curve is vertical.[13]

Phillips curve analysis provides a pessimistic "stag-flation" outlook for the politician who hopes to reconcile price stability with low unemploy-

---

[13] See Milton Friedman's Presidential Address delivered at the eightieth meeting of the American Economic Association, "The Role of Monetary Policy," *Proceedings of the American Economic Association*, March 1968. Also, E. S. Phelps et al., *Micro-Economic Foundations of Employment and Inflation Theory*, Norton, 1970.

ment. But instead of living with the Phillips curve, several strategies may be tried in an attempt to shift it to a more favorable position. In particular, the wage-price guideposts enunciated during the Kennedy Administration constituted an effort to shift the Phillips curve downward. And focusing the force of public opinion on "inflationary" wage and price increases in key industries may have had an effect; Perry's investigations suggest that under the Kennedy-Johnson guideposts the annual rate of wage increase may have been $\frac{3}{4}\%$ less than would otherwise have been generated with the same level of unemployment and rate of price change; and the longer-run relationship, taking the feedback of rising prices on wages into account, may have been lowered by 1.2%.[14] If accurate, Perry's estimates suggest that the guideposts constituted a highly potent strategy for increasing our nation's output without paying a high price in terms of high inflation. But there remains the suspicion that the guideposts may have been exploiting the lower portion of the Phillips curve loop.

Shifts in the Phillips curve may result from imbalances in relative wages and changing expectations about the likelihood of inflation. The curve may shift in response to policy measures designed to improve the inflation-unemployment tradeoff. And the Phillips curve also may shift in response to long-run demographic trends. Over the last 15 or 20 years there have been substantial shifts in the composition of the work force. Prime-age white males now constitute a much smaller proportion of the total labor force than they did before the Korean War; teenagers, females, and blacks have grown in importance. And the unemployment rate for these groups has grown, while that for prime-age white males has remained relatively stable. This means, Perry argues, that labor markets are much tighter today than they would have been with the same official unemployment rate in the mid-1950s; he estimates that 4% unemployment would now generate 4.5% inflation instead of the 2.8% of the mid-1950s.[15]

As an alternative to moral suasion and direct price controls, steps to improve the efficiency with which labor markets operate can reduce the inflationary effects of low unemployment. Unfilled job vacancies and frictional unemployment persist simultaneously for several reasons. First, there may be an actual mismatch in that the skills of the unemployed may not mesh with the requirements of unfilled job openings. Manpower retraining programs help to upgrade workers so as to mesh job skills with manpower requirements. But frictional unemployment also arises because those without jobs may not know of the existence of job opportunities

---

[14] See Perry, op cit. Also his "Changing Labor Markets and Inflations," *Brookings Papers on Economic Activity*, 1970, p. 428.

[15] George L. Perry, "Changing Labor Markets and Inflation," in *Brookings Papers on Economic Activity*, 1970, pp. 411–441.

requiring the particular skills they possess. The application of electronic computers to the task of matching the skills of the unemployed with the right job opening should help to reduce frictional unemployment. And frictional unemployment also results from unrealistic job expectations; the length of time that many workers remain without jobs might be reduced if they become reconciled more promptly to the realities of the current job situation by accepting a current offer instead of continuing to search for an ideal position paying an unrealistically high salary; and the pool of unemployed might be further reduced if management had better information concerning the amount they will have to pay workers with particular characteristics; otherwise they may turn down a series of applicants in a vain search for the ideal employee. Improved job counselling and better sources of information may facilitate a more prompt adaptation of expectations to the realities of current labor market conditions.[16]

13.4 THE PACE OF INFLATION AND EFFECTIVE DEMAND

Inflation has a double impact on effective demand. As explained in Chapter 11, the rate at which prices are *changing*, $\dot{p}/p$, must be distinguished from the level of prices, p. Only in the comparative-statics analysis of the long-run effects of a disturbance on the level of prices may the effects of $\dot{p}/p$ be neglected. In asking how long it will take the price level to adjust to its new static plateau attention must be paid to the effect of rising prices on effective demand as well as to the Phillips curve relationship linking $\dot{w}/w$ and $\dot{p}/p$ to the unemployment rate.

It is the impact of $\dot{p}/p$ on effective demand that explains how inflation may release resources for the government sector. For example, Keynes argued:[17]

". . . the use of money is taxable, and although for various reasons this particular form of taxation is highly inexpedient, a Government can get resources by a continuous practice of inflation, even when this is foreseen by the public generally. . . ."

And Friedman has explained:[18]

"The price rise imposes, as it were, a tax on the holdings of . . . those net obligations of government that are expressed in nominal monetary units. The payment of this

---

[16] Techniques for shifting the Phillips curve by improving market efficiency are discussed by Charles C. Holt, "Improving the Labor Market Tradeoff Between Inflation and Unemployment," *Proceedings of the American Economic Association*, May 1969.

[17] *A Tract on Monetary Reform*, London: Macmillan and Co., 1923, p. 49.

[18] "Discussion of the Inflationary Gap," *American Economic Review*, June 1942, as revised in *Essays in Positive Economics*, University of Chicago Press, 1953, pp. 254–255.

tax, as of any other, reduces the income available to consumers . . . and so tends to reduce the fraction of their income . . . that they want to spend on consumer goods. . . ."

It is necessary to explore the impact of $\dot{p}/p$ on investment and consumption spending in order that we can understand the incidence of the inflationary tax.

a. Consumption Spending

Particularly during the early stages of inflation the public may not anticipate the inroads being made on their consumption by rising prices. For example, suppose not only that the current level of consumption is determined by last month's income, but also that the number of dollars allocated to this function is decided on under the misapprehension that current prices as well as dollar income will remain at yesterday's levels.[19] Thus, if in the absence of inflation, real consumption is determined by $C_t = c_0 + c_1 Y_{t-1}^d$, where Y_{t-1}^d is last period's real disposable income, we suppose that only $C_t^n = p_{t-1} C_t = p_{t-1}(c_0 + c_1 Y_{t-1}^d)$ dollars are allocated to consumption. Then real consumption spending will be

$$C_t = \frac{p_{t-1}}{p_t}(c_0 + c_1 Y_{t-1}^d)$$

$$= c_0 + c_1 Y_{t-1}^d - \frac{\dot{p}}{p}(c_0 + c_1 Y_{t-1}^d) \tag{4.1}$$

where $\dot{p}/p = (p_t - p_{t-1})/p_t$. Note that this consumption function reduces to the traditional expression $C = c_0 + c_1 Y_{t-1}$ when $\dot{p}/p = 0$. That is, it involves "inflation illusion" in that behavior is modified by the process of rising prices, but it is free of "money illusion" in that real consumption is not regarded as sensitive to the *level* of prices. The presence of inflation illusion reduces real consumption spending, and the more rapid the un-anticipated inflation, the greater the reduction in consumption. Both terms in Equation 4.1 use the same coefficient, the propensity to consume out of disposable income, which may be reasonable during the early stages of inflation when it is neither fully recognized nor expected to continue. But the longer the inflation persists, the larger the proportion of the population that will recognize its presence, and this may reduce the coefficient of $(\dot{p}/p) Y_{t-1}^d$.

Rising prices reduce the purchasing power of assets of fixed nominal value—for example, government bonds and currency. To see how the magnitude of the capital loss is determined, let W_{t-1}^n denote last period's

---

[19] Tjalling C. Koopmans analyzed the implications of such behavior in "The Dynamics of Inflation," *Review of Economics and Statistics*, February 1942, pp. 53–65.

nominal wealth holdings. If prices rise from p_{t-1} to p_t its purchasing power will fall from W_{t-1}^n/p_{t-1} to W_{t-1}^n/p_t; that is, the capital loss will be

$$L_t^r = \frac{W_{t-1}^n}{p_{t-1}} - \frac{W_{t-1}^n}{p_t} = \frac{p_t - p_{t-1}}{p_t} \frac{W_{t-1}^n}{p_{t-1}} = \frac{\dot{p}}{p} \frac{W_{t-1}^n}{p_{t-1}} \qquad (4.2)$$

Although this capital loss is not taken into account by the national income accountant in computing disposable income, Milton Friedman's suggestion that it will influence consumption spending certainly appears reasonable. And we may revise Equation 4.1 to read

$$C_t = c_0 + c_1 Y_{t-1}^d - c_0' \frac{\dot{p}}{p} - c_1' \frac{\dot{p}}{p} Y_{t-1}^d - c_1'' \frac{\dot{p}}{p} \frac{W_{t-1}^n}{p_{t-1}} \qquad (4.3)$$

If consumers regard the capital loss as equivalent to a reduction in income it might well be subtracted from disposable income, in which case its impact on consumption will be measured by the propensity to consume out of income (i.e., $c_1'' = c_1$). When inflation is expected to be temporary instead of permanent, the capital loss is similar to a transitory loss in income, and c_1'' may be small; if the inflation is regarded as permanent, c_1'' will be larger, although this affect will be mitigated if consumers are induced to escape the tax that inflation imposes by shifting out of assets of fixed nominal value, that is, by selling their municipal bonds and buying real estate or stocks. However, even the holder of real assets cannot entirely escape loss during periods of inflation, because the realized gain will be subject to taxes, although at a favored rate, if and when he sells his assets.

The effect of inflation on consumer spending in the United States has been studied intensively by F. Thomas Juster and Paul Wachtel,[20] who make extensive use of household attitudinal data generated by the Survey Research Center of the University of Michigan. They find that when inflation is unanticipated there is little impact on durable expenditures, although nondurable spending may be stimulated. However, consumers who anticipate inflation, far from hoarding in advance of the price rise, are inclined to reduce their expenditures on durables, including cars, and increase consumption of nondurables. This startling empirical finding may occur, according to Juster and Wachtel, because inflation generates uncertainty and uncertainty in turn generates a conservative spending policy because consumers fear that they will become overextended. Be that as it may, Juster and Wachtel report that, at least in the United States, periods of high inflation have never been fully anticipated.

---

[20] "Inflation and the Consumer," in *Brookings Papers on Economic Activity*, 1972, pp. 71–122. See also their "Note on Inflation and the Saving Rate," op cit., 1972, pp. 765–778.

b. Investment Spending

The retailer who anticipates inflation may try to increase his inventories in advance of the price rise. The manufacturer who fears rising prices may try to expand his factory in advance of need; furthermore, when higher wages are expected in the future, it may be worthwhile to install capital-intensive labor-saving equipment. Borrowers who anticipate rising prices tend to discount the rate of interest charged by banks for borrowed funds. In other words, it is the real rate of interest, displayed in Table 11.3, that matters, not the nominal rate. The analysis in Chapter 6 of the determinants of investment spending may still be valid during inflationary episodes if we regard r as denoting the real rate of interest; that is, $r = r^n - (\dot{p}/p)$.

This distinction suggests that those who argue that investment is insensitive to the rate of interest should also conclude that the rate of price change does not matter much either: they should conclude that the rise in the real rate of interest that took place as a result of the falling price level in the 1930s probably did not have an adverse effect on investment spending; again, the acceleration of inflationary forces at the end of the 1960s probably did not induce much investment spending. However, those who argue that the interest rate is a decisive determinant of investment spending should also conclude that the inflationary process will have a strong tendency to feed on itself, because rising prices lower the real cost of borrowed funds, given the nominal interest rate, and thereby encourage further investment spending and add to the inflationary gap. But it also follows that falling prices are a grossly unsatisfactory cure for depression, whatever the effect on the ultimate equilibrium, because the declining prices will discourage investment spending and precipitate a downward deflationary spiral.

To the extent that inflation is not correctly anticipated, firms will not know the real rate of interest; they can guess, but there may not be unanimity of opinion. If uncertainty is generated by price instability the prudent entrepreneur may be induced to adopt a more conservative investment policy than would be justified if he knew with certainty the real rate of interest; thus there may be a tendency for both inflation and deflation to discourage investment spending by some firms.[21] But less prudent investors may be misled during inflationary episodes. As business cycle theorists have long recognized, many businessmen become overly optimistic because of the paper profits they realize as a result of the price rise taking place between the time when raw materials were purchased and their transforma-

---

[21] Even if there is no bias in the rational firm's estimate of the rate of interest it will be inclined to adopt a more restrictive investment policy because the penalty for erroneous over extension, which may involve bankruptcy, is considerably larger than the opportunity abandoned by failing to invest when the extent of inflation is not fully anticipated.

tion into final product ready for the marketplace;[22] if and when the cycle peaks and the upward spiral of prices terminates, the profit picture becomes bleak, and overextended firms may be forced into bankruptcy. Thus the ultimate effect of price uncertainty may be to generate less investment than would occur in a period of stability in which the real rate of interest can be judged with greater precision.

c. The Demand for Money

And how will inflation influence the demand for money? First of all, with rising prices, given the nominal rate of interest, the cost of holding money balances increases. While the effect of this "tax" is similar to an increase in the nominal rate of interest with stable prices, it may not be quite so strong. Inflation increases the cost of holding *all* assets of fixed nominal value—the variable W^n of Chapter 4, Section 7—the government debt as well as coin, currency, and demand deposits. So there will be a tendency to cut back on all assets of fixed nominal value, and it is not obvious that money will become either a larger or a smaller proportion of this reduced stock. In contrast, a rise in the nominal rate of interest leads to the substitution of *both* nominal and real assets for money. In other words, it is reasonable to write the demand for money equation as

$$\mathbf{M}_{d^n} = p\mathbf{M}_d \left(Y^r, \frac{\dot{p}}{p}, r \right)$$

$$\frac{\partial \mathbf{M}_{d^n}}{\partial r} < \frac{\partial \mathbf{M}_{d^n}}{\partial \dot{p}/p} < 0 \qquad (4.4)$$

---

[22] A number of alternative accounting procedures are employed by business firms in evaluating their inventories. Some use first-in-first-out (FIFO); others use last-in-first-out (LIFO). Since the FIFO procedure evaluates inventories of raw materials at the price paid for the earliest purchases not yet used up, it yields a larger markup and bigger profit figure for the firm during inflationary episodes. In contrast, the LIFO procedure uses the price paid for the most recent purchase of raw materials in figuring the cost of goods sold; this procedure will yield a lower profit figure during inflation, thus reducing the firm's tax liability. Because of the rich variety of accounting procedures employed by business firms, the National Income Accountants must exercise meticulous care in computing the inventory investment component of GNP; they must make sure that their estimate reflects an actual change in the magnitude of inventories instead of a reevaluation of existing stocks. For example, if the book value of inventories rises by 10% when prices have also gone up 10%, the inventory investment figure in the GNP accounts should be zero; and if the book value of inventories had remained constant the GNP accounts should show negative inventory investment because stocks have obviously been reduced in magnitude even though they have the same dollar value on the firm's balance sheet; the Inventory Valuation Adjustment (IVA) of the national income accounts corrects for such distortions. While it is ordinarily small in magnitude, the IVA is quite large during inflationary episodes; it was only $.2 billion in 1960, but it was −$7.0 in 1946, −$6.1 in 1950, and −$7.2 billion in 1972. In computing national income, profits are "written down" by the amount of the IVA in order that the estimate of income earned through participating in the production process will not be distorted by paper profits arising from inflation.

Note that the demand for money balances is proportional to the price level, given Y^r, $\dot{p}/p$ and r. This means that if an equilibrium characterized by stable prices is disturbed by an increase in the nominal money supply, a proportional rise in the price level can ultimately reequate the demand for money with the supply; the inflationary gap is eliminated and $\dot{p}/p$ returns to zero. But, during the transitional inflationary period, prices are rising rapidly enough to equate continuously the demand for money with the supply.

d. Determining the Speed of Inflation

How do inflation illusion, capital loss adjustment behavior, and the distinction between the nominal and the real rate of interest, by their influence on effective demand, help in conjunction with monetary and fiscal policy to determine the rate of inflation? To begin the discussion of this complicated issue, we must consolidate our earlier analysis of how spending is influenced by the speed of inflation. Suppose that investment spending is determined by the nominal rate of interest, the speed of inflation, the level of output, and the inherited capital stock.[23]

$$I\left(r^n, \frac{\dot{p}}{p}, Y, K_{t-1}\right) \tag{4.5}$$

Furthermore, let us write the implicit relationship for the money rate of interest implied by Equation 4.4 as

$$r^n\left(\frac{\mathbf{M}^n}{p}, Y, \frac{\dot{p}}{p}\right) \tag{4.6}$$

The rate of interest is determined by the real money supply, output, and the speed of inflation. Putting it all together along with consumption function 4.3 yields the following expression for effective demand.

$$C + I + G = c_0 + c_1 Y_{t-1}^d - \frac{\dot{p}}{p}\left(c_0' + c_1' Y_{t-1}^d + c_1'' W_{t-1}^n / p_{t-1}\right)$$

$$+ I\left[r^n\left(\frac{\mathbf{M}^n}{p}, Y, \frac{\dot{p}}{p}\right), \frac{\dot{p}}{p}, Y, K_{t-1}\right] + G \tag{4.7}$$

The curve labeled $E(\dot{p}/p, \mathbf{M}/p, \mathbf{G}, Y^d, K_{t-1})$ on Figure 13.3 reveals effective demand as a function of $\dot{p}/p$, given the real value of the money supply, government spending, and so forth. The effective demand curve is drawn with a negative slope under the presumption that rising prices reduce spending; that is, it is presumed that the combined effects of inflation illusion and capital-loss adjustment behavior dominate the tendency for

[23] A special but interesting case of Equation 4.5 has investment depend on the real rate of interest, $r^n - \dot{p}/p$, as well as Y and K_{t-1}.

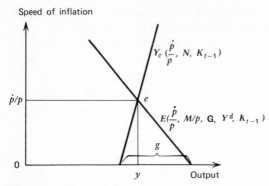

Fig. 13.3 *Determination of the speed of inflation. The speed of inflation is determined by the intersection of the effective demand and capacity curves. Distance* **g,** *the inflationary gap, is influenced by the real money supply and the level of government spending.*

rising prices, by reducing the real rate of interest, to stimulate investment spending. The upward rising $Y_c[(\dot{p}/p), N, K_{t-1}]$ curve indicates the capacity output of goods and services that can be produced with the available labor force (N) and the current stock of capital (K_{t-1}). Capacity output is likely to be an increasing function of the speed of inflation, since the Phillips curve concept involves an inverse relationship between the rate of price change and the number of idle workers. And this effect would be reinforced if employers were misled by errors of accounting connected with inflation into confusing paper windfall profits with the actual gains of business; then workers may be paid more than their marginal product. The tendency for output to be stimulated by rising prices may be enhanced if wage increases lag behind price rises so that the real wage falls. Only to the extent that rising prices lead to production inefficiencies will there be a tendency for output to fall at higher rates of inflation. Intersection point e on Figure 13.3 reveals the rate at which prices will have to rise in order to equate effective demand with supply.

The impact of a variety of factors on the rate of price change can be readily determined with the aid of Figure 13.3. For example, an increase in government spending, by shifting the effective demand schedule to the right, will accelerate the inflationary pressure. On the other hand, the gradual accumulation of capital resulting from investment will help retard the inflation, because more plant and equipment enables the economy to produce more, and this shifts the $Y_c[(\dot{p}/p), N, K_{t-1}]$ curve to the right. This effect will be reinforced because the increased capital stock, other things being equal, discourages investment spending, thus shifting the effective demand schedule to the left. And an increase in tax rates, by lowering the level of disposable income (given total output) discourages consumption spending, thus pushing down on the effective demand schedule and slowing the pace of inflation.

A convenient shorthand summary of the effects of such factors as changes in government spending, tax policy, and capital accumulation on the speed of inflation is provided by the concept of the *inflationary gap*, which we will now define as

$$\mathbf{g} = E(0, \mathbf{M}/p, G, Y_d, K_{t-1}) - Y_c(0, N, K_{t-1}) \qquad (4.8)$$

That is, the inflationary gap is now defined as the amount by which effective demand would exceed supply *if $\dot{p}/p$* were equal to zero; it is the distance labeled $\mathbf{g}$ on Figure 13.3.[24] As can be seen from the graph, when the effective demand and supply curves have constant slope, the rate of inflation will be proportional to the size of the inflationary gap.

How much inflation will be generated by an inflationary gap will be influenced by certain factors affecting the slope of the effective demand curve. In particular, continuing inflation may lead to a stronger and more widespread expectation that it will continue. In a sense, some of the hardship of inflation may be mitigated when its presence is anticipated, but the very process of adapting to inflation can accelerate the rate at which prices rise. When rising prices are anticipated, the impact of inflation illusion is reduced; that is, coefficients c_0' and c_1' in the consumption function become smaller. Furthermore, when inflation is anticipated, the real rate of interest is perceived by entrepreneurs to be less than the money rate, and this stimulates investment spending. Both these factors will lead to a gradual strengthening of effective demand and accelerate the pace of inflation. In much the same way, escalator wage clauses may accelerate the pace of inflation by preventing the real wage from being eroded prior to the time for contract renegotiation. However, there is one offsetting factor that curtails spending: once consumers have become accustomed to inflation, they will regard the capital losses they suffer on their assets of fixed nominal value as a permanent instead of a transitory phenomenon, and this will have a negative impact on their consumption spending; but this effect will be limited if they cut back on their holdings of such assets.

[24] This definition constitutes an elaboration on more elementary concepts of the gap mentioned in Chapter 11, Section 4c. Milton Friedman has emphasized that the "inflation gap" is a virtual gap in that the process of rising prices restricts demand to the capacity level of output; see his "Discussion of the Inflationary Gap" in the *American Economic Review*, June 1942, as revised in his *Essays in Positive Economics*, University of Chicago Press, 1953. Note that the gap depends on W_{t-1}^n as well as $\mathbf{M}$. However, this subtle distinction can be suppressed under the assumption that the government consistently borrows in financing its affairs so as to keep W_{t-1}^n proportional to $\mathbf{M}$.

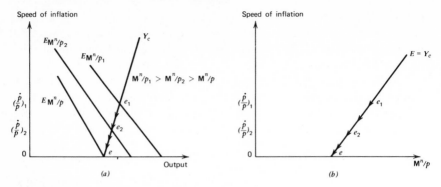

Fig. 13.4   *Self-correcting inflation. (a) Reductions in the real money supply, resulting from either a higher price level or a cut by the central bank in the nominal money supply, lower the effective demand schedule and reduce the speed of inflation. (b) When the nominal money supply remains constant, the process by which inflation cures itself may be summarized by the $E = Y_c$ curve.*

Can the very process of inflation cure itself? Changes in the real value of the money supply and other assets of fixed nominal value affect the speed of inflation by shifting the effective demand curve, as shown in the left panel of Figure 13.4. But care is required in interpreting the implications of changes in the price level on the real value of the money supply. Indeed, if the nominal money supply and W_{t-1}^n are fixed, the process of inflation will reduce their real value and eliminate the inflationary gap. The $E = Y_c$ curve on the second panel of the graph summarizes this process by which inflation may cure itself. Suppose, for example, a full-employment equilibrium at point e is disturbed by a 25% increase in the assets of fixed nominal value achieved by issuing new money and borrowing from the public.[25] Initially the economy shifts to e_1 and experiences quite rapid inflation. But as prices rise the real value of monetary assets falls, causing the economy to slide gradually down the $E = Y_c$ curve, as illustrated by the arrows. The process of rising prices is curing itself. Details of the timing of this adjustment process are suggested in Figure 13.5. The final equilibrium position, characterized by stable prices after the return of the real money supply to its initial value, was predicted earlier with the static *IS-LM* apparatus of Chapter 11, Section 4d.

---

[25] The analysis is simplified somewhat by assuming that the ratio of money to other assets of fixed nominal value remains constant.

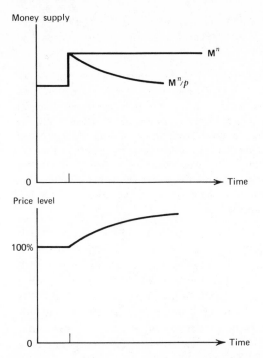

Money supply

M^n

M^n/p

0   Time

Price level

100%

0   Time

Fig. 13.5 *Chronology of an inflation. An injection of new money into a fully employed economy causes a rapid inflation initially but, as the price level rises, the pace of inflation slows; the process terminates when the price level has risen enough to restore the real money supply to its initial level.*

13.5 FORCED SAVING

The concept of "forced saving" refers to the power of inflation to reallocate resources away from consumption. The possibility of financing economic development by creating money constitutes a strong temptation for emerging nations. "Forced saving" is an intriguing doctrine of long history.[26] In the fourteenth century Bishop Nicole Oresme condemned a prince who would substitute new coins obtained by melting down the old with generous additions of lead and other base metals. He argued that debasement of the coinage was "so tyranical and fraudulent that I am un-

---

[26] F. A. von Hyeck traces the notion to John Stuart Mill and Bentham in his "Note on the Development of the Doctrine of Forced Saving," *Quarterly Journal of Economics*, November 1932, pp. 123–133.

certain whether it should be called violent theft or fraudulent exaction. . . ."[27] But Oresme also asserted that in certain circumstances the community itself might alter its coinage.[28]

". . . if the community has great need of a large sum of money for a war or for the ransom of its prince from captivity . . . it might raise it by altering the money, and this would not be contrary to nature or usurious . . . in this arrangement about all the conditions desirable for such a levy seem to be combined; it brings in a large revenue in a short time, it is very easy to collect and assess without the services of many officials, and it involves little expense or opportunity for fraud by the collectors. Indeed, no other more equitable or proportional plan can be imagined; for he who has more pays more, and being relatively less felt, it is more tolerable without danger of rebellion and complaint by the people. It is also very general, for neither cleric nor noble can escape it."

Inflation has often proved to be an expedient way of financing government spending in times of national emergency, although few advocate it as a matter of principle. Indeed, this practice led to the hyperinflations that disrupted so many European economies after World War I. Inflationary finance generated the rampant inflation in Korea in the 1950s; the inflation experienced by Viet Nam in her conflict was less than that suffered a decade earlier by Korea in large measure because of stronger economic support from the United States.[29] Nonetheless, inflationary financing does not always lead to the collapse of the currency. Professor Joseph Grunwald reports on the experience of one South American country.[30]

"The curious aspect of Chile's inflation history of close to a century is that the country never experienced runaway inflation. . . . [If] the forces that made the authorities "print money" were so strong as to maintain a 20 or more percent yearly inflation for many years, what stopped those forces from compelling a snowballing monetary expansion?"

The evaluation of forced saving must focus on the following questions. Given the proportion of real government spending to be financed by the printing press, will the rate at which prices rise converge to a particular value, or will prices spiral upward at an ever increasing rate? How will the speed of inflation respond to increases in the proportion of real government

    [27] "On the First Invention of Money," in *Early Economic Thought*, Arthur E. Monroe, Ed., Harvard University Press, 1951, p. 96.

    [28] Ibid., p. 101.

    [29] G. E. Makinen, "Economic Stabilization in Wartime: A Comparative Case Study of Korea and Vietnam," *Journal of Political Economy*, November–December 1971, pp. 1216–1244.

    [30] "The Structuralist's School on Price Stabilization and Economic Development: The Chilean Case," *Latin American Issues: Essays and Comments*, Albert O. Hirschman, ed., The Twentieth Century Fund, 1961, p. 100.

spending financed by injections of new money? What determines the response of the speed of inflation to changes in the level of government spending?

Once it is decided that a given share of real government spending will be financed by a deficit, both the nominal and the real money supply must be regarded as endogenous variables. Rising prices will reduce the purchasing power of the money already in circulation. And inflation means that more and more new money will have to be injected in order to finance a given volume of real government spending. Let us suppose that a deficit D, measured in real terms, will be maintained at a constant proportion δ of real government spending G; we have $D = \delta G$ and real tax revenue $T = (1 - \delta)G$. The presence of the deficit leads to the creation of money. Assume that the change in the nominal money supply is

$$\Delta M_t^n = M_t^n - M_{t-1}^n = \mu p D = \mu p \delta G \qquad (5.1)$$

where p is the price level and μ is the coefficient of expansion of the money supply. If the deficit is financed either by debasing the currency or with the printing press, $\mu = 1$, because the change in the money supply then is equal to the deficit; when a more advanced economy finances the deficit through the banking system, however, μ may be considerably in excess of unity.

What happens to the real money supply depends on a race between the printing press and the speed of inflation. Specifically, from the identity

$$M_t^r \equiv \frac{M_t^n}{p_t} = \frac{\Delta M^n}{p_t} + \frac{M_{t-1}^n}{p_t} = \frac{\Delta M_t^n}{p_t} + M_{t-1}^r \left(\frac{p_{t-1}}{p_t} \right)$$

one can obtain

$$\Delta M_t^r \equiv M_t^r - M_{t-1}^r = \frac{\Delta M_t^n}{p_t} - \left(\frac{p_t - p_{t-1}}{p_t} \right) M_{t-1}^r \qquad (5.2)$$

Substituting from Equation 5.1 now yields the fundamental equation for the change in the real money supply.

$$\Delta M_t^r = \mu \delta G - \left(\frac{\dot{p}}{p} \right)_t M_{t-1}^r \qquad (5.3)$$

The larger government spending, the less the reliance on taxes to finance it, and the larger the coefficient of expansion of the money supply, the more likely it is that the real money supply will increase. But an acceleration in the pace of inflation or a larger real money supply will tend to reduce it. Indeed, the real money supply will remain constant ($\Delta M^r = 0$) if

$$\frac{\dot{p}}{p_t} M_{t-1}^r = \mu \delta G \qquad (5.4)$$

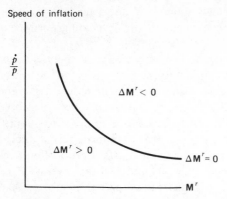

Speed of inflation

Fig. 13.6 *The real money supply. Depending on the speed of inflation and the stock of money, the process of inflationary finance can lead to either an expanding or a contracting real money supply.*

This is the rectangular hyperbola labeled $\Delta M_r = 0$ in Figure 13.6. At any point below the hyperbola the real money supply is expanding; at any point above it the real money supply contracts. An increase in μ, δ, or $\mathbf{G}$ will push it outward in the northeasterly direction.

Equation 5.3 does not suffice to determine the path of prices generated when a government resorts to inflationary finance. An additional equation is required because there are two endogenous variables to be determined, $(\dot{p}/p)_t$ and $\mathbf{M}_t^r$. It is necessary to take into account the way in which the changing money supply, via its influence on the public's spending, influences the speed of inflation; the $E = Y_c$ curve in the right panel of Figure 13.4 summarized this relationship. In the first panel of Figure 13.7 the $E = Y_c$ curve is superimposed on the $\Delta M^r = 0$ rectangular hyperbola. Their point of intersection constitutes a *forced-saving equilibrium*, because the injection of new money generated by the government's deficit is just offset by the depreciation in purchasing power of the existing currency. Note that if the real money supply is initially at $\mathbf{M}_0^r$, which is less than its equilibrium level of $\mathbf{M}_e^r$, the pace of inflation as determined from the $E = Y_c$ curve will not suffice to keep the real money supply from expanding. Thus the pace of inflation will be stepped up and the economy will move as indicated by the arrows toward forced-savings equilibrium point e. Conversely, if the money supply is initially above its equilibrium level, rapidly rising prices will cause it to contract as the economy glides down the $E = Y_c$ curve. Thus the forced-saving equilibrium in Figure 13.7a is stable. Note that an increase in government spending accelerates the pace of inflation and increases the equilibrium real money supply by

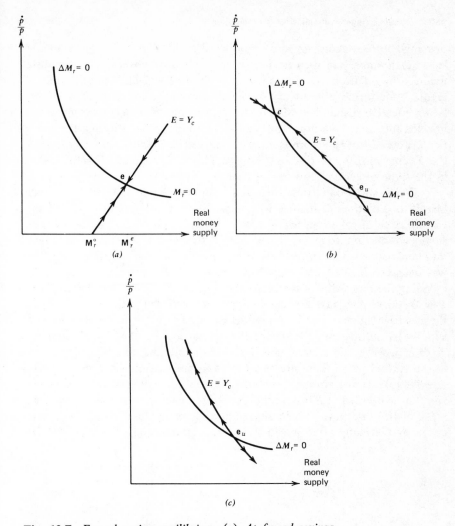

Fig. 13.7 *Forced saving equilibrium.* (a) *At forced savings equilibrium point* **e** *the real money supply and the speed of inflation remain constant.* (b) *Forced savings equilibrium point* **e**$_u$ *is unstable; the equilibrium at* **e** *is stable.* (c) *Hyperinflation occurs when there is no stable forced savings equilibrium.*

pushing the rectangular hyperbola outward and the $E = Y_c$ curve to the left. Furthermore, an increase in the proportion of government spending financed by inflationary finance will have the same effect. Not only does a greater reliance on inflationary financing reduce the tax bite, thus stimulating effective demand, it also increases the rate at which new money is injected into the economy. However, if the funds raised through the practice of forced saving are invested, the enlarged productive capacity pushes the Y_c curve in Figure 13.4 to the right. This will move the $E = Y_c$ curve in the same direction, slowing the rate of inflation.

While some countries, such as Chile, may have experienced a long history of inflationary finance without suffering from a continually accelerating pace of inflation, a government cannot count on a stable forced-saving equilibrium to insure that hyperinflation will be avoided. The longer inflation persists, the more likely it is that it will be anticipated, and this will push the $E = Y_c$ curve upward, quickening the pace of inflation and reducing the real value of the money supply. And it is conceivable that the $E = Y_c$ curve may have a negative slope, as illustrated in the second panel; the negative slope arises if the reduction in the real value of the money supply, by cutting into the size of the capital loss suffered by consumers, gives a decisive stimulus to effective demand. In the situation illustrated in the second panel there are two forced-savings equilibria; only the one at e is stable. In the bottom panel there is no stable equilibrium, and prices spiral ever upward at a faster and faster rate, leading to the inevitable collapse of the currency. This is the classic case of hyperinflation, as experienced by Germany after World War I and Hungary after World War II.

REFERENCES

1. The following papers are all concerned with the link between wage and price changes. The Phelps volume contains a variety of papers utilizing microeconomic analysis in investigating the link between unemployment, unfilled job vacancies, and the determination of money wages.

Arthur J. Alexander, "Prices and the Guideposts: The Effects of Government Persuasion on Individual Prices," *Review of Economics and Statistics*, February 1971.

R. G. Bodkin, *The Wage-Price Productivity Nexus*, University of Pennsylvania Press, 1966.

Robert E. Hall, "Prospects for Shifting the Phillips Curve through Manpower Policy," *Brookings Papers on Economic Activity*, Vol. 3, 1971.

G. L. Perry, "Wages and the Guideposts," *American Economic Review*, September 1967, and Comments by Anderson, Wachter and Throop in the June 1969 *American Economic Review*.

Edmund S. Phelps (ed.), *Microeconomic Foundations of Employment and Inflation Theory*, W. W. Norton and Co., 1970.

A. W. Phillips, "The Relationship Between Unemployment and the Rate of Change of Money Wages in the United Kingdom, 1861–1957," *Economica*, November 1958.

Paul Samuelson and Robert Solow, "Analytical Aspects of Anti-Inflation Policy," *American Economic Review*, May 1960.

C. L. Schultze, "Recent Inflation in the United States," Study Paper No. 1, Joint Economic Committee, *Study of Employment Growth and Price Levels*, 86th Congress, September 1959.

"Governmental Policies to Deal with Prices in Key Industries in Selected Foreign Countries," Joint Economic Committee, 88th Congress, 1963.

2. Dynamic aspects of inflation are discussed in the following articles.

Phillip Cagan, "The Monetary Dynamics of Hyperinflation," in *Studies in the Quantity Theory of Money*, Milton Friedman, ed., Chicago University Press, 1956.

Colin D. Campbell and Gordon C. Tullock, "Hyperinflation in China, 1937–49," *Journal of Political Economy*, June 1954.

Michael C. Lovell, "A Keynesian Analysis of Forced Saving," *International Economic Review*, September 1963.

KEY CONCEPTS

labor's share

Phillips curve

Phillips curve loop

"inflation illusion" versus "money illusion"

capital loss

inflationary gap
effective demand
forced saving
debasement

EXERCISES

13.1 Analyze carefully the following statement, pointing out both the truths and the ambiguities involved. "Wage increases that exceed the rate of productivity advance are inflationary."

13.2 Explain carefully what is meant by the "Phillips curve." Does the evidence support the Phillips curve concept? Consider the data on Tables 2.1 and 13.1.

the business cycle and economic forecasting

the business cycle: an overview

*14.1 INTRODUCTION

How old is the business cycle? How regular are the cyclical reversals that interrupt the expansion of economic output? What procedures are used to predict fluctuations in economic activity and how useful are they? What types of theories have been advanced to explain the persistence of the cycle? These issues are surveyed in this chapter. Subsequent chapters focus in greater detail on the task of explaining, predicting, and controlling fluctuations in economic activity.

*14.2 A CAPSULE HISTORY OF THE BUSINESS CYCLE

The business cycle predates the industrial revolution. Perhaps Sir William Petty (1623–1687) did not have business fluctuations in mind when he referred to the seven-year "cycle of dearths and plenties." But the bursting of the speculative South Sea Bubble in 1720 was only one of a series of financial panics that frequently harassed the money markets of Europe throughout the eighteenth century.[1] A contemporary description of one serious panic was provided in *The London Chronicle* on June 23, 1772.

"It is certain that by the failure of some capital houses . . . upward to two thousand valuable artificers and workmen are thrown out of employment and their families deprived of support. . . . It is beyond the power of words to describe the general consternation of the metropolis. . . . An universal bankruptcy was expected; the stoppage of every house in London was looked for; the whole city was in an uproar; the whole city was in tears. . . . Many of the trading people, suspicious that their money was not safe in private hands, have drawn all their cash from places where they usually kept it, and placed it in the Bank of England. . . ."

Remedy was sought in legislative reform, *The London Chronicle* arguing in August that "it is generally acknowledged" that legislation should be

---

[1] For a discussion of early thought on the business cycle, see Joseph Schumpeter, *History of Economic Analysis*, New York: Oxford University Press, 1954, pp. 738–750.

passed providing punishment for bankers who "game away the money of their creditors. . . ."[2] Banking legislation in 1773 provided for the registration of bankers, imposed restrictions on merchandise trade by bankers, and established for creditors a prior claim on the estate of deceased bankers.[3] The continued buffeting of business activity by the rhythmic forces of the cycle for over two centuries testifies to the difficulties involved in trying to legislate economic stability.

The history of the business cycle in the United States since the Civil War has been meticulously recorded by the National Bureau of Economic Research (NBER) in a protracted research project initiated in the 1920s by Wesley C. Mitchell.[4] From the NBER chronology of business cycle turning points, recorded in Table 14.1, it is clear that the word "cycle" is a misnomer if it conveys the impression that business fluctuations occur with a steady and uniform rhythm. The expansionary phases of the business cycle have averaged about two and a half years in length, but some expansions have petered out after only a year or 18 months. And contractions, while fortunately shorter on the average than expansions, have been subject to equal variability in length. Clearly, it is only as a very rough first approximation that the business cycle can be said to be represented by the smooth mathematical sine function plotted in Figure 14.1.

$y = \sin t$

Fig. 14.1   *A perfect cycle.*

Further evidence concerning recent business cycles in the United States is provided by Table 14.2. For each cycle, we have in successive rows on the table the level of GNP and its major components at the cycle peak and at the subsequent trough. Each Δ row indicates the *changes* taking place during the contraction in GNP, its major components, and unemployment. Both the magnitude of the decline and the consequent rise in unemployment have varied dramatically from one contraction to the other. How the sources of the decline in purchasing power have changed from one cycle to the next will be revealed by a comparison of the Δ rows.

[2] August 20, 1772.

[3] Op cit., May 29, 1773 and June 1, 1773.

[4] *Business Cycles: The Problem and Its Setting*, New York: National Bureau of Economic Research, 1927.

Table 14.1 NBER CHRONOLOGY

Business Cycle Reference Dates		Duration in Months			
				Cycle	
		Contraction (Trough from Previous Peak)	*Expansion (Trough to Peak)*	*Trough from Previous Trough*	*Peak from Previous Peak*
Trough	Peak				
December 1854	June 1857	(*X*)	30	(*X*)	(*X*)
December 1858	October 1860	18	22	48	40
June 1861	April 1865	8	46	30	54
December 1867	June 1869	32	18	78	50
December 1870	October 1873	18	34	36	52
March 1879	March 1882	65	36	99	101
May 1885	March 1887	38	22	74	60
April 1888	July 1890	13	27	35	40
May 1891	January 1893	10	20	37	30
June 1894	December 1895	17	18	37	35
June 1897	June 1899	18	24	36	42
December 1900	September 1902	18	21	42	39
August 1904	May 1907	23	33	44	56
June 1908	January 1910	13	19	46	32
January 1912	January 1913	24	12	43	36
December 1914	August 1918	23	44	35	67
March 1919	January 1920	7	10	51	17
July 1921	May 1923	18	22	28	40
July 1924	October 1926	14	27	36	41
November 1927	August 1929	13	21	40	34
March 1933	May 1937	43	50	64	93
June 1938	February 1945	13	80	63	93
October 1945	November 1948	8	37	88	45
October 1949	July 1953	11	45	48	56
August 1954	July 1957	13	35	58	48
April 1958	May 1960	9	25	44	34
February 1961	November 1969[a]	9	105	34	114
November 1970[a]		12	(*X*)	117	(*X*)
Average, all cycles:					
27 cycles, 1854–1970		19	33	52	52[b]
11 cycles, 1919–1970		15	42	56	60[c]
5 cycles, 1945–1970		11	49	60	59[d]
Average, peacetime cycles:					
22 cycles, 1854–1961		20	26	45	46[e]
8 cycles, 1919–1961		16	28	45	48[f]
3 cycles, 1945–1961		10	32	42	42[g]

Source. Business Conditions Digest.

Note. Underscored figures are the wartime expansions (Civil War, World Wars I and II, Korean War, and Viet Nam War), the postwar contractions, and the full cycles that include the wartime expansions.

[a] Tentative and subject to revision as more information becomes available.
[b] 26 cycles, 1857–1969.
[c] 10 cycles, 1920–1969.
[d] 5 cyclss, 1945–1969.
[e] 21 cycles, 1857–1960.
[f] 7 cycles, 1920–1960.
[g] 3 cycles, 1945–1960.

387

Table 14.2   COMPARISON OF BUSINESS CYCLE PEAKS AND TROUGHS. This table evaluates the changes in major components of gross national product at business cycle peaks and troughs, as identified by the National Bureau of Economic Research

Year	GNP	= C	+ I	+ X − M	+ G	NRI	RI	INV	G_f	Y_d	$U\%$
						Investment Components					
P 1929	203.6	139.6	40.5	1.5	22.0	26.5	10.4	3.5	3.5	150.5	3.2
T 1933	141.5	112.8	5.3	0	23.3	7.6	2.1	−4.3	6.0	112.2	24.9
Δ_{33}	−62.1	−26.8	−35.1	−1.5	+1.3	−18.9	−8.3	−7.8	2.5	−38.3	+21.7
P 1937	203.3	143.1	30.0	−0.7	30.8	18.9	5.6	5.5	11.5	153.1	14.3
T 1938	193.0	140.2	17.0	1.9	33.9	13.7	5.7	−2.4	13.3	143.6	19.0
Δ_{38}	−10.3	−2.9	−13.0	+2.6	+3.1	−5.2	+0.1	−7.9	1.8	−9.5	+4.7
P 1945	355.4	183.0	19.8	3.8	156.4	19.9	2.8	−2.9	139.7	220.7	1.9
T 1946	312.6	203.5	53.3	8.4	48.4	30.2	12.1	10.0	30.1	227.0	3.9
Δ_{46}	−42.8	+20.5	+33.5	+4.6	−108.0	+10.3	+9.3	+12.9	−109.6	+6.3	+2.0
P 48–4	328.7	212.8	59.7	5.5	50.7	38.5	16.8	4.4	27.3	234.0	3.8
T 49–4	323.3	219.7	46.0	3.8	53.8	32.7	19.8	−6.5	27.1	232.7	5.9
Δ_{49}	−5.4	+6.9	−13.7	−1.7	+3.1	−5.8	+3.0	−10.9	0.2	−1.3	+2.1
P 53–3	413.7	251.1	61.5	1.1	100.0	41.1	19.3	1.2	70.0	275.9	2.9
T 54–3	407.2	256.9	59.8	3.3	87.2	39.9	22.4	−2.5	54.6	278.5	5.6
Δ_{54}	−6.5	+5.8	−1.7	+2.2	−12.8	−1.2	+3.1	−3.7	−15.4	+2.6	+2.7
P 57–3	455.2	289.3	70.9	6.0	89.1	48.0	19.9	3.0	51.3	317.7	4.3
T 58–2	439.5	287.5	56.0	2.5	93.6	41.3	19.7	−5.0	53.4	314.5	6.8
Δ_{58}	−15.7	−1.8	−14.9	−3.5	+4.5	−6.7	−0.2	−8.0	2.1	−3.2	+2.5
P 60–2	489.8	317.8	73.5	3.9	94.7	47.6	22.0	3.8	51.0	341.2	5.6
T 61–1	482.7	316.3	62.4	6.4	97.6	44.9	20.9	−3.4	52.2	341.8	6.7
Δ_{61}	−7.1	−1.5	−11.1	+2.5	+2.9	−2.7	−1.1	−7.2	1.2	+0.6	+1.1
P 69–3	729.2	469.5	114.0	0.7	145.1	80.9	23.7	9.4	72.3	517.3	3.5
T 70–4	719.3	477.5	102.1	2.0	137.8	73.5	24.1	4.5	61.8	537.4	5.8
Δ_{70}	−9.9	+8.0	−11.9	+1.3	−7.3	−7.4	+0.4	−4.9	−10.5	+20.1	+2.3

Note. All figures (other than unemployment) are measured in billions of dollars at 1958 prices. GNP denotes Gross National Product, C consumption, I gross private domestic investment, $X − M$ net exports of goods and services, G government spending, NRI nonresidential investment, RI residential structure, INV inventory investment, G_f federal government expenditures on goods and services, Y_d disposable income, and U the unemployment rate. Postwar figures are quarterly data at annual rates.

Consider first the 1929–1933 contraction. From the Δ_{33} row we note that three of the four components of GNP contributed to the $62.1 billion decline in output.[5] Consumption fell by $26.8 billion, investment by $35.1 billion, and the foreign trade balance by $1.5 billion. Only the

---

[5] Because of the national income identity, we must have $Y = C + I + G + X − M$ at both the peak and the trough of the cycle; therefore the sum of the changes in the components must equal the change in output.

government sector mustered an increase in expenditure, and this was an insignificant contribution of $1.3 billion; although federal expenditures increased by $2.5 billion, this was offset partially by a drop of $1.2 billion in state and local governmental spending. All three components of investment spending declined. Residential housing construction fell to one fifth the level of 1929. Nonresidential investment (e.g., factories and machinery) collapsed to only slightly more than one fourth the boom levels of 1929. Inventory investment became negative, because producers and retailers were emptying their warehouses and unloading stocks from the shelf instead of meeting sales with new production. Finally, the substantial decline of $38.3 billion in disposable income explains the decline in consumption.

How about the problem of converting from a war to a peacetime economy? The Δ_{46} row reveals that government spending on goods and services declined by a drastic $108 billion at the end of World War II. Although most economic projections had emphasized that conversion would be achieved only at the expense of a severe recession, the task of postwar readjustment was eased by substantial gains in consumption and investment spending and an improvement in the foreign trade balance.[6] Consumption spending was stimulated by a substantial boost in disposable income brought about by an augmented flow of federal transfer payments in the form of a variety of veterans' benefits. Thus, the G.I. Bill of Rights provided educational and unemployment benefits to help returning veterans adjust to civilian life; these benefits also provided a healthy boost to aggregate purchasing power. Consumer demand was stimulated further by the backlog of unsatisfied demand accumulated during the years of wartime shortages and rationing, the wherewithal to make up for lost time being provided by the substantial holdings of liquid assets saved during the war. All components of investment spending increased markedly. Manufacturers were eager to replace worn-out machinery and to expand productive capacity, the demand of returning veterans for housing helped to stimulate a major construction boom financed under easy credit conditions, and the need to replenish stocks depleted during the war led to positive inventory investment of sizable proportions. A substantial rise in exports, financed in large measure by grants and loans designed to finance the rebuilding of devastated Europe, contributed further toward the maintenance of effective demand. The alacrity with which the United States converted from war to peacetime production after World War II testifies to the ability of our economic system to drastically shift the focus of industrial activity—provided effective demand is maintained.

[6] For a discussion of the factors leading to erroneously pessimistic projections, see Lawrence R. Klein, "A Post-Mortum on Transition Predictions of National Product," *Journal of Political Economy*, August 1946.

The five remaining reversals in economic activity reported in Table 5.1.2 are customarily called "inventory recessions," because each of these downturns, including the decline that followed the close of hostilities in Korea, was characterized by drastic reductions in inventory investment. It is not that inventory investment is such a large component of GNP; instead, it is the fact that this category of investment is subject to more erratic fluctuations, moving abruptly from positive accumulation to drastic liquidation. Clearly, any explanation of the recessions that interrupt the expansion of the American economy will have to account for the movements of inventories.

*14.3 BAROMETRIC FORECASTING OF THE CYCLE

From this capsule history of the business cycle it is clear that the task of forecasting economic fluctuations cannot be handled easily by any naive projection techniques, such as simply projecting that the current boom will be of the same duration as the last. The business cycle is much too variable in both length and intensity for that. But, as an alternative, amateur and professional forecasters alike often employ "barometric" procedures. The barometric approach involves an attempt to identify one or more indicators or barometers that will signal change in advance of actual developments. Practitioners of the art of barometric forecasting are inclined to use past experience more than theory in selecting their arsenal of indicators; success is said to depend less on the application of any particular theory than on the skill with which the indicators are identified and the experience of their user in interpreting them.

Historically, barometric forecasts are marked by more failures than successes. Relying largely on three separate barometric time series measuring speculative, business, and monetary developments, the *Weekly Letters* published by the Harvard Economic Society may be credited with correctly anticipating the 1929 peak in business activity. In April 1929, four months before the cycle peak, the newsletter noted that there had been a marked reduction in general construction and a falling off in commodity prices; readers were warned that "continuance of this current downward movement would foreshadow a recession in the volume of basic manufacture. . . ." And, on October 19, the newsletter confirmed that "business is facing another period of readjustment, rendered necessary, in part, by the long period of expanding production which culminated in the summer." But it was also argued that "if investment should threaten serious consequences for business (as is not indicated at present) there is no doubt that the reserve system would take steps to ease the money market and to check the movement." On November 2, 1929, after a precipitous collapse of the stock market, the readers of the *Weekly Letters* were told that "the next six months will probably bring a substantial recovery of stock prices"; they were assured further that the fall in interest rates was "in itself evidence of the soundness of the present business situation" and that "the present recession, both for stocks and business, is not the precursor of business depression, but will prove intermediate in character." In December 1929 the readers of the *Weekly Letters* were advised:

"The economic effects of the decline in stock prices are of course not yet spent, and two or three months of slack business lie ahead. . . . In some directions, however, recession may soon come to an end, if only because contraction has already been so drastic. . . . Reviewing these facts, one must conclude that neither the optimistic opinion expressed in some quarters nor the alarm of those who look solely at the stock market or basic industry is justified. . . . Today a depression seems improbable, and continuance of business recession is all that is in prospect. This justifies a forecast of recovery of business next spring, with a further improvement in the fall. . . ."

Although the *Weekly Letters* had forecast correctly the upper turning point, it had failed to anticipate the stock market crash. Equally serious, it gave a false signal of recovery in the face of what turned out to be the most serious depression in our country's history. Many forecasters have done worse than miss two out of three, but this economic newsletter shortly ceased publication.

Memories are short, and the quest for an ideal barometric indicator persists. The dashed *II* line on Figure 14.2 indicates how an ideal barometric indicator should behave. The ideal indicator turns down in advance of the cycle peaks and starts to rise in advance of the lower turning point in general economic activity. In contrast, the dotted *EO* line on the same graph commits a serious error of omission that obviously disqualifies it. But sins of omission are not the only type of error; a second type of error involves false signals. Thus, the *FS* line on the figure leads all the turns in

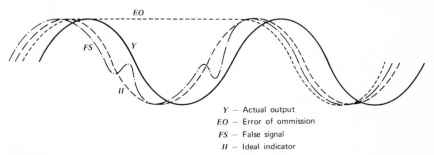

Y — Actual output
EO — Error of ommission
FS — False signal
II — Ideal indicator

Fig. 14.2 *Types of cyclical indicators.*

actual business activity, but it erroneously indicates several additional turns that do not materialize. Everyone remembers the fable of the ill-fated shepherd boy who cried "wolf" when there was no wolf. Surely the indicator that calls turns when none occurs is unlikely to be believed when it finally signals an actual turning point in economic activity. While it should be obvious that in appraising turning point indicators it is necessary to keep both types of errors in mind, partisans of particular indicators often praise them for their ability to turn down in advance of recession while failing to mention numerous false signals.

Changes in stock prices are sometimes cited in the financial press as a precursor of movements in general business activity. But inspection of Figure 14.3 reveals that stock prices are not an ideal barometric indicator. True, the series does peak in advance of the 1948, 1953, 1957, and 1960 upper turning points. But as can be seen from the graph, stock prices gave a number of false signals in the 1960s. For example, the market decline of 28% from December 1961 to June 1962 was not followed by recession. As can be seen from the plots of the unemployment rate and the industrial production index on the same graph, the 1960s were characterized by more or less steady expansion instead of by the erratic fluctuations that had shaken the economy in the preceding decade; nonetheless, the stock market continued to fluctuate in the absence of recession. Thus the traumatic downturns in stock prices in 1961 and 1966 constituted false signals of recessions that never really materialized. Stock prices reached another peak at the end of 1968, and this time the business analysts who still watched this indicator were correctly forewarned of forthcoming recession.

The rate of change in the nominal money supply is regarded by many as a useful barometric forecaster. The dotted line plots the percentage increase in the money supply over the same month of the preceding year. This series is quite erratic, and it has been smoothed statistically by taking a six-month moving average, which is plotted as a solid line.[7] In retrospect, one can find movements in the smoothed series that anticipate the major business cycle swings of the 1950s. But, if anything, the rate of change in the money supply fluctuated more in the 1960s than it had in the preceding decade; these were false signals, since there were no corresponding recessions in business activity. Admittedly, there was a slight hesitation in the rate of growth in industrial production in 1967, and a corresponding pip in the unemployment rate but, at worst, this was a "minirecession" that

[7] A six-month centered moving average for month t is simply

$$\frac{m_{t-3}}{12} + \frac{m_{t-2} + m_{t-1} + m_t + m_{t+1} + m_{t+2}}{6} + \frac{m_{t+3}}{12}$$

An unfortunate effect of taking a six-month moving average is that it involves an additional three-month publication lag before the smoothed indicator is available.

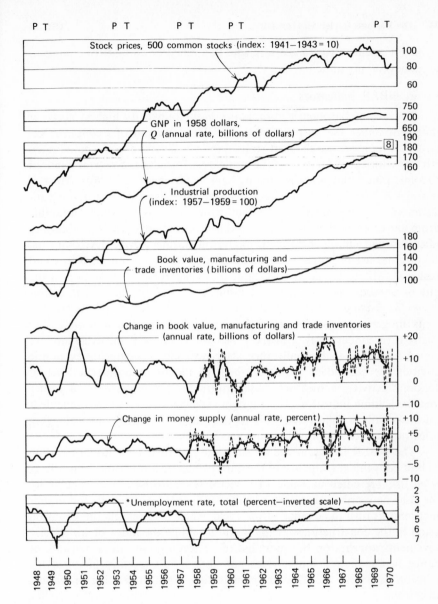

Fig. 14.3 *Cyclical indicators for the United States economy.*

was much smaller than forecasters who had relied on the rate of change in the money supply anticipated.

a. NBER Indicators

The art of barometric forecasting has attained its highest stage of refinement under the auspices of the National Bureau of Economic Research.[8] A major research effort stretching over several decades culminated with an historical evaluation of the cyclical performance of several hundred economic time series, some stretching back as far as the Civil War. Most of the series did not behave in precise cyclical patterns; indeed, a major conclusion of the investigation was that while there is no single infallible barometer of cyclical movements, a skillful practitioner would find certain indicators particularly helpful in analyzing business cycle developments. The original list of indicators, published in 1938 by Arthur F. Burns and Wesley C. Mitchell,[9] has been subject to considerable modification in the light of subsequent successes and failures. Currently the NBER distinguishes 37 *leading indicators* that tend to turn in advance of the turning points in general business activity, 25 *roughly coincident indicators* that usually turn concurrently with the peaks and troughs of the cycle, and 11 *lagging indicators* that usually turn after reversals in aggregate economic activity. The coincident indicators help to identify the current level of economic activity; sometimes they confirm the prognosis derived earlier from the leading indicators; a false signal is suggested when the coincident indicators fail to follow the shift in the leading indicators. The lagging indicators help to confirm the previous diagnosis.

The NBER has identified a "short list" of their indicators providing the best convenient summary of the current business situation. This abbreviated list, presented in Table 14.3, yields few surprises. In particular we note that new orders, building permits, and orders for plants and equipment tend to turn in advance of the cycle—their lead reflects the gestation period in the construction of capital goods. While the index of stock price movements appears on the short list of 12 leading indicators, the rate of change in the money supply does not—but it has recently qualified for inclusion as one of the 37 series constituting the complete list of leading indicators.

The indicators identified by the National Bureau, together with a large number of other measures of current business activity, are conveniently graphed in *Business Conditions Digest*, a monthly publication of the

---

[8] For a summary of National Bureau research achievements, see Geoffrey H. Moore, "Tested Knowledge of Business Cycles," reprinted from the *1962 NBER Annual Economic Report in A.E.A. Readings in Business Cycles*, Gordon and Klein, editors, Richard Irwin, 1965.

[9] *Statistical Indicators of Cyclical Recessions*, National Bureau of Economic Research, 1938.

Table 14.3   NATIONAL BUREAU CYCLICAL INDICATORS—SHORT LIST

Leading Indicators
   Average workweek, production workers in manufacturing
   Average weekly initial claims, state unemployment insurance
   Net business formation
   New orders, durable goods industries
   Contracts and orders, plant and equipment
   New building permits, private housing units
   Change in book value, manufacturing and trade inventories
   Industrial material prices
   Stock prices, index of 500 common stocks
   Corporate profits after taxes
   Ratio, prices to labor costs in manufacturing
   Change in consumer installment debt

Roughly Coincident Indicators
   GNP in current dollars
   GNP in 1958 dollars
   Industrial production index
   Personal income
   Manufacturing and trade sales
   Sales of retail stores
   Employees on nonagricultural payrolls
   Unemployment rate (unemployed/labor force)

Lagging Indicators
   Long-term unemployment rate (15 weeks or longer)
   Business expenditures on new plant and equipment
   Manufacturing and trade inventories
   Labor cost per unit of output in manufacturing
   Commercial and industrial loans outstanding (large commercial banks)
   Bank rate on short-term business loans

Department of Commerce. With only a short compilation and publication lag, business analysts who subscribe to this publication can follow the latest wiggles of the indicators. Anyone who casually inspects the graphs is likely to be particularly impressed by the number of false signals of recession. Many of the leading indicators turned down toward the end of 1950 and continued to decline in 1951, and numerous other false signals of contraction were displayed in subsequent upswings. Indeed, statistical studies by such investigators as Arthur Okun[10] and Michael Evans[11] suggest that

[10] "On the Appraisal of Cyclical Turning-Point Predictors, *Journal of Business*, April 1960.

[11] *Macroeconomic Activity: Theory, Forecasting and Control*, Harper and Row, 1969.

when proper debits are deducted for false signals and missed turns, the leading indicators are of no net use in forecasting business developments. The issue is still open to debate, and some would interpret the statistical evaluations as nothing more than confirming the National Bureau's caveat that reading the indicators is an art that cannot be delegated to a mechanistic formula. As a practical matter, it is interesting to note that, regardless of changes of administration in Washington, members of the Presidential Council of Economic Advisors are inclined to cite the indicators from time to time. It is hard for practical men of affairs to resist the temptation to rely on them, particularly when they indicate favorable economic developments.

Regardless of how useful a business analyst may find the leading indicators, it is necessary to resist the temptation to conclude that timing implies causation. That a *post hoc ergo proctor hoc* approach to the problem of determining causation can lead to serious difficulties is suggested by a simple example. The book value of manufacturing and trade inventories, according to the NBER, qualifies as a lagging indicator, and a naive investigator might be inclined to say that the cycle in general business activity causes the movement in inventory stocks. Furthermore, the time series of changes in the book value of manufacturing and trade inventories (inventory investment) is classified as a leading indicator, and it may be tempting to argue that this supports the hypothesis that inventory investment causes the cycle. But both these propositions can hardly be true, because the leading series is simply the *change* in the lagging series. In Figure 14.4, where both series are plotted, it is clear why the change leads the stock: when stocks level out, inventory change is zero; when stocks decline, inventory investment is negative; when stocks are rising more rapidly late in the 1950s, investment peaks. There is, as a matter of mathematical necessity, a tendency for changes in relatively smooth cyclical series to lead the series itself. Figure 14.5 illustrates how a perfectly smooth cycle is led with mathematical precision by its first derivative. The same argument may explain why changes in the money supply, but not the stock of money itself, serve as a leading indicator. Certainly, evidence on the timing of inventory investment and the rate of change in the money supply does not *in and of itself* imply causation.

b. Diffusion Indices

The diffusion indices developed at the NBER provide another barometric forecasting device, and a number are graphed each month in *Business Conditions Digest*. The diffusion index reports the proportion of industries in which the component series are expanding. For example, the manufacturing diffusion index for new orders stands at about 75% when more new orders are being received in 26 of the 35 component industries;

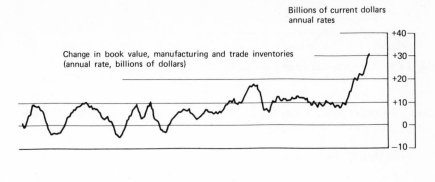

Fig. 14.4 *Inventory investment and inventory stocks.*

it would stand at 100% if the expansion were diffused throughout all 35 industries, and at zero if all were contracting. What the diffusion index does not do is weigh the contribution of the various industries in accordance with their general importance or the magnitude of the change. It is in this respect that it differs from the results of looking at changes in a series.[12] While many analysts feel that the diffusion indices have been quite useful when evaluated in conjunction with other barometric indicators,

---

[12] To see the relationship between a diffusion index and the time series obtained by looking at changes in the aggregate, let X_{it} denote the level of the variable in industry i at time t. Furthermore, let sign $(\Delta X_{it}) = 1$ if $(X_{it} - X_{it-1}) > 0$, and -1 otherwise. Then the level of diffusion index in the quarter t is $\sum$ sign $(\Delta X_{it})/2n + \frac{1}{2}$. In contrast, the ith change in the series at time t is $X_{it} - X_{it-1} = $ sign $(\Delta X_{it})|\Delta X_{it}|$. Therefore the change in the aggregate may be written as $\Delta X_t = \sum_i (X_{it} - X_{i,t-1}) = \sum_i$ sign $(\Delta X_{it})|\Delta X_{it}|$; thus the change in the aggregate series weights the sign of the change in each of the component series by the magnitude of the change. If all industries changed by the same magnitude the diffusion index and the change series would move in strict proportion to each other. *Business Conditions Digest* reports a diffusion index for inventory stocks and, as a leading indicator, the change in inventories; obviously, this involves a degree of redundancy.

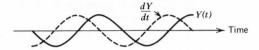

Fig. 14.5   *The cycle and its first derivative.*

their usefulness as a forecasting device has been subject to serious question by a number of investigators.[13]

c. Anticipatory Data

It is possible to buttress impressions gained from diffusion indices and leading indicators by looking at anticipatory data revealing what businessmen expect to happen. For example, *Business Week* publishes each fall the results of the McGraw-Hill business survey of anticipated capital expenditures. Periodically, the *Survey of Current Business* reports on businessmen's plans for new plant and equipment expenditure, as revealed by a sample survey of business firms. The *Survey of Current Business* also reports every three months on how businessmen expect their sales to change in the immediate future, whether current inventories are in excess of requirements, and how they plan to change their inventory in the immediate future. Of course, businessmen frequently revise their investment plans in the face of changing economic conditions. It is primarily for this reason that surveys of business intentions have not provided particularly precise guidance on actual developments.[14]

d. Summary

The barometric procedures widely employed by business analysts are far from reliable guides to short-run business cycle developments. Even their strongest advocates must concede that in and of themselves they do not explain why cyclical movements occur. And when they do indicate in which direction the economy is going to move, they do not tell what policy should be prescribed and what dosage is appropriate in order to achieve economic stability. Theory as well as vision is required in formulating economic policy. As we will see, econometrics—the art of applying sta-

---

[13] Sidney Alexander has concluded that the diffusion index is no better than the first difference of the aggregate as a predictor of turning points. See his "Rate of Change Approaches to Forecasting—Diffusion Indexes and First Differences," *Economic Journal*, June 1958, as reprinted in *A.E.A. Readings in Business Cycles*, Gordon and Klein, editors, Richard D. Irwin, 1965.

[14] For an analysis of the investment anticipations survey see Arthur Okun, "The Predictive Value of Surveys of Business Intentions," *American Economic Review*, May 1962, p. 221. Albert Hirsch and Lovell analyze the Department of Commerce inventory survey data in *Sales Anticipations and Inventory Behavior*, John Wiley, 1969.

tistical techniques in the implementation of economic models—has come into its own as an alternative approach to forecasting.

*14.4 THE SCOPE OF BUSINESS CYCLE THEORY

The difficulties encountered in over two centuries' effort at achieving economic stability are not caused by a failure to focus sufficient attention on business cycle phenomena. Over the years an amazing variety of theoretical arguments have been advanced to account for the recurrence of cyclical fluctuations in business activity in terms of overinvestment, underconsumption, monetary complications, and/or psychological factors. In 1878, during the most severe depression of the nineteenth century, the distinguished William Stanley Jevons commented[15]

"It is curious to notice the variety of the explanations offered by commercial writers concerning the cause of the present state of trade. Foreign competition, beer-drinking, overproduction, trade-unionism, war, peace, want of gold, superabundance of silver . . . , the Government policy, the Glasgow Bank directors, Mr. Edison and the electric light, are a few of the happy and consistent suggestions continually made to explain the present disastrous collapse of industry and credit."

Jevons also raised the following complaint about the incompleteness of John Stuart Mill's argument that psychological factors explain the periodicity of crisis.

"Assuming that variations in commercial credit and enterprise are essentially mental in their nature, must there not be external events to excite hopefulness at one time or disappointment and despondency at another."[16]

To Jevons, an acceptable theory must explain the periodicity of the business cycle.

Jevons attributed the regularity of the business cycle to sunspots. By their influence on the harvests in India and elsewhere the sunspots affected England's foreign trade and ultimately caused reversals in the pace of overall economic activity. While in all modesty Jevons did not claim to be the originator of this theory, which can be traced back into the eighteenth century, he can be credited with having taken more pains than any of his predecessors to muster empirical evidence in support of the proposition. Indeed, he may well have been the first economist to cite probability theory in support of his explanation of the business cycle. He asserted that "trade

[15] *Investigations in Currency and Finance*, Macmillan and Company 1884, as reprinted by Augustus M. Kelley, p. 221. This quotation is from an article originally published in 1878 and reprinted in the Jevons volume.

[16] Op cit., pp. 203–204.

had probably reached a maximum of activity on the following dates: (1701?), 1711, 1721, 1731–32, (1742? 1752?), 1763, 1772–73, 1783, 1793, (1804–5?), 1815, 1825, 1836–39 (1837 in the United States), 1847, 1857, 1866, 1878."[17] On the basis of this list, he concluded:[18]

". . . the principal commercial crises do fall into a series having the average period of 10.4666 years. Moreover, the almost perfect coincidence of this period with Broun's estimate of the sunspot period (10.45) is by itself strong evidence that the phenomena are causally connected. . . . Judging this close coincidence of results according to the theory of probabilities, it becomes highly probable that two periodic phenomena, varying so nearly in the same mean period, are connected as cause and effect."

In fact, however, the coincidence arises from a regrettable error. Jevons used a monthly series on bankruptcies as a major guide in attempting to identify the dates at which the downturns occurred. Unfortunately, the time series he examined was interrupted from 1785 through 1790. If he had filled in the gap in his data by consulting issues of *Gentleman's Magazine* or the *London Chronicle* for those years, it seems certain that the exceptionally large number of bankruptcies recorded for 1788 would have led him to identify that as a year of crisis. Thus there were probably 18 instead of 17 cycle peaks from 1701 to 1878, and the average cycle length was 9.88 years, a figure that deviates substantially from Broun's estimate that the average period between episodes of high sunspot activity is 10.45 years.

Jevons was neither the first nor the last economist to emphasize the effect of meteorological factors in explaining the periodicity of the cycle.[19] And meteorological explanations are only one example of exogenous theories that attempt to explain the rhythm of the cycle in terms of noneconomic factors. Some exogenous theorists emphasize political events. And, of course, we usually do find that postwar periods of readjustment are troubled by recessions in business activity. Since depressed business conditions may at times contribute to military conflict, it might well be argued that the line of causation involves interaction between economic and noneconomic factors.

[17] Ibid., p. 230–231.

[18] Ibid., pp. 231 and 215.

[19] Henry L. Moore (1869–1958), one of the two or three most important pre-World War II pioneers in econometric work in the United States, pointed out in discussing the regularity of the cycle that the planet Venus "thrusts itself at intervals of eight years almost exactly in the direct path of radiation from the Sun to the Earth" in his *Synthetic Economics*, Macmillan Co., 1929, p. 102, as quoted by George J. Stigler in "Henry L. Moore and Statistical Economics," *Econometrica*, January 1962, p. 11. And to this day some say that sunspot disturbances influence the rate of admissions to mental hospitals, the spawning of codfish, the reception of radio and television signals, and also contribute to great vintages in Burgundy wines.

Endogenous cycle theorists attempt to explain the cycle in terms of economic factors. For example, R. G. D. Hawtrey argued that the business cycle is essentially a monetary phenomenon. He said that the upper turning point of the cycle is caused by the restriction of credit, which occurs once the banking system becomes loaned up. As long as the gold standard or other legal restrictions limit the capacity of the banking system to expand, the boom must inevitably come to an end. In contrast, psychological theorists are more inclined to emphasize the role of errors of pessimism. For example, Keynes argued that the business cycle is largely psychological in origin, the boom being generated by excessive optimism concerning the profitability of investment opportunities.[20]

". . . an essential characteristic of the boom (is) that investments which will in fact yield, say, 2 per cent in conditions of full employment are made in the expectation of a yield of, say, 6 per cent and are valued accordingly. When the disillusion comes, the expectation is replaced by a contrary "error of pessimism," with the result that investments, which would in fact yield 2 per cent in conditions of full employment, are expected to yield less than nothing; and the resulting collapse of new investment then leads to a state of unemployment in which the investments, which would have yielded 2 per cent in conditions of full employment, in fact yield less than nothing. . . ."

Of course, Jevons might object, albeit posthumously, that such psychological arguments do not account for the observed periodicity of the cycle. But Keynes argued that there were two stable time factors that explain why downturns are of fairly regular duration. First, recovery hinges partly on a wearing out of the excess capital stock, and this will be governed by the average durability of capital; he went on to mention that the length of the downswing would be lengthened if the economy passed from a period of expanding population growth to an epoch characterized by contraction, since this would cause a decline in the equilibrium stock of capital. The second stable time factor is that only a limited amount of time is required to liquidate surplus inventories.

The extent of professional disagreement concerning the causes of the business cycle has been matched only by the variety of remedies that have been advanced. While many economists have argued that interest rates must be raised in periods of boom in order to snub excessive spending and limit the impact of the ensuing depression, Keynes argued that this was a very dangerous strategy.[21]

". . . the remedy for the boom is not a higher rate of interest but a lower rate of interest! . . . an increase in the rate of interest, as a remedy for the state of affairs

---

[20] John Maynard Keynes, *General Theory of Employment, Interest and Money*, Harcourt Brace, 1935, p. 321.

[21] Ibid., p. 322.

arising out of a prolonged period of abnormally heavy new investment belongs to the species of remedy which cures the disease by killing the patient."

Keynes was an underconsumptionist. He argued that income should be redistributed from the rich to the poor on the supposition that this would raise the aggregate consumption function; higher consumption would provide a market for the increased output made possible by the investment projects erroneously undertaken during the upswing.

In opposition to underconsumptionism, the overinvestment school of thought held that much of the investment generated during the upswing was of the wrong type, and that recession is necessary to liquidate the mistakes of the boom. Joseph Schumpeter (1883–1950) argued that the cycle was an inevitable aspect of the process by which technological progress is realized in a capitalistic society. While inventions may take place in a more or less continuous random process, the actual adoption of new techniques of production must wait until entrepreneurs sense that the time is ripe, which is after the economy has recovered from the preceding slump. The investment of innovators, financed in large measure by the banking system, contributes to an expanding money supply and a more rapid pace of economic activity. Once the cumulative upswing is underway, rising prices contribute to unwarranted optimism and excessive investment as the expansion feeds on itself. The cumulative forces generating the expansion cannot continue indefinitely. For one thing, as the banking system gradually becomes loaned up as a result of excessive borrowing, interest rates begin to rise, investment is choked off, and the slump inevitably must follow. But this does not mean that the ultimate *cause* of the cycle is monetary in nature, argued Schumpeter. The overinvestment stimulated by the boom means that once the task of building the capital projects is completed, the existence of excess capacity will become all too apparent. Even if monetary factors do not terminate the boom, investment spending must eventually collapse, and the depression inevitably must follow. The downturn, the running down of surplus inventories, and inevitable unemployment are characteristic of a necessary phase that must run its course before equilibrium can be restored.[22]

The technique of business cycle research has been subject to marked change within recent years. However bitter their disagreements may have been, the literary arguments in the 1930s of Hawtrey, Keynes, and Schumpeter may bear a closer resemblance to each other, and perhaps to the research strategy of Jevons in the preceding century, than to modern studies of cyclical phenomena. A pioneering paper by Ragnar Frisch on

---

[22] Schumpeter's theory of the cycle was clearly articulated in his *Theory of Economic Development*, Harvard University Press, 1934. An exhaustive research effort led to his monumental two-volume *Business Cycles*, McGraw Hill, 1939.

"Propagation Problems and Impulse Problems in Dynamic Economics"[23] failed to earn mention in Gottfried Haberler's League of Nations sponsored survey of the state of business cycle theory as of the eve of World War II.[24] But Frisch's contribution is recognized today as a precursor of dynamic models characterizing much recent business cycle research, because he explicitly specified the equations constituting a dynamic model capable of generating quite regular fluctuations when excited by external random shocks. And, in the 1930s, Jan Tinbergen was pioneering the empirical testing of business cycle theories and the construction of econometric models of the cycle. Frisch and Tinbergen were to share the first Nobel Prize in economics in 1969. As we will see in subsequent chapters, modern business cycle research focuses on the appropriate specification of the equations of dynamic models, on the perfection of econometric techniques for estimating their parameters, and on the experimental simulation of alternative economic policies on the electronic computer.

[23] In *Economic Essays in Honor of Gustav Cassel*, George Allen and Urwin, 1933.

[24] *Prosperity and Depression, A Theoretical Analysis of Cyclical Movements*, 3rd ed. enlarged by Part III, George Allen and Unwin, 1952.

REFERENCES

1. Gottfried Haberler's monumental contribution summarized the history of business cycle theory up to World War II.

    Gottfried Haberler, *Prosperity and Depression*, 3rd ed., United Nations, 1952.

2. The techniques developed at the National Bureau of Economic Research for analyzing business cycles are discussed in the two contributions by Geoffrey H. Moore. Professor R. A. Gordon's article evaluates the techniques developed at the Bureau.

    Geoffrey H. Moore, "Statistical Indicators of Cyclical Revivals and Recessions," in G. H. Moore, ed., *Business Cycle Indicators*, Princeton University Press, 1961.

    ———, "Tested Knowledge of Business Cycle," in *Annual Report*, National Bureau of Economic Research, 1962.

    R. A. Gordon, "Alternative Approaches to Forecasting: The Recent Work of the National Bureau," *Review of Economics and Statistics*, August 1962.

KEY CONCEPTS

business cycle

NBER

inventory recession

barometric forecasting

leading indicators

coincident indicators

diffusion index

anticipatory data

false signals

underconsumption

overinvestment

CHAPTER 15

simple dynamics
of the business cycle

*15.1 INTRODUCTION

The time has come to explain how cyclical phenomena are generated. In an earlier era economists focused their attention on the characteristics of business cycle turning points in attempting to explain the cycle. But we will find that it is not necessary to advance separate explanations of the upper and lower turning points in order to account for cyclical phenomena. And it is not necessary to invoke a *Devil's Theory* explaining the occurrence of economic downturns in terms of the unfortunate timing of critical errors made by either the monetary or the fiscal authorities. Instead, we will see that a simple dynamic aggregative model based on elementary assumptions about the determinants of consumption and investment behavior is capable of generating the business cycle. It has often been said that the economy may respond to disturbances in a fashion similar to that with which a child's rocking horse responds when its master hits it with a stick. Just as the rocking horse rocks repeatedly to and fro in response to a single blow, so an economy shocked by a major disturbance, such as a war, may experience a number of cyclical maladjustments as it gradually returns to equilibrium. The shape of the horse's rockers will affect the length of time elapsing before the rocking horse comes to rest. Similarly, we will find that how rapidly the economy returns to equilibrium may be influenced by the parameters of the functions determining consumption and investment behavior.

Our discussion will begin with a simple model developed by Alvin Hansen and Paul Samuelson[1] in the years immediately preceding World War II. In a later chapter we consider a slightly more complicated inventory cycle theory developed by Lundberg[2] and Metzler[3] and evaluate a more elaborate monetary model of the business cycle. Such models should

---

[1] Paul A. Samuelson, "Interactions Between the Multiplier Analysis and the Principle of Acceleration," *Review of Economic Statistics*, Vol. 21, pp. 75–78, May 1939.

[2] Erik Lundberg, *Studies in the Theory of Economic Expansion*, London: P. S. Green and Sons, 1937; reprinted in New York by: Kelley and Millman, 1955.

[3] Lloyd A. Metzler, "The Nature and Stability of Inventory Cycles," *Review of Economic Statistics*, Vol. 23, pp. 113–129, August 1941.

be regarded as prototypes hopefully capturing certain essential features of cyclical phenomena. While they are too simple to constitute useful forecasting devices, an understanding of how they work will provide insight into the properties of more involved econometric models that have been created by teams of economists interested in developing sophisticated procedures for forecasting economic developments and guiding economic policy. The models discussed in this and the following chapter are analytically tractable, and an appendix on difference equations will guide the reader interested in learning the mathematical techniques involved.

*15.2 MULTIPLIER-ACCELERATOR INTERACTION

We will consider what may well be the simplest economic model capable of generating cyclical movements. As the price of simplicity, we neglect depreciation, foreign trade, and tax complications; we will also ignore monetary variables for the time being.

As our first assumption, suppose that consumption is determined by last period's income.

$$C_t = c_0 + c_1 Y_{t-1} \tag{2.1}$$

Second, suppose that the capital stock (machinery, plants, and equipment) that entrepreneurs desire to possess is also proportional to output.[4]

$$K_t^d = k Y_{t-1} \tag{2.2}$$

Third, suppose that firms always undertake enough investment to keep the capital stock at this desired level.[5] That is,

$$I_t = K_t^d - K_{t-1} \tag{2.3}$$

so that the actual capital stock is

$$K_t = k Y_{t-1}$$

This condition is supposed to be satisfied in every period; in particular, in period $t - 1$, we had

$$K_{t-1} = k Y_{t-2}$$

---

[4] The crucial assumption that k is constant will be relaxed in a later chapter when the time comes to introduce monetary complications. Samuelson made the desired capital stock proportional to consumption, implicitly assuming that capital goods are produced without capital as an input, but this approach turns out to make the analysis of stability conditions that follows more complicated.

[5] For a relaxation of this assumption, see Exercise 15.3.

Substituting this last equation and Equation 2.2 into Equation 2.3 yields net investment.

$$I_t = K_t - K_{t-1} = k(Y_{t-1} - Y_{t-2}) \tag{2.4}$$

Thus investment spending is proportional to the *change* in income according to this simplest version of the principle of acceleration. Finally, we will use the national income accounting identity in order to complete the model

$$Y_t = C_t + I_t + G_t \tag{2.5}$$

Government spending G_t is exogenous.

Simple as this model is, it is capable of generating the damped oscillatory movements displayed in Figure 15.1 when disturbed by the indicated step upward in government expenditure. That is, the motion displayed by

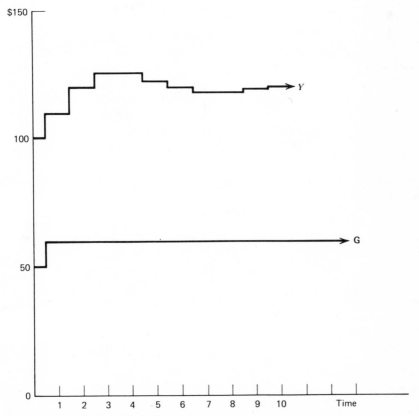

Fig. 15.1 *Multiplier-accelerator interaction. A step increase in government spending generates a cycle in output.*

output on the chart was generated by a step increase in government spending from 50 to 60 units per period. From this business cycle simulation it appears that the oscillations in income generated by the shock of higher government spending are damped; is the system converging to a new output level of 120 units?

Table 15.1 presents the hypothetical data that were plotted on the graph, and the interested reader can verify that all of the entries in the table satisfy the equations of our model for $c_1 = k = 0.5$ and $c_0 = 0$. Take period seven, for example: $C_7 = 60 = 0.5 Y_6$, since Y_6 was indeed 120. Similarly, $K_4 = 62.5 = 0.5 Y_3$, since Y_3 was 125. Furthermore, we always have I_t equal to the change in the capital stock. Also, the national income accounting identity is always satisfied.

While inspection of the table verifies that the simple model is capable of generating cycles, it does not answer a number of interesting questions. Will cycles of this form be generated for disturbances in government spending of whatever magnitude? Will the system really converge to the equilibrium level of income, $Y^e = 120$? How are the dynamic properties affected by changes in the magnitude of parameters c_0, c_1, and k? One way to answer such questions is by trial and error. We could experiment by creating a number of sets of tables for alternative values of the parameters, different disturbances, and so forth. Such experimental *simulation* of the economy eventually proves tedious to even the most persistent investigator. Of course, it is easier to simulate with a desk calculator than by doing the calculations on the back of an envelope, and the whole table may

Table 15.1 HYPOTHETICAL MULTIPLIER-ACCELERATOR CYCLE DATA. $c_0 = 0$, $c_1 = 0.5$, $k = 0.5$

Time Period	Output	Consumption	Investment	Government Spending	Capital Stock
t	$Y_t = C_t + I_t + G_t$	$C_t = c_1 Y_{t-1}$	$I_t = K_t - K_{t-1}$	G_t	$K_t{}^d = k Y_{t-1}$
0	100	50	0	50	50
1	110	50	0	60	50
2	120	55	5	60	55
3	125	60	5	60	60
4	125	62.5	2.5	60	62.5
5	122.5	62.5	0	60	62.5
6	120	61.25	−1.25	60	61.25
7	118.75	60	−1.25	60	60
8	118.75	59.375	−0.625	60	59.375
9	119.375	59.375	0	60	59.375
10	120	59.6875	0.3125	60	59.6875
.	.	.	.	.	.
.	.	.	.	.	.
.	.	.	.	.	.
∞	120	60	0	60	60

be generated with a suitable program on an electronic computer.[6] But even with the largest computer it is not possible to consider every conceivable possibility. Certain critical values of the model's parameters that generate particularly interesting types of behavior might be overlooked. And, with the simulation approach, one can never be certain that such an oversight has not occurred. Fortunately, the simple multiplier-accelerator model now under consideration proves tractable analytically. Instead of resorting to simulation, we will analyze its properties mathematically in subsequent sections of this chapter.[7]

15.3 EQUILIBRIUM OUTPUT

As a first step toward understanding the workings of our simple model, let us search for *equilibrium output*. We ask whether there exists a particular unchanging level of output, call it Y^e, that would satisfy the basic equations of our model *if* government spending remained constant at some specified level G. In order to answer this question, we first substitute Equations 2.1 and 2.4 into Equation 2.5 to obtain

$$Y_t = c_0 + (c_1 + k)Y_{t-1} - kY_{t-2} + G_t \qquad (3.1)$$

This *second-order linear difference equation* explains output in terms of two lagged values and the magnitude of the exogenous variable, G_t. If the economy is in equilibrium, Y^e must satisfy this last equation; that is, $Y^e = Y_t = Y_{t-1} = Y_{t-2}$, and we have

$$Y^e = c_0 + (c_1 + k)Y^e - kY^e + G$$

Solving this equation reveals that equilibrium income is determined by government spending; that is,

$$(1 - c_1)Y^e = c_0 + G$$

or

$$Y^e = \frac{1}{1 - c_1}(c_0 + G) \qquad (3.2)$$

The *multiplier* times the sum of government spending plus c_0 yields the equilibrium level of income. Thus, for our numerical example ($c_0 = 0$,

---

[6] Exercise 15.4 presents an elementary *FORTRAN* computer program for simulating the multiplier-accelerator model.

[7] An alternative strategy is to simulate the behavior of the model for values of the parameters estimated empirically. This strategy must be resorted to when more complicated models that are not tractable analytically are under consideration.

$c_1 = k = 0.5$), increasing government spending to 60 raised equilibrium income to

$$Y^e = \frac{1}{1 - 0.5} 60 = 2 \times 60 = 120$$

That is, if fluctuations cease while government spending remains at 60, income must be 120. The curve in Figure 15.1 suggests that output is gradually converging with the passage of time toward this equilibrium level. Note, however, that our economy is not necessarily in equilibrium whenever output equals the equilibrium value. Thus, in Table 15.1, we see that income is at the equilibrium level of 120 in periods 2, 6, and 10. But the fluctuations continue. Fortunately, the economy overshoots the equilibrium by smaller and smaller amounts with each successive cycle. The economy overshoots because further investment is required in order to adjust the capital stock to its equilibrium level, $K^e = k Y^e$. In equilibrium, $Y_t = Y_{t-1} = Y^e$, and, as Equation 2.4 reveals, this condition means that investment must be zero in equilibrium.

Observe from Equation 3.2 that our model's equilibrium level of output depends only on the propensity to consume and the level of government spending. Thus, the long-run level of economic activity may be influenced by changing **G**; it may also be influenced by tax adjustments that change the marginal propensity to consume out of total income. But as long as we restrict our attention to the long-run equilibrium level of income, we may neglect the possible influence of tax policy on the accelerator coefficient, k. That parameter does not enter into the determination of long-run output, Equation 3.2 reveals. We will find when we turn to dynamic problems of adjustment that the magnitude of k may be of critical importance in influencing the nature of the short-run process by which the system adjusts to equilibrium.

15.4 MODES OF DYNAMIC BEHAVIOR

That the multiplier-accelerator mechanism is capable of generating damped cyclical behavior was made clear from our examination of the particular numerical example displayed in Figure 15.2. But this is not the only possibility. The multiplier-accelerator model constitutes only one example of a second-order linear difference equation, and equations of this type are capable of generating any one of the various types of behavior displayed in Figure 15.2. That is, for certain values of c_1 and k the multiplier-accelerator system might converge to equilibrium without oscillation, as indicated by the curve "m-s" on the graph;[8] but we might find, for cer-

---

[8] Try $c_1 = 0.5$ and $k = 0$, and repeat the numerical exercise of Table 15.1.

tain other values of c_1 and k, that the system explodes in the unstable cycle illustrated by the "c-u" curve instead of converging to equilibrium.[9]

The fact that the dynamic behavior of the economy is sensitive to the numerical values of the parameters is of fundamental importance from a policy viewpoint. We know that changes in tax policy may influence the marginal propensity to consume out of total output. Furthermore, the accelerator coefficient may also be sensitive to various types of governmental policy. Therefore, the proper evaluation of economic policy requires that one consider its influence on the stability of the economy as well as its effect on equilibrium output.

A simple graphical device developed by William Baumol[10] facilitates the analysis of second-order linear difference equations, such as the one that arises from combining the multiplier and accelerator equations. Let us write our second-order difference equation in the form

$$Y_t + \beta Y_{t-1} + \gamma Y_{t-2} = G + \alpha \tag{4.1}$$

For our first application, the multiplier-accelerator, we have

$$\beta = -(c_1 + k)$$

and   (4.2)

$$\gamma = k$$

as the coefficients of the difference equation. As explained in more detail in the appendix, how such a system behaves when disturbed from equilibrium depends entirely on the magnitude of the coefficients β and γ. The situation is summarized graphically in Figure 15.3. Note that the axes of the graph are β and γ; thus a single point on the graph indicates the coefficients of our difference equation. For the particular numerical example plotted in Figure 15.1 we had parameter values $c_1 = k = 0.5$, and so $\beta = -1$ and $\gamma = 0.5$; this is point "x" on the graph. The type of dynamic path that will be generated for specific numerical values of the coefficients of the difference equation can be read off the graph by inspection with the aid of certain propositions established in the appendix. First,

The difference equation will be subject to oscillatory behavior if and only if the point $\langle \beta, \gamma \rangle$ falls inside the CUP OF CYCLICAL MOVEMENTS formed by the parabola on the graph.

Second, it is established in the appendix:

The system will converge to equilibrium if and only if the point β, γ is inside the ISO-STABILITY TRIANGLE plotted on the figure.

---

[9] Try $c_1 = 0.5$ and $k = 2$.

[10] "Pitfalls in Contracyclical Policies: Some Tools and Results," *Review of Economics and Statistics*, Vol. 43, pp. 21–26, February 1961.

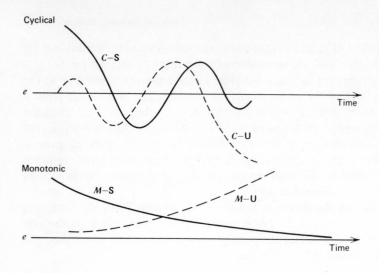

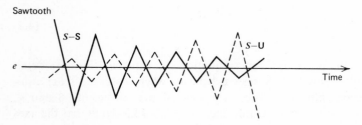

Possible Modes of Dynamic Behavior

	Stable (Convergent)	Unstable (Divergent)
Cyclical	c-s	c-u
Monotonic	m-s	m-u
Sawtooth	s-s	s-u

Fig. 15.2 *Types of movement generated by second order linear difference equations.*

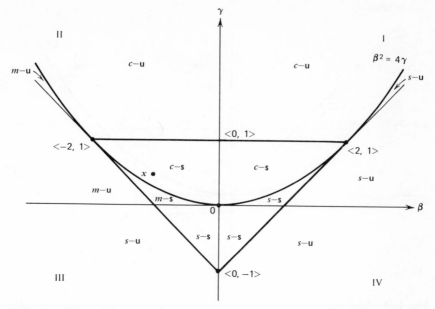

Fig. 15.3 *The stability triangle.*

Since point "x" is inside the triangle and within the cup, cyclical convergence to equilibrium is generated for the particular values of the marginal propensity to consume and accelerator coefficient used for the numerical example of Figure 15.1.

The sawtooth-type movements illustrated by curves "s-s" and "s-u" of Figure 15.2 are generated for certain combinations of β and γ. The combinations are indicated in Figure 15.3.

As our first application of these propositions, let us now inquire as to what values of the propensity to consume and accelerator coefficient will lead to explosive behavior instead of to convergence to equilibrium. Remember that the hypothetical cycle data plotted in Figure 15.1 were generated with parameter values of $c_1 = k = 0.5$; hence the difference equation has coefficients $\beta = -1$ and $\gamma = 0.5$, which is point "x" of Figure 15.4. More generally, we know that both the accelerator coefficient and the propensity to consume must be nonnegative; furthermore, the propensity to consume is less than unity. These economic restrictions suggest that we may confine our attention to the case

$$0 < c_1 < 1$$

and

$$k > 0$$

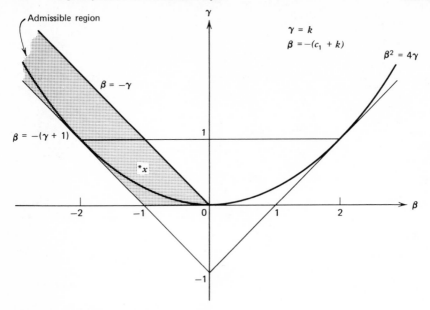

Fig. 15.4 *Multiplier-accelerator model.*

These restrictions, Equation 4.2 reveals, insure that the point $\langle \beta, \gamma \rangle$ must lie within the shaded stripe of Figure 15.4; that is,

$$0 \leq \gamma$$

and

$$-(\gamma + 1) < \beta < -\gamma$$

The lower portion of this shaded stripe is contained within the left-hand half of the iso-stability triangle. But if $k > 1$, we will be *above* the iso-stability triangle, and the system will diverge from equilibrium. Thus

A necessary and sufficient condition for the stability of this simple model is that the accelerator coefficient be less than unity.

In the next section we will consider how certain policy changes may influence the adjustment process.[11]

---

[11] A difficulty with the model discussed in the present chapter arises from the fact that the accelerator coefficient relates a stock (capital) to a flow; consequently, the length of the time period—presumably reflecting the reaction time of business firms—is critical. Thus, if the capital/output ratio is $\frac{1}{3}$ when measured by the ratio of capital to annual output, it will be $\frac{4}{3}$ when measured on a quarterly basis. And, in applying the stability theorem mentioned in the text, it is necessary to determine whether we should use quarterly or annual data. In generalizing this model in the next chapter we will circumvent this problem by using a distributed lag version of the accelerator. See exercise 15.3.

15.5 AUTOMATIC STABILIZERS AND TAX ADJUSTMENTS

It is frequently argued that certain *automatic stabilizers* may contribute to stability even in the absence of deliberate discretionary intervention on the part of fiscal authorities and the Federal Reserve System. For example, the Council of Economic Advisors argued in their 1963 *Annual Report*:[12]

"Automatic fiscal stabilizers increase the stability of the economy. . . . Any weakening in private spending will reduce incomes, causing tax revenues to fall and transfer payments to rise. Thus disposable incomes will decline less than pre-tax incomes, and will be partially cushioned against the decline in private demand. . . . The greater the extent to which a fall in government revenues cushions the decline in private incomes, the less the flow of spending for output will be curtailed. Automatic stabilization operates in reverse when private demand increases. Additional income is generated, but part of it is siphoned out of the spending stream in higher tax payments and lower transfers. . . .

Thus the effect of a progressive tax policy and the transfer payments generated by unemployment compensation and welfare programs are said to contribute to economic stability.

The most enthusiastic advocates of automatic stabilizers argue that they constitute our first line of defense against the business cycle. They go into operation more promptly than *discretionary* stabilization measures; time is not lost in recognizing the onset of recession, in debating the most appropriate course of action, and in enacting legislation. Many distinguished advocates of automatic stabilizers, in an argument deserving full attention in the next chapter, assert that so-called discretionary efforts at "stabilizing" economic activity have in practice contributed to instability because of the difficulties inherent in attempting to forecast economic developments and in trying to prescribe the appropriate dosage of the right medicine.

Those who stress the limitations of automatic stabilizers often mention two basic points. First, the automatic stabilizers cannot eliminate entirely the business cycle. Like the shock absorbers on an automobile, they at least may dampen the impact, but they will not eliminate completely all response to disturbing forces. Second, members of the stagnation school in particular are inclined to stress that automatic stabilizers may contribute to the stabilization of the economy at the *wrong* level of output.

In advocating the personal income tax cut early in the 1960's the Council of Economic Advisors recognized a fundamental conflict.[13]

". . . in the present (1963) situation—with the American economy laboring for over five years well below its potential rate of output—automatic stabilization

[12] p. 67.
[13] Op cit., p. 68.

becomes an ambiguous blessing. The protection it gives against cumulative down-ward movements of output and employment is all the more welcome. But its sym-metrical 'protection' against upward movement becomes an obstacle on the path to full employment, throttling expansion well before full employment is reached."

The Council went on to argue:[14]

". . . high employment can be restored—as is being proposed under the 1963 tax program—by a reduction in taxes. When this is done the need is not primarily to lessen the responsiveness of tax receipts to changes in GNP. Rather, the whole schedule of taxes should be lowered—so that, at any given GNP, taxes siphon off less private purchasing power—while leaving the response of tax receipts to *changes* in GNP about as great as before. To be sure, it is almost impossible to lower taxes without lessening to some degree their sensitivity to changes in GNP. But the pur-pose of such a change should be to lower the level of taxes—and hence their per-sistent drag on purchasing power—rather than to reduce their automatic counter-cyclical response."

Thus the Council hoped that the primary effect of the tax cut would be in the form of a lump-sum increase in the intercept of the function relating consumption to total output, although some change in the marginal pro-pensity to consume was unavoidable. They wanted c_0 to be larger, but they felt it desirable for c_1 to be unchanged so that there would be no weaken-ing of the automatic fiscal stabilizer.

From our discussion of equilibrium income in Section 15.3 it is clear that increases in either c_0 or c_1 will stimulate the level of economic activity. Equation 3.2 revealed that the stimulative effect of an increase in c_0 is magnified by the full amount of the multiplier. But any policy change that makes c_1, the marginal propensity to consume out of GNP closer to unity will also stimulate the economy, because it enlarges the multiplier. However, these are long-run equilibrium effects, and the policymaker, because of the impatient nature of the political process, must worry about the short-run impact of policy change. Indeed, if the economy were unstable, the long-run equilibrium effects of the policy change would be of no relevance whatsoever, since they would never be realized.

Simulation constitutes one technique that can be used to contrast the dynamic implications of policy alternatives. In Table 15.2 we have analyzed the effect of an increase in the marginal propensity to consume out of GNP from an initial value of $\frac{1}{2}$ to $\frac{7}{12}$, everything else constant. This change in the MPC is of precisely the amount required to raise equilibrium income from 100 to 120. It will be observed that Y again follows an oscillatory path and appears to be converging toward the equilibrium solution. From our earlier analysis it is clear that the effects of an increase in c_0 of 10, with no change

[14] Op cit., pp. 68–69.

Table 15.2 HYPOTHETICAL MULTIPLIER-ACCELERATOR CYCLE
DATA, II. (INCREASE IN MPC.) $c_0 = 0$, $c_1 = 7/12 = 0.58333$, $k = 0.5$

Time Period	Output	Consumption	Investment	Government Spending	Capital Stock
t	$Y_t = C_t + I_t + G_t$	$C_t = c_1 Y_{t-1}$	$I_t = K_t - K_{t-1}$	G_t	$K_t^d = k Y_{t-1}$
0	100	50	0	50	50
1	108.33	58.33	0	50	50
2	121.51	63.19	4.16	50	54.16
3	127.47	70.88	6.59	50	60.75
4	126.44	74.36	2.08	50	63.73
5	123.25	73.76	−0.51	50	63.22
6	120.30	71.90	−1.60	50	61.62
7	118.68	70.17	−1.47	50	60.15
8	118.41	69.22	−0.81	50	59.34
9	118.93	69.07	−0.14	50	59.20
10	119.64	69.38	0.28	50	59.46
.	.	.	.	.	.
.	.	.	.	.	.
.	.	.	.	.	.
∞	120	69.78	0	50	60

in c_1, would also raise equilibrium income by 20. And a comparison of
Tables 15.1 and 15.2 reveals that the adjustment paths are quite similar.[15]
Indeed, they are so similar as to suggest that it is immaterial whether the
tax policy works through a change in the intercept or the slope of the
function relating consumption to gross output.

Let us now utilize Baumol's iso-stability diagram to evaluate the
effect of the change in the marginal propensity to consume. In Figure 15.5
we indicate two points, "x" and "x^*." The first has coordinates $\langle -1, 0.5 \rangle$,
and applies to the initial example in which $\beta = \gamma = 0.5$. Point "x^*" has
coordinates $\langle -\frac{13}{12}, 0.5 \rangle$ and reflects the increase in the marginal propensity
to consume from $\frac{1}{2}$ to $\frac{7}{12}$. The effect of the increase in the marginal propensity to consume on the point $\langle \beta, \gamma \rangle$ is obviously small, even though it
was sufficient to cause a substantial increase in equilibrium output. It is
not surprising, then, to find that the dynamic paths traced out in the two
simulations (Tables 15.1 and 15.2) are so similar. Would a larger change
in the marginal propensity to consume have a more dramatic effect?
Inspection of Equation 4.2 reveals that an increase in the marginal propensity to consume causes the system to shift, as shown by the arrow on
Figure 15.5; that is, the point "x" necessarily moves due west, but it is
confined within the stripe, since c_1 must be less than unity. And it may move

[15] In our initial discussion of Table 15.1 we were concerned with a step of 10 in
government spending. But a moment's reflection will reveal that Table 15.1 also shows the
effects of a 10 unit increase in c_0. After all, it is the sum of c_0 plus G that enters into Equations 3.1 and 3.2.

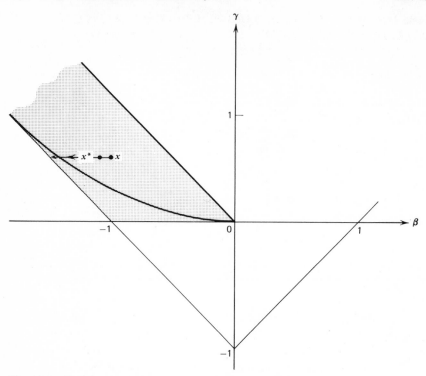

Fig. 15.5   *Stability-triangle analysis of a change in the* MPC.

the system so far as to take it outside the cup of cyclical movements. Thus a stable economy might be converted from an oscillatory to a monotonically convergent system as a result of increases in the marginal propensity to consume. However, changes in the marginal propensity to consume cannot convert it from a stable to an unstable system, at least if the implications of the Samuelson-Hansen model are to be believed, since we have already seen that the issue of stability hinges only on k.

Slightly stronger statements regarding the effects of changes in the consumption function can be made with the aid of certain additional propositions concerning the properties of second-order linear difference equations. It is shown in the appendix:

So long as the system is within the cup of cyclical movements, the speed of convergence toward equilibrium is determined only by γ.

Thus the movement to the west generated by an increase in the propensity to consume out of total output will not affect how rapidly the system moves toward equilibrium, unless it is sufficiently large to convert the system from an oscillatory mode of behavior to monotonic convergence. Once the system is outside the cup yielding oscillatory motion, however, further westward movement will cause the system to converge less rapidly when disturbed from equilibrium. It is also demonstrated that the periodicity of the cycle is reduced as a result of westward movement within the cup yielding cyclical movements; for example, the length of time elapsing between successive business cycle peaks will be reduced by an increase in the propensity to consume.

Obviously, the multiplier-accelerator mechanism achieves simplicity at too high a price; it neglects many important complications so that the resulting model of the business cycle will be analytically tractable. For what it is worth, our analysis has suggested that moderate movements in the marginal propensity to consume out of GNP that are of sufficient magnitude to increase decisively the equilibrium level of income may still be small enough to have only a moderate impact on the dynamic properties of the economy. The analysis has also suggested two alternative strategies that may be used in more sophisticated studies based on more complicated models. In analyzing the questions of comparative dynamics it is sometimes possible to derive analytical results even when the system is considerably more complicated than that discussed here. And when the models are too complicated to yield to this line of attack, it may be necessary to revert to simulation procedures (as in generating the data in Table 15.1) in tracing out the effects of alternative stabilization strategies.

REFERENCES

1. Nobel laureate Paul Samuelson published his analysis of multiplier accelerator interaction at the age of 24.

   Paul A. Samuelson, "Interactions Between the Multiplier Analysis and the Principle of Acceleration," *Review of Economics and Statistics*, May 1939.

2. Graphical procedures for analyzing second-order difference equations are presented in the following paper.

   William J. Baumol, "Pitfalls in Contracyclical Policies: Some Tools and Results," *Review of Economics and Statistics*, February 1961.

KEY CONCEPTS

multiplier-accelerator model

simulation

accelerator coefficient

cyclical, sawtooth, monotonic behavior

explosive versus convergence movements

cup of cyclical movements versus iso-stability triangle

automatic stabilizer

comparative dynamics

EXERCISES

15.1   Determine whether the Samuelson-Hansen multiplier accelerator model will be stable and whether it will generate cycles if the marginal propensity to consume (c_1) is 0.8 and the accelerator coefficient (k) is 0.2. (*Hint.* Use Figure 15.4.) What if $k = 1.2$ and $c_1 = 0.8$?

15.2   Suppose that the Samuelson-Hansen multiplier accelerator is modified by introducing an intercept into the desired capital stock equation; specifically, suppose that Equation 2.2 is modified to read $K_t{}^d = k_0 + k_1 Y_{t-1}$; show that the static and dynamic properties of the multiplier-accelerator model are not sensitive to this complication.

15.3   Suppose the original Samuelson-Hansen multiplier accelerator model is complicated by modifying the assumptions concerning investment behavior. Specifically, suppose that Equation 2.2 is retained, but that we allow for delayed adjustment investment behavior by specifying

$$I_t = \delta(K^e - K_{-1}) \qquad 0 < \delta \le 1$$

Note that in our earlier analysis we implicitly assumed $\delta = 1$.

a. How will Equations 2.4 and 3.1 be modified as a result of this change in specification?

b. Does the magnitude of δ influence the equilibrium solution of Equation 3.2?

c. How will the dynamic properties of the system be influenced by reductions in δ below unity?

d. How must the analysis of the effect of changes in the marginal propensity to consume be modified once the assumption that $\delta = 1$ is relaxed?

15.4 A simulated 50-period history for a multiplier-accelerator model as generated on the Wesleyan University DEC 10 computer is presented in Table 15.3. As in Exercise 3.14 of Chapter 3, a 10-unit step in government spending in period 3 disturbs an initial equilibrium position. Observe that a cyclical path of GNP is generated. After peaking with an output of 670.1 in period 9, the economy slumps to a trough of 624.1 in quarter 19, and the cyclical movement persists.

a. Compare the computer program with that used for the multiplier in Exercise 3.14 of Chapter 3. Note that while none of the behavioral equations have been changed, a few additional instructions have been inserted (these are underlined). What is the form of the accelerator used in the new model?

b. The output generated by the multiplier model of Exercise 3.14 of Chapter 3 revealed that the ultimate effect of the 10-unit increase in G was to raise GNP by 30.0; that is, the multiplier was 3.0. In precisely what limited sense is this multiplier concept pertinent in the analysis of the effects of an increase in G on this multiplier-accelerator model?

c. Investigate whether the multiplier-accelerator mechanism would be more or less stable if business firms attempted an immediate adjustment of the capital stock to the target level instead of only a 30% correction each period. (*Hint.* You can examine the second-order difference equation describing the behavior of GNP. Alternatively, if you have access to a computer, you could determine experimentally how the data generated by the computer is influenced by changes in the model's parameters.)

Table 15.3 Simulation of a multiplier-accelerator model

QTR	GNP	INVS	CON	TAX	REAN	YD	GOVT	CAP	CAPDESIRED
0						435.2		918.4	
1	612.3	0.0	397.3	146.5	30.6	435.2	215.0	918.4	918.4
2	612.3	0.0	397.3	146.5	30.6	435.2	215.0	918.4	918.4
3	622.3	0.0	397.3	148.5	31.1	442.7	225.0	918.4	918.4
4	633.5	4.5	404.0	150.7	31.7	451.1	225.0	922.9	933.4
5	644.6	8.2	411.4	152.9	32.2	459.4	225.0	931.1	950.2
6	654.6	10.7	418.8	154.9	32.7	466.9	225.0	941.8	966.9
7	662.5	12.0	425.5	156.5	33.1	472.9	225.0	953.8	981.9
8	667.8	12.0	430.8	157.6	33.4	476.8	225.0	965.8	993.8
9	670.1	10.8	434.3	158.0	33.5	478.6	225.0	976.6	1001.7
10	669.4	8.6	435.9	157.9	33.5	478.1	225.0	985.1	1005.1
11	666.1	5.7	435.4	157.2	33.3	475.6	225.0	990.8	1004.1
12	660.7	2.5	433.2	156.1	33.0	471.5	225.0	993.4	999.2
13	653.9	-0.7	429.6	154.8	32.7	466.4	225.0	992.7	991.1
14	646.5	-3.5	425.1	153.3	32.3	460.9	225.0	989.1	980.9
15	639.4	-5.8	420.1	151.9	32.0	455.5	225.0	983.3	969.8
16	633.1	-7.3	415.3	150.6	31.7	450.8	225.0	976.0	959.0
17	628.2	-7.9	411.1	149.6	31.4	447.2	225.0	968.1	949.6
18	625.2	-7.7	407.9	149.0	31.3	444.9	225.0	960.4	942.3
19	624.1	-6.8	405.9	148.8	31.2	444.1	225.0	953.6	937.7
20	624.9	-5.2	405.2	149.0	31.2	444.7	225.0	948.3	936.1
21	627.4	-3.3	405.7	149.5	31.4	446.6	225.0	945.1	937.4
22	631.2	-1.2	407.4	150.2	31.6	449.4	225.0	943.9	941.1
23	635.8	0.9	409.9	151.2	31.8	452.8	225.0	944.8	946.8
24	640.7	2.7	413.0	152.1	32.0	456.5	225.0	947.4	953.7
25	645.3	4.1	416.2	153.1	32.3	460.0	225.0	951.5	961.0
26	649.2	4.9	419.3	153.8	32.5	462.9	225.0	956.4	967.9
27	652.2	5.2	421.9	154.4	32.6	465.1	225.0	961.7	973.8
28	653.9	5.0	423.9	154.8	32.7	466.4	225.0	966.6	978.2
29	654.3	4.3	425.0	154.9	32.7	466.7	225.0	970.9	980.8
30	653.5	3.2	425.3	154.7	32.7	466.1	225.0	974.0	981.4
31	651.6	1.9	424.8	154.3	32.6	464.7	225.0	975.9	980.2
32	649.0	0.5	423.5	153.8	32.5	462.8	225.0	976.4	977.5
33	645.9	-0.9	421.8	153.2	32.3	460.5	225.0	975.5	973.5
34	642.8	-2.0	419.7	152.6	32.1	458.1	225.0	973.5	968.9
35	639.8	-2.8	417.6	152.0	32.0	455.9	225.0	970.7	964.1
36	637.4	-3.3	415.7	151.5	31.9	454.0	225.0	967.4	959.7
37	635.6	-3.4	414.0	151.1	31.8	452.7	225.0	964.0	956.0
38	634.7	-3.2	412.8	150.9	31.7	452.0	225.0	960.8	953.4
39	634.6	-2.6	412.2	150.9	31.7	451.9	225.0	958.2	952.0
40	635.3	-1.9	412.2	151.1	31.8	452.4	225.0	956.3	951.8
41	636.6	-1.0	412.6	151.3	31.8	453.4	225.0	955.3	952.9
42	638.4	-0.1	413.5	151.7	31.9	454.8	225.0	955.1	954.9
43	640.4	0.7	414.7	152.1	32.0	456.3	225.0	955.9	957.6
44	642.5	1.4	416.1	152.5	32.1	457.9	225.0	957.3	960.7
45	644.4	1.9	417.5	152.9	32.2	459.3	225.0	959.3	963.8
46	645.9	2.2	418.7	153.2	32.3	460.4	225.0	961.5	966.6
47	647.0	2.2	419.7	153.4	32.3	461.2	225.0	963.7	968.9
48	647.4	2.0	420.4	153.5	32.4	461.6	225.0	965.7	970.4
49	647.4	1.6	420.7	153.5	32.4	461.5	225.0	967.3	971.2
50	646.8	1.1	420.7	153.4	32.3	461.1	225.0	968.5	971.1

Table 15.3 *(Continued)*

```
COMMENT: THIS PROGRAM SIMULATES THE MULTIPLIER-ACCELERATOR
         REAL INVS
         YD=435.2
         GOV= 215
         INVS=0
         GNP=612.3
         CAP=918.4
         TAXR=0.20
         WRITE(5,35) YD,CAP
35       FORMAT(' SIMULATION OF A MULTIPLIER ACCELERATOR MODEL'//
        1' QTR    GNP      INVS    CON    TAX    REARN    YD     GOVT
        2  CAP    CAPDESIRED',//
        3'   0',35X,F7.1,7X,F7.1)
COMMENT: THE DO COMMAND REPEATS 50 TIMES ALL INSTRUCTIONS THROUGH 300
         DO 300 I=1,50
         CAPDESIRED= 1.5*GNP
         INVS= .3*(CAPDESIRED-CAP)
         CON =9.94 + 0.89*YD
         IF(I-3) 101,99,101
99       GOV=GOV+10
101      GNP=CON+INVS+GOV
         TAX=24+TAXR*GNP
         REARN = 0.05*GNP
         YD=GNP-TAX-REARN
         CAP=CAP+INVS
         WRITE(5,201) I,GNP,INVS,CON,TAX,REARN,YD,GOV,CAP,CAPDESIRED
201      FORMAT(1H ,I3,9F7.1)
300      CONTINUE
COMMENT: THIS ENDS THE ITH ITERATION
         END
```

†APPENDIX 15.A   SOLUTION OF LINEAR DIFFERENCE EQUATIONS

†15.A.1   INTRODUCTION

The simple models of the business cycle considered in this chapter constitute examples of linear difference equations. We saw that their dynamic properties are determined by the coefficients of the difference equation, and the coefficients in turn depend on the parameters of the economic model. In this appendix we will see why this is so. We will begin by considering the properties of a *first-order* difference equation model.[16]

$$Y_t + \beta Y_{t-1} = Z_t \tag{1.1}$$

This will suggest a strategy for examining the more complex *second-order* difference equations of the form

$$Y_t + \beta Y_{t-1} + \gamma Y_{t-2} = Z_t \tag{1.1'}$$

Second-order difference equations are harder to solve because they involve a two-period lag. Later, in Appendix 15.B, we explain Figure 15.3.

Inspection of Equation 1.1 reveals that if we know the value of Y_t at a particular point of time (say $t = 0$), we could find the value of Y_1 if we know Z_1; then, given Y_1, we could solve for Y_2 if we were told the magnitude of Z_2. By iterating in this way, the time path generated by the first-order difference equation can be calculated, provided one knows the magnitude of the coefficient β and two additional facts: one needs to know the time path of the sequence of values assumed by the exogenous (forcing) variable, the sequence $Z_1, Z_2. \ldots$ In addition, one needs to know as an *initial condition* the magnitude of Y_0.

Precisely this same iterative procedure can be used for second-order difference Equation 1.1', although it is obvious that we now need to know *two* initial conditions, Y_0 and Y_1. Indeed, this is exactly what we did when we analyzed the response of the Samuelson-Hansen multiplier-accelerator model to a *step increase* in government expenditure; that is, we observed how the system responded when disturbed from equilibrium by an increase in exogenous spending to the new value $G = 60$. In principal, one could determine by repeated application of this iterative procedure the effects of changes in the difference equation's coefficients on the time profile of the response. But this is a laborious way to proceed, and we will find it useful to learn how to *solve* second-order difference equations. By a *solution* we mean a function

$$Y_t = Y(t, Y_0, Y_1, Z_t) \qquad t = 2, 3, \ldots$$

that satisfies *both* the initial conditions and the difference equation itself. A function of this form will be useful, since it enables us to solve directly for Y_t without having to worry about Y_{t-1}.

---

[16] A model of this form is obtained by simplifying the Samuelson-Hansen multiplier accelerator model by making investment exogenous; per example, if $k = 0$ in equation 2.2, we find that Equation 4.1 simplifies to

$$Y_t = c_1 Y_{t-1} + G$$

The task of finding a solution is simplified by breaking it down into two easier problems. The first simplified problem we will consider is that of finding an equilibrium solution by *ignoring the initial conditions* (see Section 15.3). The second simplified problem we will examine yields a solution satisfying the initial conditions but *neglecting the forcing term Z*. Fortunately, it will turn out that the *sum* of the solutions to these two simplified problems constitutes the solution of the difference equation.

†15.A.2 SOLUTION OF FIRST-ORDER DIFFERENCE EQUATIONS

For the *first* step we seek the equilibrium (steady state) solution, as in Section 15.2. That is, we look for a specific number Y^e (which will depend on Z) that will satisfy the difference equation, although not necessarily the initial conditions.[17] For the first-order case we must have

$$Y^e + \beta Y^e = Z \tag{2.1}$$

or

$$Y^e = \frac{1}{1 + \beta} Z \tag{2.2}$$

For the *second* step we look at the deviations of the system from the equilibrium solution. Subtracting Equation 2.1 from Equation 1.1 reveals

$$(Y_t - Y^e) + \beta(Y_{t-1} - Y^e) = 0$$

or, if we work in terms of deviations from equilibrium by defining $y_t = Y_t - Y^e$,

$$y_t + \beta y_{t-1} = 0 \tag{2.3}$$

Note that the equation is *homogeneous*, since the forcing term Z has conveniently dropped out of the picture.

The solution of first-order homogeneous difference equation 2.3 is easily derived. The initial deviation is dictated by the initial condition

$$y_0 = Y_0 - Y^e \tag{2.4}$$

Substituting into Equation 2.3 with $t = 1$ yields as the first period's deviation

$$y_1 = -\beta y_0$$

Similarly, we apply Equation 2.3 with $t = 2$ to obtain

$$y_2 = -\beta y_1 = (-\beta)^2 y_0,$$

---

[17] This appendix only considers the case of fixed Z. The extension to the case in which Z grows exponentially is straightforward. For a detailed treatment, see R.G.D. Allen, *Mathematical Economics*, Macmillan, 1956.

where the second equality follows on substitution from the preceding equation. Successive substitution in this way reveals[18]

$$y_t = (-\beta)^t y_0 \qquad t = 1, 2, \ldots \tag{2.5}$$

Since this expression may be rewritten as

$$(Y_t - Y^e) = (-\beta)^t (Y_0 - Y^e) \qquad t = 1, 2, \ldots \tag{2.6}$$

we have on adding Y^e to both sides the solution

$$Y_t = (-\beta)^t (Y_0 - Y^e) + Y^e, \tag{2.7}$$

where Y^e is, of course, given by Equation 2.2. Note, by letting $t = 0$, that the initial condition is satisfied. Also, it is clear that the process of adding the equilibrium solution to the homogeneous solution does indeed solve Equation 1.1; after all, Equations 2.1 and 2.3 sum to the original first-order difference equation, Equation 1.1.

Equation 2.7 allows us to solve directly for Y_t without worrying about Y_{t-1}, Y_{t-2}, and so forth. And it yields very useful information about the behavioral properties of first-order difference equations. First, it is obvious from Equation 2.7 that the system will approach Y^e as t approaches infinity if and only if we have

$$-1 < \beta < 1,$$

for then $(-\beta)^t \to 0$. Otherwise, the initial deviation, $Y_0 - Y^e$, will not wash out of the solution. Second, we can see immediately from Equation 2.6 that if and only if $\beta > 0$ will successive powers of $(-\beta)^t$ be alternately positive and negative. Then the deviations will flutter in a sawtooth fashion around the equilibrium solution. Third, the behavior of the system when disturbed from equilibrium is proportional to the magnitude of the initial disturbance, $Y_0 - Y^e$; for example, if the initial disturbance from equilibrium is twice as large, *all* disturbances will double in magnitude. And a system that initially deviates by 10 units from an equilibrium of 100 will have successive deviations from that equilibrium of precisely the same magnitude as it would if it deviated by 10 units from an equilibrium of 200.

†15.A.3 SECOND-ORDER LINEAR DIFFERENCE EQUATIONS

Let us now attempt to follow the same strategy in solving second-order linear difference equation 1.1'.

$$Y_t + \beta Y_{t-1} + \gamma Y_{t-2} = Z \tag{1.1'}$$

The first step, finding the equilibrium solution, is easy. Y^e must satisfy Equation 1.1'; that is,

$$Y^e + \beta Y^e + \gamma Y^e = Z \tag{2.1'}$$

or

$$Y^e = \left(\frac{1}{1 + \beta + \gamma}\right) Z \tag{2.2'}$$

---

[18] The cautious reader may want to complete the second step of the proof by mathematical induction. That is, we have seen that Equation 2.5 holds for $t = 1$. Showing that if the equation holds for any positive integer t', it also holds for $t' + 1$ now verifies that it holds for all positive integers t.

The second step is to solve the following homogeneous difference equation, which is obtained by subtracting Equation 2.1′ from Equation 1.1′. If we again define $y_t = Y_t - Y^e$ the homogeneous equation is

$$y_t + \beta y_{t-1} + \gamma y_{t-2} = 0 \qquad (2.3')$$

Again, the forcing term Z has conveniently dropped out of the picture, but there are now *two* initial conditions that must be satisfied.

$$Y_0 - Y^e = y_0$$
$$Y_1 - Y^e = y_1 \qquad (2.4')$$

Let us first try an obvious strategy that does *not* quite work but will prove suggestive. Suppose that we find a number λ satisfying the characteristic equation

$$\lambda^2 + \beta \lambda + \gamma = 0 \qquad (3.1)$$

Multiplying through by $\lambda^{t-2} y_0$ yields

$$(\lambda^t y_0) + \beta(\lambda^{t-1} y_0) + \gamma(\lambda^{t-2} y_0)$$

This suggests that a possible solution of the homogeneous equation would be of the form

$$y_t = \lambda^t y_0 \qquad (2.5')$$

Substitution of this expression into the preceding equation reveals that with the aid of Equation 3.1 the homogeneous equation is satisfied. We can also have for $t = 0$ that $y_0 = \lambda^0 y_0 = y_0$, so as to satisfy the first initial condition. Unfortunately, Equation 2.5′ does *not* constitute a general solution because it will not necessarily satisfy the second initial condition. It is easily seen that this strategy would only work in those applications in which it fortuitously happened that $y_1 = \lambda y_0$. Clearly, a general solution of the second-order equation requires a slightly more sophisticated approach.

The important thing to note is that since Equation 3.1 is a quadratic equation, it has *two* roots. With the aid of the quadratic formula from high school algebra it can be shown that

$$\lambda_1 = -\frac{\beta}{2} + \sqrt{\left(\frac{\beta}{2}\right)^2 - \gamma}$$

$$\lambda_2 = -\frac{\beta}{2} - \sqrt{\left(\frac{\beta}{2}\right)^2 - \gamma} \qquad (3.2)$$

Remember also that there are *three* possible cases. *First*, $(\beta/2)^2 - \gamma > 0$, implying that the two roots are distinct. Second, if $(\beta/2)^2 - \gamma = 0$, the two roots are identical. Third, we may have $(\beta/2)^2 - \gamma < 0$; in this case there exist no real numbers satisfying Equation 3.1, and the two imaginary roots are most conveniently written as

$$\lambda = -\frac{\beta}{2} \pm i \sqrt{\gamma - \left(\frac{\beta}{2}\right)^2} \qquad (3.3)$$

where i denotes $\sqrt{-1}$.

a. Distinct Real Roots

For the case of *distinct real roots* note that since

$$\lambda_1^2 + \beta\lambda_1 + \gamma = 0$$

multiplication of both sides by $c_1\lambda_1^{t-2}$ yields

$$[c_1\lambda_1^t] + \beta[c_1\lambda_1^{t-1}] + \gamma[c_1\lambda_1^{t-2}] = 0 \qquad t = 1, 2, 3, \ldots$$

regardless of the value of c_1.

Consequently, the sequence of numbers c_1, $c_1\lambda_1$, $c_1\lambda_1^2$, $c_1\lambda_1^2$, ... satisfies homogeneous equation 2.3′, although not necessarily the initial conditions. Similarly, for the other root, we have

$$[c_2\lambda_2^t] + \beta[c_2\lambda_2^{t-1}] + \gamma[c_2\lambda_2^{t-2}] = 0 \qquad t = 1, 2, 3, \ldots$$

as another solution of the homogeneous equation not necessarily satisfying the initial conditions. Finally, if we sum these last two equations we obtain

$$[c_1\lambda_1^t + c_2\lambda_2^t] + \beta[c_1\lambda_1^{t-1} + c_2\lambda_2^{t-1}] + \gamma[c_1\lambda_1^{t-2} + c_2\lambda_2^{t-2}] = 0$$

Here is a third solution of the homogeneous equation. That is, for any arbitrary c_1 and c_2, the expression

$$y_t = c_1\lambda_1^t + c_2\lambda_2^t \tag{3.4}$$

satisfies the homogeneous equation for all positive integers t. By judicious selection of c_1 and c_2 can we also satisfy *both* initial conditions as well? To satisfy the first initial condition, we observe from Equation 3.4 that when $t = 0$, we must have

$$c_1 + c_2 = y_0$$

Furthermore, when $t = 1$, we must have

$$c_1\lambda_1 + c_2\lambda_2 = y_1$$

in order to satisfy the second initial condition.

We solve these two simultaneous equations for c_1 and c_2.

$$c_1 = \frac{y_1 - \lambda_2 y_0}{\lambda_1 - \lambda_2}$$

$$c_2 = \frac{y_1 - \lambda_1 y_0}{\lambda_2 - \lambda_1} = y_0 - c_1 \tag{3.5}$$

With these particular values of c_1 and c_2, Equation 3.4 constitutes a solution of the homogeneous equation that satisfies both initial conditions. That is,

$$y_t = (Y_t - Y^e) = c_1\lambda_1^t + c_2\lambda_2^t \tag{3.6}$$

is the solution of the second-order homogeneous difference equation satisfying both initial conditions, where c_1 and c_2 are from Equation 3.5. Adding Y^e to both sides yields the solution of the second-order difference equation for this case of distinct real roots.

$$Y_t = c_1\lambda_1^t + c_2\lambda_2^t + Y^e \tag{3.7}$$

The types of dynamic behavior generated in the case of distinct real roots are easily found by inspection of Equation 3.7. First, the sequence of deviations from equilibrium generated by the system will necessarily converge to zero if and only if both λ_1 and λ_2 are less than unity in absolute value. If $\lambda_1 = 1$, for example, the system cannot converge to equilibrium unless it happens fortuitously that initial conditions are such that $c_1 = 0$ and, with $\lambda_1 > 1$, we would have an explosive growth (or collapse) in output. It is also obvious from Equation 3.7 that sawtooth oscillations will be generated if either λ_1 or λ_2 is negative. Certain of these possibilities were illustrated in Figure 15.2. That the specified regions in Figure 15.3) did generate the indicated type of behavior will be verified later by showing that they indicate combinations of β and γ yielding roots with the appropriate characteristics; but first we must consider the cases of identical and imaginary roots.

b. Identical Roots

Only one root of quadratic equation 3.1 exists when it happens that $\beta^2 - 4\gamma = 0$, because then the expression under the radicals of 3.2 vanish and $\lambda_1 = \lambda_2$. In precisely this situation, Equation 3.2 reveals

$$\beta = -2\lambda$$

and

$$\gamma = \left(\frac{\beta}{2}\right)^2 = \lambda^2 \tag{3.8}$$

Now a possible solution of the homogeneous equation is provided by Equation 2.5′ but, since there are no longer two distinct roots, we no longer have sufficient flexibility to satisfy any two arbitrary initial conditions. However, another possibility exists, thanks to Equation 3.8.

$$y_t = t\lambda^t \tag{3.9}$$

To verify that this will indeed satisfy the homogeneous equation, first substitute into Equation 2.3′, obtaining

$$t\lambda^t + \beta(t - 1)\lambda^{t-1} + \gamma(t - 2)\lambda^{t-2}$$

Using Equation 3.8 to eliminate β and γ, now confirms:

$$t\lambda^2 + (-2\lambda)(t - 1)\lambda^{t-1} + \lambda^2(t - 2)\lambda^{t-2} = 0$$

Thus Equation 3.9 does indeed provide a second solution to the homogeneous equation, and the linear combination with Equation 2.5′

$$y_t = c_1\lambda^t + c_2t\lambda^t \tag{3.10}$$

also satisfies the homogeneous equation. In order to satisfy the initial conditions we have to solve

$$y_0 = c_1$$

$$y_1 = (c_1 + c_2)\lambda$$

Hence

$$c_1 = y_0$$

$$c_2 = \frac{y_1 - \lambda y_0}{\lambda} \tag{3.11}$$

Again y_t approaches zero if and only if

$$-1 < \lambda < 1$$

c. Complex Roots

Examination of Equation 3.2 reveals that the expression under the radical sign will be negative whenever $\beta^2 < 4\gamma$. The problem is complex because, while the solution is still of form 3.4, the c_i and λ_i are complex numbers. While the analysis proves tedious, it is of considerable economic interest, because it is in precisely this situation that the solution to the difference equation generates cyclical oscillations. We will see that with complex roots, cycles of fixed periodicity will be generated, such as c–s or c–u of Figure 15.2. Whether the cycles are damped or explosive depends entirely on λ_1 and λ_2 which, in turn, are determined by β and γ; so does the periodicity of the cycle (time elapsing between successive peaks). The initial conditions (y_0 and y_1), however, determine both the magnitude of the oscillations and the phase (precise dating of peaks and troughs) of the cycle.

We may write the two roots as

$$\lambda_1 = a + bi$$

$$\lambda_2 = a - bi \tag{3.12}$$

where

$$a = -\frac{\beta}{2}$$

$$b = \sqrt{\gamma - \beta^2/4}$$

$$i = \sqrt{-1}$$

The situation is clarified by inspection of the Argrand diagram (Figure 15.A.1), where the roots λ_1 and λ_2 appear on a graph in polar coordinates, the real part of each root being plotted on the abscissa and the imaginary part as the ordinate. If we recall from elementary trigonometry that

$$\cos \theta = \frac{a}{\gamma} = \frac{-\beta}{2\gamma}$$

$$\sin \theta = \frac{b}{\gamma}$$

$$\tan \theta = \frac{b}{a} = \frac{-\sqrt{4\gamma - \beta^2}}{\beta}$$

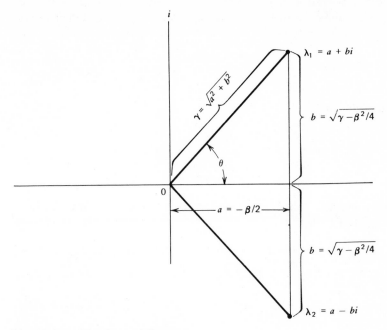

Fig. 15.A.1   *The Argrand diagram.*

we have on substitution into Equation 3.12

$$\lambda_1 = \gamma(\cos \theta + i \sin \theta)$$
$$\lambda_2 = \gamma(\cos \theta - i \sin \theta)$$

(3.13)

By *DeMoivre's theorem,*[19]

$$\lambda_1{}^t = (a + bi)^t = \gamma^t(\cos \theta t + i \sin \theta t)$$
$$\lambda_2{}^t = (a - bi)^t = \gamma^t(\cos \theta t - i \sin \theta t)$$

Substituting into Equation 3.4 yields as the solution of the homogeneous equation

$$
\begin{aligned}
y_t &= c_1\lambda_1{}^t + c_2\lambda_2{}^t \\
&= c_1\gamma^t(\cos \theta t + i \sin \theta t) + c_2\gamma^t(\cos \theta t - i \sin \theta t) \\
&= \gamma^t[(c_1 + c_2) \cos \theta t + i(c_1 - c_2) \sin \theta t]
\end{aligned}
$$

(3.14)

Of course, the actual y_t generated by Equation 3.14 must be real instead of complex numbers; after all, our model makes no sense if it ever generates a level of GNP with an imaginary component. In practice, the initial conditions assure this. For

---

[19] Abraham DeMoivre (1667–1754) was a friend of Newton and a Fellow of the Royal Society. His theorem states

$$(\cos \theta + i \sin \theta)^t = \cos \theta t + i \sin \theta t$$

example, real y_t will be generated by Equation 3.14 if it happens that initial conditions are such that $c_1 = c_2$, but this is by no means necessary. Suppose we define

$$A_1 = c_1 + c_2$$

and

$$A_2 = i(c_1 - c_2)$$

Then we may note that

$$c_1 = \frac{A_1 - A_2 i}{2}$$

$$c_2 = \frac{A_1 + A_2 i}{2}$$

are complex conjugates. Substituting into Equation 3.14 now yields as the solution to the homogeneous equation

$$y_t = \gamma^t (A_1 \cos \theta t + A_2 \sin \theta t) \tag{3.15}$$

A slightly more convenient solution is obtained by transforming directly into polar coordinates; setting

$$\tan \epsilon = \frac{A_2}{A_1}$$

and

$$A = A_1{}^2 + A_2{}^2$$

yields

$$y_t = A\gamma^t \cos (\theta t - \epsilon) \tag{3.16}$$

The initial conditions determine A and ϵ; that is, we solve

$$y_0 = A \cos (-\epsilon)$$

$$y_1 = A\gamma \cos (\theta - \epsilon)$$

for ϵ and A simultaneously.

From Equation 3.16 it is obvious that stability requires $|\gamma| < 1$, because then limit $y_t = 0$.[20] Furthermore, we note that the magnitude of the deviations are strictly
$t \to \infty$
proportional to A, which is determined by initial conditions. To see how the dating of successive peaks of the business cycle is determined, we recall that cos (0) = 1, and so the first cycle peak occurs when $\theta t - \epsilon = 0$, or $t = \epsilon/\theta$; thus initial conditions, by determining ϵ, establish the date of the first cycle peak. Since cos $(2\pi) = 1$ also, the second cycle peak occurs when $\theta t - \epsilon = 2\pi$, or $t = (2\pi + \epsilon)/\theta$, which is exactly $2\pi/\theta$ units of time after the first peak. It is easily verified that subsequent peaks also occur at intervals of $2\pi/\theta$. Thus it is the angle θ, indicated in Figure 15.A.1, that determines how frequently cycle peaks occur, and θ in turn is determined by the parameters of the difference equation.

[20] Recall that $\gamma > 0$ for imaginary roots.

†APPENDIX 15.B   GRAPHICAL ANALYSIS OF SECOND-ORDER DIFFERENCE EQUATIONS

†15.B.1   CYCLES

As Appendix 15.A revealed, the dynamic properties of a homogeneous second-order linear difference equation of the form

$$Y_t + \beta Y_{t-1} + \gamma Y_{t-2} = Z \tag{1.1}$$

are intimately related to the roots λ_1 and λ_2 of the characteristic equation

$$\lambda^2 + \beta \lambda + \gamma = 0 \tag{1.2}$$

And the roots depend on β and γ; in other words, the point $\langle \beta, \gamma \rangle$ categorizes the dynamic properties of Equation 1.1.

a.   Oscillatory Behavior (Imaginary Roots)

From Equation 15.A.3.2 it is clear that imaginary roots yielding oscillatory behavior require that $\beta^2 < 4\gamma$. That is, the coefficients of the difference equation must lie within the *cup of cyclical movements* that was formed by the parabola

$$\beta^2 = 4\gamma \tag{1.3}$$

in Figure 15.3. Thus, the system will oscillate instead of move monotonically if the parameters β and γ of difference equation 1.1 are inside the parabola, which is symmetric about the γ-axis.

b.   Sawtooth Cycles (Negative Real Roots)

Suppose the point $\langle \beta, \gamma \rangle$ is outside the cup; sawtooth fluctuations are still possible, inspection of Equation 15.A.3.6 reveals, if at least one of the roots is negative.

From Equation 15.A.3.2 we see that

$$\lambda_1 + \lambda_2 = -\beta \tag{1.4}$$

This means that if the difference equation parameter β is positive, the largest root of Equation 1.2 must be negative. Thus a system with real roots will be dominated by sawtooth cycles if the point $\langle \beta, \gamma \rangle$ is in quadrant I or IV of Figure 15.B.1.

We also find from Equation 15.A.3.2 that the product of the two roots is

$$\lambda_1 \lambda_2 = \left[\frac{-\beta}{2} + \sqrt{\left(\frac{\beta}{2}\right)^2 - \gamma} \right] \left[\frac{-\beta}{2} - \sqrt{\left(\frac{\beta}{2}\right)^2 - \gamma} \right] \tag{1.5}$$

$$= \gamma$$

Consequently, precisely one of the roots will be negative if γ is negative. Thus, in either quadrants III or IV of the figure, we have one negative root.

By considering the implications of Equations 1.4 and 1.5 concurrently, the following statements concerning the case of real roots are easily verified (Table 15.B.1).

Table 15.B.1 SIGN OF ROOTS OF CHARACTERISTIC EQUATION (CASE OF REAL ROOTS)

Quadrant	$\beta = -(\lambda_1 + \lambda_2)$	$\lambda_1\lambda_2 = \gamma$	Sign
I	Positive	Positive	Both real roots negative (sawtooth fluctuations inevitable)
II	Negative	Positive	Real roots positive (no sawtooth fluctuations)
III	Negative	Negative	Only dominant root positive (monotonic movements dominate but sawtooth fluctuations possible)
IV	Positive	Negative	Only dominant root negative (sawtooth fluctuations dominate but monotonic behavior possible)

In recording this information in Figure 15.3, only those areas in which both roots were necessarily positive were marked with an $m-$.

†15.B.2 ISO-STABILITY TRIANGLES

In order to see how Baumol's isostability triangles are constructed, let us plot in Figure 15.B.1 all points $\langle \beta, \gamma \rangle$ yielding a root with absolute value r. If the roots are real, we must have either $\lambda = r$ or $\lambda = -r$, and substituting into Equation 1.2 yields two equations linear in β and γ.

$$\gamma + \beta r + r^2 = 0 \tag{2.1}$$

and

$$\gamma - \beta r + r^2 = 0 \tag{2.2}$$

The two *iso-root lines* specified by these equations for given r are plotted on the figure, and labeled $\lambda = r$ and $-\lambda = r$. The iso-root lines obviously intersect at the point $\langle 0, -r^2 \rangle$ in Figure 15.B.1; the reader can verify that each iso-root line just "kisses" the parabola.

These two iso-root lines reveal the *real* roots of modulus r; what about the imaginary roots? From Equation 2.5 we know that an imaginary root of Equation 1.2 has absolute value $r = \gamma^2$. Hence the roots are imaginary with absolute value r if they are inside the parabola and have $\gamma^2 = r$; that is, they must lie on the horizontal line passing through point $\langle 0, r^2 \rangle$ in Figure 15.B.1.

The three lines that we have plotted in Figure 15.B.1 form a triangle. We will use an *indirect proof* to show that any point $\langle \beta, \gamma \rangle$ inside this iso-r triangle must have absolute value less than r. We have already seen that no point with absolute value equal to r can lie inside the triangle; such a root must be on one of the three lines in Figure 15.B.1. It remains to be established that if the point $\langle '\beta, \gamma' \rangle$ yields a root with modulus $r' > r$ it must lie *outside* the iso-r triangle. To verify this fact, suppose that $\langle \beta', \gamma' \rangle$ is some point constituting a root with modulus $r' > r$. Now, if this is an imaginary root, it must have a value $\gamma' = r'^2$, which is obviously above instead of inside the triangle. On the other hand, if $\langle \beta', \gamma' \rangle$ yields real roots, it

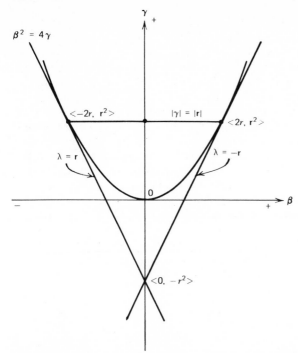

Fig. 15.B.1 *Iso-root lines. Consider any positive number* r.
All points yielding r *as a root are on the line labeled* $\lambda = r$; *all points yielding* $-r$ *as a root are on the line* $\lambda = -r$; *all imaginary roots of absolute value* r *are on the line segment connecting points* $\langle -2r, r^2 \rangle$ *and* $\langle 2r, r^2 \rangle$.

must be on one or the other of two iso-root lines passing through point $\langle 0, -r'^2 \rangle$ and just kissing the parabola; but it is clear that all points on these lines are outside the iso-r triangle. Since no point inside the iso-r triangle can have a modulus greater than or equal to r, all such points must have modulus less than r, as was to be shown.

Of course, the most interesting triangle involves $r = 1$, since this "iso-stability triangle" serves to demarcate the points inside the triangle leading to stability from the explosive roots, which are outside the triangle. A moment's reflection reveals that in order to be inside this iso-stability triangle the parameters β and γ must satisfy the following three inequalities.[21]

$$1 + \beta + \gamma > 0$$
$$1 - \beta + \gamma > 0 \qquad (2.3)$$
$$1 - \gamma < 0$$

[21] For a discussion of these "Routhian conditions" and their generalization to the roots of nth order systems, see Paul A. Samuelson, *Foundations of Economic Analysis*, Cambridge: Harvard University Press, 1947, pp. 436–437. Also E. I. Jury, *Theory and Application of the z-Transform Method*, John Wiley, 1964, pp. 93–94.

†15.B.3 ISO-FREQUENCY CURVES

Iso-frequency curves revealing the particular combinations of β and γ within the cup of imaginary roots that will yield cycles of any specified duration are easily obtained. That the period of the cycle (the length of time between successive peaks) depends on θ is obvious from Equation 15.A.3.16. Indeed, the periodicity of the cycle will be $2\pi/\theta$ if we measure the angle θ in radians. For example, if $\beta = 0$, the cycles must be precisely four periods in length; this follows at once, because $\beta = 0$ implies $\cos\theta = 0$, which in turn implies $\theta = \pi/2$. Note, too, that if $\beta = 2\sqrt{\gamma} > 0$ (anywhere on the *right* half of the parabola of Figure 15.B.1), we have $\cos\theta = -1$; hence $\theta = \pi$, and the cycles are of period 2. On the other hand, if $\beta = -2\sqrt{\gamma} < 0$ anywhere on the *left* half of the parabola in Figure 15.B.1, then $\cos\theta = 1$, $\theta = 0$, and the cycles are of infinite duration. Indeed, for any given value of γ, the larger β, the shorter the periodicity of the cycles generated by the difference equation—provided, of course, that we remain within the cup. Now, in order to find the loci of all points yielding the same cycle period, note that $[\cos\theta]^2 = -\beta^2/2\gamma$; the set of all points yielding cycles of identical duration and hence satisfy this expression for given θ must lie on a parabola passing through the origin and nested inside the parabola already plotted in Figure 15.B.1.

a portfolio of cycle models

*16.1 CATALOG

Two elaborations on the simple multiplier-accelerator model are presented in this chapter. The first model introduces monetary complications. While the multiplier-accelerator mechanism sufficed to demonstrate that the cycle *may* be the product of "real factors" instead of a monetary phenomenon, the introduction of financial variables will yield a framework capable of explaining the cyclical movements typically displayed by money and interest rates over the course of the business cycle. And the model will reveal how difficult it is to design a policy rule-of-thumb that will effectively guide the central bank in stabilizing the cycle. The second model is quite different. In concentrating on the way in which inventory adjustments lead to the generation of cyclical reversals in economic activity, it suppresses monetary complications entirely. Thus this model emphasizes once more that cycles can occur even in the absence of money.

The task of designing optimal linear decision rules for achieving economic stability is discussed in an appendix to this chapter. The optimal strategy minimizes the losses the policymaker incurs from manipulating *control instruments*, such as **G** and **M**, as well as losses from departures of such variables as real output and the rate of inflation from their target levels. It is shown that the appropriate mix of control instruments depends on the relative costs of manipulating the control instruments and their potency. While much of the appendix is complicated, the policy implications of the analysis are summarized in a nontechnical fashion in Section 16.A.4.

16.2 MONEY AND THE BUSINESS CYCLE

A *money* multiplier-accelerator model generated the computer simulation reported on Figure 16.1 and Table 16.1. As with the simplest multiplier-accelerator, a marked cycle in output results when the initial equilibrium is disturbed by a step increase in government spending. And both

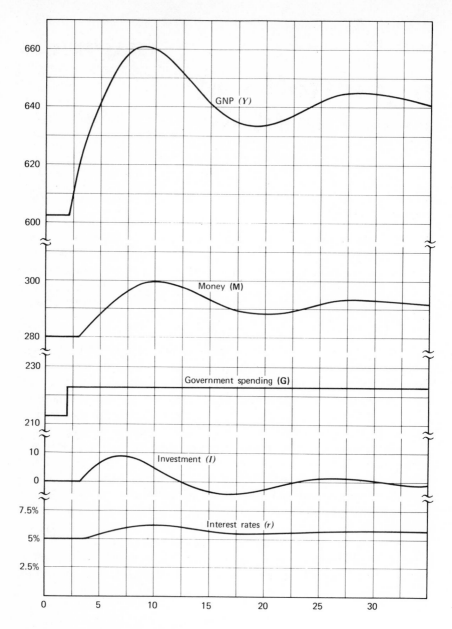

Fig. 16.1 *Simulation of a monetary cycle.*

Table 16.1 Simulation of a monetary cycle

Qtr.	GNP (Y_t)	I_t	C_t	G_t	Capital (K_t)	Desired Capital (K_t^d)	r	M
0					918.4	918.4		
1	612.3	0.0	397.3	215.0	918.4	918.4	5.0%	281.0
2	612.3	0.0	397.3	215.0	918.4	918.4	5.0	281.0
3	622.3	0.0	397.3	225.0	918.4	918.4	5.0	281.0
4	632.7	3.8	404.0	225.0	922.2	930.9	5.2	284.8
5	642.4	6.5	410.9	225.0	928.7	944.0	5.5	288.4
6	650.6	8.2	417.4	225.0	936.9	956.1	5.8	292.2
7	656.7	8.8	422.9	225.0	945.8	966.4	6.0	295.2
8	660.4	8.5	426.9	225.0	954.2	974.0	6.1	297.4
9	661.7	7.3	429.4	225.0	961.5	978.6	6.2	299.0
10	660.9	5.6	430.3	225.0	967.1	980.2	6.2	299.3
11	658.3	3.6	429.7	225.0	970.7	979.2	6.2	298.9
12	654.6	1.6	428.0	225.0	972.3	976.0	6.2	298.2
13	650.2	-0.3	425.5	225.0	972.0	971.3	6.1	296.7
14	645.7	-1.9	422.6	225.0	970.1	965.8	5.9	295.3
15	641.6	-3.0	419.6	225.0	967.2	960.2	5.8	293.3
16	638.3	-3.6	416.9	225.0	963.6	955.1	5.7	291.8
17	635.8	-3.8	414.6	225.0	959.8	950.9	5.6	290.8
18	634.4	-3.6	413.0	225.0	956.2	947.8	5.6	289.6
19	634.0	-3.0	412.1	225.0	953.2	946.1	5.6	289.2
20	634.5	-2.3	411.8	225.0	950.9	945.6	5.5	289.3
21	635.7	-1.4	412.1	225.0	949.5	946.2	5.6	289.2
22	637.4	-0.5	412.9	225.0	949.0	947.7	5.6	289.6
23	639.3	0.3	414.0	225.0	949.2	949.8	5.6	290.4
24	641.2	0.9	415.3	225.0	950.1	952.2	5.7	291.1
25	642.9	1.3	416.6	225.0	951.5	954.6	5.7	291.9
26	644.3	1.6	417.7	225.0	953.0	956.7	5.8	292.2
27	645.3	1.6	418.7	225.0	954.7	958.5	5.8	293.0
28	645.8	1.5	419.3	225.0	956.2	959.7	5.8	293.4
29	645.9	1.3	419.7	225.0	957.4	960.3	5.8	293.3
30	645.6	0.9	419.7	225.0	958.3	960.5	5.8	293.3
31	645.1	0.5	419.5	225.0	958.9	960.1	5.8	293.3
32	644.3	0.2	419.2	225.0	959.0	959.4	5.8	293.4
33	643.5	-0.2	418.7	225.0	958.9	958.5	5.8	293.0
34	642.7	-0.4	418.1	225.0	958.5	957.5	5.8	292.6
35	642.0	-0.6	417.6	225.0	957.9	956.5	5.8	292.2
36	641.4	-0.7	417.1	225.0	957.2	955.6	5.7	291.8
37	641.0	-0.7	416.7	225.0	956.5	954.8	5.7	291.9
38	640.8	-0.6	416.5	225.0	955.8	954.4	5.7	291.9
39	640.8	-0.5	416.3	225.0	955.3	954.1	5.7	291.4
40	641.0	-0.4	416.3	225.0	955.0	954.1	5.7	291.4

interest rates and the money supply as well as investment spending move cyclically. In reviewing the record the central bank might claim that it had effectively "leaned against the wind" by raising interest rates in boom and reducing them in the trough. But monetarists are likely to object that the drastic expansion of the money supply fed the expansionary forces, contributing to instability.

a. Alternative Simulations, an Exercise in Comparative Dynamics

On the computer, in contrast to the "real world," it is possible to compare alternative types of policy by repeating history. Three alternative stabilization strategies are simulated in Table 16.2. *Simulation A* supports the central bank's argument, because it reveals that the hypothetical economy would have experienced a much more pronounced cycle if interest rates had been kept constant. On the other hand, *Simulation B* shows that a more drastic application of the monetary breaks, an actual decline in the money supply, might have led to monotonic convergence instead of to a cycle, in accordance with the argument of the money critics. Finally, the sawtooth flutter displayed in the last simulation shows that it is possible for the central bank to overrespond to recently experienced fluctuations in output.

While these various simulations show that quite provocative results can be obtained in comparing alternative stabilization strategies on the computer, caution is required. Because the types of fluctuations obtained through computer simulation depend critically on the behavioral assumptions underlying the model, the equations used in generating the simulation data must be carefully looked at. We will find that our model is so simple as to be far from realistic. And we will also discover that the type of monetary policy that best stabilizes the system depends critically on the parameters of the equations. This means that the simulations reported in Table 16.2 should be regarded as only suggestive of the types of policy that might best contribute to stability in practice. Detailed econometric investigation involving much more complicated models is required in order to determine what type of policy would, in practice, serve to stabilize the American economy. The next chapter will review this line of research.

b. Model Details

The money simulations were generated by slightly modifying the basic multiplier-accelerator model. The primary change involved the introduction of the interest rate as an additional determinant of the desired capital stock. In terms of the analysis of the determinants of investment spending in Chapter 6, Section 2, it is assumed that

$$K_t{}^d = k_0 + k_1 Y_{t-1} - k_2 r_t \tag{2.1}$$

If net investment at least partially adjusts the inherited capital stock toward the desired level,

$$I_t = \delta(K_t{}^d - K_{t-1}), \qquad 0 < \delta \le 1 \tag{2.2}$$

Table 16.2 Alternative stabilization policies

Qtr.	Simulation A Y_t	I_t	r_t	M	Simulation B Y_t	I_t	r_t	M	Simulation C Y_t	I_t	r_t	M	Qtr.
1	612.3	0.0	5.0%	281.0	612.3	0.0	5.0%	281.0	612.3	0.0	5.0	281.0	1
2	612.3	0.0	5.0	281.0	612.3	0.0	5.0	281.0	612.3	0.0	5.0	281.1	2
3	622.3	0.5	5.0	281.0	622.3	0.0	5.0	281.0	622.3	-0.2	5.0	281.0	3
4	633.5	4.5	5.0	286.0	627.5	-1.5	7.0	276.0	614.7	-14.2	11.2	254.8	4
5	644.6	8.2	5.0	291.5	630.6	-1.8	8.7	273.3	624.7	-13.7	6.5	274.4	5
6	654.6	10.7	5.0	297.0	632.8	-1.7	9.1	271.7	616.9	-13.6	12.9	248.2	6
7	662.5	12.0	5.0	302.0	634.4	-1.5	9.4	270.5	626.9	-1.6	17.9	268.0	7
8	667.8	10.8	5.0	306.0	635.7	-1.3	9.7	269.6	618.9	-13.2	14.1	242.3	8
9	670.1	8.6	5.0	308.5	636.8	-1.1	9.9	269.1	628.9	-1.2	19.4	263.4	9
10	669.4	5.7	5.0	310.5	637.7	-1.0	10.1	268.5	620.6	-12.7	15.4	237.1	10
11	660.1	2.5	5.0	309.5	638.4	-0.8	10.2	268.1	630.7	-2.9	10.2	258.9	11
12	660.7	-0.7	5.0	308.0	639.1	-0.7	10.4	267.7	622.2	-12.2	11.2	232.4	12
13	653.9	-3.5	5.0	305.0	639.6	-0.6	10.5	267.2	632.4	-3.5	17.1	255.1	13
14	646.5	-5.8	5.0	301.5	640.0	-0.5	10.6	267.3	623.6	-12.0	18.5	228.2	14
15	639.4	-7.9	5.0	298.0	640.4	-0.4	10.7	266.9	633.9	-11.4	12.9	251.0	15
16	633.1	-7.7	5.0	294.5	640.7	-0.3	10.7	266.6	624.0	-11.8	13.6	224.1	16
17	628.2	-6.8	5.0	291.0	641.0	-0.3	10.8	266.4	635.2	4.5	20.1	247.5	17
18	625.2	-5.3	5.0	289.0	641.2	-0.2	10.8	266.4	626.5	-11.5	20.8	220.8	18
19	624.9	-3.3	5.0	287.5	641.4	-0.2	10.8	266.3	636.5	5.3	14.8	245.1	19
20	624.1	-1.2	5.0	287.0	641.5	-0.1	10.9	266.1	627.6	-11.3	21.3	217.4	20
21	627.4	0.9	5.0	285.5	641.7	-0.1	10.9	266.09	637.6	-11.4	15.3	214.3	21
22	631.2	2.7	5.0	288.5	641.8	-0.1	10.9	265.9	628.6	5.8	22.8	235.0	22
23	635.6	4.1	5.0	292.0	641.9	-0.1	10.9	265.9	639.6	-11.2	22.6	237.3	23
24	640.7	4.9	5.0	295.0	642.0	-0.1	10.9	266.3	629.4	-6.2	16.2	235.6	24
25	645.3	5.2	5.0	297.5	642.1	-0.1	11.0	266.2	639.4	-10.9	23.1	207.1	25
26	649.2	5.0	5.0	299.5	642.1	0.0	11.0	266.2	629.4	-10.8	16.6	234.0	26
27	652.2	4.3	5.0	301.0	642.1	0.0	11.0	266.1	630.2	-6.9	22.6	205.2	27
28	653.9	3.2	5.0	302.0	642.2	0.0	11.0	266.1	641.9	-10.4	16.2	234.0	28
29	654.3	1.9	5.0	301.5	642.2	0.0	11.0	266.1	630.8	-7.3	23.1	205.2	29
30	653.5	0.5	5.0	300.5	642.2	0.0	11.0	266.1	631.3	-10.7	16.9	232.0	30
31	651.6	-0.9	5.0	299.5	642.2	0.0	11.0	266.100	642.6	-7.6	23.5	203.0	31
32	649.0	-2.0	5.0	299.0	642.3	0.0	11.0	266.0	631.8	-10.7	23.9	231.4	32
33	645.5	-2.8	5.0	297.5	642.3	0.0	11.0	266.0	643.2	-7.9	17.2	201.4	33
34	642.6		5.0	296.0	642.3	-0.0	11.0					229.7	34
35	639.8				642.3								35

441

where δ denotes the speed of adjustment.[1] Hence, the capital stock at the end of the period will be

$$K_t = \delta(k_0 + k_1 Y_{t-1} - k_2 r_t) + (1 - \delta)K_{t-1} \qquad (2.3)$$

Obviously, if this equation also held for the preceding period,

$$K_{t-1} = \delta(k_0 + k_1 Y_{t-2} - k_2 r_{t-1}) + (1 - \delta)K_{t-2}$$

Subtracting into Equation 2.3 now yields

$$I_t = K_t - K_{t-1} = \delta k_1(Y_{t-1} - Y_{t-2}) - \delta k_2(r - r_{t-1}) + (1 - \delta)I_{t-1} \quad (2.4)$$

The interested reader can verify that the investment data reported in Tables 16.1 and 16.2 were generated with $k_0 = 50$, $k_1 = 1.5$, $k_2 = 1000$, and $\delta = 0.3$. Consumption was generated with the familiar lagged relationship:

$$C_t = c_0 + c_1 Y_{t-1} \qquad (2.5)$$

with $c_0 = 9.94$ and $c_1 = 0.89$.

The interest rate movements recorded for the various simulations were all generated under the supposition that monetary policy is determined by a very simple rule. Specifically, it was supposed that the central bank instructs the Open Market Committee to buy and sell government bonds as required in order to make the rate of interest depart from a long-run target level r^* in proportion to the gap between actual output Y_{t-1} and its target level Y^*. Specifically,

$$r_t - r^* = \pi(Y_{t-1} - Y^*) \qquad (2.6)$$

If this mode of behavior is consistently followed, Equation 2.6 also holds in period $t - 1$, and we obtain, by subtraction,

$$r_t - r_{t-1} = \pi(Y_{t-1} - Y_{t-2}) \qquad (2.7)$$

If the policy parameter π were zero the interest rate would remain constant and the behavior of the system would be adequately described by the multiplier-accelerator model. But with π positive, the rate of interest rises in the boom and falls in recession. The simulation on Table 16.1 was obtained with $\pi = 0.025$. The three alternative simulations were obtained by first setting $\pi = 0$, then $\pi = 0.2$, and then $\pi = 0.625$.

The movements of the money supply recorded on the tables were generated under the assumption that the supply of money always equals demand, where the demand for money is determined by

$$M_t{}^d = m_0 + m_1 Y_{t-1} - m_2 r_t \qquad (2.8)$$

---

[1] This "delayed adjustment" or "flexible" accelerator was developed in detail in Chapter 6, Section 2. In order to simplify the development of the multiplier-accelerator in Chapter 15, it was presumed that $\delta = 1$.

Thus, substituting r_t from Equation 2.6 into the demand for money equation revealed the way in which the central bank must adjust the money supply in order to obtain the desired movements in the rate of interest.[2]

$$\mathbf{M} = m_0 - m_2(r^* - \pi Y^*) + (m_1 - m_2\pi)Y_{t-1} \qquad (2.9)$$

In all simulations $m_0 = 0$, $m_1 = 0.5$, and $m_2 = 500$.

c. Analysis of the Dynamic Properties of the Model

Although the numerical simulations recorded in Table 16.2 are of obvious interest, it is important to find analytically what factors determine the nature of the cycle generated by the model. In this way the full range of results obtainable from the model can be determined and the precise conditions for stability specified. More important, the factors determining the optimal value of policy coefficient π can be determined.

Appropriate substitutions with Equations 2.4 through 2.7 eventually yield the fundamental difference equation

$$Y_t + \beta Y_{t-1} + \gamma Y_{t-2} = \delta c_0 + \mathbf{G}_t - (1 - \delta)\mathbf{G}_{t-1} \qquad (2.10)$$

where

$$\beta = \delta(1 - k_1 + k_2\pi) - 1 - c_1$$

$$\gamma = c_1 + \delta(k_1 - c_1 - k_2\pi) = \delta - 1 - \delta c_1 - \beta$$

Note that it is possible for the central bank, by changing π, to adjust the two coefficients of this second-order linear difference equation. The "control ray" on Figure 16.2 illustrates the way in which the difference equation's coefficients can be changed by manipulating π. While difference equation coefficients β and γ are both sensitive to the value of the policy parameter, they necessarily sum to a constant; specifically, $\beta + \gamma = \delta - 1 - \delta c_1$. This convenient property means that the point $\langle \beta, \gamma \rangle$ must necessarily fall somewhere on a control ray with slope minus one and intercept $\delta - 1 - \delta c_1$; the control ray plotted on the graph corresponds to $\delta = 1$ and $c_1 = 0.7$. Precisely where the point $\langle \beta, \gamma \rangle$ falls on the control ray depends on the policy coefficient π as well as the parameters of the behavioral equations. In particular, point $\mathbf{S}(\pi = 0)$ indicates the two coefficients of difference equation 2.10 when $\pi = 0$. $\mathbf{S}(\pi = 0)$ would coincide with point a where $\gamma = 0$ only if $(\delta - 1)c_1 = \delta k_1$; otherwise γ is positive when π is zero and $\mathbf{S}(\pi = 0)$ lies in the northwest quadrant of the graph.[3] Since γ is

---

[2] The effect of having the interest rate depend on current instead of a lagged output will be considered in a later section.

[3] Point $S(\pi = 0)$ is plotted on the graph for $\delta = 1$, $c_1 = 0.7$, and $k_1 = 0.5$; hence it has coordinates $\langle -1.2, 0.5 \rangle$. These parameter values were suggested by G. H. Fisher's study, "Comments on Stochastic Macro-Economic Models," *American Economic Review*, September 1952.

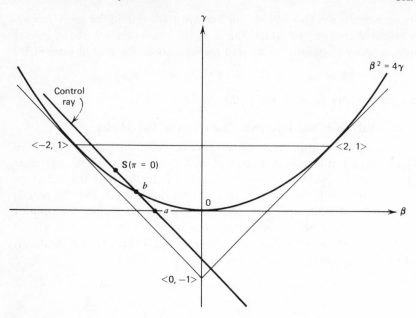

Fig. 16.2 *Stabilization strategy. The control ray indicates combinations of difference equation coefficients β and γ that can be attained by manipulating π. If $\pi > 0$ the point will lie southeast of* $S(\pi = 0)$. *The economy will oscillate if the point is inside the cup of cyclical movement above $\beta^2 = 4\gamma$); it will converge if the point is inside the stability triangle.*

a decreasing function of π, a positive π leads to a point on the control ray southeast of $S(\pi = 0)$; conversely, with a negative π the coefficients of the difference equation would be denoted by a point on the control ray northwest of $S(\pi = 0)$.

The circumstances under which the system will be stable, necessarily converging to equilibrium output Y^e, can also be visualized in Figure 16.2, since the isostability triangle and the cup yielding cyclical movements have been reproduced from Figure 15.3. It will be remembered that stability requires that point $\langle \beta, \gamma \rangle$ on the control ray be inside the isostability triangle. Substituting from Equation 2.10 establishes that the policy parameter must fall within the range

$$\frac{(1 - \delta)c_1 + \delta k_1 - 1}{\delta k_2} < \pi < \frac{1 + c_1 + \delta k_1 - 0.5\delta(1 + c_1)}{\delta k_2} \qquad (2.11)$$

if the system is to be stable. Only if $\delta(k_1 - c_1) > (1 - c_1)$ must π be positive in order to obtain convergence to equilibrium. It can be shown that the value of π leading to most rapid convergence to equilibrium corresponds to point b on the control ray, which is just on the boundary of the cup generating cyclical movements;[4] this yields, as the optimal policy coefficient,[5]

$$\pi^\circ = [c_1 + \delta(k_1 - 1) - 1 + 2\sqrt{\delta(1 - c_1)}]/k_2\delta \qquad (2.12)$$

Substituting π° into Equation 2.9 reveals how the money supply would have to respond to changes in income.

$$M_t^s - M_{t-1}^s = (m_1 - m_2\pi^\circ)(Y_{t-1} - Y_{t-2}) \qquad (2.13)$$

The proposition that a money supply moving countercyclically would best contribute to economic stability could be validated only by empirical evidence demonstrating that $m_1 - m_2\pi^\circ < 0$. In the absence of such evidence categorical statements cannot be made concerning the appropriate way in which the monetary authorities should respond to fluctuations in income.

d. A More Responsive Monetary Policy

Policy equation 2.7 specified that changes in the interest rate lag one period behind changes in the level of net national product. This is reasonable. Time is required to digest the information provided by the economic indicators. Once an appropriate course of action has been agreed on, additional time will elapse before the actions of the Federal Reserve System influence interest rates. An improvement in forecasting techniques may partially offset the lags inherent in the execution of monetary policy. A simple example will illustrate that our intuition is not correct if it suggests that a reduction in the monetary lag would necessarily result in a more stable economy.

With a more responsive monetary policy, fluctuations in the interest rate will be proportional to current instead of lagged changes in income; that is, Equation 2.7 becomes

$$r_t - r_{t-1} = \pi(Y_t - Y_{t-1}) \qquad (2.14)$$

With this alternative to Equation 2.7 the coefficients of the second-order difference equation are affected; in particular, if $\delta = 1$, we have $\beta = -(k_1 + c_1 + k_2\pi)/(1 + k_2\pi)$ and $\gamma = k_2/(1 + k_2\pi)$. As before, both of

---

[4] See the discussion of isostability triangles in Section 15.B.2. That π^0 determined by Equation 2.12 is indeed optimal can be verified by showing that the corresponding values of β and γ are on the cup formed by the parabola $\beta^2 - 4\gamma = 0$.

[5] This is the optimal value of the policy coefficient when the objective is to converge to equilibrium as rapidly as possible. But an alternative criterion, minimizing the variance of income, would involve a larger value of π, as is explained in Appendix 16.B.

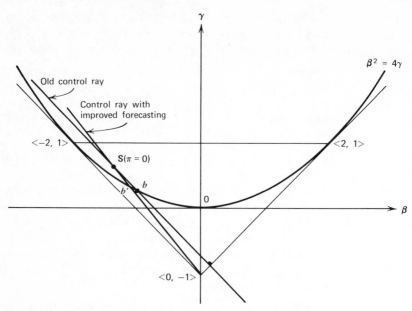

Fig. 16.3 *More responsive monetary policy. If an improvement in forecasting technique allows a prompter response of monetary policy, the control ray will rotate through point* $S(\pi = 0)$ *so as to go through* $\langle 0, -1 \rangle$. *The optimal point on the new control ray is* b′, *not* b.

the coefficients depend on the magnitude of the policy parameter π. But substitution reveals that the equation for the control ray is

$$\beta = \left(\frac{1 - c_1 - k_1}{k_1} \right) \gamma - 1 \qquad (2.15)$$

Thus the control ray for the more responsive monetary policy is a straight line, as before. In order to evaluate the effects of a responsive policy, note, in terms of Figure 16.3, that the new control ray approaches the point $\langle 0, -1 \rangle$ as π approaches infinity. A second point on the control ray is $S(\pi = 0)$, because with $\pi = 0$ the speed of response does not make any difference—either way the interest rate is constant.[6] From the point of view of maximizing the speed of convergence towards equilibrium, π should be set so as to place us at the intermediate point at which the new control

---

[6] Figure 16.3 was drawn for Fisher's values for the marginal propensity to consume ($c_1 = 0.7$) and the accelerator ($k_1 = 0.5$). The best point on the control ray characterizing the more responsive monetary policy yields a dominant characteristic root of 0.56, with the less responsive control ray; on the other hand, the dominant root was 0.45.

ray crosses the parabola. In the situation illustrated in the graph the employment of improved forecasting techniques in order to achieve a more rapid adjustment of interest rates to changes in economic conditions leads to less rapid convergence.[7] As explained in the appendix to this chapter, a more complicated mechanism for determining policy, instead of the simple response pattern of form 2.14, is required if the improved forecasting techniques are to enable the central bank to stabilize the economy more effectively.

16.3 THE INVENTORY CYCLE

In the 1930s members of both the psychological and the monetary schools of business cycle theory pinpointed inventory investment as a particularly critical factor in the generation of the business cycle. While R. G. Hawtrey[8] argued that the monetary authorities had their primary effect on the economy through their influence on inventory investment, the models of Lundberg[9] and Metzler[10] stressed the role of expectational errors in the generation of the inventory cycle.

Empirical confirmation of the critical nature of inventory investment was provided a decade later by the important contribution of Moses Abramovitz.[11] Now it is generally appreciated that inventory investment is subject to more violent fluctuations than other components of investment spending, as indicated in Figure 16.4. A closer inspection of the historical record will reveal that during recessions, when high inventory investment would have generated income and added to effective demand, stocks have moved in the wrong direction. In periods of boom, when excess demand prevails, inventory investment has been large in magnitude, contributing to inflationary pressure.

An estimate of the extent to which the recessions of recent decades have been the consequence of changes in the level of inventory investment

[7] Of course, if the accelerator coefficient were sufficiently small the more responsive policy might be preferable. In particular, if $k_2 = 0$, the more responsive control ray would go through the origin, while the less responsive control ray would be unaffected. But it can be shown that if the accelerator is so small as to make a more rapid response of monetary policy to changing income preferable to Equation 2.7, the policy parameter π° would be negative, and interest rates should fall as income rises, and conversely.

[8] *Trade and Credit*, London: Longman, Green and Co., 1928; *Capital and Equipment*, London: Longman, Green and Co., 1937.

[9] *Studies in the Theory of Economic Expansion*, London: P. S. King and Sons, 1937.

[10] "The Nature and Stability of Inventory Cycles," *Review of Economic Statistics*, pp. 113–129, August 1941.

[11] *Inventories and Business Cycles*, New York: National Bureau of Economic Research, 1950.

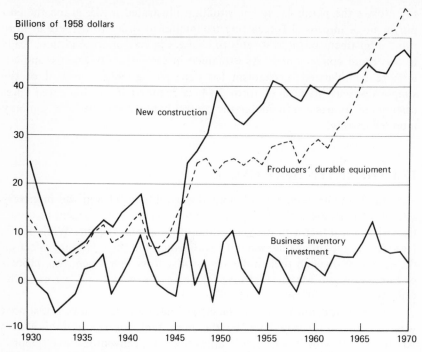

Fig. 16.4   *Components of gross private domestic investment.*

is provided by Figure 16.5, where fluctuations in actual gross national product are contrasted with a hypothetical GNP series corresponding to the path that effective demand would have followed if there had been no fluctuations in inventory stocks. The hypothetical series is obtained by subtracting from actual GNP both inventory investment and an estimate of the consumption it generates.[12] If there had been no inventory liquida-

---

[12] The curve suggesting the way in which effective demand would have behaved if there had been no inventory investment or disinvestment was derived by subtracting the effects of inventory investment on GNP, as estimated with the Klein-Goldberger econometric model of the United States, from actual GNP. A brief description of the procedure used is provided in Lovell, "The Contribution of Inventory Investment to Cyclical Reversals in Economic Activity," in *Inventory Fluctuations and Economic Stabilization, Hearings,* Joint Economic Committee, Congress of the United States, p. 261, July 1962. For more sophisticated simulations of the 1953–1954 and 1957–1958 recessions, see Klein and Popkin, "An Econometric Analysis of the Postwar Relationship Between Inventory Fluctuations and Changes in Aggregate Economic Activity," in *Inventory Fluctuations and Economic Stabilization,* Part III, Joint Economic Committee, Congress of the United States, pp. 71–89, 1961. Note that the simpler procedure of utilizing "final sales" (GNP less inventory investment) to measure the impact of fluctuations in inventory investment on GNP is only a rough approximation, because it neglects the impact of changes in income on consumption spending.

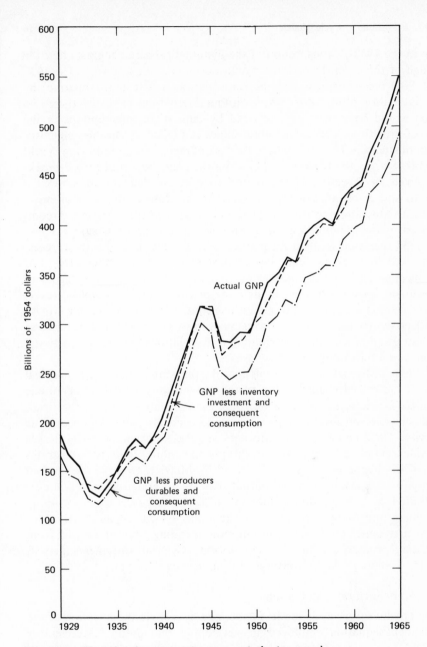

Fig. 16.5 *The role of inventory investment in business cycles.*

tion in the 1930s, an inspection of the hypothetical series suggests that the trough of the Great Depression would not have been so severe. The 1937 and 1949 recessions can both be explained, as a first approximation, by the liquidation of inventory since, without fluctuations in stocks, these two years would have been characterized by only slight interruptions in the rate of growth instead of definite declines in GNP. The sizable replenishment of stocks in 1946 did smooth the task of reconversion following World War II. During the Korean mobilization the contribution of record-breaking levels of inventory accumulation to effective demand constituted a serious source of inflationary pressure. At the close of the Korean emergency a reduction in inventory investment deepened the recession. A comparison of the hypothetical series with actual developments suggests that the 1958 recession resulted from inventory liquidation. In contrast, recessions remain in the second hypothetical series, which shows GNP less producer's durables and consequent consumption; this second category of investment spending has not made a major contribution to cyclical reversals in economic activity, although it has contributed to the secular growth in effective demand.[13] In sum, investment in inventories has been perverse in timing and magnitude, contributing to fluctuations in economic activity, booms, and unemployment.

This historical review reveals that fluctuations in stocks are a critical link in the causal chain leading to the generation of cycles in economic activity. But it says nothing concerning the complex of factors that lead, by their effect on inventory investment, to cyclical reversals in economic activity. The Lundberg[14] and Metzler[15] aggregate inventory cycle models provide a simplified explanation of this phenomenon. Figure 16.6 illustrates one of the hypothetical cycles described by Metzler. Observe the marked fluctuations in inventories and output that are generated when this model is excited by a single disturbance in autonomous government spending. Lundberg and Metzler maintained that induced fluctuations in inventory investment and consequent consumption spending prevent output from adjusting promptly to the new equilibrium. Cyclical movements persist, but the system gradually converges to the new equilibrium.

a. Behavioral Assumptions

The inventory cycle model is obtained by a slight modification of the investment equation employed in developing the multiplier-accelerator models. The argument focuses on the way in which sales expectations are

---

[13] The effect of zero investment in plant and equipment on capacity is suppressed in analyzing the contribution of this category of investment spending to effective demand.

[14] Op cit.

[15] Op cit.

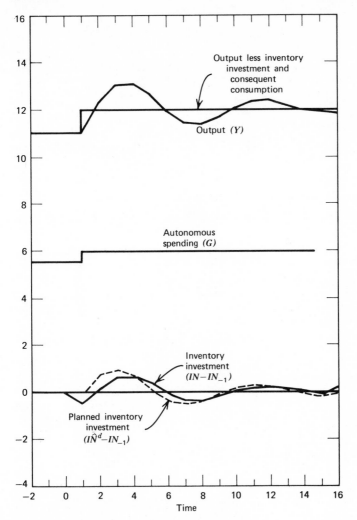

Fig. 16.6 *The Lundberg-Metzler inventory cycle.*

formed and on the impact of errors made in predicting sales on inventory and output.

Suppose that desired inventory, IN_t^d, is a linear function of actual sales volume, A_t.

$$IN_t^d = k_0 + k_1 A_t \qquad (3.1)$$

This line, which indicates a long-run objective, is plotted in the upper panel of Figure 16.7. But at the time when production decisions must be

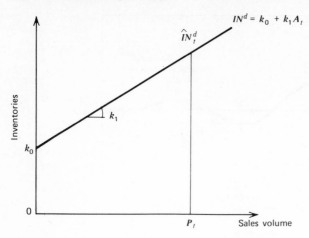

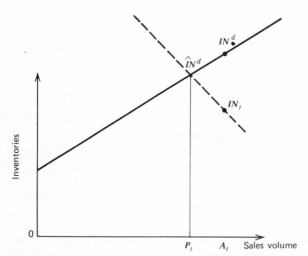

Fig. 16.7   *Planned and realized inventory investment.*

made, actual sales may not be known precisely. If the firm predicts sales of P_t, its *anticipated* desired inventory level will be

$$IN_t^d = k_0 + k_1P_t \tag{3.2}$$

How errors in anticipating sales will, in practice, cause actual inventories to depart from the planned level is revealed by the lower panel of the graph; thus, if actual sales exceed P_t, inventories may be drawn down below $\hat{IN}_t^d$ by the full amount of the forecast error, leaving actual end-of-period inventories of

$$IN_t = I\hat{N}_t^d - (A_t - P_t) \tag{3.3}$$

as indicated on the lower panel of the graph. The line with slope -1 on the graph indicates actual inventory as a function of realized sales, given sales anticipations of P_t. Substituting Equation 3.2 into Equation 3.3 yields as the "reduced form" equation for inventory investment

$$IN_t = k_0 + (1 + k_1)P_t - A_t \tag{3.4}$$

Now an equation explaining the generation of sales expectations is needed. The simplest hypothesis is to suppose that firms expect no change.

$$P_t = A_{t-1} \tag{3.5}$$

With the aid of this hypothesis, Equation 3.4 reduces to

$$IN_t = k_0 + (1 + k_1)P_t - A_t = k_0 + (1 + k_1)A_{t-1} - A_t \tag{3.6}$$

Inventory investment is simply

$$IN_t - IN_{t-1} = -A_t + (2 + k_1)A_{t-1} - (1 + k_1)A_{t-2} \tag{3.7}$$

This inventory investment equation corresponds to investment Equation 15.2.4 of the elementary multiplier-accelerator model.

The next step is to link sales with output. Since all output must be either sold or added to inventory, there is also an identity for output

$$Y_t \equiv A_t + (IN_t - IN_{t-1}) \tag{3.8}$$

and substituting from Equation 3.7 reveals

$$Y_t = (2 + k_1)A_{t-1} - (1 + k_1)A_{t-2} \tag{3.9}$$

Since aggregate sales are the sum of an endogenous consumption component and an exogenous term G_t representing the sum of government spending and fixed investment,

$$A_t = C_t + G_t \tag{3.10}$$

Furthermore, if consumption is simply $C_t = c_0 + c_1 \imath_t$,

$$A_t = c_0 + c_1 Y + G_t \tag{3.11}$$

Substituting this last sales expression into Equation 3.9 yields the following equation for output.

$$Y_t = c_0 + c_1(2 + k_1)Y_{t-1} - c_1(1 + k_1)Y_{t-2}$$
$$+ G_{t-1} + (1 + k_1)(G_{t-1} - G_{t-2}) \tag{3.12}$$

This second-order linear difference equation has as its equilibrium solution

$$Y^e = \frac{1}{1 - c_1}(c_0 + G)$$

which is the product of the multiplier times autonomous spending. The cyclical movements in income that were illustrated in Figure 16.3 were generated by Metzler with the above equation, hypothetical parameter values of $c_1 = k_1 = 0.5$, by having an initial equilibrium with $G = 550$ and $Y_1 = 1100$ disturbed by an increase in autonomous spending to $G = 600$; the data are recorded on Table 16.3.

b. Dynamic Properties

The inventory cycle model summarized by Equation 3.12 is conveniently rewritten in the standard form of the preceding chapter.

$$Y_t + \beta Y_{t-1} + \gamma Y_{t-2} = Z_t$$

where

$$\beta = -(2 + k_1)c_1$$

$$\gamma = (1 + k_1)c_1 \qquad (3.12')$$

Since $k_1 \geq 0$ and $0 \leq c_1 \leq 1$, the coefficients of this second-order linear difference equation are subject to the following restrictions.

$$\beta \leq 0$$

$$\gamma > 0$$

$$\gamma + \beta = -c_1$$

$$\gamma \geq \frac{-\beta}{2}$$

These restrictions demarcate the range of admissible values of the coefficients displayed in Figure 16.8.

Comparing this graph with Figure 15.4 reveals that the coefficients of the Metzler model are constrained to a subregion of the admissible values of the multiplier-accelerator scheme. Since the admissible region is within the V area on the graph, as with the elementary multiplier-accelerator model, the question of convergence or divergence hinges on whether γ is greater or less than unity. If γ is less than unity the system converges, and the smaller γ the more rapidly it approaches equilibrium. If γ exceeds unity, the system is unstable, and the larger γ the more violent the divergent

Table 16.3 HYPOTHETICAL INVENTORY CYCLE DATA

Time Period t (1)	Autonomous Spending G_t (2)	Predicted Sales $P_t = A_{t-1}$ (3)	Desired Inventory $\widehat{IN}_t = 0.5 P_t$ (4)	Planned Inventory Investment $\widehat{IN}_t - IN_{t-1}$ (5)	Production $Y_t = $ cols $3 + 5$ (6)	Consumption $C_t = 0.5 Y_t$ (7)	Realized Sales $A_t = $ cols $2 + 7$ (8)	Inventory Investment $\Delta IN_t = IN_t - IN_{t-1} = Y_t - A_t$ (9)	Inventory Stock $IN_t = \Delta IN_t + IN_{t-1}$ (10)
0	550	1100	550	0	1100	550	1100	0	550
1	600	1100	550	0	1100	550	1150	-50	500
2	600	1150	575	75	1225	612	1212	13	513
3	600	1212	606	93	1305	652	1252	53	566
4	600	1252	626	60	1312	656	1256	56	622
5	600	1256	628	6	1262	631	1231	31	653
6	600	1231	615	-38	1193	596	1196	-3	650
7	600	1196	598	-52	1144	572	1172	-28	622
8	600	1172	586	-36	1136	568	1168	-32	590
9	600	1168	584	-6	1162	581	1181	-19	571
10	600	1181	590	19	1200	600	1200	0	571
11	600	1200	600	29	1229	614	1214	15	586
12	600	1214	607	21	1235	617	1217	18	604
13	600	1217	608	4	1221	610	1210	11	615
14	600	1210	605	-10	1200	600	1200	0	615
15	600	1200	600	-15	1185	592	1192	-7	608
16	600	1192	596	-12	1180	590	1190	10	598
· · · ∞	600	1200	600	0	1200	600	1200	0	600

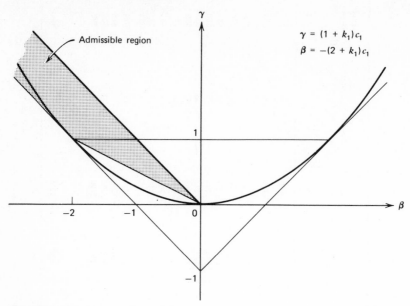

Fig. 16.8 *Inventory cycle model.*

movement. For Metzler's model, $\gamma = (1 + k_1)c_1$, while for the elementary multiplier-accelerator we have $\gamma = k_1$. Thus the inventory cycle model is *less* stable, unless $(1 + k_1)c_1 < k_1$; that is, $c_1 < k_1/(1 + k_1)$. In sum, the errors of foresight incorporated in the inventory cycle model make the system less stable unless the marginal propensity to consume is small relative to the accelerator coefficient.

REFERENCES

1. Metzler's analysis of the inventory cycle appeared on the eve of World War II. Eight years later, in a paper designed to clarify certain aspects of Roy Harrod's growth theory, Sir J. R. Hicks outlined his theory of the business cycle.

   Lloyd Metzler, "Nature and Stability of Inventory Cycles," *Review of Economics and Statistics*, August 1941.

   John R. Hicks, "Mr. Harrod's Dynamic Theory," *Economica*, May 1949.

2. The following papers are all concerned with evaluating stabilization strategy. A. W. Phillips considers a variety of stabilization strategies. Lovell and Prescott focus on the effects of alternative monetary rules. Holt and Theil both consider optimal discretionary policy of the type described in the appendix to this chapter; while Holt's paper is theoretical, Theil proceeds to present a number of practical applications, including the formulation of an optimal antidepression policy for the United States in the 1930s and planning policy for the Netherlands in the 1950s. Friedman argues that stabilization efforts should be less vigorous the greater the degree of uncertainty. Chow also discusses stochastic control problems. Cooper and Fischer evaluate alternative rules that the Fed might follow within a deterministic framework.

   A. W. Phillips, "Stabilization Policy and the Time-Forms of Lagged Responses," *Economic Journal*, June 1957.

   Michael C. Lovell and Edward Prescott, "Money, Multiplier Accelerator Interaction and the Business Cycle," *Southern Economic Journal*, July 1968.

   Michael C. Lovell, "Monetary Policy and the Inventory Cycle," in *Trade, Stability and Macroeconomics: Essays in Honor of Lloyd A. Metzler*, Academic Press, 1974.

   Charles C. Holt, "Linear Decision Rules for Economic Stabilization and Growth," *Quarterly Journal of Economics*, February 1962.

   H. Theil, *Optimal Decision Rules for Government and Industry*, North Holland, 1964.

   Milton Friedman, "The Effects of a Full-Employment Policy on Economic Stability: A Formal Analysis," in his *Essays in Positive Economics*, University of Chicago Press, 1953.

   Gregory C. Chow, "Problems of Economic Policy from the Viewpoint of Optimal Control," *American Economic Review*, December 1973.

   J. Phillip Cooper and Stanley Fischer, "Simulations of Monetary Rule in the FRB-MIT-Penn Model," *Journal of Money, Credit and Banking*, May 1972.

KEY CONCEPTS

control instruments
inventory cycle

anticipated versus realized sales
control ray
planned inventory investment
Metzler and Hawtrey

EXERCISES

16.1   Draw a flowchart for the simple Samuelson multiplier-accelerator model described in Chapter 15. Now show how the flowchart can be modified in order to reflect the effect of interest rates on the desired capital stock; complete the new feedback loop by showing the effect of the money supply and the pace of economic activity on the interest rate.

16.2   Consider the investment equation used in the computer program of Exercise 15.4. That equation lends itself to the following interpretation. Firms wish to have the capital stock equal to 1.5 times the value of GNP; in planning investment they presume that GNP will remain at its current level, and firms attempt to eliminate 30% of the gap between the desired and actual capital stock. Show how the computer program must be modified in order to run simulations revealing the effects of the following elaborations.

   a.   Make the desired capital stock depend on anticipated sales, where anticipated sales are based on the assumption that the *change* to next period's GNP will equal the immediately preceding GNP change.

   b.   Following Metzler, modify your simulation model by having the capital stock (inventories) drawn down by any excess of GNP over the anticipated level.

   c.   Make government spending endogenous by supposing that this period's government spending equals 20% of the most recent change in GNP.

16.3   In *Contribution to the Theory of the Trade Cycle*[16] Hicks presented a number of modifications of the basic multiplier accelerator model. Analyze each of the following modifications of the model developed

---

[16] Oxford, 1950. For a capsule presentation consult an earlier paper by Hicks, "Mr. Harrod's Dynamic Theory," *Economica*, pp. 106–121, May 1949.

in Section 15.2, either analytically or by modifying the computer program model presented in Exercise 15.4.

a. Growing government spending: suppose that government spending, instead of being constant, grows at a constant rate.

$$G_t = (1 + \rho)G_{t-1} = (1 + \rho)^t G_0$$

Show that output cannot remain at any constant equilibrium level, but that it can grow along an equilibrium growth path at rate ρ. Indeed, if output grows at a constant rate, it must be at rate ρ.

b. The one-way accelerator, first approximation: suppose that it is impossible to disinvest the capital stock; investment cannot be negative. Thus investment equation 15.2.3 is modified to read

$$I_t = \max(K_t^d - K_{t-1}, 0)$$

Of course, we still have $K_t = K_{t-1} + I$. Note that as long as the economy is growing, this model is identical to the multiplier-accelerator model of Section 15.2. But when the economy declines, the system switches into a different regime characterized by zero investment. What determines output when $I_t = 0$?

c. The one-way accelerator, second approximation: as a refinement of part b, suppose that negative investment can take place, but that the rate of disinvestment is limited by the speed with which the existing capital stock depreciates. Specifically, suppose that depreciation in period t is dK_{t-1}. Therefore,

$$K_t = (1 - d)K_{t-1} + I_t$$

Further suppose that net investment is

$$I_t = \max[K_t^d - K_{t-1}, -dK_{t-1}]$$

Analyze the implications of this alternative to the investment equation in part b.

APPENDIX 16.A OPTIMAL LINEAR DECISION RULES

16.A.1 INTRODUCTION

Simplistic rules of thumb may at times offer a useful guide to policymakers concerned with stabilizing the economy. Considerable professional support has been mustered for the proposition that the nominal money supply should expand at a constant rate per annum in both prosperity and depression. But, given the vital stake we all have in achieving economic stability, it makes sense to try and work out an *optimal* stabilization strategy. This appendix presents examples showing how optimal decision rules may be derived in some particularly simple cases. The approach uses a quadratic loss function of a form pioneered by H. Theil and Herbert Simon in studies of the optimal way in which a profit-maximizating firm should schedule production.[17] But, as Charles Holt has emphasized, the same analytical technique can be employed in designing the most appropriate strategy for stabilizing the economy.[18] Indeed, van den Boggard and Theil worked out as a historical exercise the strategy that Roosevelt *should* have followed in expediting the United States recovery from the Great Depression of the 1930s.[19] And, as a demonstration of how this strategy can be used in practical macroeconomic planning, Theil and his associates have shown how the procedure is employed in planning economic policy for the Netherlands.[20] In the next section a few examples will illustrate the basic approach used in all these studies. A nontechnical summary in the concluding section of this appendix reviews the basic macroeconomic implications of this mode of analysis.

†16.A.2 SOME SIMPLE EXAMPLES[21]

a. Adjustment Costs

The task of the decision maker will initially be explored under conditions of certainty. He knows the path of the exogenous variables and the parameters characterizing the economy. His problem is to pick the time path of certain decision

---

[17] Herbert A. Simon, "Dynamic Programming Under Uncertainty with a Quadratic Criterion Function, *Econometrica*, 1956; H. Theil, "A Note on Certainty Equivalence in Dynamic Planning," *Econometrica*, 1957; Holt, Modigliani, Muth, and Simon, *Planning Production, Inventories and Work Force*, Prentice-Hall, 1960.

[18] C. C. Holt, "Linear Decision Rules for Economic Stabilization and Growth," *Quarterly Journal of Economics*, pp. 20–45, 1962.

[19] P. J. M. van den Bogaard and H. Theil, "Macrodynamic Policy-Making: An Application of Strategic and Certainty Equivalence Concepts to the Economy of the United States, 1933–1936," *Metroeconomica*, pp. 149–167, 1959. This analysis is presented by Theil in his *Optimal Decision Rules for Government and Industry*, Rand McNally, 1964.

[20] The study by P. J. M. van den Bogaard and A. P. Barten on "Optimal Macroeconomic Decision Rules for the Netherlands, 1957–1959" is reviewed by Theil in his *Optimal Decision Rules for Government and Industry*, North Holland, 1964.

[21] The reader interested only in a summary of the argument may skip over the more technical material in this section.

variables so as to minimize his total loss.[22] In principle the loss function might be of quite general form, but, in the interests of simplicity, a quadratic loss function is used.

$$L_t = \frac{\theta}{2}(Y_t - Y_t^*)^2 + \frac{\Psi}{2}(Y_t - Y_{t-1})^2 \tag{2.1}$$

This function says that the penalty imposed on the decision maker depends on the gap of actual output Y_t from its target level Y_t^*; but it also depends on the rate of change in output, $Y_t - Y_{t-1}$, because abrupt changes can be disruptive to the economy. In multiperiod analysis the decision maker is concerned with what happens over a longer planning horizon. The total loss to be minimized over a horizon of T periods may be taken to be:

$$L = \sum_{t=1}^{T} L_t = \sum_{t=1}^{T} \frac{\theta}{2}(Y_t - Y_t^*)^2 + \frac{\Psi}{2}(Y_t - Y_{t-1})^2 \tag{2.2}$$

(For notational convenience we are counting time from *today*; that is, $t = 1$ for the first planning period; $t = 2$ for the second, etc.)

Consider first the one-period planning horizon case, the decision maker having to worry only about the loss in period 1. With $T = 1$, the problem is to minimize $L = L_1$, and differentiation yields as a necessary condition for a minimum

$$\frac{\partial L}{\partial Y_1} = \theta(Y_1 - Y_1^*) + \Psi(Y_1 - Y_0) = 0 \tag{2.3}$$

Consequently, the solution to the *one*-period problem is simply

$$Y_1 = \left(\frac{\theta}{\theta + \Psi}\right) Y_1^* + \left(\frac{\Psi}{\theta + \Psi}\right) Y_0 \tag{2.4}$$

Loss minimization involves a compromise between the desire to minimize changes in output and the desire to obtain output level Y_1^*. And the relative magnitude of θ and Ψ determines the extent to which output is adjusted toward its target level. While this is a simple solution, only the most myopic of decision makers would fail to look into the future. It is necessary to consider the implications of a longer planning horizon.

As a first step toward setting up the T horizon problem, notice that the costs of adjusting Y_t influences L through its impact on L_t and on L_{t+1}. Differentiation of Equation 2.1 yields $\partial L_t / \partial Y_t = \theta(Y_t - Y_t^*) + \Psi(Y_t - Y_{t-1})$ and $\partial L_{t+1} / \partial Y_t = -\Psi(Y_{t+1} - Y_t)$; also $\partial L_t / \partial Y_\tau = 0$ for $\tau \neq t$ and $t + 1$. This suggests that

$$\frac{\partial L}{\partial Y_t} = \frac{\partial L_1}{\partial Y_t} + \frac{\partial L_2}{\partial Y_t} + \ldots + \frac{\partial L_T}{\partial Y_t}$$

$$= \theta(Y_t - Y_t^*) + \Psi(Y_t - Y_{t-1}) - \Psi(Y_{t+1} - Y_t) = 0 \tag{2.5}$$

Of course, for a planning horizon of length T, there are T such conditions to be satisfied simultaneously. Note that the initial level of output, Y_0, is determined

---

[22] The problem may be formulated in terms of a decision maker interested in maximizing utility instead of minimizing loss; simply define $U = -L$ in the following argument.

historically and must be regarded as fixed; also, the influence of Y_T on L_{T+1} may be ignored, because that is beyond the end of the planning horizon.

Now consider the almost trivial case of $T = 2$. The two equations constituting the first-order conditions for a maximum are[23]

$$(\theta + 2\Psi)Y_1 - \Psi Y_2 = \theta Y_1{}^* + \Psi Y_0 \tag{2.6}$$
$$-\Psi Y_1 + (\theta + 2\Psi)Y_2 = \theta Y_2{}^*$$

Alternatively, one may consider the equivalent matrix expression

$$\begin{bmatrix} \theta + 2\Psi & -\Psi \\ -\Psi & \theta + 2\Psi \end{bmatrix} \begin{bmatrix} Y_1 \\ Y_2 \end{bmatrix} = \begin{bmatrix} \theta Y_1{}^* + \Psi Y_0 \\ \theta Y_2{}^* \end{bmatrix} \tag{2.6'}$$

There are two simultaneous equations to solve, and the optimal first period output is easily shown to be

$$Y_1{}^\circ = w_0 Y_0 + w_1 Y_1{}^* + w_2 Y_2{}^* \tag{2.7}$$

where the weights are defined as

$$w_0 = (\theta + 2\Psi) \frac{\Psi}{(\theta + 2\Psi)^2 - \Psi^2}$$

$$w_1 = (\theta + 2\Psi) \frac{\theta}{(\theta + 2\Psi)^2 - \Psi^2}$$

$$w_2 = \frac{\theta \Psi}{(\theta + 2\Psi)^2 - \Psi^2}$$

More generally, with a horizon of length T, the problem involves solving the system of T simultaneous equations

$$\begin{bmatrix} \theta + 2\Psi & -\Psi & 0 & 0 & \cdots & 0 \\ -\Psi & \theta + 2\Psi & -\Psi & 0 & \cdots & 0 \\ 0 & -\Psi & \theta + 2\Psi & -\Psi & & 0 \\ \cdot & \cdot & \cdot & \cdot & & \cdot \\ \cdot & \cdot & \cdot & \cdot & & \cdot \\ \cdot & \cdot & \cdot & \cdot & & \cdot \\ 0 & 0 & 0 & 0 & \cdots & \theta + 2\Psi \end{bmatrix} \begin{bmatrix} Y_1{}^\circ \\ Y_2{}^\circ \\ Y_3{}^\circ \\ \cdot \\ \cdot \\ \cdot \\ Y_T{}^\circ \end{bmatrix} = \begin{bmatrix} \theta Y_1{}^* + \Psi Y_0 \\ \theta Y_2{}^* \\ \theta Y_3{}^* \\ \\ \\ \\ \theta Y_T{}^* \end{bmatrix} \tag{2.8}$$

Premultiplication by the inverse of the $T \times T$ matrix on the left yields the desired solution; the computations are tedious, but the linear nature of the simultaneous equations generated by the quadratic form of the loss function makes the problem manageable. The solution for the first period can be shown to be of the form

$$Y_1 = w_0 Y_0 + \sum_{t=1}^{T} w_t Y_t{}^* \tag{2.9}$$

---

[23] That is, the equations are derived by setting $\partial L/\partial Y_1 = 0$ and $\partial L/\partial Y_2 = 0$. Because the loss function is quadratic, the second-order conditions are trivial.

where

$$\sum_{t=0}^{T} w_i = 1$$

That is, regardless of the length of the planning horizon, the optimal level of activity in the first period is a weighted average of last period's output plus the desired outputs of the next T periods. Similar equations can be used to obtain the entire optimal path of outputs for subsequent periods, $t = 2, \ldots, T$. Linear decision rules are obtained because the loss function is assumed to be of the simple quadratic form specified by Equation 2.1.

Having derived the target level of output for the first period, the appropriate monetary and/or fiscal policy depends on what model of the economy is deemed most appropriate. Suppose, for example, that the interest rate is to be manipulated in order to stabilize the multiplier-accelerator economy of Section 16.2. Instead of using the rule provided by Equation 16.2.7 to determine the interest rate, one can now calculate the rate of interest that would generate the desired level of output specified by Equation 16.A.2.9, given the level of government spending and the inherited capital stock.

b. Control Costs

Consider a decision maker concerned with obtaining an optimal level of aggregate economic activity by manipulating government spending. But having G, the *control instrument*, depart from its desired level is not costless. Thus our decision maker must seek an appropriate compromise between the desired level of economic activity and a targeted rate of government spending, where the government spending target may be dictated by defense needs and so forth. For simplicity suppose that the decision maker's problem is to minimize the quadratic loss function

$$L = \frac{\theta}{2}(Y - Y^*)^2 + \frac{\Omega}{2}(G - G^*)^2 \tag{2.10}$$

where Y is actual output and Y^* is its desired level, while G and G^* are actual and target government spending. Now output is the sum

$$Y = C + I + G \tag{2.11}$$

where I is exogenous and consumption is

$$C = cY \tag{2.12}$$

Therefore, output is determined by the multiplier to be

$$Y = m(I + G) \tag{2.13}$$

where $m = 1/(1 - c)$. The problem is to minimize Equation 2.10 subject to linear constraint 2.13. From Equation 2.13 we have

$$G = \frac{Y}{m} - I \tag{2.14}$$

and substituting into Equation 2.10 yields

$$L = \frac{\theta}{2} (Y - Y^*)^2 + \frac{\Omega}{2} \left(\frac{Y}{m} - I - G^* \right)^2 \tag{2.15}$$

Differentiating with respect to Y provides a necessary condition for a minimum.[24]

$$\frac{\partial L}{\partial Y} = \theta(Y - Y^*) + \frac{\Omega}{m} \left(\frac{Y}{m} - I - G^* \right) = 0 \tag{2.16}$$

Hence, the optimal level of Y is

$$Y^\circ = \left(\frac{\theta m^2}{\theta m^2 + \Omega} \right) Y^* + \left(\frac{\Omega m}{\theta m^2 + \Omega} \right) (I + G^*) \tag{2.17}$$

which is achieved, as may be seen from Equation 2.14, with the following value of the control instrument:

$$G^\circ = \left(\frac{\theta m}{\theta m^2 + \Omega} \right) Y^* + \left(\frac{\Omega}{\theta m^2 + \Omega} \right) G^* - \left(\frac{\Omega m^2}{\theta m^2 + \Omega} \right) I \tag{2.18}$$

In this example the optimal policy involves a compromise between keeping G at the optimal level and adjusting Y to its target. Again, the rule determining the optimal policy is linear in terms of the relevant variables: G^*, Y^*, and I in this case.

c. Adjustment and Control Costs

The problem of control is slightly messier, but no more difficult in principle, when the policymaker is concerned about both adjustment and control costs. Suppose that the loss in each period is

$$L_t = \frac{\theta}{2} (Y_t - Y_t^*)^2 + \frac{\Omega}{2} (G_t - G_t^*)^2 + \frac{\Psi}{2} (Y_t - Y_{t-1})^2 \tag{2.19}$$

Over a planning period of length T the total loss may be written as

$$L = \sum_{t=1}^{T} L_t = \frac{\theta}{2} (Y_t - Y_t^*)^2 + \frac{\Omega}{2} \left(\frac{Y_t}{m} - I_t - G_t^* \right)^2 + \frac{\Psi}{2} (Y_t - Y_{t-1})^2 \tag{2.20}$$

where we have eliminated government spending with the aid of Equation 2.14. Differentiation with respect to Y_t yields

$$\frac{\partial L}{\partial Y_t} = \theta(Y_t - Y_t^*) + \frac{\Omega}{m} \left(\frac{Y_t}{m} - I_t - G_t^* \right)$$
$$+ \Psi(Y_t - Y_{t-1}) - \Psi(Y_{t+1} - Y_t) = 0 \tag{2.21}$$

as a necessary condition for a maximum. Fortunately, this expression may be rewritten in a form that is identical to Equation 2.5 by a suitable redefinition of variables.

$$\frac{\partial L}{\partial Y_t} = \bar{\theta}(Y - \bar{Y}_t^*) + \Psi(Y_t - Y_{t-1}) - \Psi(Y_{t+1} - Y_t) = 0 \tag{2.22}$$

---

[24] It is easily shown that the second-order conditions are satisfied.

where

$$\tilde{\theta} \equiv \theta + \frac{\Omega}{m^2}$$

and

$$\tilde{Y}_t^* \equiv \frac{\theta}{\tilde{\theta}} Y_t^* + \frac{\Omega}{\tilde{\theta}m} (I_t + G_t^*)$$

Since this is equivalent to Equation 2.5, it is intuitively clear that the final solution must involve a linear decision rule of form 2.9.

†16.A.3 CERTAINTY EQUIVALENCE

In the simple control problems in the preceding section it was presumed that the government policymaker had precise knowledge of the future level of private investment spending. But the government is not clairvoyant. It is not reasonable to presume that investment spending can be predicted with great precision. One possible *certainty equivalence* strategy for dealing with uncertainty would be to plan government spending by substituting the best investment spending forecast available for I in the linear decision rule. Thus, in the second control example, one would replace I in Equation 2.18 with the best forecast available at the time that government spending must be determined. This *certainty equivalence* approach may not be intuitively appealing; after all, one might think that the degree of forecasting precision that is attainable would influence the stabilizing strategy followed in planning fiscal policy. But it turns out, thanks to the Certainty Equivalence Theorem of Simon and Theil,[25] that this is indeed the optimal strategy under rather general conditions! Their theorem, in full generality, is quite complicated, but it can be illustrated with a simple example.

The optimality of the certainty equivalence strategy is easily established for the simple one-period control problem considered in part b of the preceding section. Suppose that at the time when government spending must be determined, only a forecast I of actual investment spending $\tilde{I}$ is available. That is, actual investment spending will turn out to be

$$\tilde{I} = I + \epsilon \tag{3.1}$$

where the random variable ϵ is the forecast error. Equation 2.13 now shows what the planned level of output (Y) will be, given the forecast I of actual investment spending and a decision to undertake government expenditure **G**. Actual output, in contrast, will be

$$\tilde{Y} = m(\tilde{I} + G) = m(I + \epsilon + G) = Y + m\epsilon \tag{3.2}$$

Since ϵ is a random variable, actual output $\tilde{Y}$ is, too, and this means that the loss is random also.

$$L = \frac{\theta}{2} (\tilde{Y} - Y^*)^2 + \frac{\Psi}{2} (G - G^*)^2$$

$$= \frac{\theta}{2} (m\epsilon + Y - Y^*)^2 + \frac{\Psi}{2} \left(\frac{Y}{m} - I + G^* \right)^2 \tag{3.3}$$

[25] Op cit.

Now the policymaker cannot plan to minimize the random variable L because he obviously does not know I (or ϵ) at the time when he must determine $\mathbf{G}$. In making decisions under uncertainty the policymaker should attempt to minimize his loss on the average—his expected loss; that is, he should pick $\mathbf{G}$ so as to minimize:[26]

$$E(L) = \frac{\theta}{2} E[m\epsilon + (Y - Y^*)]^2 + \frac{\Psi}{2}\left(\frac{Y}{m} - I + \mathbf{G}^*\right)^2$$

$$= \frac{\theta}{2} m^2 E(\epsilon^2) + \theta m E[\epsilon(Y - Y^*)] + \frac{\theta}{2}(Y - Y^*)^2 + \frac{\Psi}{2}\left(\frac{Y}{m} - I + \mathbf{G}^*\right)^2 \quad (3.4)$$

Only the first two terms of Equation 3.4 involve the forecast error complication. Now $E(\epsilon^2)$ reduces to σ_ϵ^2 (the variance of ϵ) because the forecast should be unbiased; otherwise, it could have been improved by correcting for the systematic error. And the second of the two terms *must* vanish, according to the argument of Theil and Simon, because the correlation between ϵ and $(Y - Y^*)$ is zero; after all, Y^*, I, and Y are all nonrandom because they are known at the time the decision maker commits the economy to the chosen level of government spending (it is ϵ and I that are random).[27] As a consequence, the problem of decision making under uncertainty is reduced to the problem of picking $\mathbf{G}$ so as to minimize the expected loss.

$$E(L) = \frac{\theta}{2} m^2 \sigma_\epsilon^2 + \frac{\theta}{2}(Y - Y^*)^2 + \frac{\Psi}{2}\left(\frac{Y}{m} - I + \mathbf{G}^*\right)^2 \quad (3.5)$$

Now the first term represents the inherent loss to be expected as a result of the imperfect knowledge concerning the future level of investment—this burden cannot be influenced by adjusting $\mathbf{G}$. And the last two terms, which do not involve the measurement error, are old friends encountered in Section 16.A.3b; indeed, they constitute the loss to that problem, as can be seen from Equation 2.15. And that loss was minimized by picking the level of government spending specified by linear decision rule 2.18. Thus using the certainty equivalent strategy of substituting the forecasted value of investment spending into the linear decision rule will minimize Equation 3.5.

16.A.4   SUMMARY AND IMPLICATIONS

Starting with a quadratic loss function, the optimal stabilization strategy was found to involve the setting of policy variables (e.g., government spending) in accordance with linear decision rules. Furthermore, it was demonstrated that in

---

[26] The symbol "E" in the following equation denotes the expected value operator, which was briefly explained in Appendix 4.A.3a. In a loose molar sense, $E(\epsilon^2)$ means to take the average value of the expression inside the parentheses. Precisely the same strategy for dealing with uncertainty by minimizing expected loss (i.e., maximizing expected utility $U = -L$) was employed in analyzing the portfolio selection problem in Appendix 5.B.

[27] Jack Muth calls "rational" those forecasts that have the property of being uncorrelated with the forecast error; we return to this concept in the next section of this appendix. See his "Rational Expectations and the Theory of Price Movements," *Econometrica*, July 1961.

one particular simple case the linear decision rule for determining government spending is optimal, even when private investment spending is not known at the time that fiscal policy must be formulated. These results can be shown to hold with considerable generality. The loss function may involve lagged as well as current values of the control and endogenous variables, but provided it is quadratic, linear decision rules follow even in the presence of uncertainty. This is true even if a large number of policy variables can be manipulated simultaneously. And it is true even if the underlying behavioral model, instead of involving the simple multiplier mechanism, encompasses a large number of simultaneous linear equations.

Perhaps the most ambitious application of this approach was the analysis by P. J. M. van den Bogaard and A. P. Barten for the Dutch Social and Economic Council.[28] The behavior of the Netherlands economy was summarized in terms of a 40-equation econometric model. There were five control instruments: the general wage rate, indirect taxes less subsidies, direct taxes on wage income, direct taxes on nonwage income, and government expenditures on commodities. The loss function also involved private employment, the price level, the share of wages in national income, and the balance of payments. But the derivation of optimal strategies was sufficiently straightforward computationally that it was possible to work through the analysis three times, once for each of three alternative specifications of the coefficients of the quadratic loss function. The first loss function represented the preferences of employees in that it laid particular stress on high wages and employment. The second, intended to represent the desires of employers, emphasized lower taxes and a surplus in the balance of payments. And the third, representing the Crown, involved a compromise between these two extremes. Clearly, this approach constitutes an extremely powerful mode of analysis.

The optimal decision rule approach has certain implications for macroeconomic policy that warrant attention, even in a brief survey of the topic. Consider the problem of choosing between alternative control instruments. The debate between monetarists and "Keynesian" viewpoints has often been expressed in terms of the alleged impotence of either the fiscal or the monetary instruments. But, if the moderates are correct in believing that both weapons are indeed capable of influencing the pace of economic activity, how is the policymaker to choose between the two instruments? With a quadratic loss function it will generally turn out that no one instrument should be used to the exclusion of others. However, the dominant role will be assigned to the instrument that has a low cost of manipulation relative to its potency. Monetary instruments should bear the primary stabilization burden if, as seems likely, the cost of having government spending deviate from desired level G^* is high relative to that incurred in having the monetary instrument depart from its optimal level. The case for placing major reliance on monetary policy might be better stated in terms of the relatively small social costs involved in having the money supply and interest rates, instead of government spending or tax rates, depart from target levels.

A major issue concerns the Theil-Simon proposition of certainty equivalence. That is an extremely powerful result. But certainty equivalence is not consistent

[28] Their study is concisely summarized by Theil in *Optimal Decision Rules for Government and Industry*, North Holland, Chapter 6, 1964.

with an alternative proposition, refined by Friedman in a classic theoretical contribution, that the less perfect our knowledge about the economy, the less vigorous should be our efforts at stabilizing it.[29] And it appears to be inconsistent with certain of the results of portfolio theory; we found in Appendix 5.B that the greater the degree of uncertainty about the future value of a stock, the less of it an investor is likely to want to include in his optimal portfolio; clearly, the optimizing investor does not adopt a certainty equivalence approach. The distinction arises because, for Theil and Simon, the risk element in the expected loss function is of constant magnitude regardless of the values of the policy instruments (see Equation 3.4); the risk is inescapable. But the investor is able to escape risk by purchasing fewer risky stocks and diversifying his portfolio. It turns out that only a slight modification of the optimal decision rule approach suffices to undermine the certainty equivalence proposition. If the marginal propensity to consume and hence the multiplier (m) is not known precisely, the variance adding to expected loss will rise in proportion to the magnitude of government spending. With this type of uncertainty the control problem becomes much more complicated, even in the one-period case. With uncertainty about the magnitude of such parameters as the marginal propensity to consume, a more conservative stabilization strategy is required. Furthermore, uncertainty about the parameters provides an additional incentive for relying on more than one control instrument, since this provides a means for diversifying the control-instrument "portfolio." In the presence of uncertainty about the magnitude of government spending and monetary multipliers, the optimal policy is likely to involve a mixture of the two instruments.[30] With a longer planning horizon, the introduction of uncertainty about the magnitude of the system's parameters complicates the problem still further because of the opportunity for learning. Added information about the system is gained each period and can be used to improve the effectiveness of control policy in subsequent periods. The optimal policy will involve an element of experimental design in order to capitalize effectively on this learning possibility but, in designing the experiment, the costs involved in having abrupt changes in output and of departures of control instruments and output from target levels cannot be neglected. Because a difficult compromise is involved in designing the optimal control strategy, uncertainty about the magnitude of the parameters of the system complicates the control problem by whole orders of magnitude.[31]

[29] Milton Friedman, "The Effects of a Full-Employment Policy on Economic Stability: A Formal Analysis," in *Essays in Positive Economics*, Chicago University Press, 1953.

[30] William Brainard, "Uncertainty and the Effectiveness of Policy," *American Economic Review*, 1967; also Edward Prescott, "Adaptive Decision Rules for Macroeconomic Planning," *Western Economic Journal*, December 1971.

[31] See Edward Prescott, op cit.; also Arnold Zellner, "Analysis of Some Control Problems," Chapter 11 in his *Introduction to Bayesian Inference in Econometrics*, John Wiley, 1971.

†APPENDIX 16.B   STOCHASTIC DIFFERENCE EQUATIONS

In analyzing the role of money in the business cycle in Section 16.2 it was presumed that the objective was to find the value of the policy parameter π facilitating most rapid convergence to equilibrium. But this is not necessarily the only criterion for judging policy. It was argued long ago by Ragnar Frisch that the business cycle may persist because of the impact of erratic shocks on an inherently stable system.[32]

"[It is] particularly fruitful and promising to study what would become of the solution of a deterministic dynamic system if it was exposed to a stream of erratic shocks that constantly upset the continuous evolution, and by so doing introduced into the system the energy necessary to maintain the swings."

Such shocks may arise from the fickleness of consumers or investors, possibly from the impact of Schumpeterian innovations, or from erratic fluctuations in monetary and fiscal policy. And it turns out that if behavior is influenced by random factors, the appropriate response of the monetary authorities should be somewhat more aggressive than the analysis of the deterministic case suggested. In particular, the optimal value of the policy parameter π is larger than that prescribed in Equation 16.2.12.

The problem is to find the value of π that will minimize the variance of Y_t. As a first step, we rewrite Equation 16.2.10 as

$$Y_t = -\beta Y_{t-1} - \gamma Y_{t-2} + \epsilon_t + \delta G \tag{1}$$

Here ϵ_t is the erratic shock. It is presumed that ϵ_t has zero expected value and finite variance.[33] The variance of output will be finite if and only if the deterministic counterpart previously considered is stable; that is, the point $\langle \beta, \gamma \rangle$ must be inside the stability triangle.[34] As a first step toward determining the value of the policy parameter $\pi_s{}^\circ$ serving to minimize $\sigma_Y{}^2$, given the other parameters of the model, note immediately that under stationarity

$$\sigma_Y{}^2 = (\beta^2 + \gamma^2)\sigma_Y{}^2 + 2\beta\gamma \operatorname{cov}(Y, Y_{-1}) + \sigma_\epsilon{}^2 \tag{2}$$

Furthermore, we evaluate the covariance term by noting that if we take the expected value of Equation B.1 after multiplying both sides by Y_{t-1}.

$$(1 + \gamma) \operatorname{cov}(Y, Y_{-1}) + \beta\sigma_Y{}^2 = \operatorname{cov}(\epsilon, Y_{-1}) \tag{3}$$

---

[32] "Propagation Problems and Impulse Problems in Dynamic Economics," in *Economic Essays in Honor of Gustav Cassell*, 1933, as reprinted in the A.E.A. *Readings in Business Cycles*, Gordon-Klein, eds., 1965.

[33] We will assume for simplicity that the disturbance is free of autocorrelation. This precludes random variation in government spending, for example, as may be seen from the way in which both G_t and G_{t-1} appear in Equation 2.10. A moving average disturbance generates a higher-order stochastic process less amenable to qualitative analysis.

[34] This proposition was proved within a much more general context by H. B. Manne and Abraham Wald, "On the Statistical Treatment of Stochastic Difference Equations," *Econometrica*, July–October 1945.

But $\text{cov}\,(\epsilon,\,Y_{-1}) = 0$; therefore,

$$\text{cov}\,(Y,\,Y_{-1}) = \frac{-\beta\sigma_Y{}^2}{1+\gamma}$$

Substituting back into Equation 2 yields the fundamental equation

$$\sigma_Y{}^2 = \frac{1}{1 - \gamma^2 - \beta^2\left(\dfrac{1-\gamma}{1+\gamma}\right)}\,\sigma_\epsilon{}^2 \tag{4}$$

Note that this expression is symmetric in β; as illustrated by the "iso-variance" curves plotted on Figure 16.B.1.

Although $\sigma_\epsilon{}^2$ must be taken as a fact of life that cannot be influenced by monetary policy, $\sigma_Y{}^2$ is subject to manipulation because it is sensitive to variations in β and γ. Tangency point B reveals the point on the control ray yielding minimum $\sigma_Y{}^2$. Let $\mathbf{k} = \beta + \gamma$ which, from Equation 2.10 is a constant regardless of π. Differentiation of Equation 4 with respect to γ after eliminating β now yields a condition for an extremum:

$$(\mathbf{k} - \gamma)\left(\frac{1-\gamma}{1+\gamma}\right) - \gamma + \left(\frac{\mathbf{k}-\gamma}{1+\gamma}\right)^2 = 0$$

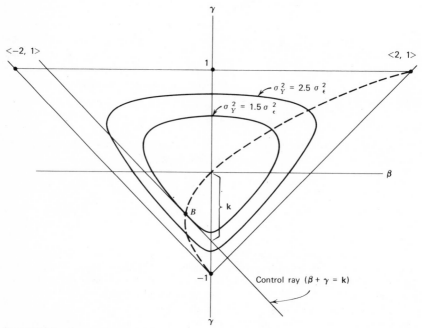

Fig. 16.B.1 *Iso-variance curves.*

which vanishes when

$$\gamma = \sqrt{1 + k} - 1 \tag{5}$$

The dotted line on the figure reveals the set of possible tangency points; the relevant one can be determined by plotting a line with slope minus one through point $\langle 0, k \rangle$. Alternatively, we find on substitution from Equation 2.10 that

$$\gamma_s^\circ = \sqrt{\delta(1 - c_1)} - 1 < 0$$

Finally, the variance minimizing value of the policy coefficient is

$$\pi_s^\circ = \frac{\sqrt{\delta(1 - c_1)} - 1 + (1 - \delta)c_1 - \delta k_1}{\delta k_2}$$

which is larger than the value maximizing the speed of convergence of the deterministic model. Returning to Equation 2.13, we see that the money supply *should* move countercyclically, contracting in boom and expanding in recession, if $\pi_s^\circ >$ m_1/m_2. Thus a central bank concerned with minimizing the variance of income is more likely to want a countercyclically moving money supply; still, for certain values of the model's parameters, it might be better to have the money supply expanding in booms and contracting in recession.

macroeconometric models

*17.1 HISTORY

Jan Tinbergen's *Statistical Testing of Business-Cycle Theories*, published in 1939 under the sponsorship of the League of Nations, was an attempt "to submit to statistical test some of the theories which [economists] have put forward regarding the character and causes of cyclical fluctuations in business activity."[1] In the introduction he explained that his method of study, "econometric business cycle research," constituted "a synthesis of statistical business cycle research and quantitative economic theory." Tinbergen built an econometric model for the United States economy, based on annual data from 1919 to 1932. His model involved 32 behavioral equations, including several consumption and investment functions, and a variety of monetary relationships; additional equations explained wages, capital gains, and stock market prices. Tinbergen rightly earned the Nobel Prize, because his pioneering contribution marks the dawn of a new era in macro-economic research.

Tinbergen's work has been superceded by a continuing stream of macroeconometric models. While some models have constituted the work of individual economists, most are so complex that they require team effort. Indeed, the fruitful interaction of ideas sparked by collaborative effort makes it difficult to trace the genealogy of econometric models.[2] A chain of models of increasing complexity was authored by Lawrence Klein, first at the Cowles Commission at the University of Chicago, then at the University of Michigan, and more recently at the University of Pennsylvania's Wharton School. At the University of Michigan, a graduate student seminar under the guidance of Professor Daniel Suits prepared annual econometric forecasts, beginning in the early 1950s, of the coming years' economic developments. Perhaps the most involved team effort was

---

[1] *Statistical Testing of Business Cycle Theories*, League of Nations Economic Intelligence, Geneva, 1939, I, p. 11.

[2] Marc Nerlove has published a convenient capsule description of 25 models in "A Tabular Survey of Macroeconometric Models," *International Economic Review*, 1966. A number of recent models are included in the list of references at the end of this chapter.

the Brookings-Social Science Research Council sponsored model of the United States economy. Twenty experts, each modeling the segment of the economy with which he was most familiar, contributed to the Brookings— SSRC edifice, which involved more than 125 behavioral equations. The Federal Reserve Board and the Commerce Department now have their own econometric models. Numerous business firms subscribe to the predictions generated periodically by the Wharton School. The forecasts of Dr. Michael Evans, a former collaborator of Klein, are now marketed by a subsidiary of the Chase Manhattan Bank. Some modern models include more than 1,000 equations.

Tinbergen's system of 32 simultaneous equations was of such complexity that its equilibrium and dynamic properties could not be determined analytically. And the larger macro-econometric models are even more involved.[3] The strategy of the econometrician involves two steps. First, the parameters of the model are estimated from historical data. At this stage considerable trial and error may be involved in determining precisely what form of the structural equations yield reasonable estimates. Thus, if the wrong sign is obtained for a key parameter (e.g., a negative marginal propensity to consume), the econometrician will try an alternative specification of the equation. Furthermore, each equation should provide a reasonably good fit if we are to obtain a model that will be useful for predictive purposes. The second step assembles the system of simultaneous equations so that it can be used for prediction. But the model can be used for more than just trying to predict next year's endogenous variables. Simulations are run in order to see if the model exhibits reasonable dynamic properties. The procedure is similar to that used in generating the multiplier-accelerator sequences, such as that recorded in Table 15.1. But, of course, with so many more equations, the calculations are quite involved and are best executed on an electronic computer.

*17.2 THE FEDERAL RESERVE BOARD—MIT ECONOMETRIC MODEL

An excellent example illustrating how econometric models work is provided by the team effort of economists at the Federal Reserve Board and the Massachusetts Institute of Technology. As with most econometric models, the Fed-MIT model has been in a state of constant modification and refinement, but we will be looking at a relatively early version of the model published in 1968. The model involves about 75 equations, two thirds

---

[3] An exception is the application of linear decision rules to a large scale model of the Dutch economy, discussed in Appendix 16.A. But that procedure is applicable only if all the equations in the model are linear.

of which are behavioral relationships and the remainder definitional.[4] A particularly attractive feature of the model, at least from a pedagogical viewpoint, is that it can be conveniently summarized in three separate blocks of equations that can be examined in isolation before consolidation into the complete model. One block focuses on consumption and inventory behavior; the second block looks at construction, producers' durable equipment, and state government expenditure; the other block analyzes financial markets. Each of these blocks will be considered in turn.

a. Consumption-Inventory Block

The consumption-inventory block generates predictions of consumption, inventory investment, and GNP. The main variables initially regarded as exogenous to the block' are fixed investment spending, exports, tax revenues, and the expenditures of federal, state, and local governments. Within the controlled environment provided by the consumption-inventory block a variety of multiplier effects can be investigated in experimental simulations. Thus, in analogy with the simple multiplier of Chapter 3, the effect of an increase in government expenditure on the American economy is investigated, given the magnitude of the remaining exogenous variables, including investment spending. Later, when the consumption-inventory block is combined with the other two blocks, the effects of an experimental increase in government expenditure will be considered again, but within an environment that allows for a more involved response, including the effects on investment spending of the induced increase in output and of monetary developments.

The effect on the consumption-inventory block of a $5 billion step-up in spending on defense is illustrated in Figure 17.1. The simulation reveals how a variety of variables would have deviated from actual developments in 1963 and 1964 if defense expenditures had been $5 billion higher. Recorded in Figure 17.1 are the differences obtained by subtracting from the experimental simulation obtained with the $5 billion increase in government expenditure the results of a "control" experiment provided by actual developments over the 1963–1964 period. That is, the graph shows the effect of the step-up in defense spending, given the historical conditions of 1963 and 1964. Presumably, the multiplier effects would have been different in a situation characterized by a greater initial degree of capacity utilization. But, within the context of the 1963–1964 situation, the simulation suggests that GNP gradually grows by about $15 billion because of the stimulus of increased defense spending. Thus the long-run multiplier is

---

[4] Because of their complexity, the details of the underlying equations are not presented here. The equations are discussed at length in Frank deLeeuw and Edward Gramlich, "The Federal Reserve Board-MIT Econometric Model," *Federal Reserve Bulletin*, January 1968. See the appendix to this chapter for additional references.

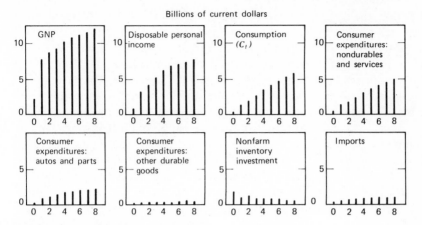

Fig. 17.1 *Defense expenditure increase of $5 billion, consumption-inventory block.*

$\Delta Y/\Delta G = 15/5 = 3$ for the Fed-MIT model, given that investment remains fixed.

The consumption-inventory block can be used to simulate the effects of a variety of other policy changes, and Figure 17.2 shows how an increase in the personal tax rate of 0.02 would affect GNP and a variety of other variables. Apparently, the 0.02 increase in the tax rate would not quite suffice to offset the effect on GNP of a $5 billion increase in defense spending, since the increase of GNP reported in Figure 17.1 is about $3 billion

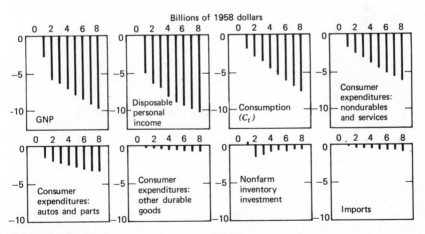

Fig. 17.2 *Personal tax rate increase of 0.02, consumption-inventory block.*

larger than the cutback revealed in Figure 17.2. But, of course, both simulations tell only part of the story, because they are artificially confined to the consumption-inventory block and presume that a number of other factors, including fixed investment spending, are constant.

The response captured by the consumption-inventory block is more complicated than that portrayed by the simple multiplier mechanism of Chapter 3, Section 5. Instead of a single function to explain consumption expenditure, the Fed-MIT model focuses on both the consumption of nondurables and the flow of services provided by consumer durables; this is in accordance with the theory of Modigliani and Brumberg, explained in Chapter 4, Section 3. The inventory equation has desired stocks dependent on consumer expenditures, new orders for producers' durable equipment, and defense spending.[5] The inventory equation allows for the negative effect of a surprise increase in consumer spending, in accordance with the Metzler theory of inventory cycle described in Chapter 16. Other equations explain automobile expenditures, investment in other consumer durables, imports, and so forth.

b. The Investment Block

The investment block looks at the effect of changes in GNP and/or interest rates on plant and equipment spending, housing construction, and state and local government expenditures. The simulations reported in Figures 17.3 and 17.4 suggest that housing is insensitive to the accelerator effect of an increase in GNP. But housing is more responsive than producer's durables to changes in the interest rate. While the effects are obviously partial in that there is no allowance for the feedback of increased expenditures on GNP, they are based on sophisticated treatment of each expenditure category.

The equations for producers' durable equipment and nonresidential structures allow for the impact of tax regulations and long-term interest rates (measured by the corporate bond rate), and the dividend-price ratio. An increase in the bond rate leads to the adoption of less capital intensive techniques of production—the substitution of labor for capital. But the adjustment will be protracted, since the capital intensity of equipment cannot be reduced once it is installed. This means that the interest rate

[5] Defense spending is singled out as a separate category of spending in the Fed-MIT model. But this was also done in certain of the Michigan models developed by D. B. Suits and in the Brookings Model. Defense procurement of military hardware is presumed to have an impact on the economy in advance of purchase. That is, when the orders are placed by the Pentagon, people are put to work producing the defense goods in advance of acquisition by the Department of Defense. This process was described in detail by Lovell, "Factors Explaining Manufacturing Inventory Investment," in *Inventory Fluctuations and Economic Stabilization*, Part II, Joint Economic Committee, 1961.

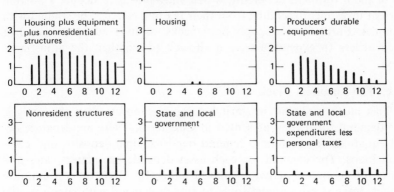

Fig. 17.3 *GNP increase of $10 billion, investment block.*

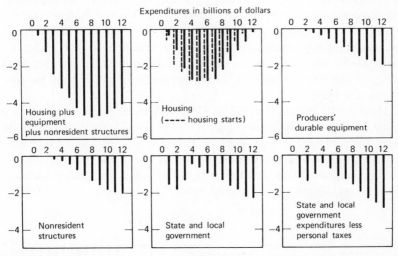

Fig. 17.4 *Corporate bond rate increase of 1%, investment block.*

effect is spread out as it gradually influences the capital stock over the time span involved in the wearing out of the existing equipment.[6] The

---

[6] This "putty-clay" assumption about the capital stock deserves a fuller explanation. New equipment is built with the current cost of investment funds influencing the type of machinery installed; for example, when interest rates are low, durability and labor-saving features will be emphasized. But, once constructed, the machinery cannot be changed drastically if an increase in interest costs means that a less capital-using type of machinery would have been more economical.

effect of the investment tax credit, which allows firms to deduct a portion of current investment spending from their tax bill, can also be studied with this model. Furthermore, supply-bottlenecks, as indexed by the ratio of unfilled orders to expenditures, are allowed to lengthen the adjustment process.

c. The Financial Block

This block is similar in spirit but more elaborate than the analysis of the demand for money presented in Chapter 5. There are separate demand equations for currency, demand deposits, time deposits, and commercial loans. The demand for each asset depends on interest rates and the pace of economic activity, indexed either by GNP or consumption spending. Interest rates adjust so as to equate demand with supply in the market for each financial asset. The supply of certain financial assets is determined partly by factors exogenous to this sector. For example, the level of economic activity, particularly the rate of inventory accumulation, influences commercial loan activity. The Federal Reserve System regulates the system by adjusting its portfolio of government securities through open market operations so as to achieve a specified reserve target for member banks; that is, the Fed exogenously determines the member bank holdings of unborrowed reserves (total reserves less member bank borrowings from the Fed).

How a $10 billion increase in GNP influences financial markets is revealed by the simulation in Figure 17.5. There is a marked rise in the demand for commercial loans because they are used to finance inventory investment, which in turn is a substantial part of the rise in GNP. The increased demand for loans, coupled with the enlarged transactions demand for money, causes the rise in interest rates. The response of the Treasury

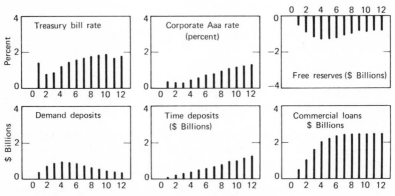

Fig. 17.5 *GNP increase of $10 billion, financial block.*

bill rate is quite sharp, but the corporate bond rate involves a somewhat longer lag. Note that the increased return provided on interest earning assets induces the commercial banks to reduce their holdings of excess reserves. Thus the rising transactions demand for money is partially accommodated by the banking system through a rise in demand deposits, and this is so even though the Fed does not increase the reserves of the member banks through open market operations.

A $1 billion increase in bank reserves prompts the financial block changes reported in Figure 17.6. The Fed's decision to enlarge bank reserves means a very sizable initial increase in free reserves, because time is required before the banks can put the funds to work. The banks continue to tolerate additional excess reserves because of the dramatic initial drop in the bill rate. Such a sharp fall in the bill rate was necessary to equilibrate financial markets, because the demand for monetary assets is relatively insensitive to interest rates in the short run. When the public's demand for money responds to the reduced interest cost of holding funds, required reserves increase, cutting into the free reserves of the banks. Demand deposits ultimately grow by about four times the $1 billion increase in bank reserves. And time deposits, which are also subject to reserve requirements, expand substantially because their interest yield falls by less than that provided on alternative financial assets.

d. The Three Blocks Combined

How will the three blocks interact when they are combined into a single group of simultaneous equations? The resulting econometric model

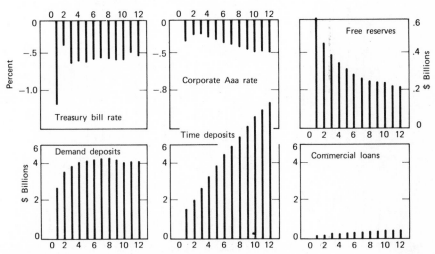

Fig. 17.6 *Reserve increase of $1 billion, financial block.*

is in many respects similar to the *IS-LM* apparatus, which was obtained by combining the multiplier mechanism, the investment mechanism, and the demand for money equation. But, of course, the much larger number of equations means that the Fed-MIT model cannot be summed up in terms of a simple two-dimensional graph. However, the effects of simulated policy changes can be plotted, and these are recorded in Figures 17.7, 17.8, and 17.9. As before, it is assumed that the policy changes were implemented at the beginning of 1963. The charts report the departure from actual developments resulting from the policy change. The simulations again reveal the effects of increases in defense spending, tax rates, and the reserves of the banking system—but they generally show a larger impact because interactions throughout the entire model are taken into account.

The increase in government defense expenditures of $5 billion results in a substantial pickup in GNP, which peaks after about a year. An induced rise in investment and consumption contributes to the expansion. The increased transactions demand for money causes a substantial rise in the Treasury bill rate, which induces an increase in rates on other financial assets, including the long-term bond rate, as it gradually percolates through financial markets. The high cost of capital eventually causes a turnaround in investment in housing, equipment, and plant. And this reduction in investment, when it comes, causes GNP to fall off somewhat from its second-year peak. As a result, consumption spending levels out in the third year instead of continuing to increase in a gradual response to the initial

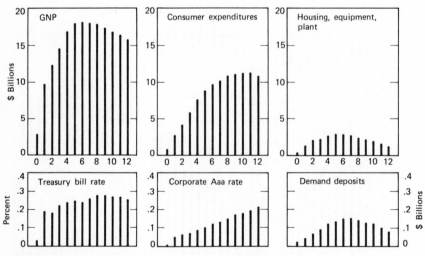

Fig. 17.7 *Defense expenditure increase of $5 billion, three blocks combined.*

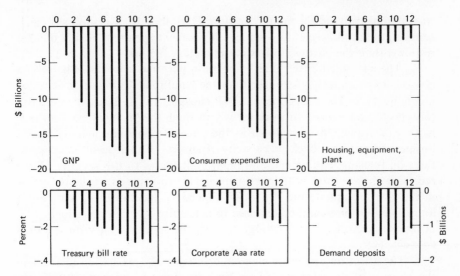

Fig. 17.8 *Personal tax rate increase of 0.02, three blocks combined.*

surge in output. Note that demand deposits increase in the first year and a half because the increased transactions demand dominates the rise in the bill rate. Indeed, it is the rising bill rate, by inducing banks to cut back on excess reserves, that allows the money supply to increase without any encouraging open market operations on the part of the Fed. But, toward the end of the simulation period, the cutback in GNP leads to a fall in the

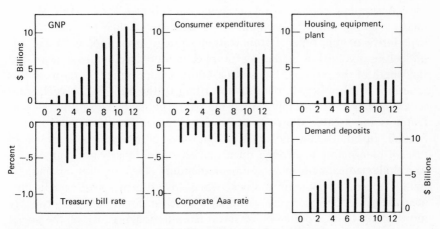

Fig. 17.9 *Reserve increase of $1 billion, three blocks combined.*

transactions demand for money. In sum, GNP initially overshoots because consumption and accelerator-induced investment spending have a quicker response than the partially offsetting monetary factors.

The simulated effect of an increase in personal tax rates, Figure 17.8 reveals, is substantially stronger than the "multiplier" simulation reported in Figure 17.2. The reduction in GNP causes a fall in interest rates. But this effect takes a while to work its way through the financial markets and, in the meantime, the slowdown in the pace of economic activity causes business firms to cut back on capacity expansion. The drop-off in expenditures on housing, equipment, and plant contributes to the severity of the recession. In the third year investment begins to respond to the reduction in the cost of capital, and it appears that GNP has bottomed out. But a longer simulation would be required to determine whether investment will, of its own accord, pick up enough to start the economy back on the road to recovery.

The effect on aggregate economic activity of a $1 billion increase in the reserves of the banking system brought about by open market operations is reported in Figure 17.9. As expected, interest rates fall substantially. And the resulting step-up in investment spending causes a substantial rise in GNP, which is further reinforced by the feedback of induced increases in consumption spending. The effect builds up gradually because of the lags involved in financial markets and in the delayed nature of the investment spending response, but after three years the $1 billion increase in reserves has induced an $11.2 billion increase in GNP. This contrasts with a $16 billion increase in GNP resulting after a year from a $5 billion increase in government defense spending. Dollar for dollar, an increase in reserves provides a bigger ultimate stimulus than an increase in defense spending, at least if the Fed-MIT simulations are to be believed.

A simple comparison of the dollar magnitudes of long-run government spending and reserve multipliers does not suffice to establish the superiority of one type of stabilization strategy over another. First, the difficulties involved in predicting future economic developments mean that the length of the response lag is of paramount importance. In terms of this criterion, fiscal policy dominates, according to the Fed-MIT model, since it takes effect more promptly than monetary policy. That is, the relevant factor is the greater short-run response of the economy to fiscal policy. Second, in comparing the dollar magnitudes of multipliers, a dollar of reserve manipulation through open market operations is not comparable to a dollar adjustment in government spending. They are not comparable units; indeed, reserves are a stock, while government spending is a flow measured in dollars per year. A dollar's worth of fiscal policy is probably more costly than a dollar of reserve manipulation because of the social costs incurred when government spending departs from the desired level prescribed by efficiency and welfare considerations. To some extent, government spending on certain projects can be accelerated in times of slump or postponed if the economy is overheating. And, on occasion, income tax refunds have been accelerated in order to stimulate the economy. But such flexibility is limited. On balance, a mixed strategy involving both monetary and fiscal policy probably dominates a pure strategy relying exclusively on either fiscal or monetary policy.[7]

e. Critique

How accurate are the simulations obtained with econometric models? A direct test would be possible if we could experiment on the real world by turning the clock back and reliving 1963–1964 with an additional $5 billion in government expenditure. But economists cannot conduct controlled experiments on the real world. Since it is possible to relive history only on the computer, there is no *direct* procedure for determining the precision with which simulation experiments reveal the effect of policy changes. However, there are a variety of testing strategies that help determine how much faith one should place in an econometric model's simulation results.

One test is simply to ask how reasonable the underlying equations of the model are. Of course, it will be recalled from the discussion of methodology in Chapter 1, Section 2 that no model can hope to capture the full complexity of reality. But other things being equal, we will be more inclined to believe the results of simulations derived with econometric models whose behavioral equations are consistent with what we know about the behavior of economic agents. In practice, however, the test almost inevitably results in controversy, because judgments concerning the realism of assumptions are inherently subjective.

A second test is to ask how well the model works when used to predict historical events. Dynamic predictions derived with the Fed-MIT econometric model for the last part of 1965 and 1966 are reported in Table 17.1. When two predictive series are presented, the second is based on only those equations included in the consumption-inventory block. For example, the second row of GNP change predictions are based on actual instead of predicted plants, equipment, and residential construction figures, because these variables are exogenous to the consumption sector. Since the second row of GNP predictions were derived with the actual values of the variables exogenous to the consumption sector, they should be more accurate than those obtained with the full model, but perhaps because of offsetting errors this expectation is not always realized.

All things considered, the Fed-MIT model predictions look fairly impressive. But, for comparison purposes, consider a naive forecaster who

[7] The more detailed discussion of the dynamics of stabilization policy in Appendix 16.A.4 reinforces the case for a mixed strategy.

Table 17.1   DYNAMIC PREDICTIONS, Fed-MIT MODEL (IN BILLIONS OF DOLLARS)

Item	1965 QIII	1965 QIV	1966 QI	1966 QII	1966 QIII	1966 QIV
GNP changes						
Actual	14.6	18.4	17.5	10.8	12.1	13.3
Calculated	15.3	18.7	16.0	10.7	9.5	7.4
Calculated, con-inv block	16.4	21.0	17.1	9.6	12.7	11.1
Consumer expenditures						
Actual	436.4	447.8	458.2	461.6	470.1	473.8
Calculated	441.1	450.3	460.1	466.7	473.8	479.7
Calculated, con-inv block	441.6	451.4	461.5	468.1	476.6	483.6
Residential construction						
Actual	26.4	26.2	26.5	25.3	23.2	20.4
Calculated	26.6	26.3	25.7	25.1	24.2	23.3
Producers' equipment and nonresidential structures						
Actual	71.9	75.8	78.3	78.7	81.3	82.8
Calculated	71.2	74.2	76.3	77.1	76.9	76.4
Inventory investment						
Actual	7.9	8.7	9.6	14.4	12.0	19.0
Calculated	5.4	9.8	10.4	10.6	7.0	6.6
Calculated, con-inv block	5.4	10.1	10.8	10.8	7.6	9.3
Demand deposits						
Actual	128.9	131.1	133.3	132.8	132.2	131.6
Calculated	129.1	130.8	132.2	132.3	132.5	132.8

always predicts same-as-last-quarter. For example, he predicts that GNP in 1966-1, will change by $18.4 billion because that was the 1965-4 change. In this quarter the naive forecaster will have done better than the dynamic prediction of $16.0 billion derived with the three blocks combined. Indeed, inspection of the table reveals that the naive forecaster would have done better than the model about half the time! While this is a disconcerting fact, it should be noted that the naive forecaster will never predict turning points in economic activity! And the naive forecaster provides an unfair yardstick with which to evaluate the model's performance, since his predictions are based on actual developments in the immediately preceding quarter. In contrast, the model's predictions were, in effect, all made in 1963, although the subsequent movement of the policy variables and other exogenous forces were presumed to be known precisely. Thus, with a longer forecasting horizon ranging from one to six quarters, the Fed-MIT model does about as well as a naive forecaster could in predicting one quarter into the future. Judged in this light, the forecasting achievement is not unreasonable, although there is obvious room for improvement.

A third test of an econometric model is to compare its simulations with those derived from other models. The simulations derived with any

Table 17.2 COMPARISON OF THREE-YEAR MULTIPLIERS OF DIFFERENT MODELS (RATIOS)

Model	Unborrowed Reserves	Defense Spending	Personal Tax Cut
Fed–MIT model	11.2	3.2	4.2
Brookings model	8.2	2.7	1.2
Wharton School model	2.9	2.9	2.4
Michigan model	n.a.	2.5	1.7

one model are likely to look quite impressive. But the policymaker who finds himself confronted with simulations from a variety of models is likely to feel uneasy if they yield quite different policy prescriptions. The authors of the Fed-MIT model compared three-year multipliers derived from their model with multipliers obtained with several other econometric models. The results are summarized in Table 17.2. All three of the Fed-MIT multipliers are larger than those of the other models. Evidently, the policy-maker who relied on the Fed-MIT model would be inclined to make less dramatic adjustment in his control variables—whichever stabilization weapon he decided to use—because less medicine would be required to achieve any desired impact. However, it is disconcerting to find such a wide range in the estimated tax-cut and bank-reserve multipliers. In part, the discrepancies may have arisen because the other models did not give sufficient consideration to the role of monetary factors. Furthermore, the simulations may not all have been based on precisely the same historical time period, and the degree of excess capacity at the time they are run will obviously influence the magnitude of the multipliers. Also, the Fed-MIT model used in these simulations—but not the more recent versions—treats price movements as exogenous, and this could lead to a discrepancy.[8]

*17.3 ACHIEVEMENTS AND PROSPECTS

How much has actually been accomplished by the econometric revolution sparked by Tinbergen's pioneering research? Thirty years ago it might not have seemed overly optimistic to hope that by now considerable

[8] See, for example, the simulations reported by Albert Ando and Franco Modigliani in "Econometric Analysis of Stabilization Policies," *American Economic Review*, pp. 296–314, 1969. Also, Frank de Leeuw and Edward M. Gramlich report the effects of additional simulations with an expanded Fed-MIT model incorporating a price sector in "The Channels of Monetary Policy" *Federal Reserve Bulletin*, pp. 472–491, June 1969.

progress would have been made in learning about the causes of the business cycle, in resolving questions of controversy concerning the structure of the economy, and in perfecting forecasting procedures. Hopefully, the perennial debate concerning the relative effectiveness of monetary and fiscal policy would have been resolved. And, perhaps most important of all, it might have been expected that econometric models would be providing an effective and reliable guide to fiscal and monetary policy, enabling us to achieve full employment without inflation. But it turns out that in all these areas the revolution is as yet incomplete. While substantial progress has been made, the complexities of the task are now more apparent than ever.

A major accomplishment has been achieved in the use of macroeconomic models in the simulation of the business cycle. Samuelson's simple multiplier-accelerator model, analyzed in Chapter 15, had provided a neat illustration of the way in which a set of linear structural equations can generate cyclical movements. But econometric models provide a much more realistic "rocking horse" for testing the degree of instability inherent in the modern industrial economy. A major contribution in this area was made by Irma and Frank L. Adelman in their investigation of "The Dynamic Properties of the Klein-Goldberger Model."[9] They found when they ran a 100-year simulation that there was no tendency to generate oscillatory movements; the cycle is not inherent in the economy's structure. They then subjected the Klein-Goldberger model to a very sharp shock by cutting government spending by about 25% for one year. This caused a very abrupt depression, and it took six years for the level of output to rise back to its former level, overshooting very slightly and reaching a very minor boom eight years after the initial drop in government spending. This cycle was unrealistic, because it was longer than those observed in practice and it was too highly damped. A third type of experiment did explain the cycle. By subjecting the economy to a stream of random shocks instead of a single disturbance, they generated a cycle which reproduced with remarkable clarity the major features of the business cycle as experienced by the American economy.[10] Subsequent research has confirmed as a major implication of econometric research that the cycle does not come about because of any inherent instability on the part of the economy. Furthermore,

---

[9] *Econometrica*, October 1959; see also John Cornwall, "Economic Implications of the Klein-Goldberger Model," *Review of Economics and Statistics*, May 1959; and Arthur Goldberger, *Impact Multipliers and Dynamic Properties of the Klein-Goldberger Model*, North Holland, 1959.

[10] The effects of random shocks on a money version of the multiplier-accelerator model were discussed in Appendix 16.B. Techniques developed at the National Bureau of Economic Research for measuring the duration, frequency, and intensity of the American cycle were used by the Adelmans in analyzing the data generated by their simulations.

the economy is so stable that it would not generate a chain of cyclical fluctuations from a rare and isolated large disturbance, for example, a war.
Instead, the cycle comes about because of a tendence for the economy's
structure to translate a stream of relatively minor and erratic shocks arising
from a variety of sources into roughly cyclical movements.[11]

There has been some progress in the direction of concensus on the
fundamental question of the relative potency of monetary and fiscal policy.
Many of the very early econometric models focused completely on fiscal
policy, leaving the central bank out of the story entirely. And this in itself
led to heated debate. Thus, at an NBER-sponsored conference in 1962,
Franco Modigliani, while observing that Lawrence Klein's latest econometric model included a number of equations devoted to a description of
money markets and the role of interest rates, objected that an insufficient
role was assigned to monetary forces. In response Klein argued:[12]

"My theoretical predilections are very much in favor of a theory of the *real* economy. The monetary economy, *if in good housekeeping order*, will not have a dominant influence on real affairs. Nevertheless, I have tried hard over the years, in
several models, to give the benefit of every doubt to money and interest rates when
making statistical estimates. My empirical verdict, thus far, is that little evidence
can be found for the actual influence of money or interest on real activity."

More recent investigation, much of it under the direct guidance of
Klein, has assigned a more prominent role to monetary variables, and it
is reasonable to say that the potency of monetary policy is no longer in
question. Monetary and fiscal variables both play an important role in
simulations obtained with more recent versions of the Wharton econometric
model. For example, Michael Evans reports that a rise in the discount rate

---

[11] Ragnar Frisch anticipated this explanation in a fundamental theoretical paper,
"Propagation Problems and Impulse Problems in Dynamic Economics," in *Essays in
Honor of Gustav Cassel*, George Allen and Unwin, Ltd., 1933, and reprinted in A.E.A.
Readings in Business Cycles, Klein, Gordon, eds., Irwin, 1965. Earlier it had been shown by
Eugen Slutsky that the successive averaging of a sequence of purely random numbers
could generate cyclical like waves: "The Summation of Random Causes as the Source of
Cyclical Processes," Conjuncture Institute of Moscow, 1932; also *Econometrica*, April
1937. For his simulation study Slutsky used random numbers generated in the execution of
the state lottery. Replications of the Adelmans' study on a variety of econometric models
were reported at a 1969 conference on *Econometric Models of Cyclical Behavior*, Studies
in Income and Wealth, No. 36, Bert G. Hickman, ed., NBER, 1932. It was found that
realistic fluctuations could be obtained if the disturbances were autocorrelated, which is a
property often indicated by the residuals of the behavioral equations. While the shocks
might be the result of wars and erratic fluctuations in fiscal and monetary policy, they
might arise as the consequence of innovations, in conformity with Joseph Shumpeter's
hypothesis about the origins of the business cycle.

[12] "A Postwar Quarterly Model: Description and Applications," in *Models of Income
Determination*, National Bureau of Economic Research, p. 56, 1964 (italics added).

of 2% coupled with a 5% increase in required reserves would induce a recession similar in magnitude to the ones actually observed in the post-World War II period. He warns, however, that in comparing alternative strategies for stimulating the economy, one must note that monetary policy takes much longer to work its way through the system, its largest effect not being induced until a year after the policy change. Furthermore, when monetary policy is used to stimulate the economy, the reduction in interest rates will involve the substitution of capital for labor, once the new machinery has been installed, which contributes to higher unemployment rates in the longer run. The case against monetary policy is not that it is ultimately ineffective, argues Evans, but that it is too slow and leads to an unfortunate substitution of capital for labor.[13]

Simulations with the Brookings-SSRC econometric model also support the potency of monetary policy. Gary Fromm ran a rich variety of simulations involving six types of policy changes: (1) an increase of $3.2 billion in government durable good purchases; (2) a reduction in personal income tax rates; (3) a cut in the discount rate of 1%; (4) a reduction in time deposit reserve requirements; (5) a reduction in demand deposit reserve requirements; and (6) an increase in unborrowed member bank reserves achieved through open market operations.[14] Fromm stresses that any one of these strategies can yield substantial gains in GNP. However, they involve substantial differences in the composition of GNP: about 90% of the increased GNP generated by a tax cut ends in higher consumption spending: only about 40% of the rise in GNP stimulated by an increase in government spending is available for consumers. Fromm considers a variety of competing criteria that might be used in ranking alternative stabilization strategies, and he concludes that the discount rate is a particularly fruitful policy weapon; he considers income tax rate adjustments as an inferior technique for stabilizing the economy.

A very different viewpoint has been set forth by Leonall C. Anderson and Keith M. Carlson of the St. Louis Federal Reserve Bank.[15] They present a monetarist model involving only five behavioral equations. The money supply summarizes monetary policy; they exclude such details as the discount rate, bank reserve ratios, and so forth—their effects are presumed to be captured by movements in M_1. The only fiscal variable in their model is the change in high-employment federal expenditures; that is, it is the level of federal spending on goods and services plus transfer pay-

---

[13] Michael Evans presents a lucid account of the Wharton School model in Chapter 20 of *Macroeconomic Activity: Theory, Forecasting and Control*, Harper and Row, 1969.

[14] See Gary Fromm, "An Evaluation of Monetary Policy Instruments," in *The Brookings Model: Some Further Results*, J. S. Duesenberry, G. Fromm, and L. R. Klein, and E. Kuh, eds., Rand McNally, 1969.

[15] "A Monetarist Model for Economic Stabilization," *Review, Federal Reserve Bank of St. Louis*, April 1970.

ments that would occur if the economy were operating at full employment.[16] Thus the fiscal variable ignores changes in the composition of government expenditure. And, while the cyclically induced movements in the government variable are removed, they remain in the money supply. Anderson and Carlson conclude that their estimates indicate a large and rapid influence of monetary actions on total spending relative to that of fiscal actions. On the other hand, with the money stock held constant, government spending has little or no net effect; specifically, an increase in government spending acts initially with positive force on total spending, but this is more or less offset by negative influences that leave little or no net impact after three quarters. In support of their model, they claim that while it is not designed for short-term forecasting, it performed reasonably well, relative to the Wharton school model, in ex post forecasts of the 1963–1964 period.[17]

In addition to questions of structure, there is room for disagreement with regard to the proper mix of policy weapons. If the lag between the application of the stabilization medicine and its effect is sufficiently long and variable, it may be advisable to pursue a hands off policy instead of trying discretionary stabilization strategy. Precisely this argument is used by the monetarists who contend that while the money supply is powerful, its lag is so long and variable that its discretionary adjustment in an attempt to stabilize the economy may do more harm than good. But, given the improvements that have been made in forecasting ability, the argument against discretionary policy has weakened somewhat over the years, although it is still not without force. But even if discretionary policy is to be abandoned, there is a question of *what* rule is most appropriate. J. Phillip Cooper and Stanley Fischer of the University of Chicago used a recent version of the Fed-MIT econometric model in analyzing this issue, concluding:

"A monetary rule using derivative controls—a systematic policy of leaning against the wind—would have reduced the variability of the rate of inflation and unem-

---

[16] Full-employment surplus concepts were discussed in Chapter 3, Section 6.

[17] In a subsequent paper Keith M. Carlson reported on their model's forecasting performance from the fourth quarter 1969 through the second quarter of 1971. He emphasized that the St. Louis model was not designed for quarter-to-quarter forecasting or predictions of the movement of the indivudual components of GNP. See his "Projecting with the St. Louis Model: A Progress Report," *Review*, Federal Reserve Bank of St. Louis, February 1972. A second "monetarist model" by Arthur B. Laffer and R. David Ranson also indicated that monetary policy has an immediate effect while federal purchases of goods and services have only a temporary impact. Both Laffer and Ranson served in the Office of Manpower and Budget, Washington, D.C. at the time their model appeared and it attracted a fair amount of attention within the administration; unfortunately, the predictive achievements of the model did not live up to expectations. Their paper, "A Formal Model of the Economy," appeared in the *Journal of Business*, July 1971.

ployment over the period 1956-1 to 1968-4 as compared with a constant growth rate rule. . . ."

Their simulations indicated that moderate departures from the constant growth rule are appropriate whenever the pace of inflation accelerates or the unemployment situation changes.[18]

To summarize, we now have a smörgasbord of econometric models representing a wide range of viewpoints, including contributions from the monetarists. And considerable improvement has been made in forecasting ability; while some of the earlier prototype models were so primitive that they did no better than naive same-as-last-period forecasts, the best of current models stand up very well against all but the most sophisticated extrapolative techniques.[19] Nonetheless, there is obvious disagreement concerning the appropriate structure of models and the relative effectiveness of alternative stabilization techniques. In prescribing policy it is necessary to consider what mix of policy will minimize uncertainty and how rapidly the medicine will take effect. One can also worry about how the policy will change the size of the government sector, the pace of investment spending, and the balance of payments. But, while monetarists still choose on occasion to condemn "Keynesian" viewpoints, in fact there is no strong support—if there ever was—for models denying the potency of monetary variables. The dominant position is occupied by models that regard *both* monetary and fiscal policy as powerful weapons.

[18] Their interesting results are reported in "Simulation of Monetary Rules in the Fed-MIT-Penn Model, *Journal of Money, Credit and Banking*, May 1972. Stochastic disturbances were not incorporated in their model, and the Adelman argument suggests that this may have affected the ranking of alternative monetary rules.

[19] The predictive abilities of econometric models have been appraised by both their authors and the critics. Carl F. Christ reported at length on the forecasting ability of Klein's model in "A Test of an Econometric Model of the United States, 1929–1947" in *Conference on Business Cycles*, National Bureau of Economic Research, 1951. His conclusion was contested because of certain deficiencies in the GNP accounts created by inflation for the years immediately after World War II. And, in a parallel study, executed 20 years later, Ronald L. Cooper provides a detailed report on "The Predictive Performance of Quarterly Econometric Models of the United States" in Bert G. Hickman, ed., *Econometric Models of Cyclical Behavior*, NBER, 1971. He found that no single model dominated the others in predicting all components of the GNP accounts; furthermore, no model dominated in all respects a purely mechanical forecasting procedure involving extrapolation from past experience. One index of the improvement achieved over the years is suggested by the fact that Cooper required a much more sophisticated "naive" forecaster in order to beat modern econometric models. Furthermore, his comparisons involved predicting only one quarter ahead, and it may well be that the econometric models do better than the extrapolative techniques when the forecasting horizon is longer.

REFERENCES

1. The art of econometric model building is cleverly displayed by Carl Christ, who shows, step by step, the practical problems involved. Klein discusses forecasting and simulation procedures. Kuh and Schmalensee develop a pedagogically oriented econometric model.

Carl Christ, "A Simple Illustrative Model of the United States Economy," Chapter 11 of *Econometric Methods and Models*, John Wiley and Sons, 1966.

Lawrence R. Klein, "Forecasting and Policy Evaluation Using Large Scale Econometric Models: The State of the Art," in *Frontiers of Quantitative Economics*, Michael D. Intriligator, ed., North Holland, 1971.

Edwin Kuh and Richard L. Schmalensee, *An Introduction to Applied Macroeconomics*, North Holland, 1973.

2. The Adelmans' study used the Klein-Goldberger model in simulating long-run properties of the business cycle. A number of papers in the work edited by Hickman update their results.

Irma Adelman and Frank Adelman, "The Dynamic Properties of the Klein-Goldberger Model, *Econometrica*, October 1959.

Bert G. Hickman, ed., *Econometric Models of Cyclical Behavior*, National Bureau of Economic Research, 1971.

3. How econometric models can be used in evaluating the economic effects of policy change is explained in two papers, both based on the Wharton econometric model.

Lawrence R. Klein, "Econometric Analysis of the Tax Cut of 1964," Chapter 13 of *The Brookings Econometric Model, Some Further Results*, Duesenberry, Fromm, Klein, and Kuh, eds., Rand-McNally, 1969.

Lawrence R. Klein and Kei Mori, "The Impact of Disarmament on Aggregate Economic Activity—An Econometic Analysis," in *Adjustments of the U.S. Economy to Reductions in Military Spending*, B. Udis, ed., U.S. Arms Control and Disarmament Agency, December 1970.

4. Here is a sample of econometric models.

James Duesenberry, Eckstein and Fromm, "A Simulation of the U.S. Economy in Recession," *Econometrica*, October 1960.

Daniel Suits, "Forecasting and Analysis with an Econometric Model," *American Economic Review*, March 1962.

T. C. Liu, "An Exploratory Quarterly Econometric Model of Effective Demand in the Postwar U.S. Economy," *Econometrica*, July 1963.

James Duesenberry, Fromm, Klein and Kuh, eds., *The Brookings Quarterly Econometric Model of the United States*, 1965.

Maurice Liebenberg, Albert Hirsch, and Joel Popkin, "A Quarterly Econometric Model of the United States," *Survey of Current Business*, May 1966.

Gregory Chow, "Multiplier, Accelerator, and Liquidity Preference in the Determination of National Income in the United States," *Review of Economics and Statistics*, February 1967.

Frank deLeeuw and Edward Gramlick, "The Federal Reserve-MIT Econometric Model," *Federal Reserve Bulletin*, January 1968.

Michael Evans and Lawrence Klein, *The Wharton Econometric Forecasting Model*, Studies in Quantitative Economics No. 2, Wharton School, University of Pennsylvania, 1968.

Leonall C. Andersen and Keith M. Carlson, "A Monetarist Model of Economic Stabilization," *Review of the Federal Reserve Bank of St. Louis*, April 1970.

KEY CONCEPTS

Jan Tinbergen

Brookings-SSRC

Fed-MIT

naive forecast

EXERCISES

17.1 Evaluate the following statement.

"In contrast to the entrepreneur of an earlier era, the business manager of the future will find his environment untroubled by periods of boom and bust; the business cycle is dead. Thanks to the computer, advances in the field of econometrics, the decisive evidence accumulated from empirical studies, the results of computer simulations, and the success in applying principles of control theory and techniques of production smoothing to macro-economic problems, economists now know how to stabilize the economy, to prevent depressions and control inflation. The fiscal and monetary authorities are now in a position to provide business with an environment characterized by full employment with stable prices."

growth and technological change

characteristics of the growth process

*18.1 INTRODUCTION

Modern economic growth dates as a distinctive epoch in economic organization from the eighteenth century. It has been said that in those economies now characterized as "developed," the majority of the population has experienced within the last 100 years a greater advance in material well-being than has occurred in any previous century in human history. Arnold Toynbee (1852–1883) coined the phrase "industrial revolution," arguing that the marked changes in social and economic conditions occurring in England from the mid-eighteenth to mid-nineteenth century deserve analysis as a unique historical event. The epoch of modern economic growth is distinguished by the fruition of the process of mechanization, the harnessing of energy resources, and the development of techniques of mass production. Simon Kuznets reports that output per capita in the United States has been growing at a per decade rate of 17.2% for more than a 100 years; in England output per decade grew at 14.1%; in Japan at 26.4% per decade; and since the Russian Revolution output in the Soviet Union has been growing at 27.4% per decade.[1] But the sweeping changes in our way of life involve much more than dramatic increases in the material standard of living. The proportion of the population enrolled in school in the United States has increased by 50% since early in the nineteenth century, while the death rate per 1000 has fallen by two thirds. There have been dramatic changes in occupational pursuits. Thus the percentage of the United States work force engaged in agricultural employment has fallen from about 70% to less than 5% during the last century or so.

During the past decade it has become more and more evident that growth may not be an unmixed blessing. As problems of pollution and crowding have become more and more obvious, it has frequently been suggested that growth itself may be obsolete. Certainly, the rates of growth

[1] Simon Kuznets, *Modern Economic Growth: Rate, Structure and Spread*, Yale University Press, 1966, pp. 64–65. The figures for the U.S. are for the period 1829 to 1960–62, for England from 1855–59 to 1957–59, for Japan from 1879–81 to 1959–61, and for the U.S.S.R. from 1913 to 1958.

in national product must not be confused with growth in economic welfare. The distinction has been analyzed by Professors Tobin and Nordhaus[2] of Yale, who derive a measure of economic welfare by subtracting from the standard national income accounts certain "instrumental" expenditures, such as defense and sanitation expenditures and an allowance for disamenities of urbanization, while adding on imputations for leisure and certain government services. According to their calculations, per capita economic welfare has been growing at 1.1% per annum since 1929, which is considerably less than the 1.7% per annum growth in per capita net national product. But, if the national income accountants have been overly optimistic, Tobin and Nordhaus have not found evidence to support the opposite fear that the gradual depletion of natural resources means growing shortages that will exert a severe drag on economic growth. Substitution of capital and labor for nature's resources plus the resource-saving characteristics of innovations will permit, if anything, a slight acceleration in the growth of per capita output.

In this and the following chapter we will look at four major macroeconomic contributions to our understanding of the process of economic growth. First, a discussion of Evsey Domar's analysis of the burden of the government's debt illustrates how certain events that appear inevitable within a stationary economy may be postponed indefinitely as long as the economy keeps expanding. Second, a look at Sir Roy Harrod's analysis of the "warranted rate of growth" will provide insight into circumstances in which the economy may be expected to grow exponentially. Third, we will look at the results obtained by Robert Solow in analyzing the extent to which the growth of the American economy should be attributed to capital accumulation and the extent to which it is the product of research and technological progress. The next chapter looks at the neoclassical analysis of the growth process in a fully employed economy. Then we will see how the rate of technological progress and the saving habits of consumers would influence the growth process if the central bank were to succeed in preserving the economy at full employment.

*18.2 THE BURDEN OF THE DEBT

One of the benefits of living in a growing economy is that it enables us to postpone indefinitely certain apparent consequences of our actions! As an example of this wondrous proposition, consider a government that continues to "live beyond its means" by spending each year more than it raises in tax revenue. The government debt thus increases without limit.

---

[2] James Tobin and William Nordhaus, "Is Growth Obsolete?" in *Economic Growth*, NBER's 50th Anniversary Colloquium Series, Vol. V, 1972.

Table 18.1   DEBT OF THE FEDERAL GOVERNMENT (AGGREGATE FIGURES QUOTED IN MILLIONS OF DOLLARS)

Year	Total Government Debt	Debt per Capita	Real per Capita Debt (1957–1959 = 100)	Debt/GNP Ratio %	Ratio of Interest Payments to Debt %	Ratio of Interest Payments to GNP %	Ratio of Interest Payments to Government Expenditure %
1900	$1,263	$17	$57.6	6.4	4.0	0.2	7.7
1905	1,132	14	45.3	4.3	2.8	0.09	4.3
1910	1,147	12	35.9	3.3	2.3	0.06	3.1
1915	1,191	12	33.89	3.0	2.4	0.06	3.0
1920	24,299	228	32.66	27.0	4.2	1.1	15.9
1925	20,516	177	289.7	22.0	4.4	1.0	28.8
1930	16,185	132	226.8	18.0	4.1	0.7	19.2
1935	28,701	226	472.8	40.0	3.0	1.1	12.6
1940	42,968	325	666.0	43.0	2.5	1.0	11.5
1945	258,682	1,849	2,949.0	122.0	1.4	1.7	3.7
1950	257,357	1,697	2,003.6	90.0	2.3	2.0	14.5
1955	274,374	1,660	1,779.2	69.0	2.3	1.6	9.9
1960	286,331	1,585	1,537.3	57.0	3.2	1.8	11.9
1965	317,274	1,631	1,484.1	46.0	3.6	1.6	11.7
1970	370,900	1,806	1,336.0	38.0	5.2	2.0	9.8

Sources. Statistical Abstract of the United States and *Long Term Economic Growth, 1860–1965*, Bureau of the Census.

But this means that the burden of interest payments to the country's creditors must also grow without limit. Deficit financing seems fraught with danger. Indeed, precisely this argument has been used by generations of conservative politicians in protesting that an imprudent government that insists on living beyond its means must inevitably end up spending its way into bankruptcy (Table 18.1). But Evsey Domar has argued:[3]

"A rising income is of course desired on general grounds, but in addition to its many other advantages it also solves the most important aspects of the problem of the debt. The faster income grows, the lighter the burden of the debt."

Let us investigate his argument.

Suppose that the government borrows a sum B_t each year to pay for the excess of its spending over revenue. Then the government's debt at the beginning of year t will be

$$D_t = D_{t-1} + B_{t-1}$$

$$= D_0 + B_0 + B_1 + \ldots + B_{t-1} = D_0 + \sum_{\tau=0}^{t-1} B_\tau \qquad (2.1)$$

---

[3] "The 'Burden of the Debt' and the National Income," *American Economic Review*, December 1944, as reprinted in his *Essays in the Theory of Economic Growth*, Oxford University Press, 1957.

where D_0 is the debt at time 0 (e.g., 1970). Suppose the amount borrowed is always some constant fraction of income

$$B_t = b Y_t \qquad (2.2)$$

so that

$$D_t = D_0 + b \sum_{\tau=0}^{t-1} Y_\tau \qquad (2.3)$$

Then, if income grows at a constant rate

$$Y_t = (1 + g) Y_{t-1} = (1 + g)^t Y_0 \qquad (2.4)$$

the government's debt at time t will be

$$D_t = D_0 + b Y_0 \sum_{\tau=0}^{t-1} (1 + g)^\tau \qquad (2.5)$$

Clearly, the debt is expanding without limit.

A government could try to evade the growing debt burden by lowering the rate of interest toward zero or by letting prices rise so that inflation can wipe out the purchasing power of its obligations. But, according to Domar's argument, it is not necessary for the government to "defraud" its creditors. The right-hand side of Equation 2.5 involves the sum of a geometric series, and this means that the expression for the debt simplifies to[4]

$$D_t = D_0 + b Y_0 \left[\frac{(1 + g)^t - 1}{g} \right] \qquad (2.6)$$

provided $g \neq 0$. So the ratio of the national debt to output will be

$$\frac{D_t}{Y_t} = \frac{D_0}{Y_t} + b \left(\frac{Y_0}{Y_t} \right) \left[\frac{(1 + g)^t - 1}{g} \right]$$

Substituting from Equation 2.4 yields

$$\frac{D_t}{Y_t} = \frac{D_0}{(1 + g)^t Y_0} + b \left[\frac{(1 + g)^t - 1}{g(1 + g)^t} \right]$$

$$= \frac{D_0}{(1 + g)^t Y_0} + b \left[\frac{1}{g} - \frac{1}{g(1 + g)^t} \right] \qquad (2.7)$$

[4] See footnote 7, p. 63.

Therefore, as we look further and further into the future, we find that $g > 0$ implies[5]

$$\lim_{t \to \infty} \frac{D_t}{Y_t} = \frac{b}{g} \qquad (2.8)$$

Thus, in the long run, the ratio of government debt to output approaches the ratio of the fraction of output borrowed by the government sector divided by the rate of output growth.

To summarize, the interest cost paid by the government for servicing the debt obviously grows without limit but, if the rate of interest remains constant at level r, the ratio of interest payments to the tax base approaches rb/g; this is the ratio of the interest cost of servicing the debt to output. As long as the economy continues to expand, deficit financing creates no major difficulty but, if the economy stops growing ($g = 0$), the ratio of debt and its servicing cost to the nation's output will be unbounded. If there is a limit to the nation's output, the government must sooner or later abandon its policy of deficit spending.

*18.3 THE WARRANTED RATE OF GROWTH

Is the economy likely to grow at a constant geometric rate? Sir Roy Harrod argued that it may have to if consumers and entrepreneurs are to be "content with what they are doing"—that is, if the public is to succeed in consuming the desired proportion of income and firms are to succeed in preserving the desired relationship between their stock of plant and equipment and the level of production.[6] How $(Y_t - Y_{t-1})/Y_t$, the growth rate, is influenced by the consumption habits of consumers and the desired capital/output ratio is explained by Harrod's model.

Harrod's proposition may be illustrated with a simple set of assumptions. Suppose that consumption is proportional to last period's output

$$C_t = cY_t \qquad (3.1)$$

---

[5] Because $1 + g > 1$, the expression $(1 + g)^t$ grows without limit as t gets larger and larger. Therefore, the first and last terms in Equation 2.7, which have $(1 + g)^t$ in the denominator, become insignificant (i.e., approach zero) with the passage of time.

[6] R. F. Harrod, "An Essay in Dynamic Theory," *The Economic Journal*, March 1939, pp. 14–33; see also Evsey D. Domar, "Capital Expansion, Rate of Growth, and Employment, *Econometrica*, April 1946, and Eric Lundberg, *Essays in the Theory of Economic Expansion*, 1937, fn., p. 185. A multi-sector growth model allowing for substitution was developed independently by John von Neumann, "A Model of General Economic Equilibrium," *Review of Economic Studies*, 1945.

Furthermore, in accordance with a very simple form of the accelerator (Chapter 6, Section 2), suppose that the desired capital stock is proportional to output

$$K_t^d = k Y_t \tag{3.2}$$

that is, k is the desired capital/output ratio or "capital coefficient." Finally, let us neglect government and international complications, so that aggregate demand is

$$Y_t = C_t + I_t \tag{3.3}$$

To see that this economy must grow at a constant rate in order to preserve the desired capital/output ratio k, first recall from Equation 3.2 that if $K_t = K_t^d$ at all times, net investment must be

$$
\begin{aligned}
I_t &= K_t^d - K_{t-1}^d \\
&= k(Y_t - Y_{t-1})
\end{aligned}
\tag{3.4}
$$

Furthermore, since Equations 3.1 and 3.3 give

$$Y_t - C_t = (1 - c)Y_t = I_t \tag{3.5}$$

the two behavioral equations imply

$$(1 - c)Y_t = k(Y_t - Y_{t-1}) \tag{3.6}$$

or

$$\frac{(1 - c)}{k} = \frac{Y_t - Y_{t-1}}{Y_t} \tag{3.7}$$

Our simple economy *must* grow at this specific rate if entrepreneurs are to preserve the desired capital/output ratio—if, as Harrod said, they are to "remain content with what they are doing."[7] This *warranted rate of growth* equals the marginal propensity to save $(1 - c)$ divided by the desired capital/output ratio (k).

One implication of Harrod's analysis is the proposition that rapid output growth requires a high propensity to save and/or a low desired capital/output ratio. The lower the capital/output ratio, the smaller proportion of output that must be set aside for investment instead of consumption. Thus Harrod's argument is just the reverse of the "underconsumption" theorists, who were concerned about a tendency for the economy to save too much. But, of course, Harrod was providing a description of how the economy would have to grow if entrepreneurs were to continuously preserve the desired capital/output ratio. In periods of economic depression this is not achieved; quite the contrary, the problem is one of coping with an excessive stock of capital.

[7] Ibid., p. 81.

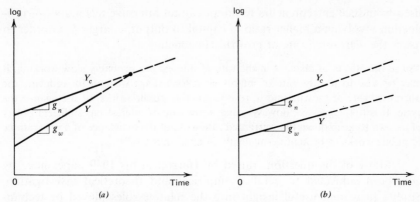

Fig. 18.1 *The natural versus the warranted rate of growth.* (*a*)
*Collision course: if the warranted growth rate exceeds the
natural rate, the warranted path inevitably collides with the
full-employment ceiling.* (*b*) *Stagnation course: if the natural
rate exceeds the warranted rate, the gap between capacity and
warranted output inevitably increases.*

Harrod was very pessimistic about the likelihood that a modern industrialized economy would succeed in maintaining the desired capital/
output ratio. He distinguished the *warranted rate of growth* required to
preserve the desired capital/output ratio from an alternative concept.[8]

". . . the *natural rate of growth* . . . is the maximum rate of growth allowed by the
increase in population, accumulation of capital, technological improvement and
the work/leisure preference schedule, supposing that there is always full employment. . . ."

The empirical counterpart to the natural rate of growth is the slope of the
path of potential GNP. Harrod could see no reason why the warranted
and natural rates would coincide. If the natural rate were less than the
warranted rate, the economy must sooner or later hit the capacity ceiling—
this collision course is illustrated in Figure 18.1. On the other hand, if the
natural rate exceeds the warranted rate, the growing gap between potential
and realized output must involve rising unemployment and stagnation.
Harrod did not believe that there were equilibrating economic forces contributing to full-employment growth by making the two rates coincide.
He thought that technological change would, on the average, be *neutral*
in that it would not change the desired capital/output ratio, at least given
the rate of interest. He did recognize that a low rate of interest might be

[8] Ibid., p. 30 (italics added).

used to induce entrepreneurs to adopt capital intensive techniques of production involving a higher ratio of capital to output, a larger k, in order to lower the warranted rate of growth. He concluded[9]

"Since the effects of changes in the rate of interest are probably slow-working, it may be wise to use the rate of interest as a long-range weapon for reducing the warranted rate of growth, and to reserve suitable public works for use against the cycle. It is not suggested, however, that a low rate of interest has sufficient power of its own to keep down the warranted rate without the assistance of a programme of public works to be kept permanently in operation. . . ."

Many of the questions raised by Harrod in his 1939 paper have by now been subjected to detailed empirical and theoretical investigation. Studies providing useful insight into the relative roles played by technological change and capital accumulation in explaining the growth of output achieved by the American economy are considered in the next section of this chapter. And Chapter 19 examines the way in which changes in the capital/output ratio may help to reconcile the natural and the warranted rates of growth.

†18.4 ON THE SOURCES OF CAPACITY GROWTH

A nation's output depends on its productive capacity as well as the proportion of its resources effectively put to work. Only in the short run can capacity be treated as given. For certain purposes it is both simple and useful to follow Okun's assumption that the gap between capacity and actual output is proportional to the unemployment rate. But any explanation of the long swings in a nation's development must involve a more detailed investigation of the sources of capacity growth. Professor Robert M. Solow has investigated the extent to which the growth of the American economy from 1909 to 1949 should be attributed to capital accumulation and the extent to which it has resulted from improvements in the techniques of production.[10] This question is of considerable policy interest. Definitely establishing that technological change plays the major role would imply that an increase in taxes used to subsidize research and development might make a decisive contribution to greater growth. But, if it turns out that investment is the decisive factor, then higher taxes, by discouraging thrift and investment, might also discourage economic development. If investment is the critical determinant, rapid growth might be encouraged by the investment tax credit and related subsidies to private investment spending.

[9] Ibid., p. 32.

[10] "Technical Change and the Aggregate Production Function," *Review of Economics and Statistics*, August 1957.

The problem posed by Solow is most easily visualized with the aid of Figure 18.2. Aggregate output and man-hours of labor, as shown in the first panel, were both much larger in 1949 than in 1909. In part, this added output is explained by the growing work force. But another input, the capital stock, was larger also. The data Solow used, which had been compiled by Raymond Goldsmith, indicated that the stock of capital had more

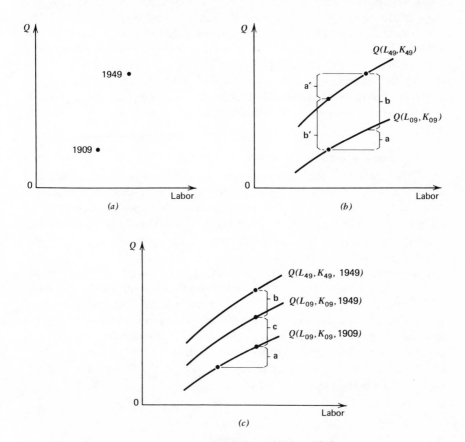

Fig. 18.2   *Sources of capacity growth.* (a) *From 1909 to 1949 the labor input increased by 54% and output increased by 216%.* (b) *If the growth in the capital stock of 102% shifted the production function as indicated,* a *would measure the contribution of increased labor and* b *the contribution of increased capital;* a' *and* b' *are alternative measures.* (c) *If part of the shift in the production function was due to technological change,* a *might indicate the contribution of increased labor,* b *the contribution of increased capital, and* c *the contribution of improved techniques of production.*

than doubled over the 40-year period under study. Because of the larger capital stock, the total product curve going through the 1949 point must be considerably higher than that going through the point for 1909. This is illustrated in the second panel of Figure 18.2. If the total product curve shifted as indicated on the figure, distance a (or a') might be attributed to the contribution of labor and distance b (or b') to the increase in the capital stock. But, in analyzing growth, it is essential to take the effects of improved ways of doing things into account. Because of technological advance the production function of 1949 might be quite different from what it was in 1909. If the total product curve had shifted as indicated on the third panel, c would measure the effect of technological change and a and b would be the revised estimates of labor and capital contributions. The empirical problem is to devise a reasonably precise way of decomposing the gains in output into the distinct contributions of labor, capital, and technological advance.

a. The Estimation Procedure

The procedure used by Solow is to estimate how much of an increase in output would have occurred from the increased inputs *if* they had been used without any improvement in technology. Subtracting this estimate from the observed increase in output leaves as a residual the improvement attributable to technological advance. But, in estimating the growth in output arising from the increased application of inputs, it is necessary to devise some way of combining the effects of increases in capital and in labor. Solow used a weighted average, with the weights determined on the basis of labor's and property's shares in national income. That is, instead of just taking a simple average of the 54% increase in labor and 102% increase in capital to obtain an estimate of the increase in combined inputs, it is assumed that each factor's relative contribution to the growth in output can be measured by the share of output received by labor and property owners.[11] Thus the basic formula is

$$\frac{\Delta Q}{Q} = \rho + \lambda \frac{\Delta L}{L} + \lambda' \frac{\Delta K}{K} \qquad (4.1)$$

where

λ is labor's share in national income
$\lambda' = 1 - \lambda$ is capital's share in national income
ρ indicates the contribution of technological advance

All elements of this equation are observable with the sole exception of ρ, the technological change residual. Output grew by 216% over the 40-year

---

[11] The rationale underlying this approach, which involves the assumptions of constant returns to scale and perfect competition, will be presented in a moment.

period (according to the data assembled by Solow). And λ, while ranging from a low of 0.603 in 1932 to a peak of 0.688 in 1946, averaged about $\frac{2}{3}$. Substituting the relevant information into Equation 4.1 yields

$$216\% = \rho + \tfrac{2}{3}\,54\% + \tfrac{1}{3}\,102\% \qquad (4.1')$$

Thus, growth in inputs would account for $\frac{2}{3}\,54\% + \frac{1}{3}\,102\%$ or 70% of output growth. Since output increased by 216% we have left a residual $\rho = 216\% - 70\% = 146\%$ as the estimated contribution of technological change. This means that the technological change factor accounted for about $\frac{2}{3}$ of the growth in output. Labor and capital made equal contributions, each accounting for about $\frac{1}{6}$ of output growth.

These estimates have to do with the growth of total output, but what about output per man-hour? This is the relevant concept for explaining improvements in the standard of living. The excess of the rate of increase in output over the rate of growth of manhours worked approximates the growth in output per worker.[12] Also, the excess of the rate of growth in the capital stock over the population growth rate approximates the growth in capital per worker. Therefore an expression for output per man-hour can be obtained by subtracting $\Delta L/L$ from both sides of Equation 4.1.

$$\left(\frac{\Delta Q}{Q} - \frac{\Delta L}{L}\right) = \rho + \lambda'\left(\frac{\Delta K}{K} - \frac{\Delta L}{L}\right) \qquad (4.2)$$

or more concisely

$$\frac{\Delta q}{q} = \rho + \lambda'\frac{\Delta k}{k} \qquad (4.3)$$

---

[12] That the excess of the rate of growth in output over the rate of growth in manhours is approximately the same as the rate of change in output per worker can be seen from the following calculation.

$$\frac{\Delta Q}{Q} - \frac{\Delta L}{L} = \frac{Q_t - Q_{t'}}{Q_{t'}} - \frac{L_t - L_{t'}}{L_{t'}} = \frac{Q_t}{Q_{t'}} - \frac{L_t}{L_{t'}}$$

$$= \left[\frac{Q_t/L_t}{Q_{t'}/L_{t'}} - 1\right]\frac{L_t}{L_{t'}} = \left(\frac{q_t - q_{t'}}{q_{t'}}\right)\frac{L_t}{L_{t'}}$$

$$= \frac{\Delta q_t}{q_t}\frac{L_t}{L_{t'}}$$

Here the change is taken over the period t' to t and we define $q_t = Q_t/L_t$. The approximation is inexact when the ratio of $L_t/L_{t'}$ departs substantially from unity; thus it is not likely to be close over the 40-year period used here for illustrative purposes. This is one reason why Solow's calculations, based on annual data, are more exact; his results are discussed later in this section. And elementary calculus assures us that the relationship holds exactly in the limit as $t-t'$ approaches zero. Precisely the same argument yields

$$\frac{\Delta K}{K} - \frac{\Delta L}{L} = \frac{\Delta k_t}{k_t}\frac{K_t}{K_{t'}}$$

where $k_t = K_t/L_t$.

where

$$q \text{ is output per worker } (Q/L)$$

$$k \text{ is capital per worker } (K/L)$$

and

$$\frac{\Delta Q}{Q} - \frac{\Delta L}{L} = \frac{\Delta q}{q}$$

$$\frac{\Delta K}{K} - \frac{\Delta L}{L} = \frac{\Delta k}{k}$$

Using the same data as before,

$$\frac{\Delta q}{q} = 216\% - 54\% = 162\%$$

$$\frac{\Delta k}{k} = 102\% - 54\% = 48\%$$

$$\frac{\Delta q}{q} = 162\% = \rho + \tfrac{1}{3}\,48\% \qquad (4.3')$$

According to these calculations, about $\frac{1}{2}$ of the increase in the capital stock was absorbed in simply keeping pace with the expanding labor force. Capital accumulation increased output per worker by only

$$\lambda' \frac{\Delta k}{k} = \tfrac{1}{3}\,48\% = 16\%$$

That the technological change residual left in this expression must be precisely the same as that obtained before, $\rho = 146\%$, can be seen from Equation 4.2. Thus about $\frac{9}{10}$ of the 162% increase in output per worker is attributable to technological advance (ρ); only a relatively small proportion was the contribution of the rise in capital per worker.

b. Results, Qualifications, and Elaborations

Solow's computations were more precise than these illustrative figures because he worked on a year-to-year basis with annual data. This meant that he was able to take account of the variation in labor's share from one year to the next. It also meant that he was able to construct a time series revealing annual fluctuations in the rated technological advance. His computations, based on Equation 4.3, revealed that about $\frac{7}{8}$ of the increase in gross output per man-hour should be attributed to technological change and only $\frac{1}{8}$ to increased capital per worker. And he found that the rate of technological advance was about 1% per annum during the first two decades and about 2% during the last half of the 40-year period.

Solow's estimates are startling, because they suggest that economic growth is to be explained largely by improved production techniques instead of by the thrift of savers and the courage of investors. Does this mean that developing nations need only borrow our technological know-how in order to catch up? Does it mean that high taxes to finance increase government subsidies of research and development—R&D expenditure—will add a further stimulus to growth? Because these policy issues are as controversial as they are important, Solow's research strategy deserves careful scrutiny.

First, is it appropriate to weight the change in each input by its share in national income? That is, are these factors rewarded in proportion to their contribution to the growth process? The answer is yes, provided the economy is competitive and characterized by constant returns to scale; but the proof is tedious, since it involves three distinct steps. Consider first the aggregate production function $Q(L, K, t)$. Then if one is familiar with the "chain rule" of calculus, the change in output with respect to time is easily verified to be

$$\frac{dQ}{dt} = \frac{\partial Q}{\partial L}\frac{dL}{dt} + \frac{\partial Q}{\partial K}\frac{dK}{dt} + \frac{\partial Q}{\partial t} \tag{4.4}$$

Here dQ/dt, the total growth of output, is the result of three components of the growth process. The first component is caused by the growth of the labor force, dL/dt; this is multiplied by the partial derivative $\partial Q/\partial L$, which is the marginal product of labor. The second component, $(\partial Q/\partial K)$ (dK/dt), is the marginal product of capital times the change in capital stock. The final term shows the amount by which output would have increased even in the absence of labor and capital growth; that is, the partial derivative $\partial Q/\partial t$ is the technological shift in the production function. The second step in deriving Equation 4.1 is to obtain the rate of change in output. Dividing Equation 4.4 by output leads to

$$\frac{dQ/dt}{Q} = \frac{\partial Q}{\partial L}\frac{L}{Q}\left(\frac{dL/dt}{L}\right) + \frac{\partial Q}{\partial K}\frac{K}{Q}\left(\frac{dK/dt}{K}\right) + \left(\frac{dQ/dt}{Q}\right) \tag{4.5}$$

The third and final step is to suppose that labor and capital markets are competitive. Under competition workers are hired to the point at which the real wage is equated with the marginal productivity of labor; that is, $w^r = w^n/p = \partial Q/\partial L$. But this means that the coefficient $(\partial Q/\partial L)(L/Q)$ in Equation 4.5 is labor's share (λ). Similarly, with competitive capital markets we must also have $(\partial Q/\partial K)(K/Q) = \lambda'$. All this means that Equation 4.5 reduces to Equation 4.1, as required.[13]

A second and quite profound issue raised by Solow's approach concerns the proper interpretation of the "technological change" residual. Because the labor input is measured in terms of man-hours, there is no allowance for changes in worker efficiency. The man-hour measure makes no allowance for a gradual upgrading of workers—fewer laborers and more skilled craftsmen, the gains arising from improved managerial techniques, and so forth. Also, when the labor input is measured in terms of man-hours, the gradual increase in the number of years that the average worker has attended school is left to be picked up by ρ. One alternative would be to regard education as an investment in "human capital" and include it in K; but a preferred procedure is to abandon the manhour labor measure in favor of units appropriately adjusted for improvements in worker productivity. Dale Jorgenson and Zvi Griliches argue that when both the labor and the capital inputs are measured in efficiency units that adjust for improvements in quality practically all of the growth in output can be explained without resorting to a "technological change" residual.[14] That is, when the effects of technological change and quality improvement are appropriately taken into account in measuring inputs, shifts in the production function are not required to explain the growth in aggregate output.

A third question involves the interaction between technological change and capital accumulation. The adoption of technological improvements often requires entirely new plant and equipment. In the absence of

---

[13] Strictly speaking, the calculus justifies the use of Equation 4.1 only for infinitesimal changes; presumably, changes from one year to the next are small enough to yield a reasonably good approximation. This helps make the detailed calculations done by Solow with annual data more reliable than those used for illustrative purposes with data covering the entire 40 years. It should be noted, however, that several difficulties are encountered if the production function does not involve constant returns to scale. If there are increasing returns to scale the "technological change" term will slop up part of the gains resulting from increasing doses of capital and labor that should rightfully be attributed to increasing returns: the distinction between technological change and increasing returns to scale is an operational one, since the gains from increasing returns to scale would be lost if the economy shrunk, because of recession or a decline in population, while the gains from improved technology are irreversible. A second problem, discussed in detail in microeconomic textbooks, arises because with either increasing or decreasing returns, $\lambda + \lambda'$ would depart from unity if the factors were rewarded, as under competition, in proportion to their marginal product. Indeed, in an industry characterized by a production function homogeneous of any degree other than one the optimal size of a price-taking (competitive) firm is either infinitesimal or infinite.

[14] "The Explanation of Productivity Change," *Review of Economic Studies*, July 1967; see also the subsequent discussion with Edward F. Denison in *The Survey of Current Business*, May 1972.

net investment, such "embodied" improvements could be adopted only as rapidly as the wearing out of old plant and equipment called for replacement. Part of the contribution of capital accumulation is to allow for the adoption of new techniques of production.

When such qualifications are taken into account, it becomes clear that the estimates provided by Solow probably place an upper bound on the magnitude of the contribution made by technological advance to the process of economic growth.

REFERENCES

1. All of the following papers are concerned with measuring the contribution of technological change to economic growth.

   M. J. Beckmann and R. Sato, "Aggregate Production Functions and Types of Technical Progress: A Statistical Analysis," *American Economic Review*, March 1969.

   Edward F. Denison, "How to Raise the High-Employment Growth Rate by One Percentage Point," *American Economic Review*, May 1962.

   Robert Solow, "Technological Change and the Aggregate Production Function," *Review of Economics and Statistics*, August 1957.

   D. W. Jorgenson and Z. Griliches, "The Explanation of Productivity Change," *Review of Economic Studies*, July 1967.

2. The following papers are concerned with the burden of the national debt.

   Peter Diamond, "National Debt in a Neoclassical Growth Model," *American Economic Review*, December 1965.

   Franco Modigliani, "Long-run Implications of Alternative Fiscal Policies and the Burden of the Debt," *Economic Journal*, December 1971.

KEY CONCEPTS

debt burden

servicing the debt

warranted rate of growth

natural rate of growth

technological change residual

human capital

embodied technological change

EXERCISES

18.1 If the desired capital/output ratio is 2 and 90% of output is consumed, what is the warranted rate of growth?

18.2 Evaluate each of the following statements.

   a. "Only a matter of lags distinguishes the Harrod growth model from the Samuelson multiplier-accelerator business cycle model."

   b. "A penny saved is not a penny earned, since an increase in the propensity to save will reduce the equilibrium growth rate of the economy."

growth under full employment

*19.1 INTRODUCTION

Explaining the process of economic growth is a task that has attracted the attention of economists from the very beginnings of our science. The Reverend Thomas Malthus (1775–1834) argued that population, when unchecked, grows geometrically—2, 4, 8, 16—while the means of subsistence at best increases arithmetically—2, 4, 6, 8. Unless preventive measures check the rate of population growth, war, famine, and pestilence must serve to restrict the growth of population to the limit imposed by the arithmetic rate of growth of the means of subsistence. Malthus also opposed the Poor Laws on the grounds that charity, public or private, only aggravates the problem of overpopulation. In more refined analyses, Ricardo (1772–1823) and Mill (1806–1873) argued that the law of diminishing returns meant that in the long run the economy would inevitably stagnate in a stationary state characterized by a zero rate of growth and a subsistence standard of living. Karl Marx (1818–1883) argued that the capitalistic system contains the seeds of its own destruction, that the process of capital accumulation leads to a growing army of unemployed, to economic crises of increasing intensity, to the inevitable collapse of the capitalistic system, revolution, and the establishment of the communist society.

In the depths of the Great Depression many interpreted the rising tide of unemployment as verification of the Marxist predictions. And Sir Roy Harrod warned of the obstacles involved in reconciling the warranted with the natural rate of growth. But the happier experience of the American economy since World War II has led to a more optimistic "neoclassical" theory of economic growth. The pioneering contributions in the 1950s of James Tobin,[1] T. W. Swan,[2] and Robert Solow[3] allowed the capital/output

---

[1] "A Dynamic Aggregative Model," *Journal of Political Economy*, pp. 103–115, April 1955.

[2] "Economic Growth and Capital Accumulation," *Economic Record*, pp. 334–361, November 1956.

[3] "A Contribution to the Theory of Economic Growth," *Quarterly Journal of Economics*, pp. 65–94, February 1956.

511

ratio to adjust so as to equate the warranted and natural growth rates. The neoclassical analysis suggests that even with diminishing returns, sufficiently rapid technological advance may insure the arrival of a "Golden Age" characterized by full employment and a continuing growth of real output.

In order to summarize the major themes of neoclassical growth theory it will first be necessary in Section 2 to spell out the basic behavioral assumptions underlying the analysis. Then we will describe how the economy would develop with the passage of time *if* prices and interest rates continuously adjusted so as to always maintain the economy at full employment. In particular, we will inquire into the factors that determine how rapidly the economy would grow and how income per capita would change if the fiscal and monetary authorities successfully pursued a full-employment policy.[4] Considerable effort must be invested in mastering the analysis of full-employment growth equilibrium presented in Sections 3 and 4. But the effort is amply rewarded in Section 5, where the apparatus will be focused on fundamental questions of economic policy. We will investigate the way in which wages and prices must adjust if the postulated full-employment conditions are to be maintained. We will examine the proposition that a money supply expanding at the long-run equilibrium rate of economic growth would contribute to stable expansion without inflation. We will also analyze the type of monetary and fiscal adjustments that would be required in order to preserve full employment if the pace of technological advance accelerates or the rate of population growth declines.

19.2 ASSUMPTIONS

In order to demonstrate the possibility of full-employment growth, let us follow Malthus in assuming that the population grows geometrically. Let P denote population and n its natural rate of growth;[5] then, letting a

---

[4] How difficult a task this is, constitutes a matter for debate that need not detain us at this point. While the question of how an economy would evolve under conditions of full employment is of obvious interest to anyone who adheres to Jean Baptist Say's dictum that "production creates its own demand," one need not assume that full employment is a natural state of affairs that would be maintained if only the government would pursue a hands-off policy. The neoclassical growth model is particularly relevant for anyone interested in the question of what would happen if the Fed were successful in executing a full-employment monetary policy.

[5] When Malthus wrote the world had only 1 billion inhabitants. The population had doubled to 2 billion by 1930, after more than 100 years. The world had three billion by 1960, and the United Nations estimates that the fourth billion inhabitant is due in 1975, the fifth in 1989, and the sixth 10 years after that. In fact, then, the world's population may grow at an increasing rate instead of geometrically.

dot over a variable indicate its first derivative with respect to time, we have

$$\frac{\dot{P}}{P} = \frac{dP/dt}{P} = n \qquad (2.1)$$

Furthermore, suppose that η, the proportion of the population in the labor force, is constant. Then, if the economy is to remain at "full" employment, characterized by say a 4% allowance for frictional factors, the level of employment at any point of time,[6] denoted by N, must be

$$N = (1 - 0.04)\eta P \qquad (2.2)$$

But, from Equation 2.1, we have at once that $\dot{N}/N = n$, and by integration,

$$N = N_0 e^{nt} \qquad (2.3)$$

where N_0 denotes full employment at time zero.[7] Thus Equation 2.3 reveals the number of workers who must have jobs if full employment is to be maintained in a society whose population grows at rate n. Obviously, in the special case of *zero population growth*, $n = 0$ and $N = N_0$.

The potential output that can be achieved by utilizing these N workers depends on both the form of the production function and the supply of other productive resources. It is convenient to be explicit about the form of the production function; suppose that aggregate output Q, net of depreciation, is

$$Q = ae^{\rho t}N^{\lambda}K^{\lambda'}R^{(1-\lambda-\lambda')}, \qquad \rho \geq 0$$
$$0 < \lambda < 1$$
$$0 < \lambda' < 1$$
$$\lambda + \lambda' \leq 1 \qquad (2.4)$$

Here K is the physical stock of capital (e.g., machinery). R is the supply of fixed resources, traditionally conceived of as land but lending itself to a more generic interpretation incorporating other limited resources, such as the atmosphere. The term $e^{\rho t}$ allows for technological advance; because of improvements in the state of the arts, the level of output that can be obtained with a given amount of capital, labor, and land increases at rate ρ with the passage of time. Note that this production function is homogeneous of degree one (constant returns to scale) with respect to labor, capital, and land; if at any point of time the quantity of these factors could be doubled, output would double as well. But, since the supply of land is fixed, the pro-

---

[6] The rate of 4% is optional, since the analysis that follows holds for any fixed unemployment rate.

[7] For a discussion of geometric growth and the constant e see Appendix 2.C, particularly Section 4.

514   Growth Under Full Employment   CH. 19

duction function is not homogeneous of degree one with respect to the variable resources, labor and capital (unless $\lambda + \lambda' = 1$). Furthermore, we have diminishing returns with respect to both variable resources; for example, given the quantity of K and R, output will increase at a slower rate than N. Because R is fixed, it proves convenient to rewrite the production function as

$$Q = Ae^{\rho t}N^\lambda K^{\lambda'} \tag{2.4'}$$

where $A = aR^{(1-\lambda-\lambda')}$.

Finally, let us make consumption and government spending proportional to net output Q. Specifically, suppose that disposable income $Y_d = (1 - \tau)Q$; where τ is the tax rate; consumption is $C = c_1 Y_d$ and government spending is $G = c_2 Q$. Then, neglecting foreign-trade complications, the national income accounting identity becomes $Q = C + I + G = c_1(1 - \tau)Q + c_2 Q + I$, and we have net investment of

$$\dot{K} = I = sQ \tag{2.5}$$

where $s = 1 - c_1(1 - \tau) - c_2$ is the *gross savings ratio*. Needless to say, Equation 2.5 is *not* an equation explaining the behavior of those who make investment decisions. Instead, it prescribes how investment must behave if effective demand is to equal full-employment output Q. It will be useful to note that, since $\dot{K} \equiv dK/dt = I$, we have, on dividing Equation 2.5 by K:

$$\frac{\dot{K}}{K} \equiv \frac{dK/dt}{K} = s\frac{Q}{K} \tag{2.6}$$

The rate of change of the capital stock depends on the gross savings ratio and the output/capital ratio.

19.3 FULL-EMPLOYMENT GROWTH EQUILIBRIUM

Let us now analyze the nature of the growth process under the assumption that the market mechanism, aided by appropriate monetary policy, succeeds in inducing the precise amount of investment required to keep the economy always at full employment. We will find that if sufficient investment is forthcoming, output can grow at a constant equilibrium rate, call it q^e, given the magnitude of the tax rate, government spending, and the other parameters of the equations of Section 2. Not only is this equilibrium growth rate unique; it is also stable. This result implies that, if a full employment policy were successfully followed, the economy would eventually grow at the rate q^e. In a later section we will examine how wages and interest rates must behave if the economy's full-employment growth potential is to be realized.

How rapidly output grows can be determined by summing the effects of three fundamental forces.

$$q \equiv \frac{\dot{Q}}{Q} - \frac{dQ/dt}{Q} = \rho + \lambda n + \lambda' \frac{\dot{K}}{K} \qquad (3.1)$$

This basic equation explains the rate of growth in output in terms of technological change (ρ), labor force growth (n), and the rate of growth of the capital stock ($\dot{K}/K$). The equation can be obtained by differentiating Equation 2.4' with respect to time.

$$\dot{Q} = \rho Q + \frac{\partial Q}{\partial N}\frac{dN}{dt} + \frac{\partial Q}{\partial K}\frac{dK}{dt} = \rho Q + \lambda \frac{Q}{N}\frac{dN}{dt} + \lambda' \frac{Q}{K}\frac{dK}{dt} \qquad (3.2)$$

Dividing by Q yields Equation 3.1.

Only the last term in Equation 3.1, the rate of growth of capital, is endogenously determined. How rapidly capital grows depends on the level of output and the fraction of it that is saved; remembering from Equation 2.5 that $\dot{K} \equiv I = sQ$, we have

$$q \equiv \frac{\dot{Q}}{Q} = \rho + \lambda n + \lambda' \frac{sQ}{K} \qquad (3.3)$$

How rapidly output grows depends on the rate of technological advance, the rate of growth of the labor force, the savings rate, and the output/ capital ratio. And unlike Harrod's model, the output/capital ratio is itself free to change instead of being exogenously determined.

The analysis is clarified by considering Figure 19.1. Rates of growth are measured on the ordinate and the output/capital ratio on the abscissa. We will plot various curves indicating the contributions to economic growth of the various forces summarized by Equation 3.3. The distance "0-n" indicates the rate of growth of the labor force and the horizontal line λn the contribution of this growing labor force to expanding output; the labor contribution line is horizontal because this contribution is insensitive to the output/capital ratio. The positively sloped line starting at point λn indicates the combined contribution to economic expansion made by the growing labor force and investment, where the latter contribution hinges (given the savings ratio) on the magnitude of the output/ capital ratio. Finally, the line $\dot{Q}/Q$ which adds the contribution of technological change, shows how the rate of economic growth depends on the Q/K ratio.

It is clear from the graph and from Equation 3.3, that if output is to grow at a constant rate, the output/capital ratio must be constant as well. But if the ratio of output to capital is to remain constant, both capital and

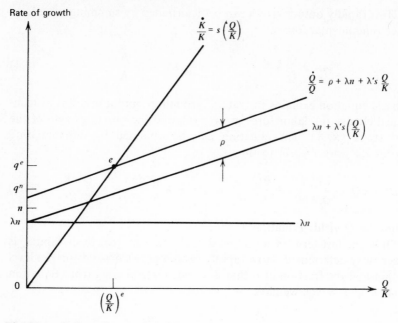

Fig. 19.1   *Full-employment equilibrium growth rate.*

output must be growing at the same rate.[8] Now Equation 2.6 reveals that the rate of growth of the capital stock depends on the output/capital ratio; specifically, $\dot{K}/K = I/K = sQ/K$. This is the steeply sloping line in Figure 19.1. Only at point e, where the $\dot{Q}/Q$ and $\dot{K}/K$ lines intersect, can the output/capital ratio remain constant. Thus q^e is the equilibrium full-employment growth rate. All this may be seen more formally by substituting q^e for $\dot{Q}/Q$ and $\dot{K}/K$ in Equation 3.1.

$$q^e = \rho + \lambda n + \lambda' q^e \qquad (3.4)$$

or

$$q^e = \frac{\rho + \lambda n}{1 - \lambda'} \qquad (3.5)$$

Clearly, there exists only one constant rate at which the economy can grow under conditions of full employment. Note, too, that this equilibrium rate of growth may be faster or slower than the rate of growth of population. Specifically, for output to grow faster in equilibrium than the popu-

[8] To verify that

$$\frac{d(Q/K)}{dt} = \frac{dQ}{dt}\frac{1}{K} - \frac{dK}{dt}\frac{Q}{K^2} = \frac{\dot{Q}}{K} - \frac{\dot{K}Q}{K^2} = 0$$

implies $\dot{Q}/Q = \dot{K}/K$, simply multiply through by the ratio K/Q.

lation, we must have $n < q^e = (\rho + \lambda n)/(1 - \lambda')$ or $\rho > (1 - \lambda - \lambda')n$. However, with zero population growth ($n = 0$), per capita output necessarily grows if there is technological progress. In the absence of technological change, the fully employed economy is capable of growing steadily at the same rate as the labor force only if the production function is homogeneous of degree one with respect to capital and labor, the two variable inputs. If $\lambda + \lambda' < 1$ and technological change were absent ($\rho = 0$), output would grow less rapidly than the labor force and per capita output would fall with the passage of time. Eventually, the Malthusian checks of hunger, pestilence, and war would have to intervene in order to drive the population growth rate below its natural rate, n.

The surprising thing about the equilibrium growth rate is that it depends only on the parameters of the production function and the rate of population growth. The gross savings rate (s) has no effect on the equilibrium growth rate! But this does *not* mean that changes in s, induced by fiscal policy or other forces, are of no importance. First, the gross savings ratio influences the magnitude of the equilibrium output/capital ratio. This may be seen by dividing both sides of the second equality of Equation 2.5 by Ks, obtaining, with Equation 3.5,

$$\left(\frac{Q}{K}\right)^e = \frac{I}{Ks} = \frac{\dot{K}}{Ks} = \frac{q^e}{s} = \frac{\rho + \lambda n}{s(1 - \lambda')} \tag{3.6}$$

as the output/capital ratio that must prevail if the economy is to grow at the equilibrium rate. Furthermore, s affects the level of output at any point of time at which the economy is growing at its equilibrium rate. To see this, note that Equation 2.4' implies

$$Q = A^\alpha e^{\rho \alpha t} N^{\lambda \alpha} \left(\frac{K}{Q}\right)^{\lambda' \alpha} \tag{3.7}$$

where we define

$$\alpha \equiv \left(\frac{1}{1 - \lambda'}\right)^9$$

Now, if our fully employed economy is growing at a constant rate, the *capital-output* ratio is s/q^e from Equation 3.6; therefore we have from the right-hand side of Equation 3.7 that the equilibrium output is

$$Q^e = A^\alpha e^{\rho \alpha t} N^{\lambda \alpha} \left(\frac{s}{q^e}\right)^{\lambda' \alpha} = A^\alpha e^{\rho \alpha t} N^{\lambda \alpha} \left[\frac{(1 - \lambda')s^\alpha}{\rho + \lambda n}\right]^{\lambda' \alpha} \tag{3.8}$$

which clearly depends on the gross savings ratio, s.

---

[9] To see this, write the production function as $Q = Q^{\lambda'} Q^{(1-\lambda')} = A e^{\rho t} N^\lambda K^{\lambda'}$. Dividing both sides of the second equality by $Q^{\lambda'}$ yields $Q^{1-\lambda'} = A e^{\rho t} N^\lambda (K/Q)^{\lambda'}$. Equation 3.7 now follows at once by raising both sides to the power α.

†19.4 STABILITY OF THE FULL-EMPLOYMENT GROWTH PATH

The equilibrium full-employment growth path, characterized by a constant rate of economic expansion, would be of little interest if it were unstable. Fortunate it is stable, and this means that the equilibrium growth path is of interest even for a "young" country characterized by a high output/capital ratio. In Figure 19.2, where the dotted line represents the equilibrium growth path given by Equation 3.8, point a represents the position of an economy with an output/capital ratio above the equilibrium value. Since Q/K is excessive, the country's actual output must be below the equilibrium path, as Equation 3.7 suggests, for the exogenously determined work force is being utilized with insufficient capital. But it is easy to show that the economy's output will be growing more rapidly than the equilibrium rate q^e, and that with the passage of time the path of actual output will tend to catch up with the equilibrium growth path—line Q^e in Figure 19.2. To verify this, consider Figure 19.3, where the $\dot{Q}/Q$ and $\dot{K}/K$ lines are reproduced from Figure 19.1. If the output/capital ratio is too high, as at point a, both output and capital grow faster than the equilibrium rate q^e. But the capital stock is growing even faster than output, and so the Q/K ratio gradually falls towards the equilibrium value, $(Q/K)^e$.

The fact that the output/capital ratio necessarily converges to its equilibrium value can be seen more formally as follows. From Equations 3.3 and 2.6 we can obtain

$$\left(\frac{\dot{Q}}{K}\right)\bigg/\left(\frac{Q}{K}\right) \equiv \frac{d(Q/K)}{dt}\bigg/\frac{Q}{K}$$

$$= \frac{\dot{Q}}{Q} - \frac{\dot{K}}{K}$$

$$= \rho + \lambda n + \lambda' s \frac{Q}{K} - s \frac{Q}{K} = \rho + \lambda n - s(1 - \lambda')\frac{Q}{K} \quad (4.1)$$

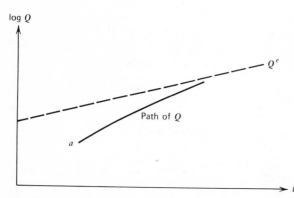

Fig. 19.2   *Full-employment growth path.*

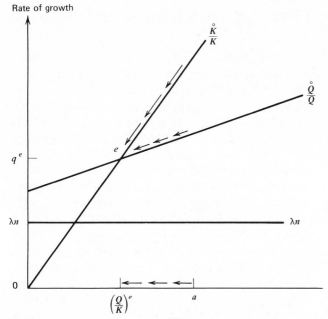

Fig. 19.3 *Convergence to equilibrium.*

Substitution from Equation 3.6 reveals

$$\left(\frac{\dot{Q}}{K}\right)\Big/\left(\frac{Q}{K}\right) = s(1 - \lambda')\left[\left(\frac{Q}{K}\right)^e - \frac{Q}{K}\right] \qquad (4.2)$$

Thus the rate of change of the output/capital ratio is proportional to the gap between the equilibrium and current magnitude of the ratio. This is the famous *Logistic Law of Growth*, employed as early as 1838 in biological investigations by the Belgian mathematician Vehulst, by biometricians Pearl and Reed in their studies of the growth of animal populations, and by econometricians in studies of economic time series and innovational activity.[10] The solution of this standard differential equation is the logistics curve

$$\frac{Q}{K} = \left(\frac{Q}{K}\right)^e \frac{1}{1 + be^{-(\rho+\lambda n)t}} \qquad (4.3)$$

as may be verified by differentiation; the magnitude of b depends on

[10] For a discussion of the logistic, see G. Tintner, *Econometrics*, John Wiley, 1952, pp. 208–211, where applications to industrial production and wholesale price indices are reviewed. Also, E. Mansfield and A. D. Bain discuss its application to the task of explaining the pace of technological innovation and the rate of adoption of television sets. See A. D. Bain, "The Growth of Demand for New Commodities," *Journal of Royal Statistical Society*, Series A, 1963, pp. 285–295; also Mansfield, "Technical Change and the Rate of Product Innovation," *Econometrica*, pp. 741–766, 1962.

initial conditions.[11] Substitution of this last equation into Equation 3.7, remembering Equations 3.6 and 3.8, yields

$$Q = Q^e[1 + be^{-(\rho+\lambda n)t}]^{\lambda'/1-\lambda'} \tag{4.4}$$

Clearly, both the output/capital ratio and output itself necessarily converge to their equilibrium values as t approaches infinity.

Since the system is stable, and the equilibrium rate of growth q^e is independent of the gross savings ratio s, it is tempting to conclude that changes in s, such as fiscal policy produces, have little effect upon the growth process. But Ryuzo Sato[12] has pointed out that the process of adjustment to equilibrium is extremely slow. How slow depends on the magnitude of the various parameters. Suppose, Sato suggests, a change in tax policy disturbs the economy from the equilibrium full-employment growth path by increasing the gross savings ratio from 11.66% to 12.54%, while $n = 0.015$, $\rho = 0.013$, $\lambda = 0.65$ and $\lambda' = 0.35$. Then, Sato shows, 30 years must elapse before the adjustment process is 50% completed; and only after 50 years will the process of adjustment be 70% completed.[13] Clearly,

[11] At

$$t = 0, \quad \frac{Q(0)}{K(0)} = \left(\frac{Q}{K}\right)^e \left(\frac{1}{1+b}\right)$$

therefore,

$$b = \left(\frac{Q}{K}\right)^e \Big/ \frac{Q(0)}{K(0)} - 1$$

the relative gap between the equilibrium and initial output/capital ratios.

[12] "Fiscal Policy in a Neo-Classical Growth Model: An Analysis of the Time Required for Equilibrium Adjustment," *Review of Economic Studies*, February 1963.

[13] Sato determined how much time will be required in order to achieve a given degree of adjustment if the system is disturbed from equilibrium at time zero. He defined the extent of adjustment achieved at any point of time t as

$$\delta(t) = \frac{q(t) - q(0)}{q^e - q(0)}$$

The task is to find the value of t for which $\delta(t) = \delta$, the specified degree of adjustment (e.g., 50%). From Equations 3.3 and 4.3 we note that

$$\delta(t) = \frac{Q(t)/K(t) - Q(0)/K(0)}{(Q/K)^e - Q(0)/K(0)} = \left[\frac{1+b}{1 + be^{-(\rho+\lambda n)t}} - 1\right]\Big/ b$$

The first equality reveals that the output/capital ratio adjusts *para pasu* with the rate of growth of output. The second equality reveals that the extent of adjustment achieved by time t depends on b, the gap between the equilibrium and initial output/capital ratios and the parameters ρ, λ, and n. Simple algebraic manipulation now yields

$$e^{(\rho+\lambda n)t} = \frac{b\delta(t) + 1}{1 - \delta(t)}$$

Hence, to achieve the specified fraction of adjustment δ requires the passage of

$$t = \frac{1}{\rho + \lambda n} \log_e \left[\frac{b\delta + 1}{1 - \delta}\right]$$

changes in the gross savings ratio significantly influence the process of economic development. However, research by Dale Mortensen with a more realistic specification of the consumption function reveals that the adjustment process may not be as long as Sato suggests.[14]

†19.5 WAGE, PRICE, AND MONETARY ADJUSTMENTS FOR FULL-EMPLOYMENT GROWTH

The growth model Roy Harrod developed in the 1930s was based on the assumption of an inflexible capital-output ratio, since it seemed unreasonable at the time to hope that the central bank would be able to reduce the rate of interest enough to achieve long-run, full-employment growth.[15] In contrast, neoclassical growth theorists presume that the required adjustments in the capital-output ratio will take place continuously. But what are the adjustments that must be made if full-employment growth is to be achieved? More precisely, how must wages adjust if profit maximizing competitive firms are to hire the growing supply of workers? And how must the rate of interest move in order to induce sufficient investment spending? Furthermore, is it true that a money supply expanding at the long-run equilibrium growth rate will best contribute to stable full-employment growth without inflation? Finally, what type of monetary and fiscal adjustments will be required if the pace of technological advance increases, or if the rate of population growth declines?

a. The Wage Rate

Under competitive conditions, profit maximizing firms adjust the size of their work force to the point where the marginal productivity of labor is equal to real wage rate w. Differentiation of Equation 2.4′ yields the familiar condition

$$\frac{\partial Q}{\partial N} = \lambda e^{\rho t} A N^{\lambda-1} K^{\lambda'} = \frac{\lambda Q}{N} = w \qquad (5.1)$$

Hence the total real income received by workers is $wN = \lambda Q$, and labor's share of total output is simply $wN/Q = \lambda$; the distribution of income to workers is completely determined by the production function. From the

---

[14] Mortensen considered the effect of incorporating wealth into the consumption function on the speed of adjustment, as well as a variety of other specifications. See "The Macro-Dynamic Implications of the Life Cycle and the Permanent Income Savings Hypotheses," unpublished Ph.D. dissertation, Carnegie-Mellon University, 1967.

[15] Harrod's model was presented in Chapter 18, Section 3.

last equality of Equation 5.1 we have for the rate of change in the real wage:

$$\frac{\dot{w}}{w} = \frac{\dot{Q}}{Q} - n \tag{5.2}$$

In equilibrium, when output grows at rate q^e (as prescribed by Equation 3.5)

$$\left(\frac{\dot{w}}{w}\right)^e = q^e - n = \frac{\rho + \lambda n}{1 - \lambda'} - n \tag{5.3}$$

Clearly, for a young country with a high Q/K ratio, $\dot{w}/w > (\dot{w}^e/w)$ because output will be growing more rapidly than the equilibrium rate. The precise time path that the wage rate must follow if full-employment conditions are to be maintained is

$$w = \lambda \frac{Q^e}{N} \left[1 + be^{-(\rho+\lambda n)t}\right]^{\lambda'/1-\lambda'} \tag{5.4}$$

as may be verified from Equation 4.4 and 5.1.

b. The Interest Rate

As for the rate of interest, it is appropriate in analyzing long-run behavior to assume, as a first approximation, that entrepreneurs always adjust the capital stock so as to maintain its marginal productivity equal to the rate of interest. This means that

$$\frac{\partial Q}{\partial K} = \lambda' \frac{Q}{K} = r \tag{5.5}$$

Thus $K = \lambda'Q/r$, implying that investment is simply

$$\frac{I}{K} = \frac{\dot{K}}{K} = \frac{\dot{Q}}{Q} - \frac{\dot{r}}{r} \tag{5.6}$$

But how must the rate of interest adjust through time if this type of behavior on the part of investors is to yield the expenditure required to maintain the economy at full employment? The answer is provided by substituting the explicit expression for Q/K provided by Equation 4.3 into Equation 5.5.[16]

$$r = \lambda' \left(\frac{Q}{K}\right)^e \left(\frac{1}{1 + be^{-(\rho+\lambda n)t}}\right) \tag{5.7}$$

From this last expression, and indeed from Equation 5.5, it is clear that for a "young" country characterized by a Q/K ratio above $(Q/K)^e$, the

---

[16] The magnitude of b is the relative gap between equilibrium and initial output/capital ratios, as was explained in footnote 11, p. 520.

rate of interest must be high. This is consistent with our intuition, because with Q/K large, capital is scarce relative to the supply of labor. But, if full employment is maintained, the rate of interest gradually falls as the country matures, and the output/capital ratio approaches its equilibrium level. In equilibrium we must have

$$r^e = \lambda' \left(\frac{Q}{K}\right)^e = \lambda' \frac{q^e}{s} \qquad (5.8)$$

Note that this "natural" rate of interest corresponding to full-employment growth equilibrium is influenced by the parameters of the production function, the rate of population growth, and the gross savings ratio. Since the gross savings ratio is affected by fiscal policy, the natural rate of interest is also subject to policy control.

Whether or not the interest rate can continue to fall as the young economy matures hinges on the Keynesian liquidity trap, an issue discussed in Chapter 8, Section 3. If the floor to the rate of interest provided by a liquidity trap were above the long-run equilibrium rate of interest, r^e of Equation 5.8, the maturing economy would eventually reach a point where the level of investment would fall short of the amount required for full-employment growth. Fiscal policy would be required in order to avoid stagnation and rising unemployment. As explained in Section 2, the gross savings rate, s, might be decreased by a reduction in tax rates or an increase in the proportion of total output utilized by the government. Also, Equation 3.6 reveals that a reduction in the savings ratio would increase the equilibrium output/capital ratio which, by Equation 5.8, serves in turn to increase the equilibrium rate of interest. Sufficient application of expansionary fiscal weapons might raise the equilibrium rate of interest above the floor provided by a liquidity trap.

c. Monetary Policy for Full-Employment Growth

Quite apart from the liquidity trap issue, there is another question of monetary policy that demands attention. Let us consider the assertion, advanced by such Chicago School economists as Henry C. Simons[17] and Milton Friedman,[18] that the rate of growth of the money supply should equal the long-run rate of economic growth. Specifically, how must the nominal money supply behave if full employment is to be maintained without inflation? Suppose, for example, that the demand for money equation is of the simple form

$$\mathbf{M}_d = Qr^{-\sigma}, \qquad \sigma > 0 \qquad (5.9)$$

[17] "Rules versus Authorities in Monetary Policy," *Journal of Political Economy*, 1936, as reprinted in *Readings in Monetary Theory*, Blackiston, 1951.

[18] "A Monetary and Fiscal Framework for Economic Stability, *American Economic Review*, 1948, as reprinted in *Readings in Monetary Theory*, Blackiston, 1951.

and that $\mathbf{M}_s = \mathbf{M}_d$. Then, if r is to behave in accordance with Equation 5.5, as required for the maintenance of full employment,

$$\frac{\dot{\mathbf{M}}_s}{\mathbf{M}_s} = \frac{\dot{Q}}{Q} - \frac{\sigma\dot{r}}{r} = \frac{\dot{Q}}{Q} - \sigma(1 - \lambda')s\left[\left(\frac{Q}{K}\right)^e - \frac{Q}{K}\right] \qquad (5.10)$$

where the second equality follows from Equations 5.6, 4.1, and 4.2. Hence the money supply must grow more rapidly than output for an immature economy with a ratio of output to capital above the equilibrium level, at least if prices are to remain stable. And since an immature economy's actual output grows faster than the equilibrium rate, it is clear that the Chicago rule leads to an insufficient expansion of the money supply. Only when the economy is in long-run equilibrium should the money supply grow at the same rate as output.[19]

Price adjustments—inflation or deflation—may still operate to permit the real rate of interest to move in the fashion required for the preservation of full employment even if the monetary authorities do not adjust the *nominal* money supply in accordance with Equation 5.10. Suppose, for example, that the economy is growing at rate q^e along the long-run full-employment equilibrium growth path, but that the monetary authorities keep the nominal money supply constant. Remembering that it is the nominal rate of interest, $r_n = r + (\dot{p}/p)$, that is customarily employed in empirical studies of the demand for money, we have

$$\mathbf{M}_n = p\mathbf{M} = pQr_n^{-\sigma} \qquad (5.11)$$

where $\mathbf{M}_n$ denotes the nominal money supply and p the index of prices. Clearly, this equation will be satisfied even if $\dot{\mathbf{M}}_n = 0$, provided that prices fall at the same rate that output is rising. Note, however, that if money wages were rigid downward, the rate of deflation required to make the real money supply grow at rate q^e would not be attainable. The money wage is $w_m = wp$; since, from Equation 5.2, $\dot{w}/w = (\dot{Q}/Q) - n$, it is obvious that

$$\frac{\dot{w}_m}{w_m} = \frac{\dot{w}}{w} + \frac{\dot{p}}{p} = q^e - n + \frac{\dot{p}}{p} \geq 0$$

implies

$$\frac{\dot{p}}{p} \geq n - q^e$$

Thus, if money wages cannot be reduced, price changes can make only a limited contribution to the required adjustment of the rate of interest.

[19] This condition would be weakened if the income elasticity of the demand for money were less than unity, money being an inferior good.

d. An Optimal Propensity to Save

Is there an optimal value of s, the gross savings ratio? We have already seen that it influences the level of output (cf. Equations 3.8 and 4.4), although the equilibrium rate of growth is unaffected. To find the best s, note first that $C + G = (1 - s)Q$; therefore, the sum of consumption plus government spending at any point of time is obviously sensitive to s; more precisely

$$\frac{d(C + G)}{ds} = (1 - s)\frac{dQ}{ds} - Q \qquad (6.1)$$

Let us now consider the following question, analyzed by Phelps.[20] What magnitude of s will maximize the sum $C + G$ when the economy has settled down on the full-employment equilibrium growth path? Differentiating Equation 3.8 with respect to s reveals[21]

$$\frac{dQ^e}{ds} = \left(\frac{\lambda'}{1 - \lambda'}\right)\frac{Q^e}{s} > 0 \qquad (6.2)$$

Thus, the larger the gross savings ratio, the larger will be the equilibrium full-employment level of output, once the economy settles down to a constant rate of growth. But this does not mean that a high propensity to save is a desideratum, even in the long run. This is illustrated in Figure 19.4, where two full-employment growth paths are compared. All the curves have the same slope because the rate of growth is independent of the savings ratio. Also, the equilibrium output growth path is higher when $s = 0.3$ instead of 0.2, as Equation 6.2 prescribes. But for $s = 0.2$ the equilibrium level of consumption is slightly higher than that for $s = 0.3$, because a larger fraction of the higher level of output is saved. Thus, too high a savings ratio may lead to a drop in the height of the equilibrium consumption path. This may be seen more formally by substituting Equation 6.2 into Equation 6.1.

$$\frac{\partial(C + G)^e}{\partial s} = \left[\left(\frac{1 - s}{s}\right)\left(\frac{\lambda'}{1 - \lambda'}\right) - 1\right]Q^e \qquad (6.3)$$

If $C + G$ is to be maximized, then $[\partial(C + G)^e/\partial s] = 0$; but this means that $s = \lambda' = (\partial Q/\partial K)(K/Q)$. From Equation 5.8 we see that this implies

$$sQ = r^e K \qquad (6.4)$$

---

[20] "The Golden Rule of Accumulation: A Fable for Growthmen," *American Economic Review*, pp. 638–643, September 1961.

[21] Differentiation is facilitated by noting that by appropriately defining ψ Equation 3.8 may be written $Q^e = \psi s^{\lambda'\alpha}$; therefore, $\partial Q^e/\partial s = \lambda'\alpha\psi s^{(\lambda'\alpha - 1)} = \lambda'\alpha\psi s^{\lambda'\alpha}/s = (\lambda'\alpha/s)Q^e$, which reduces to Equation 6.2 since $\alpha = 1/(1 - \lambda')$.

log

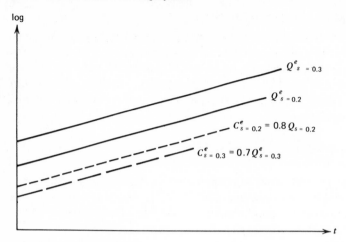

$Q^e_{s\ =\ 0.3}$

$Q^e_{s\ =\ 0.2}$

$C^e_{s\ =\ 0.2} = 0.8\,Q_{s\ =\ 0.2}$

$C^e_{s\ =\ 0.3} = 0.7\,Q^e_{s\ =\ 0.3}$

t

Fig. 19.4   *The golden rule.*

Thus investment spending is precisely equal to the return on the capital stock; investment precisely equals profits.

An economy growing along its highest achievable equilibrium consumption growth path has been characterized by Phelps[22] as living in accordance with the *Golden Rule*. If society is to agree on a fixed savings ratio that will hold for all generations, this is the one.[23] But the suggestion that the optimal equilibrium path is obtained when $s = \lambda'$ and profits just suffice to meet investment spending leaves a number of questions unanswered. First, it does not prescribe the optimal proportion of output that should be utilized by the government sector; there are a host of different tax ratios and government propensities to spend that are compatible with the optimal gross savings ratio. Thus the proportion of output utilized by the government sector may be determined either by the objective of achieving a balanced budget or on the basis of welfare considerations without violating the conditions prescribed by Phelps' Golden Rule. Second, per capita consumption may well be growing with the passage of time,

[22] Op cit.

[23] I. F. Pearce has argued that for reasonable utility functions each generation might prefer to reap a larger aggregate consumption over their life span by consuming less in their early years in order to consume even more when they are older. "The End of the Golden Age in Solovia: A Further Fable for Growthmen Hoping to 'One Up' Oiko," *American Economic Review*, December 1962, and the "Comment" by Phelps in the same issue. And it has been argued that the maximization of discounted value of future utility may involve periodic binges instead of persevering with a constant savings ratio; see, for example, David Cass, "Optimal Growth in an Aggregative Model of Capital Accumulation," *Review of Economic Studies*, July 1965.

and it might be argued that it is only reasonable for our generation to save a smaller proportion of income, to consume part of profits, in order that we can enjoy a per capita income closer to that of the next generation. Finally, if we are not yet moving along the Golden Age equilibrium growth path, optimization of the adjustment process may require a quite different gross savings ratio in the short-run from that which should prevail once the economy has adjusted to the long-run equilibrium growth path.

e. Adjustment to Accelerating Technological Change and Population Growth

How will the time path of the real wage and interest rates required for preserving full-employment growth be affected by an increase in the rate of technological advance? We will see that our intuition is mistaken if it suggests that a less restrictive monetary policy would be required to offset technological unemployment. Let us first consider the effects of an increase in the parameter ρ of Equation 2.4 on the long-run equilibrium full-employment growth path. From Equation 3.5 we have $\partial q^e/\partial \rho = 1/1 - \lambda' > 0$; the equilibrium rate of growth is increased. Differentiating 5.8 now reveals that $\partial r^e/\partial \rho = (\lambda'/s)/(\partial q^e/\partial \rho) = \lambda'/(1 - \lambda')s > 0$. Thus the equilibrium rate of interest is *increased* as a result of a rise in the rate of technological advance. This is, of course, the long-run effect. Equation 5.5 reveals that, since the current value of Q/K is given, there is no effect on the current *level* of r. But the instantaneous effect, before Q/K has time to change, will be to make r *increase* more rapidly than would be the case in the absence of the accelerated pace of technological advance; indeed, inspection of Equations 5.6 and 4.1 reveals that the instantaneous effect is $\partial \dot{r}/\partial \rho = 1$. Thus an increase in the pace of technological advance requires a *tighter* monetary policy if full employment is to be maintained.

Note however, that adjustment to technological change may be achieved by fiscal instead of monetary policy if the economy is initially moving along the long-run, full-employment equilibrium growth path. Inspection of Equation 3.6 reveals that an appropriate increase in the gross saving rate, s, achieved by an increase in taxes or a reduction in government spending could keep the equilibrium output/capital ratio at its original value; Equation 5.8 then demonstrates that under these circumstances the equilibrium rate of interest would remain at its former level.

Let us now consider the implications of a reduction in the rate of population growth. From Equations 3.5 and 5.8 we obtain $\partial q^e/\partial n = \lambda/1 - \lambda'$ and $\partial r^e/\partial n = \lambda\lambda'/s(1 - \lambda')$. Since both these derivatives are positive, a reduction in the rate of population growth implies that the equilibrium rate of growth of output will fall and an *expansionary* monetary policy will be required. As for the effect on the real wage, we find from Equation 5.3 that $\partial(\dot{w}/w)^e/\partial n = (\lambda + \lambda' - 1)/(1 - \lambda')$. If there are constant

returns to scale, the rate of growth of the equilibrium real wage is independent of the rate of growth of population. But if there are diminishing
returns to scale, $\lambda + \lambda' < 1$, a reduction in the rate of population growth
causes an *increase* in the rate of growth of the equilibrium real wage.
Of course, if a liquidity trap or ineptness on the part of the monetary
authorities prevented the required movements in the rate of interest, an
increase in government spending or a tax reduction would be required to
preserve full-employment conditions. But the combined efforts of fiscal
and monetary authorities cannot forestall the inevitable reduction in the
long-run equilibrium growth rate that would be brought about by a decline
in the rate of population expansion.

REFERENCES

1. A particularly helpful analysis of the process of long-term economic growth is provided in Chapters 10 through 16 of an advanced textbook by R. G. D. Allen.

   R. G. D. Allen, *Macro-Economic Theory*, St. Martin's Press, 1967.

2. Here is a small sample from the neoclassical growth literature.

   E. S. Phelps, "The Golden Rule of Accumulation, A Fable for Growthmen," *American Economic Review*, September 1961; I. F. Pearce, "The End of the Golden Age in Solovia," *American Economic Review*, December 1962, with response by E. S. Phelps.

   Frank P. Ramsey, "A Mathematical Theory of Saving," *Economic Journal*, December 1928.

   K. Shell, ed., *Essays on the Theory of Optimal Economic Growth*, Massachusetts Institute of Technology Press, 1967.

   Robert M. Solow, "A Contribution to the Theory of Economic Growth," *Quarterly Journal of Economics*, February 1956.

   Jerome L. Stein, *Money and Capacity Growth*, Columbia University Press 1971.

   Joseph E. Stiglitz and Hirofumi Uzawa, eds., *Readings in the Modern Theory of Economic Growth*, Massachusetts Institute of Technology Press, 1969.

3. A multisector analysis of the growth process was developed by John von Neumann. His contribution spawned a fascinating literature concerning the optimality of balanced growth.

   John von Neumann, "A Model of General Economic Equilibrium," *Review of Economic Studies*, 1945.

   Robert Dorfman, Samuelson and Solow, *Linear Programming and Economic Analysis* (especially Chapter 12), McGraw-Hill, 1958.

   Roy Radner, "Paths of Economic Growth that Are Optimal With Regard Only to Final States: A Turnpike Theorem," *Review of Economic Studies*, February 1961.

KEY CONCEPTS

Malthus

Golden Age

Golden Rule

gross-savings ratio

full-employment growth path

EXERCISES

19.1 Suppose that $\rho = 1.3\%$, $\lambda = \frac{2}{3}$, $\lambda' = \frac{1}{3}$, $n = 1.5\%$, and $s = 10\%$.
   a. Find q^e, the equilibrium rate of growth and $(Q/K)^e$, the equilibrium ratio of output to capital.
   b. Suppose that the savings ratio changes to $33\frac{1}{3}\%$ but the other parameters remain at the values specified in part a; how will this influence the equilibrium rate of growth and the equilibrium ratio of output to capital?
   c. Would the path of consumption be higher or lower in equilibrium if the savings ratio were 50% or $33\frac{1}{3}\%$ instead of 10%?
   d How long will it take the economy to achieve a 50% adjustment toward equilibrium when the savings ratio changes from 10% to 35%.

19.2 How will the equilibrium growth process be affected if consumption and saving depend on wealth, as indexed by the capital stock K, as well as income. That is, suppose that Equation 19.2.5 is modified to read

$$\dot{K} = I - sQ = s'K \qquad (2.5')$$

How will Figure 19.1 have to be modified in order to reflect this complication? What is q^e?

19.3 Evaluate the following statement.
   "Was Ben Franklin right in saying that 'a penny saved is a penny earned'? Each generation of economists provides a different answer to this question. In the 1930s the Keynesian economists said no, since an upward shift in the propensity to save schedule would serve only to generate more unemployment and reduce income. In the 1940s Harrod and Domar argued that a high savings rate was necessary for rapid growth. And in the 1960s the neoclassical growth theorists argued that the savings ratio is of no importance for it has no effect on the long run rate of economic development."

19.4 When Ragnar Frisch and Jan Tinbergen were awarded the Nobel Prize in 1969, Harry Schwartz wrote in the *New York Times:*

"The dominant position of mathematics in modern economics was brought home forcefully last week when the first two Nobel Memorial Prizes in Economics went to two econometricians. . . . In economics and many of the social sicences—political science, sociology, economic history and even some areas of anthropology—top status now is increasingly held by men whose competence is in advanced mathematics as well as in the subject fields themselves. . . . In the world of business today, increasing influence is being exerted by management scientists, operations researchers, and systems analysts. . . . Matrix algebra, vector analysis, Fourier series, topology and the calculus of variations are no longer strangers in the executive suite. . . ."

"If Adam Smith and Karl Marx were young would-be economists these days, one suspects that they would make sure they knew matrix algebra and other types of mathematics very well before applying for graduate school."

Suppose that you are writing the part of the article explaining the use of econometric and mathematical techniques in macroeconomic analysis. Write several paragraphs in a style understandable to the layman (remember, the *New York Times* carries "All the News that's Fit to Print").

index

Abramovitz, Moses, 447
Accelerated depreciation, 205
Accelerationists, 364
Accelerator, 193-198
  flexible, 196-7
  one-way, 197, 459
Adelman, Irma and Frank, 486, 487, 491
After-change equation, 68
Aggregate demand schedule, 320-321
  interaction with supply, 328-330
Aggregate supply schedule, 321-325
Aldrich Commission, 251
Alexander, Arthur J., 381
Alexander, Sidney S., 248, 398
Allen, R. G. D., 351, 425, 529
Almon, Clopper, Jr., 83, 95
American Economic Association, 3
Anderson, Leonall C., 488, 492
Anderson, Paul S., 361
Anderson, W. H. Locke, 207
Ando, Albert, 125, 138, 230, 228, 311, 485
Andreano, Ralph L., 36
Andrews, P. W. S., 202
Annual rates, 28
Anticipations, consumer, 119, 129
  inflation, 290
  sales, 451
Anticipatory data, 398
Antitrust legislation, 334
Archibald, G. C., 10, 345
Area Redevelopment Act, 40
Arrow, Kenneth, 83, 351
Automatic stabilizer, 415-418
Average propensity to consume (APC), 113
  long run stability, 106, 130

Bach, G. L., 311
Bain, Andrew D., 519
Balanced-budget multiplier, 304
Balance of payments, accounts, 233-236
  deficit, 233, 241
  equilibrium, 239
  and full employment, 239
Bank debits, 158

Bank holiday, 251-252
Bank of England, 250, 385
Banks, central, 134, 250-251
Barometric forecasting, 390-394
Barten, A. P., 460
Baumol, William J., 164, 199, 207, 411, 420
Bay Area Collective of Socialist Economists (BACSE), 8
Bear, Donald, 125
Beckmann, M. J., 510
Bernoulli, Daniel, 192
Bischoff, Charles W., 207
Black unemployment, 22
Bodkin, R. G., 381
BofP (Y, r), 237-239
Boggard, van den, 460
Bonds, constant purchasing power, 292
  government, 165, 260-61
  price versus yield, 173
  yields, 168-171
Brainard, William, 357, 468
Bridge, J. L., 138
Brimmer, Andrew, 311
Bronfenbrenner, M., 7, 311
Bronstein, Morris, 315
Brookings-SSRC Econometric Model, 473
Brown, E. Cary, 138
Brown, T. M., 131
Brumberg, R., 115, 121, 125
Budget deficit, 496-497
Budget studies of consumption, 110-111
Bureau of Employment Security, 40
Burgess, W. Randolph, 263
Burns, Arthur F., 14, 29, 276, 302, 394
Business cycle, history, 385-390
  NBER chronology, 386-387

Cagan, Phillip, 284, 381
Campbell, Colin D., 285, 288, 381
Capacity, McGraw-Hill survey, 22
  utilization, 23
  see also Potential GNP
Capital consumption allowances, 57

533

Capital budgeting, 199
Capital gains and losses, 119, 133, 367-368, 370
  on bonds, 172
Capital movements, 233
Capital stock, desired, 193
  inherited, 196
Carlson, Keith M., 488, 489, 492
Cass, David, 526
Census undercount, 22, 40
Central bank, 134, 250-251. *See also* Bank of England
Certainty equivalence, 465-466
Characteristic equation, 433
Chase Manhattan Bank poll, 3, 6
Chau, L. C., 135
Check clearing, 258-259
Chenery, Hollis, 95, 351
Chicago Mercantile Exchange, 246
Chicago School, 7, 272
Chow, Gregory, 72, 457, 491
Christ, Carl, 97, 490, 491
Civilian labor force, 17
Clapham, John, 250
Clark, John J., 29
Clark, Paul G., 95
Classical model, 336-340
Clearing house, 259
Cobb, C. W., 203, 349
Cobb-Douglas production function, 203, 214, 349-50, 357
Cohen, Morris, 29
Cole, Rosanne, 37
Commerical paper, 274
Comparative dynamics, 440
Compound interest, 42-44
Conrad, Alfred H., 311
Constant purchasing power bonds, 292
Consumer interest payments, 59
Consumer price index (CPI), 293
  sampling error, 297
Consumption (C), 50
  alternative definitions, 125
  and distribution of income, 109-15
  and interest rates, 122-125, 140
  and wealth, 134-136
  effect of tax cut, 121-122
  habit and inertia, 128
  life-cycle hypothesis, 117-122
Consumption function, 56
  estimates, 148-149

Control problems, targets and instruments, 237, 437, 463
  uncertainty, 469-471
Control ray, 443-444, 446, 470
Cooper, J. Phillip, 457, 489-490
Cooper, Richard N., 236
Cooper, Ronald L., 490
Core sections, 12
Cornwall, John, 486
Corporate retained earnings (undistributed profits), 58-59, 79
Correlation, 144, 187-188
Cost-push inflation, 300-302, 332-334
Council of Economic Advisers, 2, 76, 353, 396, 415-416
Covariance, 188
Cowles, Alfred, 180
CPI, *see* Consumer price index
CPI-Futures Market, 292
Cup of cyclical movements, 411
Curley, M. Louise, 36
Currency devaluation, 93, 236, 242-243, 300
Currency drain, 259-60
Current dollar GNP, 28
Current Population Survey, 35

Data sources, 35-36
Debasement, 375
Debt burden, 496-499
Defense expenditure, 92-93, 476
  Viet Nam War, 70-71
Deficit financing, 496-499
deLeeuw, Frank, 207, 474, 485, 491
δ (delta) speed of adjustment coefficient, 129
Demand deposits, 156
Demand-pull inflation, 302-304
DeMoivre, Abraham, 431
Denison, Edward F., 32, 508, 510
Denton, F. T., 37
Dependent variable, 142
DePrano, Michael, 228
Depreciation, 57, 205
Dernburg, Thomas F., 120
Descriptive statistics, 142-145
Desired capital stock, 193
Devaluation, currency, 92, 236, 242-243, 300
Diamond, Peter, 510
Difference equations, equilibrium, 409
  first order, 424-426

second order, 409, 424
  solution, 424-32
Diffusion indices, 396-398
Diminishing returns, 26, 328
Discount rate, 254-256, 273
Discretionary stablization policy, 415
Disposable income (Y_d), 48
  equation, 57
  line, 65
Dissavers, 115
Distributed lag, consumption, 125-131
  investment, 196
Dolde, Walter, 138
Domar, Evsey, 496-499
Dorfman, Robert, 97, 529
Douglas, P. H., 203, 349
Duesenberry, James, 131, 138, 140, 491
Durable goods, 125, 132
Durbin-Watson statistic, 147-148
Dynamic analysis, 12, 126-131, 197, 309,
  352, 410-414

e $\doteq$ 2.718 (base of natural logs), 46-47
Eckstein, Otto, 491
Econometric models, 472-492
  Brookings-SSRC, 472-473, 485
  Fed-MIT, 473-485
  Wharton, 4, 83, 485
Economic Report of the President, 2, 35,
  353, 356, 415-416
Eisner, Robert, 183, 207
Employment Act of 1946, 1
Endogenous variables, 48, 220, 319
Equilibrium, 65, 128
Estimation, 146
Esculator wage clauses, 287, 373
Evans, Michael, 83, 138, 207, 395, 473,
  487, 488, 492
Excess capacity, 22-23
Excess Reserves (R_e), 254, 268
Exchange rates, creeping, 247
  flexible, 244-246
Exogenous cycle theories, 400
Exogenous variables, 48, 220, 319
Expected value, 466
Explanatory variable, 143
Explosive movements, 413
Exponents, 44-45
Export subsidies, 236

Fallacy of composition, 75-82

False signals, 391-392
Fama, Eugene F., 180, 192
Farber, Evan I., 36
Farrell, Michael, 121, 138, 246
Federal Deposit Insurance Corporation
  (FDIC), 252
Federal Funds Market, 260
Federal Housing Authority (FHA), 204
Federal Reserve system, 5, 134, 204, 220,
  250-252
  gold holdings, 232
  reserve requirements, 252-256
Fed-MIT Econometric Model, 473-485
Feedback loop, 60
Feige, Edgar L., 215
Ferber, Robert, 207
FIFO (First-in-first-out), 370
Final product, 49
Financial intermediaries, 291
Fiscal drag, 81
Fiscal policy, 4, 222
  versus monetary policy, 222-229
Fischer, Stanley, 457, 489
Fisher, Franklin, 298
Fisher, G. H., 443
Fisher, Irving, 156, 180, 315, 316, 358
Fisher, Janet A., 138
Flaim, Paul O., 42
Flowcharts, 61, 91, 211, 221
Forced savings, 375-380
Foreign trade balance, 236
FORTRAN, 88, 219, 402, 421-423, 459
Franklin, Benjamin, 74, 530
Free reserves, 255
Frictional unemployment, 24
Friedman, Milton, 4, 5, 9-10, 115, 138,
  158, 180, 226, 228, 230, 248, 364,
  367, 373, 457, 468, 523
Frisch, Ragnar, 402, 469, 487, 530
Fromm, Gary, 488, 491
Full employment, 24, 26
  budget, 76-82, 85
  growth rate, 516
  output level, 516-517
Fundamental disequilibrium, 247

Gallik, Dimitri M., 103
Geometric series, sum of, 63
German monetary conversion, 307
Gesell, Silvio, 215
Glass-Steagall Act, 232

GNP gap, 25-31
Gold, reserves, 232
  standard, 232, 240-242
Goldberger, Arthur, 448, 486
Golden rule of accumulation, 526-527
Goldenweiser, E. A., 232
Goldsmith, Raymond, 503
Gordon, R. A., 404
Government, interest payments, 59, 499
  spending on goods and services (G), 49,
    70-73, 261-2
  Subsidies, 59
  total expenditure (G_{exp}), 77-81
  transfers, 49
Gramlick, Edward, 474, 485, 491
Great Depression, 17, 33, 63, 161, 232,
    244, 251, 267, 291, 460
Griliches, Zvi, 138, 298, 508, 510
Gross national product (GNP, Y), current
    dollar, 28, 295
  definition, 48
  gap, 25-31
  identity, 49
  potential (Y^c), 26
  real, 28, 295
  revisions, 37-38
  versus economic welfare, 496
Gross-savings ratio (s), 76, 514
Growth, arithmetic versus geometric, 42
  capital stock, 503
  full employment, 514-517
  geometric, 42
  sources of, 502-509
Grunwald, Joseph, 376
Guideposts, wage price, 353-354, 365
Gurley, John, 311

Haavelmo, Trygve, 207
Haberler, Gottfried, 342-343, 403, 404
Habits of payment, 162
Hall, Robert E., 381
Hansen, Alvin, 216, 405
Harris, Seymour E., 311
Harrod, Sir Roy, 496, 499-502, 511
Harvard Economic Society, 390
Hauser, Philip M., 36
Hawtrey, R. G. D., 401-402, 447
Heller, W. W., 14, 72
Help wanted ads, 360
Hester, Donald D., 180, 228
Hickey, Joseph A., 32

Hickman, Bert G., 491
Hicks, Sir J. R., 197, 457
Hirsch, Albert, 398, 491
Holt, Charles C., 366, 457, 460
Holzman, F. D., 285, 311
Homogeneous equation, 425
Hoover, Ethel D., 281
Housing loans, 204
Houthakker, H. S., 311
Huang, D. S., 135
Human capital, 50, 508
Hume, David, 241
Hyeck, F. A. von, 375
Hyperinflation, 283-284, 286, 287, 376-380
Hypothesis testing, 147

Ideal indicators, 391
Immigrant remittances, 133
Implicit price deflator (IPD), 293, 295
Imports (M), 234-235
  equation, 86, 211
Imputed rental income, 51
Income, permanent, 129
  profiles, 117, 123
Income redistribution, 109-15
Incomes policy, 301
Income velocity of money, 158
Indexing, 287-88, 292, 373
Index number construction, 313-317
Indirect business taxes, 59
Inflation, and balance of payments, 236
  anticipations, 285-6
  cost and wage push, 330-334
  demand-pull, 302-304
  hyper-, 284-285, 380
  IS-LM analysis, 304-305
  and monopoly, 332
  self-correcting, 304, 339, 374
Inflationary gap, 302-304
  IS-LM analysis, 305
  speed of inflation, 371-3
Inflation illusion, 367, 371, 373
Initial conditions, 128, 424
Input-output analysis, of defense spending,
    92-93
  and material balance, 102-104
  predictive accuracy, 97
  price implications, 101, 357
  two sector example, 92-95
  viability, 101-2
Interest payments,

consumer and government, 59
Interest rate, and balance of payments, 236-237
   and demand for money, 163-165, 175-179
   effect on consumption, 122-125, 130, 140, 218
   and investment demand, 197-202
   natural, 123
   negative, 215
   real, 290-393, 369
   and supply of money, 267-270
   versus bond prices, 173
Internal financing, 199, 202
International capital movements, 233-237
International Monetary Fund (IMF), 233, 246-47
Intriligator, Michael D., 491
Inventory, cycle theory, 447-456
   investment, 197
   recessions, 390, 398
   survey data, 398
   valuation adjustment (IVA), 58, 370
Investment (I), 193-206
   gross, 49-50
   tax credit, 205, 478
IS curve, derivation of, 212-214
   and multiplier, 214
   shifts of, 214
   slope of, 213
IS-LM apparatus, 220-222
Iso-root lines, 434
Iso-stability triangle, 411

Jevons, William Stanley, 399-402
Job vacancies, 24, 360
Johnson, Leland, 26, 122, 346
Johnston, J., 87, 142, 148
Joint Economic Committee, 2
Jorgenson, Dale W., 203-204, 207, 216, 508, 510
Jury, E. I., 435
Juster, F. Thomas, 32, 368

Kahn, Richard F., 63
Kaldor, Nicholas, 230
Kane, Edward J., 142
Kaysen, Carl, 298
Kennedy, John F., 1, 2, 24, 122, 242, 301, 365
"Key" industries, 357

Keynes, J. M., 8, 138, 165, 177, 183, 184, 198, 215, 224, 326, 340-344, 359, 367, 401, 402
"Keynesian" theory, 8, 63, 224, 228
Kindahl, James, 299
Klein-Goldberger econometric model, 486-487
Klein, Lawrence R., 70, 83, 105, 389, 448, 472, 487, 491-492
Koopmans, T. C., 10-11, 14, 83, 367
Kostinsky, Barry L., 103
Korean War, 17, 281, 306
Kramer, Gerald H., 2
Krupp, Sherman, 10
Kuh, Edwin, 491
Kuhn, T. S., 14
Kuznets, Simon, 106, 495

Laboratory, nature's, 6
Labor force (L), 17
   time lost, 20-21
Labor productivity, average, 353, 357
Labor's share (λ), 350-351, 352-3, 357, 521
Laffer, Arthur B., 489
Lange, Oscar, 340
Laspayres index, 314-316
Law of exponents, 44
Laursen, K., 286
Leading indicators, 394-396
Least-squares, 60, 228
Lender of last resort, 250
Leonard, William R., 36
Leontief, Wassily, 83, 92, 97, 197
Lepper, Susan J., 191
Levy, Michael, 32
Liebenberg, Maurice, 491
Life-cycle hypothesis, 117-122
LIFO (last-in-first-out), 370
Lintner, John, 141
Lipsey, Richard G., 345
Liquid assests, 134-136
Liquidity preference, 161. See also
   Money, demand for
Liquidity trap, 177, 182, 226, 523
Liu, T. C., 491
LM curves, and the liquidity trap, 177
   derivation of, 175-179
Logarithms, 44-47, 159
   common, 45
   natural, 47
Logistic Law of Growth, 519

Lubell, H., 138
Lucas, Robert, 138
Luce, Duncan, 191
Lundberg, Erick, 405, 447, 450, 499

Machlup, Fritz, 10
Maddala, G. S., 138
Makinen, G. E., 281, 376
Malinvaud, E., 138
Malthus, Reverend Thomas, 511, 512
Manne, H. B., 469
Manpower Development and Training Act, 40
Mansfield, Edwin, 519
Marginal efficiency of investment, 198-199
Marginal product of labor, 323
Marginal prepensity to consume (MPC, c_1), 56
  out of disposable income (c_1), 76
  out of GNP (c_1), 76
  short and long run, 129
Marginal propensity to save (MPS), 76
Markowitz, Harry, 186
Marshall, Alfred, 158, 315
Martin, William McChesney, 5, 274
Marx, Karl, 511
Material balance in planned economies, 102
Mature economy, 133
Mayer, Thomas, 228
McGraw-Hill survey of capacity utilization, 22
Meade, J. E., 202
Meiselman, David, 226, 228, 230
Meltzer, Allan, 158
Methodology, 6
Metzler, Lloyd A., 198, 345, 405, 447, 450, 457
Military transactions, 234
Mill, John Stuart, 399, 511
Miller, H. Laurence Jr., 7
Minhas, B. S., 351
Mitchell, Wesley C., 394, 396
Models, sequence of, 11, 319
Modigliani, Franco, 115, 121, 125, 131, 138, 228, 230, 345, 485, 487, 510
Monetary base (B), 265
Monetary conversion, 306-308
Monetary policy, 4, 272-273, 523-524
  rules versus discretion, 275
Money (M), definition of, 153
  demand for, 175

in multiplier accelerator model, 437-447
M_1, M_2 and M_3, 154-6
speculative and precautionary balances, 165-75
transactions demand for, 161-165
see also LM curve; Velocity of money
Money illusion, 367
Money market equilibrium, 221-222
Money multiplier, see Money supply expansion coefficient
Money supply, exogenous, 220
  interest elasticity of, 267-270
  nominal, 320
  potential, 267
  rate of change, 392-394
  real, 304, 320
Money supply expansion coefficient (μ), 264-265
Montias, Michael, 102
Moore, Geoffrey H., 394, 404
Moore, Henry L., 400
Morgan, Alison, 83, 92
Morgenstern, Oskar, 37, 191
Morgenthau, Henry, 307
Mortensen, Dale, 521
Mori, K., 70, 491
Moving average, 392
Multiplier, balanced budget, 72-73
  effects of increased government spending, 65
  effects of tax cut, 66-67, 70-72
  estimates, 70-71, 485
  family, 69
  foreign trade, 89-92
  graphical analysis, 64-67
  impact, 214
  multisector, 89
Multiplier-accelerator model, 406-409
  and money, 437-447
Mundell, Robert A., 248
Muth, Jack, 466

Nagel, Ernest, 10
Naive forecast, 483-484
Napier, John, 47
National Bureau of Economic Research (NBER), cycle chronology, 386-387
  indicators, 394-396
National income accounting identity, 49
National Industrial Conference Board, 360
Natural rate of growth, 501

Negative income tax, 4
Nerlove, Marc, 472
Net Liquidity Balance, 235-236
Neumann, John von, 191, 499, 529
Nixon, Richard M., 2, 301
"Noninflationary" wage settlements, 352-358
Nordhaus, William D., 32, 311, 496

Occam's razor, 9
Official Reserve Transaction Balance, 233, 237
Oksanen, E. H., 37
Okun, A. M., 14, 26-29, 32, 72, 395, 398
Okun's law, 26-30, 60
O'Leary, James, 138
Open market operations, 256, 262-3
Operation twist, 242, 274-275
Operationally meaningful theorem, 9
Optimal linear decision rules, 460-468
Oresme, Bishop Nicole, 375-376
Overemployment, 24
Overinvestment, 133, 402

Paasche index, 315-316
Packer, Arnold H., 363
Papandreou, Adreas G., 10
Pardox of thrift, 73-75
Parameters, 60
Park, Seong H., 363
Parkin, Michael, 215
Patinkin, Don, 135, 343-344, 345
Pearce, I. F., 526, 529
Permanent income, 115, 119-120
Perry, G. L., 361-363, 365, 381
Petersen, J., 286
Petty, Sir William, 385
Phelps, E. S., 364, 381, 525, 526, 529
Phillips, A. W., 358, 361, 381, 457
Phillips curve, 358-366
  loop, 363-64
Pifer, Howard, 183
Pigou, A. C., 158, 342-3, 345
Polenski, Karen, 83, 92
Poole, William, 230
Popkin, Joel, 448, 491
Population growth, 501, 503-506, 513
  effect on consumption, 121, 137, 139-140
Portfolio selection, 184-191
Postulates, self-evident, 10
Potential GNP (Y_c), 25-31

Predictive accuracy, 9
  of econometric models, 483-484
  of input-output analysis, 97, 100
Prescott, Edward, 457, 468
Price controls, 301
Price indices, quality improvements, 298, 300. See also Consumer price index; Implicit price deflator; Wholesale price index
Process analysis, 100
Production function, 349-351. See also Cobb-Douglas production function
Productivity, average (output/worker), 353, 357
  marginal and the wage rate, 321-324
Projector, Dorothy S., 116
Propensity to consume, 111
Proxmire, William, 276
Putty-clay, 476-477

Quadratic loss function, 461
Quadratic utility functions, 191
Quantity theory of money, 45, 306, 339
  cash balance approach (k), 158, 175
  crude, 226-227
  graph of components, 159

Radner, Roy, 529
Raiffa, Howard, 191
Ramsey, Frank P., 529
Ranson, R. David, 489
Ratio scale, 28, 42-46
Rationing, 301-2
Reagan, Michael, 276
Real-balance (wealth) effect, 135-136, 342
Real-bills doctrine, 273-274
Real GNP, 28
Reduced form equation, 86, 212
Rees, Albert, 281
Regression coefficient, 142
Rehiring costs, 26
Rental value of owner occupied housing, 50, 132
Repressed inflation, 301
Resek, R. W., 207
Reserves (R), borrowed, 255
  excess (R_e), 254
  free, 255
  required (R_r), 254-256
Retained earnings, 199
Reuss, Representative Henry S., 85

Reynolds, Sabron, 36
Ricardo, David, 511
Rigid money wages, 325-328, 342
Risk, 185
Robbins, Lionel, 10
Rocking horse, 405
Roosevelt, Franklin D., 251
Rosett, Richard, 120
Ross, Arthur M., 300
Ross, Leonard, 311
Richter, M. K., 191
Ruggles, Nancy, 57
Ruggles, Richard, 57, 298
Rules of the Game, 241

Sampling error, in price indices, 295
  in unemployment estimates, 39-40
Samuelson, Paul A., 4, 9, 57, 216, 359,
  381, 405, 406, 420, 435, 529
Sato, Ryuzo, 510, 520
Saving, 76
Say, Jean Baptiste, 340
Say's law, 340
Schmalensee, Richard L., 491
Schultze, C. L., 381
Schumpeter, Joseph, 385, 402
Seasonal unemployment, 23
Self-equilibrating specie flow mechanism,
  241
Semilogarithmic (ratio) charts, 42-46
Servicing the debt, 499
Shannon, David A., 32
Shaw, Edward S., 158, 230
Shaw, George Bernard, 3
Shell, K., 529
Siegel, Jacob S., 22
Silk, Leonard S., 36
Simon, Herbert A., 10, 460
Simpson, David, 83, 92
Simons, Henry C., 276, 523
Simulation, 408-490, 416-417, 474-483
Slutsky, Eugen, 487
Smith, Adam, 156
Smith, Warren L., 345
Soligo, Ronald, 29
Solow, Robert, 29, 359, 381, 502-509, 510,
  511
Sorrentino, Constance, 24, 32
South Sea Bubble, 385
Speculative balances, see Money
Stagnation, 133

thesis, 29, 215-217
Standard deviation, 186-188
Standard error of estimate, 144
Stans, Maurice H., 85
Static analysis, 12, 309
Statistical discrepancy, 39
Statistical inference, 142, 146-148
Stein, Herbert, 2, 14
Stein, Jerome L., 529
Stigler, George, 7, 299, 400
Stiglitz, Joseph E., 529
Stock market, 133, 137
Stock prices, 392
Stock versus flow, 153
Strong, Benjamin, 251
Strotz, Robert H., 207
Subjective probability distribution, 186
Suits, Daniel B., 70-71, 472, 476, 491
Sunspots, 399-400
Superscripts n, r and t, 12
Surplus of government enterprises, 59

T-accounts, 257
Taft, Robert A., 3
Targets and instruments, 237
Tariffs, 236
Taxes, and disposable income—GNP gap,
  58, 78-82
  effect on consumption, 121-122
  in GNP accounts, 58
  indirect business, 59
  lump-sum, 70
  multiplier effects, 70-73
  surtax, 137
  war, 137
Tax the rich, 109
Technological change, 334, 347
  embodied, 509
  neutral, 501
  residual, 504-6
Theil, H., 457, 460, 467
Thrift, the paradox of, 73-75
Throop, Adrian W., 361
Time deposits (TD), 254
Tinbergen, Jan, 403, 472, 530
Tintner, G., 519
Tobin, James, 32, 138, 164, 180, 186, 230,
  311, 496, 511
Total spending line, 65
Tower, Edward, 83, 92
Toynbee, Arnold, 495

Transactions demand for money, 161-165
  and interest rates, 163-165
  see Money, demand for
Transfer payments, 49, 59
Treasury bills, 167
Treml, Vladimir G., 103
Truman, Harry S., 301
Tullock, Gordon C., 285, 288, 381

Udis, B., 70
Ullman, Joseph C., 40
Uncertainty, 370
  decision making under, 185
Underconsumption, 133, 137, 402
Undistributed profits, *see* Corporate
  retained earnings
Unemployment, by sex, age and race, 20-21
  frictional, 24
  insurance benefits, 289
  international comparisons, 24
  natural, 364
  percent of labor force, 17
  regional estimates, 40-41
  sampling error, 39
  seasonal, 23
  targer rate, 22-25
  transitional, 23
Union for Radical Political Economics
  (URPE), 8
Unstable cycle, 411
Uzawa, Hirofumi, 529

Variance, 144
Velocity of money (v), 45, 156, 222, 339
  income (v_y), 158
  transactions, 156
Veritas Foundation, 8
Veterans Administration (VA), 204
Viet Nam War, effect of war on

U.S. economy, 70-71
  inflation, 281, 356
Vogel, Robert C., 292

Wachtel, Paul, 368
Wachter, Michael L., 361
Wage inflation, 300-302, 330-331. *See
  also* Phillips curve
Wage-price guideposts, 3, 301
Wage rigidity, 325-326, 340-342
Wages, and full-employment growth, 521-
  522
  real versus money, 323
  and supply of labor, 337
  and unemployment, 336-338
  see also Wage rigidity
Wald, Abraham, 469
Wallace, Neil, 138
War, demobilization, 389
  finance, 274, 278
  inflation, 302
  see also World War II; Viet Nam War; and
    Defense expenditure
Warranted rate of growth, 500
Wealth, and demand for money, 183
  "effect," 134-37
  nonhuman, 132
  nominal, 135
Weber, Warren, 125
Wholesale price index (WPI), 293
Wilson, Woodrow, 250
Wonnacott, Ronald J. and Thomas H., 87,
  142
World War II, 220, 274, 301, 303
  consumption, 105
  financing, 274

Zellner, Arnold, 37, 135, 468
Zero population growth, 121, 139-140, 513

67.12